# ENQUIRE WITHIN

# ENQUIRE WITHIN

*upon everything*

124th, NEW, COMPLETELY REVISED EDITION

HERBERT JENKINS
LONDON

© 1967, 1969 by Herbert Jenkins Ltd

This 124th edition published 1969
by Herbert Jenkins Ltd
2 Clement's Inn, London WC2

SBN 257 65052 0

Printed in Great Britain by
Cox & Wyman Ltd
London, Reading and Fakenham

# PREFACE

TO THE ONE HUNDRED AND TWENTY-FOURTH EDITION

This 124th Edition of ENQUIRE WITHIN, called for so soon after the publication of the completely revised 123rd Edition, has been even further revised and brought up to date by the inclusion of sections on decimal currency and the metric system. More than ever it justifies its claim to be the most famous book of domestic reference in the world, providing a mine of practical information and knowledge indispensable to the needs of modern men and women and their families.

By far the greater part of the information and advice offered in this volume will be found to be of permanent service and utility. Certain information, however, correct as we go to press, may be subject to change at any time – for example, international currency rates, addresses of organisations, Income Tax requirements and National Health and National Insurance benefits. Such details, when need arises, should be checked with current Press quotations, the appropriate Ministry or through one of the sources of information indicated herein. It is sensible, too, in such as legal and medical matters to seek professional advice in specific cases: the information offered here is for general guidance only.

The contributors to this 124th edition include Roy Hay, the well-known garden authority; Dr. E. Anthony, M.D., J.P.; Alan Chalkley, B.Comm., A.C.I.S., financial author and journalist; Iain Wickenden, M.A., LL.B.; Paul Martin, the travel expert; Pamela Vandyke Price, author and journalist specialising in food and wine; Professor H. C. Dent, B.A., F.R.S.A., Hon.F.E.I.S., formerly Editor of *Times Educational Supplement*, and many others.

To these and to all who have in any way shared in the preparation of this new edition the Publishers express their grateful thanks.

# CONTENTS

# BEAUTY AND FASHION

Beauty in women is an idea that is capable of many different interpretations. At one period in history the buxom blonde was the type most admired, at another the angular brunette. What would have been considered the disfigurement of freckles in the nineteenth century is nowadays thought of as an additional charm on certain faces. Of course, the outstandingly beautiful woman may well be outside the currently fashionable idea of what is beautiful in her type, but there are very few people likely to be worried or to require advice about this! Certainly, there have probably never been so many different types of beauty admired at one time as there are today, and therefore, although fashions do change, ideas are very liberal on this point. Study of the fashion magazines will give an idea of what is currently smart.

What is perhaps even more important, however, is that never before has it been so easy for a woman to make herself pleasing and attractive and to create an impression of beauty. As it is always more agreeable to be surrounded by people who are good looking, it may be regarded as part of a social duty to make the best of oneself and it is noticeable that often the women who give the impression of being outstanding in this respect are usually well aware of their own limitations and short-comings and not vain even about their good points.

**Self-Respect.** The presentation of the individual as pleasing to the senses is also of definite value as regards maintaining morale. The great physician, Sir William Osler, once said "for a woman, there is nothing much more important in life than to look well", and those who have charge of the sick are frequently able to remark on the improvement in health and spirits that is given by quite simple means, such as a new hair-do, a becoming bed-jacket, a manicure or lavish use of scent or cologne. No one can look radiant throughout their life and for twenty-four hours of every day, but a moderate pride in the appearance is instrumental in the maintenance of self-respect.

## CLEANLINESS

Although there are great beauties whose charms are not impaired even when they are dirty from some domestic task, there can be none who achieve or maintain beauty when they are never clean. A clean and healthy face and body has a natural attraction. This sort of cultivation of beauty is something that every mother can inculcate in her daughter from an early age. Different people require different attention, both according to their physical types and ages and to the lives they live and some ideas for basic beauty and cleanliness will be given later on. At this point it is enough perhaps to say that many minor complaints about which people consult their doctors may well be the result of insufficient personal cleanliness.

## WHEN TO CONSULT THE DOCTOR

There are, however, some conditions and beauty problems that require expert advice and treatment. Fortunately the medical profession nowadays recognises the right of every woman to look her best and the general practitioner will usually be sympathetic about recommending a specialist to deal with certain disabilities that impair attractiveness.

**Bad Skin and Acne.** Any serious disfigurement due to recurrent spots, boils and pimples can be very depressing. The teenager, in particular, may well need specialised attention relating to this problem and parents should not hesitate to ask advice, as the scars left on the face by bad attacks of acne can remain for a lifetime, although (see pp. 11 and 21) it is now possible even to deal with these to the benefit of the sufferer. Advice on cleansing and making up the skin of an acne sufferer should also be sought from either a skin specialist or a qualified beautician. Nowadays there are many medicated preparations which can heal and prevent the spread of any infection and it is worth while getting the benefit of these.

**Allergies.** Strictly speaking, one is only "allergic" to shellfish, but the term has come to assume the significance of anything which produces certain undesirable reactions in the body – for example, people who get puffy swellings immediately after eating certain foods, those who develop rashes or sores, those who evince some signs of internal irritation, and so on. Something that may not be appreciated is that, at different times in one's life, one may develop an intolerance to certain foods that have previously been enjoyed without any ill effects. It is some consolation to know also that the bad reaction may, in a few years, cease to work in this way. People who have any history of allergies in their families, whose relations suffer from skin complaints, hay fever, asthma, migraine, should mention this to their doctors if they begin to suspect that they themselves are developing an intolerance to certain substances. Ranges of cosmetics for people whose skins are irritated by even the best of ordinary preparations are now fortunately not scarce and, again, advice should be taken about obtaining and using these, either for good or until the condition that has produced the reaction is brought under control.

**Falling Hair (Alopecia).** Sometimes as a result of an illness, accident or severe shock, people lose their hair, either generally or from patches in the head, at an alarming rate. Medical advice should definitely be sought and, although this is a most unpleasant complaint, the sufferer should be reassured that the hair nearly always grows again, though the time this takes may seem interminable. The excellent wigs, wiglets

and switches of hair now widely available are a tremendous help in enabling anyone to cope with social life at such a time.

**Superfluous Hair.** Some advice will be given farther on about dealing with the minor manifestations of this, but there are two periods in a woman's life – the onset of puberty and the menopause or change of life – when she may be troubled by unexpectedly heavy growths of hair on body or face. This is again a matter about which medical advice should be sought to avoid any distress incurred during this happening and very often the growth can be controlled or banished, purely by medical means. Take your doctor's advice before trying to do anything about the problem yourself.

**Chilblains and Bad Circulation.** When chilblains are severe, they can be disfiguring as well as painful. The doctor will not only advise immediate treatment, but can give much help to enable the chilblain-prone person avoid letting them develop seriously. It is bad luck that many people in this category have the fine, delicate skin so greatly envied by others.

Bad circulation can be related to the chilblain problem and the woman whose nose turns purplish red as a result either of this or some similar condition, also requires advice from her doctor.

**Bad Digestion and Bad Breath.** The one does not necessarily mean the other but the two can be related and as bad breath (halitosis) in its severe forms can affect sufferers, especially at times when they are under any nervous strain, it is a grave social disadvantage. The person who is a severe sufferer should certainly consult the doctor.

**Constipation.** The British people tend to be rather fanatical on this subject – rather as the French are about their livers. In general a great deal of unnecessary fuss is made about being "regular" and the person who lives a moderately active life and eats a reasonably balanced diet should not worry that the body may not eliminate the substances which it does not require with clock-like precision. If you feel and look well, it is advisable to leave the gut alone! If, of course, there is discomfort or any side effects from what seems to be a chronic state of constipation, the doctor must be consulted. Usually, a reasonable amount of liquid in the diet, plus the sort of "bulk" taken by means of brown bread and vegetables, will keep this part of the body working satisfactorily. The occasional dose of "health salts" especially if one has been eating and drinking heavily, is of course helpful, but the regular use of an aperient or laxative is about as sensible as tying up a perfectly healthy arm in a sling or putting a healthy leg in a splint. Anyone who rushes to "take something" when they feel the slightest internal discomfort may risk damaging the delicate interior membranes and no one who is in the slightest degree gastrically upset should take a laxative without their doctor's approval, as this may do definite damage.

**Warts and Blotches.** These again may appear with greater frequency at the time of puberty and the menopause or after and sometimes they merely disappear again. In fact, they are seldom as unsightly as the owners often seem to think and sometimes pass quite unnoticed as far as friends and even relations are concerned. But it is better, if you feel worried about them, to seek the advice of an expert through your doctor rather than risk damaging your skin by trying to get rid of them yourself.

**Puffy Ankles.** Anyone who suddenly has to do a lot of standing may find her ankles swell and this can also occur during pregnancy. But if it seems in the slightest degree serious, or the kind of condition that has come to stay, seek medical advice at once, as it may be an alarm warning of a possibly more serious trouble.

**Varicose Veins.** This is something which no longer need distress any woman. Ideally, of course, it is a condition which should be dealt with in its early stages before the legs are seriously disfigured, but modern surgery, with minimal pain involved, can not only remove the disfigurement completely, but bring new life to the tired leg. See your doctor as early as possible if you have trouble of this kind.

**Plastic Surgery.** Enormous advances are made in this field of specialised surgery every few months. It is now even possible to shorten a too-tall person. The correction of features such as large or mis-shapen noses, outstanding ears, pendulous breasts and severe scarring may, of course, involve considerable expense, but as doctors now recognise the grave distress suffered by people with such disfigurements, which can really warp their approach to life, some of even the most complicated plastic operations can sometimes be achieved through the National Health Service. It is worth noting that naturally the younger a person is at the time of major plastic operations, the more successful will be the healing and the easier for the subject to adjust to being more attractive.

Face-lifting and nose remodelling are in rather a special category. At one time the former tended to take away the mobility of the face, but this is no longer true. It is a minor operation which can have a wonderfully rejuvenating effect if, once again, it is not carried out when age has advanced. It is also one that can be repeated, even several times. Many women would rather have a present of this kind for their fiftieth birthday than a piece of jewellery. As far as nose bobbing or remodelling is concerned, this may be very important to a woman whose appearance plays an important part in her work. Someone who is a model, anybody having to be repeatedly photographed, or appear at certain types of public function when her attractiveness is of paramount importance, should pay for the best advice she can afford in this respect.

**Dentistry.** As will be mentioned in the routines for regular beauty care, visits to the dentist are a "must" both for health and attractiveness. But cosmetic dentistry is something that can be very helpful to people who have malformed jaws or unattractive teeth – and again, the younger a person is when work of this kind is undertaken, the more satisfactory and long lasting will be the results. It is not necessary nowadays for anyone to have a violently receding chin, aggressively protruding teeth, or irregular and discoloured teeth.

**Glasses.** Glasses today are definitely an important fashion accessory, whether or not they are required to improve or correct the sight of the wearer. No disadvantage of any kind is attached to wearing them – indeed, as they invariably enlarge the eyes as far as other people are concerned, the wearer of glasses has this distinct advantage! It is also worth pointing out that very often people who appear to develop defects of sight in youth may have these corrected and completely cured by the right advice given early on – something for mothers to remember. When choosing spectacle frames, it is worthwhile investing in the best you can afford and choosing these with the aid of someone experienced in advising on the type likely to be not only the most comfortable, but enhancing to the face. Indeed, a "wardrobe" of different types of frames for different conditions is something that the person who wears glasses continually should try and acquire.

For those who are rarely comfortable with the ordinary type of spectacles, contact lenses are now in a very advanced stage, and may even be worn for long periods of time. They are not cheap, of course, as they are a highly individual precision product, and anyone planning to invest in them should seek the advice of an authority on the subject, have them properly fitted and generally experiment as to see whether they will be satisfactory for him or her. The abandonment of even the most comfortable glasses can make a tremendous psychological difference and therefore the use of the contact lens should never be regarded as either too expensive or too complicated to consider.

## EXERCISES, MASSAGE AND CORSETRY

Lack of proportion in the body can be helped considerably by keeping this healthy, with muscles toned-up and firm (though not over-developed), cultivating graceful deportment and wearing the right kind of clothes over appropriate foundation garments. The whole shape of the body, however, cannot be radically changed if certain features are a matter of heredity; if your parents and grandparents are all short people, inclined to be pear-shaped, it is unlikely that you will achieve the height and lean frame of a professional model. But exercises can be very useful in a society where so many people either lead sedentary lives or else only make use of a limited number of muscles in the body in the ordinary course of the day's routine, and massage can also be of great help in relaxing severe tension and encouraging people to avoid the unattractive deportment that tension often produces.

As regards corsetry, this can often adapt and redispose the flesh of the body so as to provide the right kind of "clothes horse" for certain garments, but it should be emphasised that the healthy body has a built-in system of supports for itself which, properly used and kept in trim, will provide a better foundation for all but the extremes of fashion than anything man-made. The idea that the healthy body "needs support" is erroneous, except for people who, as a result of disabilities of various kinds, have received medical advice in this respect.

## SOME BEAUTY ORGANISATIONS

**Beauty Farms (or Health Hydros).** In recent years, these have taken the place of the elaborate public baths of classical times and the spas of the pre-1914 era. They provide an opportunity for complete relaxation, combined with advice from expert beauticians and frequently a certain amount of medical treatment such as the ordinary person may find helpful in general. Some of these establishments are very luxurious and expensive, others more reasonable and they also vary considerably according to the type of treatment involved. For example, some are vegetarian.

Most do have, either on their staff or as a supervising consultant, a qualified medical practitioner, though it should be noted that some of these may not be doctors whose qualifications are recognised by the British Medical Association. This does not mean they are not perfectly adequately qualified for their job, but it may be that their ideas do not coincide with standard medical practice in the United Kingdom, so anybody considering visiting a beauty farm should mention the matter to their own doctor and show him or her a prospectus indicating what is involved, and, in the event of being already undergoing treatment, should get him to contact the consultant at the establishment concerned, in case any specialised adaptation of procedure is necessary.

**Beauty Clinics.** Most cities and large towns have clinics where highly trained and qualified beauticians are able to give specialised advice and treatment both about make-up and general beauty care and certain specific problems such as skin blemishes, superfluous hair, and similar matters. It is important, of course, to consult such establishments only if you are sure that they are responsible and ethical organisations, and that the individuals concerned with smaller clinics have the necessary qualifications.

**Beauty Salons.** Most of the large cosmetic houses have salons in cities and large towns, some of them very elaborate, in which one can spend as much as a day at a time undergoing a complete beauty treatment and where detailed advice on any of the establishment's products may always be obtained.

Even if it is not an economic proposition to visit either a beauty salon or a beauty clinic regularly, many women (especially those whose careers necessitate their appearance being kept at its best), find enormous benefit, both physical and psychological, if they are able to treat themselves to a session on certain oc-

casions. If you have recovered from an illness, or even a long period of strain, had a baby, or are a bride in the hectic state of being about to be married, or a woman who has recently suffered a shock, even a single session or perhaps a series of short treatments can be enjoyable and beneficial.

Even if you have no reason to make frequent use of the services of a beauty salon or clinic, it is worth knowing that they will usually create a special make-up for a particular occasion, i.e. for a party or an evening when something out of the ordinary is required to go with a special dress, and so on. This can often be combined with a hair-do by the same establishment. This kind of thing is very helpful from time to time in a woman's life, so that she avoids sticking to the sort of make-up she adopted in her youth, which may sometimes give her a more elderly and dated appearance than she realises.

**Beauty Advisers.** Most large stores either enjoy the regular services or frequent visits of specialist beauty advisers from the different cosmetic companies. Very often a free make-up or one for which only a nominal charge is made will be given to customers. This can be of great use for people wanting to try out new preparations or a different range of cosmetics from those they usually buy. Some concerns, too, send representatives travelling around to visit women in their own homes, to advise them and give them an opportunity of sampling products. Recently there has been an increase in the practice of this, along American lines, whereby the cosmetics may be offered at what seems a very much lower retail price, simply because they are not advertised in any way and do not incur the sort of expenditure involved when marketed through ordinary shops.

## ALLIES TO BEAUTY

It is first and foremost in the interests of everyone to keep themselves clean. It is not necessary to be fanatical about this in order to achieve the healthy ideal, and cleanliness is possibly the greatest single

factor contributing to beauty. With
cleanliness goes fragrance, because
everyone has an individual bodily smell,
however slight, and the fragrance of
clean healthy skin and hair is in itself an
attraction.

Below are listed some routines for
basic cleanliness and health, all of which
should be used as a check list by anyone
who wishes to be and remain attractive.
It is, of course, not necessary for the
very young to adopt the same routines
as the middle-aged or elderly, nor for
those living in the clean air of the
country to follow the same stringent
rules for cleansing which are obligatory
to those living in a town, but if reasonably cared for, the body should function
efficiently and be pleasing – surely
sufficient justification?

Although many great writers have
attempted to define charm, this is an
elusive quality, one that overrides all
considerations of mere physical beauty,
achievements of any kind, and even the
ravages of time. Many women who have
earned tremendous reputations for being
beautiful have kept these into extreme
old age and very often their admirers are
incapable of describing their beauty,
only being able to delight in the charm
emanating from them. The vivacity of
someone in health and good spirits, who
retains a lively mind, receptive to what
is going on in the world and willing to
interest others, creates a type of charm
that is invaluable.

**BEAUTY ROUTINES**

**Deodorising.** Everyone, as has been said,
has an individual bodily smell (this is
neither pleasant nor unpleasant, but
individual) and everybody gets dirty,
however much or little their activity.
But the combination of that dirt which
arrives on the person from outside and
the excretions from the skin in the form
of sweat are never attractive if allowed
to remain. A daily bath should be considered as a matter of course, though if
for any reason this is not possible the
body should at least be sponged all over
with soap and water. It is a matter of
personal taste and convenience whether
the bath is taken in the morning or

evening, but it is important that, after
you have removed the dirt from your
body in the water, you should rinse your
skin, either by means of a shower, or
merely by pouring clean water over
yourself.

Use of cool or cold water with which
to do this closes the pores and stimu-
lates the circulation, as does vigorous
rubbing with a rough towel and this can
also remove more dirt and grease that
the ordinary bathing procedures have
not shifted from the skin. The use of
either a deodorant (which removes the
risk of the offence of the smell of stale
perspiration) or an anti-perspirant (which
actually checks a heavy flow of sweat) is
an essential part of daily bathing procedure, both for men as well as women.
Those whose work involves their wearing dark or black clothing constantly
should take particular care in this respect as, when one cannot see that a
garment is dirty, it is all too easy to go
on wearing it when it is decidedly not
fresh. It is worth while pointing out at
this stage that very few people have
their clothes cleaned as often as is required, but the amount of grit and grease
held in garments, especially those worn
in towns, is damaging to the most expensive fabric, and therefore it is a false
economy to postpone having them
cleaned. Whenever possible, of course,
clothes worn next to the body should be
washed and washed frequently.

Particular care should be taken to
preserve personal freshness at the time
of menstruation – a woman's monthly
period. Ideally, it should be possible for
her to wash herself every time she
changes whatever form of sanitary
protection she uses, and to dispose of
this immediately. For those whose professional activities make it impossible
for them to wash in this way, the use of
tissues impregnated with a mild disinfectant is recommended as both refreshing
and deodorising. There are also excellent
spray deodorising preparations made
specifically for the purpose of counteracting bodily odour in the anal and
vaginal regions. Mothers should take
particular care to inform their daughters
about these, as young women often
suffer great embarrassment at the be-

ginning of menstruation and need both reassurance and information. Many chemists and manufacturers of sanitary equipment of this kind also issue excellent booklets of information which parents and young women may find of great help.

**Scent.** The use of a particular scent which becomes associated with the individual who wears it is a most powerful charm. As, however, the individual skin and its natural oils have the effect of slightly changing even the most expensive scent, toilet water or cologne, it is essential to try and use scent on your own skin before deciding whether or not to buy it. Put a little either in the palm of the hand or the pulse point at the wrist, allow it to dry and then see what it smells like. Toilet waters and colognes are lighter versions of the concentrated scent and can be used when a very heavy fragrance is not required. When testing scents, try only a few at a time, or you may find your sense of smell becomes confused after three or four different fragrances.

Many people like to choose one scent for daytime and another for evening wear, possibly with other toilet preparations to match. It is a good idea, anyway, to change around occasionally, because the wearer of a particular scent gets so accustomed to it that she is unable to enjoy it herself when she wears it.

Scent should always be kept out of the light, in a drawer and not on the dressing-table, and unless you use a great deal, it is better to buy a comparatively small bottle at a time, rather than risk the last drops in a bottle deteriorating, which even the best can do with constant exposure to the air. The best way to apply scent is with a spray, but this should always be directed on to the skin or the hair and not on to clothes or furs, which may become stained and on which any smell of stale scent can be very disagreeable. If you want your underwear, furs or handkerchiefs to be lightly scented, however, you can keep them in close contact with the scented sachets specially made for the purpose, or use pads of cotton-wool on which you

sprinkle a few drops of the scent. The ideal places for the application of scent are the pulse points, where the skin is thin – the wrists, under the ears, at the temples, throat, elbows and, most curiously, the inside of the knees, where the scent will remain for longer than at any other part of the body.

**Cleansing.** Somebody once said that cleansing cream was the most useful cosmetic – certainly, very few people realise, until they see a professional clean their faces, how much dirt remains on the skin. This, in the end, inevitably produces open or blocked pores and wrinkles. Even for those who use a minimum of make-up, this must be removed as thoroughly as possible every night.

Many people find the use of soap on their skin to be drying. There are, however, superfatted and other medicated soaps which need not have this effect, and a preliminary cleansing with soap and water is something that should only be avoided in extreme cases. One caution, however – the face-flannel can be both a source of infection and an inadequate face-cleanser. Unless you can boil this every other day and be sure of rinsing it thoroughly after use, it is better either to apply the soap and water with the fingertips or, best of all, with one of the small complexion brushes (rather like a soft shaving-brush) which really let the soap do its work and at the same time stimulate the skin. After drying, the face should be cleansed, not once but as many times as is necessary to remove all traces of make-up, either with cream or with cream and a cleansing lotion. Never be uneconomical about using plenty of cotton-wool (it need not be the most expensive kind) or tissues for this purpose. You don't want to spread back on the skin the old make-up you have removed. After removing every trace of make-up, paying particular attention to such danger spots as the sides of the nose, along the hairline, the eyebrows and under the eyes, the skin should be refreshed with a light tonic or similar lotion, and it is then up to the individual to decide whether she needs a skin food, or one of the moisturising creams or lotions now so popular. Older women have a tendency to dry skin and younger ones to greasy skin and advice should be sought as to what is most suitable at different times of life.

An elementary but essential part of beauty care is the regular cleaning of anything in close contact with the face, hair and body. Powder-puffs should be washed frequently and brushes and combs likewise.

At the same time that the face is cleansed, attention should be paid to the neck. Too often the neck betrays the age of a woman whose face still looks young! The routine for the face should be followed for the neck, but as the use of dark clothes and certain forms of necklines can really stain the neck and throat, it is sometimes necessary to use even more cleansing preparations, and also to ask advice about some of the mildly bleaching preparations now on sale for the throat. In all cleansing operations, care should be taken not to stretch the skin too much, while being sure to remove all traces of dirt or make-up.

Most people find it helpful, at intervals varying to the type of skin and life and age of the individual, to use some kind of toning and stimulating lotion and a face-pack. The toning lotion is perhaps most helpful to people who are obliged to spend a lot of time indoors (a walk on a mild, slightly rainy day will do almost the same thing for the skin) especially in centrally heated houses. They will also probably require richer creams for the face. A face pack, of course, of which there are many kinds available for home use, can be wonderfully helpful before a special date or to give the skin a bit of a holiday at regular intervals.

**Eye Care.** Whether you do or do not wear glasses, your eyes should occasionally be treated to an eye-bath or one of the soothing medications applied with a proper medicated pad which are specially refreshing for people who do a lot of close work or who have been driving. These pads are also very efficacious in banishing the swelling induced by a fit of crying. Any inflammation of the eyes or eyelids, is a matter that requires expert and immediate attention. Those who spend a lot of time indoors should seize the chance of enjoying long vision whenever they can.

**Teeth.** Ideally, the teeth should be brushed (with an up-and-down as well as a side-to-side movement) after every meal. Those for whom this is not possible should be extra scrupulous about morning and evening brushing. It is also worth while experimenting with tooth powder as well as toothpaste, as sometimes the one seems to give more satisfactory results than the other. Tooth brushes should be frequently renewed and, if possible, not left exposed to dust and flies when they are not in use. A great variety of tooth brushes are available at low cost and one with the right type of bristle and of the right size should be selected for the individual mouth. If you cannot get the advice of your dentist about this, a good chemist will usually be helpful. Dental floss should be used regularly by people who have spaces between their teeth in which food tends to collect; some people believe that the reason why certain continental countries have good teeth is because it is not considered bad mannered to employ a tooth-pick after meals. Whether you do this or not, the removal of every kind of foodstuff from the mouth and the regular cleansing of the mouth and teeth is of great importance.

Exactly the same sort of care should be taken with false teeth and plates of any kind, and the dentist will always advise on the most up-to-date preparations for cleaning them and for treating the mouth of the wearer.

Economy practised on your teeth is invariably a false economy and anyone who loses teeth which are not quickly replaced will find that the shape of the face alters considerably, usually giving an impression of age.

**Hair.** Whether the hair is long or short, it must be regularly brushed and regularly washed. For greasy hair, especially if the owner lives in a town, it may be necessary to shampoo the head every four to five days; those with a dry scalp can usually go a little longer, but this is a matter for the individual to decide. The type of shampoo used and any preparation with which the hair is dressed afterwards is also very much a matter of individual taste, though fortunately most of these preparations are available in individual or small-sized packs so that one can experiment.

If a woman is not able to have her hair done professionally very often, it is of the greatest importance that she chooses a style she can easily manage for herself, and this nearly always means that the initial cut must be of as high a standard as it is possible for her to afford. The same applies to permanent waving (ideally, this should be carried out three or four times a year, so that the hair never gets out of hand) and to any tinting and colouring that is more than a rinse, which can be easily used at home. All preparations applied to the head can have a definite effect upon the skin and therefore anything strong should only be used under the supervision of an experienced hairdresser, or with milder products, with strict adherence to the manufacturers' instructions.

The whole question of hair-colouring has recently undergone a tremendous change. Very attractive effects may be produced by slightly changing even the natural colour of the hair of an older woman (whose skin will probably have changed anyway) and, for those who feel inclined, exotic effects such as streaks, highlights, and the application of actual colours, such as blue or even green, can, when skilfully carried out, be charming. It should be borne in mind, however, that it is very rare for a head of hair in its completely natural state to be absolutely of one colour, and therefore if a solid colour is applied to the hair this can look definitely artificial. A hair-colouring that contrasts sharply with the skin can be very beautiful in a young woman, but may produce an effect of hardness and age if the skin and contours of the face have begun to age.

As regards style, this must be studied in accordance with what is currently fashionable and also to suit the individual at different times of her life. With the many wigs and hair pieces now avail-able a complete change of style is easily possible for special occasions. One important point, however, is that, for the older woman, hair falling below the jawline is rarely becoming, even if by some means it can be kept impeccably groomed. The way in which the head is set on the neck can be a charm that it is a pity always to hide and any woman who has longish hair into middle age will find that the collars of her coats and dresses tend to become grubby.

With the adolescent, or anyone who has spots or skin troubles on their face, particular care should be taken to ensure that the hair is both clean and does not come into contact with the affected piece of skin. Hair is very difficult to keep completely clean and therefore anyone running their hands through their hair and afterwards touching their face, or letting their hair fall over their faces, risks spreading infection from one place to another.

**Hands.** In these days when every woman's hands tend to be subjected to a certain amount of severe wear and tear, extra care and protection of them is advisable. If you can, make regular use of a barrier cream before embarking on a lot of washing, dusting or heavy cleaning, or any particularly dirty work, wear gloves for rough work wherever possible (rubber ones for preparing vegetables, cotton or old leather ones for household cleaning) and, when you have cleansed your hands after work, automatically use some cream or lotion. Do not use very hot water to wash with immediately before going out or exposing the hands to the wind.

Whether or not you have your nails professionally manicured, it is important to keep them trimmed and clean, with the cuticles pushed down. If you have trouble with splitting nails, use one of the many good preparations now available to remedy this, and of course see that any stains are removed from hands and nails and that nail-varnish, if used, is always immaculate. Unless you can be sure of keeping it so, it is better merely to polish your nails, as nothing looks worse than chipped, unkept nail-varnish.

Some people regard the use of even brilliantly coloured lacquer as routine as that of lipstick, while others find such accentuation of the finger nails unpleasant. It is a matter of personal taste, but it is worth noting that the use of a brilliant nail-varnish on a short, square or plump hand can give the effect of the fingers having been abruptly cut off. If you are in any doubt, the best course is to experiment for yourself inexpensively and, if you like the result, to take advice and use the professional services of a manicurist when possible. Ideally, only emery-boards should be used for filing the nails, and scissors only for any cutting of cuticles that may be necessary.

The use of many different washing preparations these days can present problems for the hands, either by causing actual skin irritation or excessive drying and splitting. If this happens, change the detergent you think responsible, treat your hands to extra care with a softening lotion and, if the matter does not clear up within a few days, consult your doctor.

**Superfluous Hair.** Hair under the arms should be regularly removed if you wear sleeveless dresses. The same applies to unsightly down on the arms or legs which are, of course, exposed or seen through transparent fabrics. There are a variety of preparations to remove hair, and a wax treatment will also do this professionally. You may also use a razor, though this can seem to increase the toughness of the hair that grows afterwards. It is of supreme importance that any preparations used should only be applied in exact accordance with the manufacturers' instructions, which usually include the advice to make a preliminary test on the skin.

Unsightly odd hairs on the face may either be bleached into inconspicuousness or carefully removed with tweezers. Both the tweezers and the area of skin involved should be scrupulously clean. With unruly eyebrows, the plucking should always be done from underneath the brow. Professional brow-shaping is something that a good hairdresser or beauty salon will undertake for you if required.

If hair growing on any other part of the body is such as to be unsightly or a source of embarrassment, it can usually be removed by any of the methods suggested above, and pubic hair, which can be unsightly to the wearer of a very brief bathing costume, can be trimmed with scissors. Thick growths of bodily hair should be treated only by the qualified expert.

The criterion is entirely one of what is pleasant and seemly and it is worth pointing out that in many countries hair on the arms, legs or breasts of a woman is considered attractive.

## BEAUTY CARE IN SPECIAL CIRCUMSTANCES

**Travelling.** Perhaps the greatest problem about preserving a fresh-looking appearance when travelling is to keep clean. If the journey involves visiting cities or industrial areas, it is best to wear dark clothes and keep the hair and hands covered, with a fresh pair of gloves to put on when you arrive. There are many preparations – impregnated pads and tissues – with which the hands and face may be cleaned or blotted, even if a cloakroom is not readily accessible, and the use of a cologne or toilet water can be particularly refreshing and stimulating.

If possible, avoid wearing clothes that crush or mark easily when travelling and anything that is tight, which can tire you. If, for a plane journey, you can put on a pair of soft slippers, this can be a great help, and if anyone has to travel overnight on a plane, it is a good idea to blot off any surplus make-up before trying to go to sleep, loosen anything tight around the waist (and release at least the back suspenders of any girdle, even if you do not roll your stockings down) and try and choose a light silk or jersey garment, which will be soothing and uncrushable, for the basis of your travelling outfit. For anyone travelling in a country with a hot climate, it should be borne in mind that anything tightly fitting will increase the feeling of heat. Absorbent materials, such as cotton, and smooth ones, such as silk, are more suitable than 100 per cent synthetics, which can be very hot, though nowadays there are many materials made combining the advantages of natural and synthetic fibres. For travelling in hot countries especially, it is often more comfortable to have at least part of the arms and neck loosely covered by some soft material than to leave them completely exposed, and of course comfortable shoes on any journey are essential, especially if, due to heat or atmospheric changes, the feet are likely to swell.

Many women find trousers or ski-pants particularly suitable for travelling and nowadays such outfits can be very smart as well. If you do wear them, however, it is worth while making sure that they will not cause critical comment in the country in which you are to arrive or to any hosts who may be meeting you.

**Heat and Sunshine.** No one accustomed to the temperate, rather humid climate of the British Isles should expose themselves suddenly to long hours of sunshine and heat without taking precautions against this. The skin needs protection, by means of any of the numerous good preparations available against burning, and sun-bathing should be undertaken gradually. Remember that, even on a dull-seeming day, you may get seriously burnt unless your skin is protected, and this is particularly true of anyone by the sea or on a boat. Preparations for promoting a sun-tanned appearance do not always have the protective ingredients that protect against sunburn, so check this when you are buying them. This applies also to leg and arm make-up and any of the "quick tan" preparations.

Even with the skin thoroughly anointed, though, continuous exposure to sun and wind can be harmful until you are used to it, so a little judicious covering up from time to time with a loose jacket, light blouse or skirt can prevent trouble. Excessive sun-tanning can have a coarsening and ageing effect on the skin of any woman past her first youth and there are some people, who are definitely better-looking while they remain pale-skinned, who do not court tanning indiscriminately.

It goes without saying that your feet, when exposed in sandals or barefoot, should be sightly and well cared for. If you cannot manage this, keep them partly covered with soft slippers – which are kinder to the unhardened soles of the feet, anyway, on many beaches brought up to high temperature by constant sun.

Although sun-glasses are useful for people reading or driving in a strong light or for counteracting the glare of water, the eyes benefit by a moderate amount of sunlight and should not be over-protected from it. It is refreshing, however, to make occasional use of eye-drops or eye-masks, especially in these conditions.

**Extremes of Cold.** Anyone going on a winter sports holiday or to any part of the world where they will meet with extremes of cold, should invest in the special preparations now widely available to protect the skin both against the cold and, where there is likely to be sun as well, against this, too. The body and particularly the extremities must be kept warm, of course, and it is usually easier and more comfortable to do this by means of several comparatively light layers of clothing than a single heavy one. Any store stocking winter sports equipment will have experts to advise on this, down to details such as underwear and gloves and caps. Special goggles for use in snow are also easily obtained.

**Housework.** Mention has already been made of the advisability of making use of barrier creams and gloves to protect the hands in any kind of wet, dry or dirty work – ironing, as well as dusting, can really dry up the skin of the hands harmfully. The hair, likewise, should be covered when you are dusting or doing heavy cleaning and also, if possible, when any cooking involving smells is undertaken, as the hair picks up and retains cooking odours unpleasantly.

The woman who is very tired by housework should try and get even a short period of rest in between her various activities and this will be most effective if she can sit or lie down with her legs raised above her body; there are special chairs in which the foot-rest can be raised to achieve this, or you can lie on the bed with only a flat pillow under your head and several under your legs. Even fifteen minutes of relaxation in such a position can be very refreshing. Whenever you sit down, put your feet up if possible and, if you are working at a desk or sewing-table, either rest them on a cross-bar, hassock or footstool – this can make a tremendous difference.

Shoes chosen for housework should have low or flat substantial heels and give the foot some support; never get into the habit of doing your housework in soft slippers, as this can result in the feet spreading and, especially with older people, many dangerous falls are caused by people stumbling, slipping or being unsure of their footing because they are wearing bedroom slippers.

Finally, it cannot be too strongly emphasised that every woman will find housework less monotonous and herself in better spirits if, no matter what she is doing, she is wearing practical but reasonably attractive clothes – overalls and house-dresses these days are usually very pretty and far more morale-raising than one's worn-out sweaters and skirts – with a moderate amount of care devoted to her face and hair during these activities. Then, no matter who comes to the door, she will have no need to apologise for her appearance.

**Pregnancy.** It is an old tradition founded on considerable fact that very often women look radiantly beautiful during pregnancy and when they are lactating. But at a time of such great changes in the body, it is both soothing and helpful to the morale to pay extra attention to the regular beauty routines and, of course, to let your doctor know if you notice any major change in, say, your hair, your nails or your skin. Your dentist, too, should check on your teeth and, even if you do not make regular use of a professional chiropodist, extra attention to the feet can be very relaxing when the weight of the baby begins to make you tired. Your hairdresser should be consulted about a style that is going to be

both becoming and easy for you when you are actually having the baby and immediately afterwards. Maternity clothes these days are not only becoming, but high fashion, so there need not be any difficulty about an expectant mother looking attractive. But it is generally considered that, as one tends to get very bored with the same clothes at such a time, it is better to have several outfits that are comparatively inexpensive and that may be then either worn out or passed on to friends rather than two or three "good" things that provide no variety.

In general, clothes should be chosen of a style to take the attention of the beholder away from the waistline and direct it on the head and shoulders. The change in the bodily proportions also means a reappraisal of the choice of accessories, particularly hats and shoes. The latter, in particular, should be carefully chosen so that fatigue is avoided and so that the wearer does not risk losing her balance.

## BEAUTY PROBLEMS THAT CAN BE SOLVED OR HELPED

**Overweight.** The overweight person, as well as being less attractive than she might be, runs a considerable risk to the maintenance of health. There are a number of serious complaints which the overweight person risks incurring, and in addition, anyone expecting a baby or having to undergo an operation, suffers from a serious disadvantage if overweight. Even only a few pounds over the healthy average can cause tiredness.

The seriously overweight person should, of course, consult a doctor about this condition but generally the adoption of a sensible diet and a reappraisal of eating habits, so as to make the daily intake of food only what the particular individual requires, should produce the desired result. "Crash" slimming is something that can be highly inadvisable for the active person. There are many different diets, but the most sensible and medically approved are based on the restriction of the intake of the carbohydrate foods (starches and sugars). If anyone is in doubt as to whether she is genuinely overweight, most chemists have scales or charts of weights appropriate for men and women of different heights; if you are more than 5 to 7 lbs. in excess of these, it is time to take a critical look at yourself in the glass, and do something about your diet. It is not, as is commonly supposed, inevitable that, with age, surplus weight and fat are bound to accumulate. The fact that, as people get older, they tend to lead more sedentary lives while still eating in the same way as when they were young and very active, with the addition of many "between times" snacks if they are at home all day, is, as far as the healthy person is concerned, the main reason for "middle-age spread".

Anybody with a tendency to top-heaviness, with a big bust or very square shoulders, should avoid clothes that, either by cut or pattern, draw attention to the upper half of the body.

If you tend to be pear-shaped – and large numbers of people are – choose clothes that take the attention away from the hips and up to the shoulders and head.

People who are above or below the average in height may have special problems in choosing clothes sized for them, but it should be stressed that both smallness and tallness can be tremendous assets and it is far better to dress up to either of these than to try and minimise them.

Short people in general should avoid large-patterned and heavily textured materials, and an impression of bulkiness caused by a lot of folds of material; they should also not wear clothes that stress the line of the body – very short jackets, heavily indented waists, or puffed-out skirts. They should avoid big handbags, and the sort of fussy accessories that often tend to be thought suitable for the woman who is described as "petite".

Those who are tall should avoid very small handbags and tiny pieces of jewellery. The tall or large-boned woman should take care not to give an impression that her clothes have shrunk on her – three-quarter sleeves, clothes that are tight around the shoulders and neck, and skirts and slacks that accentuate the hip bones.

**Underweight.** This tends to be more difficult to remedy than overweight, and medical advice should be taken, especially if the condition has arisen suddenly as a result of some illness or strain. But no underweight person should merely eat in abundance all the foods forbidden to the fat person; health will be improved and maintained with an increased intake of protein foods and, possibly, by some alteration in eating habits so that, for example, people may take more milk by having a glass or two at intervals during the day.

**Scarred Skin.** If this is not a matter for surgery, then expert advice should be taken about make-up. There are now several preparations that give virtually total concealment of scars. Some of the cosmetic houses make preparations suitable for this purpose and a good beauty clinic should also be able to advise.

For a temporary blemish, such as the scar after a boil or a bad spot, or a minor cut, once the skin has healed, the discoloration may be concealed by make-up. If the ordinary foundation is not sufficient, use a heavier cream or liquid on the particular area affected, bearing in mind that a darker shade will make any mark less conspicuous, whereas a very light tone will highlight it.

For those who have any scars on their legs, either temporary or permanent, and who do not wish to wear thickish stockings all the time, the many types of leg make-up can be very helpful. Care should be taken, of course, in choosing the colour of the stockings to go over the made-up leg, as these can change the way they look considerably.

**Problem Legs and Feet.** Very few people have completely straight legs, but anyone who has serious bandiness or knock-knees should avoid wearing straight and tight skirts, which inevitably emphasize the legs as these emerge from them. Even a single pleat or slight fullness can draw the attention away satisfactorily. For very fat legs, stockings of slightly dark shades should be chosen – naturally in accordance with what is fashionable and the colour of the clothes being worn

– and those who have very thin legs can give an illusion of slight plumpness by choosing lighter stockings. There are even leg cosmetics, which can give the impression of more shapeliness – the principle being that shading of a pinkish tan can create an impression of the leg going in and a highlight of pale colour can bring the shin or ankle bone into greater prominence.

People who have thick ankles or fat feet should avoid wearing any type of shoe that draws the eye to these features; straps and elaborate fastenings should not be worn and an elongated or slightly pointed shoe will make the foot look slimmer. If your feet have become unsightly, do not wear shoes that expose toes or heels and take care to remove rough skin regularly, as well as pedicuring your feet and giving them regular applications of a body or hand lotion. This will not only keep them soft, but is remarkably refreshing. Indeed, it may be said with a certain amount of truth that if you look after your feet, your face will look after itself.

**Dingy Skin.** Even the most scrupulously clean person may well find that, after the winter, the neck, arms and shoulders appear sallow and almost grimy in the first brilliant sunshine. This is the time to cleanse the surface of the body with additional care and thoroughness, either by means of a Turkish bath or Sauna, which will get rid of a tremendous amount of accumulated grime, or for a routine of special cleansing and toning and bleaching packs, such as are made by most good cosmetic houses. The feet and legs should not be overlooked in this bodily spring-cleaning process. People with a sallow or dark skin, or the kind of very fair skin that tends to darken with age, should avoid choosing clothes that too nearly approximate to their skin colour. A contrast – of a soft kind where older people are concerned – will have the effect of lightening and brightening the skin. It can also make a face look very washed out if the colour of the eyes is too exactly repeated by the predominant colour of the clothes; try always to choose a lighter or a darker shade.

**The Shape of the Face.** A face that is too round, too square, with too heavy a jaw, or too prominent a chin, can have its proportions subtly adjusted by the right kind of hair style and make-up. Shading of the face is, of course, something which requires a little skill and practice, but in general dark tones of make-up tend to sink and minimise contours, light tones to bring out areas into prominence. Anybody who wears spectacles should be careful to note how they, too, may change the proportions of the face.

**Short Neck.** Anyone who feels this is a problem should avoid wearing choker style necklaces, high-necked dresses, high round collars and any neckline that directly cuts across the throat. Care should also be taken with the choice of scarves and hats, so that these do not give an impression of muffling the wearer's neck too much or, as it were, sitting down on the top of the head.

## GROOMING AND FASHION

In these days of clothes which are both reasonable in price and well styled and finished, there is no need for anyone to be dowdy, even on a tiny dress allowance. Of course, a wardrobe should be planned so as to include clothes appropriate for the life of the individual, and things such as winter coats, walking-shoes and anything that has to take constant hard wear – even if this only involves a coat and skirt being worn regularly to an office – should be carefully chosen and considered as a long-term investment. Gimmicky garments, likely to go out of fashion within months, and specialised clothes – such as sun-dresses, evening clothes and play clothes – need not be costly, as they may be worn less often.

The fashion magazines and window displays in the major stores and smart dress shops give guidance on fashion trends, and it is for each woman to observe these, take note of what suits her and adapt or adopt according to what is likely to be becoming and useful. However big your dress allowance, it is never necessary to be a slave to fashion to be well dressed. What is important is to have an open mind and be willing, at all ages, to experiment; nothing is more unsuccessful than the effect produced by a woman who dresses at 40 as she did at 25. Her proportions and individual style and mannerisms may have changed considerably, her skin may have darkened, or she may (indeed she should) be wearing quite a different kind of make-up and she may have altered the colour of her hair, or it may have altered of its own accord.

**Shopping.** Ideally, one should never go shopping for clothes in a hurry, but take time. If you are of the type who tends to be hustled into buying something by a forceful saleswoman, take a friend with you who will help you to say "No," until you are absolutely sure that the garment you buy both pleases you and does something for your appearance. You should, of course, also have made up your mind to a certain extent as to what you want to buy and for what purpose, and know approximately how much you are prepared to spend. Look at yourself in the garment in a full-length mirror and also from the back and sides – this is the view of you many people will see. Try to wear the same sort of underwear and accessories that you may be wearing with your ultimate purchase – strapless bra for a low-cut evening dress, town shoes for a town dress, a coat and skirt of the sort that will go on under your winter coat or raincoat if you're planning to buy one, and the right kind of foundation garment for anything close fitting. And, unless you are skilled at doing your own alterations or have found a shop with a fitter you can really trust, beware of having any major changes carried out on a garment in the hope that it may then suit and fit you – very often the result will be unsatisfactory and you would have done better (and saved money) by choosing something different.

**Choice of Clothes, Colours and Styles, and Accessories.** Although your clothes must be practically suitable for the kind of life you live, they need never be dull. The young woman may have a more

extensive wardrobe than her mother, simply because she is still experimenting with fashion and trying to find her individual style, but she need not spend more money; indeed, the young can often dress smartly and very cheaply, simply because a young woman does not usually need as much help from clothes and accessories (or wish them to last as long) as the woman of thirty plus. Fine fabrics, subtle cutting and details of finish, such as hand-sewn button-holes, lined skirts, hand-made gloves and shoes are all things that cost money. But there are certain general rules useful as guides in considering how to make the best of what one has, both as regards money and natural gifts.

*If you pass most of your time at home, with the family,* choose clothes that can be easily washed or cleaned, that will stand up to reasonably hard wear, and that are not so expensive that you tend to wear them long after they have ceased to be attractive or smart.

*If you have a job,* depending on what it is, choose either clothes that are inexpensive but smart and therefore can be frequently replaced, or else buy a few in number of good quality and basic good style, so that you can always be sure of being at your best.

**Care of Clothes.** All repairs, such as threads coming undone, buttons or fasteners getting loose, tiny holes or catches in hems, should be attended to at once, or they may become major problems. If you do have an accident that tears or burns any garment, wonders can now be performed by a good invisible mender.

Otherwise, clothes should always be hung up when they are taken off, and should not be put away at once, but allowed to air, either overnight or for a few hours. When putting them into drawers or cupboards, they should not be squashed, and when putting winter clothes away for the summer you should be careful to make sure that any woollens or furs are clean and that – even if they are moth-proofed – your place of storage has an effective anti-moth preparation in it.

Clothes that have become creased, of

course, must be pressed (use either a steam iron or an ordinary iron with a pressing cloth to avoid making textured cloths shiny) but generally hanging up will free a garment of creases and too-frequent pressing can take the life out of it. Clothes that cannot be washed should be regularly cleaned; this, how-ever expensive it seems, is a real saving, for it preserves the life of the fabric to have it freed from the grit and grease falling on it in all towns today. It is also much harder to achieve satisfactory cleaning of a garment that has been allowed to get very dirty. Odd marks and spots, can be removed by any of the preparations made for this purpose,

With all cleaning and washing, how-ever, care should be taken to follow any instructions given by the manufacturers on the garment's label – whether it is to be dry-cleaned, or whether any specific washing preparation should be used, temperature of the iron, and so on. If these instructions are followed and there is still some mishap, inform both the shop and the manufacturer, who will appreciate hearing from you.

Regular brushing of clothes, shoes and handbags is of great importance in keeping them clean day by day. Differ-ent brushes should be kept for dark and light materials, delicate fabrics and for leather. If a garment gets wet, hang it up to dry in gentle heat, never directly before a fire or on a radiator. Shake furs free of surplus wet and shake them again when dry. Clean leather shoes and bags with good-quality cream or polish – if you use a coloured cream on a bag, rub it over with a little white cream after-wards, or you may stain gloves and clothes. Always clean new shoes and bags before you wear them, as if they get wet marks may remain. Special cleaners are now made for plastics and synthetic leathers if these cannot be sponged or wiped clean. Ideally, put your shoes on trees, but at least always do this if they have got very wet, and let them dry slowly, before cleaning them and putting them away. Clean leather belts like shoes and bags. Gloves should either be washed – even the most delicate-seeming leather ones can now be washed – or professionally cleaned;

again, if they are not allowed to get too dirty, they will come up like new, but nothing will shift a lot of grime from light-coloured leather. If either gloves or shoes do get badly stained, it is often worth having them dyed, though econo-my on dyeing is usually a false economy. Suède clothes require professional clean-ing, though they may be kept very satis-factorily with the aid of regular light brushing and the use of one of the india-rubber-like cleaners; on no account use spirit or spot-remover on suède.

With all cleaners or dyes for home use, study the instructions very carefully before using them.

Furs should also be regularly cleaned – even fur collars benefit enormously – and bulky coats, that have to be put away for the summer, may be placed in cold storage, where they are not only perfectly safe from burglars, but protec-ted from moths. The charge for this is small and any good furrier will advise about it. Greasiness – as occurs round collars and the edges of stoles – or wear, such as is often seen near fastenings of coats or on cuffs, detracts greatly from the appearance of even a costly fur, and should be promptly remedied.

## AIDS TO ELEGANCE

*If you have a fairly busy social life*, choose your evening or "special oc-casion" clothes of simple colours and cut, so that they can eventually be altered or dyed to give you a more variable wardrobe. And don't overlook the advantages of the many excellent firms hiring out evening clothes and furs.

*If you have a problem figure* and can't do more than adjust to it, spend time finding an intelligent and sympathetic shop, and, if possible, a good dressmaker as well. Should you want to be very smart, you will certainly save money and time if you can have your clothes made or make them yourself.

*Choose the colours of your clothes within the same range*, if you want to be able to combine different garments – a topcoat over a suit or dress, or a sweater with an odd skirt. It is, however, better to have two different tones of the same colour than a would-be match of colours that doesn't quite succeed.

*Choose the colours of your accessories* so that these can be interchanged. For example, you might decide on black shoes and bag and black or white gloves for winter, and cream shoes and bag for summer. Even if you then replace any of these, the scheme will still be maintained. Remember that, just as there are browns and browns, navies and navies, so even blacks and whites can look startlingly unmatched and unco-ordinated if chosen in very different materials – a white nylon glove can look almost blue against a white cloth coat and the coat can look almost cream or off-white. So be careful!

*Never choose* a material, a colour, a pattern or a style just because you like it – in itself it may be fine, but it may do nothing for you. A fondness for flowers has resulted in far too many English ladies putting flowers on their hats instead of leaving them in their gardens! If you are essentially a "pretty" woman, beware of swamping your prettiness with too many frills, fussy ornaments and dainty patterns. If you are essentially "smart", don't give yourself a hard, aggressive look by wearing everything this is very severe in style, colour and cut.

*Unless you are very rich, very beautiful, and very self-assured* (when you won't need advice anyway) it is always a safe policy to dress simply. If a particular occasion is a grand one, either the invitation card or your hostess will let you know. Elaborate clothes date quickly, one gets tired of them and friends tend to comment: "Here comes Mary in her yellow and black striped coat." It was once said of the clothes made by a great couturier that, once worn, they were seldom remarked on – but that everyone complimented the wearer on how well she looked. That is what good dressing should achieve – something for you rather than your dress maker or your dress shop.

**Jewellery and Ornaments.** At one time it was considered more elegant to have a pinhead-sized diamond than any costume jewellery. Nowadays the only criterion is attractiveness and suitability; a single semi-precious stone or chain-store brooch can be more effective than an heirloom.

Even if you have a lot of real jewels, it's worth taking a critical look to see whether their settings have become old-fashioned (better two wearable clips than a hideous tiara living in the bank), as often is the case with inherited jewellery. A single piece, made up from others, is generally more useful and attractive than lots of little bits. Costume jewellery is often very beautiful and worthy of being worn on any occasion, but there are other kinds that are purely "fun" jewels, meant only to fashionable for a short while. Don't buy these unless you are strong-minded enough to throw them out once they are no longer in vogue.

All jewellery should be kept scrupulously clean – dirty pearls and grubby diamonds are inexcusable. Most pieces can be polished gently with a piece of silk to remove powder or neck make-up, and some precious stones (though not pearls) can be washed, or cleaned with spirit. Any jeweller will advise you on how to do this or do it for you, and of course valuable necklaces should be regularly professionally restrung.

Whatever jewellery you wear, avoid the "Christmas tree" appearance of too much, especially in the daytime. But the single strand of tiny pearls, the little brooch or minute ring can look out of place worn by an older woman, especially if she is on the plump side; choose a single piece, or just two ornaments of fair size and importance instead.

There is no rigid etiquette about signet and wedding rings in the United Kingdom, though generally a divorced woman leaves off her wedding-ring and a widow continues to wear it; if she marries again, she can decide whether to move the first ring on to her right hand or put it away and have it remade. But some women nowadays choose not even to wear a wedding-ring and it is entirely a matter of personal choice. Few men in this country wear wedding-rings, though it is perfectly correct for a man to wear a signet; this should only be plain gold, with either a crest or monogram, and it is conventionally worn only on the little finger. A man seldom wears a pocket-watch these days, but if he does, and uses a chain for it, this should be fine and fairly thin. Although a considerable variety of choice is available as regards cuff-links, studs and tie and scarf pins, it is conventionally preferable to choose these of a simple style – which does not mean they cannot be considerably expensive and precious if required. The same applies to cigarette-cases and lighters.

**Shoes and Gloves.** The quality of these was formerly supposed to denote the type of wearer – "lady" or otherwise. Today many smart women would hold the opinion that it is better to have a few comparatively inexpensive up-to-the-minute pairs, and replace them when they get shabby, rather than costly ones that look dated long before they have even begun to wear out. But even if you are able to afford the most luxurious accessories for each outfit, it is undeniable that – with the exception of informal and "play" clothes – the simplest accessories are always the most effective. A beautiful hand and a pretty foot are enhanced by a simple glove and shoe; less attractive ones need the discreet camouflage of something inconspicuous in colour and plain in style. Light colours draw the eye and have a tendency to enlarge – so, if you have large feet or hands, choose cream rather than white, black rather than light navy or a colour such as red or yellow. Gloves or shoes that exactly match a dress or coat can look very smart, but beware of having too much matching up – gloves, shoes, bag and hat all of the same colour can either look dreary (if in a dark or neutral colour), or stridently eye-catching if in any kind of contrast or vivid shade. A set of white accessories – shoes, gloves, bag and hat – can look disastrously "bitty", as well as making the feet and hands of the wearer look large and conspicuous.

## THINGS TO AVOID

Although fashion often brings into favour styles, colours and colour combinations and fabrics that may not previously have been regarded as smart at all, there are a few "don'ts" that may be applied to dress in general, whatever may be currently in vogue. These – and the reasons why they can never be smart – are:

*Walking or country-style shoes with town clothes* – and vice versa. The height of a heel may make all the difference to the look of a skirt and the way a woman walks – and the incongruity of the feet being dressed for one set of surroundings when the rest of the woman is dressed for another kind makes the discrepancy look like combined carelessness and sloppiness. Informal shoes, such as sandals, can make the smartest formal clothes look dowdy, and formal shoes with casual clothes make the wearer seem bent on showing off in an undesirable way.

*Fussy gloves.* These merely draw attention to the hands without enhancing them. With an ultra-smart ensemble it is sometimes possible to wear decorated or vividly coloured gloves – but anyone who deliberately contrives this kind of effect has usually the fashion knowledge to achieve complete success with it. Net gloves, frilly gloves and so on should, generally, be avoided. Choose basic colours – white, black, cream, tan, brown, caramel, navy or grey. It is better to have a good-quality fabric glove in impeccable condition than a shabby leather pair. And gloves should always be worn – not carried. They are, after all, to protect your hands.

*Stockings of the wrong shade.* Although fashions in stocking colours change, it is still wrong to pair, for example, a dress or skirt of a green or yellow shade with stockings that are basically pink. Nor do very pale stockings look correct with ultra-formal day wear. Evening stockings should be chosen under the artificial light under which they will be worn. Textured and coloured stockings can be very effective with the appropriate clothes, but they must either match exactly or contrast effectively. And, no matter how beautiful or how brown her legs, no woman of 25 and over should ever do without stockings for town or even the most lightly formal of occasions – the leg needs the "finish" of a stocking, just as the face needs the "finish" of make-up.

*Fussy or elaborate hats on shoulder-length hair.* Not only does the hair hide the neck – and spoil the proportion of the hat as it sits on the head – but loose hair blurs the effect of an elaborate hat. To put a hat that is a pretty thing in itself on top of a face that is past its prime is to make a direct – and inevitably unflattering – comparison. A hat that exactly matches the hair can make the head look enormous, and a fussy hat worn with spectacles or a hearing aid is simply too much of a good thing. White and flowered hats are, in general, only to be worn to advantage by the very young or those who are still very beautiful – and even if this is the fact, they should not be combined with flower or patterned clothes.

*High heels with shorts or slacks and absolutely flat shoes with straight skirts.* Either of these change the proportions of the clothes and also involve a way of walking that is unbecoming to the clothes worn.

*Too low décolletage.* Even if you are not plump, a neckline or shoulder-straps that cut into the flesh gives a most unpleasant effect. In the older woman especially, great care should be taken when choosing evening or resort clothes involving low necklines, to see how these look from the back and sides, also bearing in mind the fact that the part of the arm immediately below the shoulder is the one which tends to show signs of age first of all.

*Grubby, chipped, down-at-heel or cracked shoes.* However expensive these may have originally been, once they cease to present an immaculate appearance, they nullify a large amount of the effect of the smartest outfit.

*Bulging or grubby handbag:* see as for *Shoes,* above.

*Corsages.* A single flower (minus any fern or frill) may look attractive on the lapel of a plain coat or dress, but a spray of flowers rarely enhances an outfit. The woman who is presented with one can avoid pinning it on her clothes if she can attach it to her handbag, but only a very young and beautiful woman can wear flowers in her hair without looking absurd.

*Lack of make-up on the neck and arms under artificial light.* Few things look more absurd than a well-made-up face sitting on top of an unmade-up neck and shoulders. Artificial light has the effect of making even the most beautiful skin look slightly off colour and the texture is not improved. The appearance of anyone in evening dress is enormously enhanced by arms, neck and shoulders being lightly made up with one of the preparations made for this purpose, which do not come off against clothes; anything like this should, of course, be removed when the evening is over.

*Nipped-in waists over 42-inch hips.* Even if you think you look all right, you will change your mind if you catch sight of your back view in a mirror! A bunchy, full skirt increases the impression of fatness around the hips if it is suddenly cinched in. Anyone with a waist over 30 inches, too, should beware of belts which are very wide, very narrow, or of a violent colour contrast to the garment on which they are worn.

*Cardigans or non-matching jackets worn with dresses.* This can ruin the style of a dress, make a smart outfit look unsuccessfully informal and usually makes the wearer look plump into the bargain.

*Too many matching accessories.* There is something too studied and contrived about this, and the number of blobs of colour dotted about on the figure when hat, gloves, shoes and bag, and possibly a scarf as well, are all of the same shade, is disastrous. If the accessories are of very light colours, or white, they can draw undesired attention to the extremities and feet.

**A Golden Rule.** A couturier once remarked that it was an ideal policy for smartness if a woman, looking at herself in the glass before leaving her bedroom, always removed one thing. "When in doubt, don't" is a sound piece of advice for the hesitant.

# GOOD MANNERS AND ETIQUETTE

Although etiquette derives from good manners, it has come to have a slightly specialised meaning. Good manners are based on consideration for other people, convenience and practicality. Etiquette is the specific good manners accepted in a particular society. It is, of course, of prime importance to base all one's social conduct on good manners, but a knowledge of what is accepted as conventionally correct in the social circles in which one moves can increase self-assurance and enable one to break the rules when necessary. But rigid adherence to what is "done" and "not done" is becoming a thing of the past and slavish adherence to convention is as foolish as the wilful flouting of it for no good reason. As one wise diplomat once remarked, apropos the question of precedence being debated, "Those that matter don't mind, and those that mind don't matter".

**Etiquette in detail.** This is not the place to find tables of precedence for the different ranks of nobility, the clergy, officers in the services or matters of diplomatic protocol. There are plenty of good books on all these subjects which may be consulted in a public library and, as far as any special routine is concerned, you can always consult either the person for whose convenience certain rules have been devised, or their secretary, ADC, or similar official. When any occasion involves meeting or receiving royalty, those responsible are usually informed as to what will be expected of them. Anyone concerned about receiving distinguished foreign guests, whether or not these are diplomats, should refer the matter to the appropriate embassy, who will always give advice both on etiquette and matters such as any special dietary conventions followed because of religious reasons. Should a very distinguished personage, who does not come into the category of those mentioned above, not have a secretary or anyone who may be consulted in advance of the occasion on which they are to be met, you can try and get advice from one of their friends, the readers' information services of any of the quality magazines or newspapers or, as a last resort, from the person concerned. If you are giving a party or being presented to anyone of importance, ensure your own peace of mind by finding out in advance all you can about how to make the occasion easy and agreeable; uncertainty is perhaps the chief social problem and as goodwill counts for more than anything, sensible persons will do their best, if necessary making a joke at their own expense should anything seem to go wrong, and concentrate on good manners rather than etiquette.

## EVERYDAY MANNERS

People from different countries, different regions and different types of home all have individual ways and in particular individual ways of speech. It is often possible to deduce, from the vocabulary that someone uses, the type of family to which they belong and the kind of education they have had, just as one might deduce a regional accent in their speech. The use of vivid phrases and a way of speaking that is vigorous and sincere enhances all conversation, just as the meaningless repetition of a few words and over-indulgence in current slang weakens the power of speech. But there are some words and phrases which, to the snob, indicate that the speaker has had a different type of upbringing from the one the snob (male or female) hopes to give the impression of having enjoyed. Although this type of person is not worth serious consideration, it is good sense to endeavour to know and avoid phrases and expressions (mentioned elsewhere) which can give rise to comment in snobbish company – that is of course if it is considered worth while playing up to the snobbish preferences of the company.

**Introductions.** Conventionally, a younger person is introduced to an older one, and a man to a woman. But as there is also the convention that a less important person is introduced to a more important one, the situation could arise that a young woman would be introduced to a distinguished public man. People distinguished professionally, or holding high official posts are, even in informal introductions, considered "important" and therefore many people will be introduced to them. Clergymen count as "important" in this way because of the respect due to their calling. An unmarried woman is usually introduced to a married woman, although a very distinguished or elderly unmarried woman might be considered the more important person by comparison with a very young married woman. Strictly, the prefixes Mr, Mrs or Miss, or of course titles or ranks, are used when making introductions, but young people today often prefer to omit them.

Traditionally, when an introduction is made, it is for the woman to extend her hand if she wishes to shake hands. Women do not always shake hands with each other and in the United Kingdom it is also quite usual for men being introduced to omit the handshake. But we are perhaps the only country in the world to be casual in this respect and therefore it is perhaps a good idea always to offer to shake hands in case one should be thought rude by omitting to do so.

If you are introduced to someone on an occasion when a number of introductions are being made to them, it is considerate not to give them a firm handshake; shaking hands with large numbers of people can be both tiring and very painful for those who have to do it. Consideration of this kind is also appreciated by anyone wearing rings.

The usual phrase when being introduced is "How do you do?" The reply is also "How do you do?" though the informal "Hello" is now very usual. "Pleased to meet you" is to be avoided if in doubt, though of course you may say "I am delighted to meet you" or "I am so glad to have the chance of meeting you."

**Conversation.** With people whom you hardly know or have only just met, conversation can present problems. Usually, the older person in a twosome should initiate the conversation, but, however great your respect for the person to whom you are talking, you need not merely reply "Yes" or "No" but will help them if you add personal comments or even questions of your own. It is no longer considered unsuitable to discuss serious subjects in general conversation, though personal talk, either about yourself or friends, is ideally only indulged in in small doses–it can be very boring–and controversial subjects such as religion, politics or anything similar should likewise only be introduced with caution in case you inadvertently start an argument or upset whoever you are talking to.

**How to Refer to People in Conversation.** Husbands and wives refer to "My husband" or "My wife", or use Christian names. "Mrs Brown" and "Mr Jones" are only used by their wives and husbands when speaking to tradespeople. Pet names and the use of "fun" names for one's husband or wife are not really suitable for using on moderately formal occasions.

Excessive use of the word "lady" or "gentleman" instead of "woman" and "man" tends to be affected.

**Speaking to Older People.** It has been conventional for any man addressing one older than himself, even when of exactly the same social and professional standing, to call the older man "Sir". This is still current practice – even with a comparatively older man to a very old man – among people of traditional and upper-middle-class education. Omission of the "Sir" need not imply disrespect, however, though older men do usually appreciate the additional courtesy. A man of senior rank in one walk of life may be called "Sir" by his juniors, and this applies particularly to officers in the services, governors, ambassadors and diplomats (women holding high office of this kind are addressed as "Ma'am", pronounced "marm"). A young woman, married or single, who meets a very senior man, holding some important post or rank, at a party, refers to him by his rank or title, but, suppose he has neither, she may please him by the cautious and very occasional use of "Sir" in conversation unless he immediately asks her to refer to him less formally. The age at which a woman stops doing this sort of thing is left to the individual! But deference, which is all that is involved, is invariably acceptable. In any case, if you are in the slightest doubt, ask your hostess.

**Ministers of Religion.** Unless these hold high office or a doctor's degree, they are introduced as "Mr. Smith" and referred to as "Vicar" or "Rector" as the case may be. If the vicar holds an academic doctorate he is referred to as "Doctor". Wives are "Mrs Smith". Roman Catholic clergymen are introduced as "Father John Brown" and referred to as "Father", or sometimes, especially by service people, as "Padre".

A Jewish minister is introduced as "Reverend Joseph Cohen" and referred to as "Mr Cohen". His wife is Mrs Cohen. If he is a Rabbi, he is referred to as "Rabbi".

A qualified medical practitioner is usually given the courtesy title of "Doctor" although strictly speaking he is only entitled to this if he has an MD or a FRCP after his name. A surgeon is always referred to as "Mr William Sawbones" unless he has a doctorate of surgery in which case he, too, is entitled to be referred to as "Doctor". You can look these up in the medical directory in the library if in doubt.

Very important doctors often have titles as well, and in this case, of course, are addressed as "Sir John Brown" and "Lord Sawbones".

**Heads of Schools and Academic People.** These are introduced or referred to as "Mr Jones" and "Miss Smith" and referred to as "Headmaster" and "Headmistress" unless they have an academic doctorate, in which case they are entitled to be called "Doctor Jones". If the head of a teaching establishment is known as "the Principal", "the Master", "the Rector", exactly the same procedure is followed.

**Officers in the Services.** These are introduced by their rank and title (if they have one) and referred to in speech by their rank if they have no title, but by their title (i.e. Sir George) if they have one. Their wives are addressed as "Mrs Jenkins" or, if the title is involved, "Lady Jenkins".

Dames of the British Empire are introduced as "Dame Henrietta Champion" and referred to as "Dame Henrietta".

**Local Dignitaries and Heads of Firms.** In ordinary informal gatherings where no announcement is being made, the Mayor is introduced as "the Mayor of Little Nightcap, Mr Blenkinsop" and referred to as "Mr Mayor" or "Mayor", even if a woman holds the position. The Mayor's wife or whoever fills the role of Mayoress for him (sometimes this may be his daughter if he is a widower, or his sister) is introduced informally as "Mrs Blenkinsop" or "Miss Blenkinsop".

Unless the man or woman holding the position of head of an organisation has a title or doctorate or similar important honour, they are addressed just as an ordinary person would be. Even if the use of Christian names is common in an organisation, however, it shows additional deference to a senior man or woman to refrain from using their first name until they specifically ask you to do so.

**Children.** Although we are far from the days when children were seen and not heard, it is nevertheless considerate to all concerned if children are brought up not to dominate any social gathering. They should be taught to shake hands and say "How do you do?", to look up to the person speaking to them and also to say "Thank you very much" (if possible without being prompted), when given any present and to say "Goodbye", adding the name, when people leave. Some parents rather like a return to the slight formality of former times, with little boys bowing or inclining their head when they shake hands and little girls dropping a curtsy. This can be very charming with children, though it is a practice that can be abandoned as they get a little older. Once children cease to be at the baby stage when adults take their hands when walking about, they should be encouraged to let a grown-up woman walk in front of them through a doorway – even if they are too small to open it for her – to give up their seats to older people and to stand up if an older person, man or woman, comes into the room.

**Standing Up and Sitting Down.** Men stand up when a woman comes into a room, gets up to leave or rejoins a party at a table (although it is for her to say, "Please don't get up" rather quickly to anticipate this); they also stand up when anyone of great seniority or holding a position deserving respect comes into a room. Any man, except someone definitely in the elderly and inactive category, stands up when being introduced to anyone else, even to another man. A young woman stands up for an older woman and for anyone – such as a member of the Church – to whom she wishes to show deference, and for a very elderly man. Usually the person for whom everyone has risen will either sit down, so that others may sit, or unobtrusively ask them all to do so.

**Hats, Gloves and Taking the Arm.** If a man wears a hat he raises it when he meets a woman and if the girl he is accompanying is greeted by another man also raising his hat. The hat is also raised when parting from a woman in the same way. It is removed when the man goes into a house, restaurant or hotel, in shops, lifts, offices and any building which the man enters in which women are present, and this includes museums and art galleries and business premises when, even if women are not present, the man he has come to see is senior to him. He takes his hat off when he goes into a place of entertainment, or in church (but he keeps it on in a synagogue), when royalty are present, at a funeral or if a funeral passes him.

If a man does wear gloves – few do nowadays – he removes them before shaking hands with a woman, but a woman never removes her gloves when being introduced or presented.

When a man and a woman are crossing the road, he either temporarily takes her arm or holds her elbow so as to make sure she does not trip. People in formal dress or present at formal functions do not usually walk arm in arm.

**Doors.** A man opens a door for a woman and allows her to precede him through it unless, of course, it is such a heavy one that he has to go first and hold it back for her. The same applies to lifts. With a revolving door, a woman goes in front of a man into this, but if it is not revolving it is considerate if he either pushes it to start it or, if necessary, goes in first.

**Stairs and Steps.** A man accompanying a woman must be guided entirely by what is convenient and most helpful to her with regard to stairs and steps. She takes the side nearest the balustrade or handrail and he either walks beside her or, if the stairs are steep, a little in front, either taking her arm or being ready to offer his at need (see also *Restaurants*). If a servant is preceding them down the stairs, however, the man drops slightly behind them. When mounting stairs, the same sort of procedure is followed.

With steps, or ladders, convenience and safety are the governing factors. A man gets out of a train or off a bus first so that he may help the woman, but he lets her get on before him, opening the door of a train or compartment for her. He follows her up a steep staircase, such as a spiral, or a ladder, ready to help her if necessary. When going down very steep stairs or steps, it is usually most convenient if he goes in front of her.

When a man and a woman are walking along a street, the man always walks on the outside of the pavement. This is both to guard against the woman getting jostled off the kerb and, if necessary, to protect her from being splashed by traffic.

**Cars.** A man opens the door of his car for a woman passenger to accompany him and, if she is the driver, he opens the driver's door for her, seeing her comfortably seated and closing the door before taking his own seat. When possible, he similarly helps her to get out of the car, but this is not always convenient if he, as the driver, is unable to park, in which case he opens the passenger door for her anyway. A woman naturally helps an older woman into or out of a car.

The "place of honour" in a car is the seat beside the driver, but there is no governing factor except convenience about where one sits in a private car. A very tall person naturally requires room, women in long dresses likewise, and anyone elderly or infirm should sit where he or she will be most comfortable.

When two married couples go out together in the car belonging to one of them, the men seat the women first before getting in themselves, but where they sit and beside whom is entirely a matter of personal preference and convenience.

With a chauffeur-driven car or a taxi the women get into the car first and occupy the back seat, with the men facing them unless there is room for one man on the back seat as well. When getting out of a taxi, a man or the men of the party go first to help the woman or women. They let the women go past them and get out first, however, if the door of a taxi or chauffeur-driven car is opened by a porter or doorman at an hotel, restaurant, night club or theatre. In a chauffeur-driven car, the chauffeur will open the door for any passengers, unless there is a doorman on duty where the car stops. In a private car arriving anywhere with a doorman on duty, the passengers will be helped out of the car by the doorman, and the driver then either parks the car or gives the keys to the doorman to do this for him or her.

The most important thing governing people getting in and out of cars is convenience. If there is someone to help a woman alight, the man lets her go first, if not, he opens the door and helps her out. The same procedure, in reverse, is followed when people get into cars. (See also *Tipping*, page 40.)

**Smoking.** A man offers cigarettes to a woman before helping himself and, if he is with his wife or girl-friend, he offers to other women in the party before handing them to her. He does the same about lighting cigarettes for a woman. Conventionally he does not smoke when accompanying a woman in the street and at all times it is considerate, wherever he is, to ask if a woman minds him smoking if he is doing it in her company. (See also *Formal Meals*.)

**Pipes.** A pipe, which may emit too strong a smell even for the person who does not mind cigarettes, should only be smoked if the hostess and the company are sincere about not objecting to it and only a very important person, feeling themselves entitled to some personal eccentricity, would smoke a pipe on a formal occasion.

**Cigars.** Permission is usually asked before a cigar is lit, but this is only really important if it happens to be a large or strong one. Again, the convenience of the company dictates what should be done.

**Going to the Lavatory.** In a restaurant or place of entertainment you ask for "the cloakroom". If coats and umbrellas are left somewhere else and this is definitely the cloakroom, then ask for "the ladies' room" or the "men's room". Some establishments use the words "powder-room" for the ladies' room.

In a private house, according to the kind of place it is, you ask if you may "have a wash", "tidy up", "go upstairs" or "use the bathroom". The thoughtful host or hostess, or whichever of their servants receives you, should indicate the whereabouts of this to you, but all these phrases are acceptable and immediately understood. The word "loo" is acceptable slang for water closet, or w.c. (which is rather outspoken for many people), but the words "toilet", "little girls' (or boys') room", and "spending a penny" are inadvisable. "John" is an Americanism, and, as the exact meaning of the word "lavatory" is a place where one only washes, those who are strict as regards the English language tend to deplore it having the same significance as "water-closet"!

**Cards, Letters and Invitations.** The use of the visiting card for social purposes has greatly declined, although, especially in the country, people do "call" on a newcomer, leaving their card and, if they are not accompanied by their husband, two of his with a corner of each turned down. Conventionally, a visiting card is engraved, not printed, and usually in copperplate, with the name in the centre and the address in the left-hand corner. A married woman using cards for social purposes is Mrs James Jones, not Mrs Mary Jones, and, married or single, her telephone number does not go on a social visiting card. A widow usually prefers, for social purposes, to keep her husband's name, i.e. Mrs James Jones, but a divorced woman may choose to use her Christian name – Mrs Mary Jones. But for business purposes, the card is virtually essential. Nowadays it is no longer considered unacceptable to have this kind of card printed instead of engraved and the telephone number must, of course, be included on the right-hand bottom corner of a business card.

A woman's visiting card is larger than a man's, but a man who uses a business card may find it necessary to have one bigger than the conventional size for social purposes. Business people may also wish to include their professional qualifications or some kind of description as to who they are, i.e. Sales Manager, Representative, Decorator and Builder, Free-lance Travel Features, Dressmaking and Alterations. If the letters after someone's name indicate sufficiently adequately what their business is, it is unnecessary to add any description and it is for the individual to decide whether honours and academic qualifications should also be added. A good stationer, with experience in preparing cards of all kinds, will be able to give detailed advice for specific purposes and show samples of what is conventionally acceptable.

**Writing Paper.** Again, a good stationer will be able to show samples of what is both acceptable and in fashion for any purpose. In general, however, writing paper should be chosen from papers of inconspicuous colours and the layout of any printed or engraved heading should be plain rather than fancy. Nowadays many people with heavy mail of a business or partly business nature, have their names printed on their writing paper as well. Correspondence cards, which are like postcards, with the name, address and telephone number, are becoming increasingly popular, and are acceptable for all but the most formal letters.

At one time it would have been considered rude to have sent a personal letter that was typewritten but nowadays people are sensible enough to prefer legibility and perhaps the only occasions on which a handwritten note is virtually obligatory are those when you wish to convey that you have paid great personal attention to the letter – as in the case of congratulations or a bereavement. (Unless, of course, you are applying for a job and are specifically requested to submit your application in your own handwriting.)

There are many decorated cards, printed specifically for different occasions, i.e. anniversaries, success in examinations, engagements, going away, moving to a new home, and so on. For close friends, it is always acceptable to send something that you think will amuse or please the recipient, but if there is any kind of formality involved, send a short letter conveying your wishes instead. A printed card should never be sent in the event of bereavement. Although letters of condolence are very difficult to write, it is always better, at such a time, to send even a visiting card with the words "deepest sympathy and love" or "we are all thinking of you and send our deepest sympathy" rather than anything printed.

**Christmas Cards.** A good stationer will provide plenty of samples of these if it is wished to have them printed, with a personal message or the name and address of the senders. Nowadays many people choose to have only their address printed and to write in their names, either first names and surnames or just the first names. This is entirely a matter of personal preference.

**Letters in General.** The variety of letters, both business and personal, is endless and if anyone finds the writing of a letter a particular problem, it is worth consulting a manual on correspondence such as may be found in any public library. The following general rules are usually to be observed:

A letter addressed to someone you do not know personally begins "Dear Sir" or "Dear Madam" and ends "Yours faithfully" or "Yours truly". A woman signs her name to this kind of correspondence giving the first name in full, and if she is "Mrs" putting this either before or after her signature, for the purposes of clarity. It may be noted that if you are writing back to someone who has omitted to do this, the reply when in doubt is to call her "Miss" on the envelope. This formal method of address, however, is often considerably modified nowadays and a letter may be received from a complete stranger, beginning "Dear Mrs/Miss Brown" or even "Dear Mary Brown". The implication is that the writer feels some personal involvement with the addressee. Such a letter should always conclude with "Yours sincerely".

For letters addressed to people with titles, honours, holding positions of importance and those with letters after their names, a detailed reference book should be consulted. The Librarian of any public library will have at least one work giving complete guidance.

Letters sent to firms, shops, hotels and institutions should be addressed to the official – whose name you may never know – for whom they are destined, i.e. the Chairman, Managing Director, Secretary, Principal, or the Manager. They should also end "Yours truly" or "Yours faithfully".

It is considered clumsy to begin the opening paragraph with the pronoun "I", and to begin a number of paragraphs with this pronoun. This, however, is purely a matter of style. Use of formerly traditional commercial terms, such as "prox.", "ult.", "inst.", "your

esteemed favour", "your goodselves", and so on are now considered clumsy and old-fashioned. It is always better to be simple and direct, using the language of polite everyday speech whenever possible.

The use of the suffix "Esquire" is peculiar to the United Kingdom, and, although it originally meant a man without title but with the rank of gentleman, and entitled to bear arms, it is now more generally a term of courtesy. An American concern or an American individual is unlikely to use it.

Similarly, the practice of indenting for a paragraph is now a matter of personal preference. Some people like the look of a letter that is not indented at all. This is again for the individual to decide.

**Postcards and Correspondence Cards.** It is traditional to begin these with the message, without any mode of address and to end them with only a brief expression of good-bye. But, as with all personal and informal correspondence, nowadays people are entitled to write as they and their correspondents like, and to set out their letters and cards as best pleases them, always bearing in mind that a letter that is easy to read is in itself a courtesy.

**Envelopes.** Envelopes of unusual sizes will soon be discouraged by the Post Office, therefore anyone ordering stationery should ascertain the acceptable sizes that will facilitate sorting.

**Telephone Manners.** Whether a personal or business telephone call is involved, it is of prime importance to be clear in diction and subject. Never answer the telephone by saying "Hello". Always give either your own number, your name, the department in which you are working, or the position you hold (i.e. "Mr Smith's secretary speaking").

It is an appreciated courtesy, should you telephone for a conversation that may either take some time, or be purely social in content, to ask whether this is a convenient moment to take up the time of the person you call. If personal telephone calls are allowed to be received or made at your place of business, they should always be kept as short as possible. When receiving a call intended for someone else, give (in a private house) either the number or say "This is Mrs Smith's house" and, unless you are quite sure that it is convenient for the call to be taken at that time, ask the caller to wait while you see whether the person they want may be found so as to come to the telephone. It is always acceptable to be told that the person one wants will call back, but it is rather rude to hear that "Mr X is too busy to speak to you now".

**Invitations.** Nowadays, except for the most formal occasions, people tend to be invited out either by means of a telephone call or an informal written note. For details about the correct layout of a card to a formal party, consult a stationer specialising in such matters. But in general such a card may read:

Mrs John Smith
At Home
Friday, May 27th.
55 Park Avenue,   Cocktails: 6 o'clock.
London S.W.1.

*RSVP*

The name of the guest or guests to whom the card is sent is written on the left-hand upper corner of this invitation – i.e. Mr & Mrs James Brown.

Many people today dispense with the slightly formal "Mr & Mrs" and merely use their first names and surnames – i.e. "George and Mary Smith" and a single person will use his or her name alone without any prefix.

For dances, the word "Dancing" followed by the time, is put in the right-hand corner of the card but the *"RSVP"* may go underneath this or above the address to which the reply is to be sent. If the occasion involves the wearing of decorations, this would usually be stated on any formal invitation, or the host or hostess may write the words "black tie" at the bottom of the card.

If the invitation is sent on the occasion of some special celebration such as a coming-of-age, an engagement party, a wedding anniversary or similar celebration, this can be included on a printed or engraved invitation card. (See also *Wedding Invitations*, page 44.)

**Replies.** The reply to a formally-worded invitation should always be in the third person and should repeat the form of the invitation, i.e.:

"Miss Mary Jones thanks Mr & Mrs John Smith for their kind invitation to cocktails on June 5th at 6 o'clock at 20 Park Avenue, S.W.1, which she has much pleasure in accepting."

If, of course, the form of the invitation is lengthy, the reply can be cut down. For example, a business invitation that begins: "The Chairman and Directors of Blank and Company and Monsieur Emile du Pont and Senor Emilio Ponti request the pleasure..." etc., can be accepted merely to "The Chairman and Directors" of the company concerned.

It is conventionally correct to accept or decline in fairly few words. When you cannot accept an invitation, only a brief excuse is needed: "...regrets that, due to a previous engagement, he is unable to accept the kind invitation of..." or "... which they are unable to accept, due to being abroad on that date."

If there should be some rather complicated reason why the invitation either cannot be accepted or may only be provisionally accepted then, if you know the host or hostess, it is better to write an informal personal letter to them, explaining the situation, i.e.:

"Dear Mr Brown,
Thank you so much for your kind invitation to the Sports Day of Fireworks and Company, followed by Cocktails at 55 Avenue Road, W.1. My wife and I hope to be able to come, but we are at present unable to make definite plans for that week, due to our eldest son having to go into hospital. As the date for his operation is not yet fixed, I am sure you will understand if I let you know a little nearer the time whether one or both of us will be present.
Yours sincerely,"

Do not go into minute detail about why you cannot accept an invitation, although always express regret for not being able to do so and gratitude for having been asked.

Should you, at the last moment, be unable to keep an appointment for even the most casual party, it is essential both to telephone to say that you will not be there and to send a written expression of regret with your excuses immediately afterwards. If, of course, a gathering such as a dinner party is involved or any occasion where your absence might inconvenience the host or hostess, a very valid excuse indeed must be presented.

Between friends who know each other well and who see each other often, it is usual nowadays only to express thanks for a party by means of a telephone call or card, but a short note is always appreciated, and the tradition that you always write your thanks after the first occasion when you visit someone still holds good in many circles. This is particularly important where the host or hostess are older people.

Traditionally, you do not need to write every time you visit a house where you are a frequent guest – though many people greatly appreciate being thanked in this way.

In some circles, it is also traditional to take a gift, such as flowers, the first time you visit someone. This can, however, be slightly awkward if a bunch of flowers is presented to a hostess on the point of coping with an elaborate dinner single-handed. It is perhaps more considerate to send flowers afterwards (or beforehand), or bring a small gift, such as chocolates, that requires no immediate attention. It is also acceptable nowadays if a small gift of food or drink is brought to the household, though this naturally depends on the circumstances.

# ENTERTAINING AND BEING ENTERTAINED

## IN PRIVATE HOUSES

**Informal Entertaining.** Everyone appreciates being received in someone's home, even if it is only for the most informal hospitality. There are numerous ways of doing this and of giving parties – tea parties, cocktail parties, New Year parties, wine and cheese parties, buffet meals of various kinds, ranging from brunch (a combination of the traditional large-scale breakfast and luncheon, usually held about midday), after-theatre suppers and special occasions such as family celebrations, anniversaries and children's parties. If you are anxious to be very up to date with what is currently fashionable, consult the appropriate consumer magazines, but the really important thing to remember is that professional advice and help for every kind of party is available in most towns and many caterers will go into even the remote country districts.

**Using Catering Facilities.** For any large-scale party, or even dinner for four, if you are short of time, it is worthwhile at least seeing what is involved by hiring professional help. The hostess editors of the better consumer magazines usually have lists of organisations who can hire staff and all equipment, decorators who will create a special effect for a party, and, if the caterers themselves do not supply all the food and drink, they can also recommend those who will. Be quite definite about the kind of party you wish to give, state at least the approximate number of guests and what you are prepared to spend. A good caterer should be able, at need, to advise you how to give a party that is perfectly appropriate to the occasion and not ruinously expensive, and you approve the estimate – get as many as you can and compare them – before you decide. Check with whoever deals with your requirements as to what you are expected to do about tipping, though a service charge is usually added to the bill. If whoever is in charge is particularly helpful, you can of course either tip them separately (though they will probably put this into a pool of tips) or increase the percentage you are willing to pay for service. Never be timid about approaching even the most superior-seeming caterer. The most important people must often be very budget conscious and the wise and considerate caterer may, for example, recommend a first-class supper of sausage and mash and kippers, with beer or an inexpensive cup, rather than a pinch-penny dinner where everything tends to be second-rate and half-hearted.

Even if you do not want the on-the-spot services of a caterer, nowadays many firms will deliver you a ready-cooked meal or single dish which greatly simplifies the preparation of a party. In these days when staff are short everywhere, there is no need to be shy about engaging a maid, a butler, or a cook for an evening, or having the whole meal sent in.

The most important thing about all entertaining is that each guest should be made to feel welcome and be looked after throughout the time they are under your roof.

**Dinner Parties.** Whether you have help or entertain single-handed or as a husband-and-wife team, the basic routine of a dinner party is the same. Guests are invited, ideally by letter (but nowadays the telephone or personal conversation is quite acceptable) a week or more in advance – much more among a group of busy professional people whose engagement diaries may be full – and the time is given as, for example, "7.30 for 8". This allows for unavoidable delays and gives sufficient time for guests to meet each other and have some refreshment before the meal. It is correct to arrive at any time during this preliminary period, but of course, if you are going to be late, you should telephone and explain, politely urging the hostess not to wait dinner for you if the delay is going to involve the meal being put back more than, say, fifteen minutes.

On arrival, guests are shown where to leave their coats and where they may wash and tidy up. If the hostess opens the door, she can show women guests to her room and then, when the men guests meet her husband, they can ask him if they wish to wash. Guests are then introduced to each other and given a drink and possibly some small snacks before the meal. In what may be described as very grand houses they will be shown into the drawing-room, announced at the door, and the hostess will come to meet them. On a very formal occasion, men and woman are allocated to each other as dinner partners at this stage, the hostess introducing a man to each woman as: "Mr Jones, Mary, who will take you into dinner". This only means that the man will escort the woman into the dining-room, pull out her chair, if there are no staff, and sit next to her. Usually, however, the hostess merely takes the women with her in a group, the more senior ones going before the younger ones.

**What to Wear.** A formal or semi-formal invitation that contains the words "black tie" means that the men wear dinner jackets and the women short or long evening dresses. Anyone in the slightest doubt about what may be appropriate should not hesitate to ask the hostess. With a verbal or telephoned invitation the query "Are you changing?" implies that the guest wants to know whether evening dress will be worn. If it is not, the men wear dark suits and women the sort of dress they would wear for an evening engagement in town. The hostess should, out of consideration for her guests, always be definite about what she is going to wear and not change her mind after she has told them. She should also, again out of consideration for them, tend to "dress down" rather than wear anything too spectacular, so that any guest who may not be able to dress smartly for the occasion is not made to feel inferior.

**Seating People.** If you have guests of rank on a really formal occasion – such as when you are entertaining a high-ranking diplomat or officer in the services, consult the secretary, equerry or ADC in advance about where each guest should go. But for all but the grandest occasions, the general rule is – the most important man sits on the right of the hostess, and the most important woman guest sits on the right of the host. Those next in importance sit on the left of host and hostess respectively. The question of who is "important" really means those who are senior because of age, rank or position. A married woman is considered senior to a spinster, though of course a distinguished single woman should be given precedence over a young married woman, but traditionally, among people of approximately the same age and social standing, precedence goes to the person who has not dined in the house before – for this occasion, they are the most important guest or guests. After a couple get married, they are similarly honoured the first time they dine again with their friends. But really this is a matter capable of infinite variations, and the most important thing is to see that people are comfortably seated and next to those they will enjoy meeting.

Husbands and wives are always separated, so that they may have the chance of meeting other people, and in a dinner party where the men and women are in equal numbers, two people of the same sex do not sit side by side, though of course where the numbers are uneven this is unavoidable.

It is generally accepted that very controversial topics, such as may risk people becoming vehement or offending others, should not be introduced around the dinner table. At one time, politics, sex, religion and money were all taboo in polite society and no one commented on the food, however good or bad. Nowadays this rigidity has been greatly relaxed and it is rather for the guest to gather what may be acceptable by the attitude adopted by the hostess or host.

**Food and Drink.** Nowadays, there are no foods specifically reserved for "dinner" as opposed to "luncheon" but it is interesting to remember that things such as *hors d'œuvres*, and the less formal foods would never be served at a dinner party and may not be met with at very formal meals in the evening today. Nor are dishes passed twice for second helpings at extremely formal meals, though an exception is usually made for the pudding. (For dealing with specific foods, see below. For detailed advice on the presentation and service of foods, see the *Food and Wine* section, page 287.)

It is considered polite to talk to people on either side of you, rather than across a very wide table, except at small parties. It is not considerate for a woman to touch up her face or for anyone to smoke before the host or hostess give permission, and at a formal meal this will not be until the end, after the service of the pudding. At a banquet or formal meal in official quarters, guests will be told after the loyal toast that they may smoke and nowadays this is often proposed in the middle of the meal, just so that those who wish to light a cigarette may do so. Among those who smoke heavily and anyone entertaining guests from the United States or any of the Spanish-speaking countries, however, it is an accepted practice to smoke in between courses, or even while food is being served. It would be very inconsiderate to do this, however, without being given a very clear indication that it was in order to do so.

**"Difficult" Guests.** However carefully chosen the guests may be, some may either have problems or pose problems to hostess and host. For example, if someone is on a diet of great strictness, it is considerate to mention this to the host and hostess beforehand either so that suitable food may be served, or so that discreetly small portions may be given to the particular dieter, without attention being drawn to this. If a dish is not liked, it is polite at least to try and eat some of it, but also to have some polite excuse ("I had such a large lunch" or "My appetite is really very small") although the hostess should not, unless all the guests are fairly close friends, draw attention to the fact that someone

has left a lot on their plate. If a guest is in any doubt as to how to eat a particular dish, the thing to do is either to ask the hostess or merely watch what she does. No one should be urged to have more to eat and drink than they wish and, ideally, the hostess should always try to keep some food on her own plate to accompany someone who has had a second helping, or who is just a very slow eater.

A guest who causes distress or inconvenience to another is a great problem. It is the duty of the hostess to try and keep an eye on everyone, so that there is no risk of this happening, but if a violent argument breaks out she has the choice of either changing the subject or trying to soothe those involved. Some hostesses have even gone to the lengths of creating the kind of diversion caused when a plate is dropped or a glass spilled, but this is rather drastic! If someone is left out of the conversation or if remarks in doubtful taste, likely to cause offence, are made, it is for the hostess to deal with this problem, too. The status of the guest is sacred, but the one who is in need of help gets priority treatment from the master and mistress of the house. Although it is extremely difficult to give general advice about a particular circumstance, an abrupt change of subject usually indicates to the offender that what he or she has said is unacceptable. One can then remember not to ask a persistent offender again! For the man or woman entertaining single-handed, it is very helpful to have a close friend among the other guests who will keep an eye on the company and, if necessary, help to deal with any problem.

## ENTERTAINING OUTSIDE THE HOME

**In the Bar.** There are bars in which no one minds if a woman sits up at the bar and those in which the barman or waiter will prefer a woman, especially one on her own, to sit at a table. The only difficult social problem connected with bars, however, is when a woman is meeting someone who is late. The best way to deal with this is to tell the barman or waiter immediately you arrive – ask them if they have seen Mrs Smith or Mr Jones, explain you are meeting there and then either order yourself a drink or say you will wait. Staff should always look after you in these circumstances and if, after a reasonable length of time, the person for whom you are waiting neither appears nor sends a message (which the barman can always relay to you), you can take yourself away, leaving any message with the barman and without the slightest feeling of embarrassment.

A man should never keep a woman waiting when he meets her in a public place. If for any reason he is likely to be delayed, he should contact someone responsible in the establishment where she will be, and ask them to find her, express his apologies, and to look after her until he is able to arrive.

**In the Restaurant.** *Who goes where?* If there is a mixed party, the host leads the way into the dining-room, so that he may show people where to sit. If a man and woman are dining, he goes after her to the table – she walks behind the head-waiter – but if he has no table reserved, he goes first to arrange a reservation with the head-waiter and then follows his guest.

**Ordering.** If you do not go straight into the dining-room, but have drinks in the bar it is nearly always possible to ask for the head-waiter to bring out the menu and take your orders, so that the food may be ready when you go to the table. At the same time, the wine list should be requested so that any drinks may be prepared as well.

People who are entertaining a party of more than six or a woman who is entertaining single-handed, often find it much more convenient to order the meal in advance. Then no one hesitates about ordering a possibly too expensive dish and the task of the staff is greatly simplified. A good head-waiter will always help you with advice about a suitable menu, though of course it is sensible not to try and consult him at the peak hours of his working day – the middle of lunch or the middle of dinner for example.

**Paying.** (See also *Tips and Tipping*,) If you do not wish to pay in cash, and do not have credit-card facilities in the restaurant you are using, it is generally possible to sign the bill and have it sent to you for payment later. But it is always wise to inquire about this in advance, as some establishments would prefer you to write a cheque on the spot. Sometimes drinks in the bar can be added to the main bill, sometimes they are settled separately, and if a host or hostess does not wish to pay the bill in front of guests, the request can be made for it to be presented during the time when he or she leaves the dining room for this express purpose. If you are in any doubt about what may be convenient, do not hesitate to ask the head-waiter or manager.

**In the Night-club.** Night-clubs vary tremendously and, in the smart ones, visitors usually have the choice as to whether they will have dinner, just drinks or the sort of light refreshments that are described as "breakfast" and probably consist of bacon and eggs, or something similar. Breakfast is usually served after midnight. If there is a floor show, there may be two editions of this, one fairly early in the evening, the other at midnight or 1 a.m. Evening dress is not required, although in the more conventional night-clubs men are expected to wear dark suits and women have the choice of wearing anything suitable for a smart late-evening engagement. If a night-club does insist on evening dress, visitors in day dress may be admitted even so, but will probably not get a table on the dance floor.

**Hats for Women.** Although hats are often worn for cocktail parties, there are still some restaurants at the smart London hotels where a woman having dinner may be asked to remove her hat.

## TIPS AND TIPPING

Tipping is a payment for services rendered, which may be small or large. It may be a way of expressing appreciation, especially if someone does something for you in excess of their ordinary work. Many people regard the tipping system as degrading, but if one can look at it as merely a way of saying "thank you" as one might do by means of, say, a small present, it need not be a source of embarrassment or worry.

**In a Restaurant.** Unless a service charge is added to the bill (when this is done you need not tip in excess of it, although if you have had excellent service it is a pleasant gesture to leave any very small change in addition) you tip a percentage of this – 10 per cent is acceptable, 12½ per cent very adequate thanks, 15 per cent thanks for exceptional service, perhaps on some special occasion. The public do not always know that generally the tips in a restaurant are pooled in what is called the "tronc" of which each member of the restaurant staff draws a percentage so that the tips are shared according to seniority. You do not tip a chef or manager, but if you are particularly grateful for their services it is possible to ask them to have a drink with you, or send one to them.

**In an Hotel.** As in the restaurant, you tip immediately for services such as those provided by page, porter or chambermaid. If the hall porter has been helpful to you during a stay in an hotel, tip him when you leave.

**In a Friend's House where there are staff.** Tip whoever looks after you – the maid who does your room, a manservant who helps with your luggage or anyone who cleans your car. In a house with a butler, tip him most of all, as he is the senior servant. (The amount you tip depends on the length of your stay, but if it is not possible to ask any other guests for guidance on this subject, it is probably fair to assume that your tips should not be less than £1 each.)

**Chauffeurs.** If a friend loans a car and chauffeur to you, or if a man sends a woman home in his car with his own driver, the chauffeur is tipped – about 5s. for a short journey, more if more time is taken up.

**Taxis.** The 10 per cent rule applies here, unless some special arrangement is made for a long journey. In general, tip 1s. to 1s. 6d. for a fare costing up to 10s., 2s. to 2s. 6d. for a fare up to £1. If a taxi-driver has to wait for you, he should be tipped to compensate for the time he has lost which might have enabled him to earn another fare.

**Other people whom you tip.** In a hairdresser's, you tip whoever does your hair, with a smaller tip to anyone who does the shampoo or manicure. If the owner of the establishment attends to you, do not tip him, though if you appreciate his services, you give him a Christmas present. In a garage, you do not tip if you are merely purchasing petrol, but if you ask for some special service, or if the staff are helpful (if they wipe the windscreen without being asked, for example) you give them a small tip.

**Cloakrooms.** Cloakroom attendants are also tipped and generally have a saucer with the amount of tip they expect lying in it. One can be sure, however, that this will be the coin of the largest value they hope for.

**On board ship.** You tip in the same way as you would do in an hotel – those who look after you, and usually at the end of the voyage. Sometimes tips are pooled and often passengers are given a note as to the sort of tips expected; if this is not done, you can always inquire of the Purser or any of his staff, whom of course you do not tip.
*NB.* In all these circumstances, it should be remembered that young men and women are either not expected to tip at all, or only small amounts so that they need never feel shy about only saying "thank you" for services rendered.

Some people are shy about handing a tip over in person. There need be no embarrassment about this, but should you be unable to find the member of the staff concerned, you can always leave the tip for him or her with the receptionist.

**You do not tip** – airline staff, staff in other people's clubs (except in the cloakroom), and of course, never offer a tip to a policeman.

## STAYING IN A FORMAL HOUSEHOLD

In an establishment where staff are still kept and work in the traditional ways, the guest will usually find that he or she will be well looked after without any problems. It is always possible to decline the offer of services; for example, if someone offers to take your keys and unpack for you, you can always say you can do this yourself. Unless a very large staff is kept, it is courteous to ask the host or hostess, should you require any special services, such as having clothes pressed.

## STAYING IN A HOUSE WITHOUT STAFF

It is for the guest to be as unobtrusively helpful to host and hostess. The simplest thing is to ask exactly how you may do this and also remember that there are times when even the most sought-after guest may get in the way of routine domestic chores – it is often easier, for example, to opt for breakfast in bed while the hostess copes with the early morning routine.

In any household (even that of a millionaire), the thoughtful guest does not make free with the establishment's drinks, cigarettes, postal and telephone facilities, nor does he or she demand numerous additional services from the staff.

## GOOD MANNERS AT WORK

Every place of work has its own set of conventions – in some, everyone is called by his or her first name, in others this is a matter dictated by seniority, and in others surnames with the appropriate prefix are invariable. There are probably more firms organized informally than otherwise today, but the newcomer should be quite sure of what is considered acceptable before addressing the chairman of the company by his first name, nickname or initials! It is a fairly general rule, however, that at a formal meeting, or when outsiders are present, business people refer to each other formally, i.e. "Mr Jones has just reported

..." even though they may be Bill and Tom to each other every day.

Traditionally, one does not knock on the door of any room that is not a bedroom, but some people like there to be a knock on an office door. Usually – and this applies to any room – if it is imperative that no one should come in, then either the door should be locked or a "Do not disturb" or "Meeting in progress" sign put outside. But individuals and firms vary as to what they consider most convenient.

Business procedure differs, also, with regard to the conventional behaviour of men and women. Obviously a man or group of men do not rise when a woman secretary comes in and anyone in a subordinate capacity, man or woman, should wait to be asked to sit down when joining a meeting. It is perhaps worth stating that, even in the most taxing business situations, with the most difficult personalities involved, politeness and comparative quietness are not only invariably appreciated, but are usually more effective in achieving what is wanted than any displays of temperament.

## ENGAGEMENTS

Although nowadays many people planning to get married do without the formality of an engagement, the traditional procedure is for the prospective bridegroom to ask the father of the bride for his permission to marry, to obtain the agreement of both families and to tell relations and close friends before making an announcement, either in the national or local newspapers or in both. The usual form of this is:

Mr A. H. Smithson and Miss E. L. Jones
The engagement is announced between Arthur Henry, eldest son of Mr and Mrs Frederick Smithson, of The Briars, Avenue Parade, Margate, Kent, and Eleanor Louise, only child of Mr and Mrs David Jones, of 72 Pont Street, London, S.W.1.

If the parents of either bride or groom are divorced, they are named (with the woman's present married name, if she has remarried), with their two separate addresses.

If any of the parents concerned are dead, the phrase "and the late Mr Jones", is used.

If the bride is a widow, her present address is given and "widow of Dr George Brown" added, before the names and address of her parents.

In the announcement of the engagement of older people, whose parents may be dead, the names of the parents are not necessarily included.

If any doubt is felt about the wording of an announcement, the clerks in charge of this section of a newspaper will usually be able to give advice as to the customary form.

After an engagement is announced, friends write to express their good wishes to the two concerned. It is traditional to congratulate the bridegroom, but to wish the bride happiness.

If an engagement is to be short and the date of the wedding is announced in the newspaper at the same time, friends may start sending presents. At one time, the sending of a gift implied that you expected to be asked to the wedding. Nowadays, this is entirely for those immediately concerned to decide. If a wedding is to be a quiet one – on account of illness, family mourning, the couple being older, or simply because they prefer it this way – then they may prefer not to make any announcement, or only make one after the wedding.

**The Breaking of an Engagement.** The announcement of this is worded as briefly as possible:

Mr A. H. Smithson and Miss E. L. Jones
The marriage arranged between Mr, Arthur Henry Smithson and Miss Eleanor Louise Jones will not now take place.

Friends refrain from inquiries about this. The girl returns the engagement ring and any presents she has received from her former fiancé that are in the nature of "valuables", and both the man and woman return to the senders any wedding presents that may already have been sent to them, accompanied if possible by a brief note of thanks and regret.

**Engagement and Wedding Rings.** This is the personal choice of the bride – having reasonable regard to the bridegroom's pocket. Many people today do without an engagement ring, and wedding rings are also a matter of personal preference as regards metal, form and style. The ideal procedure is to go to a good jeweller and ask to see a selection, stating the price range in which you are interested. The bridegroom can make a preliminary selection before inviting the bride to choose. Men in the United Kingdom do not usually wear wedding rings, although they do on the Continent. Nor do widows in Britain change their rings over to their right hands, although of course a divorced woman may simply leave off her wedding ring. The fourth finger of the left hand is traditional for the wedding and engagement rings, because of a belief that it is directly connected with the heart. But Jewish brides wear their wedding rings on the forefinger of the right hand for the religious ceremony. Nowadays, too, some women prefer not to wear a wedding ring at all.

**Wedding Presents.** In addition to asking the couple what they would like – wedding presents are usually given to them as a couple or for their home – friends may find it helpful to find out if they have made a list of what they want and have deposited this with one or more local stores. This enables people who want to give a small gift to choose something within their means, and for the couple to include purely utilitarian presents – which friends might hesitate about suggesting – as well as large-scale ones (such as dinner-services), which several friends may often group together to buy.

Ideally, wedding presents are sent out fairly soon after receiving the wedding invitation or announcement, so that the couple can write their thank-you letters (which need only be brief) before the wedding. Presents are sent primarily to the bride – who will be making the home

44

– but if you only know the groom, then your gift is sent to him.

**Wedding Invitations.** These go out ideally three or four weeks before the wedding. They are engraved or printed on a folded invitation sheet, in plain black. Silver printing is not considered conventionally "correct", but this is a matter of individual taste. The invitation gives the name of the people being married, the place and time, details of any reception and the address to which the reply should be made. It is also a matter of personal preference as to whether the name of the guest should be filled in in the middle of the invitation, or written at the top. Any good stationer will have several examples of what is usual to show prospective couples. Replies should be in the third person, briefly accepting or declining. Any personal message should be in the form of a personal letter – or even a telephone message.

If a wedding is to be held some distance away from where the couple live, then the invitation may include directions as to how guests are to get there – e.g. a footnote "Cars will meet the 10.15 a.m. train from Paddington, arriving at Reading at 11.6."

Wedding invitations are usually sent out from the bride's parents, but when older people or those who have been married before are getting married, then nowadays it is quite acceptable for them to word the invitation directly from themselves; if they are being married quietly and only invite friends to the reception or a party, then the invitation states "On the occasion of the wedding of . . ." or "Following the wedding of . . ." without giving details of the ceremony, which may be only attended by very close family and friends.

**The Wedding Ceremony and Reception.** By tradition, this is the responsibility of the parents of the bride, in particular her mother, but in practice nowadays it is a matter for mutual arrangement between both families. However, the financial conventions are as follows:

*Her parents (or the bride) pay for:* Any announcements, invitations, her dress,

trousseau and any photographs. They pay for any decorations of where the wedding takes place and at the reception, service papers, and for all catering, and for all the transport on the wedding day except the car for the bridegroom and his best man, and the car in which the couple go away afterwards.

*He pays for:* Banns, licence and any tips where the marriage takes place; fee for the certificate and for any music; transport for himself and the best man, for the bride and himself to go away, flowers for the bride, bridesmaids and for his own mother and her mother, a small gift to each bridesmaid (piece of jewellery, powder compact, handbag or something similar), and for the honeymoon.

The bridesmaids pay for their own dresses, though of course if the bride wants them to wear anything expensive, it is only considerate for her or her parents to make a contribution towards this. It is also thoughtful for the bride to choose dresses of a kind that can be useful to her attendants afterwards.

Either the minister who is to marry the couple or the registrar will be able to give detailed advice on the ceremony, and any library or bookshop will have small manuals as to what is currently fashionable in the procedure of arranging a wedding and reception.

In general, however, the bridegroom's friends act as ushers at the ceremony while the best man accompanies the bridegroom and traditionally keeps the ring until it is required. In a church wedding, guests are asked on arrival whether they are friends of the bride or groom, and seated accordingly – right of the church if they are friends of the groom, left if friends of the bride. Front pews are kept for immediate family on both sides. When the parents and any close family or friends who have been asked to sign the register accompany the bride and groom to the vestry, the families combine afterwards to come down the aisle after the newly-married couple, the bride's mother being escorted by the bridegroom's father, bridegroom's mother by bride's father and so on.

At the reception, the formal tradition is that guests are received by – in order –

the bridegroom's mother and father, the bride's mother and father, the bride and finally the bridegroom. Whether or not they are announced, they shake hands, say a few words to the effect that they are delighted to be there, and then join the rest of the party. After everyone has been received, and later, whether or not a meal is served, the bride cuts the wedding cake, which is then offered to all guests. Speeches are, traditionally, made by either the bride's father or a close friend of her family, ending with a toast to the couple. The bridegroom then replies, and may go on to thank the bridesmaids, to which the best man replies. But nowadays there may be only the speech toasting the couple, with a very brief reply. Bride and groom then go to change—unless they have been married in day dress—and leave for their honeymoon, seen off by the guests. Small portions of wedding cake may be sent to guests unable to attend the reception.

Presents are not usually displayed at the reception nowadays, unless this is held in the bride's home. If they are on show, each should be labelled as to the donor, but cheques are merely listed, without the amount being stated.

**Dress.** If the bride is wearing a full-length dress and the groom a morning suit (though it is in order for him to wear an ordinary dark suit for all but the most fashionable type of wedding), then the best man and ushers follow his example, and the guests wear formal late-day dress, unless evening dress is indicated on the invitations and the reception is held in the evening. Women wear hats and gloves (which they do not take off until they have shaken hands at the reception), but men nowadays often dispense with even carrying the hat and gloves formerly a part of morning or formal dress. Bridegroom, best man, ushers and bride's father may wear white buttonhole flowers, the women of the families concerned will look smarter if they either carry a small bouquet or posy, or have flowers attached to their handbags, rather than wear them on their dresses as "sprays".

**Deaths and Funerals.** Unless it is possible to notify all friends personally, the simplest way of announcing a death is to put a notice in the local and national newspapers. This briefly states that the person concerned has died (it may be stated whether as the result of an illness, accident, or suddenly) and if possible indicates date, place and time of the funeral, or else says "funeral private", and gives particulars as to where flowers are to be sent, or if a donation to charity is to be made instead, as well as saying "No letters, please", if the family concerned feel unable to acknowledge correspondence. Notices about memorial services may be given at the time of death or a little later.

Letters of sympathy need never be long, but they should be personally written. If they cannot be personally acknowledged, then an announcement of thanks may be put in the newspapers, or printed cards expressing thanks for the expressions of sympathy may be sent out when there are large numbers of friends. Flowers intended for a funeral should be sent either to the house or to the undertaker concerned (the address should be given in the death announcement if possible) addressed to "The late Mr Smith." They should be accompanied by a card giving the donor's name; any personal message is a matter of individual preference. Nowadays many people request that cut flowers or bunches instead of wreaths should be sent, and arrange for these to go to hospitals or nursing homes after the funeral.

After a funeral, close friends or anyone who has had a long journey may be invited back to the bereaved household for light refreshments, but this again is a matter of personal convenience.

Nowadays few people observe the conventions of drawing the blinds in a bereaved household – and those adjacent – until after the funeral, as a mark of respect, and deep mourning is seldom observed. Many announcements specify "No mourning," and few people now wear black armbands. But this again is a matter of personal taste. Black-edged writing-paper and cards are seldom seen. People wear dark clothes to a funeral, men usually wear black ties, but actual full black is not obligatory. Women usually wear hats or some kind of head covering for a religious service, but few nowadays wear veils.

At a time of grief, the real guidance for friends of the family must be what may be helpful to the bereaved – whether their company is welcome or whether solitude is preferred. It is usually possible, if in doubt, to ask someone close to those concerned for advice. The same applies to people going out for social purposes – if they feel inclined to do so, there is no good reason why they should not, and friends should therefore not hesitate to offer invitations, even to those recently in mourning, which can always be declined if people feel unwilling to accept. One would not, of course, include a recently bereaved person in the kind of hectic and high-spirited celebration that might be tiring or distressing to them.

**Family Celebrations.** Christenings, confirmations, first communions, bar mitzvahs and birthdays are all occasions for family celebrations and it is entirely a matter of individual choice as to how they are organised – some might prefer a quiet tea-party, others a full-scale dance. A good caterer should also be able to offer useful suggestions as to how best to do honour to the occasion. But wedding anniversaries are in rather a special category and although very few people would think of offering, say, real rubies for a "Ruby Wedding", presents wrapped in ruby-red paper, or something ruby-coloured – tea-service, glass vase, tray – might be appropriate and fun, so here are the traditional names for the different years:

1: paper; 2: cotton; 3: leather and straw; 4: fruit and flowers; 5: wood; 6: iron or sugar; 7: wool or copper; 8: bronze; 9: pottery; 10: tin; 11: steel; 12: silk or linen; 13: lace; 14: ivory; 15: crystal; 20: china; 25: silver; 30: pearl; 35: coral; 40: ruby; 45: sapphire; 50: gold; 55: emerald; 60 and 75: diamond.

**Divorce.** There is no stigma attached to divorced people nowadays, but there can be problems as how to address a divorced woman. Conventionally, a widow retains her husband's first name – i.e. Mrs James Brown – and a divorcée puts her first name in front of her married name – i.e. Mrs Geraldine Brown. Women in business may, of course, be using their maiden or professional names anyway. So, if you are in doubt, the best thing to do is to ask a divorced woman friend how she prefers to be introduced and addressed. The same thing applies if you are planning a party which may include divorced couples who may or may not have married again – ask if they mind meeting each other. It is also up to the person concerned to avoid any embarrassment when meeting people to explain, briefly, that she is the *former* wife of John Smith, should the company be such that some of them are about to start a conversation about him.

**Going Abroad – and Foreign Visitors.** Anyone visiting a foreign country is an unofficial ambassador for their native land. So it is reasonable to try and avoid offending any national prejudices, being unduly critical or even being too enthusiastic about the host country. Conversely, it is up to those receiving visitors to help them as much as possible, to enable them to adapt themselves when necessary to another way of life and to maintain a sense of proportion about national differences.

Even if you do not speak a foreign language, you should be able to learn a fair amount about another country's way of life from the tourist office concerned, from the public library, and from the relevant embassy or consulate. It should not be necessary for anyone to bother to imitate different styles of national manners; but it may help, for example, to know that in Denmark flowers are always brought (even a couple of blooms) to the hostess when one is invited to someone's home, that in certain Latin countries shorts or very brief bathing-suits are not approved of, and that in some Moslem countries alcohol is not served. Knowledge of what is standard behaviour in another country can make one both a better guest and more understanding host.

**Public Appearances.** If you have to open a bazaar or fête, make a speech at a prize-giving, propose a vote of thanks, receive an important guest on an official occasion, or simply sit on a platform and receive a bouquet, it is important to do honour to the occasion. If at all possible, find out in advance exactly what is expected or get someone experienced to give you some advice. Even if you are shy, remember that others may be equally so and also that nothing is more charming and disarming than a smile. The advice given to a would-be public speaker – "Stand up, speak up, shut up" – is still sound. Never be tempted to speak at length unless you are really accomplished in doing so.

A woman who is in the limelight on such a public occasion should try to look her best as regards clothes and make-up, if necessary getting professional help about this, especially if she has to be photographed, as she should not look tired or pale under artificial lighting.

Never be hesitant about shaking hands or expressing appreciation or making some interested comment, and should you feel that you have made a mistake – trip going on to a platform, have your hat knocked off by some enthusiast at a sports event – make light of the mishap and make fun of yourself, as this will put others at their ease and avoid anyone being worried or offended.

# MEDICAL INFORMATION

## THE NATIONAL HEALTH SERVICE

The British National Health Service provides for every possible necessary form of treatment for the sick, nothing is barred if it is medically necessary and available. Each patient registers on the list of a family doctor of the patient's choosing and through him is obtained all necessary treatment either provided by the doctor or through him at a hospital.

**The Family Doctor Service.** Once a patient is registered on a doctor's list certain rules apply. The patient must attend the doctor's surgery for advice and treatment unless the patient's medical condition prevents this, when he is entitled to ask the doctor to call. It has been laid down officially that it is the doctor who has to decide if a home visit is necessary and not the patient, so that when asking a doctor to call the patient must explain the medical reasons necessitating a home visit.

**Registering on a Doctor's List.** Each patient is provided with a medical card, on the front of which is the doctor's name and the patient's National Health number and name and address. The name and address of the Executive Council for the area is printed on the front of the card.

On the back of the card are printed a number of rules for patients.

Inside the card are provided schemes for changing the doctor if the doctor and patient so wishes.

A doctor is not bound to accept a patient on his list and if a patient finds difficulty in getting on to a doctor's list then he should write and explain his difficulty to the area Executive Council who will give advice and in the last resort has powers to allocate a patient to a doctor's list.

A full list of National Health family doctors can be obtained at any Post Office.

When a newborn baby has its birth registered the Registrar of Births hands the parent a card which on completion should be handed to the family doctor so that the baby can be registered on the doctor's list.

New arrivals into the country or those who have never had a National Health doctor previously can call on a doctor and fill up an application form which will register him on that doctor's list. Later a medical card will arrive through the post from the Executive Council.

Each family doctor has a self-imposed area in which he is willing to attend patients and if the patient moves out of that area he will have to register with a doctor in the new area.

A patient can only register on a doctor's list if he is going to stay in that area for at least thirty days. If staying for a shorter period he has to register as a temporary patient, see below.

**Temporary Patients.** If the patient is away from home, whether on business or holiday and in need of medical attention he can call on any doctor and register as a temporary patient. The doctor supplies the form which must be signed by the patient. This covers a temporary stay of up to three months.

**Changing the Doctor.** If the patient moves from his address, even if he only moves to a different house in the same street, he has at once the right to choose a fresh doctor. To do this he completes the appropriate space inside his medical card and presents it to the new doctor.

If the patient has moved within the same area and chooses to remain on his doctor's list then he must send his medical card to the Executive Council with a letter explaining the change of address. The Executive Council will then issue a new medical card with the

48

correct details. *The patient may not change the address on the front of his own medical card unofficially.*

Occasion may arise when the patient wishes to change his doctor and is still living at the same address. This can be done in two ways.

He can ask the doctor to consent to the change and ask him to sign the appropriate space in the medical card after which he presents the card to the new doctor for acceptance. Because of the obvious embarrassment that arises this procedure is seldom adopted.

The other method of changing is by a Transfer Slip. The medical card is sent by the patient to the Executive Council with a letter asking for a Transfer Slip to be stuck on the card so that the patient can change his doctor.

The Executive Council sends back the card with a white sticker inside (the Transfer Slip). The patient fills this in with his name and address and presents it to the new doctor. If the doctor accepts the patient the doctor sends this card back to the Executive Council who then transfers the patient to the new doctor's list fourteen days later and issues the patient with a new medical card showing the transfer.

**The Doctor's Rights.** The doctor has the right to refuse to accept any patient on his list without giving any explanation. He has also the right to rid himself of a patient by requesting the Executive Council to remove the patient from his list. However if the patient is in need of medical treatment the doctor has a duty to provide this during the period that the patient is finding a new doctor *but it is the doctor who decides whether such treatment is medically necessary.* The patient is sent a letter by the Executive Council stating the date on which the doctor will commence to have no more responsibility for him.

**Certificates.** During sickness the patient has the right to get free certificates from the doctor with which to claim Sickness Benefit or Industrial Injury Benefit. He should send in to the National Insurance local office such a certificate within three days of being taken ill and if he delays he may lose the right to some of his sickness benefit, but the patient can send in a private letter during those three days stating that a medical certificate will follow in due course which registers the actual date of the start of a sick period. The patient must then get certificates at intervals to cover the whole sickness period *and must not go back to work until the doctor has issued a final certificate.* If this last rule is broken the doctor is not allowed to give a final certificate and the patient may lose benefit.

During the period covered by these official certificates no insurance stamps have to be applied to the Insurance Card, so even if the patient does not want to claim sickness benefit, perhaps because he is self-employed or has his wages made up by his employer, he should still send in certificates to cover the period of sickness otherwise he will have to pay for unnecessary insurance stamps.

National Health certificates are issued free of charge by the doctor for the purposes of the National Insurance benefits and that is the only purpose for which they may be used.

If a patient requires certificates merely to notify an employer or to claim private benefits from a sick club then the patient has to ask the doctor for a private certificate for which the doctor will charge a fee.

**Emergencies.** If a real medical emergency occurs and the patient's own doctor is not available then the patient has the right to send for any near-by National Health doctor to get emergency treatment. This right should not be used too lightly because if the case turned out not to be an emergency but just sheer panic then the doctor attending might charge a fee.

Emergencies such as home accidents, poisoning, burns, etc., and all accidents or cases of sudden illness in the street entitle the patient to have an emergency ambulance summoned to take the patient to hospital by any member of the public without a doctor attending.

The emergency ambulance can be summoned by using any telephone and using the emergency number listed in the telephone box, or asking the telephone operator, if the phone is not on the dialling system.

**Ambulances.** The doctor can summon a free ambulance or hospital car to take to hospital a patient who is not fit to travel by public transport.

See also under *Emergencies.*

**Treatment Under the NHS.** The patient is entitled to any or all medical treatment that is necessary for his investigation and recovery and this is at the sole discretion of the doctor. If the local hospital cannot provide the treatment the patient can be transferred to another hospital where such specialist treatment is available. Whilst any doctor will try to satisfy any preference the patient has as to which hospital he would like to attend there is no obligation on the doctor to send his patient to any particular hospital especially if the distance of the hospital makes the request unreasonable.

The patient cannot insist that any particular surgeon should perform an operation though usually the surgeon who first sees the patient at his Out Patient clinic does perform the operation.

The family doctor effects treatment by giving the patient a prescription which any chemist in the country doing NHS dispensing will dispense. Provision is made in each area for one chemist to stay open late on weekdays and to be open for a brief period on Sunday mornings. Bank Holidays are the same as for Sundays.

Medicines and other treatment left over after recovery from an illness should not be stored against a future need, some medicines become useless in time whilst others degenerate and could become dangerous; eye-drops are a typical example. If any treatment is left over it should be either flushed down the toilet or taken back to the doctor and his advice sought about disposal. Drugs should not be put in the dustbin from where they can end up on a road or rubbish dump and harm children or animals.

**Eye Treatment and Spectacles.** To obtain an eye test the patient must attend his doctor with his medical card at the doctor's surgery when he will issue form OSCI. This the patient takes to an optician or a medical ophthalmologist (many of whom practise from the optician's premises) where the eye test is performed and any necessary spectacles provided. If any medical disease of the eyes is discovered the optician reports back to the family doctor so that the doctor can send the patient to an eye specialist.

Having once had form OSCI issued the patient is entitled to attend the optician for an annual eye test without further reference to the doctor.

**Dental Treatment.** Children of school age can attend the dentist at the local Public Health Clinic if one is available. Both adults and children can attend any dentist who accepts NHS patients. If patients fail to keep appointments without adequate notice so that the dentist can use the appointment for another patient he is entitled to charge a fee.

**Nursing Equipment.** Any nursing equipment that is needed for the patient at home can be loaned free of charge if certified as necessary by the District Nurse or the doctor in attendance. The local medical officer of health on receiving the application makes the necessary arrangements.

*Nursing.* Patients needing nursing attention at home of a limited kind can be visited free by the district nurse on the orders of the doctor.

**Laundry.** Patients suffering from disorder causing an unusual amount of laundry for bed linen can be given assistance by the local medical officer of health.

**Night Watchers.** Where a doctor certifies that his patient needs a person to be with him at night the cost of paying a night watcher can be reimbursed by the local medical officer of health.

**Special Equipment.** The family doctor can order the chemist to provide oxygen equipment.

If the patient is crippled by a disease which prevents his getting about by public transport the family doctor can send the patient to an Orthopaedic Surgeon for assessment after which the Ministry of Health may supply free either a mechanical chair or an invalid motor-car.

**Home-helps.** Any patient unable to do housework for medical reasons can be given a certificate by the doctor stating what is required and the reasons. This is taken to the local public health clinic where arrangements can be made for a Home Help to attend, *if one is available.* The Home Help will only attend for a set number of hours each day to do the heavy work and occasionally cook a meal. They will not be available to stay all day with the patient as a free companion and housekeeper.

**Old People ... the Geriatric Service.** Where through infirmity or old age a person is no longer able to take care of himself/herself, provision is made for the patient to be admitted to an Old People's Hospital or Nursing Home. The family doctor has to certify the necessity after which an investigation is made by the medical department of the Local Authority.

Increasingly the modern concept is to provide hostels accommodating twenty to forty old people and provided by the Local Authority.

Elderly people requiring medical treatment are admitted to a normal hospital where geriatric beds are set aside in special wards.

**Financial Hardship.** Patients in need of financial help can apply to the local office of the National Assistance Board.

## GOOD HEALTH

Medical Science has by no means learnt all that there is to know about the curing of the many diseases that attack the human species, but it probably knows something about all of them. To turn the statement round the other way, however, it can certainly be said that so far as the question of good health is concerned, if certain rules of health are adhered to, then many of the common ailments that prey upon mankind would in some cases be wiped out altogether, and in others, reduced to a minimum.

There is far too much of the situation which is known as sub-health; sub-health being that state between quite healthy and not ill. This state of health can rarely be pinned down to one particular cause, unless the whole of the patient's manner of existence is investigated closely. In some cases the patients that visit the doctor in his surgery ask for a tonic in order that they may regain that spring in their step, that healthy sleep, that wide-awake feeling, that happy outlook on life which once they knew. Far too often the cure does not lie in a bottle of medicine. Good health is a manner of living. If you do not live in a healthy way, then all the medicine in the world will not do you very much good. What you must do is to take exercise, keep clean, get plenty of fresh air, eat the correct food, make the correct use of sleep, and live as nearly as possible as nature meant you to live. In the bringing up of children their future health may rest entirely upon the wisdom of the parents in the early training stages.

## SLEEP

**What it is and how much we need** Sleep is a voluntary state of rest for the body and mind during which volition and consciousness are in partial or complete abeyance and the bodily functions are partially suspended. In the course of it we become revitalised to deal with the problems of the ensuing day, but how we go to sleep is still very much a mystery despite the vast amount of research that has been undertaken on the subject.

How much sleep do we need? It is customary to regard eight hours as the requirement for the average adult but since people differ so widely no fixed figure can be laid down, though perhaps six to eight hours is a mean average for most people. Some people never sleep more than three hours at night and yet remain perfectly fit and well, whilst others complain if they get less than ten hours. Many people who claim to suffer from insomnia do not in fact need any more sleep than they are getting.

The sleep requirements of children are somewhat different. The newborn baby will sleep for twenty-two hours of the day, waking only for meals and bathing, but as the child grows so his need for sleep declines as is shown in the chart below.

*Average Hours of Sleep required by Children*

| Age | Hours required |
| --- | --- |
| 6 months | 18 |
| 1 year | 14 to 16 |
| 2 years | 12 to 14 |
| 5 years | 10 to 12 |
| 10 years | 10 to 11 |
| 16 years | 9 |

Teenagers, with so many activities such as parties, dancing and similar entertainments clamouring for their attention, rarely nowadays get the nine hours of sleep they require each night. Many of them attempt to fight off the desire to sleep by drinking strong black coffee or one of the soft drinks claimed by the manufacturers to give "lift", an effect which they obtain by incorporating in the drink caffeine citrate – a brain stimulant and the active ingredient of strong black coffee.

Some of these young people, in their efforts to keep going, even commit the height of folly by resorting to pep-pills, little realising that by doing so they may be taking the first step on the road to drug addiction and all its terrible consequences.

## FACTORS CONDUCIVE TO NORMAL SLEEP

Mental peace, physical fatigue, warmth, fresh air, pleasant surroundings and a comfortable bed are all factors conducive to sleep, whilst pain, anxiety, noise and lack of warmth will effectively banish sleep for most people.

**The Mattress.** The essential quality of a good mattress is its ability to keep the spine horizontal and in a muscular-negative state. One that does not provide this degree of physical support allows the spine to become curved with the result that one set of spinal muscles is stretched and the other set of muscles is half-bunched and cramped.

Since people come in all shapes and sizes it is clearly obvious that no one spring-tension is suitable for everybody. A mattress suited to the wife's eight stone will be inadequate for her 15-stone husband, who will sink into it so that his wife will literally be trying to sleep on the side of a hill and neither of them will obtain proper rest.

Nevertheless, the problem is not as insoluble as it may appear, for many bedding manufacturers now produce mattresses with several spring-tensions to cater for varying weights. Even double-bed mattresses can now be obtained with different spring-tensions on each side. In some cases these mattresses actually consist of two single mattresses joined by a zip-fastener, which is virtually unnoticeable so far as it affects comfort.

A pamphlet on the subject of sleep and containing some worthwhile advice on choosing a mattress has been published by the Central Council for Health Education, Tavistock House, Tavistock Square, London W.C.1.

**Bedclothes and Warmth.** Snuggling down into a warm and comfortable bed is a luxury that can make one feel sleepy just to talk or think about it, but it is important to realise that heavy bedclothes are not necessarily warmer than lighter coverings. In fact in some people an excessive weight of blankets causes violent dreams.

For a really warm bed there is little to compare with an electric blanket. However, unless these appliances, which are designed to emit only a predetermined degree of heat, are used strictly according to the manufacturer's instructions serious consequences can result. The body normally sweats during sleep, and obviously the warmer one is the more one will sweat. If, therefore, one sleeps on a switched-on blanket that is not thermostatically controlled, and many manufacturers advise against doing so, there is a very real danger that sweat will soak into the blanket, alter its electrical resistance and cause it to become so overheated that a heavy sleeper may well suffer burns.

There are even greater dangers for those subject to diseases likely to cause coma (diabetes and epilepsy are examples), bed-wetting or any other illness which may cause the blanket, even one that is thermostatically controlled, to become moist, for in recent years there have been many cases of fatal burns from this cause.

No electric blanket should be left on during sleep, and not only should it be switched off but the mains plug should be removed from its socket.

**Fatigue and Supper-time Drinks.** If the body is not fatigued then obviously it is not ready for sleep, and just to go to bed at a fixed hour from sheer habit will only result in insomnia.

Those who do not feel tired as bedtime approaches and who for a variety of reasons are unable to stay up until the early hours, may find that a long walk after supper will help to get them pleasantly fatigued or if that is not possible then a warm bath just before getting into bed is very relaxing and conducive to sleep.

Elderly people are often poor sleepers at night, due frequently to the fact that they have had several cat-naps during the day and, in addition, have taken little exercise. Since alcohol is a sedative, a hot toddy containing whisky or rum immediately before retiring may help them to sleep, but if that does not work then it will perhaps be necessary to obtain a mild sedative from a doctor.

Coffee contains caffeine citrate, a brain stimulant, and cocoa induces the kidneys to work faster so that both are equally unsuitable as a bedtime drink for poor sleepers. Any type of drink taken late at night disturbs some people, and though this may be no more than irritating to those who sleep well, poor sleepers have little choice. Either they must forgo their supper-time beverage or suffer the inconvenience of visiting the toilet in the early hours and the consequent difficulty of resuming their slumbers.

**Freedom from Pain, Anxiety and Depression.** Pain and anxiety will both prevent sleep, so that once the causes of both have been removed the problem of insomnia also disappears.

Depression combined with insomnia is a horse of a different colour, and it indicates that the sufferer is in need of medical advice, because this combination is often the forerunner of a state of mental imbalance that could well lead to an attempt at suicide. Many of these people are so mentally sick that they refuse to seek medical help themselves, in which case it is incumbent on their relatives to consult a doctor for them.

## DIETETICS

Food is required by the body for three reasons:

    (*a*) to supply heat to the body.
    (*b*) to supply energy to the body.
    (*c*) to repair body waste.

Many factors control body heat, and among these are local temperature, clothing, movement, the condition of the skin and tissues (especially the muscles and the glands, chiefly the liver). Nevertheless there is a daily loss to the body of about 2,500 calories of heat. This is lost by the skin, 77–80 per cent; by breathing, 17–20 per cent, and by excreta, 3 per cent.

Air and food must supply to the body the chemicals needed by the tissues. These are carbon, hydrogen, oxygen, nitrogen, sulphur, sodium, potassium, calcium, magnesium, iron, phosphorus, chlorine and iodine. Food is made up of: proteins, carbohydrates, fats, vegetable acids, salts, vitamins and water. All are essential to health and growth, but not all are essential to life.

**Proteins.** Essential to health and growth, the main among which are, trytophane, tyrosine, cystine, lysine and arginine. A minimum of 37 grms. daily are required. The main sources of protein are obtained from animal products such as cheese, eggs, fish, meat and milk.

**Carbohydrates** include the monosaccharides glucose, laevulose and galactose, which are found in the sweet juices of fruits, yeast, honey, etc., the disaccharides maltose, lactose and cane sugar, which are found in malt, milk, cane sugar and some plants, and the polysaccharides which include dextrine, starch glycogen and cellulose, which are found in beer, juices of most plants, crust of bread, in seeds of cereals and potatoes, in liver, muscles, and other tissues of man and animals.

**Fats.** A combination of trivalent alcohol (glycerin) with stearic, palmitic or oleic acid. Usually taken in the form of neutral fat found in meat-oils, butter, cheese, cream, eggs, and nuts.

**Vegetable Acids** contain sufficient oxygen to oxidise their hydrogen. Form carbonates for blood and other tissues. Found in most vegetables.

**Mineral Salts.** Certain mineral salts need to be provided in definite amounts. The most common deficiency is that of calcium, although iodine is often deficient in certain areas. Calcium is to be found in cheese, egg yolk, milk, bran and green vegetable. Most of these also contain phosphorus, as also [does oatmeal. Iodine is present in fish, watercress, onion. Iron is found in egg-yolk, liver, oatmeal and green vegetable.

**Vitamins** are classified in alphabetical order, and not according to their action, as A, B complex (which comprises B1, B2, B6 and other compounds), C, D, E and K.

*Vitamin A* is the anti-infective vitamin. Deprivation is followed by septic complications. In adults, a lack may produce softening of the cornea of the eye. It is essential for the formation of tooth enamel, and for cell growth. It is present in fat, milk, butter, egg-yolk, cream, dried eggs, cod-liver oil, halibut oil, cheese, cabbage, potatoes, carrots, liver,

kidney, heart, herring and salmon. The main source is from fish oils.

*Vitamin B Complex: Vitamin B1.* Occurs in cereals, eggs, yeast, malt, liver, kidney, potatoes and wholemeal. Pork muscle contains about eight times as much as beef. It is essential for the proper utilisation of the starches. Lack of this vitamin effects the emotions and the nervous system. There is a loss of appetite, the individual becomes excessively fatigued on slight exertion or mental effort and suffers from vague, undefined, gastro-intestinal disturbances. If there is a gross deficit, the diseases which manifest themselves are Beri-Beri and Polyneuritis, with enlargement of the heart. The body needs more during growth than in maturity.

*Vitamin B2.* An important source of Vitamin B2 is egg-yolk, and in a less degree, wholemeal bread, nuts, beans and peas. A partial deficiency of this vitamin results in impaired growth. The lips and the mouth are also affected and the eyes may become inflamed. A marked deficiency produces a disease called Pellagra with a peculiar type of Eczema.

*Vitamin B6,* occurs in high concentrations in seeds, yeast and liver. A deficiency appears to be responsible for insomnia, muscular weakness, and cramp-like pains in the stomach.

*Vitamin C* is called ascorbic acid. It is found in abundance in citrus fruits, fresh green vegetables, and apples. A necessity for Vitamin C occurs in periods of epidemics. Therefore when colds, influenza and respiratory catarrhal diseases are present, citrus fruits such as oranges, grapefruit and lemons should be consumed. It prevents scurvy, and is essential for perfect health and development; lack of it may cause dental caries and gingivitis. Affects the normal health of the body, and is an important factor in the health of the gums. Deficiency causes swollen and bleeding gums, and changes in the bones. This vitamin is lost in some methods of domestic cooking, being destroyed in boiling green vegetables in soda, or carried away with the water used to cook the vegetables. Is present in fresh vegetables, cabbage, onion, lime, orange, lemon, swede, tomato, raw meat juice, wheat, peas, lentils, beans. (Note rolling or crushing will destroy the vitamin in these seeds.) Orange juice is the richest source of Vitamin C.

*Vitamin D*, found in eggs, milk and in liver. The livers of many fish contain Vitamin D in abundance. Loss of this vitamin predisposes to infections, especially of the respiratory tract. Plays a part in the deposition of lime and phosphorus in the growing bones, and is therefore needed to counteract Rickets. Has an effect on the growth and well-being of teeth and is needed to counteract the occurrence of dental caries. Vitamin D is needed especially by babies and young children. Vitamin D can be built up in the body by the influence of sunshine or ultra-violet rays. Fruit and vegetables obtain their Vitamin D content through contact with the sun. Is also present in fat fish, especially fish liver oils, fish roe, egg-yolk, and in summer milk, butter and green vegetables.

*Vitamin E* is necessary for fertility and reproduction. Prevents sterility in both sexes. Administration of this vitamin has been useful in cattle-breeding. Is present in oats, lettuces, meat, egg-yolk, liver, whole wheat.

*Vitamin K.* This occurs in the leaves of the plants, but little is known as to its distribution. It is essential to man. A deficiency of this vitamin is characterised mainly by haemorrhages, particularly in infants. Is responsible for certain allergic skin diseases, such as Urticaria and certain types of Alopecia (falling hair).

**The Normal Adult Diet**
This consists of getting an adequate daily intake of:

*Protein* (fish, meat, cheese, milk).

*Fat*, contained in oils, cream and butter, etc.

*Carbohydrate*, contained in all forms of cereal, flour, cakes, bread, sugar, honey, syrup, etc.

*Chemicals.* Adequately covered by a mixed diet.

*Water*, which needs to be drunk freely.

*Vitamins.*

As personal preference plays such a large part in deciding which food is eaten all that can be said about the adult diet is it must be carefully balanced so that meat, fish, dairy products, eggs, fresh fruit, vegetables and water are all included.

Old people tend to concentrate on items that are easy to prepare and often live on little more than bread, cakes and tea. They need iron in tablet form and vitamin capsules to reinforce their diet.

## SPECIAL DIETS

### BLAND DIETS
For those suffering with indigestion or an ulcer a special easily digested diet is required.

*Food and Drinks Allowed:*

**Milk and Eggs.** Milk prepared in any way – junket, custard, well-cooked milk puddings, milk soup. Plain cream, made-up cream, ice-cream, or cream soups. Butter. Eggs lightly cooked, beaten as egg and milk, or as custard.

**Fish and Meat.** Fish boiled, steamed, or baked, but not fried. Chicken or game roasted or baked. Tripe, brains or sweetbread, well cooked, but not fried. Meat – beef or mutton occasionally, roasted or baked but not boiled or stewed.

**Vegetables.** Potatoes well cooked and mashed. Cauliflower, spinach, carrots, well cooked and rubbed through a sieve. Tomatoes fresh or cooked if rubbed through a sieve.

**Fruit.** If raw, avoid skins and pips. If cooked, always rub through a sieve; apricot fool, apple meringue, red currant, apple or marmalade jelly, damson cheese.

**Various.** White bread, cut thin and toasted dry. Any kind of smooth plain biscuit. Plain sponge cakes, or light madeira cake without fruit. Jellies, plain chocolate, sugar, honey and golden syrup.

**Drinking.** Drink sparingly with meals. You may take plenty of water between meals. Freshly-made weak tea, especially China tea; coffee with milk. Fruit juice. Milk. A small quantity of light wine is allowed with dinner or supper.

**Instructions as to Meals:** Take your meals regularly and avoid hurrying over them. Large meals are always bad; frequent small meals should be your aim. Avoid taking a meal when you are tired or when you have cold hands or feet. Lie down, rest, and get warm first. Eat and chew thoroughly.

*Food and Drinks Forbidden:*
*Fried foods* in all forms are forbidden.
**Soups and Meat Dishes.** *Avoid* meat soups and rich gravies; twice-cooked meat, sausages, made-up dishes, pork, "high" game and all tough meat.
**Fish.** *Avoid* salmon, sardines, dried fish.
**Condiments.** *Avoid* spices, pepper, cayenne pepper, curries, vinegar, relishes, pickles, chutney and mustard.
**Vegetables.** *Avoid* cabbage, peas, beans, celery, onions, watercress, and cucumber; other vegetables must be passed through a sieve. You may add fresh butter to vegetables, but they are not to be cooked in fat. Avoid fried or chip potatoes.
**Fruit.** *Avoid* all pips or skins of fruit (whether raw, cooked or in jam). Avoid raw apples, melon, marmalade, jam, lemon peel, currants, raisins, figs, nuts, and all unripe fruit.
**Various.** *Avoid* rich pastry or puddings, new bread, brown bread, porridge, and fruit cake. All cheese, other than cream cheese, is forbidden, and so is cooked cheese in whatever form.
**Drinking.** *Avoid* cocktails, spirits. Never take alcohol on an empty stomach. Avoid strong tea, black coffee and cocoa.
**Smoking.** Give up smoking if indigestion is present.

## ANAEMIA DIET

For those suffering with anaemia and under treatment by their doctor and taking iron tablets or having injections of Vitamin B12 for Pernicious Anaemia.
**Beverage.** Tea, coffee, cocoa, Sanatogen, milk, fruit juices.
**Bread.** Whole wheat.
**Cereals.** Preferably oatmeal, bran, shredded wheat.
**Dairy products.** As desired. At least 1 pint of milk per day.

**Fruits.** Preferably oranges, lemons, grape fruit, prunes, apricots.
**Vegetables.** All kinds, cooked and raw, especially spinach, peas, beans, cabbage, asparagus and lettuce.
**Dessert.** Fruits, milk puddings and plain desserts.
**Meat.** (1) Liver. (2) Red meats, roast beef, beef heart, steak. (3) Sweetbreads, kidney and brains may be substituted for liver.
**Take Daily.** (1) Two large servings of vegetables and fruits every meal. (2) $\frac{1}{2}$ lb. liver or liver extract (directions are on the bottle).

**Sample Menu**
**Breakfast.** Fruit. Cereal. Egg and bacon. Brown bread and butter. Black treacle. Milk, $\frac{1}{2}$ pint. Cream and sugar.
**Dinner.** Broth or vegetable soup. Meat. Potato. Vegetables (green or root). Bread and butter. Dessert.
**Supper.** Cheese macaroni. Lettuce and tomato salad. Brown bread and butter. Fresh fruit. Sanatogen (2 teaspoons in $\frac{1}{2}$ pint milk).

## LOW-RESIDUE DIET

Diet for those suffering with intestinal disorders, colitis, Crohn's disease, diverticulitis, etc.
  Foods allowed:
**Beverage.** Cocoa, milk, Sanatogen, strained fruit juices, weak tea.
**Bread.** White (stale).
**Cereals.** Strained porridge and gruels.
**Desserts.** Custard, junkets, jellies, blancmange, milk puddings, plain cake.
**Eggs.** Lightly boiled, poached or scrambled.
**Fruits.** Sieved fruit, baked apple (without skin), ripe banana. All pips, seed and skins must be avoided.
**Meats.** Lamb, chicken and steamed fish.
**Vegetables.** Cooked and put through a sieve.
**Soup.** Strained vegetable soup.

**Sample Menu**
**Breakfast.** Strained porridge. Egg. Toast and butter. Sanatogen.
**11 a.m.** Orange juice and biscuits.
**Dinner.** Meat. Potato mashed. Sieved vegetable. Egg custard. Milk, 1 glass.

**Tea.** Bread and butter, honey or strained jam. Sponge cake or biscuit. Tea, milk, sugar.
**Supper.** Strained vegetable soup. Steamed fish and sauce. Bread and butter. Apple sauce and junket.
**At Bedtime.** Sanatogen, 1 cup.

## BLAND PURIN-FREE DIET

Diet for those suffering with high blood-pressure, kidney trouble or Gout.
Foods to *avoid*:
(1) Red and glandular meats.
(2) Coffee, tea, cocoa, chocolate in excess.
(3) Broths and meat soups.
(4) Rich highly seasoned food.

**Sample Menu**
**Breakfast.** Fruit. Cereal. Egg. Toast and butter. Cup of Sanatogen.
**Dinner.** Boiled fowl or fish. Potato. Vegetables. Bread and butter. Dessert.
**Tea.** Bread and butter. Jam. Cake. Weak tea, milk, sugar.
**Supper.** Cheese macaroni. Lettuce and tomato salad. Bread and butter. Fruit. Plain cake or pudding. Cup of Sanatogen.

## HIGH CALORIC DIET

Diet for those requiring to put on weight or convalescing from an illness.
Suggestions for adding food to increase calories:
(1) Use butter and cream in liberal amounts.
(2) Use mayonnaise with salads.
(3) Use foods requiring the addition of sugar and cream.
(4) Sanatogen made with condensed milk.

**Sample Menu**
**Breakfast.** Fruit. Cereal and cream. Bacon. Bread and butter. Marmalade or honey. Tea or coffee. Milk, 1 glass.
**Lunch.** 1 cup Sanatogen. (2 teaspoons Sanatogen. 1 tablespoon glucose. ¼ pint condensed milk).
**Dinner.** Milk soup, biscuits or toast. Meat. Potato (mashed with butter). Cooked vegetable. Dessert with cream. Bread and butter.
**Tea.** Bread and butter, jam. Cake. Tea, milk, sugar.

**Supper.** Cheese omelet. Hot vegetable. Bread. Salad with mayonnaise. Fruit and cake, junket, custard or cream. Milk, 1 glass.
**10 p.m.** Cup of Sanatogen. (As at lunch.)

## REDUCING DIET

For those who are overweight.
Sugar, cakes, pastries, puddings, jam, bread, potatoes, or fried food, *must not be eaten.*
Plenty of green vegetables, salad, and all fresh fruit *except* bananas, *may be eaten.*

**Sample Menu.**
**Breakfast.** Tea, milk – 2 tablespoons. 2 eggs. 1 "Vita Weat" biscuit or Ryvita. Butter – piece size of ½ a walnut. Tomatoes – ¼ lb.
**Dinner.** Lean meat or cheese – a good portion (about 3 ozs.). A good plateful of green vegetables or salad. 1 small apple, orange, pear or grapefruit.
**Tea.** Tea, milk – 2 tablespoons. 1 egg. 1 "Vita Weat" biscuit or Ryvita. Butter – piece size of ½ a walnut.
**Supper.** Steam fish – a fair portion (about 6 ozs.). Butter – piece size of 2 walnuts. A good plateful of green vegetables or salad. 1 small apple, orange, pear or grapefruit. 1 "Vita Weat" biscuit or Ryvita.

1,128 Calories.

## ACIDOSIS DIET (CHILDREN)

Digestive disturbances caused by acidosis are apt to produce a state of poor nutrition in children.
Protein foods (low in fat content):
(1) Lean beef, lamb, liver, chicken.
(2) Skimmed milk.
(3) Steamed or boiled fish.
(4) Eggs.
Suggested puddings (low in fat content):
(1) Jelly.
(2) Fruit whip (made with egg white).
(3) Blancmange (made with skimmed milk).
(4) Skimmed milk pudding.
(5) Cornflour and fruit juice combinations.

(6) Fresh, dried and tinned fruit.
(7) Sponge cake.
(8) Fruit charlotte.
(9) Bird's custard.
(10) Barley sugar.
Foods to *avoid*:
(1) Fried foods.
(2) Chocolates and toffee.
(3) Pastry.
(4) Nuts.
(5) Cream and butter.

**Sample Menu**
**Breakfast.** Fruit. Cereal and skimmed milk. Dry toast. Marmalade or honey. Sanatogen ($\frac{1}{2}$ pint skimmed milk).
**Dinner.** Lean meat. Potato. Vegetables. Blancmange and fruit.
**Tea.** Baked tomato on toast. Stewed fruit and sponge cake. Glass of skimmed milk.
**At Bedtime.** Sanatogen. $\frac{1}{4}$ pint skimmed milk. Cold water, biscuit.

## HEALTH AND AIR TRAVEL

The big airlines maintain a medical department who are there to give advice as to whether a patient ought to fly or to provide special oxygen equipment if they are fit to fly. When in doubt the airline should be consulted.

Patients with the following diseases should get advice as to their suitability before booking an air ticket:—

**Nervous Disorders.** Lack of oxygen and hyperventilation can aggravate the condition of those suffering with uncontrolled epilepsy. Mental cases might be accepted if sedated or accompanied by an attendant.

**Pregnancy.** Most airlines will carry expectant mothers up to the thirty-second week and even later on internal short air trips; the restriction is enforced to avoid the risk of a confinement when airborne. Those women liable to abortions are encouraged not to fly until after the third month lest a bumpy journey precipitates the onset of a miscarriage.

**Blood Diseases.** Any blood disorder which reduces the number of red blood-cells to under $2\frac{1}{2}$ million per cubic m.m., or the haemoglobin to under 50 per cent or causes a tendency to haemorrhages cannot fly without oxygen and may require a blood transfusion before the journey. The airline medical officer should be consulted.

**Heart Diseases.** Those suffering with angina pectoris or compensated heart disease who can take reasonable exercise without becoming distressed or out of breath should be reported to the airline medical officer who will make available special oxygen breathing equipment.

Patients with heart failure and suffering with breathing distress will have to be considered by the airline medical officer.

Those who have had a coronary thrombosis should not fly until they have been free of all symptoms for two to three months, and patients suffering with high blood-pressure should have a sedative before the flight and extra oxygen made available and in all fairness the airline medical officer should be consulted.

**Chest Diseases.** Acute head colds especially if accompanied by sinus trouble or blocked eustachian tubes causing blockage of the ear drums are a temporary contra-indication to air travel.

Asthma, bronchitis, emphysema, and fibroid lung are contra-indications if the patient is permanently short of breath but even if allowed to fly they must have oxygen available.

Cases of active tuberculosis cannot be carried whilst still rated as infectious.

Other lung conditions than mentioned may require extra oxygen and each case has to be judged on its degree of severity and amount of breathlessness.

**Gastro-intestinal Disease.** Gastric and duodenal ulcers may bleed or perforate under conditions of reduced pressure or be aggravaged by air sickness and definitely should not fly until a month after recovery from a bleed whether haematemesis or melaena. After any abdominal operation it is most unwise to fly until two weeks after the operation.

If there is any doubt about a patient's condition and suitability for air travel then no chances should be taken but the airline medical officer approached for a medical opinion.

**Inoculation.** Nowadays many countries lay down compulsory health laws such as vaccination against smallpox and if the traveller is going to or through the yellow fever belt then they insist on immunisation against yellow fever too.

One has to differentiate between what inoculations are compulsory and which are desirable. Without the compulsory inoculations the passenger will not be allowed to land from his plane and may waste a lot of valuable time being isolated and injected. As regards the voluntary inoculations it rather depends on the country of destination. If the country to be visited is somewhere like America with an up-to-date public health system then there is less need to be inoculated against typhus and plague than if one was visiting the interior of China where these diseases are alleged to be always present.

The International Sanitary Regulations specify the following periods for the validity of International Certificates for the compulsory inoculations.

| Type of Vaccination | Certificate valid for | Period validity begins |
|---|---|---|
| SMALLPOX | | |
| Primary vaccination | 3 years | 8 days later |
| Re-vaccination | 3 years | At once |
| CHOLERA | | |
| Primary vaccination | 6 months | 6 days later |
| Re-vaccination within six months | 6 months | At once |
| YELLOW FEVER | | |
| Primary vaccination | 6 years | 10 days later |
| Re-vaccination after six years | 6 years | At once |

These rules may vary from country to country and from year to year so it would be as well to make inquiries early as to the current rules in force not only for the country of destination but for all countries that the traveller intends to pass through.

These International Certificates, in blank form, have to be obtained by the traveller and taken to the doctor for completion and afterwards they have to be taken to the Local Medical Officer of Health to be stamped before they will be accepted abroad.

The blank forms can be obtained from the travel agency or air line or direct from one of the following:

Ministry of Health, Elephant and Castle, London S.E.1.

Welsh Board of Health, Cathays Park, Cardiff.

Scottish Home and Health Department, St. Andrew's House, Edinburgh, 1.

## MENSTRUATION

Menstruation is the medical term for the monthly periodic flow of blood which occurs in normal women between the approximate ages of 13 and 50, lasting from three to six days and varying in degree according to general health and occupation.

**The First Menstruation Period.** The age at which menstruation first appears varies in different races and in members of the same race. The average age for the first onset is 13 to 14 years, but it may be as low as 9 to 10 and as late as 18 to 21 years. In these latter ages it is due to delayed development of the uterus. If accompanied by severe pain or excessive flooding medical advice should be sought as these are abnormal conditions and can usually be alleviated by drugs, vitamins or surgery.

The menopause, climacteric, or change of life usually occurs between the ages of 45 to 50. It may occur as early as 40 years and as late as 52, although some healthy women continue to menstruate up to 55 years of age.

Menstruation may cease abruptly at the change of life, or it may cease gradually. It is a very dangerous fallacy which is unfortunately still accepted by many women, that the change of life is usually ushered in by excessive menstrual bleeding or flooding. Do not fail to seek medical or gynaecological advice at once in the case of excessive and prolonged bleeding during the average years when the climacteric, menopause, or "change of life" occurs.

The signs and symptoms of the menopause are "hot flushes", especially of the face and neck, lasting from a minute to several minutes, followed by cold sweats. These may be accompanied by nausea. Frontal or occipital headaches are common, accompanied by giddiness, particularly on stooping or looking up suddenly, and an irritable nervous state which the woman appreciates but cannot control. In some cases she is depressed. At the same time many women become more obese, and early arthritis of the knees is noticeable, particularly in the working woman who is a domestic, a waitress, shop assistant, or one who belongs to the great unpaid working women of the community, the housewife. Treatment by a doctor with special ovarian glandular preparations will relieve a woman very quickly of the distressing symptoms of the menopause.

The disturbances of menstruation are due to three main causes:

(a) *Amenorrhoea.* Absence of the menses which may be primary or secondary, and may be the result of pregnancy, lactation, shock, climactic change, or as a symptom of such diseases as anaemia, tuberculosis, or from a congenital condition preventing the proper exercise of the sex organs. In all these cases the patient must be under the care of the doctor.

(b) *Dysmenorrhoea.* Painful menstruation is experienced by many women, but only in a small percentage does it handicap them. In these cases it should not be considered a normal condition and medical advice should be sought. It is often a question of a slight operation, or the pain can be alleviated by drugs, or change of routine and diet, which will improve the general health. In the treatment of dysmenorrhoea, modern gynaecology has made great strides in the past decade. Women vary in their tolerance to pain, and the psychological approach is as important as the physical. In many cases dysmenorrhoea ceases after childbirth as the dilatation of the uterine canal relieves the congestion or spasm which had originally caused the pain.

(c) *Menorrhagia* is excessive loss of blood during the normal time of the period, and *metrorrhagia* is loss in between the periods. They are both often caused by the same condition.

The presence of fibroids in the womb is one of the commonest causes, other causes are some upset of the hormones; the sequel to a recent miscarriage and any form of ulceration within the womb.

Heavy loss of blood at the periods, or any blood loss between periods justifies seeking medical advice early.

**Cleanliness.** Cleanliness is essential. Liberal use of soap and water and, much more important, internal cleanliness through complete elimination of waste products in order to avoid that most chronic of all modern scourges, constipation. Do not over-eat. Vary the diet, making it as mixed and as balanced as possible. A plentiful diet of meat, fish, eggs, fresh fruit, green vegetables, salads, butter, wholemeal bread, cereals and milk will supply the necessary protein, carbohydrate, fat, vitamins and essential minerals. Eat not to fill but to nourish the body and remember that getting overfat causes more diseases than enough.

The body needs plenty of fresh air and exercise at all ages. Avoid wearing tight clothes and ill-fitting shoes.

## THE SKIN

**Care of the Hands.** The normal skin keeps healthy and supple by means of the natural oil supplied by the grease glands. Anything which degreases the skin leaves it dry and brittle and liable to crack.

All the detergents, furniture polish, oven cleansers, lavatory powders, pot scourers, turps, petrol, lime, cement, nail polish removers, etc., all degrease the skin, so protective gloves should be worn when handling these articles.

For those keen on keeping the skin of the hands soft and supple here is a hand lotion which is used after scrubbing up by surgeons.

Tragacanth powder, 44 grains.

Simple tincture of benzoin, 72 minims.

Glycerine, 5 fluid ounces.

Water to one pint.

The chemist, on request, can colour it pink and add some eau-de-Cologne to make it smell nice. A little should be rubbed into the hands after washing each time.

**Skin Disorders and Treatments applicable to the Face and Neck.** It must be emphasised that a doctor's advice is absolutely necessary if a speedy recovery is required. Affections of the skin are frequently made worse by ill-advised home treatment, and the use of proprietary medicine.

Of the disorders which may attack the face and neck, the following are the most common:

**Seborrhoea** (*excessive sebum secretion*). Sebum is the secretion of the sebacious glands of the skin and is chiefly composed of fat. Seborrhoea is not really a disease, but is most undesirable cosmetically, because of the unpleasant oily shine it gives to the face. It is most common in adolescents, and is often associated with dandruff.

The treatment lies in the removal of the stimuli which may increase the activity of the sebaceous glands, such as cold, heat, light, wind, and weather. Attempts should be made to remove the sebum from the skin by washing frequently, or by using a proprietary solvent containing spirit. A dusting powder of sulphur (5 per cent) and talcum, is very helpful in these cases.

A cream containing 4 per cent precipitated sulphur and 12 per cent solution of precipitated coal tar is very useful in cases associated with dandruff.

**Acne Vulgaris.** The actual cause is not known. Predisposing causes are puberty associated with constipation and excessive seborrhoea. Infected tonsils, teeth, and irregular menstruation may aggravate. The earliest stage is the comedone or blackhead.

In acne vulgaris, a small pustule may appear at the mouth of the skin gland. If the contents of the acne pustule erupt to the surface, healing may occur spontaneously. It is quite common for the orifice to close again, however, and fresh pus to collect. The acne may be cleared after coming to a head, by expressing it gently so as not to form a scar, remembering to heat the face first with hot water in order to open the pores.

Treatment: Wash with a super-fatted sulphur soap with resorcin. After washing, treat with a sulphur lotion.

If there are a considerable number of pustules, your doctor may prescribe penicillin treatment. An acne vaccine is helpful, and internally, Vitamin B1.

**Comedones** (*Blackheads*). The glands in the skin may become blocked with the secretion in a number of ways. If they do, almost always the common blackhead occurs. The cause of the complaint is the same as that of the acne vulgaris, either a disturbance of nutrition, or constipation or puberty with the usual secretions.

The treatment is similar to that for acne. The blackheads may be squeezed out. Remember always to open the pores as much as possible by the application of warm or hot water or towels wrung out in hot water. If the blackheads are numerous and difficult to reach, the doctor should be consulted. If there are repetitions of the complaint it may be advisable to obtain a pair of comedo forceps from the chemist. These are easy to use and may prevent undue damage to the skin.

**Megaloporia** (*dilated or enlarged pores*). Frequently found on the nose and surrounding parts of the face. Can only be cured by removing the surrounding skin, and must be done by a plastic surgeon. Relief and improvement may occur with treatment by the ultra-violet lamp which must be given under the supervision of an expert in this form of treatment.

**Milium.** Hard whitish deposits lying close under the epidermis, each about the size of a grain of sand. Treatment should be left to the doctor and consists in splitting the skin and squeezing out the small deposits.

**Hypertrichosis** (*superflous hair*). Superfluous hair is produced when the fine hairs with which the body is covered develop into hairs of ordinary size.

In order to destroy a hair, it is necessary to destroy or put out of action the hair follicle which lies well below the surface. It is, therefore, quite clear that the advertised hair removers cannot remove hair permanently, but can only remove the hair which appears above the surface. The only safe and permanent measure is by electrolysis, and since special knowledge and skill is required, it must be done by the doctor or qualified specialist. If the condition is marked, and the growth of superfluous hair excessive, it may be associated with disease of the suprarenal gland. Consult your doctor in such an event.

**Naevi** (*birth-marks*). An overgrowth of dilated capillaries in the skin.

**Soft and Hard Warts, and Moles.** Small, normally harmless tumours, these disturbances may prove to be very unsightly. The only safe method of removal is by surgical operation.

**Abnormalities of the Hair.** Falling hair may be due to several reasons. Normal hair is subject to seasonal fluctuations, and may fall a little in the spring and autumn. Following illness, or as a sign of general debility, there may be some signs of falling hair.

The common disorder causing falling hair, and probably subsequent baldness, is seborrhoea of the scalp. It is first shown by the appearance of the white fine scales that will be well known to most readers as dandruff. The head is often itchy and scurfy as a result.

**Cosmetics.** Exposure to sunshine, which, when reacting on the secretions of the skin, produces Vitamin D, is most beneficial to health. In some cases, where sunshine is either non-existent at the time, or where it is too weak for the desired effect (for example in towns when the layer of smoke prevents penetration of the rays) it may be necessary to implement the sun with artificial aids. This irradiation, as it is called, is effected by ultra-violet light or quartz light. It is useful in such diseases as rickets, skin diseases associated with diabetes, tuberculosis of the skin, and in the promotion of sleep.

In cosmetics, to promote a tan, ultra-violet rays may also be used.

Needs and fashions may vary, however, and if it is desired to stay out of doors and at the same time to keep the skin white, there are two matters wihch must be attended to. Firstly, those parts that are to be protected must be covered from the sun as much as possible, although this might be difficult when the sun is very hot, and secondly by anointing the necessary parts.

**The Nails.** White spots on the nails may be ignored. Furrows running across the nails are indicative of poor circulation, and this must be the matter of treatment before the nails can be improved. Some diseases of the skin which attack the hands, may have an adverse effect upon the nails. Eczema, ring-worm, are the most common. In all these cases the original disease must be checked before the nails will improve. Whitlows, which are most painful and may prove to be very unsightly, are best treated by surgical operation.

**Hyperhydrosis.** Excessive sweating. This disorder may vary greatly in intensity and also in type. It can effect all the skin or certain regions only. In some cases only one foot or one armpit is affected abnormally. If the sweat is not allowed to evaporate, it decomposes and gives off an offensive smell and may ruin clothes. As in the case of other disorders, the matter must first be diagnosed correctly before adequate treatment can be given.

Body sweating may be of two forms, cold, or hot, and may be the result of another bodily disorder, or simply of an increased action of the sweat glands in a particular part of the body. In any case the cause must be diagnosed. Drugs, administered either internally or externally may be used, or X-ray therapy, or medicaments in the form of paints or powders. The best anti-sweat paints are a 30 per cent solution of formalin in tap water, or a 10 per cent solution of aluminium chloride. The best powders are those containing salicylic acid or tannoform mixed with a talc base. Frequent bathing is essential for personal freshness, and frequent changes of clothing, including shoes, is necessary in order that the sweat secreted is allowed a time to evaporate.

Two useful prescriptions for powders for tender feet which are caused by excessive sweating, are:
  (1) Potash alum 15 parts
      Talc in fine powder 85 parts
  (2) Talc in fine powder 2 parts
      Boric acid 2 parts
      Orris 1 part
      Zinc oleate 1 part.

## THE EYE

**1. Black Eye** (*Ecchymosis of the eyelids*). The swelling and discoloration should be kept in check by the application of lint or cotton-wool soaked in cold water bandaged evenly and firmly over the eye. The skin should never be punctured, however large the swelling. If the condition is severe, or if the eyeball is itself damaged, the doctor should be consulted.

**2. Inversion of the lower lid.** Occurs sometimes among old people. The condition should never remain untreated, and the doctor should always be consulted as it may lead to ulceration of the cornea.

**3. Painful or watering eyes** may indicate the presence of foreign bodies e.g., grit or dust, which should be removed with a small fine camel-hair brush, or small piece of lint. The condition may be due to ingrowing eyelashes, which should be removed only by the doctor. If the foreign body cannot be removed easily, consult the doctor early in order to prevent injury to the eyeball.

**4. Conjunctivitis** is inflammation of the delicate membrane that lines the eyelids and covers the eyeball. In some cases the condition may be accompanied by a purulent discharge. This condition should never be ignored, especially in newly born infants.

In every case a correct diagnosis is necessary before treatment is commenced. Therefore, the doctor or eye specialist should always be consulted.

**5. Stye.** This is an inflammation of one of the sebaceous glands of the eyelids, or infection of the hair follicle of the eyelash.

If small and not painful, the application of hot fomentations may quickly disperse the stye. If the affected eyelash is pulled out the pus will discharge and the condition be cleared up. Large or painful styes should be treated by a doctor. A penicillin eye cream is helpful.

**6. Squint.** Modern ophthalmology is able to cure squinting in most cases. Mothers should never hesitate to seek early advice for their children.

A squint may easily develop during whooping cough. This should be carefully watched for and advice sought if the slightest sign is apparent.

**Care of the Eyes.** Sight is the most important and valuable of all the senses. It should never be abused nor its importance underrated.

Parents should be jealous of the sight of their children and never hesitate to seek advice if it is needed. The use of glasses to correct a fault in young children may avoid a need for glasses at a later stage in life.

In any case and at any age always seek specialist advice before obtaining glasses. Special treatment of eye disorders may possibly correct a fault without permanent resort to the use of glasses. The science of "Orthoptics" is the method of correction of eye defects by special exercises.

For those whose eyes may be exposed to undue strain, working long hours in artificial light, or close and detailed indoor work, care of the eyes is especially important. Cold eye pads applied to tired eyes give great relief.

It is important in view of the sensibility of the human eye that eye lotions should be non-irritant, mildly antiseptic, and physically compatible with the normal tear solution bathing the eye.

A simple normal saline made with distilled water, is very helpful. A 10 per cent distilled extract of witch hazel added to the above lotions will soothe and give a cooling astringent effect to strained eyes.

**Cataract.** A condition of milky opacity occurring in the lens of the eye which blocks the vision. The eye surgeon can remove the opaque lens and fit the patient with spectacles to restore the sight.

**Glaucoma.** A condition coming on after middle age in which the internal pressure of the eyeball rises, causing a deep boring pain in the eye-socket and headache. It needs urgent attention from an eye specialist if the sight is to be saved.

### Glossary

ASTIGMATISM. A defect of the curvature of the refractive surfaces of the eye, so that the rays of light are not focused on to a single point.
BLEPHARITIS. Inflammation of the eyelid.
CATARACT. Applies to those conditions in which the transparency of the lens is lost to a greater or lesser degree.
EMMETROPIA. From the Greek, "in proper measure vision". The normal condition of the eye with perfect vision. It is the perfect type of eye. Any variation from this standard is called:
AMETROPIA. From the Greek "irregular eye".
GLAUCOMA. The result of raised tension of the fluid within the eyeball.
HORDEOLUM. A stye.
HYPERMETROPIA. Far-sightedness. The hypertropic eye is the undeveloped eye in which parallel rays of light come to focus behind the retina of the eye, and, consequently, this type of eye, if at rest, sees everything indistinctly. Eye-strain is a predominant and common symptom. Corrected by convex lenses.
MYOPIA. Short sight.
NYCTLALOPIA. Night blindness.
OPHTHALMIA. Severe inflammation of the eye or of the conjunctiva.
OPHTHALMOLOGIST. A trained eye specialist versed in the diseases of the eye.
OPTICIAN. A maker or seller of glasses.
PRESBYOPIA. From the Greek "old eye". Long sight and impairment of vision due to old age. The power of accommodation is diminished due to loss of the elasticity of the lens, so that the near point of distinct vision is removed farther from the eye.
REFRACTION. Testing the eyes to ascertain errors of vision.
RETINA. The sense organ of vision at the back of the eye, connected to the optic nerve.
STRABISMUS. Squint.

**Headache.** Headache is not a disease in itself, but a symptom of another disorder, and while the aspirin medicaments may alleviate or cure the pain, the patient should always remember that the cause of the headache, if persistent or recurrent, must be diagnosed correctly and treated accordingly.

The following are some of the more frequent causes of headache:

**1. Eyestrain.** The pain in this case may be felt in front of the head and behind the eyes. Observation will show whether or not the brow is being "wrinkled" in order to focus the eyes. Frowning will often accompany headache, and is often associated with a tired and burning feeling of the eyeballs. Do not hesitate to consult a fully qualified ophthalmic specialist in order that the disorder may be either cured by treatment, or glasses prescribed.

**2. Diseases or Disorders of the Ear, Nose and Throat.** Mouth breathing in the case of adenoids or enlarged tonsils, or due to blocked nasal passages, a cold, sinus trouble, or blocking of the external ear passages through an over-secretion of wax or foreign bodies in the ear, may all cause a headache. The site of the pain is frequently over the forehead.

If the headache persists medical treatment must be sought and the cause of the headache treated.

**3. Teeth.** Diseased molars or wisdom teeth (those at the back of the jaw) may cause headache in adults. The pain will be felt at the back of the head. The diseased teeth must be attended to by the dentist. An X-ray may be necessary.

**4. Poisons.** Bad air owing to poor ventilation, an over-indulgence in tobacco, alcohol, or drugs, fumes from petrol, coal gas, paint, coke or other similar substances, may all cause a heavy feeling in the head and severe headache. The cause must be removed. In every case removal into clean fresh air, coupled with the removal of the poison concerned should quickly cause the headache to disappear.

Constipation and kidney disorders may produce headache. In these cases the primary disorder must be treated. Headaches may accompany menstruation.

**5. Fatigue.** In addition to bodily fatigue which may cause headache, brain fatigue in which other symptoms may not be manifest, may also produce headache. Rest will produce the cure.

**6. Organic Head and Bodily Disorders.** Tumours in the head, blows on the head, fevers and other specific diseases, blood disorders such as anaemia and high blood-pressure may all produce headaches.

**7. Nervous Headaches,** typified in migraine, epilepsy, or other nervous disorders. The cause must be treated, but in some cases the headache must be regarded as chronic and part of the disease.

Headache should never be disregarded. The cause should always be sought. Neither in children nor in adults should headache be regarded as normal. It is certainly a sign of ill-health in one way or another.

If the headache is persistent or recurrent, the doctor should always be consulted in order that an accurate diagnosis may be made, and correct treatment applied to the cause of the headache.

*Treatment.* If the headache is rare, slight, and cannot be attributed to any primary cause, one of the following analgesic medicaments may be taken:

Aspirin, Phenacetin, Veganin, Panadol. For adults the dose is about two tablets every four hours. Tablets should never be taken for weeks on end. If the headache persists a doctor should be consulted.

## THE EAR

**Cerumen (or Wax).** This is secreted from special glands in the external ear. If excessive it may vary from a semi-solid mass to a hard plug of grey or black wax. The condition is often due to over-secretion of the glands, or to allowing soap to remain continually in the ear after washing. If the wax is hard it must be softened before syringing, either by warm olive oil or glycerine drops inserted in the ear two or three times a day for a few days.

It is necessary to syringe the ears with care. Therefore consult the doctor, and do not allow an amateur to meddle with the ear.

**Foreign bodies** may be inserted in the ear by children or adults and forgotten, e.g. plugs of cotton wool. Other foreign bodies may be insects such as flies, etc.

A foreign body pressing on the drum may cause deafness, noises in the head (Tinnitus), a dry cough, and sometimes vomiting.

Do not meddle. Consult the doctor or aural specialist.

**Furunculosis** of the external auditory meatus. This condition is a boil in the ear and one due to infection of a hair follicle or gland by the staphylococcus. It is caused by scratching the ear, or as a result of boils elsewhere on the body, or by chronic discharge of the middle ear.

As a routine measure in recurrent boils of the ear, the urine should be tested by the doctor to eliminate any possible diabetic cause.

If the boil does not rupture spontaneously, the doctor may have to incise the boil under an anaesthetic.

**Eczema** of the external ear should always be treated by a doctor. Treatment should be sought in the early stages, since the condition may easily become chronic.

**Bleeding** from the ear may be present after an accident or blow on the head, and is suggestive of a fracture of the base of the skull.

**The Middle Ear.** The middle ear includes the tympanic cavity, which lies between the internal ear and the external auditory meatus, the mastoid cells and antrum and the Eustachian tubes.

Acute inflammation of the middle ear may be caused by a severe cold in the head, nasal catarrh, the infectious fevers such as scarlet fever, measles, diphtheria or small pox, influenza, pneumonia or whooping cough, from internal septic infections, or from injuries to the head.

The symptoms may vary according to the cause of the inflammation. Pain may vary from occasional twinges to acute continuous pain, which may radiate from the ear up the side of the head. Some deafness may be present, noises in the head, a high temperature, possibly a discharge from the ear.

R—E.W.—C

In children the symptoms may include convulsions and vomiting.

Children suffer greater pain and may have a higher temperature than adults suffering from the same disorder.

For practical purposes it is true to say that all earache in children is due to an inflamed eardrum and requires treatment with antibiotics started within the next 24 hours if the hearing is not to be damaged.

Repeated attacks of earache warrant a consultation with an ear, nose and throat specialist lest the tonsils and adenoids need removal.

**Chronic Suppuration of the Middle Ear** (*discharge from the middle ear*). The chief causes are persistent nasal catarrh which has remained untreated, or adenoids. The causes are aggravated usually by unhealthy surroundings and poor health.

The condition may last for years without causing undue worry and treatment unfortunately is not usually sought until deafness, headache, giddiness, neuralgia, or an increase in the discharge cause some concern to the victim or the parents.

No treatment is advisable unless prescribed by a doctor, who should be consulted early in every case.

**Polypus in the Ear.** A polypus is a smooth growth which occurs in the mucous membrane. In the ear, polypi may be single or multiple and usually occur as symptoms of another disease. Treatment is by a minor surgical operation by an aural specialist.

### Glossary

AUDITORY. Pertaining to the sense of hearing.
AUDITORY CANAL. *External:* The passage from the external meatus to the tympanic membrane or ear drum. *Internal:* The passage in the petrous bone for the auditory and facial nerves and the auditory blood vessels.
AURICLE. The ear outside the head.
CERUMEN. Ear wax. The secretion found in the external auditory canal.
DEAFNESS. *Labyrinthine:* Associated with the middle ear. *Family degenerative:* A hereditary condition of labyrinthine deafness. *Old age:* Usually accompanies hardening of the arteries. A labyrinthine type. *Syphilitic:* Occurs in acquired and hereditary syphilis. *Toxic:* A labyrinthine type caused by poisons acting on the auditory nerve. *Congenital:* due to maldevelopment of the middle ear. *Boilermaker's:* Caused by working in places where sound is deafening. *Hysterical:* Which appears and disappears with the hysteria

in affected patients. *Music:* Inability to determine musical notes (tone deafness). *Vascular:* Due to a disease of the blood vessels of the ear.
EUSTACHIAN TUBE. A tube one-and-a-half to two inches long extending from the naso-pharynx to the eardrum. Its purpose is to equalise the pressure between the ear drums and the outer air. If blocked, causes deafness with noises in the ears (*Tinnitus Aurem*).
HEARING. Sound waves travel through the external ear to the drum, which vibrates. These vibrations are transmitted across the middle ear by three small bones called the *Malleus* (Latin – Hammer), shaped like a mallet; the *Incus* (Latin – Anvil), shaped anvil; and the *Stapes* (Latin – Stirrup), shaped like a stirrup, to the internal ear, and thence to the endings of the auditory nerve and so to the brain.
INTERNAL EAR - or LABYRINTHE, is embedded in the petrous portion of the temporal bone, and contains three semicircular canals and other delicate structures, the nerve endings of the eighth cranial nerves – the auditory nerve (or nerve of hearing).
MASTOID PROCESS. The nipple-shaped portion of the temporal bone lying immediately behind the ear, containing large air spaces communicating with the middle ear.
MASTOID. From the Greek "nipple-shaped".
MÉNIÈRE'S DISEASE. A disease of the internal ear, causing giddiness and deafness, with noises in the ear. The giddiness is known as vertigo and the patient's sense of balance may be temporarily affected.
MIDDLE EAR. The cavity on the inner side of the eardrum and communicating with the outer air with the Eustachian tube.
OTITIS MEDIA. Inflammation of the middle ear.
TYMPANIC MEMBRANE. Ear drum.

## TEETH

**Pyorrhoea.** A condition in which pus exudes from the teeth sockets accompanied by swollen and inflamed gums. As the infection persists the gums recede and the teeth may become loose.

Dental treatment is essential in all cases.

**Alveolar Abscess.** Pertaining to a tooth socket. Nearly always due to sepsis originating in a decayed tooth. Several varying conditions may arise depending on the situation and the course taken by the pus so formed.

In most cases the removal of the tooth is necessary. Certainly early dental treatment must be sought.

**Dental Caries (Decay) in Children.** Dental care and treatment should start for children as soon as the teeth appear. The number of milk teeth which may be expected is twenty, and they will begin to break through the gums at any time between the sixth and thirtieth month. The centre front teeth on the lower jaw are the first to appear, followed by the corresponding teeth in the upper jaw, and then the remainder of the teeth.

The enamel and dentine of teeth are the hard coverings of the teeth (enamel is the polished exterior, and dentine the bony interior covering).

The amounts of dentine and enamel present may vary with individuals, and depends on:

(1) The nature of the first teeth;
(2) Subsequent care of the teeth;
(3) The health of the individual;
(4) The action of the saliva.

It is not difficult to ensure fine healthy teeth, provided that adequate attention is paid to their early development and care.

The following measures should be adopted by parents for infants and continued until the child adopts the measures automatically:

1. Thorough mastication of all food. Hard crusts and biscuits should be given to all infants and later followed by other hard foods which require active mastication. Biting on a plastic or bone teething ring is useful.

2. No food or sweets should be allowed between meals.

3. The mouth and teeth to be thoroughly cleaned *before retiring at night* with a soft baby toothbrush and milk of magnesia. This time is more important than in the morning.

4. At no time should particles of food be allowed to remain between the teeth.

5. After the age of three years it is essential to have regular attention to the teeth by a dentist, at not less than six-monthly intervals, whether or not any pain is felt or any decay noticed.

## COMMON MALADIES

The object of this chapter is therefore to outline the more common maladies which affect us in order that they may be readily recognized, and to mention what early precautions can be taken to alleviate the matter, and whether or not the doctor is required urgently.

**Abscess.** May occur in any part of the body. There are local signs and symptoms referable to the part inflamed, and general signs and symptoms due to the absorption of poisons into the circulation.

Locally there are heat and redness of the part, swelling, pain and the inability to use the inflamed part due to the aforementioned symptoms.

The most characteristic general signs and symptoms are a rise of temperature and a rapid pulse. Rigors or shivering attacks accompanied by vomiting in some cases. Consult a doctor early and do not procrastinate. Modern treatment by penicillin, the administration of the sulpha group of drugs, may abort or localise an abscess early, and may avoid surgical intervention.

**Adenoids.** Usually associated with enlarged tonsils. More common in children, but affects all ages.

*Symptoms.* Headache, bad breath, mouth breathing, dullness and expressionless face, deafness often with discharging ears (*Otitis media*), snoring and sniffing of the nose due to catarrh, and persistent cough at night when the child is in the prone position. There is a nasal tone to the voice.

*Treatment.* Only by operation. Therefore consult the doctor. After operation, breathing exercises are of the greatest value. The symptoms may be alleviated and the catarrhal discharge checked by spraying frequently with penicillin in a normal saline solution. Asthmatical attacks may occur, and occasional nocturnal emissions (bed-wetting) may be a symptom of enlarged adenoids. "Pigeon chest" or a "barrel" chest may result. See also page 116.

**Anaemia.** A reduction in the amount of haemoglobin (the colouring matter of the red blood corpuscles) which carries the oxygen inhaled into the lungs into the tissues. It may be primary or secondary. In the latter case it may be due to simple loss of blood by haemorrhage. In the former case it may be due to various causes which the doctor will diagnose from a complete blood examination and institute the necessary treatment accordingly.

Increasing pallor, giddiness, shortness of breath, a low temperature and fatigue are some of the common signs and symptoms which should prompt a patient to consult a doctor.

**Appendicitis – Acute.** A common disease which may prove disastrous if the signs and symptoms are misunderstood. It is most common in childhood and in adolescents, but may occur at any age.

Its onset is generally sudden, and the first symptom is primarily referred to the area around the umbilicus or navel, and later settling down in the right iliac fossa, the area between the right crest of the pelvis and the umbilicus. This is often followed by vomiting, a rise of temperature and a rapid pulse. Even if there is no rise in temperature, but sudden acute pain in the right side in a child, followed by vomiting, send for a doctor at once. *Do not* give aperients on any account.

**Appendicitis – Chronic.** This may be a sequel to an acute attack which has subsided or it may occur as a series of sub-acute attacks. There may be constant pain and discomfort in the right side which is often increased by exertion or the symptoms are referred to the stomach or duodenum and simulate a peptic ulcer.

Consult your doctor who will arrange for an X-ray and other tests.

**Asthma.** Severe attacks of shortness of breath of a paroxysmal nature due to spasm of the bronchial muscles, and associated with an over-secretion of the mucus in the bronchial tubes.

It occurs at any age and very often in nervous types. Certain conditions affecting the nose, stomach and allergic conditions may precipitate an attack. It may occur in middle-aged patients who are subject to chronic bronchitis and emphysema. Sensitivity to various proteins or pollens may precipitate an attack. Attacks frequently occur at night.

Send for the doctor early, and while waiting for the doctor's arrival relief may be obtained by giving an ephedrine tablet (half-grain). The breaking of an amyl nitrate capsule in a handkerchief and inhaling the vapour may give relief. The doctor will probably give an injection of adrenalin and prescribe the necessary further treatment.

Attention to the general health is important. Constipation, flatulence and gastro-intestinal disturbance must be avoided, and nasal obstructions treated. Chronic bronchitis must be treated by the doctor. Heavy meals should not be taken at night. Attendance at an asthma clinic for skin tests and vaccine treatment is advised. Breathing exercises, especially in the young, are very beneficial.

**Back-ache.** Back-ache is mainly a woman's complaint. It may arise through abnormal conditions of the body such as severe constipation, kidney disease, lax abdominal muscles, prolapse of the uterus, or as a symptom of such acute illnesses as pneumonia or influenza. In cases of menstrual disorders and pregnancy it can be very severe, and requires medical advice, as it is an abnormal feature in these conditions.

**Disorders of the spinal muscles.** In this category belong all the forms of muscular rheumatism, lumbago, and fibrositis which are largely due to exposure to cold and damp. Fatigue, faulty posture, or occupation which results in prolonged stooping and unnecessary curvature of the spine are also contributory causes and may result in severe pain in the spinal muscles.

**Diseases of the spinal column.** These diseases are of a far more serious nature and demand the specialised skill of the orthopaedic surgeon as the pain felt in the back is caused by the diseased joints which may need surgical skill or manipulation.

Nervous or functional back-ache may be experienced when there is no organic disorder which can justify the presence of pain, but is caused by the psychological state of the patient, who may be using physical pain as an outlet for his mental instability.

*Treatment.* The treatment for the various types of back-ache will depend on the doctor's diagnosis of the general condition of the patient or the specific disease from which he may be suffering.

If it cannot be remedied surgically the doctor will rely mainly on the correction of diet, supply the necessary vitamins, massage and electricity, surgical belts and appliances, etc., according to the location and nature of the pain.

**Prolapsed Vertebral Disks.** Between each pair of vertebrae which go to form the spinal column emerge a pair of nerves. Also between each vertebra there is a disk of gristle which acts as a shock-absorber. If this disk wears away, splits or extrudes it allows the two vertebrae to grind against each other and against the emerging spinal nerves.

The symptoms are pain in the back (lumbago) which radiates down one or both legs and sometimes with feelings of numbness and tingling in the legs or feet.

The treatment consists of consulting an orthopaedic surgeon who will X-ray the spine and be able to see that two of the vertebrae are riding close together showing that the disk has collapsed. Physiotherapy, special exercises, a surgical belt and occasionally an operation may be employed.

A similar condition which used to be called osteo-arthritis of the neck spinal joints has now acquired a new name . . . spondylosis.

The neck joints show evidence on an X-ray of being worn away.

The symptoms are neck pains, sometime travelling right up and over the skull and stiffness in moving the neck.

Treatment may be a felt collar, neck supports and physiotherapy.

**Bed Sores.** The chief causes of bed sores are neglect and bad nursing, although in cases of prolonged illness in bed-ridden patients, in illnesses associated with wasting, and in those associated with chronic pus discharge, a bed sore may be difficult to prevent.

Once a bed sore has been formed it may be a very difficult thing to heal.

The following rules should be carefully observed:

Attention must be directed to making the bed, smoothing the sheets, preventing the draw-sheet from creasing unduly, and removing crumbs from the bed. Air cushions, water cushions, and in some cases a water bed will assist in the prevention of bed sores, or, if formed, they will prevent pain. Macintoshes should not be used if possible. Avoid continuous pressure by changing the position of the patient.

Wash the lower part of the back and the buttocks with soap and water. Dry thoroughly and then bathe with surgical spirit or eau-de-Cologne, followed by dusting freely with zinc starch and boracic powder, or a powder of talc, zinc or magnesium stearate, boric acid, and starch. It is essential to pay great attention to the removal of excretions in the prevention of bedsores, particularly in those patients who suffer from incontinence of urine, or who are convalescing at home after a bladder operation when the wound is still leaking.

If the skin has become red or broken before an ulcer has occurred, strapping the affected area with Elastoplast is a useful means of preventing the sore developing.

When, unfortunately, the actual ulcer has developed, applications of the BPC ointment of Balsam of Peru, or a cream of zinc, castor oil and Friars' Balsam will assist healing. The ulcer should be kept clean with compresses of warm normal saline, and if followed by applications of gauze soaked in penicillin lotion made with normal saline, healing will be promoted. This latter treatment needs a doctor's advice and prescription.

In intractable bed sores, where all treatment has failed, an Elastoplast strapping may succeed.

**Boils.** Boils are the result of infection by the *Staphylococcus Aureus*, attacking a part of the skin or hair follicle which may have a weakened resistance to infection owing to sweating or lack of cleanliness. If you would avoid boils, therefore, the primary consideration is to remain clean, and secondly to prevent undue friction at any part of the body where sweat may accumulate. Too tight a collar, or unnecessary friction at the back of the neck is frequently the cause of there being boils at that particular spot. Boils often occur in debilitated persons or during convalescence after certain infectious diseases such as measles or scarlet fever.

*Treatment. Antibiotics.* An antiseptic should be used to paint around the boil to prevent the infection from spreading to the surrounding parts. An Elastoplast strapping over the boil will bring it to a head more rapidly. Incision should be left until the boil is pointed and full. After incision some magnesium sulphate paste should be applied, and the whole protected by lint or Elastoplast with a small hole cut opposite the head of the boil. Penicillin cream applied every four hours will assist a cure. If the boils are widespread, a daily bath with some antiseptic in the water is essential. If the boil is secondary to another skin trouble, such as eczema or dermatitis, this condition must also be treated correctly otherwise further recurrence of the boils may be the result. Apart from maintaining an adequate supply of vitamins to promote healing, very little can be done for the boils in the way of dietetic alteration.

If the boils recur in crops, examination of the urine is necessary for sugar and albumen.

**Bronchitis – Acute.** This commences as a cold with headache behind the eyes, sore throat, fullness in the head, and a general feeling of illness, pain in the back and aching joints. There may be a rise of temperature, and some patients feel sick. At the commencement the cough is dry and painful, and there is a feeling of tightness in the chest. Later the cough becomes loose, with expectoration. There is a slight rise in the rate of breathing.

Bronchitis is more common in the young and in old people, and in these cases it may become more serious. It is therefore imperative that a doctor should be consulted early. Acute bronchitis is seasonable and often recurs annually in certain susceptible persons.

The length of the illness varies, and in ordinary healthy adults it usually lasts for about two weeks.

*Treatment.* Send for a doctor early, and while awaiting his arrival the following treatment can be instituted.

An inhalation of one teaspoonful of Friar's Balsam in a pint of boiling water inhaled three times a day will relieve.

An ordinary simple linctus given frequently will ease the cough.

The doctor will prescribe the necessary medicines.

**Bronchitis – Chronic.** There are various causes of this condition and the treatment will depend upon the cause. Amateur doctoring is strongly inadvisable as skilled advice should be sought. It may be necessary to have the chest X-rayed.

Patients who are susceptible to colds and recurrent attacks of bronchitis should consult their doctor in the early autumn on the advisability of having a regular course of prophylactic vaccine injections.

**Carbuncle.** Caused by the inflammation of the skin glands, hair follicles and secondary deeper tissue, by the same organism that produces boils, namely the *Staphylococcus Aureus.* The condition is associated with a high temperature and hard brawny red stain round the area of infection. Some pain is present, preventing sleep. Usually occurs on the neck or back.

As carbuncles may be the first sign of diabetes, a careful examination of the urine for sugar must be made in *all cases.*

The treatment is the same as in boils with the addition of injections of penicillin and the administration of Sulphadiazin or one of the antibiotics. If the carbuncle is well developed a free surgical incision under anaesthetic may be necessary.

**Colic.** This is a spasmodic pain, abdominal in origin, which may be due to spasm of the intestines or the gall bladder or kidney (due to stones). In the intestinal form it is usually produced by indigestible or tainted food. It is very common in infants, particularly in bottle-fed babies. In infants it is accompanied by screams. To relieve an attack of colic in an infant apply hot fomentations to the abdomen and a half teaspoonful each of peppermint water and dill water in a little hot water will soothe the infant by dispersing the wind. If constipation is present this must be treated, and if the colic pains persist then the infant must be under supervision of a doctor. In most cases the medical officer of the local infant welfare centre will advise the mother.

In adults colic may result from gall stones, stone in the kidney, a small strangulated hernia, colic of the appendix, or it may be due to enteritis. It is vitally essential that a correct diagnosis is made apart from applying a hot water bottle to the abdomen.

Constipation (Chronic) is best defined in the words of Sir Adolphe Abrahams, OBE, MD, FRCP, in a chapter in *Minor Medicine* (The Practitioner Handbooks). "For practical purposes," he wrote, "it is assumed that constipation is present if the bowels are not opened once in forty-eight hours." Regular habits do not preclude the possibility of constipation, however, for incomplete elimination, despite regular habits, may only serve to load the lower bowel.

The symptoms are many and may, of course, be varied. There is a general malaise, although the health may be termed fair during constipation. Lassitude, lack of concentration, mental depression, headache and sleeplessness may result. The complexion may be muddy, the tongue furred, appetite poor, and the breath unpleasant. The evacuations may be insufficient, hard and, as a result of much straining, haemorrhoids may occur.

If the disease is chronic the doctor must always be consulted. The reliance on one purgative after another may fail to produce the desired effect.

## ANTI-CONSTIPATION DIETS

These consist of simple nourishing foods with little meat, but plenty of fruit, salad, vegetables, syrup or jam. Bread should be made from wholemeal. Milk and milk-puddings as little as possible. Coffee should be taken instead of tea. Plenty of water, lemonade or diluted fruit juice should be drunk at meals.

## The Diet No. 1

**7 a.m.:** A tablespoonful of paraffin in 2 oz. of warm milk.

**8 a.m.:** Coffee and milk or cream; a tablespoonful of milk sugar; porridge and cream; egg, fish or fruit; wholemeal bread; butter; honey or marmalade.

**10.30 a.m.:** A glass of fresh buttermilk, or milk, or Horlicks' Malted Milk; fruit; wholemeal bread or digestive biscuit; butter.

**1 p.m.:** Fish (cooked any way); butter sauce; salad and dressing; suet pudding; compôte of fruit; cream; wholemeal bread and butter.

**4 p.m.:** Coffee with milk or cream; a tablespoonful of milk sugar; wholemeal bread; butter; jam or honey; gingerbread.

**Dinner:** Vegetable soup; some egg dish (poached, scrambled or omelet, e.g. tomato, ham or sweet omelette, or *aux fines herbes*) vegetables; fruit; cream cheese; wholemeal bread or biscuits; butter.

**Bedtime:** A tablespoonful of paraffin in warm milk; and fruit according to season.

When a regular habit is established omit the buttermilk, add meat or bird at lunch or dinner, reduce or omit the paraffin, and take white bread or toast at times. If the bowel becomes sluggish, return to the full regime.

## Alternative Diet No. 2

**7.30 a.m.:** Liquid paraffin in water or juice of half an orange.

**Breakfast:** Wholemeal bread, 60; butter, 10; sugarless (Callard's or Keillers') marmalade, 15; milk, 90; coffee, 250; 1 egg or bacon, 15, or ham, 30.

**Lunch:** Wholemeal bread, 20; butter, 5; fish, 60, or meat, 30, or chicken, 25, or cream cheese, 12; salad, 90, or greens, 100; fruit stewed without sugar, 75.

**Tea:** Coffee, 250; milk, 60; wholemeal bread, 50; butter, 5; sugarless jam, 30.

**Dinner:** Wholemeal bread, 20; butter, 5; vegetable soup, 200; 2 eggs or fish, 170; stewed fruit, 90; cream cheese, 15.

**Bedtime:** Liquid paraffin and one piece of fresh fruit.

## Re-education of Habit

An effort should be made *at the same*

*time* every morning, either before or after breakfast, whichever is more convenient. Remain for ten minutes, by the watch, trying at regular intervals, say, every third breath, but be careful not to strain so hard as to give pain in the abdomen or in the head.

If there is no result, insert a glycerine suppository, walk about for ten minutes, and then make another effort. If successful, the suppository, when expelled, will be accompanied by a natural action.

If no motion follows, take no notice of missing one day, but carry out exactly the same routine the next day. This time, if an action has not been secured after the ten minutes of effort, followed by a suppository and another effort, as described above, an enema should be administered as soon as possible.

Even if no desire is felt to pass a stool, the efforts help the passage of material along the large bowel to the region where the suppository can lead to its expulsion.

The routine must be followed steadily every day.

*N.B.* The suppository is not to be used except immediately following an effort. The enema is not to be used except after both the effort and the suppository have failed; it should then be given as soon as possible.

**Corns (Hard).** Hard corns are produced by pressure, either permanent or intermittent, on the skin where there is not very much tissue, usually over a bone. The first thought in treatment is to remove the cause. With corns on the feet, the first cause more often than not is the use of ill-fitting shoes, socks and stockings. If the foot is deformed, corns may invariably arise unless the deformity is treated first.

An expert chiropodist should always be consulted, for although there may be some relief by home treatment with the razor blade, the treatment will only be temporary unless the root of the corn is removed. The razor-blade treatment is not recommended for home treatment, owing to the possibility of sepsis. It is dangerous for a diabetic to cut his own corns. If for any reason, treatment at home is the only answer, a collodion dressing is advised.

But later an appointment should be made to see a chiropodist.

**Corns (Soft).** These occur between the toes. The essential points in the treatment are to relieve the pressure and to keep dry. The toes should be separated by felt pads, and dusted night and morning by a powder of equal parts of starch, zinc oxide and alum.

Bathing the feet at night in normal saline, and after drying carefully, rubbing with surgical or methylated spirit to which is added distilled extract of witch hazel, will harden soft or tender feet which perspire and tend to blister.

Bathing in a weak solution of permanganate of potash, followed by drying and application of the above dusting powders is also recommended.

In cases of perspiring feet, where the odour is offensive, they can be relieved by bathing in a weak solution of Dettol or Sanitas, followed by dusting with the above-mentioned powders between the toes and in the socks.

**Coughs.** Coughing may occur for a variey of reasons.

In children, in addition to the chest coughs which may indicate an affection of the lung or the bronchial tubes, the following may be the cause of the cough: whooping cough, enlarged tonsils, adenoids, foreign body in the ear, nose or throat, laryngitis from any cause, enlarged bronchial glands, an abscess in the throat or worms. A cough having no physical cause is sometimes met with in nervous children, and a similar dry cough may be found at puberty.

It is not normal for there to be a cough. Many people will, however, ignore a cough which may last for years. This is dangerous and most unwise, for a cough may be the forerunner of another disease. On being examined, the presence of other symptoms may suggest the exact nature of the cough, but in any case, unless there is a simple explanation, the doctor's advice should always be sought. Amateur diagnosis and self-treatment are unwise and can be very harmful.

**Curvature of the Spine.** May be caused by rickets, wry-neck, the result of faulty posture, occupation, physical deformity and muscular weakness of the back which leads to overstrain on the ligaments of the spine.

It is common among girls who have grown quickly, and are physically below standard. The tall long-backed child who has weak muscles, is too tired to play, and who does not hold herself erect, develops round shoulders and some spinal curvature.

It also develops as a result of infantile paralysis where one leg is wasted and is shorter than the other. It is necessary to treat the cause. Physical instruction with Swedish remedial exercises will improve the physique. It becomes the duty of teachers at school, and parents at home to note the acts which tend to cause faulty posture, and to endeavour to counteract them by removal of the cause, exercises and massage.

**Dyspepsia.** Minor digestive disorders, commonly designated as dyspepsia, need early investigation as to the causes, as they may often hide or be the precursor of a major and a more severe disease. It is, therefore, most desirable that the doctor's advice is sought as early as possible, if the undermentioned symptoms do not subside quickly.

The common symptoms are a feeling of fullness, which may vary from slight discomfort to some pain after meals, a burning sensation after food, with flatulence, due to the presence of gas in the stomach, a bitter taste in the throat due to acid eructations and occasionally nervous vomiting, probably more prevalent in women. A sallow muddy complexion, furred tongue, bad taste in the mouth, constipation, mental depression, irritability and morning headaches, may be associated with the above symptoms.

Consult a doctor early for an accurate diagnosis to be made as to the cause of the dyspepsia, and for immediate treatment for the relief of symptoms. An X-ray examination may be necessary to exclude such causes as peptic ulcer, cholecystitis (diseased or inflamed gall bladder), or a chronically inflamed appendix.

Some of the causes of dyspepsia are irregular and ill-balanced meals, hurriedly eaten and without due attention to proper mastication, an over-indulgence in alcohol or tobacco. (See *Bland Diet*).

**Eczema.** A comparatively common skin disease which manifests itself in different forms. It may be acute or chronic, dry or scaly, or it may "weep". It may be the result of irritants used in industry, and is then designated "Occupational Dermatitis". If the cause is known, as in the latter occupational type, then it must be removed. The skin must be protected from secondary infection. *Do not use the methods of an amateur in this type of disease.*

In the acute stages, a soothing oily calamine lotion is the best application. Ointments should *not* be used, and if they are used without the medical advice of an expert in skin diseases, they may do more harm by increasing the inflammation and the discharge. Dyspepsia and constipation, if present, must be treated. Alcohol, and highly seasoned dishes are inadvisable in cases of eczema, particularly in that variety which accompanies gout. If it is present on the legs as a varicose eczema, any varicose veins must receive treatment.

**Flat Foot.** It occurs in young adults and may be due to long standing, excessive fatigue, or general bad health following rickets, rheumatic fever, or any prolonged illness. If one foot is affected more than the other in children, a curvature of the spine may result.

It is due to stretching and relaxation of the ligaments in the sole of the foot, and the head of the astragalus bone is forced downwards, the muscles weaken, and the instep disappears. As a result, the whole of the sole of the foot is lengthened, and the victim walks with a shuffling gait.

In the early stages, rest, massage, and exercises are indicated, particularly standing on the tips of the toes. Skipping and running on the toes will help strengthen the feet. Walking on the outer border of the foot with the toes turned in is another useful exercise. In later stages.

**Food Poisoning.** Some people are supersensitive to particular articles of food, and, as a result of an idiosyncrasy, they are unable to partake of those particular foods, for example mushrooms, strawberries, shell-fish.

If they partake of the foods to which they are peculiarly sensitive, they become ill with vomiting diarrhoea, and an urticarial rash of varying intensity. Treatment is firstly preventive – not to partake of the particular diet, and for an attack, consult the doctor. Externally, an oily lotion of calamine, applied freely, will help.

The anti-histamine drugs will usually be found to control the skin reaction quite quickly.

**Hallux Valgus (Bunion).** This is a painful deformity due to the displacement outwards of the big toe, the other toes being crushed together.

It is caused by ill-fitting shoes or boots. The inner border of a boot or shoe should be absolutely straight, and the toe-cap square and not pointed. The head of the metatarsal bone of the big toe is exposed to pressure of the boot or shoe, and a bursa forms on the head of the bone. This may become inflamed, and so the victim develops an inflamed bunion with arthritis in the joint, causing much pain and misery, and a hammer-toe of the second digit.

Preventive measures at an early age, and the wearing of suitable boots or shoes will prevent this painful condition.

When a bunion has developed, special surgical shoes should be worn. The bunion is protected by a suitable pad, and a special spring is worn between the big toe and the second toe to assist in pressing the big toe towards the mid-line of the body.

Surgical treatment may be necessary to excise the head of the displaced metatarsal.

**Hammer-toe.** Caused by ill-fitting footwear, secondary to Hallux Valgus and bunion, and occurs as a result of congenital defects such as club-foot. The second toe is chiefly affected, and painful pressure corns may develop.

Surgical treatment is the only cure.

**Hay Fever.** This is a malady which affects the upper respiratory air passages, and conjunctiva as a result of undue sensitiveness to the pollens of certain grasses and plants.

Attacks for the most part those between fifteen and thirty years. In some cases it may lead to bronchial asthma. It occurs at the season when the pollen is most active, May to July.

The symptoms consist of severe and frequent fits of sneezing, a profuse watery discharge from the nose, smarting and redness of the eyes, and weeping. The patient is depressed and may complain of frontal headaches.

Treatment is by immunisation which should commence in January. The victim has a weekly injection in increasing strengths of a standardised pollen vaccine, and the injections are continued until May or June. In the hay fever season, the patient must keep away from flowers and grasses.

In the winter, examination of the nose by an ear, nose and throat specialist is essential to remedy any defects, and if nasal polypi are present, they must be removed.

To be successful, immunisation should be done annually for a few years until the sufferer becomes desensitised.

During an attack the doctor will prescribe remedies to alleviate the condition.

**Haemorrhoids.** A condition of dilated or varicose veins of the lower part of the rectum.

Haemorrhoids may be in two forms, internal or external. They may become inflamed, thrombosed or swollen and strangulated. Fissure may result. In the case of internal piles, the treatment is as follows: firstly treat the cause of the complaint, e.g. in the case of constipation, take liquid paraffin. Wash the affected part gently and regularly with cold water, avoid alcohol, and apply a soothing ointment, zinc and camphor ointment or an astringent witch hazel ointment. The insertion of a soothing and astringent suppository at night is of great benefit. Medical advice should be sought if these methods fail.

In the case of external piles, treatment is by injection or operation by the doctor or surgeon, who should be consulted as soon as the condition appears.

**Herpes.** Herpes exists in two forms: Herpes Simplex, or Labialis, and Herpes Zoster, or shingles. Both infections are believed to be due to a virus. In Herpes Simplex, the manifestation is a crop of blisters or cold sores on the lips and nostrils. They remain as blisters for two or three days then dry, form a scab, and disappear in about a week. The disease is said to be contagious.

The application of a dusting powder, or of a zinc cream, is all that is necessary. The trouble may recur.

Herpes Zoster, or shingles, is stated to be caused by a virus which attacks the nerve roots. The first symptom is a feeling of malaise, and a burning pain in the region of the affected nerve, which is most common on the trunk. In severe cases there may be a fever. After one or two days the local symptoms may appear, namely redness and soreness of the skin, and after another day, the typical vesicles or blisters appear in crops around the affected part. The affected part may swell slightly, and after about five days of the blisters, they begin to dry and a scab forms over them. There may be some residual pitting or scarring although this can sometimes be avoided with careful nursing. Special forms of shingles may affect the ophthalmic division of the fifth cranial nerve and the vesicles form on the face and sometimes on the scalp. The eye may become inflamed and need careful nursing.

*Treatment.* Rest is essential. The first few days should be spent in bed. The eruption on first appearing should be covered with a collodion dressing to prevent further infection and friction, or free application of an oily calamine lotion and solution of tar is advised. Otherwise the eruption should be kept dry with the use of a dusting powder. If the pain is severe, the doctor may give an injection. Analgesic tablets may be given if the pain is less than severe, e.g. codein compound, particularly if sleep is disturbed. The doctor should always be consulted.

**Impetigo.** This is a highly contagious disease of the skin. A blister is formed which will break after the first hour or after a day or so. The serum produced from the blister may be of a thick yellow crusty type, or thin and almost colourless. The disease is most common in children, but occurs frequently in adults. If it affects the beard, it is popularly known as "Barber's Rash". The incubation period is three days. The most usual area affected is the face, but it may appear elsewhere. Being so contagious the infection may readily spread to the scalp or other parts of the body by the process of scratching or from the flannel or towel. The disease will probably clear up after about three weeks, although some cases may take much longer. Sometimes the impetigo may be mistaken for ringworm, or in some acute cases, weeping eczema, but the doctor will recognize the difference.

*Treatment.* Modern antibiotics, such as aureomycin, applied as an ointment and swallowed as tablets, make short work of this complaint.

**Influenza.** There are several forms of the disease:

(1) The epidemic form which is now ascribed to the true influenza virus.

(2) The respiratory form which may lead to bronchitis, pleurisy and pneumonia.

(3) The gastro-intestinal type colloquially referred to as "gastric 'flu".

(4) The nervous form which may occur as a primary disease, or *may* result as a sequel to the three aforementioned types.

The incubation period, that is the time that elapses from infection due to contact and the first appearance of symptoms, is usually from two to four days.

The symptoms are variable. The disease may start as a feverish catarrhal cold, or with a sudden onset of shivering rise in temperature, aching pains in all the limbs, and a severe headache located behind the eyes. In the nervous form there may be marked insomnia, delirium and prostration.

*Treatment.* A patient even with slight symptoms and signs of influenza, should retire to bed at once, to avoid spreading the disease. The bedroom should be warm, fully ventilated, but draughts should be avoided. Another potent reason for retiring to bed is to avoid any heart complications, which may arise in the epidemic form.

Owing to the severe complications which may set in, the attempt to fight on against the illness is foolish, and must be absolutely forbidden. The stay in bed should be for at least three to four days after the temperature has fallen to normal in uncomplicated cases. Avoid solid food, and give only warm drinks frequently. Send for the doctor early, to avoid the risk of complications. In the early stages, in simple cases, an aspirin and Dover's powder, 10 grains of each, or a cachet of aspirin, phenacetin and Dover's powder, given with water night and morning for twenty-four to forty-eight hours and followed by a hot drink of rum or whisky and milk, or whisky, hot lemon, with demerara sugar, will produce a good perspiration and relieve the headache and limb pains and induce restful sleep.

If bronchitis and pneumonia develop they will probably be treated by the doctor with antibiotic drugs.

**Ingrowing Toe-nail.** This is due to an ingrowing of the nail bed, and is caused by ill-fitting narrow shoes and negligence in cutting the nails.

There is an overgrowth of the soft tissue along the edge of the nail and the soft tissues are pressed more and more against the edge of the nail and grow over the nail. Inflammation occurs, and a purulent discharge forms with considerable pain.

Well-fitting, square-toed shoes or boots should be worn to avoid pressure. The skin should be disinfected, the nail should be cut evenly, and gauze or medicated wool plugs used to press back the overhanging skin. Then fill in the groove formed with some antiseptic dusting powder. A doctor may recommend a sulphonamide or penicillin dusting powder. If this treatment is not successful, or as a result of the overgrown tissue, impracticable, then a doctor must be consulted for more extensive treatment. In some cases complete excision of the nail by a surgeon is the only successful treatment.

**Laryngitis.** Inflammation of the larynx or voice box. It may occur as an acute condition following a cold or influenza, or it may be due to excessive use of the voice in actors, singers or preachers. Occasionally occurs in diphtheria. In children, owing to the small aperture, spasm and swelling of the glottis may cause difficulty in breathing with a "croupy" cough.

The symptoms are an irritation of the larynx made worse by exposure to cold air, a dry cough, a husky voice which may go entirely, and some pain in swallowing.

The patient must remain in a warm room, well ventilated but with no draughts, and the atmosphere of the room must not be too dry. This can often be avoided by the old, but well tried, method of a steam kettle in which one teaspoonful of Friars' Balsam has been added to each pint of hot water.

Warm, soothing drinks, and occasionally sucking ice relieves the pain. If there is much difficulty in swallowing, junket, custard and milk puddings are often more easily tolerated than liquids.

Aspirin, Phenacetin and Dover's powders will relieve pain and congestion. Externally, application of kaolin poultices or ice packs will be found soothing to the patient.

Frequent inhalation of Friars' Balsam, one teaspoonful to a pint of boiling water, relieves the laryngitis, but the patient should not go out after these inhalations, as there is a risk of a chill and possibly bronchitis.

Send for the doctor, who will probably prescribe a soothing linctus, and may possibly order a spray of the throat with penicillin in normal saline solution by means of an atomiser.

**Neuritis.** Inflammation of the nerve which may result from many causes such as exposure to cold and wet, occupation and injury. It may affect a single nerve or several, and in the latter condition it is known as multiple neuritis. Alcohol, diabetes, a severe attack of influenza, chronic arsenical or lead poisoning are possible causes.

The symptoms are tingling or numbness, loss of ability in the lower arms and legs, especially in the later stages, and severe shooting pains along the course of the nerve which cause agonising pain. The skin may be smooth and glossy, and the nails brittle and cracked in chronic cases.

*Treatment.* Consult the doctor, and first remove the cause of the trouble. Rest in bed is essential with an adequate diet. Vitamin B1 in large doses by the mouth and by injection may shorten an attack and hasten recovery.

Chronic alcoholism and diabetes, and the neuritis caused by metallic poisons will need the doctor's attention and advice.

**Sciatica.** A very common form of neuritis with more or less constant crippling pain, associated with swift attacks of shooting pains. Usually attacks the middle aged and the old.

The pain commences in the lower lumbar region, and passes down the buttock into the back of the thigh and often extends to the ankle. In chronic cases there may be wasting of the back muscles of the thigh and buttock. The pain is in the nerve. At first it becomes slightly worse with stretching and exercise, and at night it disturbs sleep. May extend to the whole nerve. The part is tender when touched. It may last for a short or long time, and is often obstinate to treatment.

It may be caused by exposure to cold or wet, injury and chronic arthritis of the lumbar spine. Other illnesses such as gout and rheumatism may be factors in the causation. Chronic alcoholics may develop sciatica. In women, backward displacement of the womb may cause sciatic pain. But by far the commonest cause is a prolapsed spinal disk.

*Treatment.* First treat the cause. Rest in bed is necessary, and heat to the affected parts. The doctor's advice must be sought for the treatment.

**Sickness – Air, Train and Sea Sickness.** Many experienced travellers who suffer from this annoying and often distressing disorder will have found the best remedy for themselves by trial and error. It is difficult to apply measures which will prove beneficial in every case. The treatment will often vary with the patient.

The following measures should prove useful. On the day before the journey take an aperient and glucose freely. An hour or two before the actual journey take a light meal and some strong coffee with plenty of glucose. Barley sugar, glucose or chewing gum may help in the case of air travel. In sea voyages, if possible obtain a position near the middle of the boat away from the sides, lie on a chair covered with a rug, or flat on the back, and sleep or close the eyes. A band, belt or binder applied with even pressure round the upper part of the abdomen is a very useful preventive measure.

If vomiting or nausea persists, brandy and hot black coffee or weak China tea give relief. Iced champagne if available, sips of soda water with a slice of lemon, or brandy and soda may relieve the sickness.

With so many modern drugs available treatment has centred around hyoscine with or without one or other of the antihistamine drugs.

Kwells are a well known proprietary tablet which appears to work with success for many people.

**The Common Cold.** The common cold has many complications and sequels. It is therefore very important that it should not be treated lightly. Rest in bed for a short while will soon have the desired effect, and the symptoms may be treated as they arise with aspirin, Veganin, or with Dover's powders. Regular bowel action, linctus for the cough if present, medicaments to promote easier breathing such as inhalations with menthol, eucalyptus and Friars' Balsam or nasal douches may all be used. The temperature should be watched. If colds are frequent the doctor should be consulted, in which case he may find other reasons than personal infection for the complaint, such as those mentioned above.

Inoculations against cold may be effective in susceptible people. They should be given in the early autumn, six injections at weekly intervals, and the course should be repeated in December. From every point of view prophylaxis is best. That is to say, if the body is healthy, and the normal precautions are taken at all times, there is every reason for thinking that the germ will not be effective.

In order to avoid failures in the prophylaxis of colds by the aforementioned measures, it is essential to pay attention to an infected antrum and septic tonsils and adenoids.

In convalescence iron tonics and halibut-oil capsules are very helpful in restoring the appetite and overcoming the weakness following the cold.

**Tonsilitis.** An acute inflammation of the tonsils due to infection by various germs, usually the streptococcus and staphylococcus. Affects all ages and occurs often as a mild epidemic in hospitals, when it is commonly known as "Hospital Throat".

The symptoms are sore throat, difficulty and pain in swallowing, shivering, possible pains in the back, a rise in temperature, the tongue furred, a bad breath, constipation, tonsils red and swollen, and the glands in the neck are sometimes painful. The illness may last up to a week. There is an exudation of pus from the follicles of the tonsils. It may go into ulceration or to abscess (quinsey). Complications may be an inflammation of the middle ear (*Otitis Media*) and acute rheumatism.

*Treatment.* Confine to bed. Hot fomentations or kaolin poultices may be applied to the neck, a mouthwash and antiseptic gargle used freely, and send for the doctor. The doctor may take a swab to exclude the possibility of diphtheria. Penicillin lozenges or spray, and antibiotics will abort an attack, prevent quinsey, hasten recovery and avoid complications.

**Tuberculosis.** There are two forms of tuberculosis which affect human beings:

1. Pulmonary – affecting the lungs. The bacillus responsible is peculiar to human beings with rare exceptions.
2. Bovine or non-pulmonary. This bacillus is responsible for the tuberculosis in cattle, and usually only affects man in the glands, bones and joints.

Primarily, of course, the disease must be caused by the germ, and its methods of entering the body are mainly:

(1) By inhalation.

(2) By ingestion (the taking of solids and liquids into the body via the mouth).

*Early signs and symptoms.* The importance of early diagnosis must again be stressed, for the vagaries of the symptoms are often such that tuberculosis is not discovered until the disease is well marked.

The following points should be observed:

1. No cold or cough, especially if accompanied by expectoration, to be ignored. Always seek medical advice, and if there is an associated feeling of lassitude, or a general "run-down" feeling, ask your doctor if he advises an X-ray.

2. Never forgo the opportunity of an X-ray of the chest if it occurs in your industry, employment or social group.

3. Report to your doctor at once if any of the following signs are apparent: loss of weight; night sweating; a rise of temperature and pulse rate which is higher in the evening than in the morning; a tired feeling or a tendency to tire easily, especially after exertion; any digestive disturbances; any sign of blood in sputum.

*General Preventive Measures.* The incidence of tuberculosis is higher in the undernourished and poorer classes. Poverty and poor living conditions provide the best soil for the seeds of tuberculosis. Attention must therefore be paid to an adequate diet, containing sufficient vitamins, fats and carbo-hydrates, especially Vitamins A and D. No slimming diet should be followed unless under medical supervision. As much living space as possible is necessary for each individual. Cleanliness in the home, and as much fresh air as possible, especially in sleeping quarters, are essential. Adequate exercise in the open air, the use only of pasteurised milk, and the avoidance where possible of continued contact with victims of the disease.

Dr C. H. C. Toussaint, Tuberculosis Officer for the Borough of Bermondsey, in an excellent booklet *Pulmonary Tuberculosis and the General Practitioner*, published by the National Association for the Prevention of Tuberculosis, stresses the economic and social advantages of early diagnosis.

The increasing use of mass X-ray units which tour the country X-raying the chests of all who are willing has done much to uncover early cases which are so easily cured.

The routine testing of schoolchildren with BCG vaccine and the great advance made in treatment with such drugs as PAS has transformed the whole picture so that it is not too optimistic to state that within a decade tuberculosis may well become a rare disease. Already many sanatoria and TB hospitals have had to go over to other uses for lack of patients.

**Varicose Veins.** Caused by a deficiency of the valves of the veins, a weakness of the walls of the vessels, and aggravated by increased pressure inside the veins due to long standing, hard training, or severe exertion.

Pressure outside the veins will also contribute to this condition. Tight garters, habitual constipation, pregnancy and some tumours of the pelvis may be contributing factors.

The vein becomes elongated, tortuous, and dilated. They look blue underneath the skin and are unsightly. The limbs feel heavy and full, with some swelling and puffiness of the ankles. The feet may become cold and numb. Complications that may occur are phlebitis and thrombosis, varicose eczema, varicose ulcer and haemorrhage from a burst or ulcerated vein. Treatment consists in removing any cause, excitement and relieving pressure.

Injections into the veins are painless, give very little or no reaction, and are sometimes very successful. If they fail, then operative measures such as ligaturing the large vein in the upper part of the thigh, or in several places may be necessary.

A varicose ulcer needs absolute rest in bed with special dressings and bandaging such as Elastoplast, Viscopaste, or Unna's paste.

**Blood Transfusion.** Modern surgery is only possible because of the availability of blood for transfusion; some operations can only be done with the ready availability of eight pints of blood from the Blood Bank.

Anybody willing to give a pint of blood can find the address of the nearest Blood Bank by looking up the local telephone directory.

# FIRST AID

## OUTLINES OF FIRST AID

When dealing with any casualty the first thing to do is to make a diagnosis. That means finding out what injuries are present and note that injuries is in the plural, because so often there are several things wrong. It is no use treating a broken leg if the other end of the body is choking to death, or again, it is no use bandaging a cut head if the casualty is bleeding to death from a deep wound in the thigh.

*All* the injuries must be assessed; the most dangerous treated first. Now, how do you make a diagnosis? It is done by obtaining the history of the accident either from the casualty or from witnesses; you ask the casualty of what he complains, these are called his *symptoms* and then you look for *signs* of injury. So it amounts to this, a diagnosis is made on three things, *the history*, the *symptoms* and the *signs*.

**History.** A certain amount you learn from using your eyes and ears and nose. You can *see* the smashed-up car or the broken bicycle. You can *see* the bottle of poison beside the unconscious body. You can *smell* escaping gas, and so on. Don't forget, if there is a question of poisoning, to preserve any bottles of medicine or tablets you find at the scene of the accident. Both the doctor and the police will need to see them. And if the casualty is unconscious, don't forget to look through the pocket or handbag. There may be evidence that the casualty suffers from diabetes or other disease or is taking special drugs. For instance a heart case usually carries his heart treatment in his pocket for just such an emergency.

**Symptoms** are what the casualty complains of. He feels pain, faintness, nausea, thirst etc, and nobody knows better how ill he feels and the situation of the trouble than the casualty himself.

After all it is *his* body that is in trouble.

**Signs.** The signs are the evidence which you find that proves that something is abnormal. The broken leg which is misshapen, the pallid face, the rapid pulse, the quick breathing, all these are *the signs*.

### The Golden Rules of First Aid

1. Act quickly and quietly and don't panic.
2. If breathing has stopped, clear the air passages and give artificial respiration.
3. Arrest any bleeding.
4. Handle the casualty gently and speak reassuringly all the time.
5. If signs of increasing shock are present remember that rapid removal to hospital is vital.
6. Don't take off more clothing than is absolutely necessary, but don't hesitate to remove clothes to make a proper examination or to get at a wound.
7. Send for medical aid or an ambulance or both, as seems necessary.

## BANDAGES AND DRESSINGS

A dressing is what you use to cover a wound and ideally it should be sterile, that is free from germs. If sterile dressings are not available then at least the dressings should be laundry-clean. Thus a dressing may be a piece of sterile surgical gauze or just a humble clean piece of linen. The purpose of the dressing is to keep out dirt and germs and prevent the wound from further damage. It may also be used to act as a pad over which to apply pressure to stop bleeding.

Bandages are simply a means of keeping a dressing and pad in place but they are used for other purposes, as will be described later.

In first aid two kinds of bandages are used, the roller bandage which comes in various widths from 1 inch to 4 or 5 inches wide and the triangular bandage. To make a triangular bandage you just get a square of linen or calico with each side 38 inches long. You then cut this square from corner to corner and you have two triangular bandages.

The advantage of the triangular bandage is that it can be folded to form a bandage or used open to make a sling. Thus it can be used to support a limb, cover a dressing almost anywhere on the body, tied on to keep splints in place, and even to exert pressure to stop bleeding.

**General Rules of Bandaging.** As regards using roller-bandages, here are some general rules.

When bandaging a limb apply the bandage from within outwards and from below upwards. Always secure the first turn by a second turn or the bandage will later drop off. Secure the bandage when completed either with a safety-pin or a strip of adhesive tape.

Apply the bandage so that each turn covers two-thirds of the previous turn. Never tie a knot over a wound or over the site of a fracture. The bandage must be tight enough to serve its purpose but not so tight that *it will cut off the circulation. This is extremely important.*

**Too Tight Bandaging.** How do you check that the bandage is not too tight? For an arm bandage you study the finger-nails and for a leg bandage you examine the toe-nails. Normally the nail is pink and if pressed on, the nail goes white as the blood is pressed out of the area. When you release the pressure the nail regains its previous pink colour very quickly as the blood flows back again. If you have on an overtight bandage, cutting off the circulation, all this changes. The pink nail looks dusky and a bluey colour and when the nail is pressed to squeeze away the blood, the blood does not flow back quickly when you release the pressure, and the nail colour stays blanched. This is a sure sign that the circulation has been cut off and you must at once loosen the bandage and reapply it.

## HOW TO STOP BLEEDING

All bleeding can be stopped by pressure and practically every case can be controlled by a firm pad and a firm bandage. If the bleeding is not arrested it means that the pad and bandage were not properly applied in the first place. Now more pressure will have to be applied and this is done by putting a tighter bandage over the top of the last one, if necessary first putting on more dressing over the blood-soaked bandage.

If, despite all efforts, you cannot control the bleeding, then you will have to consider using pressure with the fingers or thumbs at one of the arterial pressure points. These pressure points are to be found where an artery can be conveniently pressed against a hard near-by bone, thus cutting off the blood supply to the wound. The four important ones are the carotid, subclavion, brachial and femoral. Only as a last resort should you consider the application of a constrictive bandage above the wound for the purpose of cutting off the arteries bringing blood from the heart.

**Constrictive Bandaging.** A constrictive bandage can be made from almost anything in an emergency. A triangular bandage, a handkerchief, a man's tie, a roller-bandage, an elastic belt, all will serve.

Tie the bandage around the limb above the wound after first protecting the skin with something soft and tie it just tight enough to stop the bleeding. Actually it takes very little pressure to achieve your object; too much pressure may do harm, so the motto is "just tight enough to stop the bleeding and no more". Having stopped the bleeding, what then?

At the end of fifteen minutes you cautiously loosen the bandage and watch the wound to see if it starts to bleed again. If it doesn't, then you leave the loosened constrictive bandage in position where it is and keep a close watch on the wound. Should the bleeding recur, you just re-tighten the bandage for another fifteen minutes.

Get the casualty to a doctor or a

hospital as quickly as possible. A label should also be attached indicating when the constrictive bandage was applied.

## WOUNDS

These are of several kinds. A clean cut with a knife is called an incised wound. If the edges of the wound are torn and jagged it is called a lacerated wound. If the wound is accompanied by a lot of bruising then it is called a contused wound. A stab from a sharp-ended instrument which goes in a long way is called a punctured wound.

Apart from the risk of bleeding, a wound carries another risk, namely, infection.

In the ordinary way the first aid of a wound is to arrest any bleeding, cover it with a sterile or clean dressing and then seek medical aid.

The use of antiseptics and disinfectants on wounds is not considered part of first aid.

If the wound is over or near a joint it may be necessary to immobilise the joint in well-padded splints, otherwise every time the joint moves it will split open the cut and it will never heal.

If there is also marked bleeding from the wound then you will have to apply pressure alongside it or even apply a constrictive bandage above the wound or perhaps in some cases above and below the wound.

**Head Wounds.** There is one region of the body where a constrictive bandage cannot be applied and that is the head. Cuts of the scalp tend to bleed freely because blood vessels from both sides of the head freely mingle across the midline and a cut may have two different sets of blood vessels both bleeding at the same time. For such cuts you will have to learn to make a ring-pad. This is applied around the wound and when bandaged firmly exerts pressure on blood vessels coming from all sides.

Just a word about wounds in the chest which suck and blow as the casualty breathes. These are always serious as they obviously communicate with the chest cavity and air is sucked in, as the casualty breathes, instead of going into

the lungs by the proper route. Always cover such wounds immediately with a large dressing and bandage firmly, to prevent the casualty sucking air through his wound, and then get medical aid urgently.

## INTERNAL BLEEDING

We can bleed into our internal cavities, such as the chest, abdomen and inside the skull. Moreover, we can bleed into our soft tissues without any blood escaping through the skin.

To lessen the amount of bruising, one applies cold which slows up or stops the bleeding from small blood vessels. Thus an ice-pack is ideal, but if you haven't any ice, then a cold-water compress will do. That, plus keeping the part at absolute rest, is about the sum total of first aid.

It is easy to understand that, if a person loses three pints of blood on to the pavement from a large gash, then he is in serious trouble. It is no comfort, however, that *we see no bleeding* because it may have happened just the same but we can't see it. The inside of the abdomen may be full of blood from a crushed kidney, spleen or liver, or the inside of the chest cavity may be full of blood from torn lungs or the skull may be full of blood pressing on the brain from a torn blood vessel. Or again, the bleeding may be internal from a diseased blood vessel and then later this concealed internal bleeding may become visible when the casualty vomits or coughs up the blood.

A crushed kidney will produce blood in the urine. Bleeding in the stomach organ, whether from an injury or from an ulcer, will show up as either a bloody vomit or the blood may go on and be digested, and come out as a black tarry stool; though you must not be caught out by the near-black stools of somebody taking iron medicine and the dark grey stools of those taking bismuth mixtures. If blood from the stomach organ does not come up at once, then it may be partly digested and the patient will vomit up *altered* blood, which looks like coffee grounds.

If blood is coughed up from the

lungs it gets mixed with air and oxygenated blood, and so it is bright red. If the blood is vomited up from the stomach then it appears as either dark red blood, or clots, or as coffee grounds.

Bleeding into the inside of the skull may be due to disease, such as happens in a stroke or from an accident such as a fractured skull. The bleeding may be entirely concealed, or blood may come from the nose or ear.

## NOSE BLEEDING

Sit the patient up, and put a cork between his teeth, to prevent his closing his mouth. This stops him gulping and retching, which only serves to disturb the blood clot in the nose and increase the bleeding. Moreover, it makes him breathe through his mouth which again leaves the nose undisturbed. Now pinch the nostrils together firmly with your fingers.

Whilst you compress the nose a clot will form and seal off the bleeding point. You may have to compress the nose for as long as ten minutes before the bleeding stops. Once the bleeding has stopped then the patient must be kept at rest with strict instructions not to snort or fidget with the nose. If the bleeding won't stop, then you must get medical advice.

## BLEEDING FROM THE EAR

Bleeding from the ear may be the result of a fracture of the skull, or from disease of the ear-drum, or from scratching the ear with a sharp object. Children have been known to tickle their ear with a hairpin or a knitting-needle, adults sometimes act in this stupid way thinking they can dislodge wax by their own efforts.

The first-aid treatment is not to plug the earhole but just cover the ear with a dry dressing to catch the blood and prevent germs and dirt getting in. Turn the head so that any discharge can drain easily from the ear. All discharges, whether blood, pus, or serum, must never be dammed back, but allowed to come out freely.

## BLEEDING FROM THE MOUTH

The casualty may have bitten his lip in falling, he may have bitten his tongue during an epileptic fit, or he may have just been to the dentist and had a tooth out, the blood coming from the socket.

**The Lip.** A bleeding lip can be compressed with the fingers over a clean dressing and then taken to a doctor.

A bleeding tooth socket will respond to pressure. Just make a roll of gauze into a firm pad about 1 inch thick, or wrap a small cork in gauze and then place it over the bleeding socket and get the patient to bite down hard. The biting gives the pressure, and the hard pad compresses the blood vessels in the socket and then the bleeding stops.

**The Tongue.** The bleeding wound in the tongue is no different, it has got to be compressed. If the wound is in the fore-part of the tongue, then just wrap the fingers in gauze and nip the tongue tightly. If the wound is in the back part of the tongue it is a bit more difficult, but it can be done by wrapping two fingers in gauze and then pressing on the tongue as though trying to crush the tongue from the back towards the front teeth. This compresses the blood vessels in the tongue and stops the bleeding.

Get medical aid as the wound may have to be stitched.

## CONCEALED HAEMORRHAGE

Always bear in mind that an internal haemorrhage may be present in *any* serious accident and the moment you entertain that possibility you have to direct all your efforts to getting the casualty to hospital as quickly as possible for an emergency blood transfusion and a life-saving operation.

## COUGHING UP BLOOD

Coughing up blood may be due to injury, but if there has been no accident, then it is due to disease of the lung and the first thing to think of is possible tuberculosis. These cases must also conform to the general rule of rapid removal to hospital but if this cannot be done then the casualty should be nursed in a sitting position, kept quiet and still, and smoking forbidden.

## VOMITING BLOOD

Vomiting blood, when not due to an accident, usually means either a duodenal or gastric ulcer. As a rule there will usually be a long history of indigestion and pain after meals.

The vomiting of blood, or as doctors call it haematemesis, arrives without warning and is usually fairly copious. The proper first-aid treatment is rapid removal to hospital.

## SHOCK

To doctors shock is either some terrific *emotional* upset to the nervous system; or, "surgical shock" which is a condition following injury which may *kill* the patient.

### Emotional Shock

If someone has a really bad fright, such as seeing a relative run over, the eyes record the scene and send the dreadful message to the brain. The brain is appalled and is stricken with a nervous paralysis and the result is a severe drop in blood pressure, this in turn causes an anaemia of the brain which affects the higher nerve centres and as a result the casualty may fall in a faint.

Emotional shock is a temporary paralysis of the brain with a drop in blood pressure followed by a faint and then recovery. There has been no blood loss, and so apart from keeping the patient either horizontal, or in the head low position by raising the lower part of the body, there is no other treatment.

Just a warning. The emotional shock case may come round, moan, and weep, or become violently hysterical. In one case she will need kindness and sympathy, in the other she may need gently restraining. In any case don't leave the casualty until you are satisfied she has completely recovered.

### Surgical Shock

Depending on our size, the body holds a total of ten or twelve pints of blood. We can lose one or two pints of blood without a great deal of harm, after all you can give this quantity as a blood donor, but, if we lose more, then the centres in the brain become anaemic and surgical shock sets in.

It amounts to this, anything which grossly reduces the volume of blood circulating to the brain produces surgical shock, whether it be a large haemorrhage from a wound, a large concealed haemorrhage into one of the body cavities, a severe crush injury or extensive burns and scalds.

It is obvious what the treatment has to be, namely an urgent blood transfusion to restore the body's blood volume. Nothing must stand in the way of getting this transfusion into the casualty quickly, lest irreversible damage occurs to the brain from which it *cannot* recover.

The first-aid treatment of surgical shock is as follows:

1. If there is severe bleeding, stop it.
2. See that there is no interference with breathing, especially whilst transporting the casualty to hospital.
3. If there is a sucking wound of the chest cover it with a large dressing to close the hole.
4. Don't give any drinks, as the casualty is probably going to have an operation and that means an anaesthetic. For an operation an empty stomach is necessary.
5. If there is a fractured limb do the minimum necessary to immobilise it for transport.
6. Cover the casualty with a single blanket but don't try and warm him up, even if he appears to be shivering.
7. Don't give him cigarettes to smoke, it is a mistaken kindness.
8. If there is no head, chest or abdominal injury present, raise the foot of the stretcher so that the casualty is kept in the head low position, but above all *Hurry, Hurry, Hurry.*

Whilst hurrying and working fast, keep calm and appear unruffled to the patient; he will need a great deal of kind reassurance.

In a fully developed state of surgical shock you will find a cold clammy pale skin, the pulse will be rapid and so will the respirations. The casualty will be thirsty and restless. He may complain of feeling giddy or feeling faint. He may pass into a coma. He is dreadfully ill and looks it.

You must do only the major essentials that are called for to save life, and then quickly remove him to hospital.

## BURNS AND SCALDS

Extensive burns or scalds can cause shock.

A burn is caused by dry-heat such as red-hot metal, a flame, an electric current, a corrosive chemical, or friction.

A scald is caused by wet heat such as a boiling water, steam, or a too-hot poultice.

The two complications to be feared from such injuries are surgical shock and sepsis.

As regards shock, that depends on the area of skin involved, more than the depth of the injury. If roughly a quarter to a third of the total body surface is damaged by a burn or a scald then the casualty is dangerously ill. The danger of sepsis is very real.

Doctors speak of a 30 per cent burn as the level at which things are serious because surgical shock can be expected. As a guide, the head is 10 per cent of the body surface, the front of the trunk is 18 per cent, the back of the trunk is 18 per cent, and each arm is 9 per cent. So a burn of the front of the trunk and both legs equals 36 per cent – well over the 30 per cent serious level.

In babies and small children even a 20 per cent burn can be dangerous.

**Treatment of Burns and Scalds.** Severe ones must go to hospital. Just cover the burned area with a sterile dressing or at least a very clean piece of linen.

If in an isolated area with no hospitals or doctor available, cover the burns with sterile dressings and give copious sweet drinks to replace the fluid being lost at the injured area. Tulle gras squares make ideal dressings for burns. They consist of squares of sterile gauze impregnated with a little vaseline. These dressings do not stick so they are easily removed when the dressing has to be changed. Still assuming there is no medical aid, if you possess either sulphonamide or antibiotic tablets in an emergency medicine chest, then these should be given in appropriate doses every four to six hours. *Do not prick blisters.*

For the small burn, such as a fingertip, it is treated as any small wound by putting on a clean dressing and bandage.

**Chemical Burns.** A word about chemical burns. If it is not known what the chemical is, then just flood the burn with water to dissolve any of the chemical that remains stuck to the surface. If it is known that the burn was caused by an acid, then it should be neutralised with bicarbonate of soda. Dissolve one or two teaspoonfuls of bicarbonate of soda in a pint of clean water and just flood it on. After that, apply a clean dressing.

If the burn was caused by a corrosive alkali such as quicklime or caustic soda, then first flood it with water and then make up a solution of a weak acid such as lemon juice or vinegar diluted with an equal quantity of water, and flood this on the burn. After that apply a clean dressing. If the eyes are burned, flood with copious quantities of water and get the casualty to blink his eyelid under water. Get him to hospital as quickly as possible, lest burns on the cornea cause scars which might spoil the eyesight permanently.

## RESPIRATION

Respiration is the act of breathing by which we get oxygen from the air, so vital for the health of our bodies. When we breathe *out* we get rid of waste products like carbon dioxide.

Interference with respiration prevents the body receiving its normal supply of oxygen, and this is called asphyxia.

The causes of asphyxia can be classified under three headings, depending upon whether the respiratory tract is locally affected or poisonous gases are inhaled, or whether there is interference with the breathing mechanism; and whether the respiratory centre in the brain is depressed.

**(1) Obstruction to Breathing.** Obstruction to breathing may result from swallowing and inhaling dentures into the air passages. Sometimes pieces of food go down the wrong way and enter the air passages.

Burns, scalds, corrosives or stings in the throat, may cause swelling and oedema and this can obstruct breathing.

**(2) Interference with the Breathing Mechanism.** If the chest is wedged and crushed between heavy weights, breathing becomes impossible. This can happen in mines, quarries, railway goods yards, or in civil defence from collapsing masonry.

The germ of tetanus causes lockjaw, but it can also paralyse the respiratory muscles and of course so can an attack of polio.

**(3) Depression of the Brain Centre.** Electric currents and lightning can cause asphyxia by paralysing the respiratory centre in the brain. It is a curious fact that whenever the higher brain centres are affected, it is the centre for respiration which is knocked out before the centre that controls the heart. Thus the heart may go on beating for a short time after breathing has stopped. It is for this reason that if artificial respiration is to succeed it must be applied at once before the heart has had time to stop. Once the heart has stopped the chances of recovery are very small but not entirely hopeless, as sometimes the heart can be made to restart beating.

Some poisons act directly on the brain, morphine is an example, and carelessly administered anaesthetic vapours can knock out the breathing centre. Certain gases also damage the centre.

## SIGNS AND SYMPTOMS OF ASPHYXIA

The signs and symptoms of asphyxia depend on the degree of asphyxia present. In the early stages there is shortness of breath which goes on to gasping respirations, a rapid pulse with marked swelling of the neck veins will be seen and then the face becomes cyanosed, that is the face and lips start turning a dusky blue colour. In carbon monoxide poisoning this cyanosis of the face is not apparent because the carbon monoxide makes the blood a pink colour and so the face and lips look a healthy pink instead of the more usual congested blue/purple colour.

As the asphyxia worsens the casualty starts to lose consciousness, the embarrassed heart beats slowly and irregularly, the breathing becomes intermittent and then stops. The coma deepens until the heart stops beating and the casualty dies.

**Treatment of Asphyxia.** Treatment of asphyxia consists in eliminating the cause, if possible, ensuring that the air passages to the lungs are open, and applying artificial respiration. This can be continued in an ambulance or lorry whilst the casualty is being rushed to hospital for other means of resuscitation. Make no mistake, it is the *immediate* application of artificial respiration that saves lives.

## ARTIFICIAL RESPIRATION

At present the experts are heavily in favour of mouth-to-mouth, or mouth-to-nose breathing as the method of choice, with the Silvester Method second and others after.

There is one snag about the mouth-to-mouth method; the casualty may also have facial injuries which make this method impracticable, or have some poison on their lips or skin which might be a danger to the first-aider; then you would have to adopt the second choice, the Silvester Method.

**Mouth-to-Mouth Respiration.** The whole secret of success of the mouth-to-mouth method is that you can start it *immediately*, wherever you find the casualty and with little or no preparation. Because of the forcible pressure you yourself make, you can force air past any minor obstruction and if there is any fluid in the upper air passages as in drowning, you will force some of it up and out. You don't have to delay and upend the casualty, and try to drain out water before you start. But, if you find that you cannot get air into his lungs, then you will have to turn the casualty on to his side, thump his back to dislodge any obstruction in his throat, and clear his mouth.

The important fact to realise is the position of the tongue. If an unconscious casualty is on his back, then his tongue falls backwards and will obstruct the air passage. *But*, if you tilt his head fully backwards and push his jaw forwards and upwards towards the sky above him, then his tongue will also be pushed out of the way and there will no longer be any obstruction.

So, maintaining the grasp which keeps the head tilted backwards and the jaw jutting upwards towards the sky, you place your mouth, as an airtight fit around the casualty's mouth, and having taken a double deep breath yourself, you force *your* breath into *his* lungs. This is done once every six seconds for an adult, though the first few breaths should be given as rapidly as possible. The casualty's nose has either to be blocked by pressure from your cheek or the nostrils will have to be pinched with your fingers. An alternative method is to blow in through the casualty's nose whilst sealing off his mouth by closing his lips.

Now a word about infants and young children ... you must take very special care when you are going to blow into their lungs; you place your mouth over the child's nose and mouth and blow in gently with shallow puffs of air, and you do this rather more quickly, once every three seconds.

**The Silvester Method.** The Silvester method of artificial respiration is described in the First Aid Organisations' Supplement No. 2. on Emergency Resuscitation. Quite briefly the method consists of clearing the air passages of any obstruction that can be reached with the fingers and then laying the casualty on his back. Place something under his shoulders to raise them and allow the head to fall back. Kneel at the casualty's head and grasp his arms at the wrists. Then cross them and press them firmly over the lower chest. This forces air *out* of the lungs. Then release the pressure and with a sweeping movement upwards and outwards above his

head pull the arms backwards towards the ground. This movement should cause air *to enter* the lungs.

Repeat these movements about twelve times per minute, taking two seconds for the chest pressure movement and three seconds for the arm lift.

With the casualty on his back there is a danger of his inhaling vomit, mucus or blood. This risk can be reduced by keeping his head extended and a little lower than the trunk.

Artificial respiration must be continued until either the casualty starts to breath normally, or a doctor has pronounced further efforts to be useless.

## FRACTURES

A bone may be broken and the pieces still left in their correct position, or the two pieces may have been forced out of their proper alignment or the bone may just have a crack which does not completely divide the bone, or the bone may be smashed into many pieces, or the bone may be partly cracked and partly bent, as happens sometimes in children.

But whichever variety it may be, it is still called a fracture.

Each variety has a special name, though even a doctor cannot tell exactly which variety is present without the help of an X-ray. A first-aider has to be on his guard and sometimes treat a casualty as though a fracture is present when later an X-ray at the hospital shows that there is no fracture.

## VARIETIES OF FRACTURE

There is what is called a *"closed"* fracture. This is where a bone is broken but the skin over it is intact and has no wound however small. If there is a wound through which germs can enter then it is called an *"open"* fracture and you can readily understand that this wound, however small, is a serious complication because germs can gain entrance to the blood clot lying around the fracture and breed.

Sometimes the force that causes the fracture drives the jagged ends of the broken bones into near-by arteries or nerves or some organ, then the fracture is called a *complicated fracture*. That means complicated by other damage than just a broken bone. Almost invariably this means that the surgeon has to operate and put things right.

One cannot always tell that a fracture is *complicated* by some other injury, but it may be suspected that this has happened by the presenting signs and symptoms. For instance, a case of fractured ribs associated with the coughing up of blood clearly indicates that the broken ribs have pierced the lung. This is a serious complication because although there is no external wound, the lungs breathe in air and the air may carry germs.

## SIGNS OF A FRACTURE

Obviously if you've broken a bone it hurts, so the first sign is *pain*; the next sign is *loss of power*. If the broken bones are out of position then another sign of a fracture appears, namely *deformity*.

There is often a lot of bleeding around a fracture and there may also be extensive bruising of the skin, so in the case of a fracture there will be *swelling*, and that is another sign of a fracture.

In places where a bone lies just beneath the skin, such as the shin-bone or collar-bone, it will be possible to both see and feel an irregularity in the line of the bone when it is broken and this *irregularity* is another sign of a fracture.

You expect a limb to move at its joints but if you find movement at a spot where there is no joint then you know that this can only happen if the bone is broken, so this *unnatural movement* is still another sign of a fracture, but of course it is not a sign you go out of your way to prove it present for two very good reasons. If the casualty is conscious you will make him yell with pain and if he is unconscious you may do a lot of harm by moving the broken ends about. You might increase the bleeding round the fracture, damage nerves or blood vessels, or allow muscles to get between the broken ends and later this would interfere with the broken ends joining together.

The broken ends of fractured bones are rough and if they rub against each other they produce a grating sound which you can feel through your fingers. This sound which feels like the sound made when walking over a stony beach is called *crepitus*. For obvious reasons you don't set out to find this sign but you may feel crepitus even when examining a fracture gently and you must know what it means if you feel this grating sound.

## TREATMENT FOR FRACTURES

You stop severe bleeding and check that the casualty can breathe properly *first*, and only then do you turn your attention to wounds and fractures.

In general, the treatment of fractures is essentially that of keeping the broken bones still and this can be done by means of body bandages or by the use of splints and bandages. The quickest and easiest splint to apply is to use the casualty's own body. For instance, if one leg is broken it may be possible for the good one to be tied to it, after pads have been put between the knees and ankles.

Never tie a bandage right over the site of a fracture, it may push the broken bones out of position. If splints are used they must be well padded and long enough to go beyond the joints above and below the site of the fracture, to obtain proper immobilisation. For instance, a fracture of the thigh-bone must have a splint which goes above the hip joint and below the knee joint. A fracture of the shin-bone needs a splint that goes above the knee joint and below the ankle joint.

Another fact that must be learned about treating fractures is that treatment can produce a condition called *ischaemic contracture*. This means a contracture is produced by the cutting off of the blood supply and as a result the casualty may suffer gross disability for the rest of his life. *Remember, you must watch your casualty and check frequently that your bandages are firm without being too tight.*

## SPECIAL FRACTURES

If a person has fallen from a height or

been run over in a road traffic accident, then you must at once consider the possibility of a fractured spine or a broken neck.

If the casualty is conscious and complaining of a pain in the back or neck then suspect a fractured spine, and if he tells you that he cannot move his legs then you can be certain he has damaged his spine.

If the casualty is unconscious but been involved in a fall from a height or some other accident in which the spine could have been injured suspect a fractured spine and act accordingly. Faced with such a situation the problem becomes how to move the casualty in such a way as to prevent increasing the damage to the spinal cord. If it is at all possible, it is better not to move the casualty until a doctor has arrived to direct the proceedings.

If medical aid is not readily available and you simply have to move the casualty then you must bear in mind that the spine must be kept in a straight line like a rigid steel bar. If the spine is allowed to twist, sag, or bend in *any* direction then the spinal cord may suffer severe damage. It is as well to remember that the spine has natural curves of its own. There is a curve in the neck allowing a hollow at the back of the neck and there is another hollow in the small of the back. These hollows have to be maintained and supported when moving the casualty by suitably padding the stretcher. It is imperative that the head, neck and trunk be moved as if one rigid piece.

**Skull Fractures.** Skull fractures occur in two ways, either by direct force applied to the skull or by falling heavily on to the feet from a height, when the spine tries to shoot out of the top of the neck and fractures the base of the skull. The first type is seen commonly in road accidents, especially to motor-cyclists. The second variety is met in the docks when a stevedore falls into a ship's hold and lands feet-first on some bales.

As a result of a skull fracture the casualty may be completely or partially unconscious or just confused and bewildered. He may be unconscious for a few minutes and then come round and appear quite normal. He may later relapse into unconsciousness. This lucid interval is a trap for the unwary. Blood coming from the nose or ears should make you think of a possible fractured skull and so should the appearance of a large swelling of blood at the nape of the neck under the skin, what is called a haematoma.

**Transporting a Head Injury Casualty.** The same severe force that produced the fractured skull may also have caused other injuries and these must be looked for. It is quite possible for a casualty to have a fractured skull plus fractures elsewhere and internal bleeding as well.

Now as to transporting a head injury casualty. If his breathing is quiet and normal then slightly prop him up and turn his head to one side. If his breathing is noisy put him into the three-quarter prone position, if his other injuries permit, that is half-way between being on his face and lying on his side.

If he is bleeding from his ear then have that side lowermost so that the blood can drain out.

If he is unconscious, it is most important to keep a close watch on him lest his breathing becomes obstructed.

The moment a bone is broken the surrounding muscles go into a protective spasm. This largely disappears if the casualty is unconscious, so that in general you have to immobilise fractures in an unconscious person much more carefully than in a conscious casualty and because he is unconscious you have to pay even more attention to the splints and bandages to make sure they do not become too tight, when the fracture reaction sets in and the soft parts start to swell.

**Fractured Jaw.** The casualty is in pain and holds his jaw to support it. Blood and saliva dribble from the mouth, the powerful jaw muscles go into spasm and so he cannot talk but just makes queer noises, rather like an amateur ventriloquist trying to talk without moving his mouth. Teeth may be loosened or actually fall out and there can be little doubt about the diagnosis. Treatment consists of getting him to hospital where a surgeon will either plate the bones or else wire some of the teeth together to hold the jaw in position.

The first aid is to support the lower jaw with a double loop bandage, but in an emergency you can use a lady's nylon stocking. It is put under the jaw and tied on top of the head and this gives excellent temporary support. Let him sit with his head forward once you have done your first aid so that blood and saliva can dribble out into a bowl.

If you have to lie him down because of other injuries then keep his head turned to one side and watch that his breathing does not become obstructed; this is most important and, sometimes, the bandage may have to be removed. When the fracture is comminuted or involves both sides of the lower jaw, no bandage should be applied. The casualty should then be placed face-downwards with his chest raised and his forehead supported on a pad or on bandages running between the handles of the stretcher.

**Fractured Ribs.** The commonest cause is a crushing of the chest from front to back which causes the ribs to snap down the line of the armpit or it may be that direct force has been applied to the ribs by a blow.

The diagnosis is easy; there is pain at the fracture site and it hurts to breathe. If the lungs have been punctured then blood is coughed up.

When you apply chest bandages they must be tied on the uninjured side and the first bandage is put on the lowest part of the chest and tied when the chest is at its smallest size, that is when the casualty breathes out. The next bandage overlaps the last one and again is applied after you have asked him to breathe out whilst you tie the knot. When a fracture of the ribs is complicated by lung damage, bandages should not be used unless a sucking wound of the chest has to be closed.

**Fracture of Sternum.** Fractures of the breast-bone seldom happen on their own, there are usually some broken ribs

as well and the first aid is rapid transport to hospital on a stretcher with the casualty on his back.

**Fracture of Collar-bone.** It is easy to confirm; you can see a fractured collar-bone if you look at it. First aid is easy. Tether the arm on the injured side by inserting a pad and then binding the arm to the chest with a broad bandage and finally apply a triangular sling to support the elbow, and get him to hospital. He will be happier as a sitting case than being made to lie down.

**Arm Fractures.** Arm fractures are divided into classes, those of the upper arm or humerus and those of the forearm.

If the elbow can be bent then place the forearm of the injured side across the chest pointing towards the opposite shoulder. Apply a collar-and-cuff sling and then bandage the fractured upper arm to the chest for support. This is done by applying two broad bandages, one at the top of the arm just below the point of the shoulder and the other at the lower end of the arm just above the elbow. The chest will need some padding before the arm is fixed.

*The Elbow Joint.* If the fracture is near or involves the elbow joint the elbow joint cannot be bent, so another method has to be used. Apply a long, well-padded splint, which stretches from near the armpit to beyond the wrist and although the casualty could then be moved as a walking or sitting case he would be a lot more comfortable lying on a stretcher.

If the casualty has to be moved on a stretcher because of other injuries then the simplest first aid is to pad that side of the body and secure the broken arm to the trunk and thigh with bandages.

*The Forearm.* Fractures of the forearm usually happen from falling on the outstretched hand. Either both the forearm bones are broken about the middle of the forearm or we see our old friend the Colles' fracture of the wrist. This has the characteristic deformity like the shape of a dinner-fork with a cocked-up bend in the region of the wrist.

The simplest first aid for all fractures of the forearm is to apply a sling which includes the whole forearm, hand and elbow. The pain and muscle spasm will keep the broken bones still. An alternative method in case it is needed consists of the same method described for fractures of the upper arm, unless the wrist is injured, when the collar-and-cuff sling is omitted. It is fairly obvious when you think about it, with the wrist broken you cannot put a clove-hitch round the broken wrist.

**Fractures of the Pelvis.** Fractures of the pelvis are commonly caused by crush injuries applied to the lower abdomen and often involve extensive internal injuries, though sometimes the injury is slight, very painful and no internal organ is involved. Still in first aid one has to play for safety and treat as though it was the very worst kind.

The casualty may be in great pain and all attempts to stand prove futile, and the least movement makes him cry out in agony. Often he will describe his feelings as though his body was falling to pieces; coughing increases the pain. There may be severe surgical shock and signs of internal bleeding. The bladder may be damaged and the casualty may describe an incessant urge to pass urine. If he does pass any it may be blood-stained.

The treatment is rapid transport to hospital in the most comfortable position he can find on a stretcher. If you are out in the wilds and there is a long journey to hospital then you will have to secure the broken pelvis. This you can do by first tying the legs together, after padding has been inserted, and then using two broad bandages apply them overlapping each other round the pelvis. But by far the simplest method is to pass a large towel under the pelvis and secure it with large safety-pins.

**Fractures of the Leg.** Fractures of the lower limb are governed by the same general rules as fractures for the upper limb. If the thighbone or femur is fractured then the best first aid is to get the casualty to hospital in an ambulance and only simple first aid is required. Tying the knees and feet gently but firmly together with pads between the

knees and ankles will give sufficient temporary fixation before the casualty is carefully lifted on to a stretcher. The injured limb must be supported.

If, however, the journey is going to be long or you have to manhandle the casualty over rough ground, then you will have to immobilise the broken bone. This can be done by using a well-padded splint between the lower limbs and by applying another long splint, well padded, to the outer side of the trunk and broken femur before firmly tying the limbs and splints together with bandages. The long splint should extend from below the armpit to the foot.

Fractures of the lower leg are immobilised by placing a well-padded splint between the limbs and then tying both legs and splint together.

**Fracture of Knee-cap.** Fractures of the knee or knee-cap are going to need an operation so the sooner they are in hospital the better. The simplest first aid is to place pads between the two legs and tie them together.

## CRUSHED FOOT

There is almost certainly going to be a wound present so you will have to remove the boot and sock gently before you can get at it to apply a dressing. You will have to be gentle as there may be fractures present. Having dressed the wound, apply a padded splint to the sole of the foot and secure it in position. The casualty will prefer to have the splinted foot on its side rather than pointing straight up into the air.

## DISLOCATIONS AND SPRAINS

You simply cannot be expected to diagnose what a doctor would hesitate to diagnose before seeing an X-ray, so what you must do is to treat the condition as a fracture with or without a dislocation. Never be tempted to call it *just* a dislocation. This makes it much more simple for you to treat because you will deal with all dislocations as though they were fractures by supporting and steadying the part and getting the casualty to hospital. You may have to improvise your first aid for these cases as the limb may be at an awkward angle and you must support it in that position and make no attempt to replace the limb in its normal position. If you did try to achieve this, either, you would be attempting to reduce the dislocation which you shouldn't or you would possibly increase the disability and break the bone.

The same remarks apply to *sprains*, which are injuries to the outside of joints. It is not possible to say whether a sprain also involves a fracture without an X-ray, so all severe sprains are potential fractures until proved otherwise, and you treat all such alleged sprains as you would a fracture.

## TORN KNEE CARTILAGE

The treatment is a doctor's job. He may manipulate the joint to persuade the pad of cartilage to drop back into position and then strap up the knee to keep it in place. If the knee has recurrent attacks of this trouble then the surgeon may have to operate to remove the cartilage. The job of a first-aider is to lay the casualty down, support the leg in the most comfortable position and get medical aid. Usually the knee is found to be partly flexed and requires a good firm support, such as a rolled-up blanket, placed underneath the knee joint.
**Torn Ligaments.** The knee also often suffers from sprained or torn ligaments. The knee joint isn't a very strong one mechanically, and it depends on its powerful ligaments to keep the bone in place. Thus a sudden twisting movement may tear the inner ligament even if the pads of cartilage remain undamaged. There is great pain, the joint can't be used and there is a very tender spot over the inner side of the knee. Usually the joint reacts and blows up with what is called synovitis. The knee swells up to quite a large size. The first aid is the same as for a torn cartilage.

## STRAINS

A *sprain* means a joint has been wrenched or the joint ligaments torn,

whereas a *strain* is an injury to a muscle. Violent muscular exercise may tear a few muscle fibres and then the whole muscle goes into a protective spasm. The pain is quite severe and the muscle tender to touch. In many cases the doctor will require an X-ray before he expresses an opinion. So all that can be done is to treat as though it were a fracture by immobilising the part and obtaining medical aid.

## CRUSH INJURIES

If our soft body is caught between two crushing forces then great damage is usually caused. These cases must always be treated as grave emergencies and taken to a hospital for examination and treatment. Oddly enough, sometimes the casualty will say "I feel all right" after he has been rescued; but take no notice of that. He may be so numbed that he has not yet felt his injuries, or surgical shock may set in slowly and the man suddenly collapse. Often the casualty has multiple injuries.

The first aid is to stop any bleeding, see that he can breathe properly, and then with the utmost speed and gentleness remove him to hospital.

## UNCONSCIOUSNESS

If it is only partial it is called *stupor* and if it is complete it is called *coma*.

There are several ways of testing whether this condition is partial or complete.

If the casualty answers a shouted question then you are getting through to him and he is responding and so he is in *stupor*, unless of course he is normally deaf.

If there is no response he may be in *coma*, or *faking*, or *be hysterical*, or dead; but first-aiders must not presume a casualty is dead; that diagnosis is a doctor's job.

If you retract the eyelids and they flutter or resist then he is in stupor, if there is no response, showing the muscles are not working, then he is in coma.

If you retract the eyelids and shine a pocket torch into the eyes, the pupils will contract if he is in stupor, and when the light is turned off the pupils will dilate again.

In coma the pupils will not move when illuminated and, if the coma is very deep, the pupils will be very widely dilated as well as unresponsive to light. If the casualty is deeply under the effects of morphia or other narcotic the pupils are contracted right down to pin-points. If you see this you should be suspicious of an overdose of drugs.

## CAUSES OF UNCONSCIOUSNESS

Apart from asphyxia and shock the next common cause of unconsciousness is a head injury.

A blow on the skull may so rock the brain inside that the casualty becomes either dazed or completely unconscious, this is called *concussion*. It may last a few minutes or days, and the first sign of recovery is often an attack of vomiting. On becoming conscious he may suffer with loss of memory and be unable to recall what hit him or how he arrived at hospital.

If the only damage to the brain is concussion and a shaking-up then the casualty gradually recovers. But sometimes more severe damage has occurred. Either there has been bleeding into the skull or the brain has been lacerated. The blood collects and presses on the brain and then arises the condition *cerebral compression*. Concussion may pass into compression without the casualty regaining consciousness. Sometimes the casualty comes round from the concussion and later slips into coma from late development of compression. Whereas the concussion case is quiet and appears to be just deeply asleep, when compression sets in the whole picture changes. He becomes red-faced with a slow bounding pulse, deeply unconscious, and with stertorous breathing. The pupils may be unequal or widely dilated and do not react to light.

A man suffering with high blood-pressure may suddenly have a stroke. Either a blood vessel bursts in the brain and this is called *cerebral haemorrhage* or a blood vessel clots up and then its called *cerebral thrombosis*. The absence of any suggestion of an accident gives a clue. Never, never, be caught out by judging that an unconscious man is drunk just because his breath smells of alcohol.

## FIRST AID FOR THE UNCONSCIOUS

Ensure that there is no obstruction to breathing and if dentures are present put in a finger and remove them and put them in a safe place. Slightly raise his shoulders and keep his head turned to one side in case he vomits. If the breathing is noisy and sounds as though water is bubbling in the chest, move him into the three-quarter prone position. Don't leave the patient unattended and either send for medical assistance or get him removed to hospital.

You can cover him with a blanket but don't warm him up with hot-water bottles and, as he's unconscious, don't try to give him anything by mouth or you will choke him. Where there is any specific treatment, this will be given under each cause of unconsciousness.

## SPECIAL CAUSES OF UNCONSCIOUSNESS

**Epilepsy.** A youngish person suddenly cries out and falls to the ground. At first the body is stiff and in a convulsive spasm, this passes off and then all the muscles start to jerk and the patient throws himself about and may need gentle restraint to avoid hurting himself. This jerking gradually passes off and later a very sleepy person comes to and looks surprised to see you. During the attack he may have been incontinent and passed urine or faeces. The danger is that during the jerking stage he may bite through the tongue. The treatment is to get something between his teeth on which he can bite without hurting the tongue. A piece of wood wrapped in a handkerchief or a roller-bandage will do. If the tongue is bleeding freely then the patient must be turned into the three-quarter prone position so that the blood can run out of the mouth and not down his throat and choke him. As soon as the attack has passed off and you can get the mouth open safely you will have to see if there is any first aid required for a bleeding tongue. You will require medical aid for the tongue and the fit.

**Heatstroke.** People working in a foundry, or employed in a ship's stokehole well below decks, will sweat many pints of fluid in a day and with the sweat goes a lot of the body's salt. The result may be *heat exhaustion* and the symptoms may be any or all of the following: cramp, headache, vertigo, vomiting or collapse and unconsciousness.

The first aid for heat exhaustion is to keep the casualty cool and rapidly replace the fluid and salt lost by giving copious drinks of salt and water, one-quarter of a teaspoonful of salt to a tumbler of water, and flavoured with some fruit cordial.

If the casualty has sweated until he can sweat no more or is one of those people who cannot sweat adequately anyway, then the heat exhaustion may turn into *heatstroke*. The internal temperature goes up and up, even to 108 degrees and he feels dry and burning hot and rapidly becomes unconscious.

The treatment is to get the temperature down, though this must not be done too suddenly or he will become shocked as well. Place him in a cool spot, where there is a draught if possible, and wrap him in a wet cool sheet; an ice-bag to the head helps if one is available. Keep a check on the body temperature and when it has dropped to around 101 degrees, wrap him in a dry sheet but let him stay in a cool place in a draught. If the temperature starts to go up again, repeat the wet sheet treatment. As soon as he is conscious treat him as for a case of heat exhaustion.

**Diabetic Coma.** People suffering from diabetes are liable to two types of coma, one from the disease, the other from too much insulin; one is called diabetic coma and the other is called insulin coma.

During an attack of diabetic coma the breath may smell of acetone. It is a difficult smell to describe but it lies somewhere between the smell of nail-varnish and pear-drops. The casualty will be quiet and appear to be asleep.

Naturally in both cases you will seek medical aid or, in the case of diabetic coma, waste no time but get him straight to hospital.

**Fainting.** The fainting casualty goes deathly white, complains that he feels ill, and then collapses. Treatment is two-fold. If he is just about to faint, thrust his head well down between his knees and when he feels better give him a cold drink and take him into a cool spot where there is plenty of free-moving air. Remember, the faint may be a prelude, in some people, to a hysterical attack. If the faint is complete and the casualty unconscious, then put him lying down with his head turned to one side and watch for him to recover; they always do.

**Heart Attacks.** There are four kinds of heart attacks.

The rarest are called *Stokes Adams attacks*. In these the heart beats so slowly that there is not enough blood going to the brain and the person literally faints. The first-aid treatment is similar to an ordinary faint, lay him down and send for medical aid. The pulse may be as slow as ten beats to the minute. Relatives, if present, will know all about his liability to such attacks.

*Coronary Thrombosis.* The victim is seized with a sudden fierce constricting pain in the centre of the chest. It is severe and continuous. It is often thought to be indigestion which it never is. The pain may go down either arm or up into the neck. The patient is shocked and usually looks it. It is all due to a clot forming in one of the arteries that gives the heart muscle its blood supply. The imperative treatment is not to allow the casualty to move; so often they want to get up and go to a window.

This movement may be the last straw that stops the heart. Keep him still and send for medical aid or an ambulance, and then move him on a stretcher with his head and shoulders well raised and supported. Keep in mind that the essential of treatment is to keep him completely still where he is found.

Not all cases develop a clot of blood, some just develop a spasm of the artery. This is called *angina of effort*. The sufferer knows that exercise brings on chest pain and has usually been given, by his doctor, either trinitrin tablets to chew or glass capsules to break and sniff when in pain, so you will usually find he has one or other on him. He will not be unconscious, just standing or sitting clutching his chest and complaining of the pain. If he has his treatment on him administer it; keep him still and quiet and send for medical aid.

Finally, *Heart Failure*. Either chronic heart disease, high blood-pressure, or severe chest disease sooner or later places such a heavy burden on the heart that at length it just gives out and can't cope. The victim is blue-lipped and breathless to the point when he may not be able to speak, just gasp. Keep him still in a sitting position and send for medical aid.

## FOREIGN BODIES

**The Eye.** The first step is to examine the eye. Pull down the lower lid. The grit or insect may be there, quite loose and waiting to be removed with the moistened corner of a clean handkerchief. If nothing is seen in the lower part of the eye, pull the top lid down over the bottom lid by grasping it by the eyelashes. The lower eyelashes thus sweep clean the underside of the top lid. If that fails to bring relief then examine behind the top lid by everting it. Luckily there is a plate of gristle in the top lid which helps in this manoeuvre. Take a match-stick and place it against the top part of the upper eyelid and then grasping the eyelashes fold the lid back over the match-stick.

The match steadies the gristle plate and allows the eyelid to be folded over it. You may see the foreign body resting on the inside of the upper lid and then it can be removed with the corner of a clean handkerchief. If there is no foreign body behind the upper lid then you will have to examine the eyeball itself.

It may be obvious at first glance that the foreign body is stuck to the eyeball itself and you can see it, but often you cannot see it at first glance. To make sure, shine a small torch on the eye from the *side*, this often shows up an object when direct illumination doesn't. A magnifying-glass also helps to see tiny specks in the eye when other methods fail.

By the time you have done all this examining, the eye will have poured with tears, and if then the object is still attached to the eyeball it is probably embedded. In that case, it is a doctor's job, all you can do is bandage up the eye and take the casualty to a doctor.

**Chemical in the Eye.** If the eye has been splashed with a chemical, small bits may still remain in the lower lid. Wash the eye out with lots of tepid water or if you have one handy, make him open his eye in an eye-bath full of water and repeat this with fresh water several times.

If you have a large enough bowl handy you may be able to get the casualty to plunge his face in the water and open his eye under water as though he is looking for fish in the bottom of the bowl. Then bandage up his eye lightly and take him to a doctor.

**The Ear.** In the ear, if the object is small and light it may be possible to float it out by filling the ear with olive oil. Larger objects will not respond. The casualty will then have to go to a doctor who is faced with what shape the object is.

Some objects will come out with syringing a stream of water along the back wall of the ear, by a doctor. The water swishes along and then rebounds off the ear-drum and forces the object out. It is a job for an expert if the drum is not to suffer damage. Even that fails sometimes and the doctor has to go after the object with specially made slender instruments.

**The Nose.** Foreign bodies in the nose are usually shirt buttons or rounded beads. If the child is old enough to know how to blow his nose, then that is all that is necessary to bring it out sometimes. It is a job for a doctor if the foreign body does not drop out; certainly the object ought to be removed before the child is allowed to lie down or go to sleep, lest it falls backwards into the space behind the nose and is then inhaled into the lungs. Usually the doctor can see the object and then he can grasp it with long slender forceps and remove it. If the object is rounded he has to use a long hook, this is passed gently around it and the foreign body eased out.

**The Throat.** A fish bone in the throat causes an exaggerated amount of anxiety because the casualty makes frantic attempts to cough or retch to overcome the constant feeling of something in the throat. Often the fish bone is swallowed but the wound that it caused in the throat continues to hurt and gives the feeling that the bone is still there. If it is, removing it is a doctor's job.

## RUPTURES

An abdominal hernia, or as it is often called a rupture, is a swelling due to some of the abdominal contents, usually intestine, popping through a weak spot in the abdominal wall.

The swelling may appear suddenly following some heavy work, such as lifting, or come on gradually over a period of months getting larger and larger. The commonest place to find them is in the groins. Faced with such a swelling the question is, is it an enlarged gland or a rupture? The diagnosis can be settled by asking the casualty to cough. If with every cough the swelling enlarges or if you can feel an impulse in the swelling when coughing, then it is a rupture. At first these ruptures pop in and out fairly easily and frequently, the patient knows all about his condition and for a long time has been pushing his rupture back through the opening, and may even have been fitted with a truss. There comes a time, however, when the rupture can no longer be re-placed and then it is called *irreducible*. If intestine is present in the rupture then he may get intestinal obstruction. There is severe pain in the swelling, it is tender when touched and he may vomit. This is a serious emergency and the treatment is to get medical aid immediately as he will need an urgent operation.

## FROST-BITE

Climbers up mountains above the snow-line and those in very cold climates may get frost-bite. It usually affects the extremities, fingers, nose, tips of the ears. The area becomes waxy white and numb so that all feeling is lost, in fact the casualty may be unaware that he is suffering from frost-bite. Once upon a time, the first aid was to rush at the casualty with a handful of snow and rub the affected area vigorously. This is now considered *bad* treatment. The part must be defrosted slowly by taking him into a house or hut where his body can warm up slowly and naturally. The part must not be rubbed, and he will require medical aid as soon as possible.

## CRAMP

Cramp is a very painful spasm of a muscle or group of muscles.

It occurs in swimmers when using the muscles vigorously in cold water; it occurs in people who have sweated a lot or had severe diarrhoea and vomiting and thereby deprived their bodies of fluid and salt; it occurs in some healthy people when they get into bed at night; it can occur from getting a limb into an awkward position for a time and then again it occurs in some people for no apparent reason. If the cramp follows severe fluid loss from the body, then the casualty is going to need the treatment for heat exhaustion.

All the other cases respond to warmth and massage. The person suffering with persistent night cramp should see a doctor because these attacks can be prevented by a nightly dose of quinine.

The "stitch", as it is called, is a painful cramp in the diaphragm, and comes on in a would-be athlete who is in poor shape for the exercise he is taking. The casualty only needs to rest and it passes off. Rubbing the painful area is comforting.

## POISONS

Poisons can get into the body in several ways, they can be swallowed; breathed in, as in poisoning by household gas; or injected through the skin by means of say a snake bite or by a hypodermic syringe.

When a person is found unconscious after taking poison, the cause is seldom diagnosed at first; the casualty may be in a deep coma and that is all that is known. The treatment then is to send for medical aid and to give first-aid treatment on the spot for unconsciousness.

On the other hand, the casualty may be retching and in pain and then one has to consider so many things, it may be food poisoning, or gastric 'flu or acute appendicitis.

Suppose you have thought of poisoning and have identified the poison, what do you do then?

If the casualty is in coma, place him so that he can breathe easily, remove any false teeth, and if breathing fails start artificial respiration at once.

If he is retching or vomiting, place him in the three-quarter prone position so that he doesn't choke.

If the casualty has swallowed poison recently, then some of it may still be in the stomach. So, providing he is conscious and there is *no sign of burning of the lips* which would indicate a corrosive has been swallowed, you may possibly be able to get the poison out of the stomach by making him vomit. It is taught that putting the fingers down his throat, or giving him an emetic drink of salt water or mustard and water will induce vomiting.

Of course, if the poison was swallowed some long time previously the poison will no longer be in the stomach and so there is nothing you can do about it; making him vomit would then do little good.

The next question is, should anything be given by mouth? The first aid manuals tell you that, if the casualty is conscious, then it is safe to give copious drinks of water and bland fluids like milk. However, since most of the poisoning cases these days seem to be in a deep coma before someone seeks assistance, this treatment may not often be possible, as you must not attempt to give drinks to an unconscious person.

## EXAMPLES OF THE MORE COMMON TYPES OF POISONING

**Barbiturate.** History and symptoms. Depression, stupor or collapse, followed by: coma with failure of respiration, circulation and kidney function.

**Alcohol.** History and symptoms. The casualty smells of alcohol; confused state, co-ordination poor; pupils dilated; sleepiness, stupor, coma.

(*Note:* Barbiturate plus alcohol is most dangerous combination of poisons, send immediately for medical aid or take patient to hospital.)

**Aspirin.** History and symptoms. The casualty may be a child; pain in the abdomen (belly), nausea; depression, drowsiness, coma; sweating profusely; breathing laboured; pulse rapid and full.

**Ferrous Sulphate** (*Anaemia tablets*). History and symptoms. Retching and vomiting – frequently blood-stained; cold, drowsy, and restless; pulse rapid.

**Belladonna** – *Deadly Nightshade*. History and symptoms. Skin hot and flushed; dry mouth, intense thirst; eyes staring; pupils dilated; breathing stertorous.

## CORROSIVE POISON

If the patient has swallowed a corrosive poison – (the lips and mouth may be stained yellow, grey or white) – dilute it. Give him copious fluids or soothing drinks, e.g. milk.

History and symptoms. Burning pain from mouth to stomach; characteristic odour of breath; cold, clammy skin – collapse.

In all cases of poisoning send urgently for medical aid, or take the patient to hospital.

Remember to state the nature of poison, if known, and take or send with the patient any container, original if possible, any remaining poison and vomit.

When necessary continue or start resuscitation.

## SNAKE BITES

Snake bites are a form of poisoning.

The only poisonous snake in Britain is the adder. The commonest place to find adders is on hot dry days on heaths and commons. It is a shy snake and much more likely to slither away when approached than attack. It bites in self-defence when trodden on or cornered. The bite produces a sharp pain and inspection reveals two puncture marks about one centimetre apart on the site of the bite.

The best first-aid treatment is to keep the casualty at complete rest in a recumbent position; gently wipe away any oozing from the site of the bite and cover with a clean cloth; and then immobilise the affected part by splinting or bandaging.

Adder bites are not usually fatal, but, as they are greatly feared, it is very important to reassure the casualty, who should be taken to hospital as soon as possible.

In Britain hospitals hold emergency supplies of antivenom serum which, after the doctor has given an antihistamine drug, may sometimes be injected into the patient.

## BEE AND WASP STINGS

Stings from bees and wasps in Britain also cause a local tissue reaction and a kind of poisoning. If the sting is in the mouth then dangerous swelling can be caused which may obstruct breathing, these cases need urgent medical attention and when sending for a doctor you must tell him what has happened so that he can bring an injection of adrenalin with him. Multiple stings also require immediate medical aid.

The bee sting is peculiar in that it has a barb shaped like an anchor and the bee cannot retract it. Thus one is presented with the sting and the whole of the bee's stinging apparatus still embedded in the skin. These must be removed without squeezing the sting bag or more poison will be injected. Ease them out of the skin with the point of a sterilised needle and wipe off with a clean handkerchief. Passing the pin of a brooch through a match flame will do in an emergency. After that apply an antihistamine cream or calamine lotion and take the casualty to a doctor.

## MASS CASUALTIES

When dealing with mass casualties some system of marking is imperative. This can be done by writing a symbol on a label tied to the casualty or writing on the skin of the forehead either with a skin pencil or with lipstick.

X    this is to indicate the case needs urgent removal to a hospital and may need immediate operation for his injuries. As this implies a possible anaesthetic, X cases must be given *nothing* by mouth.

T    this is to advise that a tourniquet or constrictive bandage has been applied and on the label should be written the time of application and subsequent releases.

H    indicates that the casualty has had a severe haemorrhage even if the bleeding has now stopped. At hospital he will probably be given a blood transfusion.

M    is put on those casualties who have had an injection of morphia. The dose given and the time of administration must be stated.

C    indicates that it is a case of contamination from a persistent gas such as Mustard Gas. These cases will need decontamination before their injuries can be treated at hospital.

XX   is to suggest that the casualty has been poisoned by nerve gas or a non-persistent gas. If atropine has been injected it should be stated on the label, as well as the dose and the time of administration. XX cases need watching all the time lest they suddenly need artificial respiration.

P    indicates phosphorus burns which need special treatment. These cases must never have oil or grease put on their burns. Incendiary bombs, like napalm bombs, may produce phosphorus burns.

R    indicates radioactivity.

**The first three months of pregnancy.**
During this time the woman can expect to feel off-colour as the whole of the physiology of her body undergoes a vast change from the virgin to the pregnant state. She may feel sick in the mornings and this can be combated by eating a slice of dry toast before getting out of bed. If it persists then the doctor can give treatment which will stop this nausea and sickness.

If the expectant mother comes in contact with a case of German Measles she should tell her doctor at once. If the mother has had the disease herself in childhood she has nothing to fear. If she has never had German Measles then the doctor can give her an injection which will protect her. If she is over three months pregnant then there is no danger to her baby.

**Miscarriages.** For a variety of reasons some women lose their pregnancies and the commonest time for this to occur is round about the third month. Usually the first sign is a slight bleeding as though a period was about to commence. If this happens, *however slight the bleeding*, the mother should go to bed and lie flat and send for her doctor. Many of these threats can be stopped if the doctor is notified early enough.

If the miscarriage progresses then the woman will have "labour pains" as the womb contracts trying to empty itself. If the pregnancy comes away she will pass a fleshy-looking object the size of a small chicken's egg. It is important that anything passed should be saved for the doctor to inspect otherwise he will be unable to decide what has happened.

**Medicines.** No woman should take any medicines for constipation, apart from liquid paraffin, unless ordered by a doctor.

And that applies even to ordinary aspirin tablets.

The vitamins and orange juice sup-plied under the National Health to expectant mothers are harmless and very necessary.

**Clothing.** Each article should be loose and not exert pressure on the abdomen or breasts.

Many mothers are obsessed with the idea that they should buy expensive maternity corsets to support the pregnancy. Unless they are quite definitely ordered by a doctor for some special reason they should not be worn *nor should any other form of corset or roll-on.* The reason for this advice is simple enough. Anything that presses on the abdomen also presses on the womb and pregnancy and may interfere with the growing baby's blood supply.

**Massage.** As the pregnancy progresses it causes a tight feeling in the abdomen which may be uncomfortable. This can be relieved by massaging the skin of the abdomen with olive oil from the back towards the front.

**Diet.** It is a fallacy to believe that a mother must eat a double diet whilst she is pregnant. Her diet should be abun-dant, nourishing and digestible. It should include a daily pint of milk either as liquid or cooked in with the food, and fresh fruit and vegetables.

Food likely to cause diarrhoea should be avoided and great care should be taken about eating "left-overs" and tinned food.

Alcohol, if taken at all, should be consumed in moderation and smoking restricted to well under ten cigarettes per day.

**Teeth.** The expectant mother should arrange an early appointment with her dentist to have the condition of her teeth checked.

**Breasts.** In anticipation of breast-feeding the nipples must be hardened. There are many methods in vogue but the simplest is to scrub the nipples daily with soap and water, afterwards drying them off with a rough turkish towel. The nipples should then be dabbed all over with surgical spirit.

If the nipples are naturally indrawn and countersunk they must be encouraged to protrude, by rolling the nipple between finger and thumb to develop the muscles that erect the nipple and then using hot and cold bathing. During the day the mother should wear a nipple shield beneath the brassière; this consists of a toughened glass shield with a hole in its middle through which the nipple is encouraged to protrude.

As the breasts are enlarging throughout pregnancy larger and larger brassières will have to be bought so that adequate support is provided at each stage and because of the weight to be supported wide shoulder straps should be used; narrow ones will make cuts in the skin of the shoulders.

**Exercise.** Walking is best and essential throughout, especially during the later months. Sports and games should not be indulged in and riding bicycles avoided after the third month. Antenatal exercise classes are often provided at the local clinic.

**Notify your Doctor at once if any of the following symptoms occur:**
(1) Scanty urine.
(2) Persistent headache.
(3) Swelling of the face, feet or other parts. Sometimes the first sign is that the wedding-ring feels too tight and then it is noticed that the hands are puffy.
(4) Loss of blood *however trivial.*
(5) Obstinate constipation.
(6) Nausea or vomiting late in pregnancy.
(7) Abdominal pain.

**Quickening.** Somewhere about the eighteenth to the twentieth week the baby begins to move. At first it is a gentle sensation such as a feather brushing across the abdomen. Note the date and report it to the doctor at the next antenatal visit; it helps to confirm the date you can expect the baby to be born.

**Expected date of confinement.** This is calculated from the *first day* of the last menstrual period by adding seven days and then going forward nine months.

Not all women keep to the rule but the date works out fairly accurately for most women and represents the earliest date on which you can expect labour to commence. It does not represent the final date on which the baby could be born and many women go over this date by ten to fourteen days before producing a normal full-term baby.

**The Confinement.** This commences in a variety of ways. The usual method is for the mother to commence having regular contractions of the womb which are not unlike cramp pains. They are not severe at first and come at regular intervals. That they are labour pains can be confirmed by placing the hand over the abdomen when with each labour pain the womb can be felt to be hardening up.

It is unlikely that a first baby will be born within eighteen hours of the first mild contractions so there is little need to get worried and call out doctors and midwives if the pains start in the early hours of the night or morning.

These early pains are the womb taking up the neck of the womb or cervix thus allowing the baby to pass into the birth canal, for the next, or as it is called, second stage of labour.

If the pains become intolerable the midwife or doctor will administer an injection of pethidine which relieves the pain and makes the mother beautifully sleepy.

After some twelve hours the pains change and there is a forcing urge about them and they become much stronger. This is the second stage indicating the baby is on his way down the birth canal. To give relief the doctor and midwife administer trilene in amounts sufficient to ease the pain without making the mother unconscious. Usually a special trilene machine is employed and the mother allowed to help herself as and when she pleases.

The third stage occurs after the baby is born and consists of the passing of the placenta or afterbirth.

Occasionally the first indication that labour is commencing is the "breaking of the waters". This is the rupture of the bag of water in front of the baby. The mother should lie down, read her book and send for the midwife or doctor. It is nothing to worry about.

If near term the mother has a "show" of blood she should at once lie down and stay there until seen by the midwife or doctor.

**Minimum requirements for a home confinement:**

1 large bottle of Dettol.
1 tube of Dettol cream.
1 jar of vaseline.
1 large enamel or plastic bowl.
1 small bowl.
1 baby bath.
1 nail-brush.
Baby soap.
Face flannel.
3 or 4 towels, large size.
Plastic sheeting to protect the bed.
12 old newspapers.
1 pail with lid.
1 3-pint saucepan.
1 3-pint jug.
1 yard ¼-inch-wide white tape.
Safety-pins.
Sanitary belt.
2 nursing brassières or two that fasten down the front.
36 baby napkins.
3 baby vests.
3 baby gowns.
Matinée coats.

**The Bedroom.** Whichever bedroom is chosen for the confinement it should be prepared early and not left until the last moment. It should be cleared of all furniture, pictures, vases and other bric-à-brac which hold house dust and germs.

If there is a carpet on the floor this should be protected with large sheets of bituminised paper.

The top of the bed must be 30 inches from the floor and if necessary raised on bricks or wooden blocks to reach this height.

All lampshades should be removed and the electric light bulbs replaced with 100-watt bulbs. A standard or other portable lamp should be fitted with a 100-watt bulb and available in the room without a lampshade.

The room should be heated by an electric fire in cold weather which can be easily switched off if an anaesthetic has to be given.

One or two kitchen chairs and a small table are all the furniture required in the room.

**The new Baby.** The following are some things you can expect to see which are quite normal and need no treatment:

**Jaundice.** Most babies are a little yellow for the first ten days after which it passes off; it is due to the change-over from baby blood to adult blood.

By all means point this yellow colour out to the doctor or midwife and if they are satisfied then you can be too.

**Meconium.** The first stool the baby passes looks alarming. It is thick and dark green, this is called meconium and is quite normal and represents the substance that has lined the unborn baby's bowels.

**Sex Organs.** Sometimes baby girls during the first two weeks develop a swollen appearance between the legs and this may be accompanied by a white and even a blood-stained discharge.

This is quite normal, needs no treatment and always subsides.

**Breathing.** A new baby often breathes both quickly and irregularly, however, if the baby holds its breath for long periods or goes blue in the face, the doctor should be informed at once.

**The Baby's Cry.** The baby should cry the moment it is born to expand the lungs. Failure to give a lusty yell may be due to having only just survived from a difficult birth or from having had too much of the mother's anaesthetic. Usually these babies do far better if they are left severely alone for the first 24 hours. They should not be picked up and cuddled or disturbed in any way. They do not need feeding for the first 24 hours.

**Birth Weight.** The great majority of babies are born between 6 and 8½ lbs. with boys slightly heavier than girls.

The newborn baby loses weight during the first two to five days with large babies tending to lose more than smaller ones.

This normal loss is regained as a rule by the seventh to the tenth day.

**Fontanelles.** At birth a baby's skull is not complete and at several points there are areas where there is no bone and the brain is just covered with the scalp skin and the brain membranes. These areas are called fontanelles.

The biggest is called the anterior fontanelle and is situated on top of the head and normally bulges when the baby cries. If the fontanelle is felt gently it is quite normal to feel a gentle pulsation.

If the fontanelle is tense and bulging all the time it is a sign that the pressure within the skull is raised and if it is permanently sunken it may be a sign that the child is ill and a doctor consulted. In either case, apart from the state of the fontanelle there will be other signs that the child is far from well.

**Abdomen.** A baby is normally pot-bellied. During the first two weeks the umbilical cord shrivels leaving a scar called the navel and this should be dry and clean. If it bleeds then a doctor should be consulted.

**Skin.** At birth the skin is normally pink and there may be a variable amount of soft silky hair on the scalp which normally tends to fall out during the first week.

With the baby constantly lying on the back of the skull there tends to be a bald patch in that region. This is normal and the hair always grows normally as the baby develops.

Small pink marks are sometimes seen in the skin, especially on the front and back of the skull. These are called naevi and are a collection of small blood vessels in the skin. They disappear without treatment by the time the baby is 18 months old.

## RHESUS FACTOR

The modern mother has heard about the Rh factor and how this involves danger to the newborn baby. It needs explaining to get it into a proper perspective.

Irrespective of which blood group the mother and father belong to it was discovered that everybody can also be divided into two other groups called Rhesus Positive and Rhesus Negative.

If both parents belong to the same classification and are both either Rhesus Positive or Rhesus Negative their bloods are compatible and there is no problem.

If the mother is Rhesus Negative and the father Rhesus Positive there may be a problem as the baby may be Rhesus Positive too.

During the pregnancy some of the baby's blood leaks back via the after-birth into the mother's circulation and at once the mother's blood reacts to this "foreign invader" and makes defensive substances, called antibodies, which destroy the "foreign invader".

Unfortunately the risk is that some of the mother's antibodies may leak back via the afterbirth into the baby's circulation and set about destroying the baby's blood cells.

The result is, shortly after birth, the baby becomes deeply jaundiced.

One of the routine measures taken during the early part of the pregnancy is to have the mother's blood tested. If it happens to be Rhesus Negative then at intervals her blood is tested to see if it contains antibodies. If no antibodies are found all is well.

If antibodies are found then the mother is admitted to hospital for her confinement and if the baby is born jaundiced steps are taken to change the baby's blood by transfusion.

Not all Rhesus Negative mothers have this trouble with their babies. Some Rhesus Negative mothers have had four and five babies, none of whom have shown the sightest evidence of jaundice.

## BABY MANAGEMENT

The newborn baby's requirements are simple. It needs fresh air, food and regular nursing attention such as bathing daily and napkin changing at regular intervals. Most of the time between feeds it sleeps.

If the baby cries a lot it does not mean necessarily that it is hungry; it may be uncomfortable because it is wet or cold and merely needs changing.

If the baby is putting on a normal amount of weight each week and is taking its food and persists in crying all the time then the cry is due to something else than the feeding and to increase the feed will do no good.

Many generations of mothers have fondly imagined that wrapping up the new baby and putting it out in the pram on the back lawn, even in the depths of winter, somehow hardened the baby and was "good for it". *Nothing is farther from the truth.*

A young baby has all its systems underdeveloped, especially its heat regulating system and just cannot cope with arctic conditions or very hot weather. Moreover, in hot summer weather, flies and insects bother it and unless the pram is protected by a net the cat may jump into the pram and overlay the baby.

In the winter some form of heat must be supplied for the baby's bedroom to prevent the temperature falling below 60 degs.F. in the early hours of the morning when the parents are fast asleep. The simplest means is to employ an electric convector heater fitted with a thermostat which keeps the room at a constant predetermined heat.

Just smothering the baby in extra clothes does not help because this merely provides an insulating cocoon in which the cold baby is kept cold. In the winter always bath or undress the baby in a warm room so that when the baby is dressed *a warm* baby is covered up by clothes and is then kept warm.

**Napkin Rashes.** Many mothers are distressed by finding that their young baby has very red sore buttocks despite the fact that the napkins are changed regularly.

Undoubtedly frequent changing of wet napkins is important as well as washing the skin, drying it thoroughly and applying some bland protective grease such as lanolin or vaseline. There are now on the market silicone barrier creams for babies and these act by providing a waterproof layer over the skin and although a little expensive one such as Conotrane may well be worth a trial.

**Teething Powders.** There has been a tradition which is hard to suppress that everything wrong with the baby is due to teething.

Now what is the truth about teething? From the day the baby is born, day and night, the teeth are growing until they reach the top of the gum and then *painlessly* pop through. Just once in a while the baby may have an ache in the gum and tries to gnaw on something hard, hence the time-honoured teething ring, but this normal growth process does not cause all the symptoms blamed on it, from loose stools to temperatures.

And there is a danger in this diagnosing teething trouble. By having a ready-made diagnosis to explain away all that happens to a baby there is a real risk of not diagnosing what is really wrong with the child.

*Never diagnose the cause of your baby's symptoms as due to teething, leave that to a doctor; and never buy teething powders, they are useless.*

**The Dummy.** It is easier for the harassed mother to push a dummy into a crying infant's mouth than to take the trouble to find out what is the matter.

Some dummies have a sweetened jelly substance in the teat which the child finds attractive but this sweetened substance can cause the teeth to decay.

Constantly sucking at a dummy for hours each day can cause the arch of the palate to deform and produce a poor nasal air passage.

**Tongue-tie.** In the adult there is quite a lot of tongue which projects forwards beyond the tongue string BUT in the baby things appear different because the tongue has no forward projection and the tongue string goes right to the tip of the tongue *and this is the normal appearance in the baby.*

Years ago most babies had this tongue string snipped with a pair of scissors on the grounds of preventing tongue-tie and this caused a number of troubles.

Firstly, it gave the baby a sore mouth and put this off sucking.

Secondly, it often caused a lot of bleeding.

Thirdly, a number of deaths were caused because the untethered tongue was swallowed and choked the baby.

**Circumcision.** With the exception of Jewish babies, who are circumcised as a religious rite, very few babies need this operation on medical grounds.

There is no need to alter a condition that is normal; *if the baby can pass urine it does not need circumcising* and mothers and nurses should desist from the common practice of trying to retract the foreskin in order to wash underneath.

## POST-NATAL EXERCISES
(after the birth of a baby)

Pregnancy and childbirth between them stretch many muscles and ligaments, especially those which support the womb and bladder and the routine exercise of walking and housework will not train them to return to normal.

There is a course of special exercises which if performed for ten minutes night and morning for three months will restore all the weak muscles to normal.

**Exercise No. 1.** The birth overstretches the muscles inside the pelvis which are attached to the birth canal and act as supports for the womb, bladder and rectum. They cannot be seen but they can be made to work and tighten up by the following exercise.

Stand with the feet together and REPEATEDLY tighten up the buttocks till they are tense and hard. This movement automatically also exercises the hidden pelvic muscles.

**Exercise No. 2.** Lie on the back and push out the abdomen to its fullest extent and then draw it in to its uttermost extent and hold it in tight for a few seconds. This tightens the slack abdominal muscles.

Repeat several times.

**Exercise No. 3.** Lie flat on the back and raise one leg and then the other until they are pointing to the ceiling and then lower them as slowly as possible. Repeat several times.

**Exercise No. 4.** Lie on the back and draw up the knees, clasping them with both hands. Then raise the head as far as possible to complete making the body into a ball, then commence a rocking movement to and fro.

**Exercise No. 5.** With the legs apart and the hands raised above the head to their fullest extent bend and try and touch the floor or as near to it as possible. Whilst bent down do plunging movements towards the floor as though trying to touch it. After six plunges raise the arms to above the head and then repeat the exercise.

## BREAST-FEEDING

Obviously breast-feeding is the ideal for the human baby but the sad truth is that modern woman seems unable to breast-feed her baby for more than a month or six weeks.

The danger is that the anxious mother will have a nervous breakdown if everybody pesters her to achieve what for her is impossible. If she can feed the baby, well and good, and if she cannot then stop the fuss and bring the baby up on a bottle and get on with the job of feeding the baby. The mother need have no guilt feelings at all.

## DEMAND FEEDING

This came in as a new and modern gimmick to replace feeding the baby every four hours by the clock at 6 a.m., 10 a.m., 2 p.m., 6 p.m., and 10 p.m.

The "new idea" was only to feed the baby when he woke up and screamed for it or, what was nearer the truth, when mother was prepared to drop everything and feed her baby!

Demand feeding probably suits the woman who is naturally a poor time-keeper and comforts herself that her erratic schedule is something special called "Demand Feeding".

Experience is that it suits most mothers to have a regular schedule, so the 6–10–2–6–10 scheme is recommended unless the baby is underweight or premature, when the baby should be fed three hourly.

There is a silly superstition that still exists that if a nursing mother starts to have her monthly periods again she must immediately stop breast-feeding as the milk becomes "bad". This of course is nonsense, all the mother has to do is slightly increase her fluid intake and drink extra to replace the fluid being lost from the body.

## TECHNIQUE OF BREAST FEEDING

After the baby is one day old and providing it is healthy it should be put to the breast two or three times a day, even before the breast milk has "come in" which is usually about the fourth day. It teaches the baby to suck and the baby does get a substance called colostrum from the breast.

It is no use taking longer than twenty minutes for a breast-feed, that is ten minutes each side because either the baby has already had its quota in less than that time or it has grown too tired to suck any more.

After each feed the nipples should be washed and mopped over with surgical spirit and then greased with a little lanoline.

Between feeds the breasts should be covered with a clean cloth to protect the nipples.

If the nipples become sore and cracked the mother should seek advice from her doctor at once as otherwise infection may enter the crack and produce a breast abscess.

## TEST FEEDS

From time to time the mother may want to know whether she is producing enough milk for her baby or whether he is getting enough, and this can only be done by doing "test feeds".

In addition the mother will need to know what the baby SHOULD be getting.

For this she will need a pair of accurate baby scales and these can usually be hired from the local chemist or one of the baby food manufacturers if the mother cannot afford to buy scales.

A baby should gain one ounce per day for the first 100 days of its life, excluding the first ten days during which it loses and then regains its birthweight. After the 100 days the weight progress is about one pound per month up to the age of one year. It is necessary to know these figures because the feeding has to be calculated for what the baby OUGHT TO WEIGH and not what it weighs on the scales.

To make the figures even simpler the weight increase is 4 to 8 ounces per week, except for the first two weeks of life, the difference in the figures of four or eight ounces per week is to cover both the large vigorous baby and the smaller, weaker one.

Next, we need to know how much breast milk a baby should have each day. The baby needs $2\frac{1}{2}$ ounces of breast milk for every pound of body weight per day.

The baby should be weighed, as it is, BEFORE AND AFTER EACH FEED IN ONE DAY. The difference is the amount of milk it has swallowed and if all the figures are added up they can be compared with what has been calculated that the baby should get.

If the figures are approximately the same then the baby is getting enough food and all is well.

If, however, the figures show that the baby really requires in the day more than the breasts are providing then one has to consider making up the difference by giving a COMPLEMENTARY FEED.

## COMPLEMENTARY FEEDS

A complementary feed is an artificial feed given immediately after a breast-feed when the calculations show that the baby is being underfed.

In its simplest form it consists of making up a bottle of National Dried Milk Food according to the directions on the tin and giving the baby the requisite number of ounces AFTER the breast-feed.

It is as well not to sweeten the bottle feed as otherwise the baby may show a preference for the bottle and refuse the breast altogether.

Complementary feeds are only intended as a temporary measure whilst steps are taken to stimulate the breasts to produce more milk. If it is found that the supply of breast milk is never going to be sufficient then one has to consider whether it is really worthwhile keeping the mother on such a complicated regime and in many cases the answer is to dry off the breasts and go over wholly on to artificial feeding. Each case has to be judged on its merits and the mother's wishes taken into consideration.

## VITAMINS

In theory the breast-fed baby should not require extra vitamins as the mother should supply all that are needed.

Most authorities advise that at three months breast-fed babies should receive orange juice and cod-liver oil but many doctors tell mothers to start giving breast-fed babies extra vitamins when they are three or four weeks old.

In its simplest form this can be given either as Haliborange which contains halibut liver oil and orange juice or as Abidec Drops which contain all the vitamins and only require a few drops placed on the baby's tongue before two of the feeds when it goes down with the milk.

## CONSTIPATION

Most breast-fed babies are constipated or at least have infrequent stools and this is quite normal. If a baby is going several days without a stool or passing hard crumbling stools then it is as well to realise that giving orange juice or sugar to excess can give a baby diarrhoea, thus this knowledge can be turned to useful effect in treating constipation. Merely by giving extra amounts of sweetened orange juice and water the baby can be given the stimulus to more frequent stools without resorting to purgatives which only serve to give the baby colic.

Prune juice also acts as a natural and harmless laxative for babies.

Many mothers worry themselves if the baby does not have a daily stool. Breast-fed babies often don't have a daily stool and it is quite normal and requires no treatment.

A thoroughly bad practice amongst some mothers is the habit of giving babies and children a regular weekly purgative. *Never give purgatives as a treatment for abdominal pain or teething troubles.*

## THREE-MONTH COLIC

This is the curious name for a condition that attacks some babies round about the age of three or four months. They just get colic pains in the stomach usually after the six o'clock feed, and cry pitifully for a long time.

In many cases the cause is too much starch in the diet and it is worth trying the effect of stopping all the cereals and replacing them with one of the protein strained foods containing meat or fish.

If this change stops the colic then the child will have to keep off cereals for a time and have them introduced again when the child is a month older and perhaps better able to cope with starch.

## ARTIFICIAL FEEDING OR BOTTLE-FEEDING

If it is not possible to breast-feed, baby will have to be fed on one of the many varieties of dried milk, evaporated milk or on cow's milk. Should you be in doubt which one to choose then have a word with your doctor or clinic.

Feeds are usually calculated on the basis of $2\frac{1}{2}$ ounces per lb. body weight per day.

*Examples:*
A 6-lb. baby requires 15 ozs. per day, i.e. 3-ozs. per feed.
A 10-lb. baby requires 25 ozs. per day, i.e. 5-ozs. per feed.

These are average requirements and many babies need more. The fact that baby leaves a little at the end of a feed is evidence that he is satisfied.

It is usual to start artificial feeding with a half-cream milk and change to full-cream when baby is about a month old. It is wisest to do this gradually by substituting 1 measure of half-cream for 1 measure of full-cream, increasing the full-cream each day until a complete full-cream feed is being made.

Sugar needs to be added to most dried milk, e.g. National Dried, 1–2 teaspoons per feed; some proprietary milks have sugar already added to them and it will state this on the tin.

Evaporated milk will also require to be diluted and sugar must also usually be added. If this type of milk is chosen it is important to follow carefully the instructions which the proprietors or your doctor recommend.

**The Bottle.** There are two types of baby's bottle. The boat-shaped variety with a teat at one end and a rubber valve at the other and the bottle which has only one opening on which the teat is fitted.

*Use the boat-shaped bottle* and leave off the valve; then the milk can flow through the teat easily and without the baby having to make much effort to get the feed.

The best-shaped teats are those with a bulbous end which gives the baby something to thrust against the roof of its mouth when sucking.

The hole in the teat is important. When the boat-shaped bottle is held with the teat downwards the milk should flow out of the hole in the teat at the rate of one drop every second. If it doesn't then the hole is too small and it should be enlarged by the tip of a red-hot embroidery needle. First stick the eye end of the needle into a cork and holding the cork heat the needle tip in a flame until it glows and then gently stab the teat hole. If you overdo it then the milk will emerge in a continuous stream and that is too fast and will half choke the baby.

**Sterilising the Bottle.** There are several ways of sterilising the baby's bottle.

It can be boiled in a saucepan and then left in the boiled water to cool until required for the next feed. Alternatively, it can be sterilised by a cold method using an antiseptic such as Milton.

**Milton Method.** Make up Milton solution only once in 24 hours.

Add 1 tablespoon of Milton to 2 pints cold water in glass or pottery casserole or jug.

1. After feeding baby, rinse outside of teat and bottle under cold tap (before taking off teat).

2. Remove teat, rinse inside of teat and bottle under cold tap. Brush out bottle with a soapless cleaner (detergents) and rinse again. Turn teat inside out, clean thoroughly. Rub with salt and rinse.

3. Using teat, cover glass, fill bottle to overflowing with Milton solution. To avoid air bubbles place fingers over outlet and immerse bottle completely in the solution together with teat and teat cap. Leave in solution until next feed.

4. At next feed, first wash hands then remove bottle, teat and cover from Milton solution. Put feed in bottle, put on teat and place cap over teat until ready to feed baby.

## WEANING THE BOTTLE-FED BABY

There is no difference between breast-fed and bottle-fed babies and the advice given under weaning for breast-fed babies applies except that where it refers to a breast feed a bottle feed is substituted.

The bottle-fed baby runs a bigger risk than the breast-fed baby of developing iron deficiency anaemia especially between six and 12 months of age. If the baby looks pale, consult your doctor.

## WEANING

This is made much easier if small amounts of different foods, such as cereal, bone and vegetable broth, egg yolk, orange juice and cod-liver oil have already been introduced from about the third month. It serves to get the baby used to different tastes and textures of food.

Any different article of food is usually received by the baby at first with suspicion and it will be seen to spit it out or even turn away from the new food. *This does not mean the baby does not like the new food*, and the food must be offered again and again until the baby gets used to the idea of the new taste.

## MIXED FEEDING

**10–14 Weeks' Diet.** Start by giving baby a little lightly cooked egg yolk on a teaspoon before the third feed of the day or, alternatively buy Strained Bone and Vegetable Broth, gradually add other strained foods to the diet, until by 14 weeks the baby will be having something like this.

*Early Morning.* Orange juice or cool boiled water if the baby seems to be thirsty when he wakes, and the feed is not yet ready.

*1st Feed.* Breast- or bottle-feed.

*2nd Feed.* Before the feed, a teaspoonful of cod-liver oil. (Or this can be given when baby is in his bath. Then if any is spilt it can be easily washed away.) A little Strained Creamed Cereal mixed with milk. Breast- or bottle-feed.

*3rd Feed.* 2 or 3 teaspoonfuls of Heinz Strained Bone and Vegetable Broth, Chicken Broth, Tomato Soup or Vegetable Soup.

For a change a little lightly cooked egg yolk. Follow with breast- or bottle-feed.

*Afternoon.* Cool boiled water or orange juice if the baby wakes.

*4th Feed.* Breast- or bottle-feed.

*5th Feed.* Breast- or bottle-feed.

## BETWEEN 7–9 MONTHS

*Early Morning.* Give the baby cool boiled water or orange juice if he seems to be thirsty when he wakes.

*1st Feed.* On two or three days a week, 2 or 3 teaspoonfuls of egg, increased till a whole egg is taken – on other days, Strained Fruit or Egg Custard with Rice, with a rusk. Breast- or bottle-feed – or a cup of boiled cow's milk when the baby can use a cup properly.

*2nd Feed.* ½ can or more of mixed Strained Creamed Cereal and milk, according to the baby's appetite. Bottle-feed or a cup of boiled cow's milk, if the baby can use a cup.

*3rd Feed.* Before the feed, a teaspoonful of cod-liver oil. A can of one of the Heinz Junior Dinners OR a ½ can of Strained Beef and Liver Soup with ½ can of one of the Strained vegetables. Follow with ½ to ¾ can of Junior Fruit Dessert or Junior Pineapple Rice Pudding or one of the Strained sweets or fruits. Breast- or bottle-feed, or a cup of boiled cow's milk.

*Afternoon.* Cool boiled water or orange juice.

*4th Feed.* 2 or 3 slices of brown bread and butter with honey or seedless jam. Plain cake or biscuit. Breast- or bottle-feed.

## DIET AT 10 MONTHS

*Early Morning.* Cool boiled water or orange juice.

*Breakfast.* Porridge, Strained Fruit, or Junior Fruit Dessert. Rusks or toast with egg or flaked white fish. A milk feed or a cup of milk.

*Dinner.* Before this feed, a teaspoonful of cod-liver oil. A can of one of the Heinz Junior Dinners. Or Strained soup, broth or fish, or scraped meat, or finely broken-up fish with one of the Heinz Strained vegetables and a tablespoonful of finely mashed potato. Junior Orange Rice Pudding or one of the Heinz Strained Fruits or Sweets. A cup of milk or a milk feed.

*Tea.* 2 or 3 slices of thin brown bread and butter, with honey or seedless jam. Plain cake or biscuits. A milk feed.

*Once or twice each day*, a drink of orange juice – cool boiled water at any other time when baby seems to be thirsty.

## DIET AT 13 TO 14 MONTHS

*Early Morning.* A drink of cool boiled water or orange juice if the baby wakes early and feels thirsty, and perhaps a rusk or two.

*Breakfast.* Porridge, cereal – or fruit if the baby is not likely to have fruit for another meal. On two or three days a week an egg. On other days, a rasher of crisply grilled bacon. Rusks or toast. A cup of milk.

*Mid-morning.* A drink of cool boiled water or orange juice, if the baby feels thirsty.

*Dinner.* Before this meal, a teaspoonful of cod-liver oil. A can of one of Heinz Junior Dinners. Alternatively, strained soup, broth or fish, or scraped meat or finely broken up white fish, and about $\frac{1}{2}$ can of one of the Heinz strained Vegetables. Follow with Junior Fruit Dessert or one of Heinz Strained Fruits or sweets or milk pudding. A cup of milk.

*Tea.* Brown bread and butter, spread with honey or seedless jam. Plain cake or biscuits. A cup of milk.

*At Bedtime.* A drink of milk.

## DIET 15 TO 18 MONTHS

*Breakfast.* Porridge or Junior Fruit Dessert or Strained fruit. One two or three days a week, give an egg or crisply grilled bacon. Once a week, 2 tablespoonfuls of steamed fish. Rusk or toast. A cup of milk.

*Dinner.* A can of one of Heinz Junior Dinners, or meat or fish, with vegetables, followed by a pudding or stewed fruit. Rely on Heinz Junior Foods and Strained Foods whenever the family's food is unsuitable for baby.

*Tea.* 2 or 3 slices of brown bread and honey or seedless jam or Marmite. A grated cheese sandwich can be given on some days, it is tasty and nourishing. From $\frac{1}{2}$ to a full can of Junior Apricot Rice Pudding or one of Heinz Strained Fruits, if no fruit was given at dinnertime. A little plain cake or one or two biscuits. A cup of milk should be taken with this meal.

*Before Going to Bed,* a cup of milk – perhaps chocolate flavoured for variety.

## DIET FOR A CHILD FROM 2 TO 7 YEARS OF AGE

**On Waking.** Sweetened fruit drink.

**Breakfast.** Give a small helping of a breakfast cereal or porridge with milk and sugar but not sufficient to satisfy the appetite as the child should have a second course of either egg, fish or bacon with bread and butter or toast.

One half-pint of boiled milk to include that used with the cereal or porridge.

**Midday.** About 2 tablespoonfuls of ox-tail or stew or underdone beef or finely cut up steak or fish or fish pie or chicken or rabbit finely cut up or liver or heart or sweetbread or kidneys.

1 or 2 heaped tablespoonfuls of potato with 1 or 2 tablespoonfuls of vegetable which should be sieved for the younger child or puréed.

A second course can be steamed pudding with treacle or custard or a milk pudding with stewed fruit or blanc mange or jelly or milk jelly or ice cream, etc. Water to drink.

**Tea–Supper, 4.30 p.m. to 5 p.m.** Toast, bread and butter, seedless jam or honey, cream cheese, salad of some kind such as tomatoes, water-cress, mustard and cress, banana.

Sandwiches.

Stewed fruit, jelly, junket, custard and bread and butter according to taste.

Plain or sponge cake.

Half a pint of milk.

Extra vitamins should still be continued, especially cod-liver oil or halibut-liver oil either as Haliborange or one teaspoonful of cod-liver oil three times a day flavoured with orange drink. If halibut-liver oil is ¦preferred then the child needs only two drops three times a day as it is more concentrated.

Even these older children like rusks and these can be made at home as set out below or bought in packets from a shop.

**To Make Home-Made Rusks.** Take some stale bread and dip them in sweetened milk with or without honey and then place them in a slow oven to turn crisp and brown.

**Sleep Chart**

| At birth requires | 20–24 hours |
| --- | --- |
| At six months requires | 18 hours |
| At one year requires | 14–16 hours |
| At two years requires | 12–14 hours |
| At five years requires | 10–12 hours |
| At ten years requires | 10–11 hours |

## Growth In Weight Chart

| Age | Boys (Weight in lbs.) | Girls (Weight in lbs.) |
|---|---|---|
| Birth | 7½ | 7 |
| 6 months | 16 | 15½ |
| 1 year | 21 | 20 |
| 2 years | 27 | 26 |
| 3 ,, | 31 | 30 |
| 4 ,, | 35 | 34 |
| 5 ,, | 41 | 40 |
| 6 ,, | 45 | 44 |
| 7 ,, | 50 | 48 |
| 8 ,, | 55 | 53 |
| 9 ,, | 60 | 58 |
| 10 ,, | 67 | 64 |
| 11 ,, | 72 | 70 |
| 12 ,, | 80 | 82 |
| 13 ,, | 88 | 92 |
| 14 ,, | 99 | 101 |

## Teeth Appearance Chart

### First or Milk Teeth

| | |
|---|---|
| Lower central teeth | 5–10 months |
| Upper central teeth | 8–10 months |
| Lower and upper first double teeth | 12–14 months |
| Lower and upper "eye" teeth | 16–22 months |
| Lower and upper second double teeth | 24–30 months |

### Second or Permanent Teeth

| | |
|---|---|
| First molars | 5–7 years |
| Central incisors | 6–8 ,, |
| Lateral incisors | 7–9 ,, |
| First bicuspids | 9–11 ,, |
| Second bicuspids | 10–12 ,, |
| Cuspids | 11–14 ,, |
| Second molars | 11–13 ,, |
| Third molars | 16–21 or later |

## INOCULATIONS

Children can be offered protective inoculation against diphtheria, whooping cough, tetanus (lockjaw), poliomyelitis, smallpox and tuberculosis, and others are bound to be added to the list sooner or later. In fact already there is a vaccine available in small amounts against measles.

To those parents who have misgivings about all these injections and wondering whether they are safe and necessary all that can be said is this. Nobody knows more about the problem in all its aspects than the doctor himself and he does *have his own children inoculated.*

One of the modern schedules for inoculations is as follows:

At 2 months of age the first injection against diphtheria, whooping cough and tetanus.

At 3 months of age the second injection against diphtheria, whooping cough and tetanus.

At 4 months of age the third injection against diphtheria, whooping cough and tetanus.

At 7 months of age the first dose of oral vaccine against poliomyelitis. This is given as three drops of vaccine on some soft sugar and swallowed.

At 8 months of age the second dose of oral polio vaccine.

At 9 months of age the third dose of oral polio vaccine.

At 18 months of age a boost dose of diphtheria, whooping cough and tetanus vaccine.

During the second year vaccination against smallpox.

Age 5 a boost dose against diphtheria and tetanus.

Age 10 a boost dose against diphtheria and tetanus.

Age 12 revaccination against smallpox. After age 12 a dose of BCG vaccine against tuberculosis.

None of these procedures can be carried out at shorter intervals than three weeks.

Whooping cough vaccine is given early in life in the hope of reducing the incidence and severity of the disease in the young baby because experience teaches that it does so much harm when contracted at an early age.

## DENTAL ADVICE TO MOTHERS

Take care of the child's baby teeth, for if the permanent teeth are cut into a dirty mouth they will become diseased. Clean the teeth every morning, and every night after the last meal. Brush the teeth up and down, to clear the food from between them. Food lodged in the crevices makes teeth decay. Let the child eat hard food; hard food keeps the teeth clean. An apple a day. If the teeth are decayed and dirty, poisons are absorbed into the system and the health suffers. The child's teeth should be inspected twice a year, so that any holes can be filled while they are small; it won't hurt then.

## CHILDREN'S AILMENTS

**Convulsions.** The heat-regulating mechanism in a baby is poorly developed so that when a disease such as measles is imminent and the body temperature is rising from the effect of the infection, the baby's brain cannot tolerate the heat and a form of heat stroke develops. This is called a convulsion.

The convulsion is to the baby what the rigor or shivering attack is to the adult.

In a typical attack the child is hot, becomes drowsy or unconscious and later commences to have jerky twitchings of the limbs. As a rule the attack is over in a few seconds.

Treatment obviously consists of treating the cause and for that a doctor must be consulted. If the fit is very prolonged, and the doctor delayed in attending, then a warm bath is very efficacious. This dilates the skin blood vessels and sets it sweating and this in turn lowers the brain and body temperature.

**Sore Throat.** In a published article, The Central Council for Health Education has pointed out that "these five comforting words ["It's only a sore throat"] have been the death knell of many a child.

"It is true that many sore throats are just the first sign of a cold or some other simple illness; but how can you tell? Many other illnesses, some of them very serious, start with a sore throat. Among them are: diphtheria, scarlet fever, quinsy, rheumatic fever, kidney and heart disease. It all depends on the germ.

"Different germs cause different diseases and need different treatment. The earlier the germ is recognised, the sooner the proper treatment can begin – and the quicker will be the cure. Delay may

not matter if the germs are comparatively harmless; but if they are deadly it may be serious. Dare you take the risk of guessing wrongly? It is wisest to call in your doctor at once and let him decide. Even he, with all his experience, may not be able to tell for certain until he has collected some of the germs by swabbing the throat and has got the experts at the laboratory to find out the nature of the germs. But he will start appropriate treatment without waiting for the result of the swab.

"If your child gets a sore throat you should carry out the following rules:

1. Put the child to bed at once;
2. Keep other children away (it may be catching);
3. Give no solid food, only drinks;
4. Send for your doctor at once.

*"Don't wait until he has gone out on his rounds;* this will mean delay and an extra journey for a busy man.

*"Send him a clear message,* giving full name, age and address of the patient. Indicate when the first sign of illness appeared and what seems to be the matter. He will come as soon as he can."

**Bed-Wetting.** By the age of 2 most children have control of their bladder and no longer wet the bed. Allowing for variations in children a child should have control by the third year and if bed-wetting persists regularly beyond this period then the term enuresis is given to it and it is considered as abnormal behaviour.

The problem of cure may be simple or very complex as will be seen by the following list of causes:

Associated with mental deficiency.

Lack of proper training.

Irritation within the urinary tract.

Infection in the urinary tract.

Organic disease of the nervous system.

Psychogenic.

It must be emphasised that what we are discussing here is persistent and regular bed-wetting, not the occasional lapse following an illness or some special excitement.

Thus each case has to be treated on its merits but in the vast majority of cases the cause lies in a mixture of faulty training, too deep a sleep, and psycho-genic causes.

In some cases the bad habit is the result of jealousy or nervous unhappiness, and he bedwets to draw attention to himself *or to punish his parents*. A review of the child's background may be necessary and an experienced child guidance doctor consulted.

**Scarlet Fever.** Compared with thirty years ago this is now a mild disease and with modern drugs so easily cured that it is no more serious than a heavy cold. Today the child is cured in a few days.

The incubation period is short, about two or three days as a rule, after which the child complains of a sore throat and perhaps vomits and runs a slight temperature.

On inspection the back of the throat looks raw and red and the tonsils may look swollen and covered with a soft yellowish discharge which easily wipes off.

The rash appears early on the first or second day and looks as if the skin was blushing and on it are superimposed numerous small red dots or points.

The rash may appear all over the body at once with the exception of the face or start on the chest and then spread to other parts.

The cheeks are flushed but there is usually a characteristic pale area all round the mouth.

At first the tongue becomes covered with a thick white fur through which the swollen pile of the tongue is visible as red dots and the appearance is said to resemble a white strawberry.

About the third day the white fur separates leaving the tongue revealed as bright red with a marked red pile of dots which is said to resemble a red strawberry.

The patient should be put to bed and isolated from other children. The diet should be light with large volumes of drinks in any form to flood the system. The doctor's treatment will soon have the child cured.

All the child's feeding utensils should be washed up separately in the bathroom and then kept in the bedroom lest the germ be spread in the washing-up water to the rest of the family.

**Diphtheria.** This is now a rare disease but so important that it has to be diagnosed early and treatment started at once if complications are to be avoided.

The reason for the decline in this disease is undoubtedly entirely due to preventive inoculations and that is the reason that mothers are urged to have their babies inoculated early in life.

The disease may appear in a number of ways and either as a sudden onset or gradually over a period of days.

**Throat Type.** The child may not complain of sore throat at first but just complain of odd aches and pains in the limbs and be peevish, off colour, have no appetite and complain of headache.

A child in that condition *must have its throat examined*. When this is done the tonsils are seen to be swollen and forming a yellowish membrane which spreads *beyond* the tonsils on to the surrounding throat area. This membrane is adherent and attempts to move it with the handle of a spoon result in the membrane coming away with bleeding of the raw surface left.

The breath has a characteristic odour and the neck gland or glands may be enlarged and felt just below the jaw in the neck. The condition may spread to the back of the nose which results in a blood-stained discharge from one or both nostrils.

**Malignant Diphtheria.** This is a severe type of throat diphtheria which is characterised by huge enlargement of the neck glands which, considering the size of the swelling, are curiously painless. This is the so-called *bull-necked diphtheria*. The child with this variety is very ill and drowsy, has an open mouth and noisy breathing, and the breath has a marked and characteristic odour.

**Laryngeal Type.** This is usually an extension of the *Throat Type* going down into the larynx or voice box. The child has a barking kind of croupy cough and the breathing is noisy and difficult. By this time the child has a

dusky blue colour on the face and is restless as it tries to breath.

**Nasal Diphtheria.** There is at first a
watery blood-stained discharge from
one or both nostrils which after a day
or two changes to a discharge of pus and
blood; usually there is also a crusted
sore area around the skin of the nostrils
and on the upper lip. The child does not
appear very ill and may even be attending school.

For any or all the above cases the
child should be put to bed at once and
the doctor asked to call. If you have
looked down the throat and seen a
yellowish membrane right across the
throat then the doctor should be told,
without the mother telling him that it is
a case of diphtheria (which in all
probability it isn't) but the mention of
the word "membrane" to a doctor
always conjures up the remote possibility of this disease and he is likely to
make it an urgent call. If the doctor
has the slightest doubt about the nature
of the disease then he is likely to send
the child into the nearest Isolation
Hospital for observation.

**Measles.** This is caused by a virus and
the illness occurs as a local epidemic in
cycles every two or three years.

In the early stages the child seems to
be developing a severe feverish cold
with the temperature going up and up,
the eyes become pink and sore, the
nose runs and there is a persistent hack-
ing cough. An early diagnosis can be
made by looking for the so-called
Koplik Spots which appear two or three
days before the typical measles rash.
They are to be found on the inside of the
cheek near the back teeth and look like
grains of salt on a pink base. If these
are seen then the mother can be certain
that the child is incubating an attack of
measles.

The measles rash appears after the
child has been feverish and ill as
described above for 4 to 7 days. It first
appears behind the ears, around the
mouth and on the forehead close to the
hair margin. It quickly spreads over the
face, neck and front of the chest. Within
24 hours the child is smothered all over

with spots and at this stage there can be
little doubt of the diagnosis. The child
is spotted and red all over, has a hard
irritable cough, a high temperature,
red sore eyes and both feels and looks
the picture of misery.

The rash consists of brick-red spots,
irregular in size and shape which gradually merge into one another, forming
red blotches.

The child should be in bed and the
doctor asked to call.

The doctor will prescribe the treatment. The child needs good nursing
care and lots of sweetened drinks to
keep him going for a few days whilst he
feels too ill to eat.

**Whooping Cough.** With preventive
inoculation now so widespread the
child either does not get an attack at all
or gets a mild modified form which may
make diagnosis difficult.

In its typical form attacking an unprotected child the disease starts slowly
after an incubation period of 5–14 days.

The child at first seems to have a
catarrhal attack with a slight temperature and a cough. The cough gets worse
and worse and is particularly a nuisance
at night, keeping both the child and
mother awake.

The cough gradually develops into
the characteristic type from which the
disease gets its name. The child starts to
cough out in a serious of explosive
barks which won't stop, whilst his
face gets redder and redder. When the
coughing spasm comes to an end the
child has completely emptied his lungs
of air and then takes a mighty gasp of
air into the lungs which makes the
characteristic noise called a *whoop*.
The coughing attack may set up a bout
of vomiting. Almost anything may
provoke a spasm; talking, laughing or
even eating so that in a well-developed
attack the problem of feeding the child
at all may cause anxiety.

If the child vomits up its meal then a
useful trick to know is that following a
vomiting attack the stomach stays quiet
for a time and during this quiet interval
some more food should be offered in
the hope that at least some of it will
be kept down. It seems hard to push

food at a child who has just been sick but the mother must be prepared to do this if she wants to help her child.

As whooping cough goes on for some six weeks this feeding problem is a real one and all meals should be highly nourishing and well sweetened with sugar and given in small amounts very frequently. Small amounts every hour that are kept down are more useful to the child than larger amounts every four hours most of which is vomited back.

The doctor has many new drugs at his command with which to treat the child so that the picture described is unlikely to be seen these days.

The child is infectious to other children for 4 weeks from the onset of the coughing spasms.

**Chicken Pox.** This is caused by a virus which is probably the same virus that causes shingles (*herpes zoster*) in adults. For this reason elderly relatives should be discouraged from visiting the house whilst the child has chicken pox since if the elderly relative gets shingles she may go through a very distressing and painful time. If an elderly relative lives in the house already then the child should be isolated.

As has been said about other infectious illnesses of childhood chicken pox is nowhere near as severe as it used to be thirty years ago.

The incubation period varies from 14 to 21 days, after which the characteristic rash appears first on the trunk, usually the back and then comes out in successive crops of spots over a period of several days until the child is smothered with spots.

The spots start as separate pink spots which develop at their tip a tiny clear blister full of watery fluid. Over a period of days the spot and blister form a scab leaving a pink mark which later fades to a white mark.

It is important that children be dissuaded from picking these scabs lest they cause a scar which may leave a permanent mark on the skin.

The spots not only appear on the skin but may even occur in the hair, inside the mouth or in and around the eye. If they occur inside the mouth they may make swallowing difficult and the child refuse all food. Acid tasting articles such as fruit drinks hurt more than bland ones like milk.

If the spots occur round the eye or on the eye the doctor should be informed of this complication.

Treatment consists of good nursing care and at first this should be in bed where the mother can get at the rash in order to smother it in calamine lotion. *This should* NOT *be used for the spots on the face,* unless the doctor has ordered it to be used on the face. The calamine lotion should be applied freely every four hours and layer on layer put on to form a calamine crust over the spots which should not be disturbed. When the scab comes off the lotion will come too leaving the least amount of mark on the skin. The lotion should not be washed off therefore but just added to at each application.

The medical name for this disease is varicella.

**German Measles.** The medical name for this disease is rubella and it is caused by a virus. The illness is so mild that the child neither feels ill nor looks ill, and but for the rash and some enlarged glands seems perfectly well.

The disease occurs in epidemic form usually in the spring and early summer. The incubation period is about 17 days.

The rash consists of small separate pink spots which commence on the face and quickly spread all over the body within twenty-four hours. The colour of the rash is paler than the bright red rash of scarlet fever and the dark red rash of measles.

It can be differentiated from ordinary measles by the absence of *koplik spots* in the mouth, the absence of cough and sore eyes, the absence of a high temperature and the fact that in German measles the neck glands are enlarged and can be felt under the skin and the child appears so well.

There is no treatment for this mild illness which lasts but a few days, apart from keeping the child in for seven days.

If there is an expectant mother in the house or who has been a contact then she should report at once to her doctor.

**Mumps.** This is a virus disease which occurs in epidemic form and causes swelling of the salivary glands.

In its typical form one or both parotid glands swell on each side of the face giving the child a Billy Bunter appearance. There is usually little pain despite the size of the swelling.

The child usually feels quite well and only complains of the difficulty of opening the mouth and because the child does not feel ill it is often difficult to stay in bed until all the swellings have gone.

*And yet the child ought to stay in bed for a very special reason.*

The virus of mumps has a special attraction for attacking the testicles in the male and the ovaries in the female, causing them to swell and become very painful. If this complication arises there is a real risk that the child may be sterilised and later in life when married unable to produce children. This is an awful tragedy and well worth trying to avoid. We know that, rare as this complication is, it is even rarer if the patient is kept at rest in bed until the mumps have gone.

This rare complication in childhood shows itself in the male by a sudden rise in temperature and swelling plus pain in the testicles. In the female the condition shows as a sudden attack of lower abdominal pain in a patient with mumps.

There is no specific treatment for mumps but the hygiene of the mouth is important and the teeth should be cleaned and the mouth rinsed out with an antiseptic mouthwash after each meal.

Meat and acid sharp tasting drinks should be avoided.

The diet should be bland and nourishing, such as eggs, milk and fishy dishes.

**Glandular Fever.** The medical name for this disease is Infective Mononucleosis. The disease is characterised by a vague generalised constitutional upset, sometimes accompanied by shivering and a high temperature. The feverish stage lasts about two weeks. Examination reveals that many of the glands, especially those in the neck are swollen.

The usual picture is that of a child running a temperature which does not respond to treatment, and for which there is no obvious explanation. In such cases a blood test, called the Paul-Bunnell test, can be performed which usually settles the diagnosis. If the child has had a recent injection containing serum the doctor should be warned because this can negative the test.

There is no specific treatment and treatment consists in good nursing care until the temperature has settled. An odd feature of this disease is the lengthy time it takes the patient to pick up after the illness, in some cases running into many weeks and often the quickest way to recovery is a holiday in the country or at the seaside.

The doctor can provide treatment to lessen any predominant symptom such as pain, cough or vomiting, etc.

**Catarrh.** This is a condition of low-grade infection or allergy which causes the lining membrane of the nose to swell. It may spread to the chest.

In actual fact catarrh in small babies and children is probably a natural reaction of the child to meeting and combating various germs for the first time and so in a way is a natural process. Certainly most children go t hrough a "catarrhal phase" up to five years of age.

After repeated attacks of catarrh the tonsils and adenoids may swell up and stay in a swollen condition causing nasal obstruction and general ill health.

Molly-coddling children, overdressing them, having too many bed clothes and living in an overheated house or bedroom all tend to worsen the catarrh whereas an open-air life often lessens the condition. Many a weak catarrhal child has emerged from an open-air school looking the picture of good health.

In older children one or other of the nasal sinuses may have become infected and the infection there keeps up the catarrh. If this is suspected then the child will have to pay a visit to the ear, nose and throat specialist for treatment.

There are no proprietary medicines or drops which the mother can buy from the chemist which are of much use and it is far safer to seek advice about the problem from the family doctor.

**Tonsils and Adenoids.** The tonsils are the fleshy pads of lymphoid tissue situated on either side of the throat. The adenoids are similar fleshy pads at the back of the nose.

Each cause trouble in their own way but it must be realised that they represent a ring of similar tissue, the tonsils being the adenoids of the throat and the adenoids the tonsils of the nose, as it were. They are not really separate organs.

**Tonsils.** These can be seen on either side of the throat lying between fleshy bands called the pillars of the tonsil which make a kind of cradle for them. They can become so enlarged in children that they almost meet and at one time this appearance was sufficient to condemn them and insist that they be removed surgically. Now there is a wait-and-see policy because we know that many of these cases actually subside in time.

Each tonsil has a number of crypts in it and when the tonsil is inflamed or infected each crypt discharges yellow pus and this can be seen as yellow spots all over the tonsil. Often this discharge collects on the surface of the tonsil as a yellow scum which can be moved easily with the handle of a spoon, this differentiates it from a diphtheria membrane which cannot be moved without a lot of hard scraping which causes bleeding. When the tonsils are infected the neck glands enlarge in sympathy and these can be felt in the side of the neck and below the lower jaw. Inflammation of the tonsils is called tonsillitis, popularly called a sore throat. There is a raised temperature and pain on swallowing and the condition is rapidly cured by administering modern antibiotic drugs.

**Adenoids.** Enlarged adenoids cause nasal obstruction, mouth-breathing, a nasal voice, sore throats from mouth-breathing, snoring, nightmares in some children and an alteration to the facial appearance.

That is bad enough and sufficient indication for having the adenoids removed but there is an even more important disease caused by enlarged adenoids – inflammation of the middle ear.

Behind the eardrum is a space called the middle ear and this has a tube (called the Eustachian Tube) which drains the space into the back of the nose.

Unfortunately the Eustachian Tube in a child is almost horizontal and does not assume the semi-vertical position until one becomes an adult. This horizontal position of the tube in childhood plus a lot of lying on the back in a cot allows infection to spread quickly from the back of the nose to the ear resulting in inflamed eardrums (otitis media) and this can be the starting point of deafness later in life.

**Earache** (*Otitis Media*). For all practical purposes it is true to say that *earache in children is always due to an inflamed eardrum.*

The infection has got up from the back of the nose as described under *Adenoids* (which see) and the pain is due to the eardrum being distended by pus from behind. If not treated in time the drum will burst causing a discharging ear. Now this condition must never be treated lightly: it is terribly important for the child. Probably 80 per cent of the deafness in adults is due to this condition being inadequately treated in childhood.

In small babies the child will be running a temperature, whimpering all the time because of the pain and constantly putting his hand up to the painful ear; he may even have diarrhoea or tummy pain and the condition appear to be one of enteritis. Examination of the ear by the doctor shows the drum to be bright red and later it starts to distend.

To prevent permanent damage to the hearing the doctor needs to get his antibiotic treatment in early before the drum has become distended, so there is no time for the mother *to wait and see what happens. All children with earache need treatment within twenty-four hours.*

If the eardrum bursts and produces a discharge then the ear should be covered with a dressing to soak up the discharge but *on no account must the discharging ear be plugged with cotton-wool,* the ear must be allowed to discharge freely.

**Colic (in infants).** Reference has already been made to this condition under Three Month Colic on page 105.

The commonest causes of colic in infants are:

Overfeeding with the correct food. An excess of sugar. An excess of starchy foods when weaning. Not getting up the wind at intervals during a feed. Sucking at an empty breast. Sucking at a bottle which has a teat with too small a hole so that the infant sucks round the teat and swallows air. Surgical conditions producing intestinal obstruction.

**Constipation.** True constipation is either due to faulty feeding, some disorder of the intestines or poor nursery training.

Occasionally the child passes a large hard stool which splits the opening of the back passage producing what is called an anal fissure. This produces pain every time the child tries to pass a motion and so he tries very hard not to attempt to have his bowels open. A doctor can examine the back passage and if a fissure is present this can be treated.

Too little fluid in the diet or too much protein tend to cause constipation.

The best treatment for constipation is to prevent it and early training is essential. The baby should be held on his pot at regular intervals, after feeds is a good time. The baby very soon understands what is expected of it when he feels the touch of the pot. This training can be reinforced by putting an infant-size glycerine suppository in the back passage just prior to placing the infant on the pot. The suppository provides the baby with the right sensation which tells him the bowels need opening and this plus the feel of the rim of the pot is all that is necessary to train quite young babies.

In the older child constipation is usually due to faulty training and diet plays little part.

There is a normal sensation in the bowel when it is full indicating that it wants to be emptied. If the child constantly ignores this natural message then in time it is blunted and the child receives no indication at all that the bowel should be emptied.

The older child should be sent to the lavatory immediately after breakfast and again after the midday meal and given ample time to try and empty the bowel. The presence of a recent meal reawakens the natural message from the bowels and in time a regular habit will ensue which will last the child all his life.

Once the older child has become a sufferer from chronic constipation the doctor will have to be consulted as in the early stages the cure consists of prescribing a suitable aperient.

Castor oil should never be used as this only makes the constipation worse. Adding extra oranges and apples to the diet is of assistance and so are prunes. The practice of giving a child a regular weekly dose of "opening medicine" whether he needs it or not on the general principle of keeping "his inside sweet and clean" cannot be too strongly condemned; it serves no useful purpose.

Breakfast cereals alleged to provide roughage for the bowel should not be given to children. They will not cure the constipation and may irritate the intestine and cause colic.

**Vomiting.** Vomiting without diarrhoea is common in babies but it is important to differentiate between true vomiting and what is called posseting. The latter is the regurgitation without effort of a mouthful of milk at the end of a feed, usually a breast-feed. It is of no significance and requires no treatment.

True vomiting can be caused by air swallowing, whether caused by a bad bottle teat, sucking at an empty breast, by sucking a dummy or the fists. Tossing the baby about after a feed can provoke a vomiting attack.

During the first three months of life a condition (which see) called Pyloric Stenosis causes regular vomiting.

In all these conditions the baby's digestion is normal, the appetite good but the baby becomes a greedy feeder and screams a lot. The baby is usually restless and constipated.

Some babies find difficulty in digesting fat, especially the fat of cow's milk, and show this by vomiting, failure to gain weight and the passage of large pale solid stools. After a time diarrhoea may occur. A change to a half-cream mixture produces dramatic improvement.

The newborn baby that persistently vomits may have some internal obstruction or abnormality and should be seen by a doctor.

A well-recognised group of babies suffer with *nervous vomiting*. The children are usually between 6 and 12 months old who have always been difficult about their feeding and sleeping and are the restless irritable sort. This type of child usually has a highly strung emotional mother who is always being alarmed and shows it.

Usually both mother and child need a nerve sedative.

In the older child vomiting may be due to almost any disturbance whether emotional or physical. Shock, fright, excitement, being overtired or overheated may all start an attack.

Overeating, especially too much sugar or fat, or articles that irritate the stomach such as pickles, too much ice-cream and certain foods to which the child is sensitive, may all provoke an attack of vomiting or as the mother will call it a *bilious attack*.

Repeated vomiting by a child when there is no disease present may be purely psychological and may require extensive investigation by a child psychiatrist.

Any child who persistently vomits should be seen by an experienced children's doctor and not just labelled *nervous*.

Having covered the subject of vomiting in a general way mention must be made about one special variety of vomiting which has been called by various names such as Periodic Vomiting, Cyclic or Cyclical Vomiting, Acidosis Attacks and Bilious Attacks. In some degree, probably over a third of all children suffer with this condition at one time or other.

The first onset is between 3 and 7 years of age and the attacks usually stop at puberty but may be followed in the older child by migraine headaches.

The really severe cases are not so common as they were thirty years ago but in the classical case the child is off colour for a day and then commences to vomit. After a time the child becomes sleepy, restless and thirsty. He complains of headache and his temperature may go up to 101 degrees or higher. The tongue looks furred and the breath is bad and the smell of acetone can be detected. The child looks really ill.

These attacks may last from three to seven days and then the child recovers.

Children known to be subject to these attacks need careful handling if the attacks are to be reduced in number. They need more rest and sleep than average and should be in bed early.

During the attack fat should be reduced in the diet and milk not offered. The child should have sugar in various forms such as sweetened fruit drinks and barley sugar or boiled sweets to suck. To an extent the diet between the attacks should be low in fat and high in carbohydrate.

**Diarrhoea and Vomiting.** The proper name for this condition is gastroenteritis and occurring in a child under 2 years of age is quite a serious condition.

Overfeeding, especially in hot weather, can cause diarrhoea and vomiting and so can excessive amounts of intestinal irritants such as sour fruit and strawberries. Food that is going "off" is another possible cause. Excessive amounts of fat in the diet or a preponderance of sugar (sweets) can initiate an attack.

A doctor should be consulted early so that the child can start treatment before he loses too much of the body fluid and becomes what is called dehydrated.

**Asthma.** To understand the asthmatic child one has to think in terms of three items, nervous instability, infection and allergy, all of which are involved in producing the asthmatic attack.

The asthmatic attack is seen as an attack of fast breathing in which the child is out of breath together with a wheezy chest which makes a loud noise which can be heard many feet away.

The obstruction to breathing may be severe and the child may go blue in the face. Fortunately the attack is usually relieved in a matter of seconds by an injection of adrenalin.

There is usually a history of allergy in one or other parent such as asthma or hay fever.

Asthmatic children are the highly intelligent, very affectionate youngsters with something of the artistic temperament about them, in fact just the sort of child any parent would like.

These children have been born with an inherited hypersensitivity to various forms of allergens such as animal hairs, house dust and certain foods, etc., all having a protein base. In addition they have inherited this highly charged state of nervous tension.

The tendency is to mollycoddle these children and make them into chronic invalids with disastrous results to their physique and final development.

Apart altogether from the doctor's treatment which can help enormously there are certain things the parents can do.

The child should sleep in a dust-free room with the absolute minimum of furniture and bric-à-brac which can hold dust. The floor should be free of carpets and consist of just bare lino. The curtains should be either plastic or cotton. The latter must be washed every three months before they can develop cotton dust to liberate into the atmosphere.

The bed should have a foam rubber mattress which is allergen free as against ordinary mattresses which may contain horse hair, etc. No eiderdown should be on the bed as this contains animal products. The bedclothes should consist of blankets covered with a cotton counterpane which must be regularly washed.

If the child is allergic to animals then the house must be kept free of pets such as cats and dogs.

The child should not be given a heavy meal at night as the overloaded stomach may precipitate an attack. If purgatives ever have to be administered then these should not be given at night.

The bedroom should be well aired and a window kept open at night. In heavy fog or smog the child should be kept indoors.

The pillows on the bed must be either kapok filled or made from foam rubber.

The child should not be overdressed and as far as possible wool should be replaced by silk or nylon.

Attempts should be made to give the child a calm unruffled home background and nothing said to convince the child that he is not like other children and a special invalid. The child should not be prevented from playing games and without making too much emphasis on the point the parents should see that he gets plenty of rest by putting him to bed early even if he just sits there and looks at his books for an hour or two; at least he will be off his feet and not exhausting himself.

Excitable programmes on the television during the late evening prior to bedtime should be banned.

To prevent the recurrent asthma attacks spoiling the shape of the lungs and chest permanently the child can be given instructions in breathing exercises. These are cleverly illustrated for children at all ages in a booklet issued by the *Asthma Research Council;* most of them become a game which the child will enjoy doing.

These booklets are inexpensive, profusely illustrated with instructional pictures.

The medical treatment of each individual case varies quite a lot from child to child and the parents will have to consult a doctor interested in children for advice.

**Worms.** Despite popular beliefs there are practically no symptoms from the child having threadworms. Grinding the teeth, for instance, has nothing to do with the presence of worms.

The only way of diagnosing the presence of worms is to study the stools on several occasions by getting the child to use a chamber pot. Threadworms look like one-inch threads of cotton *which move.*

If only one worm is detected that is sufficient, there may be thousands inside the bowel.

Fortunately these days there are treatments which rapidly eliminate these parasites.

The problem is reinfection. The worms come out of the back passage at night and cause irritation, the child puts his fingers there to scratch and later sucks his fingers in his mouth and starts the cycle all over again.

The child should wear some close-fitting knickers or pants at night and the back passage should be anointed with dilute Ammoniated Mercury Ointment which will kill any worms that emerge.

It is seldom that only one member of the family has worms so that once a child has been found to be suffering with worms all the rest of the family have to be checked. The parents may have had worms for twenty years and not known it!

Obviously the important thing is to cure everybody in the house who has worms to avoid reinfection.

This raises the question of pets. If a dog or a cat live in the house they must be properly wormed on at least two occasions under the supervision of a veterinary surgeon and children should be stopped from kissing the muzzle of an animal.

There are other kinds of worms than threadworms and these look like the ordinary garden worm; they are rare in children in this country and tape worms are rarer still.

**Scurf.** Many quite young babies develop a crusted scurf area on the top of the scalp. This can be controlled by giving the area a soap massage with the palm of the hand, rinsing the soap off and after drying, anointing the area with the following ointment which a chemist can make up if you show him the prescription,

Hydrarg. Ammon. Chlor. grains 15
Liq. Picis. Carb. minims 15.
Paraffin Molle Flav. to one ounce.

Apply the ointment night and morning.

This ointment is not suitable for the baby's face.

The ointment should not be used indefinitely but only for a week or two at a time.

**Thrush.** This is a disease which can occur at any age but is particularly associated with babies. It is caused by a fungus parasite.

When it is seen as a white covering inside the baby's mouth it should be an indication to overhaul the nursing care of the infant. The baby's bottles must be properly sterilised, as has been explained elsewhere in this book. Any dummy in use should be burned and not replaced.

If the baby is breast-fed the mother should wash her nipples with soap and water and then mop them over with surgical spirit after each breast-feed.

A time-honoured remedy was glycerine of borax wiped over the white patches.

Much more effective is to go to the chemist and buy a bottle of glycerine and thymol mouthwash and then wrap a piece of gauze round the finger and wipe the thrush patches over with the neat mouthwash three times a day.

**Squint.** In the early months of life a squint is of little significance; if it persists then medical advice should be sought.

Usually squints first show themselves between the ages of 2 and 6 years old and are due to trouble with the tiny muscles that move the eye.

**Milk Spots.** This is the popular name given to the appearance of some small white spots on the face of young babies. They are usually breast-fed male babies of about 4 weeks old. They always disappear and if any treatment is employed it should always be something bland like Nivea Creme or Calamine Cream.

**Pyloric Stenosis.** This is a disease of the first few weeks of life characterised by the violent vomiting of all that is swallowed. It is called projectile vomiting because the baby doesn't just bring up the milk or water but projects it well beyond himself. Male babies are affected more often than females and the precise cause of the condition is not known.

What we do know is that for some reason the valve between the stomach and the intestines becomes thickened and in spasm. This blocks the hole so that food cannot enter the intestines from the stomach.

The vomiting usually starts when the baby is 3 weeks old.

The treatment consists of a simple operation to clear the obstruction.

Any baby that starts to vomit every feed should be seen by a doctor.

**Appendicitis.** The appendix in the child is different to that in an adult, its walls are thinner and it is relatively large for the size of the child. If the appendix bursts, the peritonitis that results tends to be more widespread and therefore more dangerous than in an adult.

There is often a history that the child has previously had attacks of abdominal pain or so called bilious attacks.

The chief features of an attack of acute appendicitis are four in number:
1. **Pain.** The pain is sudden in onset, often in a child that looks perfectly fit and well. At first the pain starts around the navel and later settles in the right-hand lower corner of the abdomen. The pain should *never* be treated with a purgative or opening medicine.
2. **Vomiting.** If vomiting commences it practically always starts *after* the pain.
3. **Tenderness.** If the hand is placed gently over the right-hand lower corner of the abdomen and the area gently pressed it causes pain because below this region is the site of the inflamed appendix.
4. **Abdominal Rigidity.** As the condition worsens the abdominal muscles go into a protective spasm and the abdominal wall will feel hard and rigid, *all the time*.

Depending on various reasons too complicated to discuss here there may be constipation or diarrhoea, an urge to pass water frequently, a temperature that may be only 100 degrees or as high as 103 deg.F. In the early stages the abdomen may be soft and the pain may come in waves like colic.

Persistent abdominal pain in a child requires medical attention from the family doctor *and no experimental treatment should be started such as magnesia or syrup of figs, which never cure abdominal pain in a child and may burst an inflamed appendix.*

**Growing Pains.** Small children sometimes complain of pains in their legs and the popular diagnosis is "growing pains". Parents would be wise *never to diagnose such a condition.*

The pains may very well be due to an ache from small muscles and ligaments getting over-tired but they can also be the only sign of an early rheumatic fever, especially if the child complains of leg pains when at rest or in bed. A doctor should be consulted so that the child can have a blood test at hospital to exclude rheumatic disease.

**Acute Rheumatism (Rheumatic Fever).** The onset of acute rheumatism may begin in a variety of ways.

The disease may start with an acute sore throat and a high temperature followed by one or several joints being red, swollen and painful. Some cases start off straight away as a high temperature and heart trouble, others start with an attack of St Vitus' Dance which is closely allied to rheumatic fever. In other cases the onset of the disease is slow and gradual and heart murmurs may be detected at routine examination with the stethoscope.

If rheumatic fever is diagnosed then in the interests of the child the mother must be prepared for the child to have to go to bed for a long period. Often the early stages of the disease are first dealt with by a stay in hospital but six weeks' bed rest at first is more than likely. The convalescence will have to be slow and prolonged.

**Flat Feet.** All babies and small children seem to be naturally flat-footed and this is not because the feet are abnormal *but because the bony arches of the feet are not really formed until the child is 5 or 6 years of age.*

Some children when they first start to walk turn their feet outwards and this gives the appearance of flat feet.

There is no real evidence that supports and pads put into infants' shoes have the slightest good effect and only succeed in making walking uncomfortable and the child foot-conscious.

If after 5 or 6 years of age the child appears to be flat-footed then the child should see a doctor or an orthopaedic surgeon.

**Children's Shoes.** Children's feet can be deformed by badly fitting shoes and *badly fitting socks.* When a pair of cotton socks have been washed they tend to shrink and it should not be left to the child's foot to re-expand the sock. The sock should be properly stretched by hand and if it is obviously too small then a new or different pair of socks should be obtained and put on.

When a child is taken to a shop to have new shoes fitted the *feet should always be measured for length and breadth with the child standing.*

On no account should the mother let the shop X-ray the child's feet, for two very good reasons. Firstly we know that X-rays can interfere with the growing tip of the bones and eventually so paralyse them that the bone stops growing. Secondly, it is a complete illusion that X-rays do any good for shoe fitting because all that an X-ray shows is the *bones* of the foot, the X-rays do not show the soft tissues. Thus the foot might be chubby and plump or long and thin and these soft tissues have to be enclosed in the shoe as well as the bones. The only safe practice is to measure the child's feet for length and breadth *whilst the child is standing on his feet.*

Children do not need surgical shoes to start with unless specially ordered by a doctor, and that means all those shoes advertised as having built-in wedges, etc.

**Knock-knees.** This condition, which medically has the name of Genu Valgum, is so common that it can hardly be considered as an abnormality. The vast majority of cases correct themselves as the child grows and develops his muscles and is the reason that so very few adults have knock-knees.

With the little legs held together there is often a separation between the ankles of one to two inches and only if the distance is wider than this between the ankles should one diagnose knock-knees.

**Bowed Legs.** The medical name for this condition is Genu Varum and the popular name bandy-legs.

The degree of bow-leggedness is measured by placing the ankles together and then measuring the distance separating the knees.

Many babies appear bow-legged and later appear knock-kneed. The condition is so frequent as to be considered quite normal as they recover without treatment.

If after the age of 8 the child is still bow-legged the child should be seen by an orthopaedic surgeon.

**Taking the Temperature.** The family doctor is dependent on the mother for so much when treating her baby, not the least for the taking of the baby's temperature.

A single recording of the child's temperature is quite useless, it must be taken three times a day, morning, midday and evening.

It is quite an easy task for the mother to learn. Having wiped the child's groin free from perspiration, she places the thermometer in the fold of the groin and holds the child's leg doubled up on the abdomen, thus totally enclosing the thermometer.

She leaves it there for a full minute and then takes it away and studies it.

It has been accepted that 98·4 degs.F. is a normal temperature and this point is usually marked by an arrow on the scale.

Babies often run a temperature higher than this when they are quite fit and well so that a temperature reading of 99 degs.F. is not necessarily abnormal.

A baby, having an immaturely developed temperature regulating mechanism, runs quite a high temperature for very little, an ordinary cold can produce a temperature of 102 or 103 degrees, so that the height of the temperature does not mean as much in a baby as it would mean in an adult.

Most newborn babies have a temperature of 99·6 degs.F. normally and a toddler in a passion can run a temperature of 101 degs.F. just because it is worked up.

# TRAVEL AND HOLIDAYS IN GREAT BRITAIN AND ABROAD

## INTRODUCTION

The days when a holiday was considered a luxury belong to the past, and this section aims to provide some of the essential information that may help to ensure a successful holiday.

The cost of that annual break is an important item in the budget of the individual or the family.

The advantages of taking a holiday out of season apply equally to holidays at home and holidays abroad. Resorts are less crowded and travel is easier.

It is certainly worth taking advantage of the services offered by the motoring organisations, local information offices, British Rail and coach tour operators. A self-drive car should always be booked in advance. The British Travel Association (BTA) publishes a national holiday guide and the activities of the Youth Hostels Association (YHA) are mentioned in the section dealing with specialised holidays.

Practical steps to be taken before leaving include arranging in advance for the boarding of family pets, cancelling newspapers, milk and bread and, if the house is somewhat isolated, notifying the local police. Doors and windows should be firmly latched, gas and electricity switched off and no food left in the larder or refrigerator.

It only remains to close the front door and set off to enjoy to the full that precious annual holiday. It is the author's sincere hope that these notes may help towards that end.

## SPECIALISED HOLIDAYS IN GREAT BRITAIN AND ABROAD

**Angling and Fishing.** Several centres have been established where angling and sea-fishing are taught. Experts give instruction in fly-casting, the different types of rods, reels and lines and combine these informal lectures with practical fishing experience on lakes, rivers and at sea.

Novices are made welcome at fly-fishing courses in Snowdonia by the Central Council of Physical Recreation, 26–29 Park Crescent, London W.1. The Irish Tourist Board, 71 Regent Street, London W.1, issue several publications of interest to fishermen and give information about angling holidays in Ireland. Advice about fishing holidays in Scotland can be obtained from the Scottish Tourist Board, 2 Rutland Place, West End, Edinburgh 1.

Instruction and hire of the necessary tackle and equipment is generally paid for independently of hostel or hotel accommodation. The holidaymaker can either book hotel accommodation or stay in Youth Hostels near the site. YHA Home Tours, Trevelyan House, St Albans, Herts, will give details of courses for young people. Specialised angling holidays in Norway are arranged by Bennett Travel Bureau, 48 Wigmore Street, London W.1.

**Canoeing.** Organisations that run courses in canoeing insist, rightly, that all participants should be reasonable swimmers. Instruction on handling a canoe is given on lakes, rivers and at sea and practical canoe building is also studied.

Accommodation is often in hostels where members are expected to help with day-to-day chores. Attractive centres include Snowdonia and the River Wye and, in the north, the Lake District and several Scottish centres.

The British Canoe Union is affiliated to the Central Council of Physical Recreation (CCPR) and represents British canoe interests both within the UK and abroad. A section of the Camping Club of Great Britain and Ireland, 11 Lower Grosvenor Place, London S.W.1, will provide details on request. The Youth Hostels Association (YHA) is also active in this field.

Outside the UK, canoeing holidays in several European countries can be booked through PGL Holidays, Adventure House, Ross-on-Wye, Herefordshire. These are relatively inexpensive and are based on tented accommodation or in continental youth hostels affiliated to the YHA.

**Caravans and Camping Coaches.** An inexpensive and enjoyable holiday, whether at home or abroad, can be spent in a caravan or camping coach. Those without a car can hire caravans by the week, or for longer periods, on excellent sites – many in or close to accepted beauty spots – and use public transport to explore the surrounding countryside.

Caravans for towing can also be rented as well as the very popular specially converted "Motocaravans" with either two or four berths and Calor gas stoves, wash-basins and toilets as standard fittings. In this way towing problems are avoided.

British Travel, 64–65 St James' Street, London S.W.1, issue lists of caravan and camping sites. Similar information is available to members from the Caravan Club, 46 Brook Street, London W.1, and from the Camping Club of Great Britain and Ireland.

For larger families the excellent camping coaches operated by British Rail can be recommended; sited throughout the UK in country and seaside areas they are much roomier than a caravan and can be rented throughout the summer period. Regional offices of British Rail issue brochures detailing both locations and the conditions affecting purchase of rail tickets; those travelling the greatest distance are given priority.

Booking of camping coaches opens in December. Demand is, understandably, far in excess of supply, and very early booking is essential.

**Cycling.** A rewarding holiday can be spent on two wheels exploring an unfamiliar area, whether at home or abroad.

The Cyclists Touring Club, 3 Craven Hill, London W.2, will give addresses of local associations which exist in over fifty areas and will also make reservations for members. A new section of the Camping Club of Great Britain and Ireland assists everyone making use of light-weight equipment, irrespective of the means of transport employed. CCPR arranges a course in Shropshire for those wishing to enter for the BCF Coaching Award.

YHA Travel, 29 John Adam Street, London W.C.2, arranges continental cycling holidays, normally accompanied by a YHA leader, in many European countries, among them Belgium, Germany, Poland and Yugoslavia. Holland, with no problems of severe cycling conditions, is a popular choice.

**Holiday Camps.** The holiday camp often provides the amenities of a holiday city in miniature. In big, highly organised camps a complete range of sports and entertainment is included in the cost of accommodation and full board. A closed-circuit radio station and printed programmes outline each day's programme.

Accommodation is usually in chalets located near large social centres comprising dining-rooms, dance-halls, games rooms, bars, cinemas, variety theatres and, often, both indoor and outdoor swimming-pools.

A "baby-minding" service is included without extra charge and there are nurseries where the very young can be left in the care of trained staff. Older members of the family can come and go as they please in the knowledge that the youngsters are in safe hands.

The big holiday camp can sometimes be noisy.

At the other end of the scale are smaller, quieter and more intimate camps and while they do not claim to offer a complete entertainment service, all have social centres and often a swimming-pool as well.

The individual should check exactly what is included within the weekly terms, which vary throughout the season, before making a booking. Full details are available from The National Federation of Permanent Holiday Camps, 10 Bolton Street, London W.1.

**Mountaineering and Rock Climbing.** Mountaineering and rock climbing courses held throughout the year, both in this country and abroad, cater alike for the beginner and the experienced climber. Both activities appeal primarily to the young and physical fitness is essential. Participants often live in fairly rugged conditions, buying and cooking their own meals and sleeping in huts. Great stress is laid on safety precautions and the courses include instruction on map reading, rock climbing and mountain walking.

Over a hundred clubs are affiliated to the British Mountaineering Council, 74 South Audley Street, London W.1, which acts in an advisory capacity. The Mountaineering Association, 102A Westbourne Grove, London W.2, is a non-profit-making organisation and arranges courses throughout the UK and in Austria, Italy and Switzerland. The CCPR is also active in this field while the Ramblers' Association Service, 124 Finchley Road, London N.W.3, runs hill-walking and mountaineering holidays in England, Wales and Scotland and operates as far afield as the High Tatras in Czechoslovakia and Yugoslavia's Julian Alps.

Information on suggested types of boots and clothing and other necessary equipment, and whether this should be purchased or hired by the individual or if it is included within the cost, is always obtainable from the organisers of these specialised holidays.

**Pony-trekking and Riding.** A distinction should be drawn between different types of horse-riding holidays. For those courses in which the essential rudiments of conventional horsemanship are taught the participant will need jodhpurs or breeches. Instruction and the hire of horse or pony are normally paid on weekly terms. Accommodation can be arranged at a near-by guest-house or in hostels. The CCPR lists suggested centres and Galleon Holidays, Eccleston Court, Gillingham Street, London S.W.1, arrange both riding and pony-trekking holidays in many parts of Britain.

Pony-trekking generally involves travelling long distances over fairly rough country at little more than walking pace. After basic instruction the novice can safely undertake a holiday of this kind. Popular areas include the Black Mountains in Wales, the Derbyshire Peak District and the Highlands and Lowlands of Scotland.

Outside the UK, The Ramblers' Association Service runs pony-trekking holidays in Austria, and Budapest Travel Ltd, 26 Bloomsbury Way, London W.C.1, organise tours for the fairly skilled horseman in Hungary.

On foreign pony-trekking and riding holidays accommodation and hire of horse or pony is normally quoted at an inclusive price. The holidaymaker who is free to choose his own means of travel, whether by car, rail, or air, pays for this separately.

**Sailing.** The boat-owning population of Great Britain has grown enormously in recent years but before contemplating the purchase of a craft it is important to learn the principles of navigation and sailing.

An extensive series of courses is offered throughout the spring and summer season combining instruction and practical experience both for novices and for those with some basic knowledge.

The trainee should provide his own oilskin or anorak, preferably with a hood, and waterproof slacks and rubber-soled shoes for use on deck. Life-jackets, normally provided by sailing schools, should be worn at all times.

A week's course should enable a newcomer to take out a boat on his own with a reasonable measure of confidence.

Arrangements offered can vary from bunks on an eight-berth yacht to accommodation in near-by hotels or boarding-houses. Many schools will suggest where rooms are available.

The CCPR and Holiday Fellowship, 142 Great North Way, Hendon N.W.4, run sailing courses in Great Britain and Northern Ireland. From a comprehensive list of sailing schools one address is given for each area. Sail-a-Boat Holidays, 7 Oxford Street, Dartmouth, South Devon; South Eastern Sailing

Ltd, The Enterprise, Burnham-on-Crouch, Essex; Bosham Sea School Ltd, The Old Malt House, Old Bosham, Chichester, Sussex, and Ashlake Sailing School, Ashlake Farm, Wootton, Isle of Wight.

The Scottish Council of Physical Recreation (SCPR), 4 Queensferry Street, Edinburgh 2, organises courses in Perthshire and Argyllshire.

Outside the UK, Academy Travel Ltd, arrange sailing tuition on Lake Balaton in Hungary and the Ramblers' Association Service at Estartit on Spain's Costa Brava.

Some tour operators arrange holidays combining some sailing instruction, and an all-in-price covers transport and full board as well.

**Skin-diving, Underwater swimming, and Water-ski-ing.** A course of training is advisable before attempting skin-diving. The British Sub-Aqua Club, 25 Orchard Road, Kingston-upon-Thames, Surrey, a national voluntary organisation with branches throughout the country – there are also some overseas – controls underwater swimming in the UK. Details and conditions of membership and of the standardised training are available on request. Those undertaking instruction must have their own equipment, but aqualungs, when used, are provided. Junior members (under 19) can gain experience with fins, masks and breathing tubes but are not at present allowed to use aqualungs.

Training with the most advanced equipment is given at the British Underwater Centre, Warfleet Creek, Dartmouth, Devon and the CCPR runs its own courses at Barton Hall Hotel, Torquay.

Holiday Fellowship runs general watersport holidays for young people in the Balearic Islands, and the Club Mediterranee, 40–41 Conduit Street, London W.1, provides good facilities at their many European holiday villages.

Water-ski-ing is available at several UK centres. Clubs provide necessary equipment and some cater for holiday-makers. The British Water-Ski Federation, 14 Station Road, Chertsey, Surrey, will give details of facilities to be

found at individual clubs. The SCPR has its own headquarters at Loch Earnhead Hotel in Perthshire. Temporary membership can be arranged for visitors, including beginners, staying at the hotel.

**Walking.** "Shanks's Pony" provides a very economical holiday. Beginners should preferably join a group under the guidance of a leader who knows the terrain well. In mountain areas a knowledge of local conditions and of map reading is important.

Those embarking on a walking holiday for the first time should not try to undertake too much. A pair of good, tough, and comfortable walking-shoes is indispensable and organisers will indicate where boots are considered necessary. Popular areas in Britain include the Lake District, Snowdonia, Exmoor, the Yorkshire Moors, and many parts of Scotland.

The Ramblers' Association Service supplies lists of local Rambling Clubs and also runs walking tours both in this country and throughout Europe. In addition to the YHA the YTB, Knightsbridge Station Arcade, Brompton Road, London S.W.3, issues its own "Sports Tour Programme" covering all kinds of outdoor holidays. It also arranges walking tours in Iceland.

**Winter Sports.** Before contemplating a first winter sports holiday a series of pre-ski exercises and, preferably, a course of instruction at a dry-ski school will tone up the muscles and ensure that the novice wastes little time on reaching the resort.

The special clothes required need not be very expensive but should include waterproof trousers (vorlages), anorak, oiled-wool mittens and socks, some form of headgear, one or two pullovers, a pair of goggles, and glacier cream to prevent sunburn at high altitudes. Long woollen underwear helps to ward off the cold.

"Après-ski" or leisure clothes depend on both the type of accommodation and the resort chosen. On cheaper inclusive holidays, using chalets and youth hostels, no special evening clothes need be taken.

Special ski-ing-boots are needed and while these should ideally be bought, they can be hired, together with skis and sticks, at many resorts. The equipment required for ski-touring in Norway is better bought out there. Norwegian bindings also vary from those in use elsewhere.

A special winter sports policy – and this really is an essential – is quoted by many insurance companies.

The co-ordinating body in the UK is the Ski Club of Great Britain, 118 Eaton Square, London S.W.1, which issues lists of dri-ski classes held in all parts of Britain.

The winter sports season runs from mid-December to April according to the country and resort chosen. Most centres are less crowded in January and reductions are usually offered during this period.

Those booking an inclusive holiday through a travel agent – many run special tours for beginners – should make sure what the "all-in" arrangements comprise; whether insurance is included as well as the hire of equipment and ski-ing lessons, normally arranged for groups of from 10 to 20. Several firms arrange what is known as a "Ski-Pack" to include these items at a small extra charge.

The Scottish Highlands have become increasingly popular in recent years and full information can be obtained from the SCPR.

The choice of country is, in part, dictated by price. France, Italy and Switzerland tend to be more expensive than Austria and Norway. At most centres there is plenty of evening entertainment.

Nearly all travel agents run their own inclusive arrangements and some long-established specialists in this field include F. & W. Ingham Ltd, 26 Old Bond Street, London W.1; Ski-Plan, 80 Duke Street, London W.1; and Sir Henry Lunn Ltd, 36 Edgware Road, London W.2.

**Conclusion.** In concluding this section it cannot be too strongly stressed that for those planning any kind of specialised holiday membership of the appropriate society or association, while not indispensable, will bring the advantages of specialised advice and knowledge and, in many cases, preferential terms for use of the society's hostels, etc., as well as, in some instances, reduced rates for instruction and hire of necessary equipment.

## HOLIDAYS ABROAD

**Choice of Country and Season.** Those planning a first holiday abroad should spend some time consulting the huge volume of tourist literature and information freely available both from travel agents and from National Tourist Offices. It is essential to decide before making a definite booking exactly what sort of holiday will best suit an individual or a family. An attractive resort found on arrival to have a rocky beach will inevitably raise problems with youngsters who cannot swim. The ideal location should cater for the tastes of all the members of the party irrespective of age.

Although the number of continental hotels, pensions and villas available increases each year, there remains the problem of finding good, reasonably priced accommodation in the peak summer season. Many people will find parts of Southern Europe too hot for their personal comfort in July and August.

The foreign hotelier is as anxious as his British counterpart to extend the season and there can often be a considerable financial saving in travelling early or late. There is more room to move and cafés and restaurants are less crowded with a consequently higher standard of service.

While no one would suggest taking children away during important school examinations, the 1944 Education Act does allow parents to take children away from school in term time if a family holiday cannot be arranged at any other time.

Some important points to be considered are dealt with elsewhere in this section. Time spent in careful and detailed planning will certainly not be wasted.

**The Holiday Budget.** Once a personal choice of country and season has been made a careful budget should be worked out bearing in mind any restrictions affecting the expenditure of foreign currency abroad. It is a mistake to spend so much on transport and accommodation that insufficient money is left for day-to-day spending. Out-of-pocket expenses are always higher than originally planned.

Those with a severely restricted budget who pick an inexpensive hotel will still have enough pocket money for drinks and cigarettes, ices for the children, local excursions booked on the spot and for the occasional visit to a good restaurant or night-club.

A holiday without a reasonable margin of spending money is often an unhappy holiday and a little foresight and planning can make all the difference.

## INDEPENDENT OR INCLUSIVE TOUR

The advantages and disadvantages of booking a holiday on an independent or an "inclusive" tour basis should be very carefully considered. A rugged independence can cost the inexperienced traveller a great deal in terms of both money and sometimes disastrous experience.

Whilst the travel agent is always prepared to plan an individual itinerary, this often involves considerable expense in correspondence, and cables on his part, with an hotel where he has not a block-booking of accommodation.

An "off-the-beaten-track" choice of holiday may preclude the individual from taking advantage of the preferential terms which the agent enjoys through dealing with large numbers of holidaymakers with consequent reductions in the costs of hotel accommodation, the advantages of party travel by train and boat, the chartering of aircraft and block reservations on scheduled aircraft of national airlines.

The individual who plans his own foreign holiday without consulting a travel agent can get a great deal of background information and up-to-date hotel lists from the National Tourist Offices of

the countries concerned. These organisations are primarily concerned with the promotion of holiday facilities within their own countries and offer advisory services. They will not normally undertake to book transport and hotels but may advise you as to which tour operator arranges the type of holiday for which you are looking.

Those wishing to plan independently and still employ the services of one of the bigger travel agencies will find their representatives at stations, ports and airports and offices in some main continental centres. While the local staff is principally concerned with arranging excursions and dealing with queries from holidaymakers who are on an "inclusive" basis, they will always be prepared to help the individual who has booked through their own organisation in the UK.

An entirely independent holiday in a remote, although attractive, area of, say, Yugoslavia, can become a complicated operation if no one in the party speaks the language.

## THE ROLES OF THE TRAVEL AGENT AND THE TOUR OPERATOR

The majority of those who travel abroad employ the services of a *Travel Agent*. In view of isolated instances of tourists being stranded, of completely unacceptable accommodation and of aircraft delays, it is important to choose a really reliable agent.

All large-scale organisations, whose names are household words, and many other smaller, specialised ones, belong to the Association of British Travel Agents (ABTA). Although there are a very small number of reputable firms outside the Association, membership provides a guarantee that in the event of an unforeseen breakdown of communications or, in any emergency, ABTA will take responsibility.

A good "inclusive" holiday arrangement should take into account "hidden costs" that the individual may not foresee and these will be clearly shown in a well-designed brochure. It will cover travel from London or the provincial centre listed to the holiday destination, by coach, air, or boat and train, reserved seats on trains, the visitor's tax applicable in the foreign country, porterage, (this should be checked when booking) tips in the hotel, conveyance from airport to hotel and vice versa, and where specified, the services of a resident host or hostess at the resort.

A distinction should be drawn between the travel agent, whether a member of ABTA or not, and the *Tour Operator* who plans and sells on an inclusive basis.

A careful study should be made of exactly what two equally attractive looking holidays at the same resort offer. The apparently cheaper price can be deceptive. Hotel rooms may be in an annexe, and porterage and meals in transit may be excluded. The hotel may be some distance from the beach or the town centre. In the long run the apparently more expensive holiday may offer better value.

The *Small Print* on the back of the booking form should be read carefully. It details and limits the liabilities of the agent and tour operator who act on behalf of the carriers and hotels.

The Association of British Travel Agents, 50–54 Charlotte Street, London W.1, issues a list of members in any given locality.

An agent will willingly suggest a holiday to suit the customer who, in his turn, should state his exact requirements and what he is prepared to pay. If the customer seeking sea and sun and some night life fails to mention the latter, he will return complaining that there was nothing to do at night. The agent is not to blame.

When making a telephone booking this should be followed by a completed booking form stating class of travel, meals en route if required, and alternative dates in case the first departure chosen is not available. The most popular resorts are often fully booked early in the year. January and February are not too soon to book a summer holiday.

At the time of booking a deposit is payable and the final account should be settled in accordance with the terms of the tour operator which is usually about six weeks before departure. Holidays on credit are available and agents will advise on this.

## PASSPORTS AND VISAS

**Passports.** For travel outside the United Kingdom (with the exception of Eire) a valid passport is necessary. Application to the passport offices in London, Liverpool and Glasgow is no longer essential. Local offices of the Ministry of Labour (Ministry of Health and Social Services in Northern Ireland) handle applications for new passports and renewals quickly and efficiently but, as seasonal demand coincides with the peak holiday period, it is advisable to apply a month before the intended departure date.

The application forms, obtainable from local offices of the Ministry, must be completed and details confirmed by a responsible person as designated (i.e. Minister of Religion, Bank Manager, Solicitor, etc.). A birth certificate must be produced together with photographs as specified on the forms. A married woman must produce both birth and marriage certificates.

The cost of a full British passport is £1 10s. It can be renewed after five years for a sum of £1. After ten years a new passport is required.

A simplified document, the British Visitors' Passport, has been introduced. At a cost of 7s. 6d. this is valid for one year only and cannot be renewed. Regulations concerning its use should be studied, and it can be obtained only by personal application to an Employment Exchange.

Children under the age of 16 can be entered on the passport of *one* parent or guardian only.

A travel agent will charge to arrange for the issue of a passport and will give advice on the current visa position.

A passport is a valuable document and its loss abroad should be reported to the police and to the nearest British consul.

**Visas.** The visa is an additional document required for travel in certain countries and issued on behalf of the governments concerned by their consulates in London.

Many countries have abolished visas but these are still currently required by visitors to Yugoslavia, to the countries of Eastern Europe, the Middle East, and the USA. Up-to-date information should be sought at the time of booking.

## CURRENCY

The allowance of foreign currency that may be spent abroad in a given year is announced annually by the Treasury. The exact position should be checked before applying for travel tickets and booking accommodation abroad, whether planning to travel independently or going on an inclusive holiday.

In some countries there are restrictions on the import and export of currency notes and a preferential rate of exchange applies to tourists.

The cost of travel to and from the UK is generally excluded, but all charges payable in foreign currency must be deducted from the allowance.

Within the sterling area, which includes most Commonwealth countries in addition to Iceland and Jordan, there are no restrictions.

Outside the sterling area – and this includes the most popular holiday countries in Europe – travellers' cheques, available in several denominations, are the simplest form in which to carry foreign currency. While abroad these can easily be cashed at banks, many hotels and stores, and at local exchange offices. It is inadvisable to cash them elsewhere as there may be a considerable difference in the rate of exchange offered. Travellers' cheques can be obtained from any bank. Travel agents also provide this service and make a small charge for doing so. Travellers' cheques are purchased outright by the holder and must be paid for when ordered. They must be signed by the holder at the time of issue and should be countersigned only when cashed. In some countries it is usual to ask for a passport as a means of identification.

If lost abroad, this should be reported at once to the issuing authority who will replace their value if the cheque has not been fraudulently cashed in the meantime.

The amount of sterling currency that may be taken out of the UK is also limited. This is intended for expenditure in British ships and planes but may be used abroad for genuine travel purposes.

A small amount of foreign currency, in the form of notes and coins, should also be taken to meet immediate expenses abroad. It is inadvisable to bring back foreign currency as there will be an inevitable small loss in re-exchanging this for sterling. It may be difficult to dispose of foreign coin.

Travel agents and banks keep themselves fully informed on the current regulations.

## CUSTOMS

In recent years customs procedure has been simplified and, to some extent, liberalised. Most countries permit the temporary importation of personal effects which the visitor intends to take back to the UK, including cameras, binoculars, portable radios, tape recorders, personal jewellery, camping equipment, sports equipment and essential medicines and drugs required for personal use.

In addition 200 cigarettes, or the equivalent amount in cigars or tobacco, and a small quantity of spirits – these can usually be bought duty free on ships and aircraft – can be taken into most countries.

On return to the UK all articles acquired abroad, irrespective of their value, must be declared. It is helpful to keep receipts for these handy. One cigarette lighter worth not more than £1 and £5 worth of souvenirs or other articles will be admitted free of duty by HM Customs.

Provided that all purchases are declared the returning traveller – this does not apply to day trips – may also bring in 200 cigarettes, or a comparable amount in cigars and pipe tobacco, one bottle of spirits, one bottle of light wine and a half-pint of perfume and toilet water of which not more than half is perfume.

Strict honesty is always the best policy

and those taking abroad an expensive camera or similar equipment of foreign make should keep a receipt showing the date of purchase in the UK.

Living plants may under no circumstances be imported, but in certain cases, i.e. Dutch bulbs, arrangements can be made to have them sent home. Uncooked meat is similarly restricted.

## HEALTH REGULATIONS AND PRECAUTIONS

Health regulations in force in the country or countries to be visited should be ascertained before departure. In practice there are few medical formalities although some hot countries insist on a certificate proving recent immunisation against tropical diseases (i.e. yellow fever, cholera, etc.).

Certain European countries will also insist, in the event of an epidemic within the UK, on a current immunisation certificate. Those requiring special diets either in transit or while staying abroad should notify this in advance.

It is as well to be prepared for unforeseen accidents or minor ailments while abroad.

Those taking any regular course of medicine or drugs should ensure that they have a sufficient supply to last for the period abroad. A compact first-aid kit should be taken containing aspirins, plasters, insect-repellant and, to alleviate what is often called "gyppy tummy", a proprietary brand of tablets obtainable, without prescription, from any chemist.

Excessive sun-bathing should be avoided at all times and especially for the first few days. A good suntan lotion will prevent burning and the British stomach appreciates a gentle introduction to the richness of continental food. Sun-glasses come in useful and special goggles must be worn for winter sports.

## MEDICAL FACILITIES ABROAD

In the event of serious illness requiring hospital treatment or the services of a doctor, the local tourist office can usually recommend an English-speaking physician.

Although certain arrangements have been made for reciprocal Health Service treatment in Scandinavia (Denmark, Norway and Sweden) and with Yugoslavia, the National Health Service, as it exists within the UK, does not operate abroad and there are no provisions to reimburse charges for medical services or hospital treatment on return to the UK. A comprehensive health insurance policy is strongly recommended and, for winter sports, is a virtual necessity. Many travel agents include this automatically. The independent traveller should arrange it personally.

## INSURANCE

Many British companies arrange comprehensive holiday insurance schemes for all between the ages of 6 and 70. The exact age limits should be checked as they can vary. A low premium of about £1 provides cover in the event of death or disablement up to £1,000. Personal baggage and money are similarly covered up to a maximum of £200, conditional on the reporting of the loss of money in any form to the local police within twenty-four hours, as are medical and hospital expenses up to £250 including any additional sums incurred if an escort home is necessary. If the holiday has to be cancelled through death, illness or accident, payments already made will be reimbursed up to a limit of £50 per person. Any undue risk or hazard is not covered and a separate insurance is necessary for winter sports, mountaineering, etc.

## TAKING A CAR ABROAD

The number of British cars carried abroad each year rises steeply. Regulations and documents have been simplified but the owner should ensure that his vehicle is in peak condition before departure. A comprehensive service from the local garage will reduce the risk of trouble while abroad.

Most overseas countries drive on the right and, while motorists are not obliged to make alterations to the lighting systems of their cars, it is common courtesy to make certain modifications. If detachable headlamp bulbs are fitted, vertical or right-hand dip ones are available in the UK. The use of amber-coloured bulbs or a suitable yellow disc or lacquer is recommended in France.

Sea, air, and car sleeper services increase each year and the additional cost of air transport may well be off-set by the cost of petrol, meals, and accommodation en route. Early booking is essential. Car sleeper services run direct from continental ports to many popular holiday areas. The mileage saving is considerable and the driver starts his holiday fresh after a good night's sleep.

The motoring organisations (AA and RAC) offer a comprehensive range of continental touring services. They will book transport for car and passengers by sea or air, advise on documents and insurance, plan detailed routes and offer a complete vehicle recovery service. If a major repair cannot be completed in time, they arrange for the return of passengers and car to the UK. Both the AA and RAC employ uniformed staff at ports and airports and liaise closely with their overseas counterparts. These facilities are available to AA and RAC members *only* and those taking a car abroad are strongly advised to make use of their services.

A first-aid kit should be carried and those taking a caravan abroad can obtain an international Camping Carnet, which entitles the holder to use approved sites on the Continent, before leaving the UK.

A detailed instruction manual, complete with diagrams, will help a foreign mechanic to locate the trouble quickly.

Those arranging independent vehicle transport should check that all their papers are in order. Insurance companies or brokers should be notified in sufficient time to issue a "Green Card", covering insurance outside the UK. The ruling about International Driving Licences should be sought. Petrol is available at concession rates in certain countries and the motoring organisations and National Tourist Offices can advise on this point.

Ignorance of traffic laws abroad is no excuse for infringement and the rules of the road, parking regulations, speed limits and accident procedures, which vary from country to country, should be studied.

The distance between filling stations can vary considerably and the tank should be kept full. No itinerary should envisage an excessive mileage and, if overnight accommodation has not been pre-booked, a short detour from a main trunk road may lead to a small hotel or pension where prices are lower and comfort standards higher.

## TAKING CHILDREN ABROAD

Before taking children abroad it is absolutely vital to make sure that the holiday will suit them as well as their parents. A child who does not like excessive heat will not enjoy the Mediterranean in August. The hotel or *pension* chosen should make provision for them and if, as in Spain, the evening meal is not served until 9 or 10 p.m. the manager can arrange an early supper for youngsters.

Children usually enjoy an open-air life and a caravan or camping holiday enables parents to plan the day to suit the whole family and to give children the kind of food to which they are accustomed at home. Young tummies may not appreciate continental cuisine and an overnight introduction to rich and highly spiced dishes may result in a series of "tummy upsets" which can ruin the entire holiday.

An alternative is to rent a villa or flat through an organisation specialising in this field. With very young children washing facilities are easier and "baby-sitting" can be arranged. Familiar tinned food always comes in useful and a sufficient supply of any proprietary baby foods should be brought from home. It may be difficult to find the exact equivalent abroad.

The easiest way to take children abroad is by air with a virtually door-to-door service which is far less tiring for children and parents alike.

On a continental train journey involving overnight travel couchette, compartments should be booked.

When travelling long distances by coach or car, children who show no symptoms at home may develop un-expected travel sickness and it may be advisable to do some night driving so that they can sleep for part of the journey.

Reductions for children vary from country to country and even from hotel to hotel. When booking through a travel agent the ages of children should be listed and the appropriate travel reductions will be quoted automatically. Reduced terms in hotels and pensions are usually a matter for personal negotiation with the management. The greatest saving applies when the child shares a room with the parents. Any special diets required should be in-dicated at the time of booking. While travel reductions apply to those under 14 years old (in isolated cases up to the age of 16), no hotelier is likely to give preferential rates to a healthy boy or girl of 12 or 13 who occupies the same room space as an adult and probably eats more.

## TIPS FOR THE JOURNEY

A little foresight can make any journey more pleasant. Where a family or party are travelling together one person should be responsible for all tickets and travel documents. Passports should be carried by the holder. The number of pieces of luggage and hand baggage, i.e. "hold-alls", cameras, rugs, coats, etc., should be checked at each stage. It is all too easy to think someone else has taken the camera only to find that it has been left in the rack. Each piece should also be clearly labelled and, where provided, the operator's own luggage labels should be used.

Irrespective of the means of transport chosen, there is always room for a small personal "hold-all" which should con-tain washing and toilet necessities, including a small hand towel, paper tissues, aspirin, travel-sickness pills and any personal medicines required on the journey.

A pair of comfortable shoes or slippers and a small head-cushion are always useful and books and reading matter for the journey should include a guide-book and phrase-book to whet the appetite and provide some prelimin-ary study. Room should be left for the duty-free cigarettes and drinks pur-chased en route.

When travelling by car, maps carried should contain road plans of major towns to be navigated. The *through routes* are clearly marked and should be followed.

Children can find a long journey tedious and should be armed with a liberal supply of books, comics, pencils and paper. Boiled sweets are preferable to chocolates and, as thirst-quenchers, a bag of apples and a plastic bottle of squash are easy to carry. Disposable nappies solve the problems of the very young.

Travelling clothes should be com-fortable and loose-fitting. Smart clothes are better left for wear after arrival.

## ALTERNATIVE METHODS OF TRAVEL

### BY COACH

Coach travel is the cheapest means of reaching a continental destination but a distinction should be drawn between a coach tour, with overnight stops of different durations on a journey through several countries, and the use of express overnight coach services as an econom-ical method of direct transport.

Fast coaches – usually with two drivers and a courier – set out from continental ports to reach their given destinations as quickly as possible, compatible with reasonable comfort. Many contain a small toilet and wash-room and the seats can be set back in the reclined position for overnight travel. Individual coach seats can some-times be booked in advance. Very young children cannot be carried on some overnight express services.

A recent development provides full-length bunks which can be let down from the side of the coach at night.

There are regular halts for meals (whether these are provided in the inclusive price or not should be clarified and, if not, sufficient appropriate currency to cover their cost should be carried). In addition frequent "comfort" stops enable passengers to stretch their legs and generally freshen up. The courier will advise on gratuities to drivers but this is entirely up to the individual.

For those planning independent travel the Europabus network runs services throughout the Continent. Details are available from the East Kent Coach Company, who link up on this side of the Channel, at Victoria Coach Station, London S.W.1.

**By Air–Coach.** An inclusive air–coach holiday often comes within the same price range as a cross-Channel boat journey followed by a long coach drive to the holiday destination. Travelling time is reduced by the use of inland airports on the Continent, i.e. flying overnight to Switzerland and going on to Italy with only one day's coach journey involved. Alternatively a flight to Perpignan in France cuts the coach journey to Spain considerably. On a short holiday to a distant resort any small additional expense involved may provide a considerable saving in time.

**Continental Train Travel and the Use of Timetables.** European railways provide a complete network of services throughout the Continent. Many tour operators use special trains, available only to travellers who have made bookings through them, which run direct from continental ports to the main holiday centres in summer and winter alike.

Many "all-in" prices include the cost of couchettes in specially designed compartments which, when made up for the night, provide six bunks, converting to ordinary seating for six people by day. The sexes are not segregated and, in this respect, couchettes differ from full sleeping-car services offered at a higher supplement.

Inclusive arrangements can also cover meals served on trays in the compartment as in aircraft. On cheaper "budget" holidays couchettes and meals are excluded.

The independent traveller can make through bookings to continental destinations in this country and pay for these in sterling at any travel agent or through British Rail. He will find meals served in restaurant cars on the expensive side and a packed meal should be taken where possible. Coffee, minerals and drinks are usually obtainable from corridor service and it may be possible to buy sandwiches, etc., at a station buffet en route.

On overnight journeys involving frontier crossings, customs formalities may involve the completion of a declaration form handed in by the train staff to avoid disturbing sleeping passengers.

The twenty-four-hour clock is used throughout the Continent and a few minutes' preliminary study may prevent later misunderstandings. This applies particularly to late-night departures. To give an example, a departure listed at 00.10 means ten minutes past midnight. A train listed at 12.10 leaves just after mid-day.

**By Scheduled Air**

Regular or *scheduled air* services are operated, for the most part, by the national airlines of countries throughout the world to all main centres.

Under the supervision of the International Air Transport Association (IATA) member airlines all charge the same fares on a given route and there is no price advantage in booking on one IATA controlled service than on another. Some airlines do offer competitive rates as non-members of the Association. Many routes are operated on a shared basis by British European Airways (BEA) and their overseas counterparts.

Travel agencies offering inclusive holidays are prepared to quote a supplement for flying by scheduled air if the customer finds the timing or place of departure more convenient.

The range of fares varies from the normal return, valid for twelve months, to tourist excursion rates which result in a considerable saving.

Although the regulations currently in force may be revised, the *cheapest* form of scheduled air travel is likely to remain the mid-week night tourist excursion rate. These routes are sometimes operated on a seasonal basis.

Children under the age of three, not occupying a seat, are carried free and older children qualify for half-rate fares.

Appropriate light refreshments and meals are served during the flight and are included in the price of the ticket. Passengers are specifically requested not to tip cabin staff.

While small hand luggage may be carried within the cabin, the tourist baggage allowance is restricted to 20 kilogrammes (44 lbs.) per person. Any excess baggage must be paid for, the cost rising with the distance travelled. The baggage allowance for 1st class passengers is 66 lbs. In addition to operating scheduled services, BEA and its long-distance state-owned counterpart British Overseas Airways Corporation (BOAC) offer their own inclusive holidays as do many foreign airlines operating in and out of the UK.

A restricted number of scheduled services are operated by *independent* airlines in this country of which the biggest grouping is British United Airways (BUA), who have also entered the inclusive tour market.

The regulations affecting payment, whether in this country or abroad, of airport taxes and transport from terminal to airport can be clarified at the time of booking. Local transport abroad and foreign airport tax must be paid for in the currency of the country.

## THE USE OF CHARTER AIRCRAFT

A *chartered aircraft* means an aircraft "chartered" or hired for a given purpose. Tour operators acquire the exclusive use of aircraft for departures to different destinations on pre-arranged dates throughout the period of their own inclusive tours.

There was a period when the word "charter" was thought to imply the use of obsolescent and consequently less comfortable aircraft. This no longer applies; and the aircraft employed are subject to strict safety tests and to government licence. Many are jets of modern design, while the earlier turbo-prop aircraft, the Britannia and the Viscount among them, still provide speedy and efficient holiday transport.

Just as the tour operator effects considerable savings by block booking hotel accommodation abroad, he also reserves an entire aircraft and then allocates the seats to his own customers travelling to resorts which can be reached from the same foreign airport and provides alternative transport onwards. The airline acts as a carrier for the tour operator, who fills all the available seats with his own passengers.

Travel organisations can also arrange charter flights to airports close to the resorts but not served by scheduled flights.

A high percentage of charter flights operate at night and light refreshments are usually provided without extra charge.

Baggage is normally restricted to 33 lbs. per person and this limit must be strictly adhered to. Coach fares and airport taxes, where these are an extra, are often paid by the operator in advance and added to the cost of the holiday.

The tour operator is not normally in a position to offer seats on a chartered aircraft to those wishing to take advantage of the consequent saving in cost who want to book for the flight alone.

In many cases there is no provision to extend a holiday using charter aircraft as each party of outgoing travellers arrives at the foreign airport on the same aircraft which will carry back a full complement of holidaymakers returning to the UK.

## SEA TRAVEL

**Cross-Channel and Car Ferries.** Many people prefer sea travel whether contemplating a cross-Channel trip or a cruise to the Aegean Islands. However a cross-Channel steamer can be unpleasantly crowded in high summer. There is no guarantee of a seat and there are long queues at bars, buffets and duty-free stores.

New car-ferry services, operating across the Channel and the North Sea, are being introduced each year and the congestion problem is gradually being overcome. Brand new ships, designed for speed of turn-round, afford "drive-on drive-off" systems and, for passengers, a cruise in miniature with restaurants in all price ranges.

Car-ferries also run direct to the Mediterranean, incorporating a sea journey as a prelude to a holiday. On short runs meals are not usually included.

The passenger travelling onwards by train will find that services connect at the quayside.

**Cruises.** The range of cruises operating from UK ports increases each year. The ship acts as a floating and often luxurious hotel with all amenities found on board. Most cruise ships have their own swimming-pools, games deck, nurseries, cinemas, ballrooms and impromptu night-clubs, as well as writing-rooms and small libraries.

Everything is geared to passenger comfort with shore excursions arranged at the various ports of call by qualified members of the cruising staff.

There are also specialist cruises for those interested in archaeology and natural history. A limited number of adults can be carried on school educational cruises.

Many ships now operate a "one-class" system with all facilities and public rooms open to everyone, the price of the cruise being determined by cabin suites ranging from twin-bunk inside cabin to promenade deck accommodation with private bath and toilet. The cheaper accommodation is always snapped up first so early planning is vital. It may necessary to book a year ahead.

Travel agents and cruise brochures issued by the shipping lines will give guidance on tipping and clothes. On many cruises there is no longer any obligation to dress for dinner.

**Ocean Travel.** Those contemplating a visit to the USA or to the Far East may find it possible to combine the experience of ocean travel with a holiday or business trip. Time can be saved in travelling one way by air.

On shorter journeys a similar combination may be feasible; going by air to Venice or Trieste and from there on to, say, Greece, by sea.

Many facilities listed in the section on cruises can be found on transatlantic and other long-distance services.

Passengers can also book on cargo-passenger vessels operating from many parts of the UK. Passenger accommodation is often limited and the atmosphere on board completely informal but cargo requirements come first and the shipping lines stress that itineraries are subject to change. Those with restricted holiday periods should note that the date of return to the UK cannot be guaranteed.

On a long voyage there is little room for entertainment on board and a generous supply of books should be taken.

While in port, passengers can usually live on board on a bed-and-breakfast basis. This leaves the individual free to go off sightseeing during the day, returning to the ship at night. The purser will point out local places of interest ashore but it is *imperative* to be back on board at the stated time before sailing. The ships operate on a tight schedule and sail once cargo has been on- or off-loaded.

## SOME POPULAR HOLIDAY COUNTRIES AND AREAS

**THE STERLING AREA.** A holiday abroad need not automatically involve the expenditure of "foreign currency". In any period when restrictions are in force governing how much may be spent abroad in a given year these do not apply within the "Sterling Area".

Just as no foreign currency is required on a visit to the Channel Islands or to Ireland it is equally possible to holiday in many parts of the world without making any inroads into the prescribed foreign currency allowance.

The countries of the Commonwealth (Canada is the one exception) are all in the Sterling Area, and as the practice of taking more than one holiday a year increases, the enthusiast who spends the major part of his currency allowance on a winter sports holiday in Europe can still enjoy Mediterranean sunshine in Malta or Cyprus during the summer.

In addition to the countries of the Commonwealth, Iceland Jordan and Libya are in the Sterling Area.

Air services throughout the world have grown so rapidly that the fortunate few who have no financial problems can still winter in the Caribbean. The average holidaymaker is unlikely to find the foreign currency allocation so severely reduced that a holiday outside the Sterling Area becomes impracticable.

The countries listed below are unlikely to be affected by any currency restrictions and there are no limits to the amount that may be spent there.

**Countries in the Sterling Area.** Aden, Australia, Bahamas, Barbados, Bermuda, British Africa, British Honduras, Burma, Ceylon, Cyprus, Fiji, Gambia, Ghana, Gibraltar, Guyana, Hong Kong, Iceland, India, Jamaica, Jordan, Kenya, Kuwait, Leeward and Windward Islands, Libya, Malaysia, Malta, Malawi, New Zealand, Nigeria, Pakistan, South Africa, Tanzania, Trinidad and Tobago, Uganda and Zambia.

## SOME POPULAR HOLIDAY COUNTRIES IN EUROPE

### AUSTRIA

Austria is, deservedly, one of the most popular holiday countries in Europe. She is fortunate in enjoying a virtually year-round-tourist-season. Many famous resorts, crowded with skiers in the winter months, cater also for spring and summer visitors.

Austria, slightly larger than Scotland and with a population of about $8\frac{1}{2}$ million, is divided into two distinct areas; the low-lying region around the Danube and three Alpine ranges which reach their highest point at the Grossglockner, rising to nearly 12,500 ft.

The tourist industry plays a major role in the country's economy and yet the tourist need have no fear of being exploited. At the local tourist information offices in all the main centres information and advice are readily forthcoming from English-speaking staff. Austria is certainly one of the best-run tourist countries in the world

with an excellent network of main roads, many affording spectacular mountain panoramas. Public transport is efficient and well run and there are generous reductions for children.

Following the break-up of the Hapsburg Empire in the First World War, Austria spent the years between 1938 and 1945 under Nazi occupation and only regained her full independence some ten years after the end of the Second World War. The capital of the Austrian Federal Republic is Vienna, a gay and vital city that can truly claim to be the musical capital of Europe. Here are reminders of Schubert and Haydn, of the Strauss family and, at the annual musical festival in the provincial capital of Salzburg, the years Mozart spent in the city are recalled.

Many popular holiday resorts can be found in idyllic surroundings in the Tyrol with Innsbruck at its heart. Other outstanding beauty spots include the lakes of the Salzkammergut and Carinthia.

*The monetary unit* is the schilling, currently worth about 4d. (*Rates of exchange should always be checked before departure as they may vary from year to year.*)

**Accommodation.** This varies from luxury hotels in the larger cities at rates comparable to those elsewhere in Europe to always scrupulously clean but modest accommodation in *pensions*, often listed as Gasthaus or Gasthof.

**Food and Drink.** The Austrians are fond of good food and there are five recognised meals. Continental breakfast is followed by "Gabelfrühstuck", a substantial mid-morning snack, lunch, "Jause", a further snack co-inciding with the British teatime and finally the evening meal.

A good deal of veal is eaten, often in the form of the world-famous "Wiener Schnitzel" and – a reminder of the long links with Hungary – goulash prepared with veal or beef in a paprika sauce is very popular. The Austrian cuisine is particularly rich in cream cakes of all kinds. Coffee, universally excellent, is usually served with cream. The local beer and dry white wines of the Riesling variety are relatively inexpensive.

**Camping Facilities.** Excellent sites, many on the outskirts of major cities, exist throughout the country. Members of a camping club in the UK should obtain the appropriate International Camping Documents before leaving as reductions apply to many sites.

**Presents and Souvenirs.** These reflect the centuries-old traditions of craftsmanship and range from the hand-made peasant costumes still in general use in the Tyrol to leather goods and carved wooden souvenirs.

Visitors to Vienna should include in their itinerary "The Dorotheum" a vast state-owned pawnshop with articles ranging in value from valuable paintings to petty knick-knacks which some impoverished citizen has temporarily pledged there and failed to redeem.

Austria, at virtually any season, makes the visitor feel at home. The scenery is often breathtakingly beautiful and music, happily not of the "canned" variety, can be heard in the many attractive cafés in town and village.

## BELGIUM

Within an area of approximately 12,000 square miles Belgium offers considerable variety of terrain. The country stands at the cross-roads of Europe with the fertile plains of Flanders running inland from the coastal resorts that radiate from both sides of Ostend, the country's leading seaside resort. A network of trams runs along the Belgian coast.

The two exquisitely preserved mediaeval cities of Bruges and Ghent lie within the twin provinces of East and West Flanders.

The lovely valley of the River Meuse lies south-east of Brussels, the capital, and the hill country of the Ardennes is close to the Luxembourg border.

The country has two official languages, French and Flemish, and many people have some knowledge of English.

Main roads are well signposted and modern motorways connect the coast to the capital and run on beyond Brussels to the German border at Aachen. The cobbled pavé has nearly all been replaced by tarmac roads.

The Belgian coast, where the resorts run for some forty miles in a virtually continuous string, provides sandy beaches and safe bathing for all ages. However, the weather along the Belgian coast is comparable to that in the UK and there can be no guarantee of unbroken sunshine.

*The monetary unit* is the Belgian Franc standing currently at 119 to the pound.

**Accommodation.** The coastal resorts and principal cities are well served and there are many smaller guest-houses along the coast. Local information offices can suggest approved establishments where the proprietor speaks some English. Inexpensive all-in holidays on the Belgian coast with sea or air travel to Ostend are listed in many tour operators' brochures.

**Food and Drink.** The Belgians claim to have developed many gastronomic specialities by improving on accepted French cuisine. The sauces served are extremely rich and the cooking is generally heavier than French. Specialities include the famous Jambon d'Ardennes, a succulent smoked ham, the Carbonnades Flamandes, collar of beef cooked in butter, onions and beer with brown mustard added. Fried potatoes are on sale almost everywhere at open-air stalls.

The national drink is beer which is excellent and always served ice-cold.

**Camping Facilities.** Up-to-date lists of sites and current regulations can be obtained from the Belgian National Tourist Office. The RAC and AA are associated with the Royal Automobile Club de Bélgique (RACB) and with the Touring Club de Bélgique (TCB) which maintain road patrols and a breakdown service known as Touring Secours.

**Presents and Souvenirs.** When buying Bruges or Brussels lace care should be taken to ensure that this is the genuine article. There is also excellent copper-ware and ceramics.

Belgium is only a short distance away across the Channel. Inclusive tours to the Belgian coast offer very good value indeed. The motorist will find the country very small and compact and a tour through the Meuse Valley and the densely wooded country of the Ardennes can provide a memorable holiday in an area that has been somewhat neglected.

## EASTERN EUROPE

While there has been an increase in the number of British visitors to Eastern Europe, the situation changes constantly and the intending holidaymaker should seek up-to-date information about the documents and visas required and, if planning to go by car, the routes open to tourists.

Many East European countries have their own National Tourist Offices in London (*addresses are given at the end of this section*).

Independent travellers should book hotel accommodation in the countries to be visited in advance. In many cases travel documents will not be issued without evidence of pre-booking as there are not enough hotel rooms to go round.

At the time of writing no diplomatic relations exists between the UK and Albania or Eastern Germany (the German Democratic Republic) and no consular protection can be afforded in these two countries.

Albania is gradually being re-opened and details can be obtained from Progressive Tours Ltd, 100A Rochester Row, London S.W.1, who specialise in tours to Eastern Europe.

The Foreign Office do not anticipate any problems for the bona fide traveller to Eastern Germany but accommodation must be booked before departure and road crossing points from the West are limited.

The AA issues a comprehensive Eastern Europe handbook which provides invaluable information on all aspects of motorings and details of visas, immigration and customs procedures. The motorist planning an Eastern European holiday should consult the motoring organisations.

Other Eastern European countries, Bulgaria, Czechoslovakia, Hungary, Poland, Rumania and the USSR have full diplomatic relations with the UK and the local consulate or embassy can intervene in the event of any problems.

Tour operators now run inclusive tours to Eastern Europe and handle through bookings by coach, rail or air to the USSR as a routine operation. They also advise and help to obtain any documents required.

Concession rights affecting tourist rates of exchange and the cost of petrol exist in several countries. Petrol stations are some distance apart and it is wise to travel with a full tank. There are some restrictions on the use of cameras.

The area covered is so great and conditions change so rapidly that it is impracticable to list the main holiday areas in each country. Prior consultation with National Tourist Offices of the countries concerned is essential.

## FRANCE

France, which is twice the size of Britain, provides excellent holiday facilities throughout the year. Winter Sports enthusiasts patronise the Alps and art connoisseurs visit the great cathedrals and the castles of the Loire Valley; the sophisticate favours Paris and whole families descend on the beaches of Brittany.

The French authorities are fully aware of recent complaints of excessive costs for food and accommodation and are exerting pressure to keep them under control.

Few capital cities can rival Paris and a bed-and-breakfast booking will enable those restricted by a limited budget to explore the countless cafés and restaurants. There are several inexpensive "self-service" establishments. Public transport by underground railway (Métro) is inexpensive with a standard fare irrespective of distance travelled. Glamorous night spots where it is compulsory to buy indifferent champagne at highly inflated prices should be avoided by those with limited funds.

There are many first-class camping sites throughout the country.

The "Logis de France" operates a nationwide chain of hotels and "Relais Routiers" a system of approved transport cafés where substantial and inexpensive meals are served and prices are strictly controlled.

A car tour of France offers spectacular contrasts; from the panoramic mountain roads in the Pyrenees to the savage country of the Camargue, from the unchanging wealth of the Dordogne to the exclusive resorts of the Côte d'Azur, stretching east of Marseilles through Cannes and Nice to the Italian frontier.

*The monetary unit* is the French Franc standing currently at 1s. 8d.

**Accommodation.** Comparable hotel accommodation can be cheaper in France than in the UK. The accepted practice is to pay a price, laid down by the Hotels Association, for a given room and a double room is considerably cheaper than two singles. Many hotels in coastal resorts are open only for a limited period. In high season hoteliers may insist on a minimum stay of three days on a full or demi-pension basis with bed, breakfast and one main meal taken in the hotel. As elsewhere on the Continent, baths must be paid for as an extra and soap is not provided.

**Food and Drink.** French cuisine is rightly considered the best in the world and has become the hall-mark of the finest and most subtle culinary art. The pleasures of the table are reflected everywhere in the wide variety of regional dishes. The cooking in Provence, based on the use of olive oil, differs greatly from that of Brittany and Normandy where butter is liberally employed.

Wine is served with all meals and, apart from the classic wines – Champagne from the north, Burgundy from the heart of the country, Muscadet from the Loire Valley and the fine clarets of Bordeaux – local wine ("Vin du Pays" or "Vin Ordinaire") provides an agreeable accompaniment to regional specialities.

The *Guide Michelin* is compulsory reading for those embarking on a gastronomic tour of France. Tourist menus have been introduced at varying prices and a fixed sum pays for cover charge, a three-course meal, bread, wine and gratuities. It is always cheaper to choose a "Menu Touristique" than to order *à la carte*.

**Presents and Souvenirs.** These range from frankly tawdry models of the Eiffel Tower and other famous landmarks to the traditional French exports, scent, wine, Breton lace, china and porcelain. A tour of the local market can be very rewarding.

France is not a cheap country. The motorist will find excellent roads but the cost of petrol is high. Tour operators run inclusive tours in summer and winter alike to many areas of France. As "hidden charges" can be very high these offer first-class value for money and allow the budget-conscious sufficient spending money, secure in the knowledge that all essentials have been paid before crossing the Channel.

## GERMANY

Western Germany, or, more strictly, the German Federal Republic (*for information on Eastern Germany please refer to the section on Eastern Europe*) is set in the heart of Europe. Communications with all parts of the country are provided by an extensive system of toll-free motorways, the "Autobahnen", which by-pass built up areas.

The modern outlines of the rebuilt North German ports of Hamburg and Bremen afford a striking contrast to fairy-tale castles perched high above the Rhine gorge and mediaeval townships where wine-festivals are held once the grapes have been gathered.

The Rhine combines its functions as a great commercial waterway with countlees tourist attractions. Several organisations in the UK run Rhine cruises.

The Black Forest provides skiing terrain in winter and in spring and summer wonderful walking country once the snows have cleared. Germany's highest mountain, the Zügspitze, rising to nearly 10,000 ft., can be ascended by cog and cable railways.

Another popular holiday area lies in the Harz Mountains and in the undulating Bavarian countryside; a predominantly Catholic area, there are many fine examples of Baroque architecture.

The capital of the Federal Republic is Bonn, the birthplace of Beethoven, on the banks of the Rhine. The western sector of Berlin is in the Federal Republic and those planning to visit the former capital should study the regulations in force before leaving home.

The world-famous Passion Play is staged in Oberammergau every decade (the next performance is in 1970) and very early booking is essential.

German hospitality is traditional and the cleanliness of even the smallest establishments a notable feature.

The spirit of carnival predominates in the feasting and celebrations which precede Lent and in the autumn. German folklore has been handed down in an unbroken tradition and is neither selfconscious or commercialised. Music abounds in the characteristic beer gardens where great "steins" of beer are downed to the accompaniment of chorus singing.

Conventional night life – there are few restrictions of any kind – is mainly confined to urban areas and those wishing to sample this should certainly visit Hamburg.

*The monetary unit* is the Deutsche Mark currently standing at about 2s. 1d.

**Accommodation.** Germany is well equipped to handle an ever-increasing volume of tourist traffic. Accommodation in even the smallest countryside inns is comfortable and spotlessly clean and municipal tourist offices can offer advice on staying in private houses on a bed-and-breakfast arrangement. Illuminated notice-boards outside main railway stations list hotels where there are vacancies. The German Tourist information Bureau provides up-to-date lists of the many excellent camping sites and there is also an extensive network of youth hostels and mountain châlets.

**Food and Drink.** Authentic German cooking is remarkable for the size of portions offered. Soups, often served with dumplings, provide a substantial first course, the humble herring appears in countless tasty disguises and sausages come in limitless variety. A great deal of pork is eaten and Kasseler Rippenspeer, pork spare ribs, is served throughout the country. In view of the size of the helpings – children will certainly make do on a half-portion – eating out in a restaurant is not unduly expensive.

German beer, whether light ("Helles") or dark ("Dunkles") is served very cold and on draught. The Rhine and Moselle produce the best-known German white wines, which can be ordered by the glass in the same way as beer.

**Presents and Souvenirs.** Carved woodwork, particularly in Bavaria, is still a traditional craft. Excellent and inexpensive leather goods are on sale. Watches and cameras, less expensive than in the UK, should always be declared to HM Customs and if they are of an expensive make duty will be payable.

Germany can be thoroughly recommended as a holiday country and except in remote rural districts there are few language problems.

Many travel agents operate inclusive tours to holiday areas in the Black Forest. Rhine cruises are run direct from the UK. An inexpensive holiday can be spent travelling by coach or on the Europabus network from a continental port to a small town on the Rhine and booking on a bed-and-breakfast basis.

The motorist will find a uniformly good and well-signposted road system and excellent provision for those planning a walking or camping holiday.

## GREECE

Greece, the "Hellas" of the Ancient World, welcomes a new generation of British holidaymakers each year. The population of 8,500,000 live on the Greek mainland and on the numerous and beautiful Aegean islands. Greece is a mountainous country which remains remarkably unspoilt in spite of an ever-increasing tourist traffic.

Although it can be very hot indeed in summer, the dry climate is seldom oppressive. Good weather can be relied on throughout the spring and autumn. Athens, the capital, is the best centre from which to tour both the mainland and the islands.

The main road from Athens to Thessaloniki includes sections of motorway on which tolls are payable. A good road connects Athens to Patras and leads on to Igoumenitsa, from where ferries leave for Italy.

Exploration "off the beaten track" may involve driving considerable distances on secondary roads where the surface may be poor.

Those planning a first visit to Greece will find that a few hours spent familiarising themselves with the history of the Greek City-States at the period of their greatest power and influence in the fifth century BC will heighten their interest in the countless relics that have survived from those days. Perhaps the most famous of all are the Parthenon in its incomparable setting on the Acropolis high above Athens and the home of the oracle at Delphi.

Those able to visit Greece in the spring will find the Good Friday and Easter Sunday celebrations and religious processions among the most impressive in Europe, while those professing no interest in the Greece of the past will find magnificent swimming close to Athens. Throughout the country there are few restrictions on camping or the use of caravans.

Greece, so rich in antiquities, is a relatively poor country but even in remote country villages the people are interested in meeting foreign visitors.

Using the network of steamer services it is not difficult to arrange a personal itinerary visiting not only Rhodes, Hydra and Poros but countless lesser-known islands where the tourist will be made equally welcome in unsophisticated inns and small hotels.

*The monetary unit* is the Drachma currently worth approximately 3½d. The amount of Greek notes that may be imported is limited and a bank or travel agent will advise on this. Some banks in Athens stay open late on weekdays for the benefit of foreign visitors.

**Accommodation.** The Greek Tourist Office in London will provide a hotel guide on request. Accommodation prices are fairly low in the principal hotels used by overseas visitors and there are few language problems. There are also some delightful improvised summer camps and bamboo villages where holiday-makers can stay.

**Food and Drink.** While large hotels serve the accepted international cuisine, excellent fish can be obtained in small "tavernas". Local specialities include Dolmadakia (stuffed vine leaves) and Taramosalata (fish roe served in a cream sauce). Mousaka (layers of mince and aubergines) is found everywhere.

There are no licensing hours and beer of the lager type can be obtained almost everywhere. The local aperitif, which can be deceptively strong, is Ouzo. Flavoured with aniseed it turns cloudy when water is added. Wine is drunk with all meals; Retsina, in which the resin produces the characteristic flavour and also acts as a preservative, can be rather harsh. Aretsinoto, from which the resin has been removed, is more immediately acceptable to British tastes. Excellent wines are produced in Samos, Attica and in the island of Rhodes.

The many "Tavernas" also serve excellent coffee.

**Presents and Souvenirs.** These, by our standards, are generally inexpensive. Corfu lace is famous and the locally made embroidery is both unusual and very attractive. A visitor to the islands should certainly return with an outsize in sponges.

Greece, in spite of the cost of getting there, is fully geared to handle a rapidly developing tourist trade. Many tour operators deal in all-in holidays combining a few days in Athens with visits to Corinth and Delphi.

There are good air connections between Athens and the principal islands and those booking an inclusive 14-day holiday to, say, Rhodes, will find the price quoted using charter aircraft only slightly higher than the normal air fare alone.

Several organisations run cruises accompanied by guest lecturers who are authorities on archaeology and history to both the Greek mainland and the islands.

## HOLLAND

But for the initiative and engineering skill of the Dutch who have fought a constant battle against the inroads of the sea, Holland, as we know it today, might not exist. The dykes or "Polders" guard fertile farmland wrested from the sea and the characteristic windmills, still lovingly preserved although their period of active life is in most cases now ended, were originally used for drainage.

Holland is a small country with a population of just over 12,000,000 living in a land area only a seventh of the size of Great Britain.

An intricate system of canals carries both commercial traffic and pleasure craft of all sizes.

Amsterdam, the capital city but not the seat of government – this is at The Hague – is bisected by fifty canals and elegant enclosed water-buses carrying tourists through the city navigate skilfully under some 400 bridges.

The Dutch are friendly but reserved. English is taught at an early age in the schools and is spoken very widely.

Agriculture and horticulture play a major role in the Dutch economy and the bulbfields, north of Leiden, are at their colourful best in April and early May.

Rotterdam, almost completely destroyed in the 1939–45 War, has since been rebuilt and now ranks as the largest seaport in Europe, but the old seventeenth-century town of Delft is much more typical of the Holland the tourist will want to explore at his leisure.

The local tourist offices known as the VVV (pronounced "Fi-Fi-Fi") are courteous and most helpful. Their command of English is quite admirable.

The main seaside resort of Scheveningen virtually adjoins The Hague.

Holland is a neat and tidy country with high standards of cleanliness. People take great pride in their homes and curtains are seldom drawn over windows crammed to profusion with pot-plants.

Night life, on the conventional European pattern, exists mainly in Amsterdam, The Hague, Rotterdam and at Scheveningen.

*The monetary unit* is the Dutch Guilder or "Florin" and usually written down as "fl" or "f". It is worth approximately 2s. 4d.

**Accommodation.** Accommodation varies from the luxury hotels of Amsterdam, The Hague and Rotterdam to simple boarding-houses which cater for the "Bed-and-Breakfaster". The coastal resorts get extremely full during the summer and rooms should be booked in advance.

**Food and Drink.** Breakfast in Holland is more substantial than elsewhere in Europe. Slices of ham or cheese and often a boiled egg accompany the coffee which is universally excellent. Substantial soups, in which the spoon should ideally stand upright, and the characteristic stews and hotpots should be sampled. The "Rijsttafel" – literally a "rice table" – is a gastronomic experience with as many as thirty dishes of chicken, shrimps, meat-balls and vegetables all spiced with different condiments from the former Dutch East Indies, served, as a curry is, with rice.

The Dutch brew excellent beer which is on sale at all hours. Dutch gin, usually referred to as "Jenever", is by far the most popular aperitif; served ice-cold and normally drunk neat it does not mix happily with minerals but is generally regarded as being "hangover proof". Holland produces no wine, but imported French and German wines are freely available. Cigars and pipe tobacco are cheaper than in most European countries.

**Presents and Souvenirs.** Dutch cheeses,

cigars, Delftware (verify that this is genuine), and bulbs which, in view of customs regulations, must be despatched by the grower and may not be imported by the individual.

It is a great mistake to think, because Holland is a flat country, that it is consequently dull. Prices have been kept remarkably stable and it seldom is necessary to query a bill. The traveller will enjoy being able to wonder at those fabulous skies, in which the water seems to be reflected, that were the inspiration of the Dutch masters of the past. The motorist or cyclist will find good roads and few long distances involved.

Travel agents will advise on inclusive tours to coastal resorts and to Amsterdam, while the bulbfields can be visited in April and May on pleasure cruises lasting from four to seven days or, by air, on day trips.

## ITALY

Italy has so much to offer that the first-time visitor should decide which of Italy's many faces he wishes to see. The contrasts are quite startling, from the jagged majesty of the Dolomite Mountains in the north to the lakes that lie quite close to the country's commercial capital, Milan; from the architectural glories of Florence and Siena to miles of golden beaches centred on Viareggio on the west coast and branching out from Rimini on the Adriatic.

Italy is at once one of the most ancient European countries and one of the "newest"; the former City-States were only finally united towards the end of the last century. Regional differences are marked and the Italian takes great pride in his own city or province. He is firstly a "Romano" or a "Milanese", and secondly an Italian.

The Italians communicate their love of life to the millions of tourists who go there each year. Life for them is based on the family and on the Roman Catholic Church. They take the sun for granted and, in spite of poverty in many areas, never seem outwardly deprived.

Rome combines all the amenities of a modern and exciting city with a wealth of art treasures. It also houses within the capital an independent sovereign state, The Vatican, where tourists of all denominations can attend the general audiences held by the Pope.

The motorist will find an extensive network of "Autostrade", high-speed motorways considerably extended in recent years. The magnificent Autostrada del Sole connects Milan to Florence and Rome and runs on to beyond Naples.

Naples is the most animated Italian city. Noble civic buildings, reminders of the days when Naples was an independent kingdom, stand close by narrow streets in the poorer areas. Vesuvius, the great volcano, can be visited and the ruined towns of Pompeii and Herculaneum are not far away.

Venice and the other art cities are a treasure house holding priceless and superb examples of Renaissance art.

Venice at the height of the tourist season can be unpleasantly crowded and very expensive. Her popularity is so great that an off-season visit is strongly recommended.

*The monetary unit* is the Lira standing currently at about 1,750 to the £. A wallet is almost essential as several notes can be involved in even the simplest transaction. 100 lire is worth about 1s. 4d.

**Accommodation.** The tourist industry plays a major part in the Italian economy and many hotels are brand-new. They range from the frankly luxurious hotels in Rome, Milan and Venice to simple *pensions* in country districts where the warmth of the hospitality helps to offset occasionally primitive plumbing. Advance booking in popular resorts in high season is essential. Several UK organisations specialise in renting villas and flats. The saving in May and September, when the weather is still pleasantly warm, is considerable.

**Food and Drink.** Italian food is based on "pasta", the general term used to cover spaghetti, macaroni, vermicelli, etc., which are served in a variety of ways. The tradition of regional cooking is strong. Specialities include Bistecca alla Fiorentina (Florentine steak), Saltimbocca alla Romana (slices of veal with sage and ham, cooked in butter and sprinkled with Marsala wine), Cacciucco (fish stew) and Fegata alla Veneziana (finely sliced calves' liver fried with onion and peppers).

Italy produces many fine wines but Chianti is one of the few which travels well. Local wines, drunk on the spot, are excellent. They include the white, Cinque Terre (from the La Spezia area), Valpolicella (Verona), Falerno, known to the ancient Romans (Caserta), and Lacrima Christi, a sweet white wine from the Naples area. The best beer comes from Trieste and the most popular aperitif is Campari, drunk ice cold with soda.

**Presents and Souvenirs.** Venetian glass is exquisite but expensive. Leather goods from Florence are still made by hand and silk ties and scarves cheaper than in the UK. Straw baskets and sandals are a good buy.

Italy caters alike for the winter sports enthusiast, the lover of fine art, the sun worshipper and the gastronome. Tour operators offer all-in holidays to many coastal resorts but it is imperative to ensure that all "beach charges" are included. It is normal practice to pay to go on the beach and the extra cost of a changing cabin, deck-chairs and sun umbrella can be considerable.

Coach tours with overnight stops at the main centres of historical interest can be combined with a short stay on the coast or the lakes. It is easy to book an inclusive holiday on the lovely islands of Capri, Elba and Ischia.

## PORTUGAL

In recent years British tourists have discovered for themselves the many delightful holiday areas and the superb beaches of Portugal with its five hundred miles of coastline bordering on the Atlantic. The Algarve region in the extreme south borders on to Spain.

The climate in Portugal differs considerably from that found in Spain and fresh breezes from the Atlantic help to temper the heat of the sun.

The Algarve with its white Moorish buildings – it faces out towards North Africa – enjoys a long tourist season. The sea is warm enough for bathing in April and October and the province has retained a certain independence. It is at once remote and yet essentially Portuguese.

The people are proud of their long standing alliance with Britain and the close links dating from the Peninsular War.

Lisbon is a cosmopolitan capital with a magnificent natural harbour giving access to the wide streets of the modern city and to the old town with its narrow cobbled alleyways. The resort of Estoril, with all the amenities of a modern international playground, is only a short distance away.

There is excellent skiing terrain in the mountains of the Serra da Estrela. The lovely old town of Viana do Castelo is in the north of Portugal and not far from Oporto the home of port wine. The wine lodges can be visited.

The national sport is football played throughout the winter and Portuguese bull-fighting differs in many respects from that practised in Spain. The bull, whose horns are padded, is fought by mounted cavaleiros and their brilliant horsemanship ensures that their mounts are not touched by the bull. In Portugal the bull is not killed.

*The monetary unit* is the Escudo currently worth 3½d.

**Accommodation.** New hotels have been built in popular tourist centres and particularly in the Algarve area. Comfortable and clean accommodation can be found in "Pousadas", state-run inns often set away from the main roads in areas of great natural beauty. A stay in a Pousada is usually restricted to five days. Similar facilities are available in "Estalagems", the name given to privately-owned wayside inns.

Few formalities are involved in using the many camping sites in the pinewoods inland and along the coast.

**Food and Drink.** The Portuguese provide

146

very liberal portions and at lunch time a half portion will often suffice. As a maritime country a great deal of fish is served and a typical dish is Consoada (cod baked and served with fried pork and peas). Pork is the main meat and in Carne de Porko à Alentejana it is combined with clams. Salmonete (red mullet) and Camaroes (shrimps) can often be found on the menu. Portuguese sweets are rich and highly flavoured and Bolos de Noz (marzipan and walnut sweetmeats) and Farflas (custard topped with white of egg) are for the sweet-toothed.

The excellent Mateus Rosé is among the best-known Portuguese wines now on sale in the UK. In addition to the classic wines, Port and Madeira, the Vinhos Verdes (literally green wines) are in fact red and white sparkling wines drunk very young.

**Presents and Souvenirs.** Throughout the country the visitor will find examples of a long-standing tradition of handicrafts ranging from ornamental tiles to lace-work and embroidery. Figurines made from cork are characteristically Portuguese and the cane and basketwork is both distinctive and inexpensive.

Portugal caters for the holidaymaker who wants to be assured of both warm sunshine and pleasantly uncrowded beaches. Tour operators run inclusive holidays to Estoril and to the rapidly developing resorts of the Algarve.

Main roads are good and well sign-posted. Local religious festivals are held throughout the year and in the evenings the cafés come to life as visitors and residents alike fill their glasses with local wine and listen to the repetitive but fascinating "Fados" which recount stories of unrequited love.

## SCANDINAVIA

The three Scandinavian countries most frequently visited by British holiday-makers are Denmark, Norway and Sweden, dealt with under independent headings. Although Finland forms part of Scandinavia in a geographical sense her language and culture are of Magyar origin and the country does not,

in the historical context, form part of Scandinavia. Iceland, as mentioned elsewhere, is within the Sterling Area.

## DENMARK

Denmark is at once the smallest, flattest, neatest and certainly the gayest of the Scandinavian countries. The population of 4¾ millions live on the peninsula of Jutland adjoining the German mainland and on some five hundred islands of which the largest are Zealand and Funen. An extensive network of bridges and ferries provides good communications to all parts of the country.

The capital, Copenhagen, is set on the eastern tip of Zealand and her very distinctive green copper spires and steeples dominate the skyline. The overall impression is of spaciousness and the world-famous Tivoli gardens, laid out over a century ago, are right in the city centre. Tivoli combines the conventional amenities of a giant fun fair with elegant restaurants, Chinese pagodas and a fine concert hall. The principal shopping area, which runs from the Kongens Nytorv Square into the heart of town, is now a pedestrian precinct and combines several old city streets under the name of Ströget.

Jutland's principal towns are Århus, the provincial capital, on the east coast and farther north Ålborg.

Those arriving in Denmark by sea will probably tie up at Esbjerg on the west coast of Jutland. There are regular crossings from Harwich and Newcastle and the port is linked to Copenhagen by a direct rail service.

The island of Funen lies between Jutland and Zealand, and Odense, the principal town, is the birthplace of Hans Christian Andersen. His house is now a museum and in this pleasant country town there is also an open-air folk museum which gives a vivid picture of the Denmark of the past.

*The monetary unit* is the Danish Kroner worth a little over 1s.

**Accommodation.** The Danish National Travel Association (Turistforeningen) is one of the most efficient and courteous in the world. Offices in the main cities stay open late and there are few accommodation problems.

If all hotel rooms are full, arrangements can be made with a private family at a very reasonable price.

Motels have developed rapidly and there are excellent camping sights controlled by the Health Authorities and graded according to the amenities provided. A camping licence can be bought on arrival at the site.

**Food and Drink.** The standards of cuisine are very high in Denmark. In addition to the infinite varieties of Smörrebröd, open sandwiches with slices of rye bread piled high with meat, cheese, shrimps and, always a delight to the eye as well as the palate, the many fish specialities include Heligoland Lobster and oysters and caviar from Limfjord. Pork is served more often than beef and Frikadeller (fresh meat rissoles) and Flaeskesteg med Rödkaal (roast pork with red cabbage) will be found on most menus.

Denmark differs in one important respect from Norway and Sweden. There are, for practical purposes, no licensing restrictions. Imported French and German wines are on the expensive side but excellent beer – both the Carlsberg and Tuborg breweries in Copenhagen welcome visitors – is often downed to the accompaniment of Aquavit, a fiery and potent spirit which is the Danish version of the German Schnapps.

**Presents and Souvenirs.** Danish silver and glass is world-famous and there are many attractive contemporary designs. The textiles and embroidered table linen are among the best in Europe.

The very best reason for visiting Denmark is to meet the Danes themselves. Hard-working and pleasure-loving, these excellent hosts have a happy knack of communicating to their guests a sense of unforced gaiety.

While the climate in Denmark is similar to that prevailing in the UK, Copenhagen is at all seasons an animated city with a wide range of night life. It is preferable to book on a bed-and-breakfast basis. Motoring in Denmark

involves the use of ferries which should be booked in advance, particularly in summer months. There are no Winter Sports in Denmark.

## NORWAY

Norway stands unchallenged in Scandinavia for sheer grandeur of scenery. Her long coastline is severely indented by a series of fjords, vivid physical reminders of the period when, after the ice age, the glaciers melted leaving deep clefts through which the sea penetrated inland for, in some cases, a hundred miles.

Norway's population of $3\frac{3}{4}$ million live in the few main towns and in countless village settlements on the edge of the fjords and in fertile valleys which lie in the shadow of mountains rising to over 8,000 feet.

The Norwegians like the British and go out of their way to make them welcome. There are few language problems.

The first-time visitor to Norway can combine a visit to the capital, Oslo, with a seaside holiday on the south coast. The Gulf Stream runs quite close inshore and the sea is often warmer there than anywhere else in Europe apart from the Mediterranean. Long hours of summer daylight – even in the south of Norway it gets dark for only two to three hours in high summer – enable the holidaymaker to make the most of the northern evenings.

Oslo lies at the head of the deep fjord, to which the city has given its name, in a setting of great natural beauty. In summer business-men commute by boat to their fjordside wooden houses; in winter a twenty-minute journey on the Holmenkollen Railway leads up to the wide open spaces of Nordmarka, a paradise for the skiier. The sea and the slopes are on the city's doorstep.

Oslo has sufficient accepted tourist sights to fill a pleasant three days. The Viking Ships and Thor Heyerdahl's *Kon-Tiki*, in which he and his companions made their historic journey, bear witness to the past and present of Norway's maritime tradition. Their final resting-place is only a short bus ride away.

The massive exhibition of modern

sculpture by Gustav Vigeland in Frognerpark affords a startling contrast.

The old Hanseatic town of Bergen is the country's second city. Set at the foot of seven hills Bergen still preserves some of the atmosphere of a merchant port of the Middle Ages. From the top of Mount Floyen, easily reached by a cable railway from the city centre, there is a magnificent view looking out over Bergen and the fjord. The home of Norway's greatest composer, Edvard Grieg, lies outside the town at the edge of the fjord.

Mountain roads, with occasional stretches of hairpin bends corkscrewing up the steep ascents, pass through spectacular scenery of breathtaking beauty. They are not dangerous but do considerably reduce the average day's mileage.

The Hardangerfjord, which is easily accessible from Bergen, offers a gentler beauty than the more awesome scenery of the Sognefjord farther north.

There are excellent facilities for Winter Sports in many parts of Norway.

*The monetary unit* is the Norwegian Krone worth approximately 1s. 2d.

**Accommodation.** Even the smallest country establishments are clean, comfortable and very warm in winter. Food is plentiful in the farmhouses and mountain châlets open to tourists. Prices in the so-called "Tourist Hotels", specially designed to cater for foreign visitors and often built in natural beauty spots, are comparable to those found in the UK. Inexpensive accommodation should be booked in advance at hostels affiliated to the British YHA and in châlets run by the Association for the Furtherance of Ski-ing.

**Food and Drink.** Breakfast in Norway is a substantial meal. The "Cold Table", which may reappear at lunchtime with hot dishes added, contains a bewildering variety of smoked meats, fruit, cheese, pickled fish and two or three kinds of bread. A boiled egg is usually served, and the milk, tea and coffee are universally good. In hotels lunch is usually available between 2 p.m. and 3.30 p.m. Fish is excellent and seasonal specialities include Rensdyrryg (roast reindeer rib

served with cream sauce) and Kokt Sjöörret (sea trout served with cucumber salad). Many sweets made with wild mountain berries are delicious.

The Norwegians drink mainly beer (Pils or Pilsner), often accompanied by Aquavit. Norwegian licensing laws are very complicated. Beer and wines are freely available except in some unlicensed hostels and mountain huts. Spirits, cannot be ordered before 3 p.m.

**Presents and Souvenirs.** Norwegian silver, pewter and enamel work is distinctive and of high quality. In the main tourist centres genuine Norwegian oiled wool sweaters can be found in shops run by local art societies.

Norway provides excellent facilities for the ski-er, the sailor, the motorist and the walker. Fly-fishing can be arranged through hotels; several own reserved stretches of water and cater for the salmon fisher. Inclusive holidays by sea and air include tours of the fjord country using coaches and local steamer services. Everywhere in Norway the accent is on outdoor holidays and few restrictions govern the use of tents and caravans. Many tour operators quote for inclusive winter sports holidays.

## SWEDEN

Sweden, by far the biggest of the Scandinavian countries, is the fourth largest country in Europe but one-seventh of her territory lies north of the Arctic Circle. The country is rich in history and, as one of the world's most prosperous lands, rates of exchange and consequently prices are higher than in Denmark and Norway.

Sweden is a country of great beauty with vast areas of forest surrounded by lakes and rivers. Within that great landmass there are startling contrasts; from the reindeer herds of Lapland to the province of Skäne in the south where grapes and peaches are grown.

Southern Sweden is pleasantly warm in summer and the port of Gothenburg, the country's second city, provides access to Malmö and the near-by coastal resorts.

Stockholm, the Swedish capital, is

built on islands in the extensive archipelago and on the mainland and in this "City on the Water" the modern City Hall and Royal Palace are well worth a visit. The Sweden of the past has been recreated in the open-air museum at Skansen while the university town of Uppsala is only a short distance away.

Two islands off Sweden's east coast lie out in the Baltic, Öland and Gotland where Visby is the only remaining walled town in Northern Europe.

The Swedish people are friendly but reserved. The unusually high standard of education ensures few language problems.

A comprehensive road system links all the most important towns and although main highways are well surfaced loose gravel may be found on secondary roads in the north. There is excellent skiing in Lapland but, in general, Winter Sports facilities have not been as highly developed as in Norway. The midsummer celebrations are seen at their best on the shores of Lake Siljan in the province of Dalarna, north-west of Stockholm, and in the heart of the country.

*The monetary unit* is the Swedish Krone standing at 1s. 8d.

**Accommodation.** Advance booking is advisable in the summer in the province of Skåne and in Dalarna and hotels in the north are few and far between. In the many Youth Hostels there are no age restrictions and they are open to motorists. Svenska Turistforeningen (STF) is affiliated to the YHA and publishes an annual list of hostels obtainable from the Swedish National Tourist Office. Those travelling to the far north can hire Lapp tents equipped with cooking utensils through the STF.

**Food and Drink.** Sweden's main gastronomic contribution is the "Smörgåsbord", an outsize *hors d'œuvre* served as the prelude to the main course. The crayfish season is celebrated throughout the country during the month of August and the game, including woodcock and roast roe deer, is expensive but delicious. Beer and Aquavit are the most popular drinks. Licensing laws are subject to periodical changes. A "bar" is often more correctly a snack-bar which serves meals at reasonable prices. It is not necessary to tip in a snack-bar.

**Presents and Souvenirs.** Contemporary Swedish glassware, ceramics and stainless steel cutlery are world famous. The saving in buying them in the country of manufacture is considerable. Handknitted sweaters and men's shirts are good examples of the traditional and the contemporary.

Sweden, with its very high standard of living, is not a cheap country. Inclusive tours can be arranged through travel agents in the UK to Stockholm and to resorts in the province of Skåne. There are also unusual and fascinating train cruises from Stockholm to Kiruna, the capital of Swedish Lapland.

**Special Note.** Throughout Scandinavia the rules governing drinking and driving are very strict. While foreign motorists are seldom prosecuted, the police are empowered to ask for a compulsory medical examination and it is safer not to drink at all before or when driving. Ignorance of the law is no excuse.

# SPAIN

The popularity of Spain as a holiday country visited by countless sun starved Britons is a post-war phenomenon.

Few European countries offer more striking contrasts both in scenery and temperament than Spain and her people. The climate varies greatly from the subtropical luxuriance of the coast to the deep snows of the High Sierras. With even an elementary knowledge of European history it is not difficult to trace through the differing architectural styles the successive occupations dating from the fall of Rome to the period of the Moorish settlements which bequeathed to Spain the noble palaces which have survived from those days, including the opulent Alhambra in Granada. Throughout the country the Catholic churches are richly decorated in silver and gold while the Prado Museum in Madrid houses one of the finest art collections in the world.

Madrid, originally a Moorish fortress,

set nearly 2,200 feet up on the banks of the River Manzaneres, is the highest capital city in Europe but only became so in the middle of the sixteenth century. The former capital of Toledo has been preserved as a national monument.

Spain is an intensely exciting country which, in spite of considerable poverty, suddenly flares into life in the great processions and religious festivals. The Spaniard is both proud and passionate. The annual Easter celebration of "La Feria", the religious and secular fair held in Seville, is one external symbol of Spain; another is the bullfight which plays its part in the life of even a small town. Seen at its highest art form in Madrid, Barcelona and Valencia it combines a spectacle of colourful and brilliant pageantry with a key to the Spanish character.

Most British visitors to Spain make for the Mediterranean coast in the certain knowledge that the sun will shine throughout the long hot summer. Three very popular areas are the Costa Brava, not far from the French frontier, the Costa Blanca, lying between Valencia and Alicante, and the Costa del Sol with Malaga as the principal city.

While the coast roads can be crowded in summer, considerable improvements have already been made and the government has an ambitious programme of road works in hand.

The heat is so intense that an afternoon siesta is a virtual necessity and meal times in Spain are later than in the UK. Lunch is normally served between 2 and 3.30 p.m. and dinner from about 9 p.m. onwards. Many Spanish families have their evening meal at about 10 p.m. or even later. There is no lack of evening entertainment with cafés and bars open till about 2 a.m. and it is easy to fall in with this pattern.

*The monetary unit* is the Peseta standing at approximately 167 to the £.

**Accommodation.** All hotels in Spain are classified and many new ones with showers and private toilets adjoining all rooms have been built along the coast. The State Tourist Department operates "Paradores", former palaces and monasteries in natural settings of great beauty converted into hotels. "Albergues" are inns designed primarily for use by motorists touring the country. "Refugios" are small mountain chalets providing simple accommodation and meals.

**Food and Drink.** Spanish food, nearly always cooked in olive oil, can be extremely rich and many hotels used by British holidaymakers serve an international rather than a typically Spanish cuisine. Gazpacho (iced soup from Andalucia) is ideally suited to the climate and shellfish is not expensive. The classic Paella Valenciana (chicken, seafood, snails, pimento and peas served on a mound of saffron rice) can be excellent but some Paellas included on a "tourist menu" can be very indifferent.

Jerez is the home of sherry and Spanish brandy and locally made gin is pleasantly inexpensive. It is customary to serve Tapas (appetising titbits ranging from fried squid to the more familiar olives, gherkins and potato crisps) with drinks. Locally grown wine is very cheap.

**Presents and Souvenirs.** Andalucian iron work is distinctive and attractive and many ladies will wish to return with a mantilla or shawl. Leather work and basket ware are inexpensive and wines and spirits cheap enough to make it worth while bringing some back while still observing the limits laid down by HM Customs.

In spite of some increase in prices Spain remains an inexpensive holiday country and the many inclusive tours to popular resorts based on air travel to Barcelona and Valencia represent extremely good value. Good weather can be relied on but those who do not like intense heat should not contemplate a Spanish holiday in July and August. Several organisations handle the rental of villas and apartments and off-season prices offer considerable savings.

There are good camping facilities all along the coast.

## SWITZERLAND

Within a small area, less than a quarter the size of Great Britain, and tucked away within the very heart of Europe Switzerland offers a wide range of both scenery and culture.

The Swiss are fortunate in enjoying a virtually all-the-year-round tourist season. The slopes surrounding the international resorts of St Moritz and Davos are crowded during the winter with skiers while, in summer, the motorist can cross from valley to valley over magnificent Alpine roads through a constantly unfolding panorama of incredible variety and spectacular mountain scenery.

It was no coincidence that the now legendary Thomas Cook chose Switzerland for his first escorted tour just over a century ago. The tourist industry plays a major role in Switzerland's economy and the hotel standards are among the highest in the world.

In spite of its relatively small size Switzerland, or more correctly the Swiss Federation, consists of twenty-two cantons represented on a feudal system in the parliament which meets regularly in Berne. A short visit to the Swiss capital will allow time to see the cathedral and to go across the Nydeggbrucke to meet the famous animal residents in the Bears' Pit.

Switzerland's main geographical features are the great Alpine ranges, the six hundred glaciers, one of which forms the source of the River Rhône, and the lovely lakes of Constance, Geneva and Lucerne.

Four languages are used in Switzerland; French, German, Italian and Romansch, derived from Latin, but there are few language problems as English is very widely spoken.

Transport presents no problems for those visiting Switzerland without a car. An extensive network of buses and local trains connects all the main centres and a rack railway runs up nearly 11,500 feet to the Jungfraujoch, the highest railway station in Europe. This is the starting point for the year-round skiers who set off to explore the Alpine glaciers in a landscape of stark and savage beauty which might be thousands of miles away from the lush meadows of the Bernese Oberland and the leisurely pleasure-craft on the lakes.

*The monetary unit* is the Swiss Franc currently standing at about 1s. 11d.

**Accommodation.** Hotels in all price ranges are among the best in the world, ranging from the luxury establishment found both in the urban centres and international resorts to small inns and *pensions* built in traditional alpine style. Standards of cleanliness are exemplary and while Swiss hoteliers are fairly generous in granting reductions for children, this often involves personal negotiation at the time of booking.

**Food and Drink.** While the Swiss cuisine is understandably one of the most international in the world, each canton has its own specialities. Zürich provides Geschnetzeltes (minced veal served with chicken broth) and the Bernerplatte (a substantial dish of bacon, sausage and boiled beef served with sauerkraut and potatoes) is very popular in the capital. Swiss sweets and cream pastries are extremely rich and the famous Fondue (bread cubes dipped in cheese melted with white wine to which Kirsch has been added) is eaten with a fork straight from the dish.

Switzerland produces some excellent wines among them Neuchâtel (a dry, sparkling white wine), while the best red wine is the Dôle du Valais (slightly lighter than a French Burgundy). Lager beer is on sale throughout the country and the best Kirsch (distilled from cherries) comes from Zug.

**Presents and Souvenirs.** Lace and carved wood souvenirs are on sale in virtually every shop. The mechanical toys are among the finest in Europe and clocks and watches are very reasonable. Expensive makes will be subject to duty on returning to the UK.

Switzerland, as an international banking centre, is an expensive country and out-of-pocket expenses can be on the high side. All travel agents offer inclusive tours in summer and winter alike to the most popular centres and there is often a noticeable saving in travelling on an all-in basis. Those planning a Winter Sports holiday should bear in mind the cost of ski lifts, etc., which can be booked on a season ticket basis.

The Swiss National Tourist Office will forward a list of camping sites. Those planning to take a caravan to Switzerland should seek guidance from the motoring organisations as there are regulations over weight, bearing in mind the steep mountain roads.

## YUGOSLAVIA

Within recent years Yugoslavia has made great progress in handling an'ever-increasing volume of tourist traffic and many British visitors have discovered for themselves the pleasures of spending a holiday in the biggest of the Balkan countries.

Modern Yugoslavia combines many different racial groupings, including the Slovenes, Croats, Bosnians and Macedonians, who, while jealously preserving their own traditions, were finally united at the end of the First World War. A sense of unity has now found expression in territories occupied by the Greeks, Romans and Venetians and, in more recent times, subject to the influences of both the Austro-Hungarian and the Turkish Empires.

The Yugoslavs are keen to welcome foreign visitors and to show them what has been achieved in the past half-century and particularly since 1945.

The coastline stretching south-east from the great Italian port of Trieste faces out towards the deep blue of the Adriatic and there are excellent facilities for water-sports of all kinds. Off the rocky Dalmatian coast there are countless islands and Diocletian's great palace in the rapidly developing resort of Split is well worth a visit. The summer festival held in the incomparable setting of the city of Dubrovnik attracts visitors from all over the world.

The Yugoslavs have preserved in an unbroken tradition, which makes few concessions to the tourist, the folk-songs and dances of the different regions. There are plenty of opportunities to see and hear them.

A motoring itinerary should include a visit to the Postojna Caves where the spectacular grottoes and underground passages can be explored in a small train.

The quality of the roads varies considerably. New sections of motorway link Ljubljana to the Greek frontier and pass through Zagreb, Belgrade and Skopje, while a good road connects the Italian frontier to the resorts on the Dalmatian coast. Service stations in the interior are sometimes far apart and it is advisable to call in at a local tourist office before going far off the beaten track as minor roads inland can be very indifferent. The adventurous motorist should make sure his car will stand up to pretty rugged conditions.

*The monetary unit* is the New Dinar standing currently at approximately 30 to the £. There is a tourist rate of exchange and up to 100 dinars may be imported in notes. Travellers' cheques can be changed without difficulty at banks and tourist offices.

**Accommodation.** Hotels and *pensions* are all classified and divided into categories. High-season rates apply on the coast throughout the summer months. Motels on the Belgrade–Zagreb road are about sixty miles apart.

Advance booking is advisable on the Dalmatian coast and on the islands and is essential in Dubrovnik during the summer season. There are over 100 official camping-sites, the rates varying according to the facilities provided.

**Food and Drink.** The Yugoslav cuisine includes oriental features. Specialities include Alaska Corba (fish soup), Kastradina (smoked trout) and Srama (minced pork or beef and rice wrapped in sauerkraut).

There are few licensing restrictions and Yugoslavian Riesling is excellent. Dingac and Opolo, red wines from Dalmatia, are similar to claret. The principal Yugoslavian liqueurs are the many varieties of plum brandy generally known as Sljvovitca.

**Presents and Souvenirs.** The tooled leather and copperwork and wrought-iron are fine examples of authentic peasant craftsmanship. Ceramics are relatively inexpensive.

While the motorist may find problems in attempting to undertake a comprehensive exploration of the interior, tour operators offer inexpensive inclusive holidays at the resorts on the Dalmatian coast. Air–coach holidays flying to Switzerland with onward transport by coach combine sightseeing with a week at leisure on the coast.

---

## NATIONAL TOURIST OFFICES

Austrian State Tourist Department, 16 Conduit Street, W.1.

Belgian National Tourist Office, 66 Haymarket, S.W.1

Bulgarian National Tourist Office, 45 South Molton Street, W.1

Cyprus High Commission, 93 Park Street, W.1.

Czechoslovak Travel Bureau (Cedok) Ltd, 45 Oxford Street, W.1.

Danish National Travel Association, 2–3 Conduit Street, W.1.

Finnish Travel Information Centre, Finland House, 56 Haymarket, S.W.1

French National Tourist Office, 178 Piccadilly, W.1.

German Tourist Information Bureau, 61 Conduit Street, W.1.

Greek State Tourist Office, 195–197 Regent Street, W.1.

Hungary: Ibusz, 46 Eaton Place, S.W.1.

Iceland Tourist Information Bureau, 161 Piccadilly, W.1.

Italian State Tourist Department (ENIT), 201 Regent Street, W.1

Luxembourg National Tourist Office, 66 Haymarket, S.W.1.

Malta Government Office, Malta House, 24 Haymarket, S.W.1.

Netherlands National Tourist Office (ANVV), 38 Hyde Park Gate, S.W.7.

Norwegian National Tourist Office, 20 Pall Mall, S.W.5.

Polish Travel Office (Orbis), 313 Regent Street, W.1.

Portuguese State Information and Tourist Office, 20 Lower Regent Street, S.W.1.

Rumania National Tourist Office (Carpati), 98–99 Jermyn Street, S.W.1.

Soviet Travel Agency (Intourist), 314 Regent Street, W.1.

Spanish National Tourist Office, 70 Jermyn Street, S.W.1.

Swedish National Travel Association, 52–53 Conduit Street, W.1.

Swiss National Tourist Office, 458 Strand, W.C.2.

Turkish Tourism Information Office, 49 Conduit Street, W.1.

Yugoslav National Tourist Office, 143 Regent Street, W.1.

## FLOWERS

The ideal flower garden is one which is colourful for the greater part of the year, pleasant to walk or rest in and attractive looking from the house. It should also provide some cut flowers for the home. Even a small garden, or a section of a larger garden in which the main space is given up to vegetables and fruit can still be attractive.

A lawn is very desirable, even though it may be limited in size. Grass is the perfect foil for the bright colours of the flowers. If there are children in the family, obviously one must devote a large part of the garden to grass where they can play. A sand-pit is also useful while the children are very young. Where space permits, other attractive features – such as a rock garden or a small pool – can be introduced to add greater charm.

The plants for the garden can most conveniently be considered in groups, according to their nature and purpose. The various groups and many individual plants are described and cultural advice is given in the pages that follow.

**ANNUALS.** Annuals are plants which complete their life from seed-sowing to seed-bearing in one growing season. They are divided into three groups, hardy, half-hardy and tender. Hardy annuals require no protection whatever; half-hardy kinds have to be raised in a greenhouse or frame and planted out when danger of frost is past, while tender annuals must always be in the greenhouse.

**Hardy Annuals.** The group includes calendulas, cornflowers, nigellas, clarkias, godetias, annual chrysanthemums, mignonette, Californian poppies and many others. They can be used to conspicuously good effect in many ways. For instance, a harmonious colour panel or pattern scheme can be worked out in beds or borders, one- or two-colour beds are attractive, while small clumps of hardy annuals judiciously incorporated in the herbaceous border add to the beauty of that feature.

The soil should be fairly rich, and mid-March to mid-April is the ideal sowing period. The seed may be broadcast in patches of say 18 inches in diameter, or in drills, taken out with a pointed stick, half an inch deep about 6 inches apart over the desired area. This is preferable to sowing broadcast because it makes weeding easier. Thin the seedlings to allow room for proper development, support any plants that need it and remove the faded flowers regularly.

**Half-hardy Annuals.** A valuable family of summer bedding flowers comprising stocks, asters, ageratum, lobelia, snapdragons, African and French marigolds, salpiglossis and many more. These flowers are sown in the warm greenhouse or in a frame in early March, pricked out 2 inches apart into boxes when they are big enough to handle and hardened off in the cold frame before planting in their flowering quarters in May or early June, according to the season and district.

**Tender Annuals.** These are used for greenhouse display and include such kinds as schizanthuses, balsams, celosias, petunias, *Primula obconica, P. sinensis* and *P. malacoides*, cinerarias and calceolarias. The seed is sown in shallow boxes and the seedlings are pricked out when sizeable. When large enough they are transferred to 3-inch pots and forwarded to the 5-inch, 6-inch or 7-inch size in accordance with the size of the individual plant. Generally, tender annuals require shade during the growing period and those that bloom in summer must be shaded during the flowering period.

**BEDDING PLANTS.** These are plants which are set out in early summer to provide colour until early autumn, when they are lifted to make way for other plants which will flower in spring.

Among the favourite flowers used for the summer display are geraniums, calceolarias, penstemons, centaureas, fuchsias, lobelia, echeverias and half-hardy annuals mentioned above. For the spring-flowering scheme daffodils, tulips, hyacinths, wallflowers, polyanthuses, forget-me-nots and double daisies are the most popular plants.

**BIENNIALS.** These are plants which complete their life cycle in the second year from sowing. The principal members of the family are sweet Williams, Canterbury bells, wallflowers, iceland poppies, foxgloves and Brompton stocks. They are sown in May or June in well-worked soil in half-inch-deep drills at 6 inches apart. The seedlings are transplanted at 6 inches apart into rich nursery beds when they reach the rough leaf stage and from these beds are moved into their flowering positions in September.

**BORDER PLANTS.** There are a great many plants suitable for use in herbaceous borders. With a little thought one can have a border that will provide colour from spring until the coming of the frosts. The following will provide an excellent display:

**Tall plants** (set at 3 feet apart); delphiniums, sunflowers, artemisias, rudbeckias, lupins, red-hot pokers and Michaelmas daisies.

**Medium plants** (2 feet apart); orienta poppies, phloxes, centranthus, chelones, flag irises, peonies, veronicas, incarvilleas, galegas, *Chrysanthemum maximum*, linums, coreopsis and autumn anemones.

**Dwarf plants** (18 inches apart); heucheras, geums, potentillas, doronicums, pyrethrums, campanulas, polemoniums, trolliuses, mimuluses, megaseas and nepetas.

**Making New Borders.** The soil should be dug 2 feet deep and some manure should be worked in (see Manures and Fertilizers, page 161). Before planting (at any time between early November and the end of March) the soil should be made fine and firm. Prepare plan before planting, fixing position of every plant or group. Aim for colour harmony by associating pinks and blues, pinks and yellows, reds and blues, blues and yellows, reds and whites and any colour with white. Do not grade plants stiffly, but mix heights, taking care that the tall plants do not hide the dwarfs. So arrange plants that every part of border has some colour from spring to autumn. When planting, make holes wide enough to receive outstretched roots.

**BULBS.** Bulbous flowers are so rich and varied in beauty that no flower garden can afford to be without them. Following is a resumé of this family:

**Late Winter Flowering Bulbs.** In this branch of the family are snowdrops, crocuses, chionodoxas, *Scilla sibirica* and muscari, grape hyacinths, winter aconites and early flowering daffodils. When the clumps have grown large and need dividing they can be dug up after flowering, the bulbs separated and re-planted. This job can be done usually in May.

**Spring Flowering Bulbs.** The principal representatives are daffodils, tulips, hyacinths and irises. They are invaluable for bed and border planting, for mixing with wallflowers and other spring flowers, or in mixed perennial flower borders. September and October are the planting months and the soil should be liberally manured. Set daffodils, tulips and hyacinths 8 inches apart, irises 6 inches.

**Summer Flowering Bulbs.** The lilies are the aristocrats in this group. Among the easiest are *Lilium tigrinum*, orange with black spots, *L. regale*, white and yellow, red on the outside, *L. croceum*, orange, *L. testaceum*, buff, *L. pardalinum*, orange with purple spots. The new Oregon hybrids are also excellent, especially Destiny, Enchantment and Black Dragon. Lilies like plenty of sun, shade at their roots and well-drained, rich soil. March is a good time to plant. A good average spacing is 6 inches, and

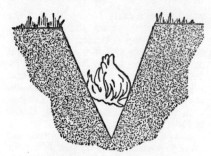

**WRONG way of planting a bulb – air space underneath is harmful...**

**RIGHT way – rest bulb on soil**

a good average planting depth 4 inches. Groups of these noble flowers are seen to great advantage in key points in the herbaceous border. Lift, divide and replant when they show signs of deterioration.

For later flowering *Amaryllis bella-donna* is a lovely pink trumpet flower which unfolds in early September. Likes a warm sheltered border and rich, limy soil. Set the bulbs 9 inches apart and 6 inches deep in August. Do not disturb the colonies once they are established.

The spire lily, *Galtonia candicans*, blooms in August, its towering spikes of cream, bell-shaped blossoms making an unforgettable picture. The herbaceous border is an ideal setting. Plant the bulbs 9 inches apart and 6 inches deep in March and lift, divide and replant every third year.

The lovely deep rose flowers of *Nerine bowdenii* appear in October and November. Treat it exactly as recommended for the amaryllis.

**Bulbs for Forcing.** The greenhouse and

home can be brightened in winter and spring by growing daffodils, tulips, hyacinths, irises, crocuses, snowdrops and scillas in boxes or pots of soil or bowls of fibre. The principal cultural factors are a rich compost of good quality bulb fibre, cool conditions for growth and flowering and copious waterings. Set the bulbs nicely clear of each other with their tips just showing. After watering, bury the pots and boxes 6 inches deep in an outdoor bed of sand or peat, or stand the bowls in a cool dark room and take no further action until the shoots are 2 inches long. Then, after gradual greening in a dim place, the bulbs may be brought forward in the greenhouse, or a light position in a genial living room. Every bulb catalogue gives a list of charming varieties for planting in September and October. The pre-cooled daffodils and tulips and specially treated hyacinths may be had in bloom for Christmas if planted in early October.

**CLIMBERS.** Plants grown alongside walls or fences and over arbours or arches for their floral or foliar effect. Examples of lovely flowering climbers are found in the clematis, rose, jasminum and lonicera families, while individual climbers of distinction are *Wistaria sinensis*, mauve, *Chaenomeles speciosa*, red, *Chimonanthus fragrans*, pink, and *Kerria japonica*, orange.

Foliage climbers include species and varieties of vitis, ampelopsis and ivy.

The correct planting period for all climbers is November to March and all, being hearty feeders, must be well supplied with manure. The pruning of flowering climbers generally consists in the removal, immediately after flowering of all or part of the growth that has bloomed. Foliage climbers must be neatly trimmed to their support in spring or autumn or both, according to the quantity of growth.

**HEDGES.** Hedges are used for a variety of purposes – to afford privacy, to shelter an exposed garden, as a background for flowering plants and to divide one part of the garden from another.

For an exposed garden oval-leafed

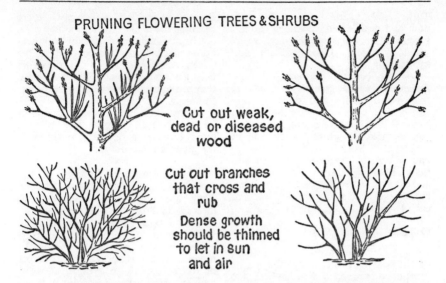

PRUNING FLOWERING TREES & SHRUBS

Cut out weak, dead or diseased wood

Cut out branches that cross and rub

Dense growth should be thinned to let in sun and air

privet or quickthorn is a good choice. For a sheltered garden something finer, such as *Chamaecyparis lawsoniana* or *Cupressocyparis leylandii* can be used.

Where a good screen of an ornamental nature is required, *Cotoneaster simonsii* could be used. Flowering subjects for use inside the garden include berberises such as *B. darwinii*, and *B. stenophylla*, *Olearia haastii*, *Escallonia macrantha* and *Fuchsia riccartonii*. Many rose species also make delightful hedges.

A hedging plant which retains great popularity is the evergreen honeysuckle, *Lonicera nitida*. It grows quickly and its glossy foliage is very attractive. The new forms of prunus, such as *P. pissardii*, *P. p. nigra* and the green myrobolan are very popular.

The soil in which a hedge is to be planted should be dug a full 2 feet deep and manured at the rate of a bucketful to each square yard.

Set plants like privet, evergreen honeysuckle and berberis at 2 feet apart; cotoneasters and cupressus at 2 feet 6 inches apart. Plant in early spring.

**SHRUBS.** A very large family of woody, comparatively dwarf-growing, flowering and evergreen subjects which should be represented in every garden. Where space permits, a shrub border might well be planted in which both flowers and evergreens are included to ensure all-the-year-round beauty. Where space is limited, shrubs may be planted here and there in flower borders.

Plant leaf-shedding shrubs from November to March, evergreens in September or April. The average spacing is 5 feet apart. Provide rich, deeply dug soil and prune intelligently. Deal with evergreens in September, removing overcrowded and straggling branches. For the most part flowering shrubs are pruned after flowering, when the growths that have carried flowers are removed.

Here is a selection of lovely flowering shrubs: Daphnes, forsythias, diervillas, lilacs, kerrias, deutzias, philadelphuses, escallonias, brooms, buddleias and hydrangeas. And here are evergreens: Cupressus, box, hollies, aucubas, junipers, and retinosporas.

**TREES, ORNAMENTAL.** A great acquisition in the larger garden. May be planted as a screen or in clumps to give ample effects, or separately as specimens. Good trees for quick screening are Ontario poplar, red-twigged lime, *Ailanthus glandulosa* (Tree of Heaven), Dutch elm, mountain ash, and whitebeam. Appropriate trees for grouping are silver birch, green and copper beech,

Turkey oak, scarlet oak, and double pink and double red hawthorn. Lovely specimen trees are scarlet oak, variegated sycamore, Deodar cedar and maidenhair tree.

Specially beautiful flowering trees are *Laburnum vossii* (yellow), *Magnolia soulangiana* (white and purple), tulip tree (white), *Garrya elliptica* (long green catkins), pink horse-chestnut, and flowering cherries in great variety. Plant ornamental trees between November and March in carefully prepared stations. Most specimens require stakes and all should be trimmed each winter, cutting out dead wood and the worst of each two crossing branches.

## OTHER FAVOURITE FLOWERS

Many other widely grown flowers which do not fall readily into any of the groups mentioned above. Following are the main points in the culture of these plants:

**Carnations.** Border carnations flower out of doors, perpetual flowering kinds in the greenhouse. The former, which should be planted 1 foot apart in rich, raised beds in September, flower in July and August. They are propagated by layering in July (see Layering, page 160).

Greenhouse plants must be grown cool and be potted in loamy, limy compost. By the third year they reach 7-inch pots, having previously passed through the 6-inch, 5-inch and 3½-inch sizes. Cuttings are inserted in November in pure sand.

**Chrysanthemums.** There are many lovely outdoor and greenhouse varieties in each section.

**Greenhouse-flowering.** There are many varieties in different flower forms – single, anemone flowered, decorative, incurved, and the huge mop-headed exhibition type. By reducing the number of shoots to say 5 or 6 to a plant, and removing all except the terminal bud, large and beautiful flowers are obtained. If the shoots are not disbudded, sprays of smaller flowers will result. Propagation is by means of cuttings inserted from December to February in sandy compost in the greenhouse. Plants go

through 3½-inch and 6-inch pots before reaching the final size of 8 or 9-inch pots.

Chrysanthemums remain in the greenhouse until April, the cold frame between April and June, out of doors between June and early October, when they are returned to the cool greenhouse to flower.

Alternatively, late-rooted cuttings may be obtained in August and planted direct into their flowering position in the greenhouse border.

**Outdoor-flowering.** Varieties in this section bloom from August to October. They are propagated from cuttings inserted in boxes in February and set out in the open garden in May at 15 to 18 inches apart. Rich, sunny quarters are essential. The plants should be moderately side-shooted, i.e. the number of stems reduced to 5 or 6, and disbudded. After flowering, plant in boxes sufficient roots to ensure cuttings for the following February. Winter the boxes in a cold frame, transferring them to the greenhouse in January.

**Dahlias.** One of the most widely grown late summer and autumn flowering plants. There are many types of dahlia, but the most popular are the medium and small cactus and decorative varieties and the pompons. The collerette dahlias are regaining popularity, and the giant cactus and decorative forms are popular with gardeners who wish to exhibit at flower shows. The dwarf mignon varieties form another section which is so much prized for summer bedding.

Being natives of Mexico, all dahlias require full sun, and in the winter previous to planting in June, the site should be liberally prepared. Space the large-flowered varieties 3 feet apart, smaller-flowered varieties at 2 feet apart.

Where large flowers are desired, allow six shoots only to develop on the large doubles, and one flower at a time on each shoot. Dahlias must be firmly supported and generously fed.

When flowering finishes, or the plants are blackened by frost, lift them and store the tuberous roots in a frost-proof place until March, when growth should be restarted in boxes of soil placed in gentle heat. Dahlias may be increased by cuttings inserted in sandy soil in a warm greenhouse in spring.

**Ferns.** A family with many attractive members both for greenhouse and garden decoration. A primary requirement is shade at all times, and during the growing season an abundance of water should be supplied. Good kinds for the average greenhouse are *Adiantum cuneatum, Asplenium bulbiferum*, and *Pteris serrulata*. Maintain a temperature of 45 to 55 degs. F., a humid atmosphere and, using peaty compost, re-pot or top-dress the plants each spring.

Hardy ferns are valuable for furnishing shady dells, or shady situations such as beneath trees. Plant them in March, mixing peat freely with the soil, and divide the roots every third or fourth March. *Athyrium filix-mas, A. filix-foemina*, and *Polystichum vulgare* are hardy and very attractive.

**Roses.** All roses are sun-lovers and draught-haters, and all like well-manured soil. There are three main sections: the bush roses, the climbers and ramblers, and the shrub roses. The bush roses consist of the hybrid teas and the floribunda types which carry many flowers on one stem.

**Hybrid Tea.** The most popular group of large-flowered roses. Of medium height and vigour. Plant 18 inches apart and prune in March, shortening branches half to two-thirds of the way back, according to the vigour of the variety. Prune weaker varieties more severely.

**Floribunda.** Also known as cluster roses because they bear their blooms in clusters. Bloom almost perpetually in summer. Are admirable for bedding. Plant 15 to 18 inches apart and prune in March, shortening branches one-third to half-way back according to vigour of variety.

**Climbing and rambler roses.** These fall into several categories. Broadly the ramblers produce many new shoots from the base each year. The stems that have borne flowers are cut out after flowering, and the new growths are tied in to take their place. The climbing

roses are more sparing in their production of new stems, and may need the encouragement of a layer of manure 6 inches thick spread around the plants for a foot or two in each direction.

Climbing roses are pruned after flowering by cutting out any old unwanted shoots and tying in new growths. In spring the tips of the long growths are shortened by a foot or so and sideshoots cut back to about 3 or 4 inches.

To promote the production of plenty of side shoots that will bear the flowers, bend over the long growths as near to the horizontal as possible. When buying climbing or rambler roses look for those that are described as "repeat" or continuous flowering. Some bloom once with great profusion, but no more.

**Miscellaneous.** There are also some large bush roses, including Penzance Briars, Bourbons, Musk, Provence, Moss, Moyesii and Scotch Briars, which are perfect as specimens on lawns or for grouping in large beds. Again look for "repeat" or perpetual flowering varieties.

**Planting.** Roses can be planted from November to March, the earlier part of the period being the better. Steep the roots in water before planting and open them out evenly in holes big enough to receive them comfortably.

**Sweet Peas.** The queen of the hardy annuals. Sow in October in boxes in cold frames, or outdoors in March. Plant October-sown batch in flowering positions in April. For really early flowers – at the end of May or early in June – sow under cloches in the first week of October. Remove the cloches and stake the peas at the end of April. Provide moderately rich, deeply worked soil. Where plants are to be grown on cordon system, space in single row at 1 foot apart. Where for ordinary garden display and cutting, in double row at 6 inches apart. From cordon plants remove tendrils and tie regularly. Growth must be effectively supported by stakes, tree branches or netting. Feed generously and remove faded flowers weekly.

## PROPAGATION OF PLANTS

**By Budding.** A method used for the propagation of roses rhododendrons, vines, peaches, and cherries, both ornamental and fruiting. There are two partners, the stock which provides the root system and the bud which supplies the variety it is desired to increase.

The stock must be well established when the bud is worked into it, or the stock and the bud will not unite. Union is achieved by making a T-shaped incision in the stem of the stock at ground level. A dormant leaf-bud with a small shield of stem is inserted in the T-shaped incision, the latter being bound with raffia, leaving the bud exposed. No further action is taken until the following spring, when the unwanted portions of stock stem are cut off and the variety is left in full possession above ground level. July is the best month for budding.

**By Cuttings.** Most bedding plants, such as violas, fuchsias, geraniums, lobelia and many more can be increased by means of stem cuttings – young, unflowered side-shoots. The shoots are cut cleanly across just beneath a joint and the lower leaves are removed. While some cuttings will root in a cold frame, the safer plan is to plant them in boxes covered with glass and placed in a greenhouse. Late summer is the usual time for taking such cuttings.

Such shrubs as buddleias, hydrangeas, and so on can be multiplied by cuttings, about 3 inches long, planted in sandy soil in a sunny border. The cuttings should be pulled – not cut – off so that they come away with a "heel" or small piece of the parent stem.

Border plants like peonies, anchusas and oriental poppies can be increased by root cuttings – pieces of root about 3 inches long – planted in a sandy border in autumn or early spring.

**By Division.** Practically all perennial plants can be propagated in this way – Michaelmas daisies, phloxes, heleniums, erigerons, doronicums and many more. The old clump is lifted, as much soil as possible shaken off, and the younger pieces on the outside of the clump eased

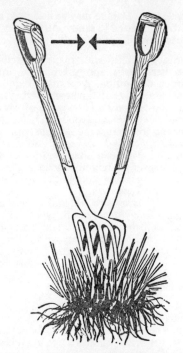

away with the aid of a hand fork, or by pushing two garden forks into the clump back to back and gently levering apart. The old central part of the plants should be discarded. With plants that have a main root-stock, such as lupins and delphiniums, the young crowns must be carefully pulled away from the old root-stock by hand.

The divisions should be re-planted in the border after the soil has been dug over. Tap-rooted plants like anchusas and lupins are best dealt with in the autumn.

**By Layering.** This method consists of pegging down a shoot or branch in the soil so that it is induced to form roots. It is then separated from the parent and becomes a separate plant.

**By Seed Sowing.** In general the sowing of flower seeds follows the same lines as the sowing of vegetable seeds (see page 167). Whatever the plants to be raised from seeds, whether they be annuals, biennials or perennials, a good seed bed is of first importance. Germination (the "coming to life" of the seeds) is always poor in rough soil; the first delicate roots have no proper contact with the soil.

The bed should be well dug over and the lumps broken down with the back of the spade. The soil should be raked level and trodden until it is reasonably firm. Finally the top inch should be raked until it is uniformly fine. That gives the seeds just what they require – fine soil in which to germinate, with evenly firm soil into which the stronger roots can delve.

Some weeds are sure to come up with the seedlings. The weeds should be withdrawn as soon as they can be distinguished. Disturbance of the seedlings must be avoided when weeding. The job should be done after rain or after the bed has been watered; the weeds will come out more easily then. If any of the seedlings are loosened they must be refirmed or they will fail.

## MANURES AND FERTILISERS (FOR FLOWERS)

Many occupants of the flower garden – particularly ornamental trees, shrubs and hedges – are hungry plants. Perennials, annuals, and the rest all need a certain amount of food. Therefore the ground in which any plants are grown needs manuring and, while making their growth, the plants also require quicker-acting fertilisers.

For almost all plants, the best manure for digging into the soil is stable manure. When sites are being prepared for trees, shrubs, hedge plants, climbers, or roses, up to a bucketful per square yard may well be worked in. For the herbaceous border, about three-quarters of a bucketful per square yard is appropriate; for annuals, bedding plants and bulbs, about half a bucketful per square yard will be sufficient.

Many gardeners, however, find it impossible to obtain even the smallest quantity of stable manure. Use must then be made of such substitutes as hop manure, available ready for use from the garden shop, or compost (rotted vegetable manure, prepared as described on page 167). Leaf-mould and horti-

cultural peat are other alternatives. Many people keep chickens using manure from the run after it has been dried, powdered with a rammer, and mixed with an equal quantity of sand or dry soil. The mixture should be dug in at the rate of 8 ounces per square yard. It is better to mix chicken manure with vegetable refuse on a compost heap. It will help to decompose the vegetable waste more quickly. Also, chicken manure used alone is often too strong for many plants.

Most convenient for use during the growing season is one of the mixed fertilisers. Such fertilisers contain all that the plants need to foster growth and flowering.

For those who would like to prepare their own general fertiliser the following is a good recipe: superphosphate of lime, 3 parts; sulphate of ammonia, 1 part; sulphate or muriate of potash, 1 part; all parts by weight. Apply at the rate of $1\frac{1}{2}$ ounces per square yard of flower-bed or border once a month during the growing season.

## COURTYARDS, TUBS AND WINDOW-BOXES

In town gardens, and in many country gardens, there are small courtyards, terraces or other formal areas which cry out for plants. In towns, it is expensive to keep buying loads of fresh soil every few years to renew beds or borders, so if a little money is spent on well-designed containers, such as tubs, fibre-glass troughs and vases, a larger amount of money is saved in the long term. The containers themselves are attractive features. They need very little soil to fill them, and only a few plants to make them colourful for many months. Window-boxes in plastics, fibre-glass and wood are available in various sizes. It is a good idea to have a duplicate set of window-boxes. One can be planted with such early flowering bulbs as daffodils or hyacinths and another with tulips and myosotis. To economise on the soil and the potting compost, so necessary for good results in tubs or window-boxes, fill the bottom third of the container with vermiculite. This is cheaper than the potting compost. Also, it retains moisture very efficiently and reduces the frequency of the waterings necessary to keep plants growing happily.

## GREENHOUSES

The owner of a heated greenhouse is potentially unlimited in his horticultural activities. He can have magnificent displays of flowers in the greenhouse at all seasons and keep the home supplied with flowers and foliage plants. He can raise plants of all kinds, including the most tender, from seeds, and provide all the bedding and other plants needed for the garden. He can do a great deal of propagating from cuttings and force many kinds of bulbs and plants into early flower.

Even without heat, a greenhouse can be very useful indeed for raising many kinds of plants and for a certain amount of propagation work. Lovely displays of flowers can be enjoyed continuously from spring until autumn in an unheated greenhouse.

The owner of an unheated greenhouse might like to extend his activities without going to the expense of a boiler and pipes, or electrical heating. The modern oil heaters made specially for greenhouse use are the answer. They are reasonable in price and oil consumption is low. They are fumeless and free from smell, and plants grow well in the houses in which they are used.

But for a trouble-free greenhouse electricity is the answer. It is not expensive if space heating is combined with soil warming. The soil is warmed by means of cables laid in a bed of sand on the benches, or buried about 6 to 8 inches deep in the greenhouse borders. If the soil is kept at a temperature of 50–55 degs.F. then the air temperature can be maintained at a very economical 45 degs.F. and most of the plants the amateur wishes to grow will grow well.

Electricity can be used also for automatic ventilation and automatic watering. Electrical vaporisers will control pests and diseases. Electricity is clean, automatic and not unduly expensive. Full information about the ways in which electricity can help the gardener is found in the booklet *Electricity in Your Garden*, free from all electricity showrooms.

## SEED AND POTTING COMPOSTS

In the old days, gardeners had their own special, often jealously guarded, recipes for seed and potting composts. Nowadays, all good garden shops sell these composts; the most popular are those made up to the John Innes formulae, usually known as JI composts. The loam in them has been sterilised, so there should be no weed seeds and no disease spores.

The latest types of seed and potting composts are based on pure peat impregnated with fertilisers. These are light to handle, and being very quick draining are almost impossible to overwater. They dry out quickly, so careful attention must be paid to watering. If they dry out, water them thoroughly and after an hour water them again.

## GROUND COVER PLANTS

Great economy in garden maintenance can be achieved by planting suitable areas with low-growing plants that will cover the ground and smother the weeds. Heathers are eminently suitable although if the soil is alkaline one is confined to *Erica carnea* and its varieties. Such low-growing and prostrate conifers as *Juniperus sabina*, *J. horizontalis*, and *J. communis prostrata* are useful for this purpose. The dwarf *Cotoneaster horizontalis* also makes excellent ground cover. Among other hardy plants are *Hypericum calycinum*, *Stachys lanata*, bergenias, *Polygonum bistorta* and *P. vaccinifolium*, ivies, and *Pachysandra terminalis*. The last-named is excellent for ground cover under trees in dry conditions.

### House Plants

In recent years, millions of house plants have been sold every year. Many die in the first few weeks after they have been placed in the living-room, largely because their needs have not been properly understood. First, when buying a house plant, whether it be a flowering plant such as a cyclamen, an azalea or an African violet, ask the shop assistant for some advice on its treatment in the home. A few points to remember about house plants: they hate draughts, a fuggy atmosphere, fumes from a boiler or from an old-fashioned gas fire. Most house plants like a temperature of around 60 or 65 degs.F.; Cyclamen like a cool room where the temperature does not rise much above 55 degs.F.

In winter, they need all the light possible, but in summer, foliage plants should be moved back into the room so that they escape the direct rays of the sun. If dust is allowed to accumulate on the leaves of foliage plants this can be very harmful. Wipe the leaves every week or two with a mixture of half milk and half water. More house plants are killed by overwatering than by under-watering, especially from October to March. Keep the soil just moist, and never stand a pot plant in a saucer of water.

In winter, never leave pot plants on a window-sill if the curtains are drawn, leaving the plants between the curtains and the glass. This could be the coldest place in the house on a frosty night.

Easy house plants are *Begonia rex* and its varieties, chlorophytums, sanse-vieria, cissus, ficus and phyllocactus.

## THE LAWN

Established lawns must be cut regularly throughout the season from the time the grass starts to grow in spring until growth ceases in autumn. For the first two or three mowings the machine should be so adjusted that it does not cut the grass very short; just the tips of the blades should be taken off. The grass box should always be used, except during the height of summer when the cuttings should be left on the turf to help to keep it moist.

Regular feeding is necessary to keep the lawn healthy and rich green in colour. Special lawn fertilisers are obtainable at garden shops. A good home-prepared dressing, for spring or autumn use, is sifted garden soil, to each barrowful of which a bucketful of old stable manure (also well sifted) is added; alternatively, hop manure can be used. The soil and manure mixture is sprinkled over the lawn to a depth of about one inch and brushed in.

For summer feeding there is a wide choice of proprietary fertilisers. It is always wise to water these in after application to avoid any risk of scorching.

Weeds, which used to be so troublesome in lawns, are now dealt with easily by means of proprietary selective weed-killers which control the weeds without harming the grass. But they must be used strictly according to the manufacturers' instructions. Also, they work best in warm weather, so they should be applied from mid-May until the end of September as necessary.

Moss will appear in lawns – usually in badly drained turf – but it is often present on light quick-draining soils. The mercuric moss-killers are the answer, watered on well before the winter, as moss can grow lustily in low light conditions when the grass is dormant.

**Mechanical Treatment of Lawns.** Besides regular mowing, feeding, and weed control, the perfect lawn needs a certain amount of mechanical treatment. After repeated mowing with a roller mower and the traffic of people walking on it, a lawn tends to become compacted. Aeration is necessary. Holes should be pierced in the lawn at 4-inch intervals with a garden fork. This will allow rain and plant food to penetrate easily to the grass roots.

Dead grass and other debris accumulates in the turf and may cause diseases to spread. A thorough raking of the lawn in autumn and spring to remove this debris is invaluable.

**New Lawns.** The site for a new lawn needs to be well dug and given a dressing of fertiliser. Immediately before sowing (in April or early September), rake the ground freely to ensure an even surface and a finely broken up bed for the seed.

Distribute the seed at the rate of 1½ ounces per square yard, and lightly rake it in. Pat down with the back of the spade or run a *light* roller over the sown area.

When the young grass is 2 inches high, clip back to 1 inch with shears, or with a mowing machine with the blades set high.

If the new lawn is to be made from turfs, prepare the site as suggested above and, during winter (frosty periods excepted), lay clean turfs close together and brush fine soil into the small channels between them. Roll occasionally to assist turfs to knit.

## THE ROCK GARDEN

Alpine and other rock garden plants add greatly to the charm of any garden. Many of them flower in spring when they are most welcome. A simple rock garden is easy to build and if skilfully made need not require a vast amount of stone. Avoid the "rock cake" type of mound with stones dotted here and there. Try to re-create a gentle slope such as one would see on the lower range of a mountain. One does not even have to build a rock garden to grow many of the lovely alpine plants. Most of them are happy in the chinks between the stones of a dry stone wall, or even in the border on top of such a wall.

The main points in rock-garden building are:

1. To choose a site which is as open and sunny as possible, away from overhanging trees and from tree drips.
2. To use good soil, best for the purpose being good loam. Where the garden soil is light and poor it can be made suitable by the addition of leafmould, peat, or garden compost. Heavy soils need to be lightened with sand and bonfire ashes.
3. To be sparing in the use of stone. The plants "make" the rock garden, the stone serves to set them off. A hundredweight of stone is enough for a rock garden covering four square yards.

When the stones are being arranged to form "pockets" for the plants each should be at least half-buried. Soil should be packed tightly behind, under and around each stone. The plants will not flourish if the soil is loose around them.

Rock gardens should preferably be made in winter, planting to begin in early spring. September is also a good planting time.

An excellent selection for a start would be the following, providing a succession of bloom from March to September; primulas, aubrietias, saxifrages, phloxes, campanulas, helianthemums (or sun roses), androsaces, alyssums, dianthuses, gentians, linarias, sedums, thymes, veronicas, armerias, and gypsophilas.

As experience is gained many other lovely, but more difficult plants, can be added.

## OTHER FEATURES

Among the many features which add distinction to a garden may briefly be mentioned:

**Arches and Pergolas.** These look particularly attractive when clothed with climbing or rambler roses, clematis, jasmine, honeysuckle or other such plants. They can be erected at the beginning or end of a path, at intervals along a path, over a gateway, as an opening in a hedge, at the end of the lawn, and so on. Arches can be bought ready made or the handyman can build them from rustic or other timber.

**Garden Ornaments.** A wide variety of garden ornaments made of stone, concrete and other materials are normally available – sundials, birdbaths, pieces of statuary and so on. These can add fresh interest to a garden; a sundial looks charming on the lawn; a bird bath in a quiet corner. Vases and tubs can also be used very effectively along a path, for instance, as a centrepiece in a large flower-bed, at the junction of paths or on a flight of garden steps.

Modern reproductions of antique lead troughs and urns in fibre-glass are also available. They are very realistic and not unduly expensive. Vases of reconstituted stone are also available at reasonable prices.

**Ornamental Walls.** These can be low walls made of brick, or of stone with "pockets" for plants. They can be built at the end of the lawn, for example, or as a dividing feature between the flower and vegetable gardens.

**Paths.** Although paths are mainly utilitarian they can also add considerably to the appearance of a flower garden. A clinker path can be quite useful, but it does not set off the flowers in the adjoining border nearly so well as one made of crazy-paving or mellow old bricks. The secret of making a successful crazy-path is to ram the foundations very firm and to pack plenty of soil between the stones. Small rock plants can be grown in the crevices between the stones if desired. A brick path must also have a very firm foundation and it is preferable that the bricks should be cemented in position.

An alternative to crazy-paving is a cement path scored while still wet in imitation of the real stones.

**Pools.** Nothing adds more to the joy of a garden than a pool in which water-lilies and other plants grow and goldfish dart to and fro. In a simple form, the pool need be no more than a hole in the ground lined with a 3-inch layer of concrete. The concrete should consist of 1 part cement, 2 parts sand, 3 parts aggregate (small shingle or broken stone).

Preferably the outline should be irregular rather than a formal circle or oval. A maximum depth of 18 inches in the deepest part will be sufficient for aquatic plants and for fish.

Plastic pools are available in various shapes and all that is necessary is to dig a hole and drop the pool in position. Alternatively a hole may be dug out and lined with plastic sheeting, anchored at the top with soil or stones. With the development of submersible electric pumps, it is now possible to have water-falls and fountains with the minimum of installation work.

Provision should always be made to flood several times a week a margin around the pool. Here can be grown primulas, rushes, mimulus and other bog-loving plants which greatly enhance the appearance of the pool.

**Screens.** A climber-covered trellis screen can be pleasant at the end of the lawn where it may divide up the garden, or to shut off the corner in which manure and the like is dumped. The trellis can be made of rustic wood or builders' laths with strong uprights. Provided the wood is treated generously with a wood preservative (not creosote), the screen will have a long life. The preservative must be allowed to dry in thoroughly before the climbers which are to cover the screen are planted.

## GARDEN TOOLS

To perform his tasks thoroughly and without unnecessarily hard work, the gardener needs an adequate kit of tools. They should be of good quality; a well-made, well-balanced tool is far easier to work with than an indifferent one. Tools, such as spades, should be chosen with a length of handle and weight to suit the individual user. Stainless or rust-resisting tools, while more expensive, are a joy to use and well worth the extra money.

The essential tools are: spade; four-pronged digging fork; draw hoe for earthing-up and taking out drills; Dutch hoe for stirring surface soil in summer; rake; trowel and dibber. A garden line is required for use when drawing drills, and one or two watering cans. Secateurs are required for pruning (most amateurs find secateurs easier to use than a knife), and a syringe, or one of the many sprayers available, for applying insecticides. Distributors for spreading lime or fertilisers on lawns, or on the soil are a great help. So are the two-wheeled trucks with a detachable body which are in many ways to be preferred to a wheel-barrow.

All tools should be freed of soil after use and wiped over with an oily rag to keep them free of rust. An occasional rub with a file will keep a good edge on spades and hoes.

## VEGETABLES

Crops straight from the garden or allotment are far fresher, crisper, better flavoured and more health-giving than the majority of those which have spent days passing through markets and shops. For this reason, it is well worth while in every garden to set aside some space for the cultivation of vegetables. Where there is a reasonable amount of space in the garden, or where an allotment can be worked, pretty well the whole vegetable needs of the family can be met for most of the year. In the small garden, room can be found, at least, for a few rows of salad crops, peas and carrots, onions and the like. Grow the crops that are expensive or liable to be of poor quality in the shops.

There are certain well-defined principles in vegetable growing and when these are followed success is assured.

## ROUTINE WORK

**Digging and Manuring.** Good digging and adequate manuring are the basis of good vegetable growing. There are two general methods of digging as here briefly described.

**Simple or Plain Digging.** Dig out a trench, a spade's depth and about a foot wide right across the plot to be dug. Barrow the soil to the other end of he plot. To save the barrowing, you might divide the plot lengthwise into two and dig out the trench, as described above, across one half of the plot. Put the soil over on to the other half of the plot, where it will be ready to fill in the last trench. Then work up the length of the half-plot, digging the soil and turning it over to fill the trench. Always drive the spade in vertically and clean out the loose soil from the trench so that there is always a neat open trench to receive the next consignment of soil as you dig.

When the end of the plot is reached, dig out another trench at the beginning of the second half and use this soil to fill the last trench on the first half. Continue digging down the second half until you reach the end. Then the soil you left there from the first trench you dug will be ready and waiting to fill the last trench. If manure or compost is available, a layer of this 3 or 4 inches thick should be thrown into the trench as the digging proceeds.

**Double Digging.** In the process of double digging, the aim is to move the soil to two spades' depth but not to bring the subsoil to the surface. This breaking up of the soil to about 2 feet deep helps to improve the drainage and allow the roots of the plants to go much deeper in search of food and moisture.

The technique is the same as described above for simple digging. Divide the plot lengthwise in two and take out a trench as advised above. Then, before turning the soil over into the trench, take a fork and loosen the soil in the bottom of the trench thoroughly. If manure or compost is to be worked in, spread this over the freshly loosened soil in the bottom of the trench. Then, with the spade, turn over the top soil to cover the manure or compost.

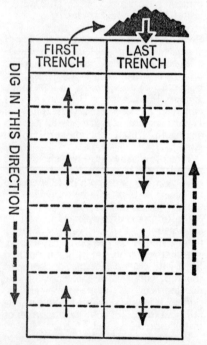

**Manuring.** Returning to the question of manure. There is nothing to beat stable manure and where this is available an appropriate allowance is a barrowful for each 25 square yards of ground.

The shortage of stable manure makes it necessary for a great many gardeners

## COMPOST HEAP FORMATION

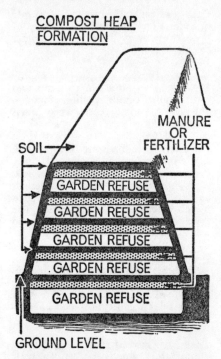

SOIL

MANURE OR FERTILIZER

GARDEN REFUSE

GARDEN REFUSE

GARDEN REFUSE

GARDEN REFUSE

GARDEN REFUSE

GROUND LEVEL

to seek some other bulk manure. Compost has come to the fore as a very effective substitute. It is used at the same rate as stable manure. Certain local authorities who have sewage farms will supply gardeners in that area with sewage manure at a very low cost, and this also is a good substitute for stable manure. Still another alternative is prepared hop manure. This is spread in the bottom of the trenches at the rate of 8 ounces per square yard. Old mushroom compost is now available and can be dug in at the same rate as hop-manure.

**Making Compost.** This consists of waste, such as unwanted leaves from cabbages and other vegetables, lawn mowings, soft prunings, annual weeds and such like, heaped up and left to rot down. Dusting the heap with sulphate of ammonia as each fresh consignment of green waste is thrown on accelerates rotting down; or one or other of the proprietary compost makers can be used.

These preparations hasten rotting down and increase the plant-feeding value of the compost.

**Seed Beds and Sowing.** Ground dug in winter should have settled down by March, when the main vegetable sowing season starts. All that is necessary then is to give the soil a good raking to level the surface and provide the seeds with fine soil in which to germinate.

Before sowing, it is a good idea to determine how the space available is to be filled. Drawing up a rough plan on paper ensures that no desired crop is overlooked or crowded out. The seeds for the various sowings should all be obtained at the same time, making them ready to hand just when they are required.

As an indication of the amount of seed to buy, it may be mentioned that typical requirements for a 30-foot row are:

| | |
|---|---|
| Beans, broad | $\frac{1}{2}$ pint |
| Beans, French | $\frac{1}{4}$ pint |
| Beans, runner | $\frac{2}{3}$ pint |
| Beet | $\frac{1}{4}$ oz. |
| Cabbage family | $\frac{1}{2}$ oz. will produce 500–700 plants. |
| Carrots | $\frac{1}{4}$ oz. |
| Lettuce | $\frac{1}{8}$ oz. |
| Onions | $\frac{1}{4}$ oz. |
| Parsnips | $\frac{1}{4}$ oz. |
| Peas | $\frac{1}{4}$ pint. |
| Spinach | $\frac{1}{4}$ oz. |
| Turnips | $\frac{1}{4}$ oz. |

With potatoes, for each of row 30 feet, allow seven pounds of "seed" of first earlies, 6 lbs. of second earlies, 5 lbs. of main crop.

When drawing drills for the seed, let them run from north to south rather than east to west. The former direction ensures for the plants maximum exposure to sunshine.

Neat, straight seed drills help to keep the plot tidy-looking, so a garden line should always be used when the drills are drawn. Most vegetables are sown in V-shaped drills which can conveniently be drawn with the corner of the draw hoe. For the very shallow drills, as for onions, a good plan is to lay a stick on the soil alongside the line and press this sufficiently to make the required quarter-inch depression.

When sowing, the aim is to distribute the seed thinly and evenly. With small seeds a good method is to tip the seeds into the palm of the left hand and take pinches with the finger and thumb of the right hand. Thin sowing helps to prevent overcrowding in the rows, reduces the work of thinning and economises on seed.

**Thinning.** Though seeds are sown thinly, there is always some thinning to be done as the seedlings begin to fill in their rows. If seedlings are left at all crowded they begin to make tall, weak growth and never do any good.

The distances to which the different crops should be finally thinned are given in the entries which follow (see pages 169 to 175). The thinning should be done by stages until the seedlings stand at the appropriate distance apart.

Thinning can best be done when the soil is moist after rain or watering, because there is less disturbance of the seedlings left in the row. The surplus seedlings can be drawn out intact, for planting elsewhere if desired. After thinning a row, it is worth while to go along it and pat down the soil around the retained seedlings.

**Feeding Vegetables.** Besides sowing or planting the vegetables in manured soil, it is necessary to feed practically all crops with quick-acting fertilizers during the growing season.

Some gardeners feed their vegetables individually, giving each of the different crops the fertiliser particularly suited to its needs. Examples of crops which like special feeding are:

**Beans, Broad.** When beans are 2 inches long, superphosphate is given, 1 ounce per yard of row, with further applications at 10-day intervals until the crop is harvested.

**Beans, Runner.** As soon as plants begin to climb their supports, a dressing of sulphate of ammonia, 1 ounce per yard, is given. Dressing is repeated 6 weeks later.

**Cabbage Family.** Sprinklings of nitrate of soda, $\frac{1}{2}$ an ounce per square yard of bed, given every 3 weeks, in summer suit these crops.

**Lettuce.** During growth, fortnightly applications of nitrate of soda in liquid form – half an ounce in gallon of water – are given. Feeding ceases when hearts have formed.

**Peas.** When seedlings are one inch tall, sulphate of ammonia is given, $\frac{1}{2}$ ounce per yard of row; when 3 inches tall, superphosphate is applied, 2 ounces per yard run. Nitrate of soda is given a month later, $\frac{1}{2}$ ounce per yard. The superphosphate dressing is repeated when flowers are forming.

**Potatoes.** Before crop is earthed up, a 1 ounce per yard dressing of the following mixture is stirred into the soil; sulphate of ammonia 1 part, sulphate of potash 2 parts, superphosphate 3 parts – all parts by weight.

**Turnips.** One dressing of superphosphate, 1 ounce per yard of row, is given after the crop has been thinned.

Nowadays, most gardeners find it more convenient and quicker to use one of the compound fertilisers which can be bought ready for application. These mixed fertilisers contain all the necessary plant foods, so can be given to all crops in the certainty that they will help to produce first-class results.

## ENEMIES OF VEGETABLES

The diseases and pests which attack vegetable crops (and flowers) are very numerous, but many of them can conveniently be grouped as follows:

**Diseases – Mildews and Moulds.** The former are known by the white parasitic down with which they cover the leaves (example, pea mildew), the latter by the brown leaf blotches and the mould which eventually overspreads them (example, spinach leaf-mould). The application of one of the proprietary fungicides will control these diseases.

Cheap and efficient hand-sprayers are available for this purpose.

**Root Diseases.** Club root, attacking turnips and members of the cabbage family, is the worst of these. It induces formation of scabs on the roots and seriously depresses growth. Control can be gained by destruction of diseased material, liming and growing the crops on different sites each season. Where club root is known to exist in the soil, make a porridge – like paste – of calomel dust and water and dip the roots of all brassica plants in this before planting. The foot rots attack a variety of crops, especially peas and beans, drying up the base of the stems, yellowing the leaves and finally proving fatal. These troubles are not likely to occur in well-drained soil, but if they do can be overcome by an early application of sulphate of iron solution ($\frac{1}{4}$ ounce in 2 gallons of water, applied at the rate of 4 pints per yard of row).

Potato blight can be very serious. It first appears on the leaves in wet humid weather in July. Then the spores can affect the tubers and cause them to rot in store. The action therefore must be preventive. It consists in spraying Bordeaux Mixture in July and repeating the spray after 3 weeks. The potato stems should be cut down and burned about 3 weeks before the crop is lifted.

**Virus Diseases.** Of widespread incidence, they are found on potatoes, tomatoes, cucumbers, vegetable marrows, lettuce, etc. Virus diseases cause distorted, unproductive growth, often marked by yellow or white leaf variegation. As the virus responsible is in the sap, external spraying is valueless. Control measures are sowing clean seed, the prompt cremation of infected crops and stern measures against greenflies, which are virus carriers.

**Damping Off.** Special mention is made of this trouble because it kills so many tomato and other seedlings raised in pots and boxes. The stems of the seedlings shrivel and the little plants collapse and die. Once attacked, seedlings cannot be saved but a sure preventive is to spray the seedlings with Cheshunt Compound fortnightly during their first 6 weeks.

**Pests.** Most of the pests which trouble vegetables (and flowers) can be dealt with either by spraying the attacked plants with insecticides or dusting them with derris, or one of the many proprietary insecticides.

Among the pests which can be dealt with by insecticide spraying are the various "fly" which worry so many crops – the black-fly that attacks broad beans in particular and the green-fly that is found on cabbages and on most other crops. Thrips, the tiny black insects which suck sap from the leaves of tomatoes, peas, beans, etc., and red spider, the minute red mites which bleach the leaves of greenhouse plants, can also be controlled by spraying.

Dusting is effective against such pests as bean and pea weevils, which eat pieces out of the leaves of these plants, turnip flea beetles, or hoppers which riddle the leaves of young turnips and the various caterpillars which appear among the crops.

## CROPS AND THEIR CULTURE

Listed below are the popular vegetable crops with the main points in their culture and the names of reliable varieties:

**Artichoke, Globe.** The immature flower heads of these artichokes are used in summer. Plant globe artichokes in April 3 feet apart in rich, sunny quarters. Divide and replant every fourth year. In November, cut the stems down to about 1 foot above the ground. Draw soil up to the top of these stems as one would earth up potatoes. Then lay a foot of straw on either side of the row, but not over the plants. In March, remove the straw and level the soil, removing the old stems.

**Artichoke, Jerusalem.** Produce tubers similar to potatoes. Plant tubers in February, 5 inches deep, 15 inches apart, in rows 3 feet apart. Reduce the shoots to 3 per plant. Cut down stems when frosted, spread straw over the bed and lift as required.

**Asparagus.** Requires a rich, deeply dug, 3-feet-wide bed. Plant 1-year old crowns in April, 5 inches deep and 15 inches apart. Connover's Colossal is an excellent sort. Cease cutting in late June and allow the beds to fill up with growth. Cut down the growth when it yellows and mulch with 4 inches of stable manure, compost, hop-manure or old mushroom compost.

## THE BEAN FAMILY

**Beans, Broad.** There are two sections, Longpod and Windsor. The former are hardy and early; the latter are less hardy, but better flavour. Sow Longpods from February to April, Windsors from April to June. Set the seeds of both in double row at 6 inches apart in flat-bottomed drills 9 inches wide, 2½ inches deep. To help pod-filling, remove growing points when the flowers fade. For an early crop, sow Sutton's Colossal under cloches in November.

**Beans, Dwarf French.** These are of sub-tropical origin and therefore cannot be sown until mid-May. They like sunny sites and liberal manuring. Sow thrice at three-weekly intervals. Set a double row of seed 6 inches apart in 9-inch-wide, 2-inch-deep drills.

**Beans, Haricot.** These are a section of the dwarf French, grown for the sake of their ripe seed for winter use. Cultivation is similar. *Variety*: Brown Dutch.

**Beans, Runner.** Can be grown in a rich trench in open garden or alongside walls and fences and can be staked or dwarfed by pinching. Set the seed in double row 2 inches deep and 9 inches apart from mid-May to mid-June. Spray the flowers with clear water daily, to encourage a good set of pods. *Variety*: Streamline.

**Beet.** Two sections – round and long. Both are grown for winter and spring use. Sow in April in moderately rich soil. Steep the seed in water for twenty-four hours to accelerate germination.

Sow very thinly in ¾-inch-deep drills, round varieties 6 inches apart, long varieties 12 inches. Thin the round variety to 6 inches, the long to 9 inches. Lift and store in a cool shed in October. For summer salad, sow the round variety in April and May and only thin those seedlings that cause overcrowding. For summer salad Crimson Globe, for winter storage Cheltenham Green-Top (Long) are good varieties.

**Beet, Spinach.** A type of beet grown for leaves alone. Sow in April for summer and autumn use, in July for winter and spring use. It likes rich soil and should be sown in drills ¾ inch deep and 15 inches apart. Thin to 15 inches and, when the plants are leafy, cut judiciously to ensure continued production.

**Beat, Seakale.** A dual-purpose crop. Soft parts of leaves are cooked like spinach, the thick midribs like seakale. Cultivation as for spinach beet.

## THE CABBAGE FAMILY

This is one of the most useful families, providing an all-the-year-round succession of green vegetables. They like rich, firm soil. They are susceptible to club root, a soil-borne disease, against which a 3-year rotation and the free use of lime are safeguards. Except where otherwise stated, the seedlings must have a period in a nursery bed before final planting.

**Broccoli, Heading.** Sow variety Veitch's Self-protecting out of doors in mid-April for autumn use. Final planting distance should be 2 feet. At the end of April, sow Snow's Winter White for winter and Late Queen for spring use. Their planting distance is 2 feet.

**Broccoli, Purple and White Sprouting.** There are early and late varieties of both. Sow the early variety in mid-April, the late at the end April. The final planting distance should be 2½ feet.

**Brussels Sprouts.** Sow the early sort like Cambridge No. 1 in boxes in the greenhouse in February. Prick out the seedlings when big enough to handle. For later use, sow Cambridge No. 5 outdoors late in April. The final planting distance is 2½ feet.

**Cabbage, Spring.** Sow early August and plant finally 18 inches apart. *Varieties:* Harbinger, Offenham and Flower of Spring.

**Cabbage, Summer.** Sow in greenhouse as advised for sprouts. Final planting distance should be 18 inches. *Variety:* Primo.

**Cabbage, Autumn.** Sow late in April out of doors. Final planting distance should be 18 inches apart. *Variety:* Winnigstadt.

**Cabbage, Winter.** Sow late in April out of doors. Final planting distance should be 2 feet. *Variety:* Christmas Drumhead.

**Cauliflower, Summer.** Sow in February as advised for Brussels sprouts. Prick out the seedlings. Final planting distance should be 18 inches. *Variety:* All The Year Round.

**Cauliflower, Autumn.** Sow mid-April out of doors. Final planting distance should be 18 inches. *Variety:* White Heart.

**Colewort.** A small, quick-maturing type of cabbage. Sow in a permanent position in the autumn for the production of "spring greens" or in spring to provide greens for late summer.

**Kales.** All kinds are sown in permanent positions in late April, setting groups of 3 seeds 2 feet apart. Seedlings are thinned to 1 per station. *Varieties:* Curled, Asparagus, Labrador, Thousand-headed, Cottager's and Ragged Jack.

**Savoy, Early.** Sow in mid-April out of doors. Final planting distance should be 18 inches. *Variety:* Ormskirk Early.

**Savoy, Late.** Sow towards the end of April out of doors. Final planting distance should be 18 inches. *Variety:* Ormskirk Late.

**Carrots: Shorthorn and Stump-rooted.** Shorthorn carrots such as Early Horn have blunt, short roots. Stump-rooted kinds, such as Chantenay Red Cored, have slightly longer thinner roots. Both grown for pulling in summer. They may be sown every 3 weeks from early March until mid-July to provide a succession. Make drills ¾ inch deep, 6 inches apart. Sow sparsely and there will be no need to thin the seedlings. It is customary to grow these carrots between rows of permanent crops.

**Intermediate.** The principal maincrop section have roots of medium length and girth. They like rich, but not newly manured soil. Sow mid-March to mid-June – the earlier the better – in drills ¾ inch deep spaced 1 foot apart. Thin the plants to 6 inches and lift in early October, storing the crop in a cool, dry shed or in clamps. *Varieties:* James' Intermediate and St Valery.

**Long.** A maincrop section with long handsome roots. It will succeed only where the soil is good and deep. Sow as intermediate, but make the drills 15 inches apart and thin the plants to nine inches. *Variety:* Long and Red Surrey.

**Celery.** Grown in 18-inches-wide, richly-manured trenches. If the plants are to be home-raised, sow white celery in February, red in March, both in a greenhouse. Prick out the seedlings. Plant white celery in May, red in June, both in a double row 9 inches apart. Water copiously and from early August earth up gradually to blanch the stems.

**Celeriac.** Turnip-rooted celery. It is sown as for white celery but is not planted in trenches. Set the plants on flat ground, a foot apart in mid-May and, as growth develops, rub off side-shoots. Lift and store at the end of October.

**Chicory.** It is eaten usually as white salad, but it can be cooked as a green vegetable. Roots are planted in November or seed is sown in May in drills, 1 foot apart. The roots are lifted for forcing from late November.

**Corn Salad or Lamb's Lettuce.** Comes in very useful when ordinary lettuce are scarce. Sow, preferably in dry soil, in spring and through summer if a regular supply is required. Make drills ¾ inch deep, 6 inches apart. Thin to 6 inches apart.

**Cress.** See Mustard and Cress.

**Cucumber.** Cucumbers may be grown in a heated greenhouse, a cold greenhouse or in a cold frame. There are varieties which can be grown in the open if the plants, raised under glass, are planted out at the end of May. Greenhouse cucumbers may be sown separately in 3-inch pots from January to July. Plant the seedlings in mounds of rich soil. Stop bearing shoots two leaves beyond fruit, non-bearers above fifth leaf. Water the plants freely, feed liberally and shade from bright sun. Telegraph is a good greenhouse cucumber. Ridge, or semi-hardy cucumbers are sown, as advised, in a greenhouse in mid-April and planted 3 feet apart out of doors in rich mounds in late May. No stopping is required, but the plants must be fed liberally and watered in dry weather.

**Endive.** A lettuce-like salad. There are two sections, curled and round-leaved. Both like rich soil. Sow the curled every 3 weeks from mid-April to the end of July in 1-inch-deep drills at 1 foot apart. Thin seedlings to a similar distance and blanch fully developed plants by tying them and covering them with dry leaves or a flower-pot. Sow round-leaved endive in late July and late August. Treat them similarly. In cold districts, lift fully matured plants and blanch them in cold frames.

**Garlic.** Useful for soup and flavouring. Set the bulbs in March, 9 inches apart and 3 inches deep in rich soil. Lift them in August, ripen well and store in a dry cool place.

**Horseradish.** Plant roots 1 foot apart early in the year. Lift them in autumn and store the crop under cover in sand. Make a fresh bed from some of the lifted roots. Treating horseradish as an "annual" crop like this prevents it spreading unduly and keeps the roots full-flavoured.

**Kohl Rabi.** Turnip-like roots with a very attractive flavour. They may be sown any time between April and August in a bed for transplanting or in a permanent position. Thin them to 9 inches. Use the roots when they are about the size of a tennis-ball; they lose flavour when left to grow larger.

**Leeks.** Best to grow an early and late batch, sowing the former in heat in February and planting out in May, the latter out of doors in June. It is customary to plant early leeks in 18-inch-wide trenches, the later batch on the flat. Feed generously during the growing period and blanch the stems by earthing up or protecting with paper collars. Musselburgh is a good early leek. The Lyon is ideal for succession.

**Lettuce.** There are two sections – cabbage and cos, and here is the cultural programme:

**Summer Cabbage.** Sow in well-worked, fairly rich soil fortnightly from mid-March to mid-July in ½-inch-deep drills, spaced 6 to 12 inches apart, according to the variety. Thin to these distances, also according to the variety, and when plants are half grown, water in around each a level tablespoonful of sulphate of ammonia. *Varieties:* Trocadero and All The Year Round.

**Winter Cabbage.** Sow early in August in fairly rich soil and when the seedlings are big enough to handle, transplant them 12 inches apart into fairly rich beds. Hoe regularly during winter. *Varieties:* Arctic King and Winter Crop.

**Greenhouse Lettuce.** Sow every 3 weeks from mid-September to the end of January in boxes. When the seedlings are big enough to handle, transplant them 7 inches apart into forked, firmed, vacated tomato border, or at a similar distance in 4-inch-deep boxes. Maintain a temperature of 45–50 degs. F., provide abundant light and ventilate carefully. *Varieties:* Cheshunt Early Giant and Cheshunt 5B.

**Summer Cos.** Sow monthly in rich soil from mid-April to mid-June in ¼-inch-deep drills 12 inches apart, to which distance the seedlings should be thinned. Blanch the mature heads for a fortnight before cutting them by binding them loosely with moist raffia. *Varieties:* Lobjoit's Green and Sugar Cos.

**Winter Cos.** Sow in early August and treat as advised for summer cos. It may be necessary to transplant the heads to a cold frame to blanch them. *Variety:* Winter Density.

**Mint.** Spearmint is the best type of this popular herb. It likes a cool, semi-shaded, fairly rich bed. Plant the roots 2 inches apart and 2 inches deep from November to February and mulch with manure each autumn. Replant every fifth year.

**Mustard and Cress.** Grow in pots or boxes in a greenhouse or frame, or even on the kitchen window-sill. Sow the seeds thickly and press them into the soil – do not cover over. To have the mustard and the cress ready for cutting at the same time, sow the cress 4 days before the mustard. Small weekly sowings will ensure a regular supply of fresh young salad.

**Onions.** Where a greenhouse is available sowings are made, in boxes, in January or February, the seedlings going into the outdoor garden in late March. Outdoor sowings are made in March, in drills only ¼-inch deep (burying seeds deeper causes the bulbs to become thick-necked) and 12 inches apart. Seedlings are thinned as they become large enough for use as "spring" onions, until they stand 6 inches or so apart. The main needs of onions are rich, well-drained soil and a really sunny situation. An easier way is to plant onions "sets" – small bulbs – 6 inches apart in rows 1 foot apart in March. Just press the "sets" into the soil.

**Parsley.** This herb can be produced for winter or summer use. Sow for winter in June, for summer in April. Make drills 6 inches apart and thin to this distance. Provide rich, firm, limy soil. Place a cloche or two over some of the plants to be sure of plenty of leaves in winter.

**Parsnips.** The soil should be as for maincrop carrots. Drills ¾ inch deep, 12 inches apart. Tnin the plants to 9 inches apart. Leave the roots in the ground and lift in winter as required. *Variety:* Offenham.

**Peas.** A succession is assured by sowing fortnightly from early March until early June in 6-inch-wide, flat-bottomed drills. Space the seeds 3 inches apart, protect from birds and support the crops with stakes or netting. Excellent first earlies (March sowing) are Peter Pan and Feltham First, second earlies (April sowing) Early Onward and Kelvedon Monarch, and maincrops (remainder of season) Onward and Autocrat.

**Potatoes.** There are three sections – first early, second early and maincrop. Soil for all of these must be worked to prime condition. Plant first early at the end of March, second early and maincrop early in April. The drills should be 9 inches deep and the spacing as follows: first early drills 24 inches, the tubers in them 12 inches; second early drills 28 inches apart, the tubers 14 inches apart; maincrop drills 30 inches, tubers 15 inches apart. Spread a 4-inch layer of manure or compost at bottom of the drills and plant the tubers on this. Earth all the sections as growth develops. Lift the first earlies from the ground when the haulm yellows. Lift the other sections at a similar stage and store in a dark, airy, frost-proof place. *Varieties of merit:* first early Arran Pilot, second early Great Scot, maincrop Majestic.

**Pumpkins.** Grown in the same way as vegetable marrows (see Vegetable Marrows).

**Radish.** Sow broadcast every 10 days from early March to the end of July in fairly rich, well-forked ground and thin the seedlings to 2 inches apart. French Breakfast is a good sort for the early

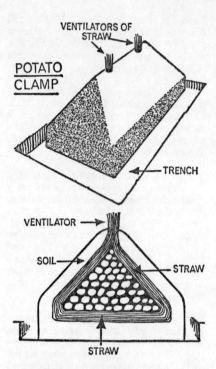

POTATO
CLAMP

VENTILATORS OF
STRAW

TRENCH

VENTILATOR

SOIL

STRAW

STRAW

in spring, will provide an adequate supply for the average household. Set the roots a foot apart.

**Salsify.** Parsnip-like root with a distinctive flavour. Sow in April or May and treat in the same way as parsnips. The roots are ready about October.

**Scorzonera.** Produces long roots which are used like carrots. Sow in March in a $\frac{1}{2}$-inch-deep drill and thin to 10 inches apart. The roots are ready in November and can be left in ground until required.

**Seakale.** A popular winter vegetable. Plant 2 feet apart in rich soil. If a warm dark shed is available, lift the roots in autumn and at fortnightly intervals until February, plant at 5 inches apart in a soil bed. Water carefully and cut when the stems are 10 inches long. Alternatively, the roots may be planted in boxes and placed in a warm cupboard in the house, under the kitchen sink for example. If watered regularly, they will provide succulent stems in about 3 weeks. In the absence of indoor forcing facilities, cover the roots with inverted boxes in January, surround them with littery manure and an excellent crop will develop.

**Shallots.** Plant them in November or from February to March in rich, deeply dug soil. "Screw" the bulbs into the soil 6 inches apart, leaving just the tips above ground. As the bulbs mature, scrape away soil until they are almost completely exposed for the sun to dry them. After lifting, lay out the bulbs in the sun until completely dry.

**Spinach.** To maintain supplies of this health-giving crop, sow summer or round spinach every few weeks from January to June; sow winter or prickly spinach in autumn. Early sowings should be made on a sheltered border, the later sowing in a semi-shaded situation.

**Swedes.** Culture is as for winter turnips.

**Sweet Corn** or *Maize.* Grown for its tasty cobs. Plants are raised from seed sown in boxes in April, in the green-

sowings, Sparkler for the later ones. There is a large-rooted winter section. Sow these in July in 6-inch-deep drills and thin to this distance. Store with other root crops in October. *Winter varieties:* China Rose and Black Spanish.

**Rhubarb.** Plant between November and March in deeply dug, rich ground, setting the roots 3 feet apart and 2 inches deep. Mulch every autumn with manure or compost, forking in the residue in spring. Divide and replant every fourth year.

Rhubarb can be forced in dark warm sheds or beneath greenhouse staging from November to February, about 6 weeks elapsing between planting and gathering. Expose lifted roots to weather for a fortnight before planting close together in a soil bed. Water copiously. When crops have been gathered, replant the roots out of doors.

**Sage.** 2 or 3 roots, bought and planted

house, or from outdoor sowings in May. Box plants are set out in late May or June.

**Thyme.** Set a few plants of this useful evergreen herb in limy soil in spring. Plant them 6 inches apart.

**Tomatoes.** This increasingly important food crop can be cultivated in the greenhouse or out of doors. For greenhouse crops, sow in January to May and plant in the fruiting quarters 9 or 10 weeks later at 18 inches apart. Remove side shoots regularly and feed generously after the fruits on the bottom truss are the size of walnuts. From the end of May artificial heat is unnecessary, but until then it must be used to maintain a temperature of 55 degs.F. Moneymaker and Ailsa Craig are excellent greenhouse kinds. Sow in the greenhouse at the end of March for planting out of doors, 18 inches apart, in early June, or buy sturdy plants for setting out then. The site should be rich and sunny. Stop the plants the second week in August and concentrate on finishing the fruit already set. *Varieties:* Harbinger and Market King.

**Turnips.** There are summer and winter sections, the former being short-season crops sown in ¾-inch-deep drills, 6 inches apart, every 3 weeks from mid-March to early June. Thin the seedlings to 6 inches apart. Snowball is a good variety. Winter turnips should be sown in June in ¾-inch-deep drills, 12 inches apart. Thin the plants to 12 inches and store in a cool, dry place after the weather becomes severe. Manchester Market is the accepted sort. Grow swedes in the same manner as winter turnips.

**Vegetable Marrows.** There are two well-defined sections, bush and trailing. Both are sub-tropical and, for that reason, are safe out of doors only from May to September. Early crops may be obtained by sowing in the greenhouse at the end of March and planting in the open in late May. For succession, sow out of doors at the end of May. Space bush kinds 3 feet apart, trailers 4 feet apart, both in sunny mounds of rich soil. Bush kinds require no stopping, but trailers should be stopped above the fifth leaf and the laterals and sub-laterals two leaves beyond the fruit. *Varieties:* bush – Green Bush and White Bush; trailers – Long White and Long Green.

## FRUIT

There is a steady increase of interest in garden fruit growing. Gardeners are finding that the smaller types of apple and other trees – the bushes and cordons – will bear generously without taking up too much space. A few soft fruits, such as currants and raspberries, can be fitted in even a small garden, while loganberries and cultivated blackberries can be grown against any piece of bare fence.

**Fruit Planting Season.** This extends from early November until early April – the earlier the better, so that the trees have a chance to become established before the hot season starts. They must not be planted when the ground is frosty. If they arrive during a hard spell, they should be placed in a shed or sheltered corner of the garden with sacking over their roots. Better still, they may be "heeled-in", that is, placed in a trench so that their roots are covered with soil, if the ground is not frozen to any great depth.

Before planting, any broken roots should be trimmed back and any branches injured in transit should also be trimmed. Deep planting should be avoided; the soil mark on the stem showing the depth at which the tree was growing in the nursery is a good guide.

Each planting hole should be large enough to allow the roots to spread out naturally. Where a supporting stake is required, this should be driven in before the roots are covered over, to avoid the root damage which might occur in staking later.

Fine soil should be used for filling in, over and around the roots. Lifting the tree up and down slightly now and again as the hole is being filled in helps the fine

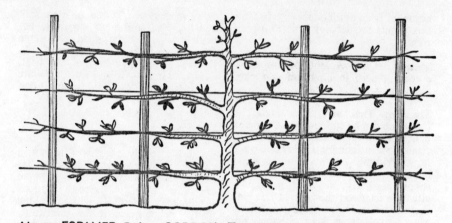

Above: ESPALIER. Below: CORDON. Two methods of training apple and pear trees

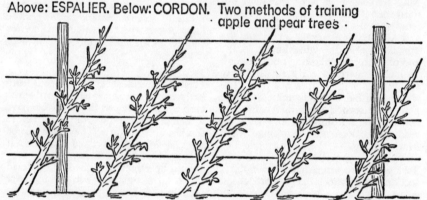

soil to work among the roots and prevents any cavities being left.

With the roots covered, the rest of the dug-out soil can be returned, each spadeful or so being trodden down firmly. Unless the soil is very poor, no manure should be worked in at planting time. The final operation is to tie the tree to its stake.

## TYPES OF TREE

**Bush.** Tree with short stem of only a foot or so, from which the branches spring.

**Cordon.** The single cordon consists of one stem furnished with fruiting spurs but with no side branches. There are also double and triple cordons. Cordons are planted upright or obliquely.

**Espalier.** Consists of a main stem with branches trained out horizontally on either side, about one foot apart.

**Fan-trained.** Trees whose branches are trained out, like the ribs of a fan, from a central stem. They are grown against a wall or fence.

**Pyramid.** A pyramid tree is one with a main stem, the branches of which are so trained as to give the tree the shape indicated by the name.

**Standards and Half-standards.** A standard is a big tree with a trunk of at least 6 feet before branching starts. A half standard is similar, except that its trunk is about 4 feet high before branching.

Bushes, as already indicated, are most

suitable for medium-sized and small gardens. Cordons likewise take up small space. They are normally grown against wires stretched between upright stakes. Espaliers are also grown against wires or against walls or fences. Apples and pears are the chief fruits grown in this form. Fan-trained trees are the type most suitable for plums, cherries, peaches and nectarines, apricots and figs when grown against house walls or fences.

Pyramids are not grown very often now, though plums and cherries in this form are occasionally seen. Standards are suitable only for orchards and the largest gardens. Half standards also require considerable space and are suitable only for good-sized gardens.

**Planting Distances.** Large bushes of apples, pears, plums and so on, should be planted about 12 feet apart, smaller bushes at 8 to 10 feet; single cordons at 2 feet, other cordons at 4 feet; espaliers at 12 feet apart, fan-trained at 15 feet; pyramids at 15 feet; half standards at 16 feet, and standards at 20 feet.

Currants and gooseberry bushes should be 5 feet apart, the same fruits in cordon form at 18 inches. Raspberries are set 2 feet apart, with 5 feet between rows, where two or more are planted. Loganberries and blackberries grown against a fence on trellis should be planted 10 feet apart.

## CULTURAL DETAILS

Following are the main points in the culture of the most popular fruits:

**Apple.** Standards and half standards require no pruning beyond removal of weak, dead and overcrowded growth and the weaker of each two crossing branches. For the first 2 or 3 years after planting, shorten the main branches of bush trees $\frac{1}{3}$ of way back and side-shoots to within 2 buds from their base. Prune cordons and espaliers by shortening side-shoots in a similar way. After second or third year, side-shoot or spur pruning is advisable for weak-growing bush apples, but judicious branch thinning is best for vigorous kinds. Prune after leaf-fall but not during frost.

Apple trees in full bearing should be fed each March with a good balanced fertiliser.

Keeping varieties should be stored in a cool, airy place up to 6 layers deep. The fewer the layers, however, the better. Gather without bruising and with the footstalk attached, when fruit separates easily from tree. Choose a dry day.

To keep down pests, trees should be grease-banded each October, to catch wingless females of winter moths, which are responsible for leaf-eating caterpillar attacks in spring, and be sprayed with a $7\frac{1}{2}$ per cent solution of tar oil wash in December or early January, to destroy eggs of greenflies, apple suckers and capsid bugs. Spray with a good proprietary spray in early June as safeguard against attack.

To control diseases, spray with lime sulphur solution (1 part in 30 parts of water) in December, and again with lime sulphur solution (1 part in 60 parts of water) at the pink bud stage, and immediately the petals fall, as a preventive of apple scab disease and brown rot.

*Varieties:* Culinary – Early Victoria, Lord Derby, Bramley's Seedling, Newton Wonder.

Dessert – Worcester Pearmain, Charles Ross, Laxton's Superb, King's Acre Pippin.

**Apricot.** This delicious stone fruit requires a limy soil and a warm, sunny wall. Is usually grown as a fan-trained tree. Fruits mostly on young wood, hence pruning consists of cutting out fruited wood as soon as fruit is gathered. *Variety:* Moor Park.

**Berries.** There are a number of berries (mainly hybrids or crosses) such as the Boysenberry, Laxtonberry, Lowberry, Newberry, Phenomenal Berry, Veitchberry and Young Berry. The culture of all these is, in general, the same as for the Loganberry.

**Blackberry.** Likes deep, fertile moist soil. Besides being grown against fences, it may also be trained to stake in the open. Prune after fruit is gathered, cutting off fruited branches at soil level.

Mulch heavily each autumn. *Varieties*: Himalaya Giant, and Merton Thornless.

**Cherry.** Likes a warm, loamy soil, preferably on limestone or ragstone. It is more suitable for growth in districts of low than of high rainfall, in which the trees make gross growth and the fruit is liable to crack.

Bush trees should be cut back in the second and third year as advised for bush apples, but afterwards very little pruning is necessary, or indeed advisable. It results in gumming, which is usually the beginning of the end. If the trees become overcrowded, thin the branches while they are in full leaf. This is a safeguard against gumming.

The most serious insect pest is blackfly, which can be controlled by tar oil spraying in December.

The worst disease is silver leaf, due to a fungus which induces the silvering of the leaves and ultimately the death of the tree. Where action is taken in time, the disease can be mastered by cutting out infected branches, making the cut immediately below the point at which a brown wood stain ends.

*Varieties:* Sweet – Early Rivers, May Duke, Black Eagle, Governor Wood, and Napoleon; Cooking – Morello and Kentish Red.

**Currant, Black.** Bears crop on one-year-old wood, hence pruning consists of eliminating a good proportion of the fruited wood immediately the crop is gathered. Fruited branches should be cut back to just above the point at which strong young shoots arise. After planting, shorten shoots to within 6 inches of soil level. There will be no crop in first year, but sacrifice must be made in interest of constitutional vigour. Mulch heavily with manure, preferably pig manure, each autumn after leaf-fall.

*Varieties:* Boskoop Giant and Seabrook's Black.

Black currants are attacked by a big bud mite, which causes buds to swell and lose fruiting capacity. After leaf-fall, hand pick and burn any infested buds and when the leaves are about the size of a florin, spray with lime sulphate solution (1 part in 20 parts water) to kill migrating mites. Reversion, a virus disease, may also be troublesome. Reversion makes the leaves become much contracted. Infection can be overcome by cutting out and burning infected shoots.

**Currants, Red and White.** Both like rich soil and a sunny situation. Red and white currants are spur bearers, hence pruning consists in shortening sideshoots to within 5 leaves from their base in July and still further shortening the shoots to within 2 buds from their base after leaf fall. Mulch with manure or compost each autumn.

*Varieties:* Red, Red Dutch, Fay's Prolific, Perfection; White, White Grape, White Versailles.

**Damson.** One of the hardiest of fruits. Grown as standard or half-standard and successful in all soils. No pruning is required, save the removal of overcrowded wood, which should be done while the trees are in leaf.

**Fig.** May be grown in a cool greenhouse or alongside a sunny, sheltered wall out of doors. It is liable to become too rampant unless its roots are enclosed in a 3-foot-square, 2-foot-deep brick chamber with occasional weep or waterholes to allow for drainage. Plant in loamy, limy compost. Prune most guardedly, removing shoots which have fruited as soon as the fruit is gathered, and thinning overcrowded branches in March.

*Varieties:* Brown Turkey, St John's and Negro Largo.

**Gooseberry.** May be grown as a bush, standard or cordon. Provide a sunny situation and rich, deeply worked soil.

Pruning may be done in two ways – by thinning overcrowded branches, taking care to keep the centre open, and by spur pruning, which involves shortening the side shoots to within 5 leaves from their base in July, and still further shortening these shoots to within 2 buds from their base after leaf-fall.

Excellent varieties are: Whitesmith,

Golden Drop, Langley Gage, Careless, Leveller, Speedwell.

The most serious disease is American gooseberry mildew, which attacks young growing shoots, spreading to the fruit, which it covers in a mass of brownish white down. The remedy is to spray with Karathane and cut off and burn distorted shoots in winter.

The most destructive insect foe, the brightly coloured caterpillars of the gooseberry sawfly, can be destroyed by dusting with DDT powder.

**Greengage.** Closely related to the plum, its culture is the same in all details.

**Loganberry.** Requires rich soil and succeeds alongside sunny or partially shaded walls and fences, or post and wire supports. Prune immediately after fruiting, cutting off at ground level branches that have fruited.

**Medlar.** Succeeds best in a somewhat moist soil. After the tree has been shaped, by pruning in the manner suggested for young apples, only dead diseased and weak wood need be removed. *Varieties:* Nottingham and Dutch.

**Melon.** Normally grown in greenhouses or in frames, or under cloches. Hero of Lockinge is a good variety to grow in a greenhouse.

Plants are raised from seed sown in heat in April and the seedlings are set out in their fruiting quarters in May.

*Varieties:* for frame or cloche culture – Charentais or Sweetie.

**Mulberry.** Does well in the open in the south, but in the north it needs the protection of a south wall, against which it should be trained. Very little pruning is required, only the removal of dead and diseased wood and growths which overcrowd any part of the tree.

**Nectarine.** Grown as fan-trained tree in a greenhouse, or in a favoured district against a sunny, sheltered wall or fence. Whether inside or out, the border should be circumscribed by bricks, otherwise roots may enter uncongenial subsoil and produce nothing but leaves. The border should be 3 feet wide, 2 feet deep, filled with rich, loamy soil containing a good sprinkling of lime rubble. Top-dress border in alternate winters, removing, before doing so, as much of top soil as can be taken off without injuring roots. Nectarines bear on one-year-old wood, hence pruning consists in maintaining an ample supply of this without allowing overcrowding.

Operation is progressive. It begins in spring, when the fore-right and fore-aft shoots are rubbed off. Later, young shoots on one-year-old shoots are reduced in numbers. Usually one young shoot is left at the tip of an old shoot and one near the base. After the fruit has been gathered, cut back the one-year-old shoot to immediately above the point at which the basal young shoot arises. Thin the fruit to 9 inches apart after stoning. Water copiously during growing season and syringe with clear water twice a day until fruit starts to ripen.

Silver-leaf is the most serious disease and should be controlled as advised for cherry.

*Varieties:* Early Rivers, and Lord Napier.

**Peach.** As for nectarine, with exception of varieties, which are Hale's Early, Dymond and Barrington.

**Pear.** Succeeds best in warm districts, though it can be grown in all districts if sheltered situation is available. Culture generally is as for apples.

*Varieties:* Dessert – Dr Jules Guyot, Williams' Bon Chrétien, Conference, Doyenne du Comice, Winter Nelis. Culinary – Catillac and Uvedale's St Germain.

**Plum.** Culture is as for cherry. Plums are, however, severely attacked by greenfly and the caterpillars of the various winter moths. The latter can be controlled by grease-banding in October and the former by spraying with tar oil wash in December or January. Summer spraying with derris or malathion may be necessary.

*Varieties:* Culinary – Rivers' Prolific,

Czar, Victoria, Pond's Seedling, Monarch. Dessert – Greengage, Early Transparent, Late Transparent, Jefferson's, Coe's Golden Drop.

**Raspberry.** Must be grown in rich soil and prefers sun, though will succeed in partial shade. Support the canes with posts and wires fixed before planting. Immediately after planting cut down canes to within 6 inches of soil level. After each crop is gathered, cut out the fruited canes. During growing season, reduce number of suckers to 6 per plant, to prevent overcrowding. Mulch each autumn with stable manure or compost. The average life of a bed is 12 years. Raspberries are frequently infested by grubs of the raspberry and loganberry beetle. Crops can be safeguarded from attack by dusting 3 times with derris powder – when the canes are in bud, full flower, and as soon as the petals fall. Virus disease is also a serious enemy. Its symptoms are yellow leaf variegation and stunted growth. Cutting out affected canes is sometimes remedial. If the disease is serious, the stock must be destroyed.
*Varieties:* Lloyd George, Norfolk Giant, or Malling Jewel.

**Strawberry.** The soil should be loamy, rich and firm. Plant in September or October or March at 14 inches apart in rows 24 inches apart. Place straw round the fruits as soon as they are set, to prevent soil splashing and cover with nets before colouring to exclude birds. After fruiting, cut off old leaves and lightly fork into the bed a dressing of equal parts superphosphate and muriate of potash at 2 ounces per square yard.

To increase the stock, if the plants are healthy, spread a layer of peat an inch or so deep around the plants and allow the first plantlet on each runner to root into the peat. When rooted, detach the plantlet from the parent plant and transplant to its permanent position. The life of a bed is 3 years. A batch of young plants should be brought forward each year to replace the 3-year-olds.

The crop is liable to be attacked by virus disease. There is no remedy for virus disease, which is less likely to attack if healthy plants are used as parents of young stock. Also, keep the plants free from aphis, which spread virus disease from plant to plant, by regular spraying.
*Varieties:* Royal Sovereign, Red Gauntlet, Cambridge Vigour.

**Walls.** Walls and fences, so often neglected, can be made into delightful features in the garden. There are only four plants in common use which will cling on to walls by themselves – Ivy, Virginia creeper, *Hydrangea petiolaris*, and *Schizophragma hydrangeoides*. But if one is prepared to affix wires, or square-meshed plastic-covered wire panels to the wall, a host of delightful plants may be grown with little trouble. Climbing roses, honeysuckles, clematis, the Russian vine, wistarias – all these and many more will clothe a wall in a year or two. Then there are many shrubs that like to grow against a wall and need no support – camellias, rosemary, Japanese quince, ceanothus, cotoneasters, or a fig tree.

**Weeds.** In recent years, chemists have come to the aid of the gardener in the control of weeds. On paths and drives simazine in one of the proprietary formulations, applied in February, will keep the area free of weeds for the rest of the year.

There are garden herbicides which will keep clean ground clean. They may be watered on the ground around the herbaceous plants, under roses or shrubs, and they will effectively stop all growth of annual weeds without harming the plants. Then there is paraquat which is remarkable because it works through the green matter, the chlorophyll in the leaves of the weeds. It does not affect the soil at all. So it can be used to kill weeds under shrubs, under roses, in beds of raspberries or black currants, under hedges and in many other places.

## GARDEN CALENDAR

**January.** Dig vacant vegetable ground. Plant rhubarb, seakale and asparagus in forcing quarters. Sow onions in a heated greenhouse. Repair defective lawns and paths. Dig, manure vacant borders, fork the shrubbery, trim shrubs. Spray all kinds of fruit trees with tar oil wash. Complete pruning.

**February.** Sow parsnips and long-pod broad beans. Plant shallots and Jerusalem artichokes. Sow tomatoes, celery, leeks, cauliflowers, cabbage, and Brussels sprouts in a heated greenhouse. Sprout seed potatoes. Plant roses, herbaceous plants, trees and shrubs. Sow primulas, gloxinias and tuberous begonias in heat. Insert outdoor flowering chrysanthemum cuttings. Roll and feed the lawn. Cut back overgrown privet hedges. Plant all kinds of fruit trees. Spray apple, pear, plum, and cherry trees with DNC washes. Fork between fruit trees in arable soil.

**March.** Sow early peas, turnips, radishes, lettuce, spinach, carrots, onions; plant early potatoes, rhubarb, mint, sage and thyme. Fork previously dug land. Fork in the residue of asparagus mulch. Fork between developing herbaceous plants. Sow sweet peas; plant gladioli and montbretias. Sow, in heat, asters, stocks, nemesias, *Phlox drummondii*, golden feather, lobelia, alyssum and ageratum. Start vines into growth. Prune gooseberries. Shorten raspberry canes to 5 feet. Give a balanced fertiliser to all kinds of fruit trees.

**April.** Sow peas, Windsor broad beans, salad beet; plant early and maincrop potatoes, Jerusalem artichokes, seakale, asparagus, cabbages and cauliflowers. In heat, sow cucumbers, melons, vegetable marrows, and plant tomatoes in their final quarters. Hoe between young crops. Sow all kinds of hardy annuals. Plant or sow sweet peas. Plant evergreen shrubs. Start mowing lawn. Hoe between wallflowers and other spring flowering plants. Sow polyanthuses and primroses. Plant vacant pockets in rockery. Protect crops from birds. Give potash dressing to strawberries. Spray caterpillar-infested apple, pear, plum, and cherry trees with a derris or DDT spray. Remove superfluous shoots from peaches and nectarines.

**May.** Sow peas, French and haricot beans, shorthorn carrots, turnips, maincrop beet, vegetable marrows, and all kinds of winter greens. Plant celery, celeriac, leeks, and Brussels sprouts. Earth early potatoes and broad beans. Stake peas. Cut and feed asparagus. In heat, plant cucumbers and melons. Plant tomatoes in cold house. Sow wallflowers, Canterbury bells, sweet Williams, Iceland poppies, aquilegias, evening primroses and herbaceous plants. Destroy lawn weeds by watering with a selective weedkiller. Prune holly and other evergreen hedges. Harden off bedding plants in cold frames. Plant outdoor-flowering chrysanthemums, penstemons, calceolarias, and violas. Destroy gooseberry caterpillars with DDT powder. Lay straw round strawberries. Reduce raspberry suckers to 6 per plant. Stop vines and thin peaches and nectarines to 9 inches apart.

**June.** Plant outdoor tomatoes, vegetable marrows and ridge cucumbers. Sow peas, runner beans, cos lettuce, curled endive, swedes, hoe between all crops and mulch where necessary. Keep all pests and diseases under control. Thin crops that need it. Plant dahlias and summer bedding subjects. Side-shoot sweet peas. Thin the hardy annuals. Feed roses. Prune forsythias, flowering currants and kerrias. Net the strawberries.

**July.** Plant all kinds of winter greens. Stop broad beans that have finished flowering. Sow French beans, winter spinach, winter parsley. Earth the second early and maincrop potatoes. Feed greenhouse tomatoes. Cease cutting asparagus. Pot chrysanthemums into final pots. Sow cyclamen. Layer border carnations. Feed the lawn. Clip hedges. Apply weedkiller to paths. Summer prune bush apples, pears, and red currants. Plant strawberry runners if large enough.

**August.** Sow spring cabbages, onions, winter spinach, Labrador kale. Feed developing crops. Hoe, mulch and water as necessary. Remove flower stems from rhubarb. Stop outdoor tomatoes. Pollinate female vegetable marrow blooms.

Remove all dead flowers. Stake and re-stake as necessary. Plant snowdrops, crocuses, grape hyacinths, scillas, *Amaryllis belladonna*. Prune raspberries, loganberries, black currants. Gather early apples and pears.

**September.** Sow winter lettuce. Lift and store onions. Earth and feed celery and leeks. Stake tall asparagus. Plant late kales. Insert geranium, calceolaria, fuchsia, heliotrope, viola, and pansy cuttings. Plant Spanish, Dutch, and English varieties of iris and *Scilla hispanica*. Clip hedges. Prune rambler roses, philadelphuses, diervillas, deutzias, lilacs. Sow new lawns. Cut down spent herbaceous plants. Gather and store apples and pears as ready. Cut damaged branches out of plums and cherries. Prune blackberries and Boysenberries.

**October.** Lift and store potatoes and other root crops. Plant spring and red cabbage. Ripen green tomatoes indoors. Earth celery and leeks. Clear spent crops. Make a compost heap. Plant daffodils, tulips, hyacinths, wallflowers, and other spring-flowering plants. Cease mowing lawn. House chrysanthemums, cyclamen, and primulas. Protect outdoor chrysanthemums from weather. After first frost, lift dahlias and outdoor chrysanthemums and place in greenhouse. Grease-band apple, pear, plum, and cherry trees. Gather and store fruit. Hand-pick and burn swollen black currant buds.

**November.** Clear spent crops and make compost. Complete lifting and storing root crops. Lime ground that needs it. Lift rhubarb roots for early forcing. Bundle and store pea and bean sticks. Obtain stable manure for winter digging. Plant herbaceous borders, roses, trees, and shrubs. Mulch established rose beds and herbaceous borders. Sweep and store leaves. Disbud late chrysanthemums. Lift and store dahlias. Prune and plant all kinds of fruit trees. See that stakes are sound and ties safe.

**December.** Dig and manure vacant ground. Earth up winter greens. Plant rhubarb, seakale and chicory in forcing quarters. Clear finished tomatoes and cucumbers. Feed cyclamen and primulas. Plant resting begonia tubers in boxes of leaf-mould and sand or peat. Dig dahlia and chrysanthemum borders. Bring bulbs into greenhouse for forcing. Spray fruit trees with tar oil washes. Examine grease-bands. Plant all kinds of fruit trees. Continue pruning.

## SHRUBS AND TREES FOR EFFECT IN GARDEN DESIGNS

In *Flower Growing for Flower Arrangement*, the authors, Arno and Irene Nehrling, give the following advice: Choose shrubs and trees first, for they are the background of every garden. Only specimen shrubs should be planted singly – the others are more effective in groups of three or five.

Filler shrubs are the quieter types used between accent plants and include such types as Chaenomeles (Japanese Quince), Cotoneaster, ground cover plants (like Pachysandra or Vinca), Ilex (dwarf hollies), Leucothoe, Spiraea thunbergii and Viburnum burkwoodii.

Accent shrubs for contrast include the colourful evergreen Azaleas, Enkianthus with its outstanding autumn foliage, Kalmia (Mountain Laurel), Pyracantha with its showy orange-red berries and the upright Taxus (dark green of the yews offers wonderful contrast to the silvery-grey of dwarf junipers).

Excellent hedge shrubs include Buxus (Box), Deutzia gracilis, Chaenomeles (Japanese Quince), Euonymus alatus compactus, Forsythia, Berberis, especially B. thunbergii, Junipers (dwarf), Lonicera (Bush honeysuckle), Philadelphus (Mock-Orange), Pyracantha, Rosa hugonis and R. rugosa (for the seashore), Spiraea in variety, Syringa (Lilac), upright Taxus group (Yews) and Viburnum in variety. Crataegus (some of the Hawthorns, especially oxyacantha), Acer campestre (Hedge Maple) and Acer ginnala (Amur Maple) are good trees for hedges.

There are many excellent specimen plants for dramatic effect such as the birch with its outstanding bark, the flowering cherries, crab-apples, dogwoods and magnolias and rhododendrons.

## ANNUALS AND PERENNIALS IN THE GARDEN

Do not plant only one annual, perennial, or bulb, use at least 5 plants, enough to make a distinctive mass of colour. Repeat the mass at intervals the length of the border. In between the masses, use flowers with complementary hues, or if you want a one-colour garden, use lighter or darker values of the same shade. Be sure to have contrasting forms and lines for accent and interest, not only in the garden, but also later for adding variety to flower arrangements.

## SPIKE FORMS

Select for height, line and accent interest in border and floral arrangement.

Campanula, Canterbury Bell
Canna
Celosia (Plume), Cockscomb
Clarkia
Delphinium, Larkspur
Digitalis, Foxglove
Gladiolus
Hollyhock
Kniphofia, Torch Lily (usually offered as Tritoma)
Lathyrus odoratus, Sweet Pea (if long stemmed)
Lavandula officinalis, Lavender
Lupinus polyphyllus, Lupin
Pentstemon, Beard Tongue
Physostegia virginiana, False Dragonhead
Polianthes tuberosa, Tuberose
Salvia, Sage
Snapdragon
Stock
Thermopsis
Veronica, Speedwell

## ROUND FORMS

Select them for centre of interest.
Anemone
Aster, Michaelmas Daisy
Calendula officinalis, Pot Marigold
Centaurea cyanus, Cornflower
Chrysanthemum, annual and perennial
Chrysanthemum coccineam, Pyrethrum (Painted Daisy)
Chrysanthemum maximum, Shasta Daisy

Coreopsis, Calliopsis
Cosmos
Daffodil
Dahlia
Dianthus barbatus, Sweet William
Dianthus chinensis, Garden Pinks
Felicia
Gaillardia
Geum, Avens
Helianthus, Sunflower
Hemerocallis
Ipomoea purpurea, Morning Glory
Lathyrus odoratus, Sweet Pea (short stemmed)
Paeonia, Peony
Papavar, Poppy
Pelargonium, Geranium
Petunia
Phlox
Ranunculus, Buttercup
Rosa, Rose
Salpiglossis
Scabiosa
Stokesia
Tagetes, Marigold
Tithonia
Trachymene caerulea, Blue Lace Flower
Tropaeolum, Nasturtium
Zinnia

## TRAILERS OR CLIMBERS

To relieve severe lines, obscure undesirable objects, cover high walls and to blend architectural masses into the garden picture. Equally useful for graceful and softening effects in floral arrangements, to relate floral design to containers or to other accessories in the room.

Clematis
Cobaea scandens, Cup and Saucers
Hedera helix, Ivy
Ipomoea purpurea, Morning Glory
Lonicera halliana, Honeysuckle
Parthenocissus quinquefolia, Virginia Creeper
Parthenocissus tricuspidata, Boston Ivy
Thunbergia alata, Clock-Vine
Tropaeolum, Nasturtium (tall)
Wisteria

## FILLERS

The smaller, fluffier blossoms of plants commonly used for edging in the border are used as fillers in indoor arrangements.
Ageratum

Anchusa capensis, Summer Forget-me-not
Cynoglossum amabile, Chinese Forget-me-not
Dianthus chinensis, Garden Pinks
Gypsophila, Annual Baby's-Breath
Iberis, Candytuft
Lobelia siphilitica, Blue Lobelia
Lobularia, Sweet Alyssum
Nigella damascena, Love-in-a-Mist
Petunia
Phlox – annual
Reseda odorata, Mignonette
Tagetes, Pot Marigold
Verbena
Viola tricolor, Pansy
*Flower Growing For Flower Arrangement* by Arno and Irene Nehrling.

## THE ROYAL HORTICULTURAL SOCIETY

The Society was founded on 7th March 1804 at Hatchard's book shop in Piccadilly. Its objects were "to collect every information respecting the cultivation of all plants and trees" and "to foster and encourage every branch of horticulture". These still remain the guiding principles of the Society.

**Fellowship in the Society.** Anyone interested in horticulture is eligible to apply for Fellowship.

**Meetings.** Meetings of the Society are held in its Halls in Greycoat Street and Vincent Square, S.W.1, at frequent intervals throughout most of the year. At these meetings there are two-day Shows of plants, flowers, fruits and vegetables, at which all horticulturists, both amateur and professional, are invited to exhibit. Lectures are given by experts on various horticultural topics.

**The Society's Garden, Wisley, Ripley, Woking, Surrey.** The Society's Garden at Wisley is under the control of the President and Council and their policy is to develop the Garden for the instruction and enjoyment of Fellows and for the advancement of horticulture.

Trials of plants and vegetables are held annually with the object of discovering the best of their several kinds and cultivars (varieties). At the same time they are described and classified. There is also an extensive collection of fruits.

A leaflet may be obtained from the Secretary giving details of the times and dates of opening the Garden. Visits to the Garden by non-Fellows are welcomed on weekdays. There is a charge for admission.

**Affiliated Societies.** Any horticultural, allotment, garden, or floral decoration society may apply for affiliation to The Royal Horticultural Society. Among the Societies affiliated are:
Alpine Garden Society
National Begonia Society
Cactus and Succulent Society of Great Britain
International Camellia Society
British National Carnation Society
National Chrysanthemum Society
The Daffodil Society
National Dahlia Society
Delphinium Society
British Fuchsia Society
British Gladiolus Society
Hardy Plant Society
Northern Horticultural Society
Saintpaulia and Houseplant Society
British Iris Society
Orchid Society of Great Britain
British Pelargonium and Geranium Society
Royal National Rose Society
National Sweet Pea Society
National Viola and Pansy Society

## KEW: THE ROYAL BOTANIC GARDENS

The origins of Kew Gardens in the sixteenth century are obscure, but the services they offer have world-wide applications and importance today. Apart from their work in tending the beautiful gardens themselves, the staff maintain and operate the herbarium, library, museums and the Jodrell Laboratory. The staff includes experts who identify rare plants, advise on economic botany (crop efficiency and suitability), identify plant pests and advise on countermeasures. Their work extends from identification of vegetable matter found in archæological research to devising new fungicides and conducting research into the physiology of various species of crop plants.

The simplest definition of investment is the purchase of an asset that gives (or that you judge will give) a future income. Inseparable from the idea of investment is the idea of risk – no income is absolutely guaranteed, but some incomes are better guaranteed than others. In general, investments which carry a high risk carry a high return – that is, not only a high income but also a chance of a high profit on the sale of the investment. So the first caution any adviser on investment will give is this: if an investment appears to show a very high rate of income, then look very closely at the risks.

Suppose you have a small sum which is surplus to your ordinary living requirements, what should you do with it? Here are some elementary rules to follow:

1. Budget for security first. Remember that your dependants, sooner or later, may have to live on what you leave them. If you have a family, insure your life, and if you are buying a house on mortgage, insure the mortgage. And make a will – it saves trouble.

2. Take precautions before investing. If in doubt about anything, see your bank manager, or an accountant, or a lawyer, or (if you have sufficient funds to invest in Stock Exchange securities) a stockbroker.

3. Keep abreast of the news that affects your investments. Read the "City" pages of your newspaper, look out for articles on your kind of investment. There are investors' magazines too, and books on various kinds of investment.

4. Do not plump for one investment alone; spread your risks. On the other hand, don't spread them so much that you have many small "parcels" of investment which are expensive to buy and sell. If your funds are very small, there are ways of spreading your investment cheaply; for instance, unit trusts (described later).

5. Watch your yields – a yield is the income you get from the amount you actually invest, expressed as a percentage. If what you paid £1 for gives you 1s. a year, then your yield is 5 per cent per annum. It's as simple as that.

6. Don't rush things; keep cool, keep well informed.

## INVESTING THROUGH THE POST OFFICE

Saving and investment through the Post Office is easy and cheap. All money used in this way is backed by the security of the Government and is virtually risk free.

**Post Office Savings Bank.** This is the most familiar form of investment in Britain. An account of your deposits and withdrawals is kept in a pass-book which you take to any Post Office when you pay in or draw out money. On every £1 left in for a complete calendar month, you get a small percentage interest. This interest is partly tax-free; you have to state the amount of the interest on your income-tax form, and the tax authorities make an adjustment automatically.

**National Savings Certificates.** These give you "interest" in a different way. You pay a sum – for instance, for the 1966 issue it was £1 – for each certificate, and this becomes worth so much more each month. You can cash it at any time, but if you hold it for its full term and beyond, then you will receive a real rate of interest higher than the rate on Savings Bank deposits. This interest is entirely free of income tax.

**Defence Bonds or National Development Bonds.** These are sold in £5 units, and pay an even higher rate of interest, but it is not tax-free, and it is paid to you twice a year. If you hold a bond for its full term, you receive an extra premium which *is* tax-free.

**Premium Bonds.** These are a straight gamble, but unlike a bet on football or racing, you never lose your stake. A certain percentage interest on all qualifying Bonds bought is put into a pool, and every month a random number machine is used to select a list of winning numbers of Bonds whose holders receive prizes, by which the interest is all paid out. You are notified by post of a win, and the prize is tax-free. You have to hold the Bond for three clear months before it qualifies for the prize draw. You can withdraw from the gamble at any time by encashing your Bond, when you receive back exactly what you paid for it.

All these Post Office investments can be encashed quickly and simply, and there is no charge for buying and selling. Any of them can be bought and sold at the nearest Post Office.

**Post Office Bank Investment Accounts.** If you have £50 or more deposited in a Post Office Savings Bank account, you can deposit further sums into an Investment Account, which pays higher rates of interest than the Savings Bank. This rate of interest will vary with the income the Post Office gets from the Government and other securities it buys with the money. You can deposit and withdraw money at any Post Office, but withdrawals are at one month's notice. You receive the interest in full, but it is subject to income tax.

**Trustee Savings Banks.** These also run savings accounts very like the Post Office (and so do the commercial banks, the ones with branches in the High Street). The Trustee Banks also have an investment department; so long as you keep at least £50 in your ordinary account, you can transfer sums into a Special Investment Account. The rate of interest you receive on this depends on the notice of withdrawal you promise to give – the longer the notice, the higher the interest rate (which is subject to tax).

**Government Securities.** Both the Post Office and the Trustee Savings Banks can help you to buy Government securities (what the stock market calls "gilt-edged") of many kinds. They charge lower rates of commission than a stockbroker does, but there is a reason for this. Unlike a stockbroker, the Post Office and the Trustee Banks will not buy and sell "conditionally" (for instance, you cannot ask them to buy only below a certain price) and they will not give you any advice.

All the forms of investment described so far are called *National Savings*, and you can get further information about them from any Post Office, any Trustee Savings Bank, or a Savings Group if your workplace has one. With the exception of the gilt-edged securities (whose price can vary from day to day), the National Savings media maintain their capital value; that is, you cannot lose your original investment. But this is not to say that they maintain their "real" value. Suppose you put £1 in the Post Office Savings Bank and leave it there for one year, you will have £1 0s. 6d. in the account, including the interest due to you. But if prices of the things you buy have risen by about 6d. in the £ during that year, then in reality you have now no more money in the account than you had at the beginning of the year. In other words, the yield on your investment has barely kept up with inflation. Always bear this in mind when calculating how well you are doing with any investment.

The rates of interest on National Savings media do change from time to time, but not very often. There is another form of simple investment account where the rate can change more often:

**Commercial Banks' Deposit Account.** If you open an ordinary account in a commercial bank, you are not paid interest on it. If you transfer sums to a "deposit account", you will receive a rate of interest which varies in two ways. First, it will vary according to how much notice of withdrawal you promise to give; and second, it will vary according to changes in "Bank Rate".

*Bank Rate* is an officially announced rate of exchange which acts as a kind of "signal" to the whole banking industry. The reasons for raising and lowering this rate are matters of Government policy, to make borrowing dearer or cheaper. The rate on bank deposit accounts rises and falls with it, and you can find out the latest deposit rates at any time by visiting any branch of any bank; they are posted on notice-boards, and the counter assistants will always give you more details. When you open a deposit account, a pass-book like a Post Office Savings book is made out, but the bank keeps it, not you.

The distinction between National Savings media and commercial bank deposit accounts lies in the way the money you invest is used. All National Savings money goes to the Government, into the Treasury, to help pay the day-to-day expenses of national government (and part of local government expenses, too). Bank deposit money is used by the bank itself, as a private business; it re-invests it in many, many kinds of activity, both in Government securities and in private and public businesses.

Finally, note that there are limits to the amount you may invest in the National Savings media (and also in the amount of gilt-edged you may buy and sell in one day through the Post Office or the Trustee Banks). There is no limit, of course, to the amount you can place in a commercial bank deposit (although, if you become very rich, your bank manager will become only too pleased to suggest to you how you can make even better rates of income out of your growing deposit).

## BUILDING SOCIETIES

For ordinary people, the most popular form of investment is the Post Office. The second most popular is the building society.

Originally, building societies were "clubs" of people who pooled their funds to build their own houses. They were special-purpose friendly societies, and their activities are still supervised by the Registrar of Friendly Societies in fact. But many of these clubs have grown to enormous size, and are big businesses, handling many millions of pounds every week. Nevertheless, their basic character remains. They are non-profit societies, borrowing from and lending to the public, for the purpose of financing dwelling-houses.

You can invest through building societies in two ways; either as a borrower, in which case you are investing in your own house, or as a lender, in which case you will receive an income from the sum you lend. There is no point in being both at once – if you already have arranged a mortgage through a building society, there is no point in investing spare sums of money in building society securities – you will get a bigger real yield by paying sums off your mortgage.

The method of investing in building society securities is as simple as investing in National Savings, and the securities themselves are similar to the National Savings media. You will receive a rate of interest which varies from time to time according to the economic situation and to Government policy. The rate does not necessarily vary with Bank Rate, but in the long run it tends to go up and down with Bank Rate, though not over such a wide range.

There are two forms of building society investment, deposits or shares, each with a slightly differing rate. The distinction is not very important; deposit investors are ordinary creditors of the building society, and in the event of a winding-up are paid off early in the proceedings; buyers of shares are a kind of owner of the society, receive a slightly higher rate of interest, and in a winding-up would be paid off among the last.

You do not have to pay income tax on the interest from a building society investment, because it is already paid for you in a unique way. Every year the societies as a whole agree with the Treasury a flat rate of income tax to be paid on all the interest. This rate is calculated according to a sample of building society investors, and is thus an average rate. So, irrespective of your own income-tax position, this is the rate which is deducted from your interest in reality.

Thus, when considering a building society deposit or share, take this rate into account. Find out what rate you are paying on your last piece of income by looking up your last income-tax assessment; if this is below the average rate being paid by the societies, then you must consider that you will not receive quite as much true yield on the building society investment as it appears, because you will be paying a heavier rate of tax on the income. This will not apply, however, to the great bulk of the working population of Britain; the building society rate of tax is significantly below the top rate of most income earners.

Money invested in building societies can be withdrawn easily and quickly. Societies have the right to ask for notice of withdrawal (one month's notice for deposits, for instance) but in practice you can take out up to £50 on demand and further sums within a few days. There are no stamp duties, brokerage or other costs in buying or selling building society securities, just the filling in of simple forms. You can operate regular savings schemes, and get a bonus above the ordinary interest rate if you keep saving for longish periods.

The capital value is fixed, like National Savings, and there are limits on the amount you can hold in any society. And if you are rich, remember that the interest is *not* free of surtax. Finally, a warning. Although all building societies are supervised by a Government department, and have to keep special laws passed for the protection of borrowers and lenders, they can be abused. Be sure the society is sound, especially if it seems to offer an unusually high rate for investments.

Details can be obtained from any branch of a building society (there is bound to be one in your nearest big shopping centre), or from the Building Societies Association (address in the London telephone directory). Failing this, a bank manager or accountant or lawyer will give you information.

## PENSIONS AND ANNUITIES

Many people invest, not to give themselves an income immediately, but to ensure an income in their later years; in other words, a pension. Apart from the State pension scheme for old age, there are many forms of privately financed schemes, both for individuals and groups.

Pensions are often part of the conditions of employment, such as in Government service and nationalised industries. Large companies also run a pensions scheme for employees, usually through a "group scheme" operated by insurance companies and special pension-fund companies.

However they are organised, pensions are based on insurance. When you pay so much a month towards a pensions scheme, you are really paying into an insurance fund, which is designed to assure the payment of sums in the future, however long you may live. Some pensions schemes include an element of life assurance; for instance, if you should die before you retire, then sums are payable to your dependants.

Because it is always unknown how long any one person may live, pensions and life assurances are based on a special kind of investment programme, calculated by professional mathematicians called "actuaries". These actuaries work with what are called "life tables" – the probable life-spans of people of certain ages and in certain places and jobs. So, when you contribute to a pension scheme, your contribution is calculated according to the general probability that you will live so many years after retirement, and therefore require payments of so much a year for so long.

So by contributing to the scheme you are in effect telling the scheme's organisers to do a complicated series of investments for you, designed to build up funds ready for your retirement, and to finance the payments that are likely to be required from that point onwards. This is why pensions scheme organisers and life assurance companies are very big investors in every way; they buy and sell all kinds of properties and securities in order to balance their investment books between sums needed now, and sums needed in the future. You could, of course, do all this yourself – invest cleverly and wisely every month so as to bring your own investments nicely into fruition just as you retired. and then maintain a target income. But the pension specialists are likely to beat you at the game; they can use large sums of money, they can spread their risks more evenly, and they can use their market power and expertise to get bargains and take opportunities.

One snag about group pension schemes operated by large companies is that they are often not transferable; thus if you leave a job with the company, you get back your payments but you may not be able to continue the scheme under the same conditions in a new job. This tends to prevent mobility of labour, especially middle-to-top-level management workers.

**Annuities.** There is, however, one quick way of "buying" a pension, and that is through an annuity. An annuity is designed for those who are getting on in years, and have at hand a significantly large lump sum from the sale of a business, a commuted pension, a legacy or hard-earned savings, and who do not want to go to the risk and trouble of investing it themselves.

For an annuity, you pay a lump sum, and in return receive a guaranteed income for the rest of your life (immediately or from a certain date) however long you may live. Naturally, the older you are, the less your expectation of life and so the more you will receive. Purely as an example, if you are aged 60, and pay £1,000 for an annuity, you might get about £95 a year immediately. The rate will vary, of course, depending on many considerations.

You can buy annuities through the Post Office or through any insurance company. There are joint annuities, too, for man and wife, payable in varying sums until the death of the longer-lived partner. Women receive slightly less than men – no, this is not sex-discrimination, but merely the fact that women tend to live longer than men. The tax position is a little complicated. You do not pay income tax on the whole of the annuity payment, but only on part of it; the rest is regarded as repayment of capital. But that will be explained when you apply for the annuity.

There are many complications possible in annuity schemes; for instance, you can couple an endowment, an annuity and a life assurance together. If you die before retirement, a lump sum is payable; if you reach retirement, a lump sum is payable as an endowment which can then be paid in whole or in part for an annuity. One thing must be remembered, however – when you have paid for the annuity, and have begun receiving the payments, you cannot then change your mind – your capital is committed for the rest of your life.

## RISK INVESTMENT

All the foregoing kinds of investment (except the gilt-edged stocks dealt in through the Post Office and Trustee Savings Banks) have a fixed capital value and a fixed income. It is now time to consider the vast array of risk investments proper. Such investments may not have any fixed capital value or any fixed income; both values may vary nearly from day to day. But again, there are many variations; some investments are far steadier in value than others. A description of the main kinds of businesses, and the main kinds of investments in those businesses, will make this clear.

**Sole Traders.** These are the one-man businesses of the simplest type. Such a business has unlimited liability; that is, in the event of a bankruptcy, the owner is liable to use all his private assets as well as his business assets to help pay his debts. He may have to sell his car, house, securities, everything except things held on trust for someone else, clothing and bedding for himself and family, and what are called the "tools of his trade".

Bankruptcy is a fearsome risk, and is closely governed by law. While a person is still bankrupt, he may not get credit from anyone without informing his intended creditor that he is an "undischarged bankrupt".

But anyone may, of course, start a sole-trader business. There is only one legal requirement; if you trade under any name which is not your own normal name, then you must register under the Business Names Act; otherwise there are no formalities.

**Partnerships.** These are businesses run by more than one person, but still with unlimited liability. In this case, if a bankruptcy occurs, all the private assets of all or any of the partners may have to be brought in to pay off debts.

Partnerships can be made very informally; a mere verbal agreement and a handshake will do. Again, if the partnership is to trade under any other name but the names of the partners (with or without initials) then it must be registered under the Business Names Act. But it is very unwise to enter into a partnership informally, whoever your partner may be. It is better to draw up a document, however simple, to govern the business, and have it scrutinised by a lawyer.

The most important legal point about a partnership agreement (whether verbal or written) is that it is "of the utmost good faith". Anyone taking part in the agreement must, by law, act in good faith, give all the information necessary for all other partners to judge the suitability of the partnership, and then act in complete trust and faith with each other thereafter.

Such an agreement should include the following points:

(1) The name and nature of the business. (2) The amounts of capital that each partner is putting in, in cash or other forms, and rules on how those capital contributions shall be increased or decreased. (3) Rules on how partners may grant loans, as distinct from risk capital, to the business. (4) How interest, if any, shall be paid on loans and capital. (5) How wages and fees shall be paid to the partners, as distinct from shares of profit. For instance, one partner may do all the day-to-day work of the business; he should, in fairness, get a regular salary. (6) How profits and losses shall be shared between the partners, and how these shares shall be affected by alterations in the capital, and how profits shall be drawn. (7) The rights and duties of each partner in the running of the business. (8) How accounts shall be kept, and be laid open for inspection for the partners, and who shall be the bankers and auditors.

A partnership agreement is only for the use of the partners themselves; the public is not expected to know anything about it. So, as far as the general public is concerned, any partner is assumed to have all the rights of the partnership, and can be sued as if he had, irrespective of what the agreement says. This is very important.

A partnership is at once brought to an end if a partner dies or is bankrupted, or wishes to take his capital out. A new partnership must be formed to continue the business (and this often leads to difficulties in finding just the right person for a new partner). If you leave a partnership, be on the safe side by giving "adequate notice" to the public at large; a notice in the *London Gazette*, in a local paper and in any trade magazines would be deemed sufficient. Otherwise, you could be regarded as continuing as a partner, merely because someone "thought you were", dealt with the partnership on that basis, and then struck some difficulty. Partnerships are rather like marriages, easily contracted, but not so easily dissolved. And remember that, while you are a partner, you are unlimitedly liable for debts.

There is one way of avoiding this liability, however; the Limited Partnerships Act. Under this, you can form partnerships in which some of the partners, but not all, limit their liability to their contributed capital. This form of business is very rarely formed; it is just as easy to form a private limited company (described below).

There is also a law which is intended to help partnerships in internal difficulties. If a dispute arises which is not covered by the partnership agreement, or if there was no agreement drawn up properly in the first place, and if the dispute is taken to court, then the court may apply the Partnership Act. In this Act is a list of "model articles" which will then be applied where necessary. In this way the dispute can be settled, but not necessarily in a way that one disputant will call "justly". For instance, the Act says that profits and losses are shared equally, irrespective of capital. So it is best to draw up a proper agreement from the very beginning. Finally, under English law, partnerships are limited in size to 20 people – 21 must form a limited company.

**Limited Companies.** The privilege of forming a limited company is that all the members of the company have "limited liability". This means that every investor in such a business knows from the beginning what his liability is, as an exact sum. This sum is called his "contribution", and it is the amount he agrees to pay in as his capital; once this is paid, he cannot be called on to pay more, however much in debt the business may get. Therefore he cannot be bankrupted for this reason alone.

But, of course, the company can be bankrupted (strictly, the verb used in this case is "wound up"). Company winding-up is hedged about with strict regulations, and it can be carried out under the control of the members, of the creditors, or of a court. Creditors have to be paid in a certain order – and the very last people to receive any money back are the providers of the capital – the lenders of loans, and the owners of risk capital (shares). But whatever happens, no lender or shareholder can be forced to put in more money (he can, of course, agree voluntarily to subscribe more under a new capital scheme if he wishes).

Any two people can form a small limited company, with some exceptions. You cannot form a limited company for an illegal or immoral purpose, of course, and some professions (lawyers, stockbrokers and Lloyd's insurance underwriters) forbid limited liability to their members.

**Private Companies.** From two to fifty people inclusive can form a private company, with relatively little legal work and at a small cost. Any lawyer will do it for you, and advise you on the form of the necessary documents and the fees to pay. Thereafter, the only legal requirement is to keep certain books of record and of account, and to render a yearly return to the Registrar of Companies. The two main returns are a list of members, showing the amounts of the capital they each hold, and a copy of the annual accounts (unless the private company is exempted from the latter).

**Public Companies.** It takes at least seven people to form a public company, but there is no upper limit to the number of members. The most important distinction between private and public companies is this – only public companies may advertise to the general public for new capital funds. Private companies must never advertise for this purpose, and in fact they must take powers to restrict the transfer of capital. Thus, if you agree to buy some shares in the capital of a private company, the directors of the company (who in most cases will be all the other shareholders) can refuse to accept your offer; in a public company, you cannot be refused so long as you can find a seller of shares.

Public companies have to render more complicated and fuller returns to the Registrar of Companies every year, and they are subject to closer legal restrictions. But they have this enormous advantage – they can draw on the whole world if necessary for their capital.

**Prospectuses.** This is the name given to an advertisement for new capital for a public company. Under the Companies Act (the very long Act that governs nearly all the formation, life and winding up of all companies) the prospectus must be in a certain form, and must contain certain minimum information. It is the basis of the contract under which all succeeding owners of the capital hold their shares or other securities.

If you wish to invest in new capital, therefore, you must read the prospectuses that appear in the Press, including a great deal of fine print. If you wish to use your own judgment, then all you do is fill in the form which accompanies the prospectus, saying how many of the new securities you want, and enclose a cheque for the necessary sum.

This is the *application form* (you need not use the one in the newspaper; you can get one from your bank or your stockbroker – and do not forget that sometimes you will be offered special consideration if you already hold some of the company's earlier securities, so get a special form from the company). With it you send the *application money*, which is often only part of the total cost.

In the prospectus will be a date on which the offer will close, and on that date the company will count up all the applications. If applications for more securities are received than the number of securities offered, the company cannot just issue more securities; it must state the maximum offer (and also, incidentally, the minimum amount). If there is a surplus of applications, (an "over-subscription") it will have to share them out by giving everyone less than they asked for, or by balloting.

Eventually you will receive either an *allotment letter* granting you all or part of your application, or (if you have failed to be granted any because of a heavy over-subscription) a *letter of regret*. As for the remainder of the cost of the securities, that will be payable according to the rules laid down in the prospectus. It may be payable immediately, or it may stretch out in instalments over the future.

A little later you will receive your *certificate*, and that becomes the document you use to sell your investment in the market. Only public companies' securities are bought and sold in the open market; private companies' shares pass privately. But note that, even before you receive your certificate, you *can* sell your security in the form of the allotment letter; on the back of this will be a form of *renunciation*, by which you can transfer the right to receive the certificate to someone else. The point about this renunciation is that it is free of the tax on transfers. You would take advantage of this if you wished to take a quick profit on a successful new issue.

**Capital Structure.** Companies often issue more than one kind of security. This is to attract different kinds of investors (some prefer risks and profits to secured loans and interest, and vice versa), and also to take advantage of different market conditions. To see how a large company's capital structure may be built up, here is a typical balance sheet:

| Liabilities | Assets |
|---|---|
| Ordinary share capital | Goodwill |
| Preference share capital | Freehold and leasehold land and premises |
| Debentures or secured loans | Plant, transport, tools |
| Notes or unsecured loans | Investments |
| | Stock in trade |
| Capital reserves | Debtors |
| Revenue reserves | Cash |
| Temporary loans | |
| Creditors | |
| Provisions | |
| Profits | Losses |

Note that capital is a liability; it is liable to be paid back to the people who own it, of course. The "reserves" are past profits put by as a kind of "buffer" against losses. The "provisions" are also a kind of reserve of profits (for instance, against bad debts, or depreciation, or future tax bills).

It may be strange to see that profits are liabilities and losses are assets, but look at this way: profits are owed to the capital-owners by the company, and so are liabilities; losses are not really assets though and are, more realistically, a subtraction from profits.

The first four items on the "liabilities" side require more detailed explanation:

**Ordinary Shares** are that part of the capital which carries the most risk. There is no guaranteed income from them. They receive a dividend, which is merely a share of any profits which are left over after all other expenses are paid. Of course, a successful business pays high dividends, and an unsuccessful one pays low dividends, or no dividends at all. The directors of the company decide what shall be paid and if the ordinary shareholders disagree, they must go to the general meeting and complain. They have this right, and it is also to be noted that it is usually only the ordinary shareholders who have any votes at general meetings.

There is a special type of ordinary share, usually called an "A" Ordinary, which has no vote, however. When buying shares, always make sure what the exact conditions of issue are.

**Preference Shares.** These shares involve slightly less risk, but only slightly. Their holders have some kinds of preference (an earlier "place in the queue") for the distribution of profits and other income. For instance, one kind of preference share may carry a 6 per cent dividend preference, and also a preference in repayment of capital if the company has to wind up. Again, when buying them, make sure what the conditions of issue were.

The "6 per cent dividend preference" means that if sufficient profits are made, then the preference shareholders will receive a payment equal to 6 per cent of the *nominal value* of their shares. Note that dividend percentages are always proportions of the original nominal value of a share or a debenture (*not* of the price you paid, *not* of the total profits, *not* of any market price at all). For instance, if you buy a share or a debenture that is called "£1" (whatever you actually paid for it) then a percentage dividend of, say, 10 per cent means that you get 10 per cent of £1, or 2s. If you actually paid 30s. to buy the security, then your true yield will be 2s. in 30s. or 6⅔ per cent.

If profits are barely enough to pay the preference dividend, then of course the ordinary shareholders will get nothing.

**Debentures and Notes** are loans. The holders receive a fixed percentage interest rate, whether the company makes profits or not. Secured loans are those "attached" to some kind of asset. For example, if the company should fail to pay the interest, the debenture-holders may have the power to seize the premises (or at least to put their own manager in to protect their stake in the company). Unsecured loans have no such certain rights. Again, when buying loan-type securities make sure what the conditions of issue were.

**Deferred Shares** are rarely issued, but should be noted. They carry the right to the "last bit" of distributed profits, after all the debentures, notes, preference shares and ordinary shares have been paid, up to a certain (usually quite high) point. The effect of deferred shares is to make the ordinary shares "underneath" a kind of large-percentage preference share.

**Participation.** Some preference shares can be issued in a very complicated way. For instance, they may carry a 6 per cent dividend preference, and then, if the ordinary shareholders get 20 per cent after that, the preference shares may come in again for another 6 per cent.

**Cumulative Shares.** Preference shares may also be issued on condition that if a dividend should not be paid in one year, the debt is carried forward. Thus, a 6 per cent cumulative preference share will become a 12 per cent share the next year. Of course, if many years go by without sufficient profits to pay the preference shareholders, the company is in serious trouble and will either have to wind up or rearrange its capital (this will require meetings of shareholders and creditors, and all kinds of negotiations). Naturally, a share on which no dividend has been paid falls in price on the market, but not right down to nothing because there may be quite good hopes for a recovery in the future.

**Gearing.** This is a colourful technical term to describe the structure of a company's capital securities. If there are a relatively large number of preference shares issued and a relatively small number of ordinary shares issued, then a moment's thought will show that when the company is doing only fairly well, the preference holders will get nearly all the profit and the ordinary holders very little if any. But as the profits begin to rise in successive years, the preference holders do not receive any more, but the ordinary shareholders get more and more. If the ordinary holders are relatively few, they will get a great deal each. This is called "high gearing", and the reverse (few preference, many ordinary) "low gearing".

**Equity Shares.** This is another name for ordinary, risk-bearing shares. An American name for the same thing is *common stock*.

R—E.W.—G

**Stocks.** In Britain, this is the name of any share or loan security which has no identifying number; when you buy stock you buy a "lump" of the capital, and not, say, Shares Numbers 1,255 to 1,355. The distinction has practically no significance.

**No Par Value Shares.** Some shares are issued without a par or nominal value. So the dividend cannot be expressed as a percentage; instead it is expressed as a sum per share (2s. per share, instead of 10 per cent of a nominal £1).

**Premiums.** Shares can be issued at a premium (say, a £1 share for 22s. 6d.). The premium is taken by the company and used as a reserve. Similarly, loans (but not shares under British law) can be issued at a *discount* (£98 for £100 nominal loan stock). Once the issue is made, these both soon become insignicant. The market price is what it is bought and sold at, and the nominal value is what dividends and interest are calculated on.

**Underwriters.** An issue of shares or loan securities can be "insured". For a percentage fee, finance groups will guarantee ("underwrite") that if the total of applications falls short, they will buy the remainder.

## THE STOCK EXCHANGES

When shares and loan securities are issued by a public company, the company nearly always applies to a suitable stock exchange for "permission to deal". The largest British exchange is in London, but there are also exchanges in all the main cities. The exchange grants permission to deal – that is, to have the securities "quoted" – only on certain conditions, and these are even more stringent than the law provides for under the Companies Act. The exchange and its members (jobbers and brokers) have a duty of professional care to protect the capital providers – the share and loan security holders.

**Jobbers** are people who actually buy and sell securities, holding stocks of them as they judge necessary, and seeking to make a profit on their deals.

**Brokers** are only agents; they carry out the orders of their customers, the general public, as best they can, and receive a commission for their work.

Only jobbers and brokers can go into the exchange (but the public can look down on the scene from a gallery in the case of the London exchange). So you need an agent, a stockbroker, if you want to buy and sell securities which are quoted there. Your bank manager or lawyer or accountant will put you in touch with one, wherever you live. Alternatively, you can write to your nearest stock exchange and ask for a list of brokers (you will find the exchange listed under the name of the city in the telephone directory).

When you give your broker an order, he (or his associate) will go to the floor of the exchange and seek out those jobbers who deal in the kind of securities you wish to buy or sell, and first find out what offers there are about. If you have given him no detailed instructions, he will accept the best bargain he can find, but you can give him limits within which to buy and sell, and he will always advise you on any aspect of your dealings. The broker may not be able to obtain your bargain straight away; some types of shares and debentures change hands only rarely. But for the big, well-known companies there are always buyers and sellers about.

Sooner or later, you will receive from him a transfer form which you sign, as either buyer or seller, and a statement of account, showing price and total amount of your bargain, tax, stamp fees and his commission. You will receive from the company or have to send to the company the certificate relating to your purchase or sale.

**Prices.** To find out at about what price the security in which you are interested is being bought and sold, you can read the lists of the main quoted securities given in the daily Press, usually under "counters" – that is, the section to which the security belongs – Government securities, bank shares, motor shares, mining shares, and so on. Always remember that the previous day's "closing price" is only an indication of what it might be by the time your broker begins to seek a bargain for you. All kinds of considerations affect the price from day to day, hour to hour, even minute to minute. The price is moved up and down by the number of buyers and sellers known to the market, the general hopes and fears for the future of the company and the industry of which it is a part, for the economy as a whole and even for the world as a whole, Government action, local authority action, demand for the company's goods and supply of the company's raw materials, labour troubles and so forth. It is finally up to you, even with all the best advice in the world, to judge the whole situation every time you consider making a purchase or a sale.

Here is a list of some of the phrases you will come across when reading about shares and other securities:

*Account.* The stock exchanges settle accounts every fortnight. If you buy a security and sell it again within this period, no stamp duty is payable and you do not receive a certificate because you are not registered as a holder of the security in the company's books. But if you only buy, or only sell, or if you have some of the security "left over" after dealing, then you will be registered or deleted as a holder, and have to pay stamp duty.

*Bear.* A speculator who thinks that prices will fail. He therefore contracts to sell a security at a certain price, for delivery later, and within the same account later on, buys that security at a lower price (if he has judged the price movement rightly).

*Bonds.* This is a general term for fixed-interest securities.

*Bonus Issues.* These are "free" shares given to existing shareholders at dividend time, instead of cash. They may not in fact be worth as much as the "old" shares, because the company has to keep up profits to keep up the dividend on the increased numbers of shares. If you would prefer cash, sell the bonus shares (but you must judge what the company's future is – it might be more profitable to keep them than to put the cash into something else).

*Break-up Value.* The value of a share in terms of the real assets of the company (land, premises, plant, stock, etc.).

*Bull.* A speculator who thinks that prices are going to rise. He will buy now and sell later.

*Capital Gains Tax.* A tax on profits (less losses) made on buying and selling shares and other securities in business, and on property. The rules are complicated, and have undergone changes. See an accountant. There is no tax on any profit made on the sale of your dwelling-house.

*Cash Flow.* A guide for investment analysts. It is the funds left after subtracting all the prior charges (see that entry) and taxes from the net profit, but before subtracting depreciation. This is the maximum amount which could possibly go to the shareholders. The market price of the share is then expressed as so many years' "purchase" of the cash flow. Example: Cash flow of £10,000, with 20,000 issued shares worth £3 each. The market price is therefore six years' purchase of cash flow.

*Certificate of Incorporation.* Certificate issued by the Registrar of Companies showing the company's name and the date of its registration. It is a company's "birth certificate" as a legal entity.

*Closing of Register.* A company closes its register of members (holders of securities) for a short period every year to prepare dividend cheques. The period is advertised, and no new registrations are made during that period; so the market price for shares "goes ex.-div." (see *Cum. and ex*).

*Contango.* A "carry-over" of a bargain from one stock exchange account to the next; this can be done for a fee.

*Coupons.* Some securities are issued to "bearer", and the holders are therefore not registered. In order to claim dividends, a coupon is detached from the security certificate and sent to the company.

*Cum. and ex.* With and without. As dividend time nears, you can buy a share only without the dividend (*ex. div.*)

because there will not be time to register you as a member. *Cum. rights* or *cum. cap.* refer to forthcoming rights and bonus issues (see those entries).

*Discount.* Used in a special sense, "discounted" means that an event has been foreseen by buyers and sellers and thus the price has moved in advance of the event itself. For instance, fears of a fall in profits will lower a price – the drop in profits has thus been "discounted".

*Dividend Cover.* The number of times the actual profit of a company would pay out the actual dividend; companies do not issue all their profits every year as dividends.

*Double-taxation Agreements.* These apply to foreign shares. Many countries have agreements with Britain that the foreign tax on profits and dividends shall be allowed to British shareholders as if it had been paid in Britain; otherwise you pay tax in both countries.

*Earnings.* A loose term, usually meaning "net profit".

*Final Dividend.* Some companies pay out dividends in instalments during a year; these instalments are called "interims", and the last one is called the "final". Interim dividends can be declared by the company's directors alone, but the final, and the total dividend, must be formally voted at the annual general meeting.

*Firmer Prices.* Prices which are rising, or tending to rise, or at least showing no signs of falling. The opposite is "*weaker*" or "*easier*". These descriptions are known as the "tone of the market".

*Flat Yield.* Yield of a loan security here and now, ignoring any premium or loss that may be made when it is redeemed; if the latter is taken into account, a "redemption yield" can be calculated.

*Grossing-up.* Making a net dividend (after tax) back into a gross figure. Formula is: multiply the net percentage by $\dfrac{20}{20 - X}$ where $X$ is the tax rate in shillings in the pound.

*Indexes* (*or indices*). A means of indicating the overall movement in a set of separate figures. Indexes are calculated for shares and other securities by taking the prices of a fixed list of securities at the end of each business day, and processing them mathematically to give a percentage of the prices that obtained on some base-date. An index of say 287 means that the prices have risen 2·87 times above what they were on the base-date when the index began.

*Kaffirs.* Stock exchange nickname for South African mining shares. There are many nicknames for markets and for individual shares.

*Margin.* Buying on margin means putting down only part of the price in cash, and borrowing the rest.

*Market Leaders.* The biggest and most significant companies in an industry, the prices of whose shares tend to affect prices of other companies' shares in that industry.

*Memorandum and Articles.* These are the "rules" of a company. The Memorandum shows the objects of the company – the activities for which it was set up. The Articles are a long series of regulations on the issue and transfer of capital, powers to borrow money, how to call and hold meetings, how directors are appointed and what they can do, how to declare dividends, and how the accounts are to be kept. In the Companies Act is a model set of articles, known as *Table A*, to which most companies closely conform.

*Middle Price.* Stock exchange prices are two-fold. Jobbers at any time quote their buying and selling prices ("bid" and "offer" respectively), and the difference is called their "turn". These two prices may be quoted in lists in the Press, but if a single price is quoted, then this is usually the "middle" of those two.

*Offer for Sale.* This phrase, appearing at the top of a prospectus, means that the company has sold the issue to a finance house, and the finance house is now selling it to the public (for a fee, given in the prospectus). This is a form of underwriting.

*Options.* Rights to choose to buy or sell a security at a given price during a given period in the future. In commodity markets, these are called "futures"

A "call" option is the right to buy, a "put" option, the right to sell. The right to choose to buy or sell is called a "put and call" or a "double" option. You pay a fee for an option. Not all securities are optionable, and there is a limit to the time period for options.

*Passing a Dividend.* Curiously, this means *not* declaring any dividend at all, although when one *is* declared, then the annual meeting of a company passes a resolution to that effect.

*Placing.* A method of issuing public company securities, not to the general public, but to finance houses and close associates, by separate arrangement. But you may be able to buy these securities just the same; the original buyers may want to sell at any time.

*Prior Charges.* Interest on loans and debentures and/or dividends on preference shares. These must be paid before any ordinary dividend.

*Rights Issues.* "Bargain" shares offered to existing shareholders as a special issue. As with bonus issues, you have to decide whether to keep them or take a quick profit.

*Scrip Issues.* Scrip means any provisional document, and in particular the provisional certificate issued with rights and bonus shares.

*Stag.* A speculator who applies for shares in a new issue, in the expectation that it will be heavily over-subscribed, and that therefore he can make a quick profit on the price at which the shares will be first dealt in.

*Take-over Bid.* A bid by another company for the whole, or most, of a company's shares. The bid will be made by an offer to all the shareholders of cash for their shares, or partly cash and partly shares in the bidding company. Shareholders can, of course, refuse, but if the bidding company succeeds in getting the great majority of the shares, then it will control the company.

*Tax-free Dividends.* No dividends are really tax-free, but a company must deduct the standard rate of income tax from a dividend before it is sent to the shareholders; it may therefore indicate what the tax-free or net percentage is. If your income is below the standard-rate level, you claim tax back from the authorities. Remember, though, that dividends are "unearned" income; they do not count towards earned-income allowances.

*Turnover or Volume.* The total number of shares changing hands during a period on an exchange, indicating the activity on that exchange.

## HOW TO FIND A BUSINESS INVESTMENT

The market for small businesses, either sole traders, partnerships or private companies, is scattered and imperfect. A great number of sales go through privately, in the "pub and club" world of the locality and between relations. Bank managers, lawyers, accountants and estate agents are obvious sources of information, and so are such people as hairdressers and garage owners, who talk with businessmen frequently.

The nearest approach to an organised market for small business is through the business transfer agencies, which are estate agents specialising in going-concern businesses rather than dwelling-houses and empty factories and workshops. They buy and sell on commission, help to arrange loans, draw up documents and give advice. The agencies advertise a great deal through the Press, and there are one or two national weekly magazines which devote sections to small businesses wanted and for sale.

Larger business opportunities, offering relatively big stakes, are advertised in the "quality" daily and Sunday Press. Partnerships are also advertised, especially in the professional magazines, but care should always be taken to scrutinise such offers with very great care – remember the unlimited liability. When considering taking part in, or taking over, a small business of the private type enlist the help of at least an accountant, and make certain that the document of transfer or sale is properly drawn up.

## YOUR RIGHTS TO COMPLAIN

A contract to buy a private business is subject to the rule of *caveat emptor* (let the buyer beware). There is no legal liability on a seller to tell you the whole story, but if he offers a guarantee and you accept, then that is another matter. Contracts to enter partnerships, however, are legally "of the utmost good faith". Both the new partner and the old ones must act openly and give full information.

Your rights as a shareholder in a limited company are laid down in the Companies Act, the Memorandum and Articles of Association of the company concerned and the prospectus under which the securities were originally issued (subject to any subsequent and properly voted amendments). Broadly speaking, as a member of a company you have the right to see these documents and the most recent annual accounts. Even if you are not a member, you can see them, or send someone to see them, at the office of the Registrar of Companies in London or Edinburgh (but in the case of exempt private companies, there will be no accounts on view).

The kind of security you hold in a company may give you the right to attend, and vote at, annual meetings. In this case, you also have the right to receive the notice of the meeting, accompanied by the agenda, with due warning. You may be able to express your vote on certain resolutions on the agenda without actually attending the meeting; you do this by filling in a proxy form.

You always have the right, of course, to make a complaint against a company stronger by joining together with other complaining shareholders, and bringing pressure to bear on the management. This does require the expenditure of time and money, however, although such movements have been quite successful in many cases. Finally, as regards all businesses, you have the right to go to court and state a case if you deem that gross mismanagement or fraud has taken place. But be careful how you make your accusations outside a court; you run the risk of a libel action against you, because an accusation of mismanagement or fraud in business causes, on the face of it, damage against the person you are accusing. If you have a serious complaint, seek legal advice at once.

## UNIT TRUSTS

This is a special and very useful form of investment for the small investor. It is a means whereby you can invest in a large number of companies without all the trouble and expense of choosing and buying and selling a large number of securities.

You do not buy unit trust units through the stock exchange but direct from the trust management. The trusts are frequently advertised in the daily and weekly Press. What happens is this: you fill in a form for a certain number of units, and send it together with your cheque. What you receive in return is a certificate, which represents a bundle of very small holdings in a relatively large number of companies. Some trusts are general, which means that your money is in effect invested in a wide range of different industries; some trusts specialise in certain types of industry.

The unit trust management uses your money and that of the other unit holders to buy and sell shares, and when it receives dividends from those investments it subtracts its management costs and a fee, and shares the remainder among all the unit holders. You can see that in effect you do not quite receive all the dividend you would have done if you had been able to invest in all the shares in the trust yourself, but, after all, you are getting the services of the management in organising the bundle of investments, and their expertise in getting you the best income they can. Unit trusts are governed by special legislation, and the managers have a professional body, the Association of Unit Trust Managers (this will give you information and advice – 306 Salisbury House, Finsbury Circus, London, E.C.2. NATional 0871).

Note that the buying and selling price of a unit varies from time to time, and is based on the market price of all the investments in the trust; so you can make a capital profit or loss on buying and selling units. The prices are advertised in the financial press.

## INVESTMENT TRUSTS

These are similar to unit trusts, but are

run on different lines. You buy shares in investment trusts through the stock exchange in the normal way, and the price varies, not only with the market value of the investments in the trust, but also with the availability of shares in each trust. Otherwise, dividends are paid over in a similar manner as in the unit trust. For an investment trust share, consult your bank manager or stockbroker.

## INVESTMENT CLUBS

This is a means of forming your own unit trust. It is a private group of people who get together regularly to subscribe a fixed amount to a fund, and decide how it shall be invested jointly. In this way, for instance, larger and more economic investments can be made (but the club members have to agree how the money shall be placed all the time).

It is best to draw up a trust deed for the club, so that the funds can be invested in the name of a trustee (say, a bank). You can make any rules you like (for instance, to plough back dividends into more investment) but you must include, of course, some rule as to how a member can withdraw his funds. Experience shows that clubs which include at least some professional investors are the most likely to succeed. Clubs, like all investors, can make losses as well as profits.

## OTHER FORMS OF INVESTMENT

**Commodity Markets.** These have not been used by the small investor a great deal, partly because the methods of investment have not been publicised, but also because the minimum investment is usually large (on the wool market, for instance, the unit of investment is 5,000 pounds weight of wool tops). All the main commodities in international trade have their own exchanges, chiefly in London, and their own methods of conducting business. They are not places for the amateur, and not for the small man.

**Money Markets.** These are the markets for credit and finance, headed by the big banks and finance houses. Here again, the unit of investment is large (a minimum bid for three-months Treasury bills – a short loan to the Government – is for £50,000 worth of bills), and the technique is – well, very technical.

**Arts and Antiques.** These can be extremely profitable markets in which to invest – old furniture, paintings, sculpture, firearms, stamps, fine glass and pottery. But wide knowledge of the articles and their availability is required. It should be always remembered that most of the articles have little intrinsic value, only a value attached to them by fashion or rarity (and that means that they have to be insured while in your care). There is no central market for fine art dealers, but each section is headed by a group of very large auctioneers and stockholders. Your local classified directory will help.

**Property.** Relatively large sums of money are needed to operate on the property market (although property can be borrowed on at relatively low rates of interest). Property is sold through many hundreds of estate agents, and advertised through the Press. Property is a relatively long-term investment, and is relatively "safe", but dwelling-houses are subject to a great deal of legislation which may raise costs and keep down income. Industrial buildings and offices can be profitable, but if demand for them begins to fall off for any reason, losses can soon pile up.

Among the snags in property ownership are the complexities of planning controls, the need to maintain the property in good repair, and the tendency for rents to rise only very slowly. If you do not want to take on the responsibilities of maintaining your own property, you can still take an interest in the property market by buying shares in property development companies, in companies supplying goods to the construction industries, and in companies in the construction industry itself.

# EDUCATION

*Preparatory Note.* While all possible care has been taken to ensure that the information included in this Section is correct *up to the time of the book's going to press*, readers are warned that throughout the United Kingdom changes are taking place continuously in the educational systems. It is advisable, therefore, to check any important item with some up-to-the-minute source. For most purposes the office of the local council's Education Department would probably be able to help. The addresses of other sources of information are included at appropriate places in the following Section.

## PUBLIC EDUCATION IN THE UNITED KINGDOM

**The State Systems.** There are three statutory systems of public education in the UK: for England and Wales, Scotland, and Northern Ireland respectively. These are regulated by Acts of Parliament, made for the two systems in Britain by the UK Parliament at Westminster, and for Northern Ireland by the Northern Ireland Parliament at Belfast.

**Central and Local Government.** As it is the policy of HM Government (of whatever party) that facilities for public education shall be broadly comparable throughout the UK, the main structure of the three systems is the same. The political head is a Minister, usually of Cabinet status, who is supported by a Government Department of Civil Servants and a Corps of HM Inspectors. The provision, equipment, and staffing of schools, colleges and other educational establishments is the responsibility of Local Education Authorities (LEAs), who are – slight differences in terminology being disregarded – the elected councils of the administrative counties and of large, or "county", boroughs. There are 162 LEAs in England and

Wales, 35 in Scotland, and 8 in Northern Ireland. They work under the "control and direction" of the Minister (who is directly responsible to Parliament), and function largely through Education Committees, which they must appoint, and to which they may delegate (in Northern Ireland must) all their powers except the power to raise money by rates or loan.

**Finance.** Arrangements differ in the three systems, but in the aggregate approximately two-thirds of the total expenditure is met by Exchequer grants voted by Parliament, and one-third by rates levied by the local authorities.

**The Three Stages.** Each system is organised in three progressive stages, of Primary education, Secondary education and Further Education. The period of compulsory education is ordinarily the same, and includes secondary as well as primary education. In none of the countries are the universities part of the statutory system of education.

**Buildings.** School buildings are provided either by LEAs or by voluntary bodies, who are usually associated with religious denominations. Schools provided by LEAs are called (except in Scotland) "county" schools; those provided by voluntary bodies "voluntary" schools. In England and Wales there are "voluntary aided" and "voluntary controlled" schools.* The latter have no financial responsibilities, everything being paid by the LEA, but only vestigial rights of denominational religious instruction. The former retain full power over religious instruction and in return are responsible for 20 per cent of all required capital expenditure. Both county and voluntary schools are called "maintained" schools, as all their recurrent

* There is also a small number of "special agreement schools" which have resulted from an Education Act passed in 1936. They resemble "aided" schools.

expenditure – their maintenance costs – are paid by the LEA. In Scotland there are no voluntary schools, an agreement having been reached in 1918 whereby they "transferred" to the LEA without loss of denominational rights. All schools maintained by Scottish LEAs are called "public" schools. In Northern Ireland most Protestant primary schools are county schools, and most voluntary primary schools are Roman Catholic schools. A majority of Grammar schools are voluntary schools, but a majority of other secondary schools are county schools.

Further Education buildings are in all three systems provided mainly by LEAs.

**Welfare Services.** All three systems provide "special educational treatment" for children handicapped by mental or physical disability. All three include a School Health Service, Milk and Meals Services, a Service of Youth providing leisure-time facilities for adolescents, and in conjunction with the Ministers of Labour a Youth Employment Service.

**Teachers.** Each system pays its teachers on a national salary scale, and each has a contributory pension scheme for teachers. No woman is disqualified for employment as a teacher, or can be dismissed, solely by reason of marriage. Every teacher (like every pupil) has the right to opt out of any form of religious instruction and/or worship arranged by the school.

**Publications.** Each government department publishes an annual Report and a variety of occasional publications. All are obtainable through HM Stationery Office or any bookseller.

**Addresses.** The addresses of the three Government Departments are:

*England and Wales.* Department of Education and Science, Curzon Street, London, W.1.

*Scotland.* Scottish Education Department, St Andrew's House, Edinburgh.

*Northern Ireland.* Ministry of Education, Dundonald House, Upper Newtownards Road, Belfast 4.

## DUTIES AND RIGHTS OF PARENTS

**Duties.** It is the legal duty of the parent of every child aged 5 years or more up to the end of "compulsory school age" (in 1967 this was 15+) to cause that child "to receive efficient full-time education suitable to his age, ability, and aptitude, either by regular attendance at school or otherwise". It will be seen that there is no statutory obligation to send a child to school; but if a parent does not he must satisfy the public authority for education that his child is actually getting "efficient full-time education" as defined above.

The term "parent" means in normal circumstances the father; otherwise, it covers the mother, a guardian, or any person who has the actual custody of the child.

If a parent sends his child to school (as practically every parent does), it is his duty to cause the child to attend regularly. Should he, "without reasonable excuse", fail to do so, the LEA can serve a notice upon him requiring him to explain why. If he ignores the notice, or his explanation does not satisfy the Authority, the latter can serve upon him an "attendance order" requiring him to send the child to a school named in the order. The parent has the right to name the school, but if he fails to do so, or names what in the LEA's opinion is an unsatisfactory school, the Authority will name a school.

Reasonable excuses for a child's non-attendance include (i) sickness or similar unavoidable cause; (ii) the child's home is not "within walking distance" (see *Transport*) of the nearest available school, and the Authority has made no suitable transport arrangements; (iii) the day is "exclusively set apart for religious observance by the religious body to which his parent belongs" (England and Wales only).

Parents offending against the law relating to school attendance are liable to prosecution and fine; and persistent offenders to fine and/or imprisonment.

**Parental Rights.** It is laid down in the Education Acts that (in the words of the English Act):

> In the exercise and performance of all powers and duties conferred and imposed upon them by this Act the Minister and local education authorities shall have regard to the general principle that, so far as is compatible with the provision of efficient instruction and training and the avoidance of unreasonable public expenditure, pupils are to be educated in accordance with the wishes of their parents. *Education Act, 1944, Sec. 76.*

The implications of this Section, and of similar ones in the Scottish and Irish Acts, have been much discussed but rarely tested in courts of law. It is agreed that parents' requests for denominational schooling must be respected, and LEAs will, if necessary, transport children long distances to particular denominational schools. A parent's preference for a particular kind of curriculum is less willingly met: the Scottish Act, in fact, says bluntly:

> A parent shall not be entitled to select a course of secondary education for his child from which in the opinion of the [local] education authority (confirmed by the Secretary of State in the event of a dispute between the parent and the authority) the pupil shows no reasonable promise of profiting. *Education (Scotland) Act, 1946, Sec. 29(2).*

In practice the same would be the case in England and Wales. In Northern Ireland, where the Grammar schools charge fees, there would be more doubt.

**Zoning.** On the other hand, the practice many LEAs follow of dividing their areas into "zones", and expecting parents to send their children to a primary school, or a non-selective secondary school, within the zone in which they are domiciled has no legal basis. The position appears to be that if a parent pays for any transport required, and if the more distant school has a place available, and if the filling of that place will not keep out a "local" child the "foreigner" may be admitted. Rather a lot of "ifs"; in practice the parent requests, the LEA decides.

(For other parental duties and rights, see *Special Educational Treatment.*)

## SCHOOLS

**Nursery Schools and Classes.** In all three systems a very small provision of Nursery schools and classes for children between the ages of 2 or 3 and 5 (and occasionally up to 7) is made by LEAs; and there are also small numbers of privately-run Nursery schools.

Nursery schools are to be distinguished from Nursery Centres, Day Nurseries and Crèches. These latter are custodial establishments, at which parents may leave young children for care; they are in the charge of Nursery nurses. Nursery schools are educational establishments, and maintained Nursery schools must by law be in the charge of trained teachers. Nursery classes are classes attached to Primary schools for children between the ages of 3 and 5; in maintained schools they also must be in the charge of trained teachers. In LEA schools and classes the number in a class is limited to thirty.

Attendance at Nursery schools and classes is voluntary for children under 5, but as the schools and classes provide education – however informal – regular attendance promises the best results. LEA schools are usually open morning and afternoon, private schools often only in the mornings.

**Primary Education.** In England and Wales the period of compulsory education begins on the child's fifth birthday; but where school places are available it is customary to accept at the beginning of a school term children whose fifth birthday falls within that term. Children may be transferred from Primary school to Secondary school as early as 10 years 6 months, and must be transferred before attaining the age of 12.

Primary schools in England and Wales are divided into two clearly distinguished parts: *Infants* (aged 5 to 7 +) and *Juniors* (7 + to 11 +). In over half of all primary schools these are separate departments in the same set of buildings, comprising an "all-through" Primary school; but there are several thousand separate Infants' schools and Junior schools in their own buildings. Almost all primary schools are co-educational. In Infants' schools practically all the teachers are women.

In Scotland there are very few separate Infants' schools or departments, and in Northern Ireland their formation is officially discouraged. In Scotland the LEA must fix two or more dates in a year for the start of compulsory education, and a child becomes of "compulsory school age" on whichever date follows his fifth birthday. Transfer to Secondary school ordinarily takes place rather later than in England and Wales, i.e. between 12 and 13. In Northern Ireland LEAs may, subject to the approval of the Minister of Education, fix by by-law the beginning of "compulsory school age" at $5\frac{1}{2}$ or 6, but this power is little used. The age of transfer to secondary education is 11+. (For methods of selection for secondary education, in all three systems, see *Examinations*.)

The maximum number of pupils in a class which is officially permitted is forty in England and Wales, and Northern Ireland, and forty-five in Scotland; but owing to shortage of teachers and/or classrooms these maxima are in practice frequently exceeded.

As part of the reorganisation of secondary education in England and Wales on comprehensive lines (see *Secondary Education*) a three-tier organisation of primary and secondary education was during the earlier 1960s being tried by some LEAs. This included a Primary school for children aged 5 (or younger) to 8 or 9, followed by a "Middle" school for ages 8–9 to 12–13, and a Secondary school from 12–13 to 18.

**Secondary Education.** At the time of writing (December 1966) the organisation of secondary education in England and Wales was being changed, at an accelerating pace, from one of separate schools for separate types of

education to one of common, or "comprehensive", schools providing all types. All that can be attempted here is to describe how this has happened and what is projected. Official definitions of the various types of schools are given at the end.

The Education Act, 1944, made no mention of separate kinds of Secondary schools, but the Ministry of Education, influenced by the historical development of post-primary education in England and Wales, and by the findings of two recent Reports, the "Spens" Report* and the "Norwood" Report† (and by the bulk of professional opinion), declared for a "tripartite" organisation comprising Secondary Grammar, Secondary Technical, and Secondary Modern schools. The first were the previously recognised Secondary schools, the second a group of Junior Technical, Junior Commercial, and Junior Art schools ordinarily recruiting at 12 or 13 for two- or three-year vocationally-biased courses, and the third the country's Senior Elementary schools, promoted by the 1944 Act to secondary status. The three parts were most unequal in size, and have remained so: a factor of critical importance for future developments. In 1947 there were just over 3,000 Secondary Modern, 1,200 Secondary Grammar, and 300 Secondary Technical schools. There were also over 8,750 "All-Age" schools, all containing pupils of secondary-school age, most of whom would need Secondary Modern courses. By 1966 practically all the "All-Age" schools had disappeared, and there were fewer than 200 Secondary Technical schools, but Secondary Moderns had increased to over 3,700, and Secondary Grammar to over 1,280.

The Ministry never precluded the possibility of different types of schools being grouped, or amalgamated into one school, on the same site, but for long regarded such organisation as excep-

* *Secondary Education with special reference to Grammar Schools and Technical High Schools.* A Report of the Consultative Committee of the Board of Education, 1938.
† *Curriculum and Examinations in Secondary Schools.* Report of a Committee of the Secondary School Examinations Council appointed by the President of the Board of Education in 1941. (Published 1943.)

tional save in special circumstances, and in the early years did not exactly encourage experiment. A few LEAs, however, notably London and Coventry, had for ideological reasons decided to organise all the secondary education in their areas in fully comprehensive schools, and a few rural areas – Anglesey and other small Welsh counties in particular – had come to the same decision because they judged the comprehensive school to be the most economical and efficient mode of providing "secondary education for all" in sparsely populated districts.

Meanwhile, the tripartite organisation was causing increasing public anxiety, because of the consuming desire of many parents to get their children into Grammar schools, and their distress if they failed to do so. After the Education Act, 1944, which abolished tuition fees in maintained secondary schools, a Grammar school education could be had only by obtaining high marks in the "Eleven-plus" (see *Examinations*) or having parents able and willing to pay independent school fees. The replacement in 1951 of the School Certificate, for which a minimum of five subject passes was required, by the General Certificate of Education, demanding at the least only one subject pass, gave the despised Secondary Modern School – dubbed "the school for failures" – the opportunity to show that its pupils, or some of them, could undertake academic courses, pass academic examinations, and secure the academic qualifications necessary to enter higher education or professional occupations. But while this greatly increased the prestige of many Secondary Modern schools it did not sufficiently diminish parental dread of the "Eleven-plus" and its segregating consequences.

When during the later 1950s sociological and psychological research demonstrated that (i) the children of professional, managerial and other middle-class parents were getting a disproportionately large number of Grammar school places, and the children of semi-skilled and unskilled manual workers disproportionately few; and (ii) that the mental ability of children, as measured

by intelligence tests, rose in the intellectually stimulating Grammar school, but tended to fall in the less stimulating Secondary Modern school; or in short that tripartitism – or any form of organisation in separate schools – was both socially and educationally divisive, public opinion began to swing steadily towards favouring comprehensive organisation of secondary education. An increasing number of LEAs established one or more comprehensive schools in their areas, and some even announced that they had "abolished" the Eleven-plus.

Labour Party policy had long ago accepted the idea of comprehensive schools, and it was therefore no surprise that the Labour Government which assumed power late in 1964 should quickly make clear that they intended to reorganise secondary education throughout England and Wales "on comprehensive lines". (The intention was extended also to Scotland, but the Scottish tradition of "omnibus" schools, and geographical difficulties, necessitated a very different approach to the practical problem.) In July 1965 the Secretary of State for Education and Science, Mr Anthony Crosland, addressed Circular 10/65 to LEAs in England and Wales. In this he "requested" them to prepare, and submit to him within twelve months, their proposals for reorganising the maintained secondary schools in their areas on comprehensive lines.

Mr Crosland declared openly his belief that the "all-through" comprehensive school, providing for all children between the ages of 11 and 18, was the best. But as this, being large, would in many places need much new building, and as no Government money was at the time available solely for the purpose of secondary reorganisation, he suggested in addition to the "orthodox" (i.e. all-through) comprehensive school five other ways in which reorganisation could be effected on comprehensive lines. Three of these were variants of the "two-tier" plan first introduced in Leicestershire in 1957, in which the secondary period is divided into two parts.

(i) All children transfer at age 11

from Primary school into a Junior Comprehensive school, stay there until 13 or 14, and then all transfer to the same (or a similar) Senior Comprehensive school.

(ii) All children transfer at 11 into a Junior Comprehensive school, and at 13 or 14 transfer *either* to a Senior school catering for pupils up to the age of 18 *or* to one taking them up to 16 only.

(iii) All children transfer at 11 into a Junior Comprehensive school. Those children intending to leave at 16 will stay in this school for the whole of their secondary education; the others will transfer at 13 or 14 to a senior school catering for children up to 18.

As (ii) and (iii) involved selection at 13 or 14, and so were not fully comprehensive solutions, they were to be regarded as interim expedients only, necessitated by the capacities of existing buildings.

The other two modes were:

(iv) Comprehensive schools with an age range of 11 to 16, followed by "sixth-form colleges" for pupils of 16 and over.

(v) A "three-tier" system combining primary and secondary education. Primary education would end at 8 or 9, a "Middle" school for children aged 8–9 to 12–13 would straddle the existing primary and secondary periods, and there would follow a Senior school with an age range of 12–13 to 18. All three schools would be fully comprehensive.

Both these plans were regarded with something less than enthusiasm by the Secretary of State, but he subsequently became more favourably inclined towards (v). By the end of 1966 most LEAs had submitted their proposals, and about fifty had had them approved. A small proportion had either refused or were "dragging their feet".

The foregoing is a highly simplified account of the progress towards comprehensive organisation of secondary education in England and Wales. Books, pamphlets and articles in the daily and periodical Press are abundant – and usually controversial. The weekly journals devoted to education are the most fruitful sources of information and comment. The chief are:

*The Times Educational Supplement*, Printing House Square, London, E.C.4. *Education* (official journal of the Association of Education Committees), 10 Queen Anne Street, London, W.1. *The Teacher* (official journal of the National Union of Teachers), Hamilton House, Hastings Street, London, W.C.1. *The Teacher's World*, Montague House, Russell Square, London, W.C.1.

## DEFINITIONS

The following definitions of types of secondary schools in England and Wales are taken from circulars or pamphlets issued by the Ministry of Education:

**Grammar School.** One providing "a general course lasting for about five years in which the treatment of all subjects and groups of subjects but notably languages (classical and modern), mathematics, and science, follows a predominantly logical development; and ... a subsequent intensive course in the "sixth form" covering a narrower range of studies, which for many boys and girls leads naturally on to studies at the university level" ... the distinguishing features of both courses being "the scholarly treatment of their content" and "the stern intellectual discipline that they afford".*

**Technical Secondary School.** This is distinguished by its "relationship to a particular industry or occupation or group of industries and occupations". Expected to recruit from the same intellectual levels as the Grammar school, it provides for "a minority of able children who are likely to make their best response when the curriculum is strongly coloured by [vocational] interests ...†"

**Secondary Modern School.** Expected to provide "a good all-round secondary

* *The New Secondary Education.* Ministry of Education Pamphlet No. 6. HM Stationery Office, 1947, page 25.
† ibid., pages 47 and 48.

education, not focused primarily on the traditional subjects of the school curriculum, but developing out of the interests of the children . . ."‡

Originally it was intended that Secondary Modern schools should be "free from the pressure of external examinations",§ but this went by the board early in the 1950s, when the schools began entering pupils in ever larger numbers for the GCE and other external examinations. Complete reversal of the original policy was achieved with the introduction of the CSE in 1965.

**Bilateral School.** One "organised to provide for any two of the three main elements of secondary education, i.e. modern, technical or grammar, organised in clearly defined sides".

**Multilateral School.** One "intended to cater for all the secondary education of all the children in a given area" and organised in three clearly defined sides grammar, modern, technical.

**Comprehensive School.** One "intended to cater for all the secondary education of all the children in a given area without an organisation in three sides".

**School Base (or "Campus").** "A group of schools, usually unilateral, in separate buildings and each with its own headmaster or headmistress, catering for all the secondary education of a given area, but having certain common facilities and possibly sharing staff resources".||

**Scotland.** Comprehensive schools, in the sense that they provide for all the children in a given geographical area, have existed since time immemorial in Scotland. But this is because the areas are sparsely populated, not because of adherence to any educational or social creed. Even today one-third of all Scottish schools have fewer than fifty pupils, and two-thirds of those with secondary pupils are "All-Age" schools

‡ ibid., page 29.
§ *The Nation's Schools.* Ministry of Education Pamphlet No. 1, 1945, page 21.
|| The above four quotations are from the Ministry of Education Circular 144, dated 16th June, 1947. HMSO.

containing pupils from 5 and under to 15 and over.

Schools containing only pupils of secondary age were (since World War II) until the early 1960s either Junior Secondary or Senior Secondary. The former offered a three-year course, and did not ordinarily present pupils for public examinations; the latter gave a five-year course, and presented most pupils for the examination for the Scottish Leaving Certificate. But in 1961 this became the Scottish Certificate of Education (SCE) with an Ordinary (O) grade, and Junior Secondary schools were allowed to develop a four-year course and present pupils for this grade. From then the Scottish Education Department has classified secondary schools – whether or not they also contain a Primary department – as "secondary schools with SCE courses" or "secondary schools without SCE courses".

The Scottish term for the large secondary school containing SCE and non-SCE departments (and frequently a Primary department as well) is "Omnibus" school. English pattern "comprehensives" have also been created, but only in recent years.

In **Northern Ireland** there are three main types of Secondary schools: Grammar, Secondary Intermediate, and Technical Intermediate. The Grammar schools – three-quarters of them voluntary schools – provide an academic curriculum. Secondary Intermediate schools, a development resulting from the 1947 Education Act, are broadly comparable with English Secondary Modern schools. The majority are provided by LEAs. Technical Intermediate schools (all provided by LEAs) are even more recent; they came into being in 1962–63, following the Government's decision to absorb the Junior Technical Schools into the secondary field by reducing their age of entry from 12 or 13 to 11+, and basing entry, as for other secondary schools, on the Qualifying Examination (*q.v.*).

**Independent and Private Schools.** The terms "independent" and "private" are often used in respect of schools as though they were synonymous or interchangeable. Strictly speaking, this is not so. Many schools which are independent as defined below are not "private" in the sense of being the private property of individuals who can run them as profit-making concerns; they are corporations conducted in accordance with conditions laid down in a trust deed or official scheme.

In the United Kingdom an "independent school" is legally defined (in exactly the same sense in all three Acts) as:

Any school at which full-time education is provided for five or more pupils of compulsory school age (whether or not such education is also provided for pupils under or over that age), not being a school maintained by a local education authority or a school in respect of which grants are made by the Minister [for Education] to the proprietor of the school.

The word "proprietor" means "the person or body of persons responsible for the management of the school".

All independent schools in the UK must be registered with the Minister for Education; it is a legal offence to open or conduct an unregistered school. The Minister has power to close a school if he is satisfied that (i) its premises or the accommodation provided are inadequate or unsuitable; or (ii) it is being conducted by a person or persons not fit to be in charge of or teaching in a school; or (iii) the education being given is inefficient or unsuitable. A proprietor can appeal against the Minister's decision; appeals are considered in Britain by an Independent Schools Tribunal, in Northern Ireland by the County Court.

All independent schools are open to inspection by HM Inspectors. In England and Wales any independent school may further apply voluntarily for a more rigorous inspection, with a view to being granted by the Minister the status of "Recognised as Efficient". (This does not mean that other schools are inefficient; the title is, however, a reasonable guarantee of good standards.)

In 1965 nearly half the independent schools in England and Wales were "Recognised as Efficient", and the proportion increases yearly.

**Direct Grant Schools** are independent schools which accept a measure of State control, especially over their entry and their tuition fees, in return for *per capita* grants paid, not by LEAs, but directly by the Department or Ministry of Education. The conditions of grant differ in the three UK educational systems. In England and Wales, where over half of all the direct grant schools are located, and two-thirds of the direct grant Grammar schools, the grant is in aid of recurrent expenditure only; all capital expenditure is the school's responsibility.

There are Nursery, Primary, Secondary, and Special direct grant schools. The ones which have caused most controversy are the English direct grant Grammar schools, many of which are "Public" schools. They must award annually free places, totalling 25 per cent of the previous year's entry, to pupils who have attended a maintained Primary school for at least two years. The tuition fees (but not boarding) for these pupils are paid either by the school governors or LEAs – in most cases the latter. LEAs may also claim up to another 25 per cent of "reserved" places, and by agreement may secure more. For the remaining, or "residuary", places the governors may charge tuition fees on a scale agreed between them and the government department concerned. The latter assists parents with the payment of fees, in accordance with a graded income scale.

It is a condition of grant that the entrance examination shall be the same for all candidates, and not less difficult than that for entry into maintained Grammar schools. Grant is paid on pupils aged 10 and upwards, with a large additional allowance for sixth-form pupils. The amounts are revised periodically; in 1965 the grant was £52 per annum, the sixth-form allowance £84.

**Public Schools.** There is no legal definition of a Public School. The title is used by schools whose headmasters have been elected members of the Headmasters' Conference (HMC), and by schools whose governing bodies are members of the Governing Bodies Association (GBA). When the British Government set up, in December 1965, a Public Schools Commission "to advise on the best way of integrating the public schools with the State system of education", it included also schools in membership with Governing Bodies of Girls' Schools Associations. This is the first time that girls' schools have been officially accorded the title.

HMC admits boys' schools only, and limits the number to 200. GBA (whose membership overlaps largely with that of HMC) accepts boys' schools and co-educational schools, but not girls' schools. It puts no limit on the number of its members, but actually its membership is little larger than that of HMC.

The constitution of HMC requires that its membership "shall consist mainly of headmasters of Independent and Direct Grant Schools", but allows that a "small number" of heads of Voluntary and Maintained schools may also be elected. A recent analysis of the 196 schools then in membership showed that 120 were independent, 66 direct grant (or comparable status), and 10 maintained schools. GBA membership is restricted to independent and direct grant schools, except that the association may admit, on its own conditions, schools not belonging to either of these categories. A count in the early 1960s showed 137 independent, 76 direct grant, and 7 maintained schools.

About four-fifths of the independent public schools are wholly or mainly boarding-schools, but only one-fifth of the direct grant schools. Features common to all public schools are that:

(i) they are controlled by governing bodies which have been created by statute, scheme, or trust deed;

(ii) a large proportion of their pupils is in the sixth form, or in other words is pursuing courses of study beyond the Ordinary level of the General

Certificate of Education, or comparable standard;

(iii) a considerable proportion of their ex-pupils goes on to university, and more especially to Oxford or Cambridge.

**Preparatory Schools.** Usually known as "prep" schools, their primary purpose is to prepare boys aged between about 8 and 13 for entry into independent "Public" schools. For this purpose their curriculum is geared to the "Common Entrance Examination" set by these schools, and therefore includes Latin as well as a modern foreign language. Most are boarding-schools (wholly or in large part), and most are privately owned – though there has been a strong trend in recent years to transfer ownership to trusts. A large number are members of the Incorporated Association of Preparatory Schools (IAPS), which accepts only schools "Recognised as Efficient". Most prep. schools are located in England, and the majority in the south. Fees, both tuition and boarding, vary widely, but are broadly comparable with those of independent "Public" schools.

**Special Educational Treatment.** Throughout the United Kingdom all children "who suffer from any disability of mind or body", yet are capable of being educated, must be given "special educational treatment" appropriate to their needs and capacities. This may be given in an ordinary school, a day or boarding "Special School", a Special School within a hospital, or individually to children in hospital or at home. The national policy is that "handicapped children", as they are officially called, whose disability is not serious enough to prevent their meeting and mixing with normal children should attend ordinary schools. If the disability is such that this is not desirable – for the sake of either the handicapped child or the other children – then resort is had to a Special School; but, again, if possible a day school, so that the handicapped child may still enjoy home life. Only when the disability is grave, or the home unable to cope with it adequately is a child sent to a boarding Special School.

**Types of Disability.** There are ten categories of disability for which LEAs must provide special educational treatment: for children who are:

| | |
|---|---|
| Blind. | Educationally sub- |
| Partially sighted. | normal (ESN). |
| Deaf. | Physically handi- |
| Partially hearing. | capped. |
| Maladjusted. | Aphasic (i.e. hav- |
| Delicate. | ing a defect of |
| Epileptic. | speech). |

*Notes.* (i) "Blind" children are those with no sight, or so little, that they must be taught by methods not involving the use of sight. "Partially sighted" children can be educated by special methods involving the use of sight.

(ii) Similarly, "deaf" children are those with no hearing, or so little, that they must be taught by methods used for pupils having no naturally acquired speech or language. But "partially hearing" children have some naturally acquired speech or language.

(iii) ESN children have a low degree of intellectual ability, but given patience, expert teachers, and appropriate methods can be taught at least the rudiments of the "3Rs" and other subjects and useful activities.

They are definitely not lunatics or idiots, but children who are capable of being educated, in the school sense of that word. Children who are judged not capable of such education are the responsibility of the Ministry of Health, not of Education.

(iv) "Maladjusted" children are so emotionally unstable or psychologically disturbed that they cannot take part normally in the ordinary everyday life of society. Maladjustment takes many forms; a child may be unduly retiring, aggressive, lazy, or legally delinquent. And he may be of any level of intelligence.

(v) "Physically handicapped" children are those, not suffering solely from a defect of sight or hearing, who because of disease or crippling defect cannot be educated satisfactorily in an ordinary school.

(vi) "Delicate" children are those, not in any other category, whose physi-

cal condition is so much below par that they cannot without risk to their health and/or their educational progress, be educated by normal methods in an ordinary school.

(vii) Many unfortunate children suffer from more than one disability.

**Parental Rights and Obligations.** Any parent can request his LEA to give his child, aged 2 or more, a medical examination to see if the child is suffering from "any disability of mind or body", and if so, how serious this is. The LEA must comply with such a request unless in their opinion the request is unreasonable.

On the other hand, it is the statutory duty of the LEA to find out what children, aged 2 or more, in their area need special educational treatment. In pursuance of that duty the LEA may serve notice upon a parent requiring him to submit his child (aged 2 or more) for examination by a medical officer of the LEA for advice as to whether the child is suffering from any disability of mind or body, and if so, how serious this is. If a parent served with such notice fails, without reasonable excuse, to comply with it, he can be fined up to £5.

If after such examination – whether initiated by the parent or the LEA – the verdict is that the child does need special educational treatment, the LEA must inform the parent, and provide the appropriate treatment – unless the parent desires, and can make, suitable arrangements for providing such treatment elsewhere.

## FURTHER EDUCATION

This term means in the United Kingdom any kind of educational study or activity, except full-time secondary education and university education, which is systematically provided by a statutory or voluntary body for persons over compulsory school age. It includes both formal and informal education, as is clearly indicated in the Education Act, 1944 (and in very similar words in the Scottish and Irish Acts), where Further Education is defined as:

(*a*) full-time and part-time education for persons over compulsory school age; and

(b) leisure-time occupation, in such organised cultural training and re-creative activities as are suited to their requirements, for any persons over compulsory school age who are able and willing to profit by the facilities provided for that purpose.

Further Education is not compulsory. Both the English and the Scottish main Acts provide for schemes of compulsory part-time education, ordinarily for one day a week or the equivalent thereto, for young persons up to the age of 18 not undergoing other forms of full- or part-time education; but neither scheme had at the time of writing (December 1966) been put into operation, or seemed likely to be in the foreseeable future.

Though there is no statutory compulsion on anyone to undertake Further Education, there is a considerable – and increasing – amount of contractual compulsion. The Industrial Training Act, 1964, specifies that apprentices and trainees shall be granted regular time off during working hours to attend organised courses of study. This can be done in the form of "day release", i.e. one day, or more, each week, or "block release", that is, the equivalent of a day a week in longer but less frequent periods: for example, one month every six months.

Further Education is not free. But many LEAs charge no tuition fees to young persons under the age of 19; and the tuition fees charged to other students represent only a small portion of the cost of providing the course of study or activity.

Further Education can be divided into three broad areas, whose boundaries tend to overlap: vocational studies; non-vocational, or cultural, studies and activities; and social and recreative activities.

**Vocational Studies.** The great majority of vocational courses are provided by LEAs, in Colleges of Further Education, Technical Colleges, Art Colleges and Schools, Colleges of Commerce, Colleges of Technology, Polytechnics, Central Institutions (in Scotland), Institutes and Colleges of Agriculture and/or Horti-culture. The agricultural and horti-cultural institutes and colleges ordinarily provide residential courses of one or two years' duration. Otherwise, vocational Further Education is almost entirely non-residential, though there has been in recent years a tendency to provide some residential accommodation for advanced or specialised courses. There are full-time courses, "sandwich" cour-ses, which involve alternating periods of some length in college and employment, part-time day courses, part-time day and evening courses, and evening only courses. Vocational education is pro-vided at every scholastic level from that of a 15-year-old school leaver to post-graduate study and research. Since the late 1950s technical colleges in England and Wales have been graded according to the level of the work they undertake: "Local", or "District" colleges provide elementary courses, "Area" colleges intermediate studies, and "Regional" colleges advanced work. In Scotland, Central Institutions concentrate on advanced studies. A more recent devel-opment is of "Polytechnics", colleges providing a wide range of higher education courses for full-time, sand-wich, and part-time students. There is also a small number of highly specialised colleges, most of them located in England, each catering exclusively for one technology, e.g. food, foundry work, leather, or a group of closely associated technologies, as do, for instance, the ILEA London College of Fashion (clothing, hairdressing, beauty culture, etc.), and the London College of Furni-ture. Half a dozen such colleges, ranging from art to agricultural engi-neering, are directly grant-aided by the Government and have the status of "National" colleges.

**Non-vocational Courses.** The provision of *non-vocational*, or *cultural*, courses – learning for its own sake – is officially known in the United Kingdom as "Adult Education". This is provided by the LEAs, by voluntary bodies – notably, the Workers' Educational Association (WEA) – and the extramural depart-ments of universities.

The very great majority of the courses provided are non-residential, and take place in the evenings. They are of various lengths, the commonest being "terminal" (about twelve meetings, once a week), "sessional" (covering one academic year, with not fewer than twenty-four weekly meetings), and, for really ambitious scholars, the famous "three-year tutorial course", begun by the WEA in January 1908, which comprises not fewer than twenty-four two-hour meetings a year over a period of three years.

**Residential Colleges.** There are some ten long-term residential colleges, provided by voluntary bodies but grant-aided from public funds, which offer courses of one or two years' duration. They range from Ruskin College, Oxford (which is not part of the University), with an emphasis on social, economic, and political studies, to Avoncroft in Worcestershire, founded to benefit agricultural and other country workers. In Wales, Coleg Harlech is closely associated with the University of Wales and the WEA; in Scotland, Newbattle Abbey is similarly linked with the universities. Both colleges are grant-aided by the Department of Education and Science.

There are also some thirty residential colleges in England, most maintained by LEAs, which provide short courses ranging in length from a week-end to a month or occasionally longer.

**Social and recreative activities** are provided by LEAs, and by a very large number of voluntary organisations, some aided from public funds, some not. Prominent among those that are grant-aided are the national organisations providing leisure-time facilities and training for young people, for example, the YMCA and the YWCA, the Boy Scouts and the Girl Guides, the Boys' Brigade, the National Associations of Boys' Clubs and Mixed Clubs, the Young Farmers' Clubs. (See also *Service of Youth.*)

## TRAINING OF TEACHERS

In Scotland and Northern Ireland it is a legal requirement that all teachers holding permanent posts in schools maintained by LEAs shall have successfully taken an approved course of training. This is not the case in England and Wales; here, such posts can only be held by persons having the status of "Qualified Teacher", but at the time of writing (December 1966) possession of a degree from a British or other approved university entitles the holder to that status, without training.

In England and Wales most universities have accepted responsibility for the academic and professional aspects of teacher-training. All the recognised (i.e. grant-aided) training establishments are grouped geographically in Area Training Organisations (ATO), which are controlled and directed by a partnership comprising the university, the training establishments, the LEAs and the teachers. To service its ATO each university has established, and finances, an Institute or School of Education. The Director of this ordinarily holds the rank of Professor.

In England and Wales teachers are trained in University Departments of Education (UDE), Colleges of Education (formerly called Training Colleges), and Art Training Centres (ATC), in Scotland in Colleges of Education, and in Northern Ireland in UDE and Training Colleges.

English UDE are maintained and staffed by their universities, but receive grants from the Department of Education and Science (DES) in respect of the "recognised" students they train (i.e. students recognised for grant by the DES). UDE admit only university graduates for training as teachers (though some accept non-graduates to study for higher degrees), and they give them a purely professional course lasting one academic year. In this, the equivalent of one term (ten to twelve weeks), or sometimes longer, is spent by the students in schools, observing and teaching. Theoretical studies range over the philosophy, psychology, sociology, history and administration of education, and students will also be advised about teaching methods in their chosen subjects. Towards the end of the course students will be examined in both theory and practice; in theory ordinarily by written papers, in practice by teaching a class (or classes) in the presence of an "external" examiner, i.e. someone not on the staff of the student's university. Successful students receive from their university a *Diploma* or *Post-Graduate Certificate in Education* (the name varies in different universities). This not only confirms the status of Qualified Teacher, but entitles the holder to a training allowance additional to his salary.

A considerable number of Colleges of Education in England and Wales provide, along with other courses of training, one-year courses on the UDE pattern for graduates. But the main business of the 170 or more colleges (the number is constantly being increased by new foundations) is the concurrent education and professional training of non-graduate students, mainly young persons of 18–19 straight from school. The course lasts three academic years, a year being ordinarily from late September to early July, with vacations of three to four weeks each at Christmas and Easter, and a "long" vacation of some twelve weeks between the years. "Mature" students, that is, older entrants into training, if they have good educational qualifications and/or experience of teaching may be permitted to attempt the three-year course in two years, or even, exceptionally, in one.

The three-year course includes the theory and practice of education, with from twelve to eighteen weeks spent in schools observing and teaching; instruction in teaching methods in specific subjects; and the study of one or two subjects (academic or practical) to as high a level as the student is capable of. The study of such "Main" subjects is intended as personal education, but many students also aspire to teach them later at specialist level.

In the 1960s a Bachelor of Education (BEd) degree was made available to non-graduate students in Colleges of Education. Different universities specify different entrance qualifications; most demand Matriculation. The degree involves one year of full-time study after the examination for the Teacher's Certificate.

**Acceptance for Training.** To qualify for entry into a College of Education as a non-graduate student one must (i) be not less than 18 years old on 1st October in the year in which entry is desired (or 1st February for a January entry, or similarly just as term opens should entry be made at another time; the great majority of students start in September); (ii) have secured at least five Ordinary-level GCE passes, *or* three "O" level and one Advanced level, *or* two "O" level and two "A", *or* three "A" level passes and evidence that the applicant has studied other subjects after the age of 16, *or* comparable approved academic qualifications, e.g. the Scottish Certificate of Education with appropriate passes; (iii) be recommended by the Head Teacher of one's school, or other responsible person in the case of older candidates; and (iv) pass a medical examination. A physical defect does not disqualify an applicant if in the opinion of the medical officer it need not handicap a teacher in the performance of his duties.

No 18-year-old candidate who does not possess these qualifications is admitted into College. And it must be emphasised that the examination requirements specified above are *minimum* requirements. For entry into a popular college, or a specialist course, higher qualifications, or "A" level passes in specified subjects, may be essential. "Mature" applicants lacking the formal academic qualifications may (i) be told to get the requisite GCE passes, *or* (ii) be given a special examination; *or* (iii) occasionally, be accepted on the strength of their previous experience. All such cases are considered individually by ATOs, and as these differ in their requirements enquiry at the college desired or its Institute of Education is advised.

All candidates for places in Colleges of Education in England and Wales must apply through the Central Register and Clearing House, not through individual colleges. Application forms are available from secondary schools and Colleges of Education.

**Provision of Colleges.** Over two-thirds of

the Colleges of Education in England and Wales are provided by LEAs. They are financed for both capital and recurrent expenditure out of a "pool" to which all the LEAs contribute in proportion to the number of children in their primary and secondary schools. There are about fifty "voluntary" colleges, most of them provided by bodies representing religious denominations, especially the Church of England and the Roman Catholic Church; these are responsible respectively for about one-half and one quarter of the fifty. Voluntary colleges can get from the Government grants of up to 80 per cent for capital expenditure, and are grant-aided for recurrent expenditure on a capitation basis. Half their student places must be available, if required, to applicants not belonging to the denomination which provides the college.

**Fees and Grants.** No fees are charged to "recognised" students in Colleges of Education, and grants for living and incidental expenses are available on the same basis as for all recognised students in approved courses of higher education.

**General and Specialist Colleges.** Most Colleges of Education train all or most of their students for general classroom duties, mainly in Primary schools. Students are given the option, often on entry into College but sometimes later, of choosing the age-range for which they wish to train. The most usual categories are:

> Infants (5 to 7), or occasionally Nursery-Infant (2 to 7).
> Infant/Junior (6 to 9).
> Junior (7+ to 11+).
> Junior/Secondary (9+ to 13+).
> Secondary (11+ to 15+ or 18+).

Only a small proportion of non-graduate students are trained for secondary school work, and these largely for teaching specialist subjects – art and crafts, music, woodwork, metalwork, home economics (housecraft, or domestic science), physical education – and less frequently subjects for which teachers are in very short supply, e.g. science and mathematics.

At the time of writing (December 1966) there are still a few wholly specialist Colleges of Education, notably some training women teachers of physical education. But the day of the exclusively specialist college seems almost over; the trend is for the specialist college to have a general "wing", and the general college to have a specialist "wing". One group of four colleges seems likely, however, to remain specialised: those training teachers for service in Further Education establishments. Their entrance requirements and training courses are very different from those of the other colleges. Ordinarily, they admit only students aged 25 or upwards, and they require responsible experience in employment as well as academic qualifications. They give a one-year full-time, or longer "sandwich", course of professional training slanted towards particular professional, industrial, or commercial occupations; and a variety of short courses for serving teachers.

**Art Training Centres** are departments in Art Colleges or, in a few cases, in universities which are recognised by the Secretary of State for Education and Science for the training of specialist teachers of art and/or handcrafts – the latter usually light crafts such as bookbinding, pottery, weaving, and not directly vocational crafts like, for example, plumbing. To qualify for entry, applicants must have specialist qualifications in art and/or crafts: the Diploma in Art and Design (Dip.AD) or its predecessor the National Diploma in Design (NDD) are the most common. ATC give a one-year course of professional training leading to the Teacher's Certificate. As the previous specialist courses require four years' full-time study, it takes a minimum of five years to qualify as a specialist art teacher.

**Scotland.** The training of teachers in Scotland differs from that in England and Wales in three important respects:

> (i) It is all carried out in autonomous Colleges of Education. The universities do not participate, and their Departments of Education do not train teachers.

(ii) Instead of there being one Teacher's Certificate entitling the holder to teach in any type of school, there are three – General, Special, Technical – each giving the holder the right to teach only in specified grades of school or specified subjects.

(iii) Professional training is compulsory for graduates as well as non-graduates.

The importance of (iii) is enhanced by the fact that all secondary school teachers in Scotland must normally hold graduate or graduate-equivalent qualifications, as must also men teachers in Primary schools.

The conditions of entry into, and the qualifications conferred by, the three Teachers' Certificates are:

(1) *The Teacher's General Certificate.* The courses leading to this can be entered by men holding Pass or General degrees, and by women non-graduates. The General Certificate entitles the holder to teach in Primary schools only, but graduates and holders of specialist qualifications officially recognised as equivalent to a degree (graduate-equivalent) can by passing a further examination secure an endorsement to this Certificate qualifying them to teach also in the lower classes of secondary schools, i.e. in practice, up to the school-leaving age of 15.

(2) *The Teacher's Special Certificate.* This is available only to holders of honours degrees. It qualifies them to teach one or more specified academic subjects throughout the secondary school.

(3) *The Teacher's Technical Certificate.* This Certificate is available only to men and women holding "graduate-equivalent" qualifications in aesthetic or vocational subjects: art, crafts (light or heavy), music, physical education, domestic science, technological subjects, commerce, agriculture, horticulture. It qualifies the holder to teach the subject or subjects specified in his/her Certificate throughout Secondary school or in Further Education establishments.

Training courses leading to the *General Certificate* last for graduates one year, for male non-graduates four years, that is, three years' preparation for a degree or "graduate-equivalent" followed by one year of professional training. For women not intending to graduate the course lasts three years.

The course leading to the *Special Certificate* lasts one academic year, and consists entirely of professional training.

Training courses leading to the *Technical Certificate* differ in length according to the specialism concerned; the range is from two terms for students with approved qualifications in art, music, commerce, or agriculture to two or three years for students wishing to teach woodwork and/or metalwork.

Two other differences between the English and Scottish systems should be noted. In England and Wales all entrants into Colleges of Education must be at least 18; in Scotland the minimum age for admission is 17, and college principals may admit girls as young as 16 years 9 months. Secondly, women taking non-graduate courses in Scotland spend considerably more time in teaching practice. Minor differences are that Scottish terms are slightly shorter than English, but the working week slightly longer.

**Northern Ireland.** The UDE at the Queen's University, Belfast, like English UDEs, accepts graduates only, and gives them a one-year course of purely professional training.

At the time of writing (December 1966) it is not known whether the new University of Coleraine, due to open in October 1968, will undertake the training of teachers.

There are three general Training Colleges in Northern Ireland: Stranmillis, a very large non-denominational establishment run by the Ministry of Education, and two closely associated Roman Catholic colleges, St Mary's for women and St Joseph's for men. There is also a tiny Ulster College of Physical Education, for women only, which is run by the Ministry of Education. Specialist teachers of domestic science are trained at the Domestic Economy Training College, Belfast.

Admission to training college is competitive. There are two modes of entry, Ordinary and Special, the former restricted to candidates between the ages of 17 and 19, the latter open to candidates between 17 and 30.

The training course for Primary school teachers lasts three years, for teachers in Secondary Intermediate schools four years. At Stranmillis a Combined Course lasting four or five years enables a student to secure both a Teacher's Certificate and a university degree – the latter (or a "graduate-equivalent") almost essential for teaching in a good Grammar school.

In Northern Ireland all teachers in maintained or grant-aided schools must have been trained.

## UNIVERSITIES

In December 1966 there were 40 universities in the United Kingdom: 32 in England, six in Scotland, and one each in Wales and Northern Ireland. There were also four "universities-designate", that is, institutions awaiting the grant of a Royal Charter, which alone confers the title and rights of a university in Britain.

Of the 40 universities 30 have been founded in the twentieth century. In 1800 there were only six universities; two in England and – surprisingly in view of the respective populations – four in Scotland.

The foundation of British universities has come in recurrent waves. Oxford and Cambridge emerged (neither was officially founded) as *studia generalia* – places of study to which scholars from anywhere could resort – in the late twelfth and early thirteenth centuries respectively; and for 600 years they preserved a monopoly of university education in England and Wales, successfully resisting all attempts to found universities in other places.

In the fifteenth century three universities were founded in Scotland: St Andrews (1411), Glasgow (1451), and Aberdeen (1494). A fourth was added in the sixteenth century: Edinburgh (1583), which was founded, and for two centuries controlled, by the town council.

In 1826 a "University of London"

(now University College, London) was established on a non-denominational basis to provide university education for nonconformists, Oxford and Cambridge being open only to members of the Church of England. This immediately provoked the foundation of King's College, London, on a strictly Church of England basis. Neither establishment got a university charter, and federation proved impossible. So in 1836 a Royal Charter was granted to a University of London that was purely an examining body, with power to affiliate colleges wishing to take its degrees. In 1858 the right to enter for London degrees was thrown open to anyone anywhere who had the required academic qualifications. Thus was established the famous London "external" degree which over the past century and more has enabled scores of institutions throughout the British Commonwealth to grow into full universities, and scores of thousands of men and women unable to attend universities to secure a university degree.

In 1832 Durham University was founded on the model of Oxford and Cambridge, that is, as a "collegiate" university – one made up of more or less autonomous colleges.

During the second half of the nineteenth centuries colleges of higher education, largely but nowhere exclusively devoted to science and technology, sprang up in large industrial towns. This led to the foundation of the "Redbrick" universities:[*] Birmingham (1900), Liverpool (1903), Leeds (1904), Sheffield (1905), Bristol (1909), and later Reading (1926). Manchester had been founded in 1880 as a federal university, as had the University of Wales in 1893. Manchester was reconstituted in 1903.

All these institutions served an apprenticeship as "University Colleges", preparing their students for London external degrees because they had not the right to grant their own. A similar apprenticeship was served by the next group of English universities, founded after World War II: Nottingham (1948),

---

[*] So called because of the dominant element in their early buildings. The term, along with "Oxbridge", was popularised if not invented by "Bruce Truscot" (the late Professor Allison Peers) in *Redbrick University* (Faber, 1943).

Southampton (1952), Hull (1954), Exeter (1955), Leicester (1957).

But during this period the pattern of foundation changed. In 1949 the University College of North Staffordshire, though a university college, was granted the right to confer its own first degrees (BA, BSc) because of its experimental character. It was the last of the "university colleges" (it became the University of Keele in 1962). The next seven universities, though all entirely new foundations, were full universities from the start: Sussex (1961), East Anglia (1963), York (1963), Essex (1964), Lancaster (1964), Kent at Canterbury (1965), Warwick (1965).

In 1963 another pattern emerged. In 1956–58 ten leading technical colleges in England and Wales were given the status of "Colleges of Advanced Technology" (CATs). In 1963 the "Robbins" Report on *Higher Education* recommended that they become technological universities. The Government agreed, and by the end of 1966 seven had received Royal Charters: Aston in Birmingham, Bath (formerly Bristol College of Science and Technology), Bradford, Brunel, City (formerly Northampton College of Advanced Technology,) London, Loughborough, Surrey (formerly Battersea College of Technology).

One other recent change in England: in 1963 the Newcastle division of Durham University became an independent university.

In Scotland, in 1964 the Royal College of Science and Technology at Glasgow (founded in 1796 as the Anderson's Institute) became the University of Strathclyde. In 1966 the Heriot-Watt College, Edinburgh, received its university charter. Two years previously the British Government had decided that Scotland should have another university, at Stirling. This expects to receive a Royal Charter in 1967.

Similarly in Northern Ireland, the Government decided to establish a second university, at Coleraine, alongside the old-established Queen's University, Belfast, which received its Charter in 1908 but was founded as a University College in 1845.

**Admission.** All applications for admission into first degree and first diploma courses at universities in England and Wales must be made through the Universities Central Council on Admissions (UCCA), whose address is 29 Tavistock Square, London, W.C.1. Applications must *not* be made direct to universities.

Applications to the Universities of Edinburgh and Stirling in Scotland, and the Queen's University, Belfast, in Northern Ireland, must also be made through UCCA. The Universities of Aberdeen, Dundee, Glasgow, St Andrews, and Strathclyde have separate arrangements for:

(*a*) Single or multiple applications.

(*b*) Applicants domiciled in Scotland or outside this country.

Information about these arrangements should be obtained from the universities concerned.

Direct application should be made to Heriot-Watt University, Edinburgh.

All applications through UCCA must be submitted to the Council's office between 1st September and 15th December in the year preceding that in which entry is desired. Applicants who include Oxford and/or Cambridge among their choices must submit their applications between 1st September and 15th October.

Applicants who are at school in the United Kingdom should obtain application forms from their school. Those who have left school should write to UCCA. *All* intending applicants are urged by UCCA to secure a copy of *the latest edition* of the Council's Handbook, which gives full, and up-to-date, particulars about application and acceptance procedures. The price, including postage, of this Handbook is: within the UK 3s., within Europe 5s., outside Europe 9s. UCCA also issues free of charge a leaflet entitled *Industrial Awards and the Universities Central Admissions Scheme.*

*Academic qualifications for entry.* It is impossible to state what academic qualifications are required to secure entry into a British university; one can only state what are the *minimum* academic qualifications which entitle an applicant to be considered for entry. These are, in terms of the English General Certificate of Education (GCE), not fewer than five subject passes, of which at least two (different from the others) must be at Advanced Level. Comparable passes in the Scottish Certificate of Education or the Northern Ireland General Certificate of Education are equally valid throughout the UK.

It must be emphasised, however, that the above are the *minimum* qualifications, and that for so long as the demand for undergraduates places exceeds the supply, as it has done for many years, and seems likely to do for many more, the minimum will rarely secure acceptance except into departments whose subjects are little known and/or little sought after. How much more than the minimum will be required depends in the first instance upon the popularity of the particular university, and secondly upon the popularity of the particular Department, Faculty or School. In addition, any Department may make specialist requirements; would-be entrants into a mathematics department, for example, may well be expected to secure an "A" level GCE pass in pure or applied mathematics, and similarly a modern language aspirant an "A" level in the language(s) concerned. Where pressure on places is heavy, high "A"-level grades will be demanded.

There are just one or two exceptions to the rule about academic qualifications. Since 1947 the British Ministry (now Department) of Education has offered annually up to thirty scholarships to "mature" students, i.e. aged 25 upwards, who have proved themselves capable of study at university level. Particulars are available from the Awards Branch of the Department of Education and Science.

In 1964 Sussex University began to offer annually a few places (nine in 1964) to applicants who left school at 16 or earlier, and lack the minimum academic qualifications.

**University Degrees.** The structure of degrees in British universities is simple, but unfortunately differences in nomenclature make it seem exceedingly complex. There is a *first* degree, usually termed a Bachelor's degree, and after this are three grades of *higher* degrees: the Master's, the Doctorate in Philosophy (PhD), and the Senior Doctorate.

In England and Wales the first, or Bachelor's, degree can be either a Pass, General or Ordinary degree requiring the study of several subjects, or an Honours or Special degree requiring study to a considerably higher level in one subject or two closely allied subjects. Most Pass, and many Honours, degree courses are of three years' duration; some Honours degrees require four years. The Master's degree is (except in Oxford and Cambridge, for which see below) a higher degree ordinarily obtainable after one or two years' study beyond the Bachelor level. It can be secured either by passing examination papers or by presenting a thesis embodying the results of the candidate's own original research. The PhD, which demands at least two years' full-time study beyond a first degree (and of course longer if taken part-time, as it can be), is obtainable only by presenting a thesis. Senior Doctorates, e.g. Doctor of Science (DSc), Doctor of Divinity (DD), are awarded to distinguished scholars who have made through their published work a substantial contribution to knowledge. Senior Doctorates are also regularly conferred, *honoris causa*, by universities on persons eminent in any field of worthwhile activity.

Most degrees, except the PhD, which can be taken in any subject, indicate clearly the broad field of knowledge in which they have been taken, e.g. Bachelor of Science (BSc), Bachelor of Commerce (BComm), Bachelor of Music (BMus). In some cases an even more precise indication is given, e.g. BSc. (Econ), Bachelor of Science in Economics. The Masters' degrees give similar indication. But the commonest of all degrees, at both the Bachelor's and the Master's level, has retained the mediaeval term "arts": the Bachelor of Arts (BA) and the Master of Arts (MA). In the Middle Ages the term "arts" meant the broad fields of scholarly knowledge –

the "seven liberal arts" – but it is now ordinarily restricted to the humanities, the subjects dealing with man and his activities: language, literature, history, geography, and so on. The restriction is not narrow; one can get, for example, BA(Admin), Bachelor of Arts in Administration, and, more frequently, MA(Ed), Master of Arts in Education. There are no senior Doctorates in "arts"; but in "letters", DLitt, that is Doctor Litterarum.

The outstanding exceptions to the grades of degrees given above are furnished by Oxford and Cambridge, and by the Scottish universities. At Oxford and Cambridge the only first degree is the BA. There is no BSc at all at Cambridge. At Oxford it is a higher degree along with other "Bachelor" degrees, e.g. BMus, BLitt (these and others are also awarded at Cambridge and some other universities). Moreover, at Oxford and Cambridge the MA (Master of Arts), which like the BA covers all subjects, is a purely honorary title. No examination is taken, no research thesis presented; all that is needed is for a BA to wait a specified period of time (about three years from taking the BA), and pay the specified fee.

In the four older Scottish universities – Aberdeen, Edinburgh, Glasgow, St Andrews – the first degree in arts is MA, but in science, commerce, engineering, agriculture, and in some universities in law the first degree is the Bachelor's. In other subjects (and in some universities in law), the Bachelor's is a higher degree, e.g. EdB (Bachelor of Education), BD (Bachelor of Divinity). Strathclyde adheres to the more usual pattern of BA, BSc, and so on for the first degree, MA, MSc for the second.

A Scottish first degree can be taken at Ordinary or Honours level. An Ordinary degree, which involves the study of seven courses, normally takes three years. An Honours degree (also involving the study of several subjects) takes four years. Higher degrees take from one to three, or occasionally more, years.

Most of England's newest universities, while keeping the normal names for their degrees, are throwing up new types of courses for first degrees, and in some cases for second degrees (MA, MSc, etc.).

The most radically different are those at the University of Keele (opened in 1950 as the University College of North Staffordshire). Here, candidates for the Bachelor's degree must spend the first year in "Foundation" studies (a general survey of Western thought, institutions, and science), and during the following three years must study four subjects, of which one at least must be a science if the others are arts subjects, and vice versa. Only in the fourth year of the four-year undergraduate course is intensive specialisation permitted. At Sussex the candidate's main subject cannot be studied alone but only in conjunction with associated or, as the university calls them, "contextual" subjects: e.g. a student who "majors" in history will also study, for example, philosophy, literature, or economics. Similarly integrated undergraduate courses are offered at most of the newer universities, and at several of the older.

The technological universities created in 1966–67, while offering some continuous full-time undergraduate courses, usually of three years' duration, mainly offer four-year "sandwich" courses involving alternate periods of some months in employment and in the university. It is to be emphasised that the periods spent in employment are just as much part of the degree course as are those spent in the university.

In addition to degrees, universities also offer "diplomas". These are of two kinds: (i) first diplomas, awarded to persons not studying for degrees, and requiring a shorter course (usually one or two years) than that for a first degree, and (ii) post-graduate diplomas. Among the latter the Diploma in Education (called in some universities the Post-Graduate Certificate of Education), awarded after a one-year course of training for teaching, attracts the largest number of students, but there are post-graduate diplomas in a wide range of specialisms from public health to classical archaeology. Some universities also offer "Certificates" for courses less demanding than those for diplomas.

## EXAMINATIONS

In one form or another, examinations began thousands of years ago. In their modern form of written examination papers to be completed within a specified period of time, they became widespread in the United Kingdom in the 1850s, with school and Civil Service examinations spreading almost simultaneously.

Examinations can be used for various purposes, of which the two main are assessment and competition. Examinations for the purpose of assessment are also of two main kinds: for the assessment of ability (actual or potential), or for the assessment of attainment in a field of knowledge or skill. Competitive examinations may be briefly defined as examinations for prizes. The "prizes" may be places in a school, college or other establishment, or the right of entry into a particular employment or grade of employment, or monetary or other material reward. The fundamental difference between assessment and competitive examinations is that in the former a specified level of attainment divides the examinees into two groups, those who "pass" and those who "fail", whereas in the latter it is the number of places or prizes available which determines success or failure.

In technical terms, examinations can be divided into two groups: *internal* and *external*. Internal examinations are those set and marked by the members of the staff of a single school or other educational establishment (or occasionally a self-selected group of establishments) for their own pupils or students. No one outside the school or college or group has any say in what is done. External examinations, on the other hand, are set and marked, and controlled throughout, by examining bodies established for the purpose. They can be taken by any school or college, and often by any individuals, who can satisfy the conditions for entry into the examination which have been drawn up by the examining body.

The foregoing paragraphs are generalisations about a very complex and complicated matter. The difficulty about being precise concerning assessment and competitive examinations is that the former are always liable to be used for the latter purpose. The English "Elevenplus" was originally intended simply to assess the attainments of elementary school children. The GCE is used to select students for university. In both cases, shortage of places in a desired educational establishment has led to an assessment examination becoming a competitive one.

The difficulty about internal and external examinations is not so serious. But while it is perfectly certain that the test set by a teacher to his class is an internal examination, and equally clear that GCE examinations are external examinations, since they are set and marked by national examining bodies which have their own offices and permanent staff (and which usually prescribe the syllabuses of work that they examine), there are examinations which exhibit both internal and external characteristics. For example, an examination may be internal to the extent that the syllabus of work prescribed, the examination questions set, and the marking of the scripts, are all done by the staff of a school or college exclusively for the pupils or students of that school or college. But the examination is external in that (i) it is taken to secure an award offered by an external examining body; and consequently (ii) the syllabus(es) of work must have been approved by that body; as must also (iii) the examination questions and/or other tests set; and (iv) a proportion at least of the scripts and/or other material produced by the examinees must be scrutinised by external examiners, or "moderators", appointed by the examining body to ensure that (*a*) the standard of those who pass is satisfactory, and (*b*) that the marking has been consistently and fairly done. In any form of external examination, should dispute arise between internal and external examiner, the latter has invariably (subject to appeal to the examining body) the last word.

Most external examinations in the United Kingdom, and a high proportion of internal examinations, consist very largely of written papers requiring "essay type" answers, that is, answers in the form of a consecutive narrative. Examinations in modern foreign languages include an oral test, in scientific subjects laboratory experiments, and in such "practical" subjects as art, architecture, cookery, handcrafts, music, shorthand and typewriting exhibits of the examinee's skill or craftsmanship. In all forms of external examination credit may be given for "course work", that is, the day-to-day exercises done by the student while following the course leading to the examination. In rare instances "continuous assessment" of "course work" is used instead of an examination at the end of the course.

The outstanding exceptions to the statement that most UK examinations demand "essay-type" answers are the tests used to select Primary school children for entry into different forms of secondary education: the "Eleven-plus" in England and Wales (officially called the "Common Entrance" examination), the Promotion Examination in Scotland, and the Qualifying Examination in Northern Ireland. Though these differ in details (as indeed do the various examinations set by individual LEAs), they are basically similar, consisting essentially of three tests, usually "objective" standardised tests, of "Intelligence" or as it is often called "Verbal Reasoning", formal English and formal Arithmetic. These tests may be, and often are, supplemented by Primary school teachers' reports, or "cumulative record cards" which trace a child's progress through Primary school. In cases where decision is difficult "course work" may be considered, parents interviewed, and/or the children given other tests, including sometimes individual tests.

The fundamental difference between "essay type" written examination papers and such tests as are used in the "Eleven-plus" is that, however carefully one tries to be consistent and impartial, it is virtually impossible to mark "essay type" answers with absolute consistency, especially in subjects, such as literature, history, geography, where opinions as well as facts are called for; but in objective tests there is one, and only one, correct answer to each question.

This is obtained by requiring only a single word, figure, or shape, to be inserted, underlined, ticked, or otherwise indicated. These answers are based on one of two principles: (i) "true–false", allowing choice between two alternatives only; or (ii) "multiple choice", in which several (word, figure or shape) answers are suggested, and the examinee must choose the correct one.

Tests of this kind are said to be "standardised" when they have been tried out on a sufficiently large number of examinees (say 10,000) of the same age, rated ability, or attainment to establish "norms" of performance, e.g. that if the "average" child gets about 100 correct answers the exceptionally able child may be expected to get 140 or more, the exceptionally dull child 70 or fewer.

A main criticism of objective tests is that they afford examinees no opportunity to exercise imagination, to show their ability to marshal (or destroy) an argument, or even to demonstrate their skill in writing their native language. There are in existence objective tests of qualities other than intellectual capacity, and batteries of tests purporting to give a "profile", or all-round estimate, of personality, but these have been little developed in the United Kingdom.

The Eleven-plus. This examination, or, more accurately, this battery of tests, so hated and feared by parents, has a much longer history than most people realise. It came into existence in the early years of the twentieth century, and became firmly established in 1907, when secondary schools were offered increased Government grant provided they reserved up to a quarter of their places for elementary school children whose tuition fees would be paid by their LEAs. The examinations, ordinarily in English and Arithmetic, held to select candidates for these "Free Places", soon became fiercely competitive, because the number of qualified candidates exceeded the places available; and this continued to be the case throughout the years.

The LEAs, who administered the examinations, gladly took up objective tests of "intelligence", and later of attainment, because these not only seemed to make the selection more fair, but could be seen to be doing so. No one could accuse the examiners of favouritism or prejudice, because all they could do was to count the correct answers. They had no power to decide which were the correct answers; that had been done for them. By 1939 practically every LEA in England and Wales was using standardised objective tests of intelligence, English, and Arithmetic to select elementary school children for transfer to secondary schools at about the age of 11 to 12.

When the Education Act, 1944, made secondary education obligatory for all children the situation was radically altered. It was no longer a matter of selecting a small minority of able elementary school children for transfer to the one form of secondary education available, the "academic" or Grammar school type, but of attempting to allocate all primary school children to suitable forms of secondary education, so that they might obtain "efficient full-time education" appropriate to their different abilities and aptitudes, as the Act required. That, at any rate, was the theory; in practice, matters worked out very differently. The same examination machinery was used for "allocation" as had been used for "selection". The children who got the best results in the examination went, as previously, to the Grammar school, and the others to the Secondary Modern school, which, as everyone knew, was only the Elementary school with a new name. Not surprisingly, parents continued to talk about "the scholarship" if a child were allotted a Grammar school place, and of "failure" if not. As the Education Act, 1944, had abolished tuition fees in secondary schools maintained by LEAs it was no longer possible to "buy" a place in a maintained Grammar school, and as over the country the maintained Grammar schools had places for only about one in five of the Secondary school population, the new "Eleven-plus" soon became even more competitive than its predecessor. As during the 1950s and early 1960s Secondary Modern schools

developed attractive courses, and in particular passed increasing numbers of pupils through the GCE parental anxiety about the "Eleven-plus" diminished considerably in many places. When in 1964 the Government decided to reorganise all secondary education on comprehensive lines the end of the "Eleven-plus" as an instrument for directing children to different kinds of schools came in sight; and during the immediately following years many LEAs openly "abolished" it, as indeed a number had done previously. In view of the suffering it (or rather its consequences) had caused, few people regretted its passing. But two points are to be remembered: (i) that while far from infallible the "Eleven-plus" tests, if accurately standardised, constitute the most accurate instrument for diagnosing intellectual ability at about the age of eleven, and (ii) that so long as the laws relating to education in the United Kingdom require children to be given education in school suitable to their "ages, abilities and aptitudes", so long must diagnosis of abilities and aptitudes be made.

The "Eleven-plus examination" (and to a considerable extent the Scottish "Promotion" and the Northern Ireland "Qualifying" examinations) consists essentially of three objective tests, usually standardised: of "intelligence" or "verbal reasoning", and of attainment in basic English and Arithmetic. The tests used come mainly from two sources: Moray House College of Education, Edinburgh, and the National Foundation for Educational Research in England and Wales (NFER), The Mere, Upton Park, Slough, Bucks. They are not ordinarily on sale to the public until they have been discarded for examination purposes.

These tests may or may not be supplemented by other means of assessment. Often, resort is had to Primary school teachers' reports and/or Cumulative Record Cards.

The individual LEAs decide whether or not they will apply "Eleven-plus" tests, what tests to use, and how these shall be administered. Ordinarily the tests are given to children in their own schools by their own teachers, who mark the scripts in accordance with instructions and convert the "raw" scores into "standard scores". The scripts and mark lists are then sent to the LEA office, where officers of the Authority rank the examinees from all the schools in the area in a single order of merit list. An Examination Board, largely of teachers, appointed by the LEA, divides this list into three parts: Grammar school certainties, a "border-zone" of doubtful cases, and non-Grammar school certainties. Great care is exercised over the "border-zone"; these children may be given further objective tests, and/or their school work and/or record may be scrutinised, or they may be given individual testing, and so on. Ultimately, of course, the allocation of the year's examinees depends upon the number of places available for each form of secondary education.

"Eleven-plus" examinations may be given all at one time, usually in spring, or in two parts, usually in autumn and spring, or at intervals during the latter part of the Primary school stage, often without the children being aware that they are being examined.

**General Certificate of Education (GCE).** The examinations for the GCE are administered by the following eight examining bodies, of which seven are based on universities:

Cambridge Local Examinations Syndicate, Syndicate Buildings, Cambridge.

Oxford and Cambridge Schools Examinations Board, 10 Trumpington Street, Cambridge.

Oxford Local Examinations, 12 Merton Street, Oxford.

The Northern Universities Joint Matriculation Board (NUJMB, or in short JMB, representing the Universities of Birmingham, Leeds, Liverpool, Manchester, and Sheffield), Manchester 15.

Southern Universities Joint Board for School Examinations (representing the Universities of Bristol, Exeter, Reading, and Southampton), 22 Berkeley Square, Bristol 8.

London University Entrance and School Examinations Board, Senate House, London, W.C.1.

The Welsh Joint Education Committee, 30 Cathedral Road, Cardiff.

The Associated Examining Board for the General Certificate of Education (AEB), 31 Brechin Road, South Kensington, London, S.W.7.

The university examining bodies are of considerable age. The AEB was introduced in 1953 because of a demand for an examination better suited than the others for candidates contemplating careers in industry or commerce rather than the professions. It held its first examinations in 1955. It is administered by the City and Guilds of London Institute (76 Portland Place, London, W.1) on behalf of various industrial and technical associations.

All the GCE examinations come under the supervision of the Schools Council for the Curriculum and Examinations (q.v.), which in 1964 took over the task of co-ordinating the various examinations from the Secondary School Examinations Council (SSEC).

The examinations for the GCE are academic examinations, adjusted to suit intellectually able pupils between the ages of 15 and 18 who have followed a fairly exacting course of general education in a secondary school. (They can, however, be taken by people of any age.) They are "subject" examinations, that is, a candidate may enter for any number of subjects, with no restrictions on his choice, and he gains a Certificate if he passes in one subject only. He can add to his list of passes at subsequent examinations. The main examinations are held in the Summer (June–July); others are held in winter (November–December).

GCE examinations are set at two levels, Ordinary (O) and Advanced (A). The "O"-level papers are intended primarily for pupils who have completed a five- or six-year Secondary school course in an academically biased school or section of a school. The "A"-level papers are intended for pupils who have completed a seven- or eight-year course, and have specialised to some extent during the last two years or so on a considerably smaller number of subjects. There are also at "A" level "Scholarship" papers, set on the same syllabuses but with somewhat more difficult questions, which are designed to test the ability of candidates for "open" scholarships (i.e. open to all-comers, not restricted to members of a school, district and so on) offered by universities and other institutions of higher education.

Most examinees take "O"-level papers first, but there is no obligation to do so; in fact, the original intention, when the GCE replaced the School Certificate and the Higher School Certificate in 1951, was that able examinees would by-pass "O" level, at least in their strong subjects, and go straight to "A" level. But that idea was killed by the condition laid down by the British universities for exemption from their "Matriculation" examinations, i.e. the passes required before they would consider applicants academically qualified for entry. These conditions differ in detail from university to university, and still more from faculty to faculty and department to department, but everywhere the irreducible minimum is at least five subject passes, of which at least two must be at A level. So, naturally, aspirants to university entry collect the easier "O" level passes first, and then concentrate upon the subjects they will take at "A" level. Many professional bodies, e.g. the Institute of Chartered Accountants, Institute of Builders, and the Engineering Associations, also exempt candidates from their preliminary examinations who have specified GCE passes. Their requirements are set out in a Circular (periodically revised) issued by the Department of Education and Science, which can be purchased from HM Stationery Office, or through any bookseller.

**Certificate of Secondary Education (CSE).** Following persistent demands over years from LEAs, teachers, parents and members of the general public for either a lower-level GCE pass, or a lower-level external examination more suited to less academically minded pupils, the English Ministry of Education took the advice of its Secondary School Examinations Council (embodied in the "Beloe" Report on *Secondary School Examinations other than the GCE*, HM Stationery Office, 1960), and in 1963 announced its intention to introduce a new set of external examinations, leading to a Certificate of Secondary Education (CSE).

The examinations for the CSE are intended primarily for Secondary school children of about average ability, or in other words the next 40 per cent or so after those who are certainly capable of taking GCE. The examinations can be taken by pupils in any type of school; the sole condition is that candidates shall have completed five years of secondary education. There is no compulsion to take the CSE examinations. Like those for the GCE, they are "subject" examinations. A Certificate can be gained for one subject, to which others can be added at subsequent examinations.

A distinctive feature of the CSE examinations is that there is no "pass" or "fail" mark; candidates are placed in one of five grades, or if hopelessly bad are ungraded, in each subject they take. Grade 1 is reckoned as equivalent in standard to a GCE "O"-level pass, and is accepted as such for exemption purposes by the universities, the Colleges of Education, the Civil Service Commissioners, and numerous professional associations. Grade 4 represents the standard that should be reached after five years by a hard-working pupil of average ability in a non-selective school or stream.

Another distinctive feature is that the examinations set and the award of Certificates are controlled by teachers serving in the schools providing the candidates. These teachers must form a majority on each of the fourteen Regional Boards – thirteen in England and one in Wales – which administer the CSE.

The first examinations (held by nine Boards only) took place in 1965, and the first full year was 1966. There are three possible modes of examining: (i) a completely external examination set and marked by the Regional Board, on a syllabus prescribed by that Board; (ii) an external examination set and marked by the Regional Board, but on a syllabus drawn up by a school or group of schools, and approved by the Board; and (iii) an internal examination set and marked by the school, on a syllabus drawn up by the school. In this case the Regional Board must approve the syllabus, and appoint external examiners to sample, or "moderate" the scripts.

The **Scottish Certificate of Education** (SCE) replaced the "Scottish Leaving Certificate" in 1962. Like the English GCE, it can be taken at two levels, called "grades", Ordinary and Higher. The ages at which candidates may sit for these is strictly controlled. The "O"-grade examination is open to pupils in the fourth year of a Senior Secondary school course, and to students who have followed comparable courses in Further Education establishments. The "H" grade examination is taken in the fifth Secondary school year, that is, one year after "O" grade, and not two years as is the usual practice in taking the GCE "O" and "A" levels. Consequently, while the SCE "O" grade is equated with the GCE "O" level for exemption purposes, the "H" grade is not considered so high a standard as the GCE "A" level.

In 1966 the Scottish Education Department announced that from 1968 onwards there would be a new examination, for pupils in their sixth year at Secondary school, that would lead to a "Certificate of Sixth Year Studies". The examination would not be marked on a pass/fail basis; candidates would be awarded "ranks" of attainment. And it would provide for aesthetic and practical interests as well as academic.

**Northern Ireland.** In some Secondary Intermediate schools there are courses leading to the Northern Ireland General Certificate of Education (*see below*). In Technical Intermediate schools two examinations (both run by the Ministry of Education) can be taken: the Junior Technical Certificate Examination, taken at about 14 or 15, and the Technical Certificate Examination, taken usually one year later. Able Technical Intermediate pupils are often entered for the

GCE (English or Northern Ireland) a year after the Technical Certificate Examination.

Grammar school pupils may or may not take the Junior Certificate Examination, which is optional. If they do, they take it at the end of their third year of secondary education. It is a "group" examination; to gain a Certificate a candidate must take English and five other subjects selected in the manner prescribed, and must pass in all six, or well enough in five to compensate for a "near miss" in the sixth. The Northern Ireland GCE is very similar to the English. It is a subject examination, and can be taken at "O" and "A" levels. Passes in appropriate subjects at specified levels qualify the holders for entry into universities, teacher-training colleges and other higher-education establishments, and to the examinations leading to professional status in many occupations. A group certificate, the Northern Ireland Senior Certificate, is also awarded on GCE results. To secure this a candidate must pass in English Language and five other subjects selected as prescribed.

The Northern Ireland GCE is controlled by a standing committee, appointed by the Minister of Education, and representative of the universities, the teacher-training colleges, the governing bodies and teachers in the Grammar schools, the technical colleges, the LEAs, and the Ministry of Education.

**Further Education Examinations.** The overwhelming majority of examinations taken by students in Further Education establishments are those giving vocational qualifications. These examinations, which are held throughout the United Kingdom, fall broadly into three main groups: those for operatives and craftsmen, those for technicians, and those giving professional status. The great majority of the examinations are offered by four examining bodies, each operating mainly at one level, and one group of examining bodies, which also operates at a single level. These are:

The Royal Society of Arts, John Adam Street, London, W.C.2.

The City and Guilds of London Institute, 76 Portland Place, London, W.1.

The University of London, Senate House, Malet Street, London, W.C.1.

The Council for National Academic Awards, 24 Park Crescent, London, W.1.

The group of examining bodies consists of various professional bodies together with the Department of Education and Science, who in partnership administer the courses and examinations leading to National Certificates and Diplomas.

There are also many educational establishments and professional associations which make their own awards, e.g. the Royal College of Art, the Royal Institute of British Architects.

The Royal Society of Arts, founded in 1754, and incorporated by Royal Charter in 1847, began organising public examinations in 1856. For twenty years it covered a very wide field, but in 1878 handed over its "technological" subjects to the City and Guilds of London Institute. Since then it has concentrated upon examinations in commercial subjects and modern languages, mainly for young students but also for teachers of shorthand and typewriting.

The City and Guilds of London Institute (CGLI), founded in 1878 "for the advancement of technical education" by the Corporation and some of the Livery Companies of the City of London, and incorporated by Royal Charter in 1900, provides a large number (some 220 in 1965) of syllabuses and examinations for operatives, craftsmen, and technicians in all Britain's basic industries, ranging from agriculture and engineering to hairdressing, cookery and computers.

The awards offered by the CGLI are the Intermediate Certificate, obtainable ordinarily after two or three years' part-time study, the Final Certificate, similarly obtainable after a further two or three years, and, in some subjects only, a Full Technological Certificate, which is accepted in English Further Education establishments as a teaching qualification. The CGLI also grants an Insignia Award in Technology (CGIA) to persons who have continued their studies,

broadened their experience, and shown outstanding ability.

The CGLI, though an independent body operating under its Royal Charter, co-operates closely with government departments, LEAs, employers' associations and trade unions. Its awards have, in effect, official status.

Four Regional Examining bodies, which are associations of LEAs and teaching institutions in their areas, also provide syllabuses and examinations in a wide range of industrial, commercial, business and domestic studies. They are:

The Union of Lancashire and Cheshire Institutes, Africa House, 54 Whitworth Street, Manchester 1.

The Union of Educational Institutions, Norfolk House, Smallbrook Ringway, Birmingham 5.

The East Midlands Educational Union, 1 Clinton Terrace, Derby Road, Nottingham.

The Northern Counties Technical Examinations Council, 5 Grosvenor Villas, Grosvenor Road, Newcastle upon Tyne 2.

Broadly speaking, the general level of the courses and examinations is approximately that of the CGLI and the RSA, with whom these Regional bodies often work in co-operation.

The external degrees of the University of London attract annually large numbers of students at home and overseas. In addition, the University gives recognition to teachers in institutions of higher education within the London area which entitles them to prepare students for its internal degrees.

The Council for National Academic Awards (CNAA) is an autonomous body created by Royal Charter in 1964 for the purpose of granting degrees, diplomas, certificates and other awards to students at "educational establishments other than universities". The power to award degrees to non-university students constitutes a unique and important departure from British tradition. The CNAA awards two first degrees, BA and BSc, two Masters' degrees, MA and MSc, and one doctorate, PhD. The Bachelors' degrees

R—I.W.—H

include Ordinary and Honours degrees, the latter awarded in three classes: first, second and third. The minimum academic qualifications required for entry into a course leading to a first degree are *either*: (i) a GCE with two appropriate passes at "A" level and three at "O" level, or in Scotland a SCE with five passes of which three are at the Higher grade; *or* (ii) an appropriate ONC at a good standard.

**National Certificates and Diplomas.**
These awards, begun in 1921, result from a characteristically British partnership between statutory and voluntary bodies; in this case, originally the Board of Education (now the Department of Education and Science) and the professional associations representative of various technologies.

National Certificate and Diploma courses are administered by joint committees representative of the DES, the professional association(s) concerned, and the teachers. The normal procedure is for individual colleges to submit syllabuses for approval by the appropriate joint committee, and to set and mark their own examinations, subject to moderation by external examiners appointed by the joint committee.

National Certificates can only be obtained by part-time study, and it is a condition of entry into a course that the candidate shall be employed in an occupation related to the subject being studied. National Diplomas can only be obtained by full-time study, either continuous from start to finish or on a sandwich basis.

Both Certificates and Diplomas are awarded on two levels, Ordinary and Higher. In most subjects a Higher National Certificate (HNC) can only be taken after the corresponding Ordinary National Certificate (ONC), but in several only HNC is awarded. Most Diplomas are awarded only at the Higher level.

A major revision of the entire scheme of National Certificates and Diplomas was begun in 1961, and was not apparently completed by the end of 1966. According to the latest available

information the following Certificates and Diplomas were then being awarded.

### National Certificates

| | |
|---|---|
| Aeronautical Engineering* | Applied Biology.* |
| Chemical Engineering.* | Business and Administra- |
| Civil Engineering.* | tion. |
| Combined Engineering. | Construction (i.e. build- |
| Electrical Engineering | ing). |
| Mechanical Engineering. | Metal Manufacture. |
| Production Engineering.* | Mining and Quarrying. |
| Shipbuilding. | Physics. |
| Textile Manufacture. | Printing. |
| | Sciences. |
| | Surveying.* |

* HNC only.

### National Diplomas

| | |
|---|---|
| Aeronautical Engineering.* | Building. |
| Combined Electrical, | Business and Admini- |
| Mechanical, and | stration. |
| Production Engineering.* | Chemistry.* |
| Metal Manufacture.* | Nautical Science. |
| Mining and Quarrying.* | Physics.* |

* HND only.

Entry into ONC or OND courses can be made direct from Secondary school provided that appropriate GCE "O" level passes have been obtained, or after a one- or two-year part-time "general" course taken during employment. General courses were in 1966 available in construction, engineering, mining, printing, science, and shipbuilding.

ONC and OND courses are somewhat more academic than other courses leading to technician status. The standard required in the examinations is broadly comparable with GCE "A" level. HND approaches first-degree (general) standard; HNC, because of the limitations of a part-time course, is somewhat lower.

**Other Qualifications.** Practically every skilled occupation has its required professional qualifications. Many are offered by the occupations, through their professional associations. *The Year Book of Technical Education and Careers in Industry*, published annually by A. & C. Black, and available in most public libraries, gives particulars of many of these associations, and lists those which conduct examinations.

**Art/Craft.** For artists and craftsmen the Diploma in Art & Design (DipAD) is broadly comparable with a first degree. It can be taken in any one of four "areas of study" – fine art, graphic design, three-dimensional design, textiles/fashion – and requires at least a three-year full-time course, open only to students possessing at least five "O"-level GCE passes.

**Business.** In business, in addition to National Certificates and Diplomas, there are available the lower level "Certificate in Office Studies" and the higher (post-graduate) Diploma in Management. Among bodies awarding their own Certificates, Pitman's Institute is widely known.

**Agriculture and Horticulture.** Five agricultural colleges—Harper Adams, at Newport, Shropshire, Royal Agricultural College, Cirencester, Glos, Seale Hayne, Newton Abbot, Devon, Shuttleworth, Biggleswade, Beds, and Studley, Warwickshire—offer (between them) National Diplomas in Agriculture, Poultry Husbandry, Poultry Technology, Dairying, and (at Harper Adams and Studley) the Diploma in Horticulture; and also College Diplomas. The 38 agricultural and/or horticultural Institutes run by English LEAs offer basic training in farming and other rural occupations.

**Monotechnics.** The six National Colleges providing full-time courses closely associated with particular industries – agricultural engineering; food technology; foundry work; heating, ventilating, refrigeration and fan engineering; leather technology; rubber technology – offer Diplomas, Associateships and other awards. In the realm of food there are also the National Diploma in Hotel Keeping and Catering, the Diploma of the Institution Management Association (IMA), and the Institutional Housekeeping and Catering Certificate.

**Music.** Most British universities offer degrees in music, some of which are concerned more with musicology than executant skill. For highest level training in the latter there are in London the Royal College of Music, the Royal Academy of Music, the Guildhall School of Music and Drama and the Trinity College of Music; in Manchester the Royal Manchester College of Music; in Scotland the Royal Scottish Academy of Music. Awards made by these bodies rank as degrees for teaching purposes.

**Drama.** Only two or three English universities offer first-degree courses in drama, for which specialist (especially executant) training must be sought at such institutions as the Royal Academy of Dramatic Art, the Central School of Speech and Drama, and the Guildhall School of Music and Drama.

Ballet and dancing have no foothold in university courses. For the first the Sadler's Wells School of Ballet has an international reputation. Dancing is taught in many LEA colleges, but for high-level training resort must be had to private establishments.

A useful short book dealing with English school, university and Further Education examinations is *A Parent's Guide to Examinations* by F. H. Pedley (Pergamon Press). Much varied information is available in *Careers Guide* (HM Stationery Office), and *Careers for Young People* (National Union of Teachers, Hamilton House, London, W.C.1.), both of which are revised periodically.

## ANCILLARY SERVICES

The **School Health Service** dates from 1907, when the Education (Administrative Provisions) Act made it the statutory duty of LEAs to provide for the medical inspection of all children attending public Elementary schools – on admission and at such other times as the Board of Education might direct – and gave them power to make arrangements, subject to approval by the Board, for providing medical treatment. The Education Act, 1918, made the provision of treatment for some ailments and defects – adenoids, enlarged tonsils, dental disease, and defective sight – a statutory duty. The Education Act, 1944 (Sec. 48), extended the LEAs' duty to cover Secondary schools and (when introduced) compulsory Further Education, and made all medical treatment free.

Every LEA must maintain a School Health Service for its area, and this must include dental as well as medical care. The LEA must appoint a Principal School Medical Officer and a Principal School Dental Officer, and sufficient other medical and dental officers, nurses, and other persons to make the service efficient. Under the National Health Service Act, 1946, LEAs may make arrangements with Regional Hospital Boards and teaching hospitals for free specialist and hospital treatment for children in maintained schools. Proprietors of independent schools may arrange with LEAs to participate in the Health Service, provided that "so far as is practicable", the expense incurred by the LEA shall not be greater, child by child, than that incurred on the inspection and treatment of children in maintained schools.

Until 1959 LEAs were required to ensure that every pupil in a maintained school had at least three general medical inspections during his "compulsory school age" (5–15), and was given a dental inspection as soon as possible after first entering school. Since 1959 the arrangements have been at the LEA's discretion. A growing number are abandoning the scheme of three routine inspections – on admission, half-way through, and towards the end of "compulsory school age" – in favour of fewer general inspections and more concentration on the re-inspection and treatment of children with physical defects.

The School Health Service in Scotland operates on much the same lines as in England and Wales. The Northern Ireland School Health Service is conducted by the Health Authorities. Medical treatment is given either at special clinics or through the general Health Service. Similar arrangements obtain for dental inspection and treatment.

It should be added that (i) the School Health Services in the United Kingdom are not responsible for treating illnesses or accidents, but only physical and mental ailments and defects; and (ii) that any parent may opt out of using the School Health Service provided he informs his LEA.

**School Meals.** The provision of meals at school for *necessitous* children has a history going back into the nineteenth century, but the offer of cooked midday meals to *all* children in maintained schools dates only from 1941, when this was made part of the national policy to safeguard children's health in conditions of total war.

The Education Act, 1944 (Sec. 49), made the provision of school meals a statutory duty for the LEAs. The original intention was that the meals should be free, but this has never been the case except for necessitous children. The charge made to parents, which increased progressively from 5d. in 1945 to one shilling in 1957, represents approximately the cost of the food supplied; it does not cover overheads. Over the years the proportion of children in maintained schools taking school meals has fluctuated from about 46 per cent to over 60 per cent. On average about 7 per cent of children taking school meals get them free.

Proprietors of independent schools may arrange with the LEA to participate in the School Meals Service, the condition being that, as with School Health Service, the *per capita* cost should not ordinarily exceed that for children in maintained schools.

**School Milk.** The provision of daily milk to children in maintained schools began on a national scale in 1934, when government subsidies enabled the "Milk Marketing Board", a government-sponsored public corporation, to start a "Milk in Schools Scheme". This enabled children to receive daily one-third of a pint of milk at one-halfpenny a time. Necessitous children were paid for by their LEA, and if undernourished were often given two-thirds of a pint daily.

During World War II the daily ration of milk became, like the midday meal, an essential part of the measures taken to safeguard children's health. Under the Family Allowances Act, 1946, it was made free, and has so remained. Exceptional cases apart, the ration is one-third of a pint. Practically all the milk supplied (99·67 per cent in 1965) is pasteurised.

Over the years an average of over 80 per cent of school children have participated. The Service is open to independent schools on the same terms as the Health and Meals Services.

**Provision of Clothing.** The Education Act, 1944 (Sec. 51) empowers LEAs to provide a child attending a maintained school with clothing (including boots or other footwear) if, in their judgment, he "is unable by reason of the inadequacy of his clothing to take full advantage of the education provided at the school"; and the LEA may continue to do so, in order to ensure that "he is sufficiently clad while he remains a pupil at the school". The Scottish Act makes this provision a duty for the LEA.

The Education Act, 1944 (Sec. 53(3) ), enables the Minister for Education to make Regulations – which he did in 1945 – empowering the LEAs to provide pupils attending maintained schools (or compulsory Further Education in County Colleges) with "articles of clothing suitable for the physical training provided".

The Scottish Act does not include this power.

**Cleanliness.** The Education Act, 1944 (Sec. 54), empowers LEAs to authorise their medical officer to have the persons and clothing of pupils attending all or any of their maintained schools examined "whenever in his opinion such examinations are necessary in the interests of cleanliness". If an LEA medical officer "has reasonable cause to suspect" that a pupil's person or clothing "is infested with vermin or in a foul condition" he can have an examination made. If the person or clothing is infested or foul, the LEA can serve a notice to the parent requiring him to have it cleansed. If the notice is ignored, or the cleansing (in the opinion of the LEA's medical officer) is not satisfactorily done, the LEA will do the cleansing. If, after cleansing, a pupil's person or clothing again becomes foul or verminous, and this condition is proved to be due to the parent's neglect, the parent can be fined up to £1.

The Education (Scotland) Act, 1946 (Sec. 52), makes almost identical provision, but specifies heavier fines, and prison for persistent offenders.

**Transport.** The Education Act, 1944 (Sec. 55), and comparable sections in the Scottish and Northern Ireland Acts, require LEAs to provide transport, or pay reasonable travelling expenses, if they consider this necessary, or they have been directed by the Minister to do so, in order to facilitate pupils' attendance at school, or at compulsory Further Education in County Colleges.

A parent's failure to cause his child to attend school regularly is legally excusable if the parent proves that the school at which his child is a registered pupil is "not within walking distance". The generally accepted definitions of "walking distance" are two miles for a child under 8, and three miles for older children, the distance being "measured by the nearest available route". Many LEAs interpret these generously.

**Youth Employment Service.** There is one Youth Employment Service (YES) for Great Britain and one for Northern Ireland. The YES for Great Britain, which in its present form dates from the Employment and Training Act, 1948, but goes back to 1910, is the responsibility of the Minister of Labour and National Service but is administered locally in most areas by the LEA. Its principal function is to provide throughout Great Britain a service of vocational guidance, job-finding, advice and after-care for young people up to the age of 18 who are seeking or in employment. This is done by Youth Employment Officers (YEOs), who must be appointed in every area, who visit the schools to talk with pupils expecting to leave soon, advise them about careers, and, if asked, place them in employment and keep them under kindly surveillance. The Central Youth Employment Executive maintains a research unit, which since 1950 has produced, and kept up to date, some 120 booklets about careers, ranging from such well-known occupations as banking and engineering to mastic asphalt spreading and woven wire manufacture.

The Northern Ireland YES, which

undertakes the same tasks as that in Great Britain, was established in its present form in 1961. It is administered centrally by a Northern Ireland Youth Employment Service Board (on which LEAs and other educational bodies are very heavily represented) appointed by the Minister of Labour and National Insurance, and locally through Youth Employment Committees each responsible for a given area, and each employing a YEO and other paid staff.

**Service of Youth.** The Service of Youth, or the Youth Service, is the name given collectively to the central Department (or Ministry) of Education, the LEAs, and numerous voluntary organisations working together in partnership, with subsidies from public funds, to offer facilities for wholesome leisure-time activities, and training where appropriate, to young people up to, in general, the age of 18+; and especially to those who have left school and are in employment.

The Youth Service is operated in such similar fashion (and to a large extent by the same organisations) in England and Wales, Scotland and Northern Ireland that a single generalised account may perhaps suffice. It came into being in November 1939, when the British Government gave the Board of Education "a direct responsibility for youth welfare", and called for a "close association of LEAs and voluntary bodies in full partnership in a common enterprise". By the English and Scottish Acts of 1944 and 1945 respectively the Youth Service became a part of the informal Further Education LEAs had a duty to provide.

The Service is provided by LEAs in youth centres, clubs and institutes, which generally meet on school premises, and by some forty national voluntary organisations. These are infinitely various but can be broadly grouped under four heads: (i) uniformed organisations with set programmes of activities; they range from the Boy Scouts to the St John Ambulance Brigade; (ii) non-uniformed club organisations offering a general range of educational, social, and recreative activities,

typified by the National Association of Boys' Clubs (NABC) and the National Association of Youth Clubs; (iii) denominational and other religious organisations, some uniformed, e.g. Church Lads' Brigade, some not, e.g. Association for Jewish Youth; and (iv) organisations having association with HM Armed or Auxiliary Forces, e.g. Army Cadet Force, Girls' Nautical Training Corps. A few organisations do not exactly fit into any of these groups, e.g. Young Farmers' Clubs, Youth Hostels Association. They have perhaps most affinity with group (ii), but they offer specialised, not general, activities.

The Service is administered centrally by the Education Department, which grant-aids the headquarters of the voluntary bodies, and locally by the LEAs, who subsidise the local units. It should be made clear that acceptance of grant or subsidy involves no loss of independence.

The Minister is advised by a Youth Service Development Council, LEAs have Youth Committees, which are ordinarily sub-committees of the Education Committee, and employ full-time Youth Officers to supervise and develop the Service in their areas.

**School Broadcasting and Television.** The British Broadcasting Corporation (BBC) has since the 1920s provided a sound radio school broadcasting service, with lesson and background programmes for all ages, supplemented by illustrated booklets for pupils and lesson notes for teachers. Both the BBC and the Independent Television Authority (ITA) began television broadcasts to schools in 1957. There are also various experiments by schools, colleges and universities in co-operation with various television organisations in the use of closed-circuit television (CCTV).

**The Schools Council.** A unique departure from English educational tradition was made in 1964 when the Schools Council for the Curriculum and Examinations was set up. This body, representative of the entire educational service of England and Wales, including the uni-

versities, the DES, and HM Inspector-
ate, and with a majority of teachers, has
as its role "to promote and encourage
curriculum study and development ...
and to sponsor research and enquiry
where this is needed to help solve
immediate and practical problems".
The Council is an autonomous body,
though financed by the DES. Its address
is: 38 Belgrave Square, London, S.W.1.

Among the problems which the Council immediately attacked were the raising
of the school-leaving age to 16, the
teaching of English, sixth-form studies,
and in collaboration with the Nuffield
Foundation the teaching of mathematics,
science and modern languages. The
Schools Council has also taken over the
work of the Secondary School Examinations Council (SSEC).

**General Teaching Council.** By an Act
of Parliament passed in 1965, a General
Teaching Council was established for
Scotland. It has the right to maintain a
register of accredited teachers, and

important powers in respect of professional discipline. It must be consulted by
the Secretary of State for Scotland about
such matters as qualifications for
admission to training as a teacher.

**Government Reports.** Among recent
reports on education the following are of
outstanding importance:

**Higher Education** (the "Robbins"
Report), October 1963. Covering Great
Britain, it proposed massive expansion of
university and other higher education
over the years 1965–1980.

**Half Our Future** (the "Newsome"
Report), October 1963. Confined to
England, it advised on the education of
children aged 13 to 16 of average and less
than average ability.

**Children and their Primary Schools** (the
"Plowden" Report), January 1967.
Ranges over every aspect of primary
education in England.

## RULES OF PRONUNCIATION

(i) C before *a, o,* and *u,* pronounce like *k.* Before *e, i* and *y, c* is equivalent to *s* in *same, this;* as in *cedar, civil, cypress, capacity.*

(ii) E final indicates that the preceding vowel is long; as in *hate, mete, sire, robe, lyre, abate, recede, invite, remote, intrude.*

(iii) E final indicates that *c* preceding has the sound of *s;* as in *lace, lance;* and that *g* preceding has the sound of *j,* as in *charge, page, challenge.*

(iv) E final, in proper English words, never forms a syllable, and in the most-used words, in the terminating unaccented syllable it is silent. Thus, *motive, genuine, examine, granite,* are pronounced *motiv, genuin, examin, granit.*

(v) E final, in a few words of foreign or classical origin, forms a syllable as *café, Nestlé, syncope, simile.*

(vi) E final is silent after *l* in the following terminations: *ble, cle, dle, fle, gle, kle, ple, tle, zle;* as in *able, manacle, cradle, ruffle, mangle, wrinkle, supple, rattle, puzzle,* which are pronounced *a'bl, mana'cl, cra'dl, ruf'fl, man'gl, wrin'kl, sup'pl, puz'zl.*

(vii) E is usually silent in the termination *en;* as in *token, broken;* pronounced *tokn, brokn.*

(viii) OUS, in the termination of adjectives and their derivatives, is pronounced *us;* as in *gracious, pious, pompously.*

(ix) CE, CI, TI, before a vowel, have the sound of *sh;* as in *cetaceous, gracious, motion, partial, ingratiate;* pronounced *cetashus, grashus, moshun, parshal, ingrashiate.*

(x) SI, after an accented vowel, is pronounced like *zh;* as in *Ephesian, confusion;* pronounced *Ephezhan, confuzhon.*

(xi) When CI and TI precede similar combinations, as in pronun*ci*ation, nego*ti*ation, they should be pronounced *ce* instead of *she,* to prevent a repetition of the latter syllable, as *pronunceashun* instead of *pronunsheashon.*

(xii) GH, in the middle and at the end of words, is silent as in *caught, bought, fright, nigh, sigh;* pronounced *caut, baut, frite, ni, si.* In the following *gh* becomes *f; cough, chough, clough, enough, laugh, rough, tough, trough;* while *bough* is *bow* (*ow* as in *cow*) and *dough* is *doh,* and so on.

(xiii) When WH begins a word, the aspirate *h* precedes *w* in pronunciation; as in *what, whiff, whale;* pronounced *hwat, hwiff, hwale, w* having precisely the sound of *oo,* French *ou.* In the following words *w* is silent: *who, whom, whose, whole.*

(xiv) H after *r* has no sound or use; as in *rheum, rhyme;* pronounced *reum, ryme.*

(xv) H should be sounded in the middle of words; as in fore*h*ead, ab*h*or, be*h*old, in*h*abit, un*h*orse.

(xvi) H should always be sounded except in the following words: *heir, honest, honour, hour,* and all their derivatives.

(xvii) K and G are silent before *n;* as *know, gnaw;* pronounced *no, naw.*

(xviii) W before *r* is silent; as in *wring, wreath;* pronounced *ring, reath.*

(xix) B after *m* is silent; as in *dumb, numb;* pronounced *dum, num.*

(xx) L before *k* is silent; as in *balk, walk, talk;* pronounced *bauk, wauk, tauk.*

(xxi) PH has the sound of *f;* as in *philosophy;* pronounced *filosofy.*

(xxii) NG has two sounds, one as in *singer,* the other as in *fin-ger.* where the *g* is hard.

(xxiii) N after *m,* and closing a syllable, is silent; as in *hymn, condemn.*

(xxiv) P before *s* and *t* is mute; as in *psalm, pseudo, ptarmigan;* pronounced *sarm, sudo, tarmigan.*

Pronounce—
—ace, not *iss,* as furn*ace,* not furn*iss.*
—age, not *idge,* as cabb*age,* cour*age,* post*age,* vill*age,*
—ain, ane, not *in,* as cert*ain,* cert*ane,* not cert*in.*
—ate, not *it,* as moder*ate,* not moder*it.*
—ect, not *ec,* as asp*ect,* not asp*ec;* subj*ect,* not subj*ec*

—ed, not *id*, or *ud*, as wick*ed*, not wick*id*, or wick*ud*.
—el, not *l*, mod*el*; novel not nov*l*.
—en, not *n*, as sudd*en*, not sudd*n*. Burd*en*, gard*en*, length*en*, sev*en*, strength*en*, oft*en*, and a few others, have the *e* silent.
—ence, not *unce*, as influ*ence*, not influ*unce*.
—es, not *is*, as pleas*es*, not pleas*is*.
—ile should be pronounced il in most cases, but in such words as ex*ile*, fert*ile*, fut*ile*, gent*ile*, infant*ile*, reconc*ile*, sen*ile*, ster*ile*, should be pronounced *ile*.
—in, not *n*, as Lat*in*, not Lat*n*.
—nd, not *n*, as husb*and*, not husb*an*; thous*and*, not thous*an*.
—ness, not *niss*, as careful*ness*, not careful*niss*.
—ng, not *n*, as sing*ing*, not sing*in*; speak*ing*, not speak*in*.
—ngth, not *nth*, as streng*th*, not stren*th*.
—son, the *o* should be silent; as in trea*son*, tre-*zn*, not tre-*son*.
—tal, not *tle*, as capi*tal*, not capi*tle*; me*tal*, not met*tle*, mor*tal*, not mor*tle*; periodi*cal*, not periodi*cl*.
—xt, not *x*, as ne*xt*, not ne*x*.

## PUNCTUATION

Punctuation teaches the method of placing points, or stops, in written or printed matter, in such a manner as to indicate clearly the pauses which would be made by the author if he were communicating his thoughts orally instead of by written signs. Correct punctuation is essential to convey the meaning intended.

**The Points or Stops** are as follows:

| | |
|---|---|
| Comma , | Hyphen - |
| Semicolon ; | Question Mark ? |
| Colon : | Exclamation Mark ! |
| Period, or Full Stop . | Parenthesis ( ) |
| Apostrophe ' | Asterisk, or Star * |

As these are all the points required in simple letter writing, we shall confine our explanations to the rules which should govern the use of them. The other points, however, are the paragraph ¶ the section § the dagger † the double dagger ‡ the parallel ‖ the bracket or parenthesis [ ] and some others. These, however, are quite unnecessary, except for elaborate works, in which they are chiefly used for notes or marginal references. The dash — is sometimes used as a substitute for the bracket.

**Points indicating Expression, Meaning and Connection.**

(i) **The Apostrophe'** is used to indicate the combining of two words in one – as *John's book*, instead of *John, his book*;

or to show the omission of parts of words, as *Glo'ster*, for *Gloucester* – *tho'* for *though*. These abbreviations should be avoided as much as possible.

(ii) **The Hyphen**, or conjoiner - is used to unite words which, though they are separate and distinct, have so close a connection as almost to become one word, as *water-rat*, *hand-saw*, etc. It is also used in writing and printing, at the end of a line, to show where a word is divided and continued in the next line.

(iii) **The Note of Interrogation** ? indicates that the sentence to which it is added asks a question; as, *What is the meaning of that assertion? What am I to do?*

(iv) **The Note of Exclamation** or of **Admiration** ! indicates surprise, pleasure, or sorrow; as *Oh! Ah! Goodness! Beautiful! I am astonished! Woe is me!*

(v) **The Parenthesis** ( ) is used to prevent confusion by the introduction to a sentence of a passage not necessary to the sense thereof. *I am going to meet Mr Smith (though I am not an admirer of his) on Wednesday next*. It is better, however, as a rule, not to employ parenthetical sentences.

(vi) **The Asterisk, or Star** * may be employed to refer from the text to a note of explanation at the foot of a column, or at the end of a letter.
*₊* Three stars are sometimes used to call particular attention to a paragraph.

**SPELLING.** The following rules will be found of assistance in writing, because they relate to a class of words about the spelling of which doubt and hesitation are frequently felt:

(i) All words of one syllable ending in *l*, with a single vowel before it, have double *l* at the close; as, *mill*, *sell*.

(ii) All words of one syllable ending in *l*, with a double vowel before it, have one *l* only at the close; as, *mail*, *sail*.

(iii) Words of one syllable ending in *l*, when compounded, retain only one *l* each; as, *fulfil*, *skilful*.

(iv) Words of more than one syllable ending in *l* have one *l* only at the close; as, *delightful*, *faithful;* except *befall*, *downfall*, *recall*, *unwell*, etc.

(v) All derivatives from words ending in *l* have one *l* only; as, *equality*, from *equal*; *fulness*, from *full*; unless they end in *er*, or *ly*; as, *mill, miller*; *full, fully*.

**(vi)** All participles in *ing* from verbs ending in *e* lose the *e* final; as *have, having*; *amuse, amusing*; unless they come from verbs ending in double *e*, and then they retain both; as, *see, seeing*; *agree, agreeing*.

**(vii)** All adverbs ending in *ly* and nouns in *ment* retain the *e* final of the primitives; as *brave, bravely*; *refine, refinement*; except *truly, acknowledgment, judgment*, etc.

**(viii)** All derivatives from words ending in *er* retain the *e* before the *r*; as *refer, reference*; except *hindrance* from *hinder*; *remembrance* from *remember*; *disastrous* from *disaster; monstrous* from *monster*; *wondrous* from *wonder*; *cumbrous* from *cumber*, etc.

**(ix)** Compound words, unless they both end in *l*, retain their primitive parts entire; as, *millstone, changeable, graceless;* except *always, also, deplorable, although, almost, admirable*, etc.

**(x)** All words of one syllable ending in a consonant, with a single vowel before it, double that consonant in derivatives; as, *sin, sinner*; *ship, shipping*; *big, bigger*; *sad, sadder*, etc.

**(xi)** Words of one syllable ending in a consonant, with a double vowel before it, do not double the consonant in derivatives: as, *sleep, sleepy*; *troop, troopers.*

**(xii)** All words of more than one syllable ending in a single consonant, preceded by a single vowel, and accented on the last syllable, double that consonant in derivatives; as, *commit, committee*; *compel, compelled*; *appal, appalling*; *distil, distiller.*

On the other hand words of more than one syllable ending in a single consonant *not* preceded by a single vowel do not double the final consonant in derivatives; as *benefit, benefited; inhabit, inhabited*; but *travel, travelled*, is an exception.

**(xiii)** Nouns of one syllable, ending in *y* preceded by a consonant, change *y* into *ies* in the plural; and verbs ending in *y* preceded by a consonant, change *y* into *ies* in the third person singular of the present tense, and into *ied* in the past tense and past participle, as *fly, flies; I apply, he applies*; *we reply*; *we replied,*

or *have replied*. If the *y* is preceded by a vowel, this rule is not applicable; as *key, keys*; *I play, he plays*; *we have enjoyed our visit.*

**(xiv)** Compound words whose primitives end in *y* change *y* into *i*; as, *beauty, beautiful*; *lovely, loveliness.*

**(xv)** The rule for verbs like *receive, believe*, etc., is that in words of this kind of more than one syllable *ei* follows *c*, when one is not sure whether to put *ei* or *ie*, or, shortly, "*i* before *e* except after *c*".

## HINTS ON WRITING FOR THE PRESS

Those who wish to write for the newspapers or magazines should observe the following rules.

Editors are very busy people.

1. All manuscripts should be typewritten on one side of the paper only. The paper should be quarto, that is to say, 8 inches by 10 inches.

2. The manuscript should be typed double-spacing, with good margins.

3. Each manuscript should have upon it the author's name and address, and the extent in words.

4. Always enclose a stamped addressed envelope for the return of the manuscript if it is not accepted.

5. See that the manuscript is neatly fastened together in the top left-hand corner with a paper-fastener, not with a clip.

6. Number the pages in the order of their succession.

7. Use no abbreviations which are not to appear in print.

8. Punctuate the manuscript as it should be printed.

9. For italics underscore one line; for small capitals, two; capitals, three.

10. Never interline without the caret (ʌ) to show its place.

11. Make your letter to the editor as brief as possible, merely stating that you are sending the manuscript and adding your name, and giving the address above with the date.

12. Do not write to an editor or publisher within a few days of sending the manuscript, asking him how he likes it.

# WORDS THE MEANING OF WHICH IS VARIED BY ACCENTUATION

| Noun, etc. | Verb, etc. | Noun, etc. |
|---|---|---|
| Ab'sent | absent' | Com'pound |
| Ab'stract | abstract' | Com'press |
| Ac'cent | accent' | Con'cert |
| Af'fix | affix' | Con'crete |
| At'tribute | attri'bute' | Con'duct |
| Au'gust | august' | Con'fine |
| Aug'ment | augment' | Con'flict |
| Bom'bard | bombard' | Con'sort |
| Col'league | colleague' | Con'test |
| Col'lect | collect' | Con'tract |
| Com'ment | comment' | Con'trast |
| Com'pact | compact' | Con'verse |
| Com'plot | complot' | Con'vert |

| Verb, etc. | Noun, etc. | Verb, etc. |
|---|---|---|
| compound' | Con'vict | convict' |
| compress' | Con'voy | convoy' |
| concert' | Dec'rease | decrease' |
| concrete' | Des'cant | descant' |
| conduct' | Des'ert | desert' |
| confine' | De'tail | detail' |
| conflict' | Di'gest | digest' |
| consort' | Dis'cord | discord' |
| contest' | Dis'count | discount' |
| contract' | Es'cort | escort' |
| contrast' | Es'say | essay' |
| converse' | Ex'ile | exile' |
| convert' | Ex'port | export' |

# PRONUNCIATION OF SURNAMES

| | |
|---|---|
| Abergavenny | Aberge'nny |
| Ayscough | As'kew |
| Bagehot | Bag'got |
| Bartelot | Bart'lett |
| Beauchamp | Beech'em |
| Beauclerc | Bo'clair |
| Beaulieu | Bew'ly |
| Bellingham | Bellin'am |
| Belvior | Beaver |
| Bethune | Beeton |
| Bicester | Bister |
| Boisragon | Bar'ragon |
| Boleyn | Bullen |
| Boucher, Bourchier | Bow'cher |
| Bourke | Burk |
| Calderon | Caldron |
| Chandos | Shandos |
| Charteris | Charters |
| Cheyne | Cheen, Chain, Chee'ne |
| Chisholm | Chizum |
| Chivas, Chives, Shives | Shee'vus |
| Cholmondeley | Chum'ley |
| Cirencester | Sis'ister |
| Claverhouse | Clavers |
| Cochrane | Coch'ran, "ch" guttural |
| Cockburn | Co'burn |
| Coghlan | Co'lon |
| Colquhoun | Co'hoon |
| Cowper | Cooper |
| Dalziel | Dee-ell' |
| Dillwyn | Dillon |
| Donoghue | Dun-no-hew |
| Drogheda | Dro-heda |
| Dumaresq | Doomer'rick |
| Dymoke | Dim'muk |
| Dynevor | Din'nevor |
| Elgin | El'gin, "g" hard |
| Enraght | En'rowt |
| Eyre | Air |
| Falconer | Fawkner |
| Farquhar | Far'har |
| Fiennes | Fynes (1 syll.) |

| | |
|---|---|
| Fildes | Filds, rhymes with wilds |
| Foljambe | Fool-jum |
| Fortescue | For'teskew |
| Foulis | Fowls |
| Furneaux | Fur'no |
| Gallagher | Gal'laher |
| Geoffrey | Jeffrey |
| Geoghegan, Gahagan | Gay'gan |
| Glamis | Glahms (1 syll.) |
| Gough | Goff |
| Gower | Gore |
| Graeme, Graham | Grame |
| Greig | Greg |
| Grierson | Greerson |
| Grosvenor | Gro'venor |
| Halkett | Hak'-et |
| Hawarden | Har'den |
| Hepburn | Heb'burn |
| Hoey | Hoy |
| Home | Home or Hume |
| Iveagh | Ivah |
| Iverach | Eeverach, "ch" guttural |
| Ives | Ivs (1 syll.) |
| Keilor, Keiller | Keel'or |
| Ker | Kar or Ker |
| Kirkby | Kir'by |
| Knollys, Knowles | Nōles |
| Leveson-Gower | Looson-Gore |
| Lygon | Liggon |
| Maclean | Mac-la'ne |
| Macleay | Mac-lay' |
| Macleod, McLeod | Mac-loud' |
| Macmahon | Mac-mahn |
| Mainwaring | Mannering |
| Marjoribanks | March'banks or Marsh'banks |
| Maturin | Match'urin |
| Maugham | Mawm |
| Maughan | Mawn |
| Mearns | Merns or Mairns |
| Meiklejohn | Mik'-el-john |
| Melhuish | Mel'-wish |
| Menzies | Meng'is |
| Methven | Meffen |
| Meux | Mews |
| Meyrick | Merrick |
| Monro | Munro' |
| Mowat | Mow'at, "ow" as in cow, or Mo-at |
| Myerscough | Maskew |
| Pole-Carew | Pool-Cary |
| Powell | Po-el or Pow'el |
| Powys, Powis | Pow'is or Po-is |
| Prideaux | Prid'o or Pree-do |
| Pugh | Pew |
| Pytchley | Pite-chley |
| Reay | Ray |
| Rees, Rhys | Reece |
| Rowton | Row'ton, "ow" as in cow |
| Ruthven | Riven or Ruffen |
| Scrimgeous | Scrim-jer |
| Skrine | Screen |
| St. John | Sin-jun |
| Strachan | Strawn or Stra-han |
| Suter | Soot-er |
| Thynne | Thin |
| Tredegar | Tread-éager |
| Tyrwhitt | Territ |
| Urquhart | Ur-hart, "quh" guttural |
| Vaughan | Vawn |
| Wauchope | Walk-up |
| Wemyss | Weems |
| Wolseley | Wools'-ly |
| Wriothesley | Roxly |

# NAMES AND THEIR MEANING
## Names of Men

Aaron, *Hebrew*, a mountain, or lofty.
Abel, *Hebrew*, vanity.
Abraham, *Hebrew*, the father of many.

Absalom, *Hebrew*, the father of peace.
Adam, *Hebrew*, red earth.
Adolphus, *Teutonic*, noble wolf.
Adrian, *Latin*, of Adria.
Alan, *Celtic*, harmony; or *Slavonic*, a hound.
Alaric, *Saxon*, noble ruler.
Alastair, Alister, *Gaelic form of* Alexander, *q.v.*
Albert, *Saxon*, nobly bright.
Alexander, *Greek*, a helper of men.
Alfred, *Teutonic*, good counsellor.
Algernon, *French*, bearded.
Alonzo, *form of* Alphonso, *q.v.*
Alphonso, *German*, ready or willing.
Ambrose, *Greek*, immortal.
Amos, *Hebrew*, a burden.
Andrew, *Greek*, manly.
Angus, *Celtic*, excellent virtue.
Anselm, *Saxon*, safeguard of God.
Anthony, *Latin*, flourishing, praiseworthy
Archibald, *German*, a bold observer.
Arnold, *German*, strong as an eagle.
Arthur, *British*, a strong man.
Augustus ⎫
Augustin ⎬ *Latin*, venerable, grand.
Baldwin, *German*, prince-friend.
Bardulph, *German*, a famous helper.
Barnaby, *Hebrew*, a prophet's son.
Bartholomew, *Hebrew*, the son of him who made the waters to rise.
Basil, *Greek*, kingly.
Beaumont, *French*, a pretty mount.
Bede, *Saxon*, prayer.
Benedict, *Latin*, blessed.
Benjamin, *Hebrew*, the son of a right hand.
Bennet, *Latin*, blessed.
Bernard, *German*, bear's heart.
Bertram ⎫
Bertrand ⎬ *German*, bright raven.
Boniface, *Latin*, a well-doer.
Brian, *Celtic*, strong.
Cadwallader, *Welsh*, battle arranger.
Caesar, *Latin*, adorned with hair.
Caleb, *Hebrew*, a dog.
Cecil, *Latin*, blind.
Charles, *German*, manly.
Christopher, *Greek*, bearing Christ.
Clarence, *Latin*, illustrious.
Claude, *Latin*, lame.
Clement, *Latin*, mild-tempered.
Conrad, *German*, able counsel.
Constantine, *Latin*, resolute.
Cornelius, *Latin*, meaning uncertain.
Crispin, *Latin*, having curled locks.
Cuthbert, *Saxon*, known famously.
Cyril, *Greek*, commanding.
Dan, *Hebrew*, judgment.
Daniel, *Hebrew*, God is judge.
David, *Hebrew*, well-beloved.
Dennis, *Greek*, belonging to the god of wine.
Donald, *Gaelic*, proud.
Douglas, *Gaelic*, dark grey.
Duncan, *Celtic*, brown chief.
Dunstan, *Saxon*, most high.
Ebenezer, *Hebrew*, the stone of help.
Edgar, *Saxon*, happy honour.
Edmund, *Saxon*, happy peace.
Edward, *Saxon*, happy keeper.
Edwin, *Saxon*, happy conqueror.
Egbert, *Saxon*, ever bright.
Elijah, *Hebrew*, God the Lord.
Elisha, *Hebrew*, the salvation of God.
Emmanuel, *Hebrew*, God with us.
Enoch, *Hebrew*, dedicated.
Ephraim, *Hebrew*, fruitful.
Erasmus, *Greek*, lovely, worthy to be loved.
Eric, *Anglo-Saxon*, kingly.
Ernest, *German*, earnest, serious.
Esau, *Hebrew*, hairy.
Eugene, *Greek*, nobly descended.
Eustace, *Greek*, standing firm.
Evan, *Welsh*, young warrior.
Everard, *German*, well reported.
Ezekiel, *Hebrew*, the strength of God.

Felix, *Latin*, happy.
Ferdinand, *German*, brave.
Fergus, *Celtic*, manly strength.
Francis, *German*, free.
Frederic, *German*, ruler, peace.
Gabriel, *Hebrew*, the strength of God.
Gavin, *Celtic*, hawk of battle.
Geoffrey, *Teutonic*, God's peace.
George, *Greek*, a husbandman.
Gerard, *Saxon*, spear power.
Gideon, *Hebrew*, a destroyer.
Gilbert, *Saxon*, bright as gold.
Giles, *Greek*, a little goat.
Godard, *German*, a godly disposition.
Godfrey, *Teutonic*, God's peace.
Godwin, *Saxon*, victorious in God.
Gregory, *Greek*, watchful.
Griffith, *British*, having great faith.
Gustavus, *Swedish*, a warrior.
Guy, *French*, a leader.
Hannibal, *Punic*, a gracious lord.
Harold, *Saxon*, a champion.
Hector, *Greek*, a stout defender.
Henry, *German*, a rich lord, home ruler.
Herbert, *German*, a bright lord.
Hercules, *Greek*, the glory of Hera, or Juno.
Herman, *Saxon*, a valiant soldier.
Hezekiah, *Hebrew*, cleaving to the Lord.
Horace ⎫
Horatio ⎬ *Latin*.
Howel, *British*, sound or whole.
Hubert, *German*, a bright colour.
Hugh, *Teutonic*, mind.
Humphrey, *German*, domestic peace.
Ian, *Celtic* for John.
Ignatius, *Latin*, fiery.
Ingram, *Teutonic*, a raven.
Isaac, *Hebrew*, laughter.
Ivan, *Russian* for John.
Jabez, *Hebrew*, one who causes sorrow.
Jacob, *Hebrew*, a supplanter.
James, Jacques, *same as* Jacob.
Jasper, *Persian*, radiant.
Jeremiah, *Hebrew*, exalted of the Lord.
Jerome, *Greek*, holy name.
Jesse, *Hebrew*, wealth.
Joab, *Hebrew*, fatherhood.
Job, *Hebrew*, sorrowing, persecuted.
Joel, *Hebrew*, acquiescing.
John, *Hebrew*, the grace of the Lord.
Jonah, Jonas, *Hebrew*, a dove.
Jonathan, *Hebrew*, the gift of the Lord.
Joscelin, *German*, just.
Joseph, *Hebrew*, addition.
Joshua, *Hebrew*, a Saviour.
Josiah, Josias, *Hebrew*, the Lord healeth.
Jude, *Hebrew*, confession.
Julian, Julius, *Latin*, soft-haired.
Kenneth, *Gaelic*, leader of men.
Lambert, *Saxon*, a fair lamb.
Lancelot, *Spanish*, a little lance.
Laurence, *Latin*, crowned with laurels.
Lazarus, *Hebrew*, God will help.
Leonard, *German*, like a lion.
Leopold, *German*, defending the people.
Lewis or Louis, *French*, famous warrior.
Lionel, *Latin*, a little lion.
Llewellyn, *Celtic*, lightning.
Lubin, *Anglo-Saxon*, friend.
Lucius, *Latin*, shining.
Luke, *Greek*, a wood or grove.
Manfred, *German*, great peace.
Mark, *Latin*, a hammer.
Marmaduke, *Saxon*, noble and powerful.
Martin, *Latin*, martial.
Matthew, *Hebrew*, a gift or present.
Maurice, *Latin*, sprung of a Moor.
Meredith, *British*, the roaring of the sea.
Michael, *Hebrew*, who is like God?
Morgan, *British*, a mariner.
Moses, *Hebrew*, drawn out.
Nathan, *Hebrew*, a gift.
Nathaniel, *Hebrew*, the gift of God.

Neal, Neil, *Celtic*, chief.
Nicholas, *Greek*, victorious over the people.
Noah, *Hebrew*, consolation, rest.
Noel, *French*, belonging to one's nativity.
Norman, *French*, a North man.
Obadiah, *Hebrew*, the servant of the Lord.
Octavius, *Latin*, eighth born.
Oliver, *Latin*, an olive.
Orlando, *Italian form of* Roland, *q.v.*
Orson, *Latin*, a bear.
Oscar, *Celtic*, eager to fight.
Osmund, *Saxon*, house peace.
Oswald, *Saxon*, ruler of a house.
Otto, *Teutonic*, rich, happy.
Owen, *British*, well descended.
Patrick, *Latin*, a nobleman.
Paul, *Latin*, small, little.
Paulinus, *Latin*, little Paul.
Percival, *French*, a place in France.
Percy, *English*, adaptation of "pierce eye".
Peregrine, *Latin*, outlandish.
Peter, *Greek*, a rock or stone.
Philip, *Greek*, a lover of horses.
Phineas, *Hebrew*, of bold countenance.
Ralph, contracted from Randolph, or
Randal, Ranulph, *Saxon*, house wolf.
Raymond, *German*, quiet peace.
Reginald, *Saxon*, ruler.
Reuben, *Hebrew*, the son of vision.
Reynold, *German*, a lover of purity.
Richard, *Saxon*, powerful.
Robert, *German*, famous in counsel.
Roderick, *German*, rich in fame.
Roger, *German*, strong, counsel.
Roland, Rowland, *German*, counsel for the land.
Rollo, *form of* Roland, *q.v.*
Rufus, *Latin*, reddish.
Rupert, *form of* Robert.
Samson, *Hebrew*, splendid sun.
Samuel, *Hebrew*, heard by God.
Saul, *Hebrew*, desired.
Sebastian, *Greek*, to be reverenced.
Seth, *Hebrew*, appointed.
Sigismund, *Saxon*, one who conquers.
Silas, *Latin*, sylvan or living in the woods.
Silvester, *Latin*, born in the woods.
Simeon, *Hebrew*, hearing.
Simon, *Hebrew*, obedient.
Solomon, *Hebrew*, peaceable.
Stephen, *Greek*, a crown or garland.
Swithin, *Saxon*, strong friend.
Thaddeus, *Syrian*, wise and prudent.
Theobald, *Saxon*, bold over the people.
Theodore, *Greek*, the gift of God.
Theodosius, *Greek*, given of God.
Theophilus, *Greek*, a lover of God.
Thomas, *Hebrew*, a twin.
Timothy, *Greek*, a fearer of God.
Titus, *meaning uncertain.*
Tobias, *Hebrew*, the goodness of the Lord.
Tristram, *Celtic*, a herald.
Uriah, *Hebrew*, light of God.
Valentine, *Latin*, powerful.
Victor, *Latin*, conqueror.
Vincent, *Latin*, conquering.
Vivian, *Latin*, lively.
Walter, *German*, a conqueror.
Wilfred, *Saxon*, bold and peaceful.
William, *German*, helmet of resolution.
Zaccheus, *Syriac*, innocent.
Zachary, *Hebrew*, the Lord hath remembered.
Zebedee, *Syriac*, having an inheritance.
Zechariah, *Hebrew*, remembered of the Lord.
Zedekiah, *Hebrew*, the justice of the Lord.

## Names of Women

Abigail, *Hebrew*, father's delight.
Ada, *German*, *same as* Edith, *q.v.*
Adela, *German*, *same as* Adeline, *q.v.*
Adelaide, *German*, *same as* Adeline, *q.v.*

Adeline, *German*, a princess.
Agatha, *Greek*, good.
Agnes, *German*, chaste.
Aileen, *Celtic* form of Helen, *q.v.*
Alberta, *Saxon*, nobly bright.
Alethea, *Greek*, the truth.
Alexandra, *Greek*, helper of men.
Alice, Alicia, *German*, noble.
Alma, *Latin*, benignant.
Althea, *Greek*, hunting.
Amabel, *Latin*, loveable.
Amanda, *Latin*, worthy of love.
Amelia, *Saxon*, industrious.
Amy, *Latin*, a beloved.
Angelina, *Greek*, lovely, angelic.
Anna, Anne, *Hebrew*, gracious.
Antoinette, *Latin*, praiseworthy.
Arabella, *Latin*, a fair altar.
Aurelia, Aureola, *Latin*, like gold.
Aurora, *Latin*, morning brightness.
Barbara, *Greek*, foreign or strange.
Beatrice, *Latin*, making happy.
Belinda, *Latin*, useful.
Bella, *Italian*, beautiful.
Benedicta, *Latin*, blessed.
Bernice, *Greek*, bringing victory.
Bertha, *Teutonic*, bright or famous.
Bessie, *short form of* Elizabeth, *q.v.*
Blanche, *French*, fair, white.
Bona, *Latin*, good.
Bridget, *Irish*, shining bright, strength.
Camilla, *Latin*, attendant at a sacrifice.
Carlotta, *Italian*, same as Charlotte, *q.v.*
Caroline, *feminine of* Carolus, *the Latin of* Charles, noble-spirited, manly.
Cassandra, *Greek*, a reformer of men.
Catherine, *Greek*, pure or clean.
Cecilia, *Latin*, from Cecil.
Celestine, *Latin*, heavenly.
Charity, *Greek*, love, bounty.
Charlotte, *French*, all noble.
Chloe, *Greek*, a green herb.
Christine, Christiana, *Greek*, belonging to Christ.
Cicely, *a corruption of* Cecilia, *q.v.*
Clara, *Latin*, clear or bright.
Clarice, Clarissa, *Latin*, clear or bright.
Claudia, *Latin*, lame.
Clementine, Clementina, *Latin*, gentle.
Constance, *Latin*, constant.
Cora, *Greek*, a girl.
Cordelia, *Latin*, warm-hearted.
Cornelia, *Latin*, meaning uncertain.
Dagmar, *German*, joy of the Danes.
Deborah, *Hebrew*, a bee.
Diana, *Greek*, Jupiter's daughter.
Dinah, *Hebrew*, judged.
Dorcas, *Greek*, a gazelle.
Dorothea, Dora, Dorothy, *Greek*, the gift of God.
Edith, *Saxon*, happiness, a rich gift.
Edna, *Hebrew*, pleasure.
Eleanor, Elinor, *Saxon*, all fruitful.
Eliza, Elizabeth, *Hebrew*, the oath of God.
Ella, *Teutonic*, elf friend; also for Isabella, *q.v.*
Ellen, *another form of* Helen, *q.v.*
Elsie, Elspeth, *Scots form of* Elizabeth, *q.v.*
Elvira, *Arabic*, white.
Emily, *corrupted from* Amelia.
Emma, *German*, a nurse, industrious.
Esther, Heather, *Hebrew*, secrets.
Ethel, *Saxon*, of noble birth.
Eugenia, *Greek*, well-born.
Eunice, *Greek*, fair victory.
Euphemia (or Effie), *Greek*, of good report.
Eva or Eve, *Hebrew*, causing life.
Evangeline, *Greek*, bearer of good tidings.
Evelina, Eveline, *Celtic*, pleasant.
Evelyn, *Latin*, hazel.
Fanny, *diminutive of* Frances, *q.v.*
Felicia, *Latin*, happiness.
Fenella, *Greek*, bright to look on.
Flora, *Latin*, flowers.
Florence, *Latin*, blooming, flourishing.
Frances, *German*, free.

Frederica, *Saxon*, abounding in peace.
Georgina, *Greek*, a tiller of the ground.
Geraldine, *Saxon*, strong, spear power.
Gertrude, *German*, spear maid.
Gladys, *Welsh*, a fair maiden.
Grace, *Latin*, favour, grace.
Greta, *short form of* Margaret, *q.v.*
Griselda, *Teutonic*, patient and firm.
Hagar, *Hebrew*, a stranger.
Hannah, *Hebrew*, gracious.
Harriet, *German*, head of the house.
Helen, Helena, *Greek*, alluring, light.
Henrietta, *fem. and dim. of* Henry, *q.v.*
Hilda, *German*, warrior maiden.
Honora, Honoria, *Latin*, honourable.
Hortensia, *Latin*, a lover of a garden.
Ida, *Saxon*, like a goddess, happy.
Irene, *Greek*, peaceful.
Isabella, Ella, *Spanish*, fair Eliza.
Jane, Jean (*Scots*), Jeanne, *feminine of* John, *q.v.*
Janet, Jeannette, little Jane.
Jemima, *Hebrew*, a dove.
Joan, *Hebrew, fem. of* John, *q.v.*
Joanna, Johanna, *form of* Joan, *q.v.*
Josepha, *Hebrew*, addition.
Joyce, *Latin*, sportive.
Judith, *Hebrew*, praising.
Julai, Juliana, *feminine of* Julius, *q.v.*
Justina, *Latin*, just.
Kate, Katherine, *form of* Catherine, *q.v.*
Keturah, *Hebrew*, incense.
Kesiah, *Hebrew*, cassia.
Laura, *Latin*, a laurel.
Lavinia, *Latin*, of Latium.
Letitia, *Latin*, joy or gladness.
Lilian, Lily, *Latin*, a lily.
Lois, *Greek*, better.
Louisa, *German, fem. of* Louis, *q.v.*
Lucretia, *Latin*, a chaste Roman lady, light.
Lucy, *Latin, feminine of* Lucius.
Lydia, *Greek*, native of Lydia.
Mabel, *Latin*, lovely or lovable.
Madeline, *form of* Magdalen, *q.v.*
Madge, *short form of* Margaret, *q.v.*
Magdalen, *Syriac*, magnificent.
Margaret, *Greek*, a pearl.
Maria, Marie, Marion, *forms of* Mary, *q.v.*
Martha, *Hebrew*, lady.
Mary, *probably Hebrew*, bitter.
Matilda, *German*, a lady of honour.
Maud, *German form of* Matilda, *q.v.*
May, *Latin*, month of May, *or dim. of* Mary, *q.v.*
Melissa, *Greek*, a honey bee.
Mercy, *English*, compassion.
Mildred, *Saxon*, speaking mild.
Millicent, *Latin*, a sweet singer.
Minnie, *dim. of* Margaret, *q.v.*
Miranda, *Latin*, admirable.
Miriam, *Hebrew*, exalted.
Molly, *dim. of* Mary, *q.v.*
Myra, *Greek*, grieving.
Mysie, Maisie, *forms of* Margaret, *q.v.*
Nancy, *a form of* Anne.
Naomi, *Hebrew*, bitterness, consolation.
Nell, Nellie, Nelly, *forms of* Helen, *q.v.*
Netta, Nettie, *forms of* Henrietta.
Nicola, *Greek, feminine of* Nicolas.
Nora, *contraction of* Honora, *q.v.*
Olive, Olivia, *Latin*, an olive.
Olympic, *Greek*, heavenly.
Ophelia, *Greek*, a serpent.
Parnell, Petronilla, little Peter.
Patience, *Latin*, bearing patiently.
Patricia, *feminine of* Patrick, *q.v.*
Paulina, *Latin, feminine of* Paulinus.
Penelope, *Greek*, a weaver.
Philadelphia, *Greek*, brotherly love.
Philippa, *Greek, feminine of* Philip.
Phoebe, *Greek*, the light of life.
Phyllis, *Greek*, a green bough.
Polly, *variation of* Molly, *dim. of* Mary, *q.v.*
Priscilla, *Latin*, somewhat old.
Prudence, *Latin*, discretion.

Psyche, *Greek*, the soul.
Rachel, *Hebrew*, a lamb.
Rebecca, *Hebrew*, a noose.
Rhoda, *Greek*, a rose.
Rita, *Greek*, pearl.
Rosa, Rose, *Latin*, a rose.
Rosabella, *Italian*, a fair rose
Rosalie, Rosaline, *Latin*, little rose.
Rosalind, *Latin*, beautiful as a rose.
Rosamond, *Saxon*, rose of peace.
Roxana, *Persian*, dawn of day.
Ruth, *Hebrew*, friend.
Sabina, *Latin*, sprung from the Sabines.
Salome, *Hebrew*, peaceful.
Sapphira, *Greek*, like a sapphire stone.
Sarah, *Hebrew*, a princess.
Selina, *Greek*, the moon.
Sibylla, *Greek*, a prophetess.
Sophia, *Greek*, wisdom.
Sophronia, *Greek*, of a sound mind.
Stella, *Latin*, a star.
Susan, Susanna, *Hebrew*, a lily.
Tabitha, *Syriac*, a roe.
Temperance, *Latin*, moderation.
Teresa, *Greek*, a gleaner.
Theodora, Theodosia, *Greek*, given by God.
Thomasine, *Hebrew*, a twin.
Ursula, *Latin*, a she bear.
Valeria, *Latin*, strong and powerful.
Vera, Vere, *Latin*, true.
Victoria, *Latin*, all conquering.
Vids, *Hebrew*, beloved
Viola, Violet, *Latin*, a violet.
Virginia, *Latin*, chaste.
Vivien, *Latin*, lively.
Wilhelmina, *Saxon*, helmet of defence.
Winifred, *Saxon*, winning peace.
Zenobia, *Greek*, the life of Jupiter.
Zoe, *Greek*, lively.

# THE PATTERN OF
# ENGLISH LITERATURE
## Fourteenth Century

| | | |
|---|---|---|
| Wyclif, John | . . | 1320–1384 |
| Langland, William | . | 1332–1400 |
| Chaucer, Geoffrey | . | 1340–1400 |

## Fifteenth Century

| | | |
|---|---|---|
| Caxton, William | . | 1422–1491 |
| More, Sir Thomas | . | 1478–1535 |
| Tyndale, William | . | 1489–1536 |
| Cranmer, Thomas | . | 1489–1556 |

## Sixteenth Century

| | | |
|---|---|---|
| Foxe, John | . | 1517–1587 |
| Spenser, Edmund | . | 1552–1599 |
| Sidney, Sir Philip | . | 1554–1586 |
| Bacon, Francis | . . | 1561–1626 |
| Drayton, Michael | . | 1563–1631 |
| Shakespeare, William | | 1564–1616 |
| Marlowe, Christopher | | 1564–1593 |
| Donne, John | . . | 1572–1631 |
| Johnson, Ben | . . | 1572–1637 |
| Fletcher, John | . | 1579–1625 |
| Beaumont, Francis | . | 1584–1616 |
| Herrick, Robert | . | 1591–1674 |
| Quarles, Francis | . | 1592–1644 |

| Herbert, George | . | 1593–1633 |
| Walton, Izaak . | . | 1593–1683 |

**Seventeenth Century**

| Waller, Edmund | . | 1606–1687 |
| Milton, John . | . | 1608–1674 |
| Butler, Samuel (*Hudibras*) | | 1612–1680 |
| Cowley, Abraham | . | 1618–1667 |
| Lovelace, Richard | . | 1618–1658 |
| Evelyn, John . | . | 1620–1706 |
| Marvell, Andrew | . | 1621–1678 |
| Vaughan, Henry | . | 1622–1695 |
| Bunyan, John . | . | 1628–1688 |
| Dryden, John . | . | 1631–1700 |
| Pepys, Samuel . | . | 1633–1703 |
| Wycherley, William | . | 1640–1716 |
| Defoe, Daniel . | . | 1662–1731 |
| Swift, Jonathan . | | 1667–1745 |
| Congreve, William | . | 1670–1729 |
| Addison, Joseph | . | 1672–1719 |
| Steele, Sir Richard | . | 1672–1729 |
| Gay, John . | . | 1685–1731 |
| Pope, Alexander | . | 1688–1744 |
| Richardson, Samuel | . | 1689–1761 |

**Eighteenth Century**

| Fielding, Henry | . | 1707–1754 |
| Johnson, Samuel | . | 1709–1784 |
| Sterne, Laurence | . | 1713–1768 |
| Gray, Thomas . | . | 1716–1771 |
| Walpole, Horace | . | 1717–1797 |
| White, Gilbert . | . | 1720–1793 |
| Smollett, Tobias | . | 1721–1771 |
| Goldsmith, Oliver | . | 1730–1774 |
| Cowper, William | . | 1731–1800 |
| Gibbon, Edward | . | 1737–1794 |
| Sheridan, Richard | . | 1751–1816 |
| Burney, Fanny . | . | 1752–1840 |
| Chatterton, Thomas | . | 1752–1770 |
| Crabbe, George | . | 1754–1832 |
| Blake, William . | . | 1757–1827 |
| Burns, Robert . | . | 1759–1796 |
| Wordsworth, William | | 1770–1850 |
| Scott, Sir Walter | . | 1771–1832 |
| Coleridge, S. T. | . | 1772–1834 |
| Southey, Robert | . | 1774–1843 |
| Lamb, Charles . | . | 1775–1834 |
| Austen, Jane . | . | 1775–1817 |
| Campbell, Thomas | . | 1777–1844 |
| Hazlitt, William | . | 1778–1830 |
| Byron, Lord . | . | 1788–1824 |
| Shelley, P. B. . | . | 1792–1822 |
| Clare, John . | . | 1793–1864 |
| Keats, John . | . | 1795–1821 |

| Carlyle, Thomas | . | 1795–1881 |
| Hood, Thomas . | . | 1799–1845 |

**Nineteenth Century**

| Tennyson, Lord | . | 1809–1892 |
| Thackeray, William | . | 1811–1863 |
| Browning, Robert | . | 1812–1889 |
| Dickens, Charles | . | 1812–1870 |
| Trollope, Anthony | . | 1815–1882 |
| Brontë, Charlotte | . | 1816–1855 |
| Brontë, Emily . | . | 1818–1848 |
| Eliot, George . | . | 1819–1880 |
| Kingsley, Charles | . | 1819–1875 |
| Rossetti, D. G. | . | 1828–1882 |
| Carroll, Lewis . | . | 1832–1898 |
| Butler, Samuel (*Erewhon*) | | 1835–1902 |
| Gilbert, Sir W. S. | . | 1836–1911 |
| Swinburne, A. C. | . | 1837–1909 |
| Hardy, Thomas . | | 1840–1928 |
| Hopkins, G. M. | . | 1844–1889 |
| Stevenson, R. L. | . | 1850–1894 |
| Wilde, Oscar . | . | 1854–1900 |
| Shaw, George Bernard | | 1856–1950 |
| Conrad, Joseph . | | 1857–1924 |
| Barrie, Sir James | | 1860–1937 |
| Quiller-Couch, Sir A. | | 1863–1944 |
| Yeats, W. B. . | . | 1865–1939 |
| Kipling, Rudyard | . | 1865–1936 |
| Wells, H. G. . | . | 1866–1946 |
| Bennett, Arnold | . | 1867–1931 |
| Galsworthy, John | . | 1867–1933 |
| Belloc, Hilaire . | . | 1870–1953 |
| Davies, W. H. . | . | 1871–1940 |
| Synge, J. M. . | . | 1871–1909 |
| Beerbohm, Max | . | 1872–1956 |
| Powys, John Cowper | | 1872–1965 |
| de la Mare, Walter | . | 1873–1956 |
| Chesterton, G. K. | . | 1874–1936 |
| Maugham, Somerset | . | 1874–1965 |
| Trevelyan, G. M. | . | 1876–1962 |
| Masefield, John | . | 1878–1967 |
| Thomas, Edward | . | 1878–1917 |
| Forster, E. M. . | . | 1879– |
| Joyce, James . | . | 1882–1941 |
| Woolfe, Virginia | . | 1882–1941 |
| O'Casey, Sean . | . | 1884–1964 |
| Lawrence, D. H. | . | 1885–1930 |
| Brook, Rupert . | . | 1887–1915 |
| Eliot, T. S. . | . | 1888–1965 |
| Wodehouse, P. G. | . | 1881– |
| Tolkien, J. R. R. | . | 1892– |
| Owen, Wilfred . | . | 1893–1918 |
| Morgan, Charles | . | 1894–1958 |
| Huxley, Aldous . | . | 1894–1963 |
| Graves, Robert | . | 1895– |

# HOUSEHOLD HINTS AND MISCELLANEOUS RECIPES

A tool-chest is useful for the smaller implements; the well-equipped cupboard should contain an axe, a hatchet, various saws, an electric drill, a hammer, a tin-opener, a tack-lifter, a spanner, a three-foot rule, a small vice, an iron last, a mallet, three or four gimlets and bradawls of different sizes, two screwdrivers, two chisels, a small plane, a jack-knife, a pair of large scissors or shears, a packing needle, a ball of twine, a carpet fork or stretcher, and a set of Rawlplugs. Also an assortment of screws and nails of various sizes, from large spikes down to small tacks, not forgetting some large and small brass-headed nails, together with hooks of various sizes, a few hinges, etc., and spare electrical parts.

The nails and screws should be kept in a wooden box, with divisions so that the various sizes may be kept separate.

**To loosen screws and nails.** If these have become rusted into their sockets, a little paraffin oil should be dropped on them. Allow this to soak in, after which they should come out with ease.

Touching the head of the screw with a red-hot poker, or inserting a screwdriver in the head and tapping it firmly with a hammer, will often succeed in starting a stiff screw.

## THE DOS AND DON'TS OF PAINTING

(*By the Home Decorating adviser to Berger Paints, makers of Magicote*)

### PREPARATION AND PRIMING

**Do make sure all surfaces are clean and sound.** No new paint can adhere properly to a dusty, greasy, cracked or oily surface.

**Redecorating** Woodwork, Plaster, Brick or Concrete previously painted with Gloss, Lustre, Eggshell, Emulsion or Flat Oil Paint inside and outside:

1. *Wash down* with warm detergent solution; rinse carefully with clean water.
2. *Remove all traces of grease, wax, oil or household polishes* with good turps substitute.
3. *Rub down* surfaces already painted with Gloss with a really fine abrasive paper. Dust off. This will give your fresh paint a sound "hold".
4. *Fill any cracks* on walls or ceilings with the appropriate filler. Leave to dry thoroughly and rub down.
5. *Prime* any bare patches or particularly "weathered" areas.
6. *Prime whole area* when applying Gloss over Emulsion on exterior surfaces.

**Redecorating** Oil-bound Distempers or Water Paints:

1. *Scrape, brush and rub down* where any flaking has occurred. Then dust off.
2. *Prime only* if finishing in Gloss or Lustre. Emulsion may be applied direct – without priming.

**Redecorating** Non-washable Distempers:

1. *Completely remove* all non-washable distemper with hot water. Rinse off thoroughly with clean water.
2. *Prime* if finishing in Gloss or Lustre. No priming is needed if finishing in Emulsion.

**Redecorating** Wallpaper; unglazed:

1. *Brush down*, first making sure all joins are sound and firmly adhering.
2. *Prime* if finishing in Gloss or Lustre.
3. *Apply Emulsion* without priming – unless your wallpaper contains water-soluble dyes. To test, paint a small area first. If dye "bleeds" the whole area must be primed.

**Redecorating** Wallpaper; Varnished or Washable:

1. *Wash down* with weak detergent solution – first ensuring all joins are sound and firmly adhering.

2. *Prime* before painting with Gloss or Lustre. Emulsion can be applied direct, without priming. This type of wallpaper is generally dye-fast. It is wise, however, to make the "dye test" (see above) if you have had to remove scuffs or particularly stubborn marks many times from this surface; and spot-prime doubtful patches even if you plan an Emulsion finish.

**Redecorating** Iron and Steel:

1. *Scrape and wire brush* to remove rust.

2. *Rub down and dust off* sound paint, and clean with turps substitute.

3. *Prime* "bare" patches.

**Redecorating** Aluminium:

1. *Gently rub down* with fine abrasive paper.

2. *Clean with turps substitute* before painting.

3. *Prime only* on bare patches.

## NEW WORK

**New Plaster, Brick, Concrete, Cement, etc.**
**Make sure all surfaces are thoroughly dried out.** *Brush down* all surfaces. Make good all cracks with appropriate fillers. New exterior brickwork should not be painted for at least twelve months. This "weathering" will improve durability when finally painted.

*All these new surfaces must be primed before painting with gloss. No priming is needed if finishing in Emulsion.*

## BARE WOOD AND METALS

**Make sure the surface is ready for painting.** Woodwork should be dry and free from grease. Iron and steel should be rust-free.

Aluminium should be lightly scuffed with fine emery paper, then cleaned with turps substitute.

*All bare woodwork and metal must be primed before painting.*

## PAINTING

**Have everything ready.** You will probably find you need: 4-in., 3-in., 2-in. and 1½-in. or 1-in. brushes. Always test the security of your ladders or trestles (remember that nearly half of all accidents occur in the home). Make sure you have enough height – if you have to paint with your arm completely extended you will tire very easily.

Make sure you have enough paint. If you have under-ordered and are tempted to skimp, *don't*. The result will be a patchy finish.

Do try to paint in natural light. This way you are least likely to miss painting a part of your surface.

## PAINTING A ROOM

The order in which a room should be painted is (1) ceiling; (2) walls; (3) windows, radiators, woodwork.

**Ceiling.** Paint in strips 12 in. to 18 in. wide, parallel to the window. Start each fresh section from the same side as you started your previous section. Use a 4-in. brush for Emulsion and a 3-in. brush for Gloss or Lustre.

**Walls.** Paint in vertical strips 12 in. to 18 in. wide. Start at the top of the wall and resume painting the next strip from the top. Never start painting from the bottom. Use 4-in. brush for Emulsion and 3-in. brush for Gloss or Lustre.

**Windows, Window-sills, and Radiators.** Use 1-in. brush, working from the top of frame to the bottom, and from side to side on cross frames and window-sills. Work from top to bottom on radiators – starting on your next section from the top.

**Woodwork.** *Picture rails:* Use a 1-in. brush and work across in unbroken line.

*Door-frame:* Use a 1-in. to 1½-in. brush, working from top to bottom on vertical frames – and across on the top frame. Do not overload door hinges.

*Plain Doors:* Remove handle and paint in 12-in. horizontal strips with 2-in. brush.

*Moulded or Panelled Doors:* Paint sections in numerical order as shown in diagram.

## AFTER PAINTING

*Cleaning Brushes:* After using Emulsion Paint wash brushes in cold water. After using Gloss or Lustre remove all remaining paint with turps substitute. When all paint is removed finish off with soap and water. Dry brushes thoroughly before storing. A piece of cotton wrapped round the bristles will help to keep their shape.

*Storing your paint:* Replace the lid as firmly as possible, and shake the can. Now the tin is air-tight, and when you next want to use it, the paint will be as fresh as when you first opened the can.

## MAKE YOUR HOUSE WARMER

*The following advice is given jointly by the Coal Utilisation Council, the Gas Council and the British Electrical Development Association.*

Experiments have shown that about two-thirds of the heat lost from a typical house leaks through the walls, floor and roof. There is little that you can easily do about the walls and floor; but you can effectively and inexpensively reduce the amount of heat lost through the roof, and this is where a good deal of it goes. It is just wasted into the atmosphere. Remember, this is heat which you are paying for with hard cash – just

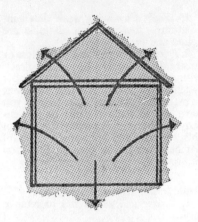

*Heat Lost*

money thrown away for all the value you get from it.

You can get greater comfort and save on coal, gas and electricity,
1. *By insulating the roof.*
2. *By stopping the draughts.*
3. *By lagging the hot-water tank or cylinder and pipes.*

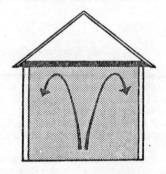

*Heat retained by Insulation*

**Choice of Insulating Materials.** If you have not been up in your loft recently, go and have a look now. Most lofts are unused except for the cold-water cistern, with the joists showing above the upper surface of the top floor ceiling. This is the best place to set about putting that tea-cosy on your house.

Three kinds of material are recommended for ceiling insulation. They are not only all light in weight, rot-proof

and unattractive to vermin, but also fire-proof, qualities which are most important. You can:

1. Lay a *blanket* of insulating material across the joists, or lay strips between them, or
2. Lay what is called a *"loose fill"* of insulating material between the joists, or
3. Lay special kinds of *aluminium foil* across or between the joists.

There is little to choose between any of these methods. Although some are a little cheaper than others, the difference is not great, and the degree of insulation you want and the construction of your loft will decide which is most satisfactory.

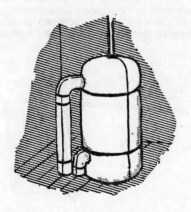

## HOW TO APPLY THESE MATERIALS

**Blanket.** This is probably the simplest way to apply insulation. These blankets are of glass wool or mineral wool, and are supplied in flexible rolls. The most usual type is 1 inch thick. They are easy to handle and to lay, and you can also take them up again if necessary. In laying a blanket unroll it across the joists so that it droops a little between them.

If it is laid taut, you may not be able to see where the joists run after you have laid it. The blankets should overlap one another at their edges by about 3 inches. Make sure that any spaces at the ends of the joists up against the eaves are filled in, or draughts may blow in underneath the insulation. The blanket should cover any water pipes if they are not lagged. Wire a layer round the cistern as well and tack a piece over the lid, but mind you leave a hole under the vent pipe. *Never* lay insulation *under* a cistern: some warmth through the ceiling here will reduce the chance of a freeze-up.

You can lay blanket between the joists instead of on the top. If you do it this way, you can use either 1-inch-thick blanket or another type of blanket, 2–4 inches thick, called "house insulation". This gives greater insulation but is a little more expensive and more bulky to deal with. Measure the distance between the joists and give this measurement with your order. The 1-inch-thick blanket should be supplied a little wider than this distance so that it will fit snugly up against the joists. Be careful to remove all wrappings and interleaving sheets of paper before laying the blanket.

**Loose Fill.** Where the spaces between the joists vary in width or where you have to deal with awkward corners and obstructions in the loft, it will probably be easier to lay a loose fill. You can use loose mineral or glass wool supplied in bags. Fill between the joists to a depth of about 2 inches. Alternatively, you can use loose vermiculite. This is a granular material, also supplied in bags and you just pour it between the joists. A depth of about 2 inches is advisable. Make sure that you get an even distribution and a uniform depth.

**Aluminium Foil.** The main advantage of foil is its lack of bulk. There are two ways of using it. One type is made up into a combined flat and corrugated sheet, only ½ inch thick, which can be laid either across the joists or between them. It is supplied in rolls. If you lay it across the joists, order it in the 2-feet width and staple or nail it onto the tops of the joists, allowing the edges to overlap. If you prefer to lay it between the joists, it should fit snugly, so order it to the measurement between them. In either case, the flat sheet must be uppermost.

The alternative method is to use two separate flat sheets of foil. One sheet should be laid, lightly crumpled, between the joists. The second should be draped across the joists and nailed down, so that it droops a little between them. The foil recommended for the top layer consists of two sheets of foil sandwiching a sheet of paper. This is supplied in rolls, 24 inches wide up to any length.

## SOME USEFUL TIPS AND REMINDERS

Select the method of insulation best suited to the conditions in your loft. Make sure the packages of insulation will not be too large to go through the trapdoor, if it is small.

Before you start, it is a sound plan to lay something solid across the joists for standing on. If you tread between the joists, you will go through the ceiling.

If you use blanket or aluminium foil laid across the joists, make sure you get a good overlap. If you lay it between, see that it fits snugly.

Never lay insulation under the cistern, but put a layer round it and over the lid. Your loft is going to be a much colder place in the future.

For the same reason, lay the insulation over the cold-water pipes if you can. If you cannot do this, lag them. Do not leave them exposed above the insulation.

Make sure that cold air cannot blow

in from outside and under the insulation, through gaps up against the eaves.

So put that tea-cosy over your house and save half the heat that is now going to waste through the roof. Whichever method or material you use, for one modest outlay you will reap dividends next winter and in the winters to come.

## OUTSIDE DOORS AND WINDOWS

If there are gaps or cracks which have nothing to do with the opening and shutting action, fill them up with putty, plastic wood or a mastic sealing compound. You can then colour the filling to match the paintwork.

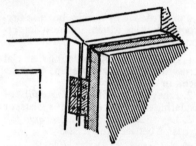

Doors and windows never fit exactly because allowance has to be made for expansion and contraction of the woodwork, otherwise they may stick. In addition, of course, some do not fit as they should owing to wear, to the woodwork warping or to bad workmanship in the first place. If gaps are really bad they need to be adjusted by a joiner.

In the normal way, you can greatly improve matters by fixing one or other

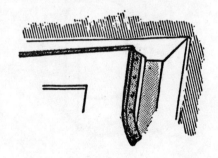

of the patent draught exclusion devices stocked by most ironmongers. Rubber piping and flexible metal strip are probably the most usual. The first is cheaper but the second lasts much longer. For draughts blowing under an inside door there are rubber mouldings, the old-fashioned "sausage" or the draught excluder which lifts up and down with the action of the door.

## DRAUGHTS AT THE SKIRTING

There are sometimes gaps between the skirting and the floorboards, through which draughts penetrate.

Trace the draughts by running a lighted match, taper or cigarette round the doors, windows, skirting and floorboards, and watch for the tell-tale flicker. You will find some without having to do this.

The best way to exclude them is to nail quarter-round strips of wood to the floor, close up to the skirting.

## DRAUGHTS THROUGH FLOORS

There is usually an air space underneath a timber floor and sometimes draughts blow up between the boards. If you suffer from this, the best solution is to close-carpet the floor, or lay linoleum. If you cannot do this, try filling up the gaps with thin fillets of wood, or a mastic sealing compound. When it is dry, you can stain it to match the floor. Another effective and inexpensive method, especially if the floor is cold as well as draughty, is to cover it with sheets of $\frac{1}{16}$-inch, $\frac{1}{8}$-inch or $\frac{1}{4}$-inch insulating fibre building board, costing a few pence per square foot, as an underlay to carpet or linoleum.

## FIREPLACES

Chimney flues of open fires are often a cause of excessive draughts. If an electric fire is used for heating the room, block up the fireplace with plywood or hardboard, but leave a small hole or you may get insufficient ventilation.

Rooms with open fires, solid-fuel stoves and fitted gas fires obviously must have flues, but often the chimney opening is much larger than it need be.

Loss of heat and execssive draughts are the result. Solid-fuel stoves and gas fires have a flue nozzle at the back. The fireplace should be filled in with sheet metal or asbestos with a hole to take the flue nozzle. In the case of a gas fire this hole should be a little larger than the nozzle to ensure proper ventilation.

## LAGGING HOT-WATER TANKS OR CYLINDERS AND PIPES

If your hot-water tank or cylinder and pipes are not properly lagged, you are throwing away more money on wasted fuel. A properly lagged hot-water installation, whether heated by solid fuel, a gas circulator or by an electric immersion heater, will be far more economical than an unlagged one. It is the old tea-cosy story again. An insulating jacket will keep the water hot much longer, even overnight. If your hot-water cylinder is in the airing cupboard, you can still air your clothes if you leave only a short section of pipe unlagged.

You would also be wise to lag the hot flow-and-return pipes if there is a run of 10 feet or more from the boiler to the cylinder. The draw-off pipes do not need to be lagged.

You can do all this yourself, quite easily. The cylinder can be lagged in one of two ways:

**Insulating Jacket.** You can order jackets made to fit any size of tank or cylinder. They are packed with mineral or glass wool and held in position with wire or tapes. If the outer covering is of American cloth or similar material, it is easier to keep clean.

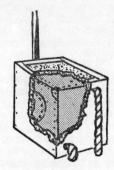

**Loose Fill.** If you have an electric immersion heater, you cannot beat loose fill for insulation. Make a boxlike casing of hardboard or plywood round the tank or cylinder, leaving a space of not less than 3 inches between cylinder and case. Fill the space with mineral or glass wool, packing it down lightly at the sides and over the top of the cylinder. The casing will need holes for the pipes and should be built up higher than the cylinder, with a lid to fit over the top.

## GAS

Many people prefer gas to electricity for cooking and heating, though few, given the choice, would prefer it for lighting. Much new gas equipment has lately been developed. Some of the new fires give great heat at little cost, and the modern gas cooker is clean, efficient and labour saving. Gas water-heaters, towel rails and drying cabinets are deservedly popular. A gas poker makes easy work of fire lighting, and a gas refrigerator runs silently and needs little attention.

A suspected leak of gas should at once be reported to your local Gas Board Offices, the leak meanwhile being temporarily sealed with soap. Never look for escaping gas with a naked flame.

Information on the use of gas in the home and the latest types of equipment can be obtained from the British Gas Council, Murdock House, 1 Grosvenor Place, London, S.W.1, or your local Gas showroom.

Country households who cannot have a gas supply can run cooking stoves, coppers, fires and lighting on Calor gas, which can be delivered regularly in large cylinders. Special gas appliances must be used. Particulars can be obtained from Calor Gas House, Key West, Windsor Road, Slough, or your local suppliers.

**How to Read the Gas Meter.** Ignore the two top dials. Commencing with dial A, write down from left to right the smaller of the two figures between which each of the hands is standing; if the hand is between 0 and 1, put down 0; but if it is between 9 and 0, put down 9. Add 00 after the figures so set down and you

have the present meter reading. Deduct the reading previously recorded and you have the gas consumption for the period between the two readings.

The index given here reads 751,900. If the reading a week before had been 749,100 the amount of gas consumed

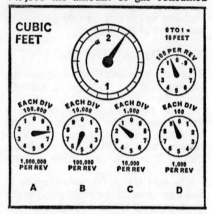

during the week would have been 2,800 cubic feet.

Some meters have a direct reading index in which the actual figures are all in a line thus:

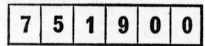

Gas is always measured in cubic feet, but it is nowadays charged for in therms.

To convert your meter reading of cubic feet to therms, you need to know the heating power or the "calorific value" (CV) of the gas. This varies in different districts, but is usually about 500 Btu per cubic foot. So one cubic foot would give $\frac{500}{100,000}$ or $\frac{1}{200}$ of a therm Therefore each therm would equal 200 cubic feet of gas.

## ELECTRICITY

It pays to have your house well wired by an expert. Poor wiring leads to constant fusing and possibly fire. All wire must be adequately insulated and properly enclosed. Advice on this will be given at your local electricity offices.

Electricity is supplied at various rates

for lighting and heating, and you should find out which tariff is best suited to the needs of your household. By paying a fixed sum each quarter for a certain amount of light and power, plus a low rate for anything used over and above that amount, it is often possible to get electricity very cheaply.

Buy good electric lamps, and keep your flexes in good condition. Watch for signs of wear, and bind with insulating tape.

Learn how to mend fuses, but be sure to switch off the current before touching the fuse-box. Use the right kind of fuse and flex for the job, and do not overload the fuses by using more lights or fires than they can carry.

When buying new equipment, study all types in the local electrical showrooms. There are fires for different kinds of rooms, water heaters of all sizes, and up-to-date cookers for large or small families. In addition there are refrigerators, irons, kettles, coffee-pots, blankets, toasters, vacuum cleaners, fans, washing-machines and many modern gadgets to aid the housewife.

Advice on the use of modern electric equipment can be obtained from the British Electrical Development Association, 2 Savoy Hill, London, W.C.2, or your local Electricity showroom.

**How to Read the Electric Meter.** Your meter is quite easy to read and you can keep a record of daily or weekly consumption of electricity.

Ignore small dials marked 1/10 and 1/100. Read the other dials from left to

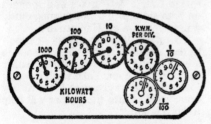

This meter reads 9,469 units.

right. The dial hand should always be read as indicating the figure it has last passed, and not the one to which it may be nearest.

When the hand is between two figures write down the lower figure. When the hand is between 0 and 9, write down 9. When the hand is on a figure, say 7, you write down 6, not 7, unless the hand on the nearest dial on the right is between figure 0 and figure 1. Go through the same process with the other dials, writing down the figures in the order left to right.

In the previous illustration below, the reading of the meter is 9,469 units. By subtracting your previous reading, the number of units used in the interval will be apparent.

## THE FAMILY WASH

Most people have washing machines. The manufacturers of them indicate precisely how they should be used, the loads they will bear and the appropriate soaps, soapflakes, chemicals and detergents that should be used in them. There is a very wide range of washing preparations available and care should be taken to use the right one for the kind of washing you are doing. Always follow the instructions on the packet or bottle.

Washing should be divided into three groups: (*a*) silks and woollens; (*b*) coloured cottons; (*c*) white cottons and linens.

Silks and woollens should be washed in lukewarm soapy water. Washing and rinsing water should be of the same temperature to avoid shrinking. Squeeze woollens rather than rub them. Support delicate fabrics with the hand as you put them through the wringer to avoid straining the threads.

Next, wash coloured cottons in hotter water, soaping and rubbing cuffs, neck bands, etc.

If the material is *not* colour-fast, the garment must be washed separately in cooler water, rinsed and pegged over the line at once.

White cottons and linens are put into warm soapy water and brought to the boil. Boil for about fifteen to twenty minutes.

If cottons have got too dry, they must be damped down with warm water sprinkled upon them, and rolled up for a short while. Silks should be rolled in a towel after washing, and not allowed to get dry.

Woollens should be ironed with a warm iron. Knitted garments are best ironed under a damp cloth. Silks should be ironed damp with a warm iron, on the wrong side. Shantung, tussore and seersuckers are ironed dry.

Care must be taken in ironing artificial silks and nylons; the iron should first be tested on a small piece of the material. Such fabrics frequently change colour when ironed, but go back to their original colour after a while. Crêpe fabrics must be stretched to their former size under the iron.

Cottons and linens are ironed damp, with a hot iron.

## TO WASH SOFT FURNISHINGS

All patterned hangings, etc., must be tested to see if the dye is fast. Dip a portion of the material in warm water and press against a white cloth. If the colour comes off, do not wash but send the article to be dry-cleaned.

Soap flakes should be used when washing soft furnishings, such as muslin and chintz.

**Thin Curtains,** such as net, should be squeezed through warm soapy water and handled very lightly. Rinse and starch a little. Stretch carefully before hanging evenly over the line. An excellent method is to re-hang them at the windows while still damp, running a rod through the bottom hem to stretch them. They will then probably need no ironing.

If curtains are frilled, iron frills first.

Net curtains are liable to shrink, and this should be allowed for by making a triple hem by hand at the bottom when the curtain is first made.

All curtains and loose covers should be well shaken to remove dust before washing.

**Velvet and Plush** should be handled as little as possible. Wash in warm soapy water. Rinse. Do not squeeze, but hang dripping wet to dry. The pile should be smoothed with a soft cloth as it dries.

Blankets should not be rubbed. See

that the rinsing water is the same temperature as the soapy water – both luke-warm. Rinse well, put through loosely adjusted wringer, hang evenly on the line, and allow to dry. When half dry hang them the opposite way on the line. When dry shake them to raise the nap.

When an ample supply of clean soft water is available, many people wash blankets without using soap.

**Feather Pillows** should only be washed on a sunny day. Have plenty of soapy water to allow for movement. Soak the pillow in the suds for an hour, then swish about and put into fresh suds. Rinse thoroughly at least twice. Hang up to drip in a sunny place, and re-peg at intervals so that the feathers are spaced out. When dry, plump up the pillows.

**Eiderdowns** are washed in much the same way, but soak only for three minutes. Iron with a warm iron when dry.

**Lace Cloths, Veils, etc.,** should be handled with great care. After washing in warm soapy water and rinsing in water of the same temperature, dry by spreading flat if possible. A veil may be lightly starched or stiffened with weak gum arabic water (a dessertspoonful of gum arabic to a pint of water). Then stretch it flat, pinning into shape. Iron on the wrong side, through muslin if it is very fragile.

**Plastic Curtains and Cloths** should be spread over a flat surface and sponged on both sides with a cloth wrung out in warm soapy water. Hang to dry.

To wash the **household chamois leather,** dissolve a large pinch of soda in a bowl of warm water. Soak the leather in this for an hour. Then wash in warm soapsuds. A little glycerine in the rinsing water worked into the leather will help to keep it soft.

## USEFUL HINTS

**To remove Grease from Silk (not Nylon).** Lay a piece of woollen cloth or baize on a flat surface and on it lay smoothly the part stained, with the right side down-wards. Having spread a piece of brown paper on the top, apply a warm iron, as for wool. About five to eight seconds is usually sufficient. Then rub the stained part briskly with a piece of tissue paper.

**To remove Stains.** Mud, blood or egg should be soaked in cold water before washing. For other stains, put the garment in lukewarm suds, and rub a little dry soap powder into the spot.

Paint, other than emulsion, is removed when fresh by the use of turpentine, applied on a piece of cloth. Ammonia should be mixed with the turpentine if the paint has been allowed to dry. Emulsion paint should be removed with tepid water, but if it is dry it may be removed with diluted methylated spirit.

Wine and tea stains can be removed when fresh by soaking in a solution of one teaspoonful of borax to a pint of warm water. If the material is not washable, rub fuller's earth or salt into the stain, and brush off.

Ink spots should be dealt with at once. Soak up as much as possible with blotting-paper. Sponge at once with milk, and then with clean water. Such ink as Quink comes out at once when washed, but again it should be done quickly. Ball point ink can be removed with methylated spirit.

**To extract Wax or Grease Spots from Fabrics other than Plastic.** Cover the spot with clean blotting-paper and lay a warm iron on it until grease is melted. Renew the blotting-paper until all the stain is removed. White spirit or petrol or a mild synthetic detergent may also be used for removing grease.

**To Take Ink out of Boards.** Apply strong muriatic acid (spirits of salt) with a piece of cloth; afterwards *wash well* with water. Spirits of salts is a poison.

If, when ink has been spilt, cold water is immediately poured over the ink to dilute it, and wiped up at once, no stains may result.

**To Take Ink-stains out of Carpets.** If the stain is still wet, cover thickly with salt, and remove with a spoon, applying fresh salt until no more ink is absorbed; then rub the spot with a cut lemon, and rinse with clean water.

**To Take Grease or Oil out of a Carpet.** As soon as possible cover the spot with clean blotting paper, and press with a hot iron, renewing the blotting-paper until the grease is absorbed. If the grease has not been completely removed rub the spot with a cloth dipped in spirits of turpentine.

**To Clean Carpets.** Carpet soaps and shampoos give excellent results. Do not get the carpet too wet, and choose a good day so that you can leave the windows open to speed the drying. Do a small portion at a time, using one cloth for the soap and another wrung in clean warm water to rinse. A few drops of ammonia in the rinsing water will brighten the colours.

**Beating Carpets.** Always beat on the wrong side first; and then more gently on the right side. Beware of using sticks with sharp points, which may tear the carpet.

**Sweeping Carpets.** Nowadays few people "sweep" a carpet other than with a vacuum cleaner or carpet sweeper. Some claim that a new carpet should not be vacuumed for a month or two after it is laid. A carpet will wear longer with an underlay of felt or plastic. Rising butts fitted to a door will enable it to clear a thick carpet.

**Sweeping Stair Carpets.** Small, handy vacuum cleaners for doing stairs are readily available. When laying stair carpets, underlay with good thick tread pads. To save wear, ensure that the carpet is long enough to permit moving occasionally.

**To Clean Furs.** The cleaning of furs, being highly skilled work, should not be lightly undertaken at home. If a fur is really dirty or greasy it should be sent to a furrier.

To freshen a fur, bran is the safest thing to use. Lay the fur quite flat upon a table; warm a quantity of new bran in a pan, taking care that it does not burn, to prevent which it must be actively stirred. When well warmed, but not too hot, rub it gently into the fur with the hand. Leave it for thirty minutes or so; then shake the fur, and brush and comb it carefully.

**To clean Hair Brushes.** As hot water and soap very soon soften the bristles, and rubbing completes their destruction, use soda, dissolved in cold water, instead; soda, having an affinity for grease, cleanses the brush with little friction. Do not set them near the fire, nor in the sun, to dry, but after shaking well, set them on the point of the handle in a shady place.

**Borax** is very useful in many household matters. If added to water in which china and glass is to be washed, it will give a sparkle and lustre. It softens water, and should be added for all cleaning purposes, as it also acts as a disinfectant.

**To Clean Windows.** First brush the dust off the window-frames, then wipe the glass with a wet chamois skin, and dry and polish with a dry chamois or linen cloth.

**Cleaning China and Glass Ornaments.** The best material for cleansing either porcelain or glass is fuller's earth; but it must be beaten into a fine powder and carefully cleared of all rough and hard particles which might endanger the polish of the surface. As articles intended solely for ornament are not so highly annealed as others, they should never be washed in water beyond a tepid temperature.

**Discoloured Varnish.** Varnish on tables, etc., is sometimes turned white by a hot vessel being placed over it. To remove the stain rub with a mixture in equal parts of linseed oil and methylated spirits till the mark disappears.

**To remove the Smell of Fresh Paint.** Pails of water will absorb the smell if left in the room overnight. Cut onions will also absorb odour.

**A Simple Mode of Annealing Glass** has been some time in use by chemists. It consists in immersing the vessel in cold water, gradually heated to the boiling point, and allowed to remain till cold, when it will be fit for use.

**To Remove Tight Finger Rings.** Pass the end of a piece of fine string under the ring, and wind it evenly round the finger upward as far as the middle joint. Then take the lower end of the string under the ring, and slowly unwind it *upward*. The ring will then gradually move along the string and come off.

Or, wet the finger, and rub it with soap, then press the ring over the knuckle, turning it on the finger meanwhile.

**To Prevent Fur in Kettles.** Water of every kind, except rainwater, will speedily cover the inside of a tea-kettle with an unpleasant crust; this may easily be guarded against by placing a clean oyster shell or stone marble in the tea kettle. The shell or stone will always keep the interior of the kettle in good order.

**To Loosen Glass Stoppers of Bottles.** With a feather rub a drop or two of salad oil round the stopper, close to the mouth of the bottle or decanter, which must then be placed before the fire, at the distance of about eighteen inches; the heat will cause the oil to insinuate itself between the stopper and the neck. When the bottle has grown warm, gently strike the stopper on one side, and then on the other, with any light wooden instrument; then try it with the hand; if it will not yet move, place it again before the fire, adding another drop of oil. After a while strike again as before; and, by persevering in this process, however tightly it may be fastened in, you will at length succeed in loosening it. Tapping round the stopper with another glass stopper will sometimes loosen it.

**Another Method.** Dip one end of a cloth in boiling water, and then wrap it round the neck of the bottle; the heat causes the neck to expand, and the stopper can generally be moved with ease; or put a piece of string twice round the neck and fix one end to a ring or hook, draw the bottle backwards and forwards sharply. The heat caused by the friction expands the neck as in the preceding case.

**Cements, Glues, Pastes, etc.** It is possible to buy these for every purpose, and a good ironmonger will advise on the most suitable make.

To mend broken china, etc., with cement it is essential to have the broken surfaces perfectly clean, and to use as little cement as possible. The closer the join, the stronger the mend.

**To Melt Glue.** This should always be done in a glue-pot or double vessel, to prevent its being burned, which injures it very materially. It is difficult to heat the glue in the inner vessel to the boiling point; this, however, can be avoided by employing in the outer vessel some liquid which boils at a higher temperature than pure water, such as a saturated solution of salt (made by adding one-third as much salt as water). This boils at 224 deg.F., or 12 degrees above the heat of boiling water, and enables the glue in the inner vessel to be heated to a much higher temperature than when pure water is employed. If a saturated solution of nitre is used, the temperature rises still higher.

**Inks.** Many kinds of ink are on the market, and should be used for their correct purpose. Children should only be allowed to use washable ink (such as *Quink*) which will wash out if spilt.

Inks for special purposes are Indian ink (for maps, plans, etc.), marking ink (for use on linen), red ink (for accountancy and clerical purposes), copying ink (whereby a copy is made of a letter or document by means of moisture or heat), and ink for use on zinc garden labels. Any good stationer will supply these and advise on their use.

## HOUSEHOLD PESTS

Pests such as bugs and fleas are not nearly as common as they used to be chiefly because of our higher standard of living and much increased cleanliness. Disinfectants and insecticides are much improved, and are still being improved. Proprietary preparations are readily available.

**To Destroy Furniture Beetles.** The grubs which destroy woodwork by riddling it with holes are the larvae of beetles, but the worm-holes which show at the surface of worm-eaten furniture are made by the beetles themselves in making their exit from the wood.

There are three varieties of furniture beetle which are common in this country, viz. the common furniture beetle, the death-watch beetle, and the powder-post beetle, all equally destructive.

The common furniture beetle emerges from the wood generally in the month of June. It is of a dark reddish-brown colour, and varies in length from about one-tenth to one-fifth of an inch. The females deposit their eggs in slits or cracks in the wood or in old worm-holes. The larvae hatch out in three or four weeks and at once begin to burrow in the wood. They are white in colour, and when full grown pupate near the surface of the wood.

The death-watch beetle comes out of the wood about a month earlier; in April and May they are most abundant, and their tapping most vigorous. They are larger than the common furniture beetle, being about one-quarter to one-third of an inch in length, and their life-cycle is about three years. They infest old oak bookcases, and sometimes the books also.

The powder-post beetle is very similar, but longer and narrower in form. They do not attack the wood of coniferous trees, but the sapwood of hard woods like oak, ash or hickory seems to have great attraction for them, and consequently this part of the wood should not be used for furniture-making.

The eggs of the beetles are usually laid in spring, and paraffin or turpentine applied to the under- or unpolished side of wood will prevent the laying of eggs. But if the grubs are already at work (and the first indication of this is often a fine powder on the floor beneath a piece of furniture) then immediate treatment is necessary by the use of such preparations as Rentokil and Cuprinol which will destroy the worms.

## IN CASE OF FIRE

Remember that fire cannot burn without air. Aim therefore at excluding air.

A spark on a rug is extinguished by putting your foot on it as this keeps out air. If a person's clothes catch fire, roll him swiftly in a rug or any material that is handy. If curtains catch fire tear them down and roll them up if possible.

If furniture or bedding is smouldering, throw water over it.

Summon the Fire Service. While the brigade is on its way try to keep the fire in check with buckets of water and rugs or blankets soaked in water. If you have no telephone send a messenger or go yourself to the nearest police station.

Close all doors and windows to prevent draught.

If you find yourself in danger of being overcome by smoke, get on the floor and keep your face near the ground while you get out of the room. The air near the ground is most free from heat, smoke and fumes.

Large houses, and all garages, should have at least one patent fire extinguisher.

Anyone running business premises or a factory should make sure that he knows the police regulations regarding fire prevention. Ignorance of the law is no defence if fire breaks out causing death or damage.

Most modern buildings intended for offices and factories are equipped with fire sprinklers fixed to ceilings. If fire breaks out, these are turned on automatically, and the fire checked. Where many people are employed, it is wise to have occasional fire drill, and to have someone in charge on each floor.

**Fireguards in the Home.** The law insists that where there are children under seven, all fires must be adequately protected so that the children cannot fall on them. There are many excellent guards to be bought, larger ones that can be firmly fixed being most suited to nurseries.

**To Extinguish a Fire in the Chimney.** Close all doors and windows to stop draughts. Throw common salt on the fire. If the fire appears to be serious do not hesitate to send for the Fire Service.

## CROCHET, TATTING AND KNITTING

Whether as a simple trimming, as an elaborate quilt, or as a fabric, almost rivalling Point Lace, it is popular with every woman who has any time for fancy work, since you only need to understand the stitches, and the terms and abbreviations used in writing the descriptions of the different designs, to be enabled to work them without difficulty.

**Stitches used in Crochet.** These, with their abbreviations, are:—*Chain stitch, Ch.; Single crochet, S.; Double crochet, Dc.; Treble stitch, Tr.,* and *Double and Treble Long.*

(i) **Chain Stitch, or Ch.** Hook the cotton into a loop, and keep on looping the cotton through each previous stitch till a succession of chains are made to form a foundation.

(ii) **Single Crochet, or S.** This occurs only in working designs; the hook is inserted in a stitch, and the cotton is pulled through that and the cotton which is on the hook at the same time; it thus makes a close tie.

(iii) **Double Crochet, or Dc.** With cotton on the hook insert the latter into a stitch, draw the cotton through; there are now two loops on the hook, take up the cotton on the hook, and with cotton again upon the hook draw it through two loops.

(iv) **Treble Stitch, or Tr.** With the loop of last stitch on the hook, twist the cotton over the hook, place the latter through a stitch, draw the cotton through, then put the cotton over the hook, draw the cotton through two loops, and again through two loops.

(v) **Double and Treble Long.** With the hook in a loop, twist the cotton twice or three times over the hook, and draw the hook successively through either two or three loops.

**Square or Filet Crochet** is also sometimes used. The squares are either open or close. An open square consists of one Tr, two Ch, missing two on the line beneath, before making the next stitch. A close square has three successive Trs. Thus, any given number of close squares, followed by an open, will have so many three Trs; consequently any foundation for square crochet must have a number that can be divided by three.

**To Increase or Decrease.** For the former two stitches may be worked in the same loop; for the latter, either miss a stitch of the preceding row, or crochet two together.

**To Join a Thread.** Joins should be avoided as much as possible in open work. In joining, finish the stitch by drawing the new thread through, leaving two inches for both ends, which must be held in. A neat join may be made by making a weaver's knot of the two ends.

**To Use Several Colours.** Hold the threads not in use on the edge of the work, and work them in. Change the colour by beginning the stitch in the old colour, and finishing it with the new, continuing the work with the latter, holding in the old. If only one stitch is wanted in the new colour, finish one stitch, and begin the next with it; then change. This method ensures the work being perfectly smooth on the reverse side, leaving no loose threads.

**To Join Leaves, etc.** When one part of a leaf or flower is to be joined to another, drop the loop from the hook, which insert in the place to be joined; draw the loop through and continue.

**Oriental Crochet, sometimes termed Tricot.** This is worked by just making a chain the length required. Then put the hook through a loop of the chain, pull the wool through without twisting it, and so continue to the end, keeping all the stitches on the hook. *In returning,* twist the wool over the hook, pull it through the first loop, twist the wool again over the hook, pull it through the next, and so continue to the end. There will now be a row of flat loops, but not on the edge. Work exactly as at the first row, which was worked with the chain row, but take up the loops instead of the chain stitches.

**Tatting Explained.** The only necessary implements are a thin shuttle or short netting needle, and a gilt pin and ring, joined by a chain. The cotton used should be strong and soft. Attention should be paid to the manner of holding the hands, as on this depends the grace or awkwardness of the movement. Fill the shuttle with the cotton (or silk) required, in the same manner as a netting-needle. Hold the shuttle between the thumb and first and second fingers of the right hand, leaving about half a yard of cotton unwound. Take up the cotton, about three inches from the end, between the thumb and first finger of the left hand, and let the end fall in the palm of the hand; pass the cotton round the other fingers of the left hand (keeping them parted a little), and bring it again between the thumb and forefinger, thus making a circle round the extended fingers. There are only two stitches in tatting, called respectively the *English* and the *French* stitch, and they are usually done alternately.

**English Stitch.** Let the thread between the right and left hands fall towards you; slip the shuttle under the thread between the first and second fingers; draw it out rather quickly, keeping it in a horizontal line with the left hand. You will find a slipping loop is formed on this cotton with that which went round the fingers. Hold the shuttle steadily with the cotton stretched tightly out, and with the second finger of the left hand slip the loop thus made under the thumb.

**French Stitch.** Instead of allowing the cotton to fall *towards* you, and passing the shuttle *downwards*, the cotton is thrown in a loop over the left hand, and the shuttle passed under the thread between the first and second fingers *upwards.* The knot must be invariably formed by the thread which passes round the fingers of the *left* hand. If the operation is reversed, and the knot formed by the cotton connected with the shuttle, the loop will not draw up. This is occasioned by letting the cotton from the shuttle hang loosely instead of drawing it out and holding it tightly stretched. When any given number of these double stitches is done, and drawn closely together, the stitches are held between the first finger and thumb, and the other fingers are withdrawn from the circle of cotton, which is gradually diminished by drawing out the shuttle until the loop of tatting is nearly or entirely closed. The tatted loops should be quite close to each other, unless directions to the contrary are given.

**Ornamental Edging.** The pin is used in making an ornamental edge, something like purl edging, thus: Slip the ring on the left-hand thumb, so that the pin attached may be ready for use. After making the required number of double stitches, twist the pin in the circle of cotton, and hold it between the forefinger and thumb, while making more double stitches; repeat. The little loops thus formed are called *picots*.

**Trefoil Tatting.** This is done by drawing three loops up tightly, close together, and then leaving a short space before making more. The trefoil is sewed into shape afterwards with a needle.

**To Join Loops.** When two loops are to be connected, a *picot* is made in the *first*, whenever the join is required. When you come to the corresponding part of the *second* loop, draw the thread which goes round the fingers of the left hand through the *picot* with a needle, pulling through a loop large enough to admit the shuttle. Slip this through, then draw the thread tight again over the fingers, and continue the work. In many patterns, a needle is used to work over, in buttonhole stitch, the thread which passes from one loop to another. Leave a long needleful of the same cotton or silk used for the tatting at the beginning of the work, and use an ordinary needle to buttonhole over bars wherever they occur.

**Knitting.** The modern tendency is towards simple designs, and the most expensive looking jerseys, etc., are often those with the least complicated pattern. This, however, is untrue of Fair Isle designs.

Buy good needles and wool, and be sure to get the exact kind mentioned in your pattern. Otherwise your work will be the wrong size when completed.

Be sure to get the right wool for your purpose. Many people use wool that is too soft for men's socks and boys' pullovers, with the result that they soon wear out. A crossbred wool is best for such purposes, while the softest of botany wool should be used for babies' clothes. Shetland wool is very fine and soft. Angora is very fluffy and extremely warm, but unsuited to babies as the long hairs are apt to get into their mouths.

When you have finished your knitting, pay special attention to the finishing. Each piece of a garment should be pinned out to shape and carefully pressed under a damp cloth on the wrong side, before being sewn up. Ribbing should not be pressed at all.

**To "Cast on".** Make a loop, and put it on the left needle, put the right needle through this loop. Twist the cotton or wool over the right needle and draw it through the loop, then transfer this loop just made from the right needle to the left; repeat this process till you have made the number required. To make a neat edge knit next row into back of loops.

**To Fasten on.** Separate the strands of the two ends of the wool for about two inches back, put one over the other, and after slightly moistening, roll between the palms of the hands to effect a join, and proceed to knit.

**Plain Knitting.** Slip the point of the right-hand needle in a loop, bring the thread round it, and with the forefinger push the point of the needle off the loop so that the thread just twisted round forms a new one on the right hand.

**Purling.** The right-hand needle is slipped in the loop *in front of* the left-hand one, and the thread, after passing between the two, is brought round it; it is then worked as before. The thread is always brought forward before beginning a purled stitch, unless particular directions to the contrary are given.

**To Increase.** There are several ways of doing this. If only one stitch is to be increased, bring the thread between the needles and knit the following stitch. This will form an open stitch or hole in the following row. To make a close increase, pick up the loop below the next stitch to be knitted, and knit it. To increase one stitch when the row is being seamed, the thread will be in front of the needle; pass it right round the needle to the front again.

**To Decrease.** Take one stitch off without knitting; knit one, then slip the point of the left-hand needle in the unknitted stitch and draw it over the other. It is marked in patterns D1. To decrease 2, knit 2 together, *as one*, twice.

**To Join a Round.** Four or five needles are used in round work, such as socks, stockings, etc. Cast on any given number of stitches on one needle, then slip another needle in the last stitch, before casting any on it; repeat for any number. When all are cast on, knit the first two stitches off on the end of the last needle. One needle is always left unused in casting on for a round.

**To Cast off.** Knit two stitches; with the left-hand needle draw the first over the second; knit another; repeat. Remember that the two before the casting off should never be very tightly knitted.

**To Knit Three Stitches Together,** so that the centre one shall be in front. Slip two off the needle together, knit the third, and draw the others over together.

**To Raise a Stitch** is to knit the bar of thread between the two stitches as one.

**To Pick up a Stitch.** With the left-hand needle pick up the loop below the next stitch to be knitted, knit it and bring it to the right needle.

**To Slip a Stitch** is to pass a stitch from the left needle to the right without knitting it.

**To Seam a Stitch.** Place the needle in the stitch to be seamed, having the point towards you. Pass the thread right round the needle, take the needle with the stitch on it out at the back, and repeat.

**Abbreviations used in Patterns.** *K, knit; P, purl; D, decrease; K 2 t, knit two together; P 2 t, purl two together; M 1, make one.*

# POULTRY, RABBITS AND BEES

## POULTRY

By keeping six good fowls or a similar number of ducks, it is possible for a family of four to have fresh eggs nearly every day of the year. Rhode Island Reds, Light Sussex, or Leghorns and their crosses that were hatched in March, if bought in late September, should lay their first eggs in early October and continue to yield unbrokenly until the following September, by which time they are due to moult and cease laying for some weeks. However, the better way would be to kill them off in August, to provide six or more good dinners, and then to replace with more young layers in September.

**Housing Fowls.** Minimum requirements of six fowls are a soundly built house, providing 4 square feet of floor space per bird; a feed-trough at least 3 feet long, 9 inches wide and 4–6 inches deep; a vessel to hold at least one gallon of drinking water, and a tin or box to hold grit. (For larger or smaller flocks, adjustments can be made pro rata.) Nest-boxes and perches are supplied as part of the essential fittings in manufacturers' houses. Style of house does not matter, so long as it provides the necessary floor-space, is well lighted by windows, and preferably has a partly netting-covered front. Height should exceed 4 feet at the highest point, in order to ensure comfortable access for cleaning out. Larger flocks may be kept on the battery system or in deep-litter houses.

**Provision of a Run.** A run in which the birds can exercise is not essential, but is desirable, and the best way is to build what is known as a covered run, as an extension to the house. This will be large enough for six birds if 6 to 8 feet long, 4 to 6 feet wide, 4 feet high at the front, with sloping roof to 3 feet 6 inches at the back. An attendance door should be provided for this, as well as the door to the house. Rear and end of the covered run are covered by boarding, asbestos sheets or overlapping strips of roofing felt (less durable), the top roofed with felt or corrugated iron sheets, and the front of the run enclosed with wire-netting, from 18 inches to 2 feet from ground level.

**House for Ducks.** Ducks (Khaki Campbells and White Campbells are the best layers) need only a shelter for nights and for windy or rainy weather, but must have a grassy run surrounding and this needs to be ample. Allow 20 square yards per duck. Shelter dimensions for six ducks should suit at 2 feet 6 inches to 3 feet wide, 4 feet long, 2 feet 6 inches high on one long side (the front) and 2 feet on the other, with roof sloping to the rear, and overhanging to shed rain water.

Ends and back are boarded, the front provided with a wire-netting-covered frame, hinged at the bottom, to let down by day and be raised for security from foxes, etc., at night. The floor would be of $\frac{1}{2}$-inch or 1-inch wire mesh netting on a removable framework, to be covered with straw, renewed as often as it becomes wet or dirty. Nest-boxes are unnecessary, the only other equipment being a feed trough as for fowls, drinking vessel such as a basin, deep enough to allow immersion of heads, and a grit box or tin. A brick in the water vessel will prevent it being overturned.

**Feeding Programmes.** Both fowls and ducks eat mash – made by mixing poultry meal with kitchen scraps, cooked potatoes and peelings – and they also like grain, especially wheat. The best feeding programmes are:

*Fowls* (in summer): Mash in the morning, 7–8 a.m.; small grain feed (about one ounce per bird) scattered in the floor litter, midday; two ounces grain per bird in floor litter at night half an hour before dusk.

In winter: Warm mash in morning; grain feed, one ounce per bird, midday; warm mash just before dusk.

*Ducks* (in summer): soaked grain (after immersion in water for twelve hours), two ounces per bird, 7–8 a.m.; dry grain, once ounce per bird, midday; mash feed before dusk.

In winter: Warm mash feed, morning; soaked grain, one ounce per bird, midday; warm mash before dusk.

(Where grain is not available, mash may be fed at each of two feeds in summer, three in winter.)

**Special Hints on Feeding.** Always give just as much mash as is cleaned up in half an hour after feeding. Appetites will vary almost day to day; be prepared to adjust the quantities supplied, as observation suggests. Make the fowls' mash fairly dry – damp enough for the poultry meal to cling to the other ingredients, but not soggy or pasty. Crumbly-moist describes the correct consistency. The ducks' mash should be wetter – pasty, but not so much so as to resemble thin porridge.

Give fowls fresh cabbage leaves and other garden greens to peck at during the day, all the year round; up to two ounces per bird is desirable. Ducks need greens too, in winter, and when the run is bare of fresh green grass. By way of variation, or if short of greens, give fowls a swede, turnip or mangold, cut into halves and placed in the trough. Pellets may also be used for feeding poultry and this allows for greater control over food requirements.

**Management Routine.** The fowl or duck house floor may be kept bare, but if floor litter (short straw for preference) can be supplied it is better. Fowls' corn can then be thrown into the litter and the birds will benefit considerably from the exercise taken in scratching for the grains. The depth of litter may have to depend upon availability of supplies, but should preferably be 3 inches. Materials other than straw that may be used are dried tree leaves (gathered in autumn and stored in sacks), dried

bracken fronds, "flights" or "cavings' (both unsuitable for the ducks' floor) that result from threshing, and dried grass or hay. Their effectiveness is in the order in which they are given. Peat moss may be bought in bales, but is rather expensive, and is no good for the ducks' netting floor. The litter should be shaken up weekly, or more often if convenient, and renewed as often as it gets damp or dirty.

Both fowls and ducks need a regular supply of grit. Two kinds should be used – flint grit, which is held in the gizzard and used by the bird in the grinding of its food, and either limestone, oyster-shell or cockle-shell grit, which supplies lime for the making of bone and egg-shells. Both grits may be put together in the one container, which should be placed under cover so as not to get wet.

Maintenance of a constant water supply is essential for all laying stock, which, in its absence, cease laying in a day or two and then may moult, remaining out of lay for weeks. In frosty weather the vessels should be emptied each night and filled early next morning or may be kept free of ice by placing a special heater lamp beneath. Vessels should frequently be cleaned out and once a week scrubbed. Periodically they should be scalded with washing soda solution.

Clearing away of the fowls' manure from the droppings-board beneath the perches is necessary at least once a week.

Litter, hay for preference, though straw will do, is needed in the fowls' nests. Not only does it encourage them to lay, but the eggs are then less likely to be broken. This litter is renewed monthly.

**Ducks and Chickens for Table.** Where the desire is simply for poultry to kill for the table the best plan is to buy eight-week-old Light Sussex cockerels and to rear them to sixteen weeks before starting to kill them off. Ducklings of the same age – preferably Aylesburys – are also a good proposition, but there is slightly more work entailed in plucking them, because after ten weeks of age there are many small stubs of feathers underneath the main coat that are laborious to remove. On the special table duckling farms they are reared to only ten weeks, but the private owner may profitably keep them another six weeks before starting to kill.

**Fattening Foods.** Both cockerel chickens and ducklings should be given an all-mash diet, four feeds a day being desirable for quick fattening. Also the mash should be slightly moister for both than for their laying counterparts. Fattening foods, such as cooked potato, Sussex ground oats when available, and milk should comprise the mash, which in the later stages may also advisedly include a proportion of fat. Drinks of milk are helpful. A little green food in the early stages of fattening is desirable. Grit of both kinds and water are necessary, although in the later stages the water may be reduced considerably and the mash made wetter, as an inducement for more to be eaten.

**Raising Geese for Table.** Goose-keeping is feasible only where a paddock or similar area of grass is available, such as in an orchard, as geese are essentially grazers, grass being necessary to their good health and growth. Four birds per quarter acre are quite as many as may reasonably be kept. The goslings may be obtained by three methods: (1) keeping a pair, or better, a trio (gander and two geese) of adults to produce eggs for hatching by broody hen; (2) buying eggs and hatching them, and rearing the goslings by broody hen; and (3) buying young goslings four to six weeks old and rearing them on their own. Of these, the last two methods are usually the most practical.

**Rearing Young Goslings.** The coop in which the birds are kept should have a small netting-covered run attached, to prevent the goslings straying, for the first two to three weeks. First feed should number five a day, reducing to four after the first week and three after a further three weeks. Give a pasty, wet mash comprising equal parts of fine biscuit meal, superfine weatings or floury middlings and Sussex ground oats. After the first week to a fortnight

they will do well on ordinary poultry meal or chick-rearing mash, mixed with a little floury cooked potato and with a good quantity of finely chopped fresh greens in it. They will need fresh water daily and chick grit. After three to four weeks they may be allowed their liberty, with the hen, by day, but should be enclosed for protection by night.

**Buying Young Goslings.** Goslings that have been weaned will need no hen, nor artificial brooder-heat. By way of housing, they, and goslings home-hatched with a hen, will be best suited at four to six weeks if a shelter of the style advocated above for laying ducks is provided. It should be borne in mind, however, that this will need to provide 3 square feet per bird by the time they are nearly full grown, hence should be big enough from the start.

The food will be poultry meal made into a mash, which suffices at three feeds a day until, at two to three months, mash feeding can be reduced to one feed daily, provided there is plenty of fresh green grass. It will be necessary to return to mash feeding in late summer, when the grass is brown and scarce, increasing to two good feeds a day for the winter. Killing can start when the goslings are twelve weeks old, if desired.

**Turkeys for Table.** Much that has been written above about raising geese for the home table applies equally to turkeys. One exception is that the mash for the poults (young turkeys) should be crumbly-moist – as given to laying fowls. Turkeys are at their best when allowed their freedom to wander at large in woodland or thickets, roosting in the trees by night, but they can be kept successfully in large grass runs, and will go into a house to roost at night if used to so doing. They need to perch, as fowls, and the perches should be two feet six inches to three feet apart, allowing each bird eighteen inches of room on a perch. They must always have a supply of fresh drinking water and grit to take at will.

Where space is limited, turkeys may be kept on the Veranda system whereby they are unable to wander. Basically the building needed consists of a roof and slatted or wire-netting platform. The sides are slatted or wire-netted with the lower part filled in. Perches are provided for roosting, the droppings fall through to the ground.

**Killing Poultry.** The usual method, with fowls, chickens and young ducks is by breaking the neck. It is quick and painless. Gripping the legs in one hand, the head is allowed to hang down and is the grasped in the other hand. Taking a firm grip around the neck at the base of the skull and pulling sharply and strongly downwards will instantly cause the neck to part.

Geese, adult ducks and turkeys are more difficult to kill. One method is to let the head rest on the ground, place a stout, strong stick over the back of the head, stand with a foot on either end of the stick and pull the bird, gripped by the legs, strongly and persistently upwards until the neck breaks. Another way is to hold the bird up by the legs in one hand and smite the back of the head strongly with a heavy stick.

Humane killers can be bought from some of the well-known firms of poultry appliance-makers.

**Plucking and Dressing.** Plucking should follow immediately after killing, as the feathers then come away easily. It is best to be seated with the bird on the lap. Begin on the breast and abdomen, taking care not to pull so hard as to tear the flesh. Working up the body sides, and over the back, next take the wings one at a time, gripping a wing with one hand and pulling the quills with the other. Work on down the neck and also pull the quills from the tail and from the thighs.

To dress a bird, place it on a bench or table. First remove the internal organs, taking care when cutting through the flesh of the abdomen (with a sharp knife) not to penetrate to the intestines. Make the incision 3 to 4 inches long and then, cutting around the vent, place the hand inside and draw out the internal organs complete. It will be necessary to cut around the diaphragm in order to get out the farthermost organs. Cut off

the head half-way down the neck and, if desired, the skin can be pulled back and the neck cut again at its junction with the body.

Cut around the legs, at the back joint, just severing the skin; break, and with care the sinews will still adhere in the back of the leg. With a sharp pull of the partly severed leg it should be possible to pull out the sinews from inside the thigh.

(With turkeys and geese, the legs must be tied to a post or other solid object so that both hands are free for pulling on the thigh.)

Tie in the legs with string, cut off the wing-tips and tie in the remainder of the wings also with string.

## RABBITS

Probably the cheapest of livestock to keep are rabbits, the outlay for hutches and the first doe or does being the main expense. Meat in plenty for the home table and pelts for the making of gloves, a cape, pram rugs or similar articles, are the return to be expected.

Breeding-stock to sell and high-class pelts for the furriers are other forms of income that can follow after experience and when first-class stock are kept.

**Providing Hutches.** Each breeding doe requires a hutch 4 feet long and 2 feet to 2 feet 6 inches wide. Height depends upon breed, the large Flemish Giant needing more head-room than the small Polish or Dutch, for example. Best procedure to produce home meat and pelts would be to keep Flemish does and mate with a buck of either the Flemish, or Dutch or English breeds. For these and the young the hutches would need to be 2 feet 6 inches to 3 feet high, even though the young from a mating of the different breeds would be medium-sized at adulthood.

Timber or asbestos sheets may be used for covering the walls, but tea-chests and similar cases can well be converted for hutches that will be kept under a roof, such as a lean-to or in a shed. Each hutch should be divided into two compartments – one for day and one for sleeping.

**Breeding Possibilities.** Mating a doe for the first time in January, it is possible to obtain three litters from her in the year without causing any undue strain. The young are born twenty-eight to thirty days after mating and weaned from the mother at six to eight weeks. Thereafter the doe can be mated after a week or two's rest and the young will take another two to three months to grow to killing size. Bucks and does amongst the young need separating at three months to prevent them mating, so that two or three additional hutches are required in addition to each doe's.

**To Feed Rabbits.** For the greater part of the year practically all the rabbits' food needs can be provided from weeds, garden greens and surplus garden produce. For breeding does after mating or when suckling young, it is advisable to give also two feeds a day of mash, made from house-scraps dried-off with bran or bran and dry tea-leaves.

In the worst of the winter months all rabbits should be fed on mash in the morning and evening, with a good handful of clover or "mixture" hay (put into a rack, for cleanliness), and swedes, turnips, carrots, or similar roots or green leaves, given in the quantity that seems by observation to be cleaned up in the day. As an alternative, a complete diet is also possible by the use of pellets, when only hay and water need to be added.

**Management Points.** Some rabbits are water-drinkers. A new doe should be given water until it is observed that she does not seem to want it. Even then, water should be given when feeding much dry food, such as hay and mash, and in hot weather, and especially when a doe is carrying or suckling young.

When a litter is being born and just after the doe should not be disturbed, as she may attack the young. She will pluck herself just before kindling (birth of young) and make a nest; to assist her, provide fine hay in the sleeping compartment.

Clean out the hutches at least weekly in winter and more often, as the need is indicated, in summer.

Where only one or two does are kept for breeding, there is little point in keeping a buck, too – mating can usually be arranged by sending the does to another rabbit-keeper's buck. If a buck is kept, he should have a hutch as far away from the does as possible, since his presence tends to upset them.

**Killing and Skinning.** Rabbits of the smaller breeds may be killed by breaking the neck. The hind legs are gripped in one hand (usually the left) and the other is placed around the rabbit's neck close behind the ears and skull. Letting the rabbit hang down, a firm grip of the legs and sharp pull of the head downwards and slightly backwards should suffice.

An alternative method is to sit the rabbit on a box or bench and then, using a stout club-like stick, to give a sharp blow at the base of the skull and root of the ears. This is followed by bleeding – pushing the point of a sharp knife up into the roof of the mouth, afterwards letting the rabbit hang for a while.

For skinning, a sharp pocket-knife is best. The rabbit is hung up by one hind leg, to a nail or hook, and the knife used to slit the skin down the inside of the hind leg. Work the skin loose and cut off around the hock (the joint half way up the legs). Skin around the vent and tail and then it should be possible to work the whole skin down the body, pulling it off with very little cutting necessary. Work the front legs back into the skin and cut around midway down the legs, then working the skin down the neck and cutting off around the neck, close to the skull.

**Treatment for Pelts.** The skin after removal from the rabbit is slit exactly down the middle, spread without unduly stretching, and tacked in that position, fur side down, on a flat, clean board. Drawing-pins are suitable to use. The skin is scraped clean of fat or flesh and then placed in moderate sun and wind to air-dry.

**Dressing Pelts.** The best method is to

send the dried skins to one of the firms that specialise in this work, but if it is desired to attempt home-curing, after removal of any adhering fat or flesh, the thin, tissue-like inner skin must be peeled off the pelt, using the back of a table-knife to assist. The dried skin should have been soaked for twelve hours in cold water with a little salt added. The curing solution is made up in two parts: (1) dissolving 1 pound of powdered alum in a gallon of water; (2) dissolving 4 ounces of soda and 8 ounces of salt in half a gallon of water. Pour the soda-salt solution into the alum solution slowly, stirring all the time. The skin is then immersed for three to five days, rinsing on removal, first in a solution of borax (one ounce to the gallon) and then in cold water.

Press and squeeze out surplus water and tack the skin out smoothly, fur side down, apply castor oil or neatsfoot oil in a thin coating, leave till the skin is nearly dry and then work and knead with the hands until absolutely soft and pliable. This may take some hours, and the skin if it dries in the process should be damped with lukewarm water. After removal of surplus oil by rubbing with sawdust, finish off the skin surface by rubbing with pumice.

## HONEY BEES

With attention to the general rules of good beemanship, a hive of bees should yield something like forty pounds of honey each season. Yields of sixty and more pounds are by no means rare, but with the variability of the seasons and the weather in the British summer, forty pounds is a fair estimate. This leaves the bees an adequate amount of honey for their own winter feeding.

The bee-keeper's year starts in April, when he makes his first brief inspection of the stock after the hibernation of winter, and that is also the best time of year to make a start with bees. The previous winter months should be spent in reading a selection of the latest, well-recommended books, and then in March or earlier contact should be made with the local or county bee-keepers' association or society.

By joining the organisation, and making the acquaintance of the association's local expert, one can have guidance free on every aspect of taking up the craft, as well as obtaining the invaluable practical help of the expert in carrying out all operations, which establishes confidence and an understanding of bees' ways.

## DOGS

The nature of the home must be considered when a house dog is being chosen. An active dog like a retriever cannot be fully fit and happy in a small flat, or with a master who is not prepared to give his dog adequate exercise. A big dog like a St Bernard can become a nuisance in restricted space.

The most suitable breeds for flats and small town houses are terriers, such as the Cairn, Sealyham, Scottish and Yorkshire, and poodles, pekinese and dachshunds. Where there is a garden or an open space near by, the above and Cocker spaniels, chows, boxers, beagles and such terriers as Fox, Bull and Manchester can be kept. In the country the bigger active breeds will be very happy – mastiffs, Alsatians and St Bernards, spaniels, retrievers and greyhounds.

With a few exceptions a licence is required for every dog aged six months or more. These exceptions are: dogs kept for leading blind persons; certain farm dogs used to "work" sheep and cattle; and certain pack hounds. Failure to take out a licence where one is required may involve a fine. The licence entitles the person named on it to keep a dog for the current year; it cannot be passed to another person, either with or without the dog. The licence, which runs for the year from January 1st, is obtainable at the Post Office. For further information consult *The Complete Book of Dog and Puppy Care*, by Harry Miller.

**Grooming.** From five to fifteen minutes should be spent each day on grooming the dog. This will not only keep the dog in good appearance; it will also help to keep it healthy and free from parasites. A thorough combing – head to tail, and down the legs – should be followed by a good brushing. The dog needs stripping every six months or so, when it changes its coat, the old dead hair being carefully plucked off.

A dog which is groomed regularly does not need bathing very often; once in three months should normally be sufficient.

**Feeding.** Puppies require a number of small meals daily; five when about six weeks old; three or four at eight weeks; two or three at three months to six months. Plenty of milk should be given as well. From six months onwards one substantial meal given preferably in the evening and a few biscuits in the morning will be sufficient. A dog's digestion is soon upset if it is constantly given titbits.

As with all animals it is essential to feed the dog a balanced diet if it is to remain in good condition. Raw meat is liked by dogs but cooked meat is preferable, either pieces from the household joint or cheaper cuts from the butcher. To this should be added dog meal and some vegetables such as greens, carrots or parsnips. Potatoes should be given sparingly as they tend to fatten the dog. Horseflesh, boiled fish (without bones) can be used and the tinned dog foods which are now so readily available are a useful addition to the diet.

A big meat bone should be given occasionally; besides providing nourishment, the gnawing is good for the dog's teeth and jaws. Small bones as from poultry and rabbits, as well as fish bones, should not be fed; they are likely to injure the dog's inside.

**Breeding.** The first season normally occurs when the bitch is nine months old. She then comes into season at six-monthly intervals. Most bitches produce their best puppies between the ages of fifteen months and about four years.

The period lasts some seventeen days, during which the bitch is hungry and restless. The parts are red and there is some discharge. The discharge lessens about the tenth day, and this is the best time for the bitch to be served.

While carrying her young the bitch should be encouraged to take regular but gentle exercise – quiet walks. Her food should be as nutritious as possible, and an occasional teaspoonful of cod-liver oil will do her good.

The normal period of gestation is sixty-three days.

**Keeping Dogs Healthy.** The main factor is adequate exercise. The smaller dogs need to walk or run two or three miles daily; the larger breeds three or four miles. Dogs love company; they will rarely take the necessary exercise if sent out alone.

Although a dog may seem perfectly fit, an occasional course of condition powders is desirable, especially in spring. These preparations, which should be given exactly as recommended by the makers, tone up the general condition of the dog.

Worms are a common trouble. The symptoms are a dry coat, evil-smelling breath, irregularity of the bowels, and irritation which the dog tries to relieve by dragging its rear part along the ground. The motions may contain eggs or small portions of worms. Tablets for worming may be obtained from pet stores or a veterinary surgeon. Starving the dog is not usually necessary before giving them.

For most minor ailments – such as coughs and colds, and constipation – specifics can be obtained from most stores, and these will soon effect a cure. Where the trouble is more serious, advice should always be sought from a pets' hospital or vet. Dogs are susceptible to hard-pad and distemper which are very serious illnesses. These may be prevented by having the puppy inoculated against them when it is eight to ten weeks old.

## CATS

To keep healthy and happy, cats require just the right amount of care and attention. Neglected and underfed they soon become thieves; they look bedraggled and probably disease starts. On the other hand cats can soon be spoilt by too much attention and overfeeding. One good meal a day is sufficient, with occasional drinks of milk. Cats should also be encouraged to drink water, and a supply should always be available to them.

Cats are subject to skin diseases and also to infectious enteritis. If there is skin disease shown by fur falling out, it is desirable to take the cat to the vet or pets' hospital for treatment without delay. If the cat is unwell or off its food, condition powders can be obtained from the chemist, but a close watch should be kept on the animal and veterinary help sought if its condition deteriorates or if the cat is obviously in distress.

**Choosing Cats.** When choosing a new cat the first consideration is the purpose for which it is wanted. If it is for keeping down rats and mice, as on the farm or other country home, there is nothing better than a good short-haired tabby of country origin. Such cats are used to an outdoor life and generally have a touch of the wild-cat in their make-up. They should not be nursed but merely spoken to in a friendly way; they are easy to keep on a light diet with sufficient milk or water to drink, and thus are always keen for their work.

The town or domestic cat betrays its Egyptian ancestry by its love of the fireside and intense dislike of damp and fog, and here we find the black, white and coloured strains which have inter-bred with the tabbies.

Related to these ordinary town cats are the more highly prized strains such as the silver greys and smokes. The golden brindle and tortoiseshell is a distinct breed, the first being the male and the second the female cat, though male tortoiseshells sometimes turn up as a rarity. This cat is also known as the orange tabby.

Anyone intending to go in for thoroughbreds should attend a Cat Show, consult experts and study the handsome breeds there displayed.

The favourites are generally the long- and short-haired Persians, which may be white, blue or brown tabby, and in a classy specimen should have bright orange eyes.

Next is the Chinchilla in pale silver with green eyes and long hair, with some varieties in short-hair blue and smoke. The curious tailless Manx cat will also be noted, usually in tabby colour, the self tones being less common.

A breed gaining rapidly in popularity is the Siamese. There are now several varieties which take their names from the colour of the darker areas of fur, e.g. Chocolate-pointed, Seal-pointed and Blue-pointed. The eyes are a beautiful blue and the full-grown cat is a very handsome and affectionate pet. The newborn kittens' fur is a very light colour, the darker areas appearing as they grow up.

**Breeding Cats.** There is considerable profit to be made from the sale of high-class kittens. A good female blue Persian is the best investment to start with. She must be mated only with a pure thoroughbred cat. Also, when breeding high-class stock, it is better not to allow a mother puss to have more than two litters a year.

The kittens generally arrive in nine weeks. During the period of gestation the cat must be kept well fed, steamed white fish being the most nourishing diet, and a week in advance a nice roomy box should be provided in a quiet corner free from draughts, and bedding of soft hay or flannel.

Cats are proverbially good mothers, with a strong maternal instinct. The mother and kittens should be left alone for the first fortnight, as some mothers are apt to be very jealous and may even destroy their offspring if interfered with too soon.

The kittens will increase in fluffiness and activity until at about two months they are fully weaned and can fend for themselves. If any are to be sold, this is the time to sell them.

## CAVIES

These little creatures, also known as guinea-pigs, make ideal pets for children. They also have a commercial value, in that experienced breeders with an assured trade connection produce them for research purposes for hospitals, experimental stations and institutions.

In the garden cavies should be kept in hutches not unlike rabbit hutches, the best method, if breeding cavies, being to have a separate hutch for each sow (female) and the boar. Dimensions for each hutch should be 2 feet wide by 3 feet long and 2 feet high, timber being the most suitable material to use. Two compartments, for exercise and sleeping, are desirable.

Food requirements are simple. For the greater part of the year weeds and lawn-clippings will suffice, but in winter a little hay and some cabbage leaves or other greens or sliced pieces of carrot, turnip, swede or similar roots will be needed.

Cavies make good mothers and the young may be left with the sow for six weeks before separating and dividing into sows and boars for keeping in separate hutches.

## CAGE BIRDS

Many kinds of birds are kept as pets, ranging from the well-known budgerigars to the lesser-known mynahs and weaver-birds. Some kinds can live in an outdoor aviary, which will add considerably to the interest of the garden; others are less hardy and need to be kept in smaller cages indoors.

The beginner should confine himself at first to the more popular birds which are easier to look after and then when more experienced he can keep and try to breed the more exotic species.

**Budgerigars.** The rise in popularity of the budgerigar since the war has been phenomenal and it is now, without doubt, the most popular cage bird. In its native Australia the wild budgerigar is grass-green in colour with a yellow mask, but breeders have produced other colours in captivity. The most popular are the various shades of blue, green, yellow and white.

They are much hardier little birds than many people imagine and may be kept quite happily in outdoor aviaries of suitable size all the year round. Such aviaries should have both sunny and shady spots and be in a fairly sheltered position. A solid roof to the aviary helps to prevent the introduction of parasites from the droppings of wild birds.

Indoors a single bird or a pair may be kept in an all-wire cage bought for the purpose, or better still in a rectangular wooden cage with a front of wire uprights about ⅜-inch apart. A removable sand tray, or sheets of sanded paper at the bottom of the cage makes cleaning easier. Cleanliness is absolutely essential if diseases are to be avoided. Water containers, food-trays and good perches are necessary. Many people like to place small toys in the cages and the birds do seem to enjoy playing with them.

Food consists of seed mixture which can be bought ready mixed, some greenstuff such as lettuce or dandelion leaves, millet spray, grit and a piece of cuttle-fish bone which can be fixed between the bars of the cage.

Sexing budgerigars is fairly easy, the cere, or swelling at the base of the beak, of the male being blue, the female brown. They will breed at almost any time of the year, in which case nest-boxes and suitable nesting material will have to be provided.

Budgerigars are prone to certain diseases and defects. The beak and claws may grow too long but these can be cut with strong scissors or nail-nippers provided great care is taken not to cut the quick. Scaly beak is the result of a mite infestation and can usually be cured by a veterinary surgeon.

In the case of an ailing bird a heated "hospital" cage is a useful piece of equipment, for warmth will often produce good results on birds which are "off-colour".

**Canaries** are the domesticated form of a finch found in the Canary Islands and first imported into Europe during the sixteenth century. From the original type fanciers have bred a number of varieties, the most popular being the Border, Norwich and Yorkshire canaries.

If a canary is to be kept simply as a song-bird, then the all-wire type of cage is suitable for housing it, but if breeding is to be attempted then a larger cage is necessary. A rectangular wooden one as described for budgerigars, about 40 inches long, 18 inches high and 12 inches from front to back is large enough to divide up into two compartments with a partition. This partition, which can be removed when required, is solid but has an oblong aperture in it which can be covered by a wire-mesh slide. Suitable perches, seed and water pots are placed in the compartments and a sand-tray at the bottom helps to keep the cage clean.

Early in the year the cock bird is put into one compartment and the hen into the other. By the beginning of April the birds will probably be feeding one another through the wire mesh of the slide. They are then ready to mate and the slide is withdrawn. A nest-box and nesting material such as cow-hair and moss can be placed in the hen's compartment. Four or five eggs may be laid. The incubation period is fourteen days.

Canaries are seed-eaters and satisfactory mixtures may be bought at pet shops. Green food should also be given two or three times a week and a piece of cuttlefish bone should be provided to supply the birds with calcium. They will probably select grit from the sand-tray at the bottom of the cage.

When the birds have young ones it will be necessary to give soft foods such as egg-yolk and breadcrumbs so that the hen may feed them. This must be fresh every day since stale egg may be dangerous. Proprietary brands of soft foods are also available.

**Other Breeds.** There are many other species which may be kept either in cages or aviaries and plenty of specialist books are available to consult if advice on housing, feeding or breeding is needed. Most of the easier ones to keep are types of finches and therefore seed-eating. Examples of these are Avadavats; Zebra Finches, Java Sparrows and Waxbills. All are extremely interesting and attractive.

Many bird-lovers find their favourites among the Parrot family. The large parrots, the cockatoos and the macaws, are known by everyone, but the smaller parakeets and lovebirds are perhaps even more delightful.

Should weaver-birds be kept, their nest-building activities will be a never-ending source of interest.

Insect- and fruit-eating birds are more trouble to keep mainly because of the messier food preparation, although the mynah is fast becoming very popular as a pet, largely because of its powers of mimicry.

For the real expert who can supply the right conditions, sun-birds are sometimes available. These exquisite little creatures are nectar feeders and need to be given a satisfactory substitute in special drinking pipes.

## HEDGEHOGS AND SQUIRRELS

Gardens in and bordering on the country are often visited by a hedgehog. This bristly little creature should be encouraged; it is a friend of the gardener, feeding principally on slugs, worms, grubs and insect pests of many kinds. It does not eat plants.

The way to encourage this animal to stay is to give it occasional titbits in the form of scraps from the table. A saucer of bread and milk is a special luxury. When it knows it is safe the animal soon becomes quite tame and ceases to roll up and set its bristles when approached.

The hedgehog sleeps through winter, and a pile of old leaves or straw in a sheltered corner will provide excellent winter quarters. On no account should the animal be disturbed once it has gone to rest. When the days brighten and warm up it will emerge, very hungry, and ready to rid the garden of a great many insects.

**The Brown Squirrel** is a nice little creature and occasionally one will come into the country garden. It, too, can be encouraged with a little treat such as an apple, a few nuts and, in particular, a little bread and milk.

The little animal, however, is becoming almost rare; it is the grey squirrel which is so abundant. This creature takes so heavy a toll of garden and farm produce that it ranks next after the rat and wild rabbit in the list of farm enemies. On no account should the grey squirrel be encouraged.

## FANCY MICE

The rearing of these lively and interesting little animals is divided into two sections, namely, the fancy pure and simple for the exhibition of choice types and colours; and the commercial side where generally the white mouse is produced in quantity for purposes of biological and medical research and other requirements of experimental science.

Thus, from what was originally a schoolboy's hobby has arisen quite an industry, where "the fancy" does its full share in selective breeding to improve types while enjoying the satisfaction of producing rarer colours and markings.

To start a small mousery is quite easy. Suitable cages can be bought at most large pet stores, or one can be made from a strong wooden box about 2 feet long, covered in front with fine wire-mesh, or part of glass and part wire, divided with a similar screen in the middle with a sliding panel so that each half can be cleaned alternately. Then horizontally there should be a narrow upper floor where sleeping boxes filled with hay or chaff are placed, the mice having a little ladder up which they will readily climb when going to bed.

A thoroughbred pair should be purchased to start with. When they have been together for a week or ten days the male mouse must be taken away and kept in a separate compartment, or he will be jealous of the litter and probably devour them.

The principal food is stale bread, either grated or softened in milk and water, with occasional oatmeal grits or other cereal as may be available. They also like canary seed and the seeds of wild plantain in the summer. A very little grated cheese may be given as a luxury.

The young mice should be taken away from the parent when they are a month old. Breeders going in for the attractive piebald and skewbald colourings, with other self colours, should get in touch with an expert who will grade them and help in their disposal, or arrange for exhibit at the next Fancy Mice Show.

Disease is not likely to cause trouble where there is absolute cleanliness all through the mousery. The compartments should be cleaned out every day with disinfectant, and if there *are* any unhealthy specimens among the stock these should be weeded out at once.

## PIGEONS

The beginner with pigeons will find two or three pairs sufficient for a start. Where a cock and hen have mated, their union generally lasts throughout their lives. The best of the squabs (baby pigeons) which will follow can be used to increase stock; or they can be sold to friends. Some pigeon-keepers raise squabs specially for table use.

**Good Breeds.** The principal breeds from which choice is made are the English Carrier, a fine bird of dun and black colouring which can also be crossed with Dragoons to produce blue and white birds. The Dragoon, formerly the Dragon, is also a fine bird, a fast racer for short distances, the colours being chiefly blues, though there are chequered and yellow strains which do well at the shows. It crosses with the Homer satisfactorily.

Homers are perhaps the most popular of show birds, and have commanded high prices, even as much as £100. The chief colours are black and chequered.

The above are some of the prime birds for racing and showing, but there are also the highly specialised breeds which look quaint and odd to any but the genuine fancier. These include the Pouters, whose chief "point" is the abnormally puffed out breast, together with the Pigmy Pouter, a real bantam among pigeons, a breed which is a favourite with lady fanciers.

Then there is the Tumbler, so called from its practice of turning somersaults in the air; a small bird with rounded head, short beak and red feet, the plumage being blues, blacks and other self colours, including the almond birds sought for in the show.

The Fantail is foremost as an ornamental dovecote sort. It can be in pure white or in colours and is fully conscious of the beauties of its fully fashioned tail, which instead of the usual fourteen, may contain as many as thirty feathers, which it is fond of displaying proudly aloft like a peacock.

If squabs or young pigeons are required for the table, the best plan is to use cross-breeds, and keep pure stock for the show bench and for sale. A breed called the Mondain is the best to rear solely for squabs; but the large crossbreds from Dragoons, Homers and Carriers give good fleshy birds and are hardy enough to breed freely from for this purpose.

**Pigeon Houses.** There are two forms of pigeon or dovecote which are suitable for a garden of moderate size – the pole house and the locker loft.

For the first, a stout larch pole not less than 4 inches thick at the base is required, on top of which is firmly fixed a barrel which has been sawn into three sections, each floored with a circular piece of wood about 4 inches larger than the barrel itself, so as to provide alighting platforms. The pole passes through the centre and the interior of each floor is divided by partitions to give four separate compartments. Entrances are then cut in the appropriate stave of the barrel to form doors to each room. The top of the barrel is covered with a cone of sheet zinc to form a roof and the pole cote is complete.

The locker loft is arranged in much the same way, but in the form of a strong wooden box with lean-to roof and divided up into four or eight rooms as the case may be, with alighting boards as before, and this may be permanently fastened to a brick wall by brackets and staples in a place where it will be safe from cats. The outside is painted with three coats of good oil colour, and the interior is lime-washed. Both kinds of cote should be made with screws and in such a way that they can easily be opened out so that the interiors can be re-washed frequently for the health of the birds and to prevent parasites harbouring there.

The size of each individual room

should not be less than 14 inches wide, 12 inches high and 12 inches deep.

**Installing the Birds.** When the stock is received, the pairs should each be put into a mating pen first, divided by a wire partition so that they can see each other. They may be shy at first, but in a few days will come to a nodding acquaintance, and soon the cock will start cooing and twirling himself about. The division is then removed and a day or so later they can be introduced to their permanent nest-box in the cote itself.

Pigeons lay only a pair of eggs, and these take sixteen days to hatch, the parents taking turns on the nest.

**Feeding Pigeons.** The birds should be given the best mixture of pulse food obtainable, consisting of peas, beans and tares for the most part. Small maize, broken wheat or crushed oats, or a few sunflower seeds, with stale breadcrumbs, will be a help in the breeding season. Plenty of fresh water must always be available.

## TORTOISES

It is a common fallacy that the tortoise eats great numbers of insect pests, and is therefore of value in the garden on that account. What it does like is young vegetables – especially seedling lettuce!

Nevertheless it is an interesting little creature, surprisingly intelligent once it becomes at home in a garden. It is therefore well worth while as a pet, so long as steps are taken to keep it, say, in a netting enclosure on the lawn, with some shade from a tree, or alternatively to net off the vegetable plot so that it cannot trespass.

Given its freedom on the lawn the tortoise will largely feed itself. Tender young leaves of vegetables – particularly lettuce, as mentioned – are much to its liking; also young dandelion leaves. Many tortoises have a great fondness for the tender top shoots of virginia creeper. A saucer of bread and milk is a great treat.

As the cold weather approaches, the tortoise's winter quarters must be got ready. This should be a wooden box with some air-holes bored in it, filled with hay and placed in a shed or other frostproof place. The tortoise will sleep safely until the warm weather of spring but it should be inspected now and again to make sure it is in the middle of the box.

## AQUARIA

A well-kept aquarium is always an item of great interest. Goldfish are general favourites, but now many semi-tropical species are kept, such as Guppies, Zebras, Platys and Angel Fish. These, however, require an artificially warmed aquarium, which is not possible in every home.

For an aquarium without heat, use can be made of some of our native pond fish such as bleak, roach or minnows. The setting up of the aquarium is the same in all cases.

The old-fashioned round bowls are not recommended; they are not very strong, and the shape is against the welfare of the inmates. It is better to get a fair-sized oblong aquarium, say 1 foot 6 inches or 2 feet long and 12 inches each way in side dimensions. This holds quite a lot of water and must be set up on a firm, strong table or bench.

A layer ½-inch thick of clean sifted soil is placed on the bottom, covered with 1½ inches of well-washed river sand. In this can be planted suitable aquatic plants such as vallisneria, potamogeton or water crowfoot, which will soon root and provide oxygen for the fish to breathe. In this way the water does not need changing but only making up as it evaporates.

Rain- or river-water should be used for preference, but clean tap water can also be used, provided the fish are not put in for a month, so as to allow the plants to settle and the water to "naturalise". A few small water-snails can be put in at first, and when these begin to lay eggs the aquarium is ready for the fish.

Do not be disturbed if the water goes very green at first. Take it off the front glass surfaces with a rubber squeegee or razor blade, and gradually the green matter will diminish and the water remain quite clear.

**Feeding Fish.** The fish are fed on prepared packeted food from the pet shops and also on small tubifex or bloodworms, which will burrow into the sand and the fish will amuse themselves by nosing them out.

To prevent dust settling on to the water, have a sheet of glass over the top, resting on square pieces of cork at the corners, so as to enable air to get in.

Much the same conditions are required for an outdoor pool, which can be shaped out in cement concrete, then filled with water and be left at first for a month or so to mature. Then empty off the old water and put a much thicker layer of soil and sand at the bottom, into which can be planted some larger plants such as water lilies and pond-rush as features. When these are settled and the water has cleared down properly, try snails again as before, and finally the fish.

## GOLDEN HAMSTERS

These small creatures make delightful pets, their lack of smell making them ideal for small houses or flats. They are nocturnal, however, and it sometimes causes disappointment to find the pet only beginning to run around in the evening, but when they are completely tame they can usually be persuaded to play at any time. Care must be taken when handling hamsters at first as they are rather nervous little animals and may bite if handled roughly but with care and patience they soon grow docile.

Unless the intention is to breed hamsters, they are best kept singly, as adult animals tend to fight. They need a cage, about 24 inches long, 12 inches wide and 9–12 inches high, covered in the front or on top with small mesh wire-netting. Remember that hamsters gnaw a great deal so hard wood should be used, reinforced at the corners. Alternatively a metal cage can be bought.

The floor of the cage can be covered with sawdust and hay or wood wool used for bedding material.

Food should consist of rolled oats, wheat, biscuit meal or one of the packaged foods which are available at pet shops. In addition grass, greens or pieces of apple and carrot should be given, but care must be taken to see that excess food is not stored by the hamster and allowed to go mouldy. Water should always be available.

Hamsters are old enough to breed by fifteen weeks. The gestation period is about sixteen days and the average number in the litter is six or seven. The young are born naked and blind but are covered by hair in just over a week. They begin to find food for themselves at about twelve days old and should be weaned at three weeks to a month.

# FOOD AND WINE

## NUTRITION & FOOD IN GENERAL

Everyone has to eat and drink each day of their lives for the maintenance of health and therefore it is sense to choose food that will preserve well-being, be appropriate to one's budget and way of life, and appear as attractive as possible – for stimulation of the appetite in this way is also conducive to good digestion.

The science of nutrition is complex and for detailed information readers are recommended to consult *The Manual of Nutrition*, and *The Composition of Foods*, both published by HM Stationery Office. The following, however, explains some of the background to nutrition as far as it affects the ordinary housekeeper.

*Carbohydrates:* provide the body with energy and may also be converted into fat.

*Fats:* provide energy and may also form body fat.

*Proteins:* provide material for growth and repair of body tissues. They can also provide energy and sometimes be converted into fat.

*Minerals:* provide the material for growth and repair of the body and for regulation of its processes.

*Vitamins:* regulate the body processes.

Although both water and oxygen are necessary for life, they are not strictly nutrients. The body needs water, and at least one and a half pints of water or other fluid should be drunk daily by the ordinary healthy person.

Almost all foods contain more than a single nutrient although one of the exceptions is white sugar, which is 100 per cent carbohydrate. Most foods contain a mixture of carbohydrate, fat and protein and as one of the principal uses of food is to supply energy to the living body, the value of such foods is with some of the energy derived from carbohydrates fat and protein. Alcohol also supplies some energy.

**Energy value of certain foods.** Very watery foods (clear soup, lettuce, cucumber, etc.) have very little energy value and foods rich in fat have more. The following table shows the energy value of certain food stuffs expressed in terms of calories per ounce:

| | |
|---|---|
| Cooking fat or lard | 262 |
| Butter | 226 |
| Cheese | 120 |
| Bacon | 115 |
| Sugar | 112 |
| White flour | 99 |
| Beef | 91 |
| Dates | 70 |
| White bread | 69 |
| Potato | 25 |
| Banana | 22 |
| Milk | 19 |
| Apple | 13 |
| Beer, draught mild | 10 |
| Orange | 10 |
| Turnip | 5 |
| Lettuce | 3 |

The energy value of meat, which is largely composed of protein and fat plus water, depends largely on the amount of fat which it contains.

**Daily Needs.** Although the amount of energy required varies from individual to individual, everybody needs food to maintain the process of living. Work of exactly the same kind may vary greatly in different sets of circumstances, but in general the approximate amounts of energy required for different kinds of activity expressed in terms of calories per hour are as follows:

| | |
|---|---|
| Sleeping | 0 |
| Sitting | 15 |
| Standing | 20 |
| Dressing or undressing | 33 |
| Walking slowly | 115 |
| Walking moderately fast | 215 |
| Walking downstairs | 290 |
| Walking upstairs | 1,000 |

It is important to realise that this is entirely concerned with physical activity; someone sitting down engaged in a highly responsible or even creative task does not require the same amount of energy as someone doing hard physical work, though of course the way in which brain work of any kind is carried out depends greatly on the physical health of the individual and his or her sense of well-being and mental condition, all of which are affected by the diet.

**Choice of Foods.** For the maintenance of health in the normal individual, it is important that a balanced diet should be planned. Anyone in doubt as to whether they need a special diet of any kind should of course consult their doctor.

**Menu Planning.** Wherever family meals or social occasions are concerned, the planning of the menu is of prime importance. In general, the first thing to choose is the main dish; in a menu of more than three dishes, the most important course should be whatever precedes the pudding, and the courses that go before or after should set off the main dish. Many meals fail to satisfy because the dishes are chosen without regard to their place in the composition of the menu.

Dishes may be either costly or inexpensive, but they should all, as it were, be in the same key. If you are building a meal around a joint with two vegetables, then the courses before and after it should be fairly simple, though this does not mean that no imagination is required in making them. A first course that is so complicated that everything that follows it is an anti-climax may occur when a very elaborate fish dish is served before roast beef and Yorkshire pudding.

If food is of prime quality it is always best served simply. If the cook should be ambitious, then any additions such as sauces, decorations or garnishes must be absolutely first-class. There is nothing that lets down the reputation of a housewife like an unsuccessful elaborate dish side by side with something good and simple. It is also important to realise that there are many dishes that are the prerogative of chefs rather than

those cooking for their family and friends, and these chef products are again best not imitated in the home, even by the most expert cook. For example, the very elaborately dressed, decorated and stuffed whole fish, such as looks magnificent in a restaurant, is really rather a waste of time and energy in the home, and the expenditure of time and money on such things is usually misplaced.

Foods made out to look unlike themselves are seldom wholly satisfying. The great Curnonsky always maintained "things must be like themselves" and deplored any disguising of good food. Appetite as well as consistency must also be taken into account. When both soup and fish are served before a meat course, the fish should not be so elaborate or so substantial that people's appetites for the main dish are spoiled.

At one time it was very fashionable to have meals all of the same colour, but although one could have either yellow or pink food for, say, a birthday party or informal celebration, especially for children's parties, the use of contrasting colours is highly important as the appetite is greatly stimulated (or discouraged) by the eye. All brown or all pale-coloured meals seldom seem completely enjoyable, which is why the use of a garnish such as parsley, watercress, a cherry on a grapefruit, or a slice of melon, a green vegetable with a piece of pale meat or fish are also important.

**Texture.** Texture is also something to be taken into account. Too many bland or smooth textures can cloy the palate, and too many crisp ones can tire it. Usually anything very smooth in texture should be garnished or accompanied by something crisp, and a meat or fish dish that is firm or hard in texture should be accompanied by smooth or light textured vegetables. Anything of a rather weighty consistency – such as something in a lot of sauce – may require "blotting-paper" by way of an accompaniment. This may be provided by potatoes, rice, some kind of vegetable puree or, with informal dishes such as casseroles, by crusty bread with which to soak up the sauce or gravy. The value of a green salad in following a fairly bland dish is obvious. It is very important not to use the same ingredients, such as cream, eggs or cheese and certain flavourings, in more than one course. This can be as boring as a number of fried dishes or a number of bland dishes. Nor should there be more than one course involving pastry. It is possible, with a well planned meal, to have, say, something with a mayonnaise at the beginning of the meal and a soufflé at the end, but if, for example, the cheese board is to be offered at the end of the meal, it would be a mistake to have a cheese soufflé as a starter.

**Formal and informal foods.** Stews, curries and dishes of a strongly regional type are only suitable for a comparatively informal meal, whether lunch or dinner. Main dishes consisting of offal or pies, savoury soups, large omelettes and similar egg dishes, grills and cold food tend to be mainly associated with luncheon or informal or family dinners or suppers, although this is naturally a matter of taste. If, however, one is planning a meal in a restaurant and ordering the dishes in advance it is worth bearing in mind the sort of foods that people expect at different times of the day and on different occasions. Very formal luncheons may include the same sort of food as formal dinners, though perhaps with only three courses instead of four, and with cheese being offered, which it is not at the most formal type of dinner party. But all of these traditions are merely founded on convenience.

The most formal type of meal may consist of a first course, a main dish and a sweet, with fruit for dessert afterwards. If it is wished to augment this, then a fish course may be put in before the main dish (in which case the opening course should not consist of fish) and sometimes people who serve game and who have large appetites would like a meat course before the principal dish, which may be venison or a fine game bird. The idea of a sorbet (a water ice to refresh and clean the palate) in the middle of a long dinner is a pleasant one that has now rather gone out of fashion, but if a sorbet is to be served, then a fresh rather than sweet flavour should be chosen; the sorbet is served in small portions, usually in cups or glasses rather like small wine goblets.

It should be emphasised that, especially in the British Isles, it is not necessary to serve only hot substantial foods in winter and cold dishes and salads in the summer. But when planning a meal in a household without staff, it is often more convenient to have the first and last courses cold and sometimes to have a main dish that can be left to wait without spoiling. Food that is meant to be served cold, however – melon, chilled consommé, vichysoisse, caviar and oysters – should be **really** cold, not tepid.

**Foods to avoid if in doubt.** Although there are very few people nowadays bound to rigid observations of days of abstinence, it is still a courtesy, when receiving guests not already well known to host and hostess, to check that the food served will be acceptable to everyone. Usually, people on any kind of special diet to which they must adhere strictly for health or other reasons, will warn those who invite them, but as it is obviously both awkward, practically and socially, to serve certain dishes to one set of guests and different ones to others, there are some foods which are better avoided if one is in any doubt.

The most obvious of these are oysters and other shellfish, game and offal, very regional dishes (especially those involving a lot of garlic and herbs), all curries and anything highly spiced or involving the use of a particularly assertive cooking medium (such as oil) or ingredient (such as caraway) not widely used in the United Kingdom. In very general terms, care should be taken to provide acceptable foods on any of the great religious fast days, about which any Almanac or Year Book in a public library will provide the information. People entertaining Jewish, Catholic or middle-Eastern friends, however liberal they may know them to be, are advised to ask either the guests themselves or a follower of the same traditions what will be acceptable and enjoyed.

**Visitors from abroad.** Anyone from

another country who is received into a private house will usually be best pleased by being offered any of the good British foods and dishes, rather than some imitation of international cuisine. Smoked fish, especially smoked salmon, is universally appreciated, also oysters and fresh salmon. Garnished joints and game birds are also treats for the foreigner. Steak and kidney pudding or pie, jugged hare, Lancashire hot-pot and Irish stew, and the various cold pies and British cheeses are usually greatly enjoyed. Traditional puddings, pies and tarts are also ideal for such occasions. The only essential is these should exemplify the best of home cooking with first-class ingredients.

KITCHEN PLANNING. Although a well-planned kitchen saves a household time and trouble, it is not possible, dealing with so individual a matter, to give more than certain guiding principles by way of advice. Anyone setting up house or moving should consider carefully the set of circumstances with which they have to deal and how much money they have to spend and then try to get as much expert advice as possible from different sources. The local gas and electricity boards are usually able to offer help with kitchen planning and so are the makers of many gas and electric cookers, as well as the Womens' Advisory Council on Solid Fuel. Local builders, too, often have kitchens built in dummy form in their showrooms. As kitchen equipment of the right kind contributes greatly to the efficiency of a household and spares the cook-house-keeper much fatigue and expense, it is well worth while taking advantage of as much information currently available as possible and also to keep oneself informed as to the very latest developments before making any major purchases.

Although the basic principles of time and motion study should be taken into account when planning a kitchen, the final decision should ideally only be made by whoever is going to use it most – in other words, the housewife. For example, colours chosen should be agreeable to her, fixtures convenient and appliances such that she can manage them without strain or worry. The following check list should serve to guide anyone setting out to plan their kitchen:

**Appearance:** The kitchen should be a pleasant place in which to work and if it is to be used for family or informal meals, this must be taken into consideration. Although a cool kitchen is basically desirable, it must obviously be able to be heated for the cook's comfort, or for that of anyone eating in the kitchen. The use of cool colours, such as blues and greens, for a room inclined to get stuffy, can be helpful, as can the use of yellows and reds to cheer up a kitchen that may tend to look "clinical" or cold. The proportions of a room may be altered by the clever use of colour, too, as for example the choice of a dark colour for a ceiling that is very high, or putting the same colour or wall covering on a wall and ceiling to give an impression of more space. Ideally, an architect or experienced decorator should be consulted about structural planning problems, but much may be learned from study of model kitchens and the way in which other people have adapted their kitchens to their requirements.

**Lighting.** It is of the greatest importance that a kitchen should be well lit. There is every likelihood, however, that even in a small kitchen, there ought to be more than a single source of light. This need not be an extravagance, because lights so positioned and directed that they provide illumination for specific areas, such as different working surfaces, can be much less powerful than a single overhead light. If the kitchen is to be used as a dining-room, a different type of lighting is advisable if the atmosphere is not to be too clinical or practical. If ironing and sewing are to be done in the kitchen, appropriate lighting should be arranged for the purpose (for example, the use of a daylight bulb or strip is practical for assessing colours that may change considerably under "artificial" light). As well as there being adequate light on all working surfaces, including sink and cooker – which should also be so positioned as to make the best use of daylight – care should be taken that the housewife does not cast shadows on any work she may be doing, or otherwise strain her eyes. Many people position the sink under a window, because, they think, it gives the worker something to look out at, but others would prefer a work or dining-table to be under a window. There can be few hard or fast rules. Special attention should be paid to ensuring that the oven, refrigerator or food store and any deep cupboards have lighting that enables their interiors to be seen clearly without shadows.

**Ventilation.** Adequate ventilation is important, both to prevent unpleasant cooking smells from accumulating and to avoid moisture condensing. This means that the main sources of ventilation should take away the smells and supply fresh air. A canopy over the cooker is possibly the most effective way of achieving the former, and some type of extractor fan or ventilator in the window the means of maintaining the latter. But the system of ventilation adopted depends on the type of kitchen and the funds available.

**Cleaning.** Ideally, everything in a kitchen, especially the working surfaces, should be able to be cleaned with the minimum of effort and time. Paint, wallpaper and all materials used for covering surfaces should be washable. Floor coverings should be chosen both for the ease with which they may be kept clean and for the comfort they provide to the housewife – a too-hard floor surface can be as tiring to the feet and legs as one that is too soft. A kitchen in the country will obviously not get as grimy as one in a town, and a household in which there are several children needs a kitchen able to cope with the wear and tear of babies and those growing up.

**Furniture.** Furniture and fittings that are built in to the kitchen should of course only be installed if a fairly long stay in the house or flat or its purchase are contemplated. But properly fitted cupboards and working surfaces not only look trim and efficient but are much easier to clean than haphazardly chosen pieces. Great attention should be paid to the height of all surfaces – the so-called "standard" height is useless for anyone even an inch or two taller or smaller than average and can result in severe physical strain on the housewife. Cupboards above shoulder level should be easy of access and all doors should be easy to open and shut, as it frequently happens that only one hand is available to do this. In planning a kitchen to be used by older people, care should be taken to see that all extremes of bending and stretching in the course of day-by-day activities are avoided and lifting of heavy objects should be avoided completely. If possible, all ledges above eye level should either be covered in or built up to the ceiling, as they harbour a great deal of often unsuspected dirt, and inaccessible corner cupboards or spaces in corners or between articles of furniture can be similar dust-traps. Handles, knobs and fastenings should all be chosen for their practicability, both as regards use and being easy to keep clean and not trap dirt. In choosing furniture and large-scale fittings for the kitchen, bear in mind that, even if the family does not move, in the course of time it may be advisable to change the kitchen – with the expansion of a family, or when the family grows up and leaves home, for example – and that the initial installation of very costly permanent fittings may not be an inevitably good long-term investment though it may be considered as such if the house or flat is to be sold or let. Psychologically, it can be very cheering to change the décor and furnishings of a room that is probably the most used in the house, and therefore the possibility of doing this should never be ruled out.

**Sinks and stoves.** If a free choice is available, it is worth while considering as wide a range as possible of what is available, before deciding. The new housewife should not automatically think that what was good enough for her mother will suit her! The height of a sink and draining boards is of major importance – the housewife, wearing the type of shoes she most usually puts on during working hours, should be able to do any washing and washing-up without any excess strain on her back or arms and, even if she has to put up with the existing heights of cupboards and work-tops, it is worth taking trouble and spending money to get the sink either raised or lowered to the ideal height. The type of sink chosen depends both on the amount to be spent and the family – for some, a single sink is adequate, others find a double sink more than twice as useful. The material – and that of the draining boards and surrounds – also depends on the length of time it is thought the sink may be in use before being replaced. A wide selection of sinks is always available.

The type of cooking stove may depend on the source of fuel, but if a choice is available, comparative costs should be worked out for the different types. A childless couple, both of them out most of the day, probably require a different type of stove from a family with several young children, who may wish to use their cooker as a means of room and/or water heating in addition. Time switches, eye-level grills, or separate grill fitments, oven doors that open out or drop down, are all features that should be given thought. If the cooker is to be bought from a store or shop, or secondhand, the opinion of the local fuel authority who may have to service it is worth consulting. Where the cooker is to be sited may also influence either the type or make, especially if a split-level cooker is being considered. Again, when deciding on a particular make, the housewife should particularly consider ease of cleaning.

**Appliances.** There are so many appliances for assisting cooking and food preparation, cleaning, washing and washing-up, that today it is possible for even the modest household to be equipped on a scale that would have seemed very extravagant only a few years ago. But the needs of the household should, always, be assessed carefully in relation to the cost and upkeep of the machine and also to the capability of the housewife and family to making the best and most economic use of the appliance. An elaborate mixer-liquidiser that spends most of the week in a drawer or cupboard, the washing machine that only adds to the amount of hand ironing the housewife dislikes, and the washing-up machine that substantially increases the bills for water heating are in the category of luxuries rather than labour-savers.

Many services are available outside the home (for cleaning, for example), that are less trouble than trying to manage oneself – and, often, virtually no more costly – and appliances for heavy cleaning several times a year may often be hired, rather than bought. Before purchase, it should be possible to see an appliance demonstrated in some detail and also to handle and use it oneself; with some, manufacturers and retailers will even arrange a period during which a portable machine of this kind may be loaned to the housewife considering buying it. Some people find that the assembly and use of certain machines is troubling to them, and elderly or arthritic people or anyone with even a slight physical disability may have difficulty in using an appliance that is suggested as a labour-saver to them. Only personal trial can decide whether the machine is going to be able to be used and liked.

**Refrigerators and food stores.** Ideally, there should be a larder as well as a refrigerator in every home, but many people have to make do with one or the other. Here, the needs of the family and the efficiency of the food store in keeping the food under hygienic conditions are the most important considerations. In some instances – with money and space virtually no object – it would be more practical to have a large larder and a smallish refrigerator in the kitchen, with perhaps another one in the dining-room or breakfast room. Or a medium-sized refrigerator might be augmented with a deep freezer, or the refrigerator incorporated in an existing larder – the individual requirements of the household must be carefully assessed. A point whch is worth making to people who either have no refrigerator or only a small one, is that it is almost more important in cold weather – when the kitchen may be heated actually to a higher temperature than in summer – than in the warmer months of the year; in the old days of stone larders with slate shelves in draughty outside walls, and ice-boxes in the ground, it was not so much a danger to health to have a warm kitchen in winter, but nowadays, when all the food may be kept in the one room, it is esential to have most perishables kept at a low temperature – lower than is usually comfortable for ordinary work.

Note: With all kitchen equipment and appliances involving moderate and substantial sums of money, care should be taken, at time of purchase, to ensure that a sound guarantee is provided and, if necessary, reliable service facilities. Reputable manufacturers and stores should always be able to do this.

Kitchen equipment. Everyone has their own ideas about what constitutes the complete batterie de cuisine – and, as this must be a matter for individual tastes and needs, it is impossible to be rigid about just what is required. Many new lines and excellent gadgets come on to the market month by month, and anyone setting up house should study the features on the subject in the quality consumer magazines and spend some time in the equipment department of a large store or, ideally, in a shop specialising in kitchen equipment of all kinds.

In general, it may be said that there are certain items – especially knives and cooking utensils such as pans – on which it is an investment to spend as much as can be afforded. The expensive goods will both last longer and give better results. But this does not mean that a great deal of money need be laid out, as there are many good medium and low-priced lines available, some with manufacturers' guarantees as well.

Pans. The type of pans chosen depends greatly on the type of cookstove and, of course, on the sort of meals that are to be prepared. Some families like a lot of casseroles and dishes that require a great deal of long, slow cooking; others prefer quickly prepared, top-of-stove dishes, many fried or grilled recipes, or roast meat several times a week. If baking is an occasional rather than a

regular event, it is clearly a waste of money and cupboard space to buy quantities of different tins, piping nozzles, icing tables and so on. Many good cookery books give lists of utensils recommended for the sort of dishes they describe.

Gadgets. With regard to kitchen gadgets, many of these can be enormously labour-saving, whereas others have only a short life. But what suits one housewife may be virtually useless to another – the woman who couldn't manage without tongs for turning food in a pan, or a garlic press, may prefer to peel potatoes with a knife rather than a peeler, the person who only fries in shallow fat will have little use for a deep fryer. With some gadgets it is worth buying cheap lines and throwing them away when they begin to rust or are past being completely efficient, but others, especially when they are made of quality materials – such as boxwood butter moulds, heavy pestles and mortars, wooden salad bowls and fine steel knives – gain in both efficiency and, somehow, "character", by being used, even over long periods of time.

Kitchen safety. The kitchen is the place where most accidents tend to occur. It is therefore important, not only to try and ensure that the likelihood of these is minimised – especially in a household where there are young children or elderly people living by themselves – but that first aid measures are always to hand. The first aid equipment should be kept in the kitchen, rather than the bathroom, which may be some distance away, and every member of the family should know exactly where the first aid box is and how to use it.

A few rules for avoiding accidents are: Never climb steps or on a high chair or table if you are alone in the house and preferably have someone to make sure steps or chair remain steady.

Never leave a pressure cooker, a grill or pan of hot fat, or any mechanical device that should only run for a short time, while you answer the door or telephone, or leave the kitchen; turn off anything of this kind if you go out of the kitchen, even if you think you are only going to be a short while.

Never go out of the home without checking that any high or unshielded source of heat – such as an iron, hotplate or fire before which clothes are airing – is turned right off, not merely down.

However well trained your children may be, never allow toddlers to be alone in the kitchen if they are big enough to climb or reach things from the table, out of cupboards above waist height, or off the stove, or touch the top of the stove, or turn on or off gas taps or other power outlets.

If an elderly or even slightly incapacitated person is to use the kitchen, make sure that he or she completely understands all the appliances in it and can manage them without risk.

## STORAGE OF FOOD IN THE REFRIGERATOR

The majority of refrigerators are sold with comprehensive instruction manuals which give full details for making the most of the storage facilities and tell users exactly where different types of food should be kept. In general, however, it is most important not to put anything into the refrigerator while it is still hot, nor to put things into the refrigerator unwrapped, or wrapped in ordinary paper; special boxes and containers for storage, as well as many different kinds of wrappings that preserve the freshness of food are available. Nothing with a strong smell should be left uncovered in the refrigerator and when the inside of the food storage compartments are cleaned, only a mild paste cleanser – nonsmelling – or bicarbonate of soda and hot water should be used, as anything with a smell will linger and affect everything stored subsequently.

**Limits of Domestic Refrigerators.** It is important to remember that even the freezing compartment of an ordinary refrigerator is *not* a deep freeze. The long-term storage of most foods requires very low temperatures indeed for safety, such as the domestic refrigerator cannot provide; foods once frozen should not,

in general, be allowed to thaw out and then be frozen again, but the instructions on the packets of most frozen foodstuffs give exact details as to how long it is safe to keep the contents in different circumstances. Although it is often possible to keep food in a refrigerator for a week or more, without either it or the consumers suffering ill effects, it is *always* unwise ever to take a chance about this kind of thing, as poisoning from food can not only be unpleasant but extremely dangerous.

Certain foods should not, ideally, ever be refrigerated: all cheeses, except the fresh cream variety; bananas; root vegetables and potatoes. If eggs are kept in the refrigerator, they should preferably be allowed to regain room temperature before being incorporated in any mixtures such as cakes or soufflés. Foods that are actually frozen, of course, should either be thawed out before being cooked or the manufacturers' instructions carefully followed as to how they should be cooked while still frozen.

## OVEN TEMPERATURES

A new cooker should be accompanied by either a cookery or instruction book, or a chart showing the different temperatures of the oven according to the markings – and what this may mean to the lay housewife. It is always worth while, however, even with a new cooker, having the thermostat checked after the cooker is installed, and with a cooker bought secondhand or taken over with the house or flat this is really important – otherwise you may think that you are a failure as a cook! Gas, electricity and solid fuel showrooms will always advise about temperatures, but here is an approximate chart for the different settings:

| Oven description | Electric Fahrenheit | Centigrade | Gas marking |
|---|---|---|---|
| Low oven | 230–250° | 110–121° | $\frac{1}{4}-\frac{1}{2}$ |
| Fairly low oven | 300–325° | 149–163° | 1–2 |
| Moderate oven | 350–400° | 177–209° | 3–5 |
| Fairly warm (or fairly hot) | 425–450° | 218–232° | 6–8 |
| Hot to very hot | 450–500° (or more) | 232–260° | 8–10 |

If by any chance your cooker has no thermostat, it is possible to buy an oven thermometer that will enable you to check whether the oven settings are correctly adjusted – or the appropriate fuel authority will come and check this for you.

## PORTIONS

It is often difficult for the beginner housewife to assess how much food may be required. Of course, appetites vary a great deal, and food that contains parts that will be wasted – bones, peel, vegetable trimmings and so on – makes it difficult always to assess exactly how much to buy. Men tend to eat more than women, growing children often appear to have inexhaustible appetites, and people who are physically active naturally tend to require larger helpings than those engaged in fairly sedentary work. Cookery books generally give some indication as to how many portions will be served by a recipe (look at the introduction if this is not stated each time), but the following give an idea of averagely fair portions for one adult: Soup: up to half a pint (slightly less if very thick soup or meat broth). Fish: 4–6 oz. if not much bone (about 3 oz. in fish pies and made-up dishes). Meat and poultry: 4–8 oz. (obviously less is eaten if the meat is very rich). Meat for pies and réchauffés: About 3 oz., depending on the recipe. Vegetables: 4–6 oz., if served with potatoes; allow up to 8 oz. potatoes. Rice and pasta: 1½–2 oz. if served as accompaniment to a dish, a little more (2½–3 oz.) if this forms the main part of the dish, or for pudding. Stewed fruit: 4–5 oz., less if in a pie or tart, or with ice-cream.

## MARKETING

In these days when air freight enables many foodstuffs to be available all the year round, and when foods formerly expensive and perishable are frozen at the peak of their freshness so as to be able to be stored for long periods and defrosted as required, it might be thought that marketing is a simple matter. It is certainly easier for anyone living in a town or the vicinity of a large market or store to enjoy a very much wider choice of all foodstuffs than in former times, but, even when the family budget is not of prime importance, wise selection can result in more enjoyable meals.

The following hints are worth bearing in mind when shopping for certain foods and also when storing them:

**Tea.** Although tea may be bought in fairly large quantities, it should always be kept in a cool, dry place, in a container, such as a caddy or tin, that is scrupulously clean and that excludes air – which may convey other smells – from the outside. Most of the tea drunk in the U.K. is blended, but some people find that, if they move and have a different source of water supply, they may need to experiment a little to get the same result from another blend from that to which they have been accustomed. Pure unblended teas available are those from India (of which Darjeeling, Assam and Dooars are the most notable types), and from Ceylon, which produces very aromatic teas. China tea, which is only drunk in small quantities in the U.K., is nevertheless much liked by connoisseurs and the most famous blend is called Earl Grey. There are also several unblended types of China tea, of which the smoky-tasting Lapsang Souchong is possibly the best known. China tea is usually drunk without milk and often without sugar, although some people like a thin sliver of lemon with it.

**Coffee.** There are many different kinds of coffee available, but the most important thing to remember, when buying, is to try and choose a retailer who roasts his own coffee and who will, on request, make up a blend for the individual customer. Coffee may be bought and ground on purchase, but as it deteriorates from the time when it is roasted and still more from when it is ground, it is essential to buy it in small quantities and either to have it ground at the time of purchase, or to be able to grind it oneself immediately before use. The type of grind – fine, medium or coarse – depends on the individual taste and on the appliance used for making coffee; in general, a very fine grind yields a dark, rich coffee, but the purchaser should state the type required and the coffee making machine used when asking for it to be ground after being bought; Espresso machines require a finer grind, for example, than coffee made in a jug. Breakfast coffee, or any with which milk is to be combined, will probably be more enjoyable if it is a medium roast; after-dinner coffee – which many people take black – may be preferable with high roast. Ideally, coffee should be kept in an air-tight container in a cool place – the refrigerator if there is room, even. Small measures are widely available for facilitating coffee making – nothing is worse than being mean with the coffee.

**Curry.** Although the ideal procedure is to make up one's own mixture of spices and grind them – cookery books dealing with the subject give detailed instructions – there are good commercial curry powders and also curry paste, which is curry powder mixed with oil. It is important to store both in an air-tight container and to use within a month or two of purchase.

**Dates.** These come from North Africa and Iraq and are available either stoned, in blocks, or packed separately still containing their stones. Tunis dates are usually more succulent and best for dessert.

**Flour.** Several types are available, ranging from white flour to wholemeal stoneground, which latter has had nothing taken away from the grain. If bread is to be home baked, it is usually worth trying wholemeal flour or wheatmeal, which is a little less "mealy". For cakes and pastries, white flour should be used, but there are various kinds of this, available from the different manufacturers. Self-raising flour, which has a raising agent incorporated in it, is liked by many people, but bread, pastry, and most classic sauces should all only be made with plain flour, and the recipes for many cakes stipulate plain flour, because the raising agent is provided by some of the ingredients. Flours from other sources – potatoes, rice, cornflour and so on – are usually obtainable at special food stores if they are required

for particular purposes. White flour keeps for longer than wholemeal flour (which lasts only about 3 months from the time it leaves the mill) and all flour should be kept in a cool, airy place, not shut up. It is important not to add new flour to old, also, if there is any doubt as to whether flour may be damp, to let it dry out before using it.

**Gelatine.** This is available in powdered or leaf form. It is always important to follow exactly the manufacturers' instructions for the use of a particular type.

**Herbs and spices.** Both should be bought in small quantities at a time, as flavours tend to deteriorate in store. The ideal thing is to buy herbs fresh and dry them oneself, but excellent dried herbs are usually to be had from most health shops and stores. For good spices, go to a specialist grocer, or a continental shop where spices will be in regular supply.

**Mustard.** This is available in powdered form, or ready-mixed in tubes. French and German mustards are usually packed in jars or tubes. The flavour of all mustard depends on the type of ingredients used in addition to the mustard itself, so experimentation is necessary to find out the preferred kind, but generally continental mustards are not as hot as the English type.

**Mayonnaise.** It is so simple to make this that it may be regarded as an emergency store if it is bought in either tubes or jars. For snacks and buffet meals, the tube type, often with different flavours, can be a great convenience. It should of course be kept cool, but lasts – in tube form – months if kept in the refrigerator.

**Oil.** Olive oil is always labelled as such. The medicinal type tends to have little flavour. The flavour derives from where the oil comes from; France, Spain, Italy all export to Britain. Some people like a rather strong oil, others a mild one, but the amount of flavour does not relate to the cost – and, especially for salads, a fine quality oil, of whatever type, is always preferable if it can be afforded. Arachis oil, which has very little flavour, is liked by some people for cooking, and there are also various cooking oils sold under brand names that are suitable both for cooking and for people who are not able to take ordinary oil. Walnut oil is a great luxury, but also very expensive and usually only available at specialist grocer's. Most oil should be kept in a place that is slightly warm but not hot; in the cold, olive oil becomes cloudy, though it will clear if allowed gradually to come up to a higher temperature, and the cloudiness is not a sign of deterioration. As oil is more economically bought in large quantities, great care should be taken, if the oil is decanted little by little from a large can or flagon into a smaller vessel, to see that the lip of the can or flagon is thoroughly wiped each time it is used, as oil left exposed in this way may become rancid and will subsequently affect all the other oil poured over or through it. Walnut oil does tend to go rancid more quickly than other oils, and therefore should be kept at a cooler temperature – or even in the least cold part of a refrigerator. Oil used for frying should not, of course, necessarily be the superior type essential for salads and other culinary purposes when the flavour and delicacy of the oil is of major importance to the dish.

**Olives.** These are either green or black – the black ones are the very ripe kind – and the green olives may also be stuffed, usually with pimentos. It is always more economical to buy them loose, from delicatessens, and if it is wished to keep them, once opened, they should have a layer of olive oil poured over them, or if they are in a jar, over the brine in which they come, and be kept in the refrigerator.

**Pepper.** Black and white pepper may be bought whole or ground. It is generally accepted that black pepper, freshly ground in a peppermill, gives a particularly good flavour, though of course it can colour a very light sauce or dish. Pepper should be kept in a cool place, or in an airtight container.

**Rennet.** This is an essence containing an enzyme of the same name, used for making junket. It should be quite clear, the bottle must be kept in a cool place, and, as rennet loses its power by being shaken up or kept in the warm, if a bottle has been in the house for some time, it may not set the junket.

**Rice.** Different types of rice are available nowadays, and whereas some are excellent for puddings, others are better when used for risottos and similar dishes. When buying, specify the purposes for which the rice is to be used; a shop where it is sold loose will be able to advise, otherwise study any specifications given on the packet. Ground rice is powdered rice, used in cakes and puddings.

**Salt.** The type suitable for salt cellars – because it will not coagulate – is not suitable for preserving, for which purpose cooking or block salt should be bought. Salt in the form of crystals – sometimes referred to as "gros sel" or sea salt – is coarse and, when used, has to be ground in a mill if it is required to be fine. It is generally thought, however, to have a more effectively "salty" flavour than any other type.

**Sugar.** The cane sugars, which are brown in colour, are either Barbados, which looks like dark sand, and Demerara, which is darkish yellow crystals. Refined sugars, including coffee crystals, are bought according to requirements – i.e. caster is useful for cakes, icing sugar for icings, preserving sugar for jam-making, granulated for table and cooking in general, and lump sugar for tea and coffee. Golden syrup is a refined sugar syrup, black treacle refined molasses. Sugar should be kept dry, as, once damp, it may set hard.

**CHEESE.** There are hundreds of different cheeses available today, but the main types are: the fresh cream cheeses, such as cottage cheese, Demi-Sel Chambourcy; the soft cheeses, such as Brie, Camembert, Pont l'Evêque; the matured cheeses, such as all the Cheddars, Gruyère, Edam, Parmesan; and the blue cheeses, such as Stilton, Danish Blue, Roquefort, Gorgonzola. A good grocer should have a selection, but the soft cheeses in particular are only to be bought when they will be absolutely in prime condition by the time of the meal for which they are required, so the advice of the expert is always helpful when buying them. Cream cheeses can be used up in spreads, most matured cheeses can be used in cooking, but the soft cheeses should really be eaten as they are and although the blue cheeses can be used, crumbled, as an addition to salad dressings, and also made into spreads, they too are best enjoyed in their plain state. Cream cheese may be kept, covered, in a refrigerator, other cheeses are best kept, covered, in a larder, but, if they must be refrigerated, then they should be wrapped in several layers of plastic film and also put in a container, and only placed in the least cold section.

**BUTTER.** Different types of butter appeal to different palates. Only unsalted butter, however, should be used for such processes as cake making. The salted butters vary from slightly to definitely salted and are often preferred for table use. Blended butter is usually cheaper than unblended, and unsalted and "farmhouse" butter will not last as long as salted butter. Butter should always be kept in a dish with a cover, as it deteriorates with much exposure to light, and, for table use, it will usually have more flavour if it is allowed to regain room temperature after being taken out of the refrigerator.

**CREAM.** Single cream has a lower butter fat content than double cream and will not whip, though it may be used in many cooking processes. Double cream can be whipped. Clotted cream, as produced in Devon and Cornwall, may be fresh or deep frozen; it is not usually suitable for cooking (although it may be added to sauces in small quantities) but of course is delicious for use with fruit and puddings. Cream should be kept in a cool place always. Creamery produced cream, which may be sterilised or pasteurised, tends to lack the flavour of the true farmhouse cream, which may be often obtained at superior food stores and health food shops.

**MARGARINE.** This must be clearly labelled as to whether or not it contains any butter. It is made mainly from vegetable fats. Kosher margarine, which many people find of superior flavour, contains no milk of any kind.

**LARD AND COOKING FAT.** Lard is refined from pork fat and is nowadays mostly sold in packs, though sometimes "bladder lard" may be bought from a butcher or pork butcher. Lard, margarine and cooking fats – which should be bought according to the cooking processes for which they are required, should be stored as butter.

**EGGS.** The food value of an egg is exactly the same, no matter what the colour of the shell – this varies merely according to the variety of hen that laid the egg. The same applies to the colour of the yolk, which varies according to the diet of the hen. The size of egg bought should be according to the purpose for which the eggs are required – standard eggs are those used in most cookery book recipes and if large and small eggs are used, this must be taken into account. Older hens tend to lay larger eggs – not necessarily better ones. Although eggs should be fresh, an egg that is absolutely new-laid (that is, within an hour or two of being laid) is it not suitable for making a meringue as the white will not whip adequately, and nor is it ideal for making a soufflé – it should be 24 hours old for this. Eggs should be kept in a cool, dry place, away from anything strongly smelling, as they tend to absorb other smells through their porous shells – if you put a truffle in a bowl of eggs and then make an omelette with them, they will have taken on the truffle flavour!

**BREAD.** There are many different types of bread and it is a matter of personal preference as to what is bought. It should be stored in a bin to which the air has access, be wrapped in a cloth and of course thrown away if any sign of mould develops. Every bread bin should be regularly scalded, as if crumbs accumulate and go mouldy, they will infect every loaf put into the bin. The bread board should, likewise, be regularly and thoroughly scrubbed.

**MEAT.** Although this can be an expensive item, there are very many inexpensive cuts which are delicious when suitably cooked, and the housewife who buys best grilling steak for a stew, or lamb cutlets for a casserole is merely being silly, as well as extravagant. Study a good cookery book and consult your butcher – preferably not at a very busy time – for advice about the most suitable cut for different types of recipe. The better-known joints for roasting and grilling tend to get in short supply at weekends, as well as being dear. Different parts of the United Kingdom use slightly different names for different cuts, and a continental butcher will divide an animal differently, too, so it is a matter of learning by experience on the spot according to what one is to cook and how much one can afford. Meat should always be kept covered – though this is not essential if it is in a refrigerator – and if it cannot be cooked soon after being bought and no really cool place of storage is available, it may be kept wholesome by being put in a "marinade" or solution of vinegar and/or wine, herbs and sometimes a little oil. Most cookery books will give suitable detailed instructions.

**POULTRY AND GAME.** With poultry, there is a big difference in flavour – though none as regards nutritional content – between the mass-produced, often deep-frozen birds, and those that are free range, though the latter tend to be dearer and may not have so much plump meat on them. When buying poultry, remember that the giblets may be inside the bird in a bag, so make sure to remove them before cooking, and, if you buy poultry direct from the farm, check that the bird will have been cleaned and drawn, as well as plucked and trussed, when you receive it. With turkeys, a "poult", or hen bird has a plumper breast than a cock bird. With ducks, a duckling only is suitable for roasting. Ducks and geese tend to be rather wasteful birds, but as a large goose – like a largish turkey – will serve a number of people, it is a good choice for a party meal. Pigeons, which are usually available most of the year, may be roast or casseroled according to whether they are very young birds or not so young.

With most game birds, the young birds are best roasted, the older ones casseroled. The same applies to rabbit. The following list shows when certain game is in season:

*Grouse:* 12th August–10th December

*Partridge:* 20th August – 10th December

*Pheasant:* 1st September–1st February

*Venison:* June–January

*Woodcock, golden plover, snipe, wild duck, capercaillie:* 1st September–28th February

*Ptarmigan:* in Scotland only–September to February

*Black game:* 20th August–10th December

*Hare:* may not be sold from 1st March–31st July

It should be remembered that nowadays many game birds are frozen and may therefore be bought at other times than those when they are in season. It is also important to bear in mind that, if game is to be enjoyed according to British tastes, it must be properly hung (as must all meat), and this implies, in the UK, that it will be kept hanging until it is fairly "high" or definitely "gamey". If you do not like it like this, however, there is no reason at all why you should not ask your game merchant to give you a game bird that is virtually fresh – the majority of Europeans prefer it like this, and the cooking methods need not be altered, although a very high bird tends to be tenderer than a fresh one.

**BACON AND HAM.** The housewife has a very wide range of different types of bacon and ham to choose from, imported from various countries, as well as from the U.K. In general, one gets the quality for which one pays, but both bacon and ham are good value. Choose, with bacon, the type of rasher required, bearing in mind that very lean rashers may be slightly tougher than fattier ones. Smoked bacon, which has a brown rind, is more definite in flavour than unsmoked or green bacon, which has a whitish rind. The "cure" or degree of saltiness is a matter of individual preference and only the man in the shop can advise as to how salty a particular rasher may be – unless one cures one's own bacon or buys it from a farm. For the different types of bacon joint, consult a good cookery book, which will indicate the types of joint and the most appropriate ways of dealing with them.

**Ham,** which is a leg of pork individually cured, varies very much. Canned hams, of mild flavour, often differing considerably according to the way the pigs have been fed (peach-fed) or how the ham has been cooked (pineapple or honey roast) are usually bought by the slice. Whole hams, which may be carved for small purchases, tend to be slightly dearer; some of these are: Suffolk ham, which is a sweet cured ham; Bradenham, which is a smoked ham: there are also many continental hams, including those from Westphalia, the Ardennes, Bayonne, the Morvan in Burgundy and the Italian proscuitto. York ham, which is probably the best-known of all hams, has a mild flavour.

**FISH.** With the tremendous advances made in freezing fish at its peak of freshness, and the speed-up of supplying markets from all over the world, it is not of such importance for the housewife to know exactly what is locally in season – unless, of course, she lives at a fishing port – as to be aware of the resources of her fishmonger. Oysters, which are traditionally only eaten when there is an "r" in the month, are in fact perfectly wholesome all the year round if you are near the source of supply, so they may often be bought at the coast even in the summer. Smoked fish of many kinds, not all of them as expensive as smoked salmon, or as well-known as the kipper, are also in year-round supply. If there should be any problem about the preparation of fish – such as the opening of oysters, splitting of cooked lobsters, dressing of crabs and so on – the fishmonger experienced in his trade will usually be able to advise and offer practical help. Fish should always be cooked and eaten as soon as possible after it has been bought; if kept at all, it must be wrapped in paper and covered and put in a cold place or the colder part of the refrigerator.

**GREENGROCERY AND FRUIT.** It is difficult to be specific about what to buy when, because obviously a greengrocer or market in a city will have more frequent supplies than one in the country, even though the latter may enjoy the benefit of very fresh local produce. Fresh fruit and vegetables may, on occasions, be less of a bargain than those that are frozen, and the amount of possible wastage is something that has to be taken into consideration when budgeting, as does the additional cost for cleaned and packed produce. What is often a problem, is to get adequate information about the source of supply of the goods and their degree of maturity; this may be easy when the retailer is personally interested and concerned, but much more difficult in a large store or supermarket. It is in the interest of the shopper to find out as much as possible about what good vegetables and fruit should be like and try to relate these findings – and any market reports of what is especially good at a certain time – to what is found in the shops. Varieties can be noted and it is not difficult to differentiate between produce that is really fresh and stuff that has been sprayed with water to give it the effect of being so. No retailer can prevent a customer buying what he or she wishes and the shopper who meekly takes goods "as they come", or who is content to telephone an order or pick up a packet in which details of the contents cannot be clearly seen is not entitled to blame the retailer if the goods prove to be unsatisfactory as the result of such careless buying. It is worth remembering that most goods can be bought one by one – with the resultant purchase being weighed, of course – which is often easier for the beginner at housekeeping to do than to calculate by the pound as to how much may be required.

Vegetables should be stored in a cool, airy place – such as a vegetable rack – which is not in direct daylight. Green vegetables such as lettuce, cress and watercress and fresh herbs deteriorate very quickly after purchase, and in general it is only potatoes (not new potatoes), root vegetables, apples and citrus fruits that can fairly be kept for several days after purchase without deteriorating appreciably, even if they can be kept in a refrigerator. They may not present any health hazard, but the flavour will decline markedly. Green vegetables that appear "tired" even soon after being brought home, may be considerably improved by being washed and allowed to rest for half an hour or so in cold water with a generous squeeze of lemon juice added. Fruit that begins to go soft must be carefully removed from contact with other fruits, which it will infect, as well as attracting flies. Potatoes that are exposed to strong light, either daylight or artificial light, tend to turn green, which gives them a bitter flavour– if the green part is too much to cut away, the potato should be discarded. Soft fruit, such as strawberries and raspberries, can be kept well in a refrigerator after being washed and sprinkled with sugar and then put in a covered container, but any fruit, cooked or raw, stored in this way must be watched for any sign of mould or fermentation. Slightly imperfect fruit is often an economical buy when it is intended to use it for cooking, but dessert fruit must be as flawless as possible and it is not usually worth while buying second-rate fruit for bottling or to use when making preserves, as the wastage will be too great. Vegetables that are not pre-packed but which have most of their outside leaves trimmed away may very well be rather stale and care should be taken to examine these closely for freshness – if they are drying up, they will lack flavour.

**CANNED GOODS.** Since the advent of frozen foodstuffs, canned goods generally form the bulk of the emergency stores. Although, if kept in a cool, airy cupboard, most cans have a long life, care should be taken to check through them regularly, in case any show signs of having "blown" – bulging at top and base. These should be discarded without hesitation, as they may present a real danger to health. Tins that seem to leak should likewise be regarded with suspicion – it is always better to be safe than sorry, and it is not always easy to taste or smell the ominous signs in the contents of a tin that has gone off. Cans of meat, pâté and fruit that is to be served cold usually improve in flavour – as well as the meat being easier to serve – if they can be chilled before being opened. When buying canned goods, avoid badly damaged cans, although a mere dent may not mean that the contents are at all affected; sometimes real bargains are offered of canned goods that may be slightly imperfect as regards labels or the actual finish of the can.

**BULK BUYING.** It is nearly always financially advantageous to buy large quantities of goods in the nature of basic household supplies, providing both that the initial outlay is not too high for the family budget and that there is adequate storage space in the home. Some firms do a large mail order business in this way, but many ordinary retailers will offer good terms and discounts to customers who will take large orders at a time, especially if they will accept the firm's own lines of goods and not insist on particular brands. It is usually easy to assess the comparative quality of such lines and considerable savings may be effected by the bulk purchase of dry groceries, certain canned goods, cleaning stuffs, soap and detergents, lavatory paper and so on, and the same applies to soft drinks, wines and spirits. People who have deep freeze cabinets will find that frozen foodstuffs may similarly be purchased in quantity on advantageous terms.

**COOKING TIMES.** Most cookers are supplied with books or instructions charts giving detailed cooking times and methods. But in general the following will serve as a guide:

**Roasting**

| | |
|---|---|
| Chicken (medium size) | $1\frac{1}{4}$–$1\frac{1}{2}$ hours |
| Duck | $1$–$1\frac{1}{4}$ hours |
| Goose | $1\frac{1}{2}$ hours |

| | |
|---|---|
| Turkey | Allow 15 minutes per pound for birds weighing up to 14–15 lb., allow 10 minutes per pound for larger birds. |
| Beef, lamb and mutton | 15 minutes per pound plus 15 minutes for small joints, 20–25 minutes per pound plus 20–25 minutes for large joints |
| Veal and pork | 25–30 minutes per pound, plus 25–30 minutes |

These times are calculated for poultry and meat roasted in an oven previously brought up to the required temperature or, when it is desired to seal the meat quickly, made hot for the first half hour, and then the temperature being reduced to what is required. If it is preferred to start cooking from a cold oven allow longer cooking time – approximately one-third more. If beef is preferred very underdone, reduce the overall cooking time. Many French and continental recipes give cooking times for lamb that give a pinkish or underdone joint, so in making use of them allowance should be made and the cooking time increased if a moderately done or well done joint is liked. Pork should never be served under-done. Veal is served slightly underdone in many continental countries, but veal available in the British Isles is usually less young and tender than that sold in Europe.

For spit-roasting, allow slightly longer for all cooking times.

**Pressure cookery:** In using most types of pressure cooker, ordinary recipes can be adapted by cutting the cooking time by one-third and cooking at 15 lb. pressure, except with most soft fruits, which usually only have to be brought up to pressure and then cooled.

## BASIC SAUCES

**White sauce**

| | |
|---|---|
| 1 oz. butter (unsalted) | 1 oz. plain flour |
| ½ pint milk | salt, pepper to taste |

Bring the milk up to the boil and put it aside. Over moderate heat, melt the butter and shake into it the flour, stirring constantly. When butter and flour have amalgamated, gradually stir in the milk, stirring or whisking through-out the process. Season with salt and pepper and, should the sauce be at all lumpy – because of the cooking process being hurried – put it through a sieve. After the milk has been added, the sauce should be cooked gently for *at least* 15 minutes to allow the flour to be properly cooked through – it is the "bring to the boil and serve" custom that makes foreigners say the British make flour and water paste instead of sauces! Seasoning to taste should be added at the end of the cooking.

**A brown sauce** is made in exactly the same way, with the butter cooked until it becomes brown first.

**A Mornay sauce** is a basic white sauce with the addition of 1–1½ oz. of grated Parmesan or similar cheese, stirred in towards the end of the cooking time.

**The basic roux** described above may be varied according to the type of sauce required: fish, meat or vegetable stock may be incorporated or substituted for the milk, herbs, spices (such as curry, mace, nutmeg, etc.), capers, pieces of meat, fish, vegetables or eggs (hard-boiled and chopped) included as liked.

**Mayonnaise**

| | |
|---|---|
| 1 egg yolk | ¼ pint olive oil |
| 1 dessertspoonful wine vinegar (or lemon juice) | ½ teaspoonful mustard salt, pepper, sugar (optional) |

Put the egg yolk in a basin with a little salt and pepper and the mustard. Stir together with a wooden spoon, then add a few drops of the vinegar and stir again. Then add a few drops of the oil, stir well and begin to add the rest of the oil drop by drop or in a thin stream. The sauce will soon begin to thicken and then the remainder of the vinegar or lemon juice may be added. When the sauce is the consistency of thick cream, add more salt and pepper to taste and, if it seems too acid, a little caster sugar. If at any stage in the process the sauce disintegrates, break another egg yolk into a fresh basin, stir it up and very gradually add the "turned" mayonnaise (which is perfectly good), which will amalgamate once more.

Add chopped parsley or watercress, a little tomato purée or ketchup, curry powder, double cream, chopped onion or garlic juice etc. as liked.

**Bread sauce**

| | |
|---|---|
| 1 onion, stuck with 2–3 cloves | 1 pint milk |
| 1 teacupful white crumbs | 1–1½ oz. unsalted butter |
| 1½ tablespoonfuls double cream | salt, pepper, nutmeg |

Simmer the onion in the milk for 25–35 minutes. Season the milk with salt, pepper and grated nutmeg, then gradually stir in the crumbs until the sauce has absorbed them. Remove the onion and, just before serving, whisk in the cream and butter in little chips.

**BASIC SHORT CRUST PASTRY.**
½ lb. flour (either self-raising or, with plain flour, add 1 level teaspoonful of baking powder to each half pound of flour).
4 oz. fat (the type used depends on the ultimate use of the pastry—butter makes a very rich pastry, margarine or margarine and lard half-and-half make a good all-purpose type, all lard or clarified dripping may be used for certain savoury dishes).

Sift the flour with ¼ teaspoonful of salt into a bowl, cut in the shortening (fat) with a knife, then, with the tips of the fingers, rub the fat into the flour until the mixture is of the consistency of fine crumbs. Then add a very little water (not more than ¼ pint to ½ lb. flour), mixing with the knife all the time, until the paste is neither sticky nor still very dry. Pick it up, put it on a lightly floured board, roll it out quickly and lightly with a floured rolling-pin to the required shape and thickness. Bake in a moderately hot oven till firm, according to whether large or small quantities used.

A *biscuit crust* is made by using 5 oz. fat and an egg yolk for the mixing agent instead of water. For sweet pastry a half teaspoonful of sugar may be added.

**BASIC ROUGH PUFF PASTRY**
½ lb. flour (as above)          6 oz. fat (as above)
¼ teaspoonful each salt and lemon juice

Sieve the flour and salt into a bowl, cut the fat into it, then add the lemon juice and water as above. Put the paste on the floured board, press it gently into three ridges, then roll out to a strip about three times as broad as it is long. Fold this into three, press the edges together with the rolling-pin to seal in the air, then turn the "parcel" of pastry sideways to the first quarter of a circle, make another three ridges in it, roll out (always avoiding unsealing the pressed-together edges), roll up, press the edges together and turn it again. Repeat until the pastry has been "turned" through the four quarters of a circle. Then fold it into two instead of three, leave it in a cool place for half an hour, before rolling it out for use as required, for pies, tarts, etc.

**DIFFERENT WEIGHTS AND MEASURES**

In countries using the decimal system, the following guide to quantities may be of use, either when shopping abroad or when adapting foreign recipes:

| | |
|---|---|
| 1 oz. | 30 grammes (gr. or g.) |
| 4 oz. | 120–125 grammes |
| 2 lb. 4 oz. | 1 kilogramme (kilo or kg.) |
| 1 lb. 2 oz. | 1 livre (in French-speaking countries) |

1 litre (liquid measure) is 1.759 pints

In American recipes there is considerable differences between measures of the same name in the United Kingdom.
British pint: 20 fluid oz.
American pint: 16 fluid oz.

16 American tablespoons – 8 fluid oz.
3 American teaspoons – $\frac{1}{2}$ fluid oz.
1 American tablespoon – $\frac{1}{2}$ fluid oz.
1 British tablespoon – $\frac{3}{4}$–1 fluid oz. approx.
1 British tablespoon – 4 teaspoons.

American measuring spoons and cups are of a standard size: It should be borne in mind that an American "spoonful" always means a level spoonful.

1 American measuring spoon (tablespoon) holds $\frac{1}{4}$ oz. of flour (Some U.K. dessertspoons are of this capacity).

1 square American chocolate – 1 oz.
1 cake American compressed yeast – 2/3 oz. fresh or equivalent dried yeast.
1 envelope American gelatine – 1/3 oz. ordinary gelatine.

| Cup sizes | USA oz. | UK oz. |
| --- | --- | --- |
| Flour | 4 | 5 |
| fresh breadcrumbs | 7 | 8 |
| icing sugar | $4\frac{1}{2}$ | 5 |
| butter or fat | 8 | 8 |
| raisins | 5 | 6 |
| syrup | 12 | 14 |

American can sizes:
Picnic: 10 oz.
No. 1: 16 oz.
No. 2: 20 oz.

American cake flour: In the UK use the best quality white flour available and take only $3\frac{1}{2}$ oz. for every 4 oz. specified. In general, use $1\frac{1}{2}$ times the amount of baking powder specified in an American recipe. Use caster sugar unless any other type is specified. For "Graham flour" use 100 per cent wholewheat flour. For "Graham crackers" substitute crispbread or unsweetened digestive biscuits.

## SETTING AND SERVING SPECIAL FOODS

## FIRST COURSES – HORS D'OEUVRES:

**Globe artichokes:** trim the stalks so that the artichokes remain upright on the plate, whether they are to be served hot or cold, and set a small knife and fork. The vinaigrette or other sauce is served separately, and as with other foods eaten with the fingers, it is pleasant to provide finger bowls for use after the artichokes have been eaten. The artichoke leaves are pulled off with the fingers and dipped in the sauce and finally the base is eaten with the knife and fork.

**Asparagus.** Usually served all together on a large dish with the asparagus heads all pointing in the same direction. Melted butter or sauce is offered separately. Asparagus is usually eaten with the fingers, though a knife and fork may be used, or a fork held in the right hand and a piece of bread in the left. Set finger bowls.

**Avocado Pear.** Usually a half avocado is sufficient, unless people are very fond of them. This must only be cut just before serving or the surface will blacken. The stone is removed and if stuffing, such as shrimps, is to be served, this is piled in the cavity left by the stone. Any sauce, such as vinaigrette, is served separately. The avocado pear is eaten with a large tea-spoon or grapefruit spoon.

**Caviar.** This may be served in individual pots or spoonfuls on a plate, but it looks best if a large pot, set on crushed ice, is offered with a spoon, for people to help themselves. It is accompanied by slices of lemon and either brown bread and butter or small pieces of freshly made toast. Some people like finely chopped hardboiled egg and finely chopped onions to be offered in little dishes as well. As with anything strongly flavoured eaten with the fingers, a finger bowl is a good idea after caviar.

**Corn on the Cob.** Although one is unlikely to serve this when any form of formality is to be observed, it is made easier to eat if the special small forks or prongs are stuck in either end of the cob, or, failing this, a skewer is put through each cob. The cob is picked up in the fingers and the kernels bitten off. Accompaniments are plenty of melted butter and salt.

**Grapefruit.** Usually served halved, and whether it is hot or cold the centre core must be cut out and the segments divided beforehand. A little caster sugar may be sprinkled on an hour or so before serving. A glacé cherry is often put in the centre of the grapefruit, which should be served accompanied by more sugar. Set a fairly large teaspoon or a special grapefruit spoon.

**Gulls Eggs.** These may either be served on individual plates, garnished with cress, parsley or a sprig of watercress, or piled in a basket, similarly garnished. They are eaten with the fingers, accompanied by pepper and salt, also celery salt if liked.

**Melon.** The small melons are usually served one to a person, a "lid" being cut off, sometimes with a jagged edge made by cutting up and down diagonally with a knife and the pips removed from the inside. The lid is then replaced. A refinement on this is to scoop out the centre of the melon with a potato ball cutter and then replace it, adding a little iced port if liked. Cantaloupe, honey-dew and water melons are served by the slice, accompanied by sugar, with powdered ginger, and salt and pepper for those who like it; the slice of melon can be cut in advance from the skin and sliced into mouth size portions, and a variation of this is to pull out the portions slightly, alternating them towards either edge of the melon, so that they stand out rather like teeth. Melon may be eaten with a large teaspoon or dessert spoon (easiest for the individual melons) or a dessert knife and fork or dessert spoon and fork.

**Lemon.** When this is served as a garnish to a dish, a half or whole fruit cut with jagged edges, or with the peel partially removed and coiled around it, is usual. But if the lemon is to be used to squeeze on to foods, a quarter of a lemon per person is easier to use than a slice.

**Oysters.** They should be opened just before serving and put on the half shell, ideally on special plates made to hold either six or twelve at a time.

Usually a half lemon is put in the centre and thin brown bread and butter and red pepper are the traditional accompaniments. As many people do not want more than half a dozen oysters at a time, and the large plates take up a lot of room, it is often a good idea to serve six at first and then change plates if people want more. If you do not have special oyster forks, any with two or three prongs will do perfectly well. The shell is held in one hand and the fork used with the other and some people like to drink the oyster liquor in each half shell. Finger bowls should be provided with oysters and, as they are fish eaten with the fingers at the beginning of the meal, it is pleasant to change the table napkins after the food is cleared away.

**Pâté.** This may either be served cut in slices from the block in which it has been turned out, or from the terrine in which it has been made. Pâté de foie gras is served in slices, cut with a silver knife dipped in hot water between each slice to ensure a clean cut. This and other forms of pâté may be garnished with a few very small lettuce leaves, a little cress or watercress, fronds of endive or small gherkins sliced at one end and pulled out to form a fan. The accompaniments are freshly-made toast or chip toast and butter. An extra knife is required for spreading the pâté on the toast, and it is either put on in bite-sized pieces and the toast eaten with the fingers, or else eaten with knife and fork or fork alone and the toast eaten separately.

**Smoked Salmon.** This is generally served on individual plates in very thin slices, accompanied by thin brown bread and butter, slices of lemon, and pepper for those who like it. Set fish cutlery.

**Snails.** There are special plates to take these, and special tongs and forks to grip the shell and extract the snail. In the absence of this equipment, serve the snails embedded in hot salt, on a large bread plate or pudding plate and eat them with a two-pronged or other small fork. Some people drink the snail liquor. Serve with crusty French bread.

**Garlic.** With garlic butter, such as is served with snails, or other food strongly flavoured with this herb, it is an idea either to serve the food accompanied by a sprig of parsley, which may be eaten afterwards, to remove the smell on the breath, or else to put out a small dish of coffee beans for people to chew, as this performs the same task.

**Soup.** The large soup tureen and shallow plates are now slightly old-fashioned and plates of this kind do let the soup get cold quickly. They may be used, however, especially for cold soups. Consommé, whether hot or cold, is served in a cup; in some restaurants this comes sitting on a soup plate and the waiter pours the consommé into the plate. When cold or in jelly form, consommé is accompanied by a slice of lemon. Onion soup and other thick soups are probably most conveniently served in small marmites with covers, standing on matching saucers. A spoon should always be provided, even for consommé in cups, although people may prefer to drink it (though it should be noted that, traditionally, soup is always referred to as being "eaten"). When soup spoons are used, the British practice is to scoop up the soup on the side of the plate away from the soup eater and to take it from the side of the spoon nearest. When the plate or cup is nearly emptied, it is either tilted away from the eater or, with a cup with a handle, picked up and drunk.

Garnishes for soup are usually offered separately, but in the case of a soup served from a tureen, they can be added to this just before serving, Croûtons – small squares of bread fried in butter – are the most usual. In a restaurant the waiter will offer these. In a private house they may be put on the table, with a spoon, for people to help themselves. A little chopped parsley or finely chopped hardboiled egg may be added to cream and vegetable soups. Gazpacho, the Spanish soup, is accompanied by a variety of garnishes, borscht, the Russian beet soup, by sour cream.

**FISH.** If fish are offered on a large dish, make sure that any sauce masking them does not prevent people from seeing how to help themselves, as great confusion may result if someone cuts across a fish that has not been boned. The usual practice is for fish such as trout, mackerel, sole and mullet to be served whole, with the heads and skin on them. Larger fish are served without the dark skin. The thick fishes, such as salmon, halibut, turbot and cod, may be served in steaks, cut straight across, but a whole salmon trout may be offered as well, with large fish servers; a really sharp knife is necessary to carve the steaks off the whole fish in this way.

**Smoked fish.** This includes smoked trout, herring, eel, and of course, smoked salmon (see above). These fish are all served accompanied by a slice of lemon and thin brown bread and butter. Some people like a little horseradish sauce with smoked fish, others think this spoils the delicate flavour, so it is a matter for the individual to decide.

**Whitebait.** Served piled on a large dish, which may be first covered with a white napkin or paper napkin, and accompanied by slices or quarters of lemon and brown bread and butter. Eaten with fish cutlery or just a fork.

**Crab, lobster, languoste and langoustines.** When these are served whole, they should be accompanied by pickers and crackers, if these are available. If not, a fork with two or three prongs and long tines is very helpful, and the lobster and crab claws may be given a preliminary crack with a hammer in the kitchen immediately before serving. The flesh is picked out from the claws and the legs – or even sucked out from the latter. Mayonnaise or any similar sauce to accompany these fish is served separately. Finger bowls and a change of table napkins are a convenience.

**Shrimps and prawns.** These are served accompanied by brown bread and butter and are shelled – if necessary – and then eaten with the fingers. If mayonnaise or another sauce is served too, then a knife and fork must also be set for eating the shellfish.

R– E.W.—K

**Whiting.** This is usually served with its tail in its mouth, but there is no real reason why it should not be presented flat.

**Mussels.** When these are served with an assortment of other fish, they are eaten with a fork, like oysters, but when served as moules marinières – a type of soup – a fork must be provided to eat the mussels plus a spoon to drink the soup.

**PASTA.** Spaghetti, macaroni, and so on, are served from one large dish, and although experts eat it with a fork alone, it is usual to provide a spoon as well. The spoon can be held in one hand and its bowl serves as a prop for the fork while this is wound up in the pasta. The sauce may be either piled on the whole dish and apportioned out, or offered separately. Grated cheese is usually offered so that individuals can help themselves.

**MEAT DISHES.** Joints are served and carved on a large dish, and casseroles offered in the dish in which they have been cooked. Steak and kidney pudding is served with a napkin around the basin in which it has been cooked. Pies are served in the pie dish, which may have either a frill around it or a folded napkin – an especially good idea if the dish is transparent glass. With lamb cutlets and crown of lamb, it is traditional to put small paper frills around the ends of the bones, but this is not essential. What is thoughtful, with all but the most formal meal, is to encourage people who wish to get the sweet meat off the cutlet bones in the most satisfactory manner to pick it up and chew it, and therefore a finger bowl served afterwards is practical.

With mutton and lamb, mint sauce and redcurrant jelly may be offered separately. With pork, apple sauce. With steak, the perfect garnish is a few sprigs of watercress dipped into a light French dressing, though a pat of parsley butter may be put on the meat as well.

For carving all joints, it is helpful to look at a good instruction book, but even more so to watch an experienced carver in action. This may be done at many restaurants, although as the largest joints are easiest to carve, the host has a harder task to present small-scale joints efficiently and economically. The essential is to have a really sharp carving knife. Those who are inexpert or slow carvers are advised to carve in the kitchen. (See also under Carving.)

**Poultry and game.** When stuffing is used, this should be spooned out in helpings as the meat is served. Small game birds are usually served whole, sometimes on a croûton of fried bread or toast, so that this catches the juices. Medium-sized birds may be split in half. Other poultry may be either carved or served in pre-carved joints. Although knives and forks are set as usual, it is in order, except at very formal meals, to pick up the joints in the fingers to get at the sweet meat when small game birds are served.

**Vegetables and salads.** In the British Isles, where main courses are seldom elaborately garnished, vegetables are usually served with this course. At one time, however, the United Kingdom followed the practice now current on the Continent of serving the vegetables separately afterwards; the only survivals of this are asparagus, which may be served as a first course or after the meat dish, and salads (see below).

**Baked potatoes.** The old-fashioned way for these to be served was either in a folded napkin or on one of the beautiful traditional silver potato rings which hold the potato firm. Nowadays, baked potatoes may be offered on a dish, in a wooden platter, bowl or basket, or on a folded napkin if preferred. When very large potatoes are served in this way it is a convenience to provide a separate small plate, like a salad plate, for them, and a separate fork, in case people do not wish to use the same fork as for their meat course; this, however, is a comparatively formal way of presenting an informal food, and really the way a baked potato is served depends entirely on the way people like it best.

**Salads.** These should not be offered at formal dinners, but may be served with or after the main course at other meals. It is a courtesy to allow people to choose when they will eat their salad. Depending on the kind of food on the dish – especially if something with a lot of sauce or gravy is served – a separate salad plate may be laid, either at the side of the main plate, or may replace the plate with the meat course when this has been cleared away. With green and simple mixed salads, the custom is for people in private houses to help themselves informally from the large salad bowl, but when some kind of a special salad, such as an orange or pear salad to accompany the main course is involved, then individual dishes of this salad can be prepared. A separate salad fork may be set.

**Cheese.** Served on a large board or platter, with several sharp knives and, if liked, small forks to facilitate service. (The practical French eat cheese with a knife and fork.) Large whole hard cheeses are often served cut across the top, swathed in a napkin, with a spoon or scoop for people to help themselves from the centre. Stilton is nearly always served like this, though many authorities prefer to be able to cut the whole cheese downwards in wedges or in slices across the top. Runny cheeses are usually served on small mats – Brie generally on straw – but individual cream cheeses, such as Petit Suisse or Demi Sel may remain on the cheese-board in their wrappings, as they are in individual portions. Other smaller cheeses must be removed from boxes or wrappings. Thick chunks of bread and a variety of biscuits and rusks may accompany cheese, also butter. In season, celery may partner cheese. The bread or side plates are put in front of the diners for this course.

**PUDDINGS.** For all puddings, a dessert spoon and fork should be laid, unless an ice cream or some kind of pudding in a small or special dish is to be served, when the spoon with which this is to be eaten may be put on the saucer of the dish, where it is replaced when the helping has been finished.

At one time it was thought correct only to use a fork for most pudding courses but the sensible thing is to eat with either fork, or spoon and fork as is convenient; at a fairly formal meal, however, a dessert spoon is never used alone, though it is perfectly correct to use any small spoon, such as an ice cream spoon, by itself.

The transatlantic custom of serving a cake for the pudding course, or a selection of pastries, perhaps at luncheon, means that either spoon and fork may be set and used as convenient, or, as is helpful at afternoon tea with rather rich pastries, a small knife and fork may be set or offered with the pudding plates.

**Yoghurt.** If this is made in the home, it may be served in any suitable individual pots. Otherwise it is eaten in the pot in which it is bought, and a large teaspoon is used.

**Savouries.** These are usually served in individual portions, and eaten with a knife and fork.

**Dessert.** When this is offered at a formal meal, the custom is for the cloth – should one be used – to be removed from the table, together with everything to do with the meal, except the glasses for port or whatever wine is to accompany dessert. The dessert plates are then laid, with a small mat and a finger bowl on each, and a dessert knife and fork at right and left, though these may arrive on the plate as it is served. People then take the mat and finger bowl and put these on the table up above the plate. Nutcrackers and grape scissors may be provided with the dish of fruit, if grapes and nuts are included. The general custom is for fruit, except grapes, to be eaten with a knife and fork at a formal meal, but the sensible thing to do is whatever is convenient.

**Finger bowls.** These should be half filled with warm or tepid water, and a thin slice of lemon may also be added, though never any scent. Some people like to float a flower head or a few petals on the surface, and this is a matter of individual taste.

**Cigarettes at the table.** It is a transatlantic custom to set small quantities of cigarettes and an ashtray for each guest or pair of guests, or arrange cigarettes and ashtrays about the table as part of the routine setting of even the most formal meal. In the Scandinavian countries, too, cigarettes are often set on the table at the beginning of the meal and in Spain people smoke between courses. But in the British Isles the tradition still holds that no-one smokes during a meal and, on formal occasions, not until the last table wine has been finished. Nowadays even some lovers of port do not object to smoking during the passage of the decanter, but in many households the host may well prefer not to offer cigarettes during the service of a fine vintage. Brandy and liqueurs are not affected by smoke, and therefore this is the stage of the meal at which people may light up if they wish to do so. At a very formal meal, or banquet it would be bad manners even to think of smoking until either the Loyal Toast to the monarch has been drunk, usually before coffee, or until the host suggests smoking.

**Finishing.** In general, when one has finished all that it is wished to eat on one's plate, the cutlery are drawn together, forks with tines pointing down, knives with blades to the left, and they are put diagonally down on the plate, with the handles at "four o'clock". If soup, seafood cocktails or ices or similar sweets are served in small cups or glasses placed on another dish, then the spoon or other utensils used to eat them with is laid on the underneath dish when the food is finished.

It should be stressed that, even if a guest leaves most of the food on his or her plate, the host or hostess should never comment on this. If second helpings are offered, people should not be pressed to have more if they definitely refuse.

## WINES AND OTHER DRINKS

Although it is never *essential* to serve alcoholic drinks when entertaining, there is no denying that they play an important part, both in breaking the initial ice in the form of apéritifs, and table wines and liqueurs, form a valuable complement to a balanced meal. Many people are nervous of serving drinks other than beer and cider and the more usual combinations, such as gin and tonic, gin and French or whisky and soda, but there is nothing really difficult about the subject once a few basic principles are grasped.

**APERITIFS.** All of these, cocktails, sherry, vermouth, white port, dry Madeira, and any of the proprietary apéritifs, such as Dubonnet, should be served refreshingly chilled and of course some mixed drinks have ice in them anyway. A tepid apéritif does not play its part in stimulating the appetite. If you do not wish to serve spirits or cocktails, a fairly dry white wine is also perfectly acceptable.

To avoid possible confusion, it is usually simplest to have a choice of drinks for guests, either a cocktail or sherry (medium or dry) plus tomato juice or a fruit drink for those who do not want anything alcoholic, rather than try and cope with a range of complicated mixed drinks – unless, for a party, you have the services of a professional barman.

A very good party apéritif and possibly the only one with which no alternative except a soft drink need be offered, is Champagne or Champagne cocktails, or a white, moderately dry, sparkling wine of good quality. Curiously, although an apéritif of this kind looks lavish, it is seldom as expensive as a range of drinks involving the use of a lot of spirits.

If you only serve sherry, it is a good idea for a large party to have a choice of an Amontillado (medium dry), and a Fino, (really dry wine).

**Drinks in-between times.** If people come to see you mid-morning – perhaps at the weekend – or during the evening, and you wish to offer them a drink not directly associated with a meal, it is always correct to suggest a glass of wine (white or rosé, but not too dry for this kind of occasion), a medium or even dessert sherry, a dessert Madeira or a glass of port (ruby or tawny), unless you keep spirits on your sideboard or in your drinks cupboard and are prepared to offer guests whisky and soda or ginger ale, brandy and water or soda, gin with tonic, lime or bitter lemon, rum with orange or grapefruit, and any of the other mixtures suitable for moderately long drinks, to be taken while people are talking. (Any good cocktail book, such as "Cocktails and How to Mix Them" in the Home Entertaining Series will tell you how to prepare drinks of this kind both simply and effectively.)

**Storage of wines and spirits.** Spirits should be kept upright in bottle, wines – except when they are to be drunk within a few days of being bought – should be

THE BORDEAUX AREA

laid on their sides, so that the wine remains in contact with the cork. Both wines and spirits should be kept in a cool place and not subjected to strong light. It does not matter much if the temperature of what serves as the "cellar' is around 50 deg.–55 deg.F., though an actual cellar would probably be cooler, providing that this temperature does not go sharply up and down. Contact with central heating or hot-water pipes should be avoided and it should be remembered that wines kept at the upper levels of the temperature recommended for storage will mature faster and be ready for drinking sooner than those kept in a cooler place.

In general, neither spirits, the fortified wines (vintage port), sherry, port Madeira nor non-vintage table wines improve by being kept long periods in bottle. They are ready to be enjoyed after being bought. Vintage wines, however, may benefit enormously by being allowed to "grow up" slowly and the advice of the wine merchant who supplies them should be sought about this. Any wine, red or white, that throws a deposit, should ideally be kept standing upright for a few days after purchase, so as to allow this deposit to sink to the bottom of the bottle and not be mixed up in the wine when it is poured. This deposit is by no means a bad thing, for many fine, slow-to-mature wines do throw a deposit, on which they "live" during part of their life in bottle, but the appearance of "bits" in the wine spoils the beautiful colour and "star bright" quality.

If both red and white wines are stored together in a wine rack or bin, it is a good idea to keep the white wines at the bottom, where the atmosphere will be cooler. Vintage port bottles usually have a splash of whitewash on one side, to indicate that this part of the bottle has been uppermost, and that therefore the "crust" of heavy deposit will be on the under-side. Table wines are usually stored label uppermost for the same reason.

**Choice of Wines.** The most important thing about wine drinking is that it should be a pleasure. The few rules that tend to be generally accepted (though they are by no means rigid) have been formed as a result of finding what gives most enjoyment in conjunction with certain foods and at certain occasions. There is nothing very complicated about this. The ideal thing to do is to consult a wine merchant about the kind of wine likely to suit your entertaining and your budget and although there are hundreds of retail outlets for excellent wines in all price ranges, it is the merchant, specialising in wine, who will be most likely to have up-to-date and informed knowledge about his stock and the time and opportunity to help you choose the appropriate bottle or half bottle for your needs.

Few occasions, however formal, call for more than one or two table wines (excluding sherry, port, liqueurs) and the order of service is: young before old and dry before sweet. There are a few exceptions – a dessert wine may be younger than, say, the red wine that accompanies the main course, and although claret is generally served before Burgundy, when two red wines are to be served a young Burgundy would probably precede an old claret. Wine should either complement or contrast with a dish; that is to say, a rich dish needs either a full-bodied wine or a crisp, dry one. For example, roast goose could be accompanied either by a light, dry white wine or a full-bodied red wine. In general, red wines do not go with white fish or shellfish, and very delicate fine wines are overwhelmed by very highly seasoned dishes. With regional recipes, the ideal choice is the appropriate regional wine, or its nearest equivalent. With Chinese food, China tea is usually the best accompaniment, with curry, a lager or similar drink.

THE VINEYARDS OF BURGUNDY

The quality of the wine should, ideally, match that of the food: plain grills and roasts of good quality will partner the finest wines, but for things such as stews and informal dishes it is better to choose a wine from the medium price ranges. Wines of "everyday" quality are for informal parties and everyday meals – although good bread, butter and cheese can be made into a meal for any gourmet if served with a fine wine.

## WHAT TO SERVE WITH WHAT.

Dry Champagne may be served throughout a meal, especially for a celebration party. If there is any doubt as to what wine to choose – suppose one is ordering in a restaurant and guests have a variety of dishes – a dry, fairly full-bodied white wine, such as a White Burgundy, will go with both meat and fish, or be offered as an alternative to a red wine. If a meal starts with a dry white wine, then guests who prefer may continue drinking it, if a red wine is to be served as well. For buffets and cold food, a dry white wine, a rosé or a fairly light red wine may be chosen.

**With first courses.** With oysters, dry Champagne, Chablis or a dry white wine such as Muscadet. With caviar, Champagne or vodka. With foie gras and pâtés, Champagne or a full-bodied white wine, such as White Burgundy, or a light dry white wine such as one from Alsace. With hors d'oeuvres, a dry white wine or a dry sherry. With individual melons, chilled tawny port. With clear soup, a dry sherry or dry Madeira, otherwise no wine. Do not serve wine with thick soup or grapefruit.

**Fish.** Dry Champagne, a dry white wine from France or Germany, or, with shellfish or salmon, a rosé is also a possible alternative. In choosing the wine for the fish, keep the very delicate wines, such as fine Moselles, for the simpler dishes; the richer fishes, accompanied by sauces, require something either full-bodied or else very dry and crisp.

**Egg dishes.** Do not serve a fine wine with eggs, but any medium-quality dry wine, red, white or rosé may be chosen, according to whether or not anything else is cooked with the eggs.

**Beef, lamb, pork. veal.** A red wine chosen in accordance with the quality of the meat – a very fine claret or Burgundy with prime cuts. With veal, a claret is usually more enjoyable unless the meat is accompanied by a rich stuffing or sauce, when a Burgundy or Rhône may be served. If liked, a white wine also may be served with a plain cut of veal. A rather robust type of wine, such as a Rhône wine, or a claret from St Emilion, is usually best with pork.

Hocks

**Offal.** A red wine of medium quality, but a medium-quality white wine may also be chosen with sweetbreads or brains unless these are cooked in a very rich sauce.

**Chicken, duck, turkey, goose.** Red or white wine or Champagne, according to preference. With a roast bird, especially one with a rich stuffing or sauce, a red wine is usually most enjoyable, but a dry crisp white wine may also be served – such as one from Alsace. With boiled chicken, a light red or dry white wine may be served.

**Game.** For fine quality game birds the fine red wines of Bordeaux and Burgundy are ideal or, if the birds are served cold, fine dry white wines or Champagne may also be served. For casseroles, a medium-quality red wine.

**Puddings.** Medium or sweet Champagne or one of the great sweet white Bordeaux or hocks – though these are rather wasted if there is a lot of chocolate or liqueur in the pudding. Keep them for the dessert.

**Dessert.** The great sweet white wines from France and Germany, port, dessert Madeira, sweet sherry or old claret.

**Cheese.** Usually the wine served with the main course of the meal can also accompany the cheese and red wine is the perfect partner for cheese. But a very strong cheese will kill the flavour of a delicate or very fine wine, so, when this type of wine is served have only a medium or creamy cheese afterwards. If white wine has been served throughout the meal, a red wine may be introduced at the cheese stage, although a full-bodied white wine or rosé will go quite well with all but the strongest cheeses.

## SERVING WINE

**White wines and vin rosé.** All these are served cold and the sweeter they are the colder they should be. 50–60 minutes in the refrigerator, or 45 minutes in an ice bucket should be ample even in warm weather and in the winter the cooling process will take less time – 30–40 minutes on a windowsill or outside step. But wines should not remain indefinitely in a refrigerator as they tend to go out of condition (a few hours is the most that is advisable), nor should they be put into a deep freeze. Ice should never be put into wine, but for anyone in a hurry, without enough time to chill a bottle, it is a help to put the wine glasses into the refrigerator, so that the first glass poured will be cool. It is always a good idea to draw the cork of a still white or rosé

MOSELLE WINES

wine for 5–10 minutes before serving the wine; the cork should be removed for a minute or two, then lightly replaced. This gets rid of any slight "bottle stink" that can spoil the initial impression of a fine wine. It is not usually necessary to decant white wines, but sometimes old white wines do throw a deposit and then the wine should be carefully poured off this into a chilled decanter or carafe before it is served.

**Red wines.** In general, these are served at the temperature of the room in which they are to be drunk, though very young Beaujolais is enjoyable when served at cellar temperature or lightly chilled. Ideally, a red wine should be stood upright for a few hours before the meal at which it is to be served, to enable any deposit to settle in the "punt" or base of the bottle and it is best if the wine can have 24 hours like this, especially if it is an old wine with a lot of deposit.

Although it is not always necessary to decant red wines, the purpose of this operation is twofold: it takes the wine off the deposit that may spoil the "star bright" appearance in the glass, and, by aeration, it brings out the wine's characteristics. The only problem is the length of time to "air" the wine and if possible, the advice of the wine merchant who supplied it should be sought. In general, a young wine, drunk slightly before its peak of maturity, benefits by being aired, and an older wine can come to life and develop amazingly by being decanted, though it may also fade and die if it is given too much aeration before being served.

**"Airing" wine.** In very general terms, red wine under five years old, of medium quality, will probably benefit by having its cork drawn – whether or not it is to be decanted – for one to three hours before it is due to be drunk. A wine of medium quality of 5–10 years old will be helped by having the cork drawn an hour before serving. A fine wine may benefit by being aired for a little longer than this, but when wines are 10–15 years old, advice should be sought as to the handling of them. Some – and this can depend on both the wine and on its vintage – may benefit by being opened for a considerable time in advance of being served; others should merely have their corks drawn just before they are to be drunk. But the decanter or carafe looks more elegant on a well-set table than a bottle, so it is well worth while taking some trouble about this, both for the sake of the appearance and the taste.

Decanting is quite a simple procedure. If you have no decanter, use an elegant carafe or even a glass jug, or, if neither are available, a scrupulously clean empty bottle will do. Remove the metal capsule covering the cork of the bottle to be decanted, wipe the top of the cork and the neck of the bottle with a clean cloth, being careful not to shake up the wine. Insert the corkscrew – choose one with a sharp, angled thread – and push it steadily through the cork. Then pull. The bottle should meanwhile be held with a cloth around it – bottles seldom do break, but they can crack and a nasty mess and a painful cut can result of holding a bottle just in the hand. If the cork is very hard to move, put the bottle gently on the floor and, while pulling with the hand holding the corkscrew, push down with the hand holding the bottle. (For opening sparkling wines, see below.)

**Wine deposit.** Wipe the inside of the bottle neck with the clean cloth, arrange a lit candle or unshaded electric light level with the top of the decanter and then pour the wine steadily into the decanter, keeping the light either underneath or behind the wine, so that it is possible to see the movement of any deposit into the neck of the bottle. When the deposit appears, stop pouring. Do not tilt the bottle up and down during decanting, or the deposit will be mixed into the wine. If you have not been able to stand a bottle up for a few hours, and it has thrown a deposit, the ideal thing it to take it carefully from the bin, without tilting it, and then put it in a decanting basket or cradle. The cork must then be drawn while the bottle lies in the basket and when the wine is poured, the ideal thing is to pour all of it out in one gradual tilting of the bottle, so that the up and down movement does not mix the deposit with the wine.

Any wine not drunk at a sitting should be re-corked or stoppered and put in a cool place. It will be perfectly fit to drink on the following day. The "heel" of the bottle, or dregs may be strained and put into a bottle kept for cooking wine – this will be usable for a couple of weeks if kept cool.

**Broken Cork.** If, while a bottle is being opened, the cork should break and prove impossible to withdraw, one may either push the remainder of the cork right into the bottle and then, holding it back with a fine skewer, pour the wine past it, or, if it crumbles, the wine may be filtered through either filter paper or a perfectly clean piece of cloth (one that has been washed in detergent or in contact with scent or kept in a drawer with cleaning materials or first-aid will not do, as it will affect the wine, but an old linen handkerchief is suitable). The presence of any small bits of cork in the wine does not make the wine "corked". If a wine smells

fresh and sweet there will be no risk of it being either corked or otherwise unfit to enjoy – the disagreeable smells indicating this are usually apparent to the discerning nose. But it is correct to pour a little of each bottle into a clean glass and for the host or hostess to try first before serving guests, just in case there should be anything wrong. This applies also to white wines.

**Opening Champagne and sparkling wines.** The bottle – previously chilled – is wrapped in a napkin, the wire is untwisted and lifted off the cork, which should immediately be held down with the thumb, in case it suddenly flies up. Never point a bottle of sparkling wine at your own face or that of anyone else, and direct it away from anything breakable, just in case of accidents. Once the wire is off, the bottle should be gently turned, while the cork is firmly held in one hand, and released gently. If the cork is very stiff, use the thumbs to ease it upwards or a pair of "nippers" which perform the same task. Should the cork actually break off before being extracted, cut off the projecting piece and then, holding the bottle carefully in a napkin, use an ordinary corkscrew to pull out the remainder, remembering that there will be the force of the wine behind it.

**Vintage port.** This is rather a special case and with both vintage port and old red table wines, the advice of a wine merchant should be sought. In general, port is handled like other wines that have thrown a heavy deposit, but as it may have spent a long time in bottle and the cork may disintegrate when the corkscrew is inserted, it is then necessary either to filter the wine – through either filter paper or a silver wine funnel with a fine mesh and a curved tip to the funnel (so that the wine runs sideways down the decanter and does not splash with superfluous aeration, straight into the middle), or else to remove the neck of the bottle. This may be done with the special bottle tongs, heated and then applied to the neck, or else, with the bottle held firmly in one hand, and covered with a cloth, and with a corkscrew inserted to the bottom of the cork, an upwards glancing blow is delivered with the back of a heavy kitchen knife to the ledge of the bottle neck, on either side. The neck of the bottle may then be broken off cleanly by merely removing the corkscrew, the edge is wiped and the wine decanted.

Port, whether vintage or tawny, is served to the host, who passes the decanter to his left, though traditionally he is allowed a "backhander", which means that he may help the guest of honour sitting at his right hand. If the women have remained at the table for the service of the port, the men usually help their women lefthand neighbours; otherwise, each person pours himself what is required and then passes the decanter to the left. It is courteous not to allow the decanter to remain in front of one for very long before sending it on.

**All table wines are served** by having the host first taste a small quantity of the wine to see if it is in prime condition. (In a household with staff, the butler should do this and of course if the host is decanting the wines, he will taste them in advance and not at the table.) In a restaurant, the bottle of wine should be presented to the host so that he can check that it is the one he ordered before the cork is drawn. If someone is to pour the wine, instead of circulating it and allowing people to help themselves, then this is done over the right shoulder of each person. The glasses are filled only two-thirds up, so that the wine can be swirled around in the glass and the lovely bouquet appreciated. If either the bottle or decanter is given a small turn to the right (clockwise) as it is lifted away from the glass, there is less likelihood of any drips falling on the table. A cloth wrapped around the bottle serves to catch any wine that may run down or, as with white wines that may have been in an ice-bucket, the drops of water.

**Care of wineglasses and decanters.** Glasses in frequent use are best stored upright, not upside down, as they can develop a "musty" smell if they are then put on the table without being washed first. Ideally, they should not be washed in anything except very hot water, and dried only with linen cloths kept specially for the purpose and which themselves are only boiled in plain water. If they do become stained, then they must be very thoroughly rinsed before being used to dry wine glasses. The trace of detergent can linger and be apparent in the taste for the wine drinker. The same applies to glasses – if for any reason they are washed in soap or detergent, they must be throughly rinsed before being dried and put away. When drying very fine thin glasses, do not put fingers into the bowl of the glass, as this tends to run the risk of breaking a piece out of it; stuff the drying cloth into the bowl of the glass and, without putting the fingers inside, turn the cloth round gently in the glass until it is dry and shining. Polish the outside afterwards.

Decanters, too, should not, ideally, be cleaned with soap or detergent, but if they are, then they must be very thoroughly rinsed, drained and dried. If a decanter has become stained, a little soda or "Milton" may be left with water to lift the stain for a few hours or overnight, If the narrow neck of a decanter presents problems about drying it, insert a skewer or neck of a straight dishmop, covered in the drying cloth, or else put the decanter upside down in a plate rack near a gentle source of heat for an hour or so. This may sound like a lot of trouble, but it is easier to clean a decanter immediately after use than to cope with one that has acquired an interior stain and smells stale with a drain of water inside it immediately before guests are due to arrive.

**HOW MUCH TO ALLOW.** People asked "for drinks" will tend to take more than if they are having a drink before a meal to which they have also been invited. But in both instances they will drink more in the evening than at midday. With cocktails or sherry offered in the half hour before a meal, few people take more than two or three helpings unless the glasses are very small.

**At a cocktail party** which will last about two hours, allow five to six drinks apiece. Some people will only have two or three, leaving the balance for the confirmed hard drinkers. (But as your wine merchant will usually be able to supply all drinks on a sale or return basis, there is no need to worry about running out of supplies.)

**At a wedding,** half a bottle of Champagne is a fair allowance, if Champagne is served throughout. It is perfectly acceptable, however, for an ordinary bar selection of drinks to be offered, and for only the toast to the bride and groom to be drunk in Champagne or sparkling wine opened for the occasion.

**At an evening Champagne party,** allow two-thirds of a bottle a head, simply because this kind of hospitality tends to last longer.

**When people are standing up at a party** they always tend to drink more than when they are sitting down. At a buffet meal, when the food will probably go on being served for longer than for an ordinary meal, allow for them drinking more than if you arranged for them to sit down at tables. If you serve cocktails and wine on such occasions, allow two to three of the short drinks each, and half to two-thirds of a bottle of wine each, slightly more if champagne or sparkling wine only is served (a bottle a head is a safe allowance).

**With a meal,** people usually drink about three glasses of wine, excluding apéritifs and port, brandy or liqueurs. If there is more than one wine, the tendency is for less of the first wine to be drunk. For example, if three wines accompany the meal, allow a glass apiece of the first wine, and two to three apiece of the second and third. With two wines served, allow one and a half glasses of the first one, and two of the second. But for a special celebration, for a meal of men alone, or when people seriously interested in food and drink are going to spend a long time at table, allow up to a bottle a head, counting all the table wines together.

**Contents of bottles.** (See also the section on Glasses for correct sizes.) Table wines – eight good glasses per bottle, using large glasses two-thirds full.

**Sherry, port, Madeira** – ten to twelve glasses to the bottle (if you get more, your glasses are on the small side, as they, too, should only be two-thirds full).

**Champagne and sparkling wines** – six to eight glasses, slightly more if the shallow saucer type of glass is used.

**Whisky, brandy and gin** – twenty-four bar measures per bottle, but obviously this will vary if people like their drinks very strong or very long.

**Vermouth** – ten to twelve helpings per bottle when drunk neat, or thirty-two measures when used for cocktails. As vermouth deteriorates after it has been opened three to four weeks or sooner in a warm place, buy half-bottles unless you are having a party or drink regularly.

**Liqueurs** – about thirty-two helpings per bottle. A miniature provides one generous glass or two small ones.

**Squash bottles** (full size) – about eighteen ordinary medium to long drinks.

Bottles of tonic, soda and the various sparkling squashes usually serve one rather long or two fairly short drinks, but small "splits" of tonic and soda are also available if you want to serve individual portions.

**GLASSES.** The ideal and all-purpose wine glass is plain and uncoloured, on a stem, and with its sides curving slightly together at the rim. It may look rather like a tulip, or an onion with its top cut off. The cost of such a glass can be a few shillings, or, if it is of fine thin crystal, a pound or more, but the shape, plainness and absence of colour are the basic essentials. This type of glass may be used for all table wines, sparkling wines and in a slightly smaller size, for sherry, port and Madeira and brandy. But very small glasses are not only mean, they prevent the drinker from enjoying the smell of the wine or a spirit if they have to be filled up to the brim (see also section on service of wine).

The only thing that is correctly drunk out of tiny glasses is schnapps or a similar digestive drink, that is served ice-cold and is intended, like vodka, to be downed at a single draught.

**Cut crystal** can look very elegant on the table, but because of the thickness of the glass, it is not suitable for the service of the very finest wines, though crystal glasses may often have cut stems and feet. Crystal may be used for mixed drinks, cocktails and water goblets, as the light reflected from fine crystal gives life to a table.

**Coloured glasses** prevent the enjoyment of the colour of the wine, although in the last century it was fashionable to have white wine glasses slightly tinted to prevent the drinkers being offended by the sight of any "flyers" in the wine – modern methods of vinification have done away with this.

Champagne and sparkling wines should ideally be served in a glass either like an isosceles triangle standing on its tip, a tulip glass or a very deep saucer. A very shallow Champagne saucer lets the wine go flat quickly.

**Brandy, both Armagnac and Cognac,** and the various fruit brandies such as kirsch, should be served in tulip or small balloon glasses. The glass should never be so large that it cannot be cupped comfortably in one hand – the enormous brandy balloons are both ostentatious and silly, because the fragrance of the spirit, when it is swirled around in the glass, is too far away from the nose.

**For sherry,** the copita type glass, like an elongated tulip on a short stem, is traditional in Spain, and for port a rather stumpy wine glass is also traditional, but it is much better to use the full sized ordinary wine glass than either the thistle-shaped glass or the very small bulbous port glass that has to be filled to the brim.

The different wine regions usually have glasses varying in shape which have evolved over the years, but it is not necessary for the ordinary household to have more than the single basic wine glass, the "Paris" goblet (the onion shaped type) found in any chain store or pub., or the tulip. When buying a glass for all-purpose use, choose the 6 oz. or 8 oz. Paris rather than the 4 oz., which is not really big enough for table wines.

If you do have more than one type of glass, the following are both traditional and suitable:

**Champagne** – elongated flûte, like an isosceles triangle standing on its tip, or the deep saucer with hollow stem down to the foot.

Alsatian wines and Moselle glasses usually have long green stems. Hock glasses usually have brown stems, though green stems are found as well.

In the neighbourhood of Trier, rather deep, saucer-shaped glasses with a particular pattern of cutting are traditional for fine wines.

**For Burgundy,** a slightly larger glass to that used for claret is often preferred but the very large Burgundy glasses are rather ostentatious.

**For sherry,** the copita glass like an elongated tulip glass on a very short stem is traditional and this is also sometimes referred to as a dock glass, as it may be used for tasting dock samples.

**Beer and cider** are served in large glasses, either big goblets or tumblers, or in tankards, and lager is traditional in an elongated tall tumbler.

## SETTING THE TABLE

**PLACE SETTINGS.** There are many variations in the way in which even a formal table is set, but the most important consideration to remember is that the cutlery is so placed that it may be used in the order in which it is required. In the following instructions standard British practice is given, but travellers should remember that every country has its own ways.

The curved side of spoons and forks rests on the cloth or table and the knives have their sharp edge pointing towards the left. As cutlery should be put where it is easy to handle, a meal of soup, meat and vegetables and pudding has the soup spoon set on the right of the place, the knife on the left of the spoon on the same side and the fork opposite on the left of the setting. A pudding spoon and fork may either be put on the inside of the knife and fork with the spoon on the right (because it will be picked up with the right hand) or above the place setting, the spoon uppermost and pointing to the left, the fork underneath pointing to the right.

If an extra knife or fork is required for a first course (such as pâté or oysters) this goes on the outside of the setting. When fish is served, the knife and fork or, traditionally, the two forks (now seldom used except by those who have old silver) are set in the order in which they will be used.

The bread knife may either be on the right of the plate, nearest to it and inside the other cutlery, or above the plate, underneath the spoon and fork (if this is placed there), with the sharp edge of the knife pointing downwards and the point to the left; or, when a bread plate is set, the bread knife may even be placed on this, either diagonally or horizontally across it.

**Formal meals.** At a formal meal, such small cutlery as grapefruit spoons, spoons and forks for seafood cocktails or ice cream spoons are usually laid on the plate in which the individual serving is brought to the table. When shellfish are served, crackers and picks may either be placed at the outside of the table setting with the other cutlery, or laid at the top of the setting, or if a service plate (see below) is included, they may be put on this.

Dessert knives and forks at a formal meal are only laid immediately before the dessert is served, or they may be put side by side on the dessert plate to facilitate the service, so that the plate, cutlery and finger bowl (see below) may all be handed to each person at once.

At very formal meals, it is not strictly correct to set a full sized spoon without its matching fork, or a fork without a knife (except of course for the soup spoon and bread knife), whether or not both pieces of cutlery are going to be used for eating. When the course is finished, the cutlery concerned with it should be cleared away, whether it has been used or not.

**Salad.** This is usually eaten with a fork alone and, rather depending on the size of the table, this may either be laid with the other forks (as salad is not served at very formal meals there is no need to worry about pairing off the cutlery), or the salad fork may be put on or at the side of the separate salad plate but if a separate salad is not served, there is no need to provide a separate fork.

**Bread plates.** Nowadays these vary considerably in size and those who do have small dining tables should take care not to buy large bread plates but rather those of the size that once would have been called a bread and butter plate. Salad plates and any small flat dishes are also perfectly suitable as side plates, but if people are going to use their side plates on which to eat fruit at the end of the meal, then very small ones should not be used.

A rather old-fashioned tradition (which it is not necessary to observe rigidly) dictates that side plates are not set at a very formal meal because bread is not served at dinner, and when it is offered at luncheon, it is put on the cloth, as was the custom in days when a large piece of damask was the only accepted suitable table covering for a formal meal. If (again in accordance with very old tradition) a course served involves the service of bread and butter, then plates are laid for this at the outside and removed when the course is finished. Nowadays, of course, these customs are seldom observed in any but the most stately homes, though it is useful to know of them, as sometimes the traditions are still kept up at formal public luncheons and dinners.

Butter is not served when bread is put on the cloth and nor is a bread knife set then because the bread is broken with the fingers. When a roll is served on the side plate, it is correct to break this with the fingers and then, if butter is taken, to spread this on to separate bite-sized portions. The butter is taken from the butter dish either with the butter knife or fork put there for the purpose, or with the individual bread knife, and put on the side of the side plate.

**Service and side plates.** In the United Kingdom the side plate is set level with place setting, on the left of it, but the American custom is to put the side plate slightly above the setting on the left, level with the top of the forks. This has the practical advantage of giving people more elbow room around a crowded table. The service plate, laid in each place at the beginning of a meal, is more usual in the United States and on the continent than in Britain. But large plates of this kind can look very decorative at the beginning of the meal, and act as "mats" on which other plates can be set until the plate underneath is used for dessert. The only thing to remember is that dishes set on top of service plates should neither wobble nor make a clatter, and therefore a small mat is often set on these and removed before the service of dessert.

**Glasses.** These are set to the top right hand corner of the place setting. If more than one glass is put out, the one on the right hand side is that to be used first. The water goblet, included in formal settings, is usually put behind the wine glasses. If the glasses are set in a line, they are arranged like the cutlery, so that the appropriate glass comes in the order in which the wine will be served, usually from right to left. Glasses for port and dessert wines are usually not put on the table until the decanters for these wines are put on and circulated at the end of a meal. As a course is finished and cleared, the glasses for the wine accompanying that course may be cleared as well if the table seemed cluttered, but usually they remain on the table until the service of dessert, when everything is removed except the cutlery and equipment required (see under Setting and Serving p. 287).

**Handing food and tableware.** By custom, when plates, glasses and cutlery have to be handed during the meal, those used by the right hand are set over the right

shoulder and those for the left hand over the left shoulder. Dishes of food offered so that guests may help themselves are offered at the left of the diner, though if someone happens to be left-handed, they may find it easier to ask to be served from the right. When plates are taken away from guests they are removed from the left of the diner. Unless a very large dish or platter is being handed, formal service means that the person offering the food holds it in the left hand only, and either offers the servers to the diner or actually serves the food with the right hand.

**CARVING.** It is always difficult to learn such a practical subject from printed text and the best advice is to watch an expert carver in action but the following general recommendations may be of use.

**Fish in general.** If separate pieces of fish are served on a large platter, arrange them so that there is space between the portions and do not mask them totally with sauce, so as to facilitate people helping themselves. Serve with a table spoon and large fork or two spoons if fish servers are not available.

In a good restaurant the waiter should ask anyone ordering fish whether they want it served on the bone or whether it should be taken off, in which case the fish will be filleted and put on a clean plate for the diner.

**Casseroles and stews.** If these are to be handed separately to each guest, it is a good idea either to have them in a holder, such as is provided with many serving dishes, or to surround the dish with a napkin pinned in place. This catches any drips of gravy or sauce and also protects the hands of anyone lifting it.

**Spaghetti and pasta in general.** Serve this from a single dish – there are special serving tongs but it is quite usual to use a table spoon and fork.

**Salmon.** If this is served whole, it must be carved right across the fish in whole steaks. A very sharp knife is necessary. The portions are put on to the plates either with fresh servers or with a table spoon and fork. It is perfectly correct, however, to have salmon cooked and served in individual steaks or portions. If this is to be filleted at the table, the head, tail and fins are removed, together with the line of small bones between the fins and the fillets.

**Turbot.** If this is to be divided at table, the tail should face the carver, pale side of the fish uppermost. Then a dividing line is made from eleven o'clock near the head through diagonally to twelve, and straight down to the tail. The right hand side is then divided, horizontally, into portions. Then the left side is divided horizontally, as the fish is thicker on this side.

**Meat and poultry in general.** A sharp knife is essential for good carving and for anything which has to be sliced in the direction of the carver it is advisable to have a fork with a guard in case the knife or the joint should slip. The use of a carving board or dish with prongs to hold the meat is an added convenience. It is correct always to ask people the type of meat that they prefer and also to offer them any of the gravy off the dish, whether or not gravy and sauce is to be handed separately.

Although the Victorian tradition established that the host would carve for each person around the table, it usually saves time if the carver does all the carving at once and then serves the different portions with a spoon and fork, as otherwise all but the biggest joint tends to get cold. A plate warmer, hot plate and the old fashioned dish cover are helpful adjuncts to the satisfactory serving of a large joint or bird. It is also worth bearing in mind that a joint should never be carved when straight from the oven. If it is allowed to "rest", being kept warm, for about five minutes, the flavour seems to concentrate and it will certainly be easier to carve.

**Sirloin of beef.** When on the bone, the thick part of the joint and the bone should be towards the carver. The meat should then be cut parallel to the bone, across the undercut or fillet as required and then lengthwise at right angles to the bone.

**Ribs of beef.** Carve as for sirloin with the undercut or fillet.

**Saddle of lamb or mutton.** This is carved like sirloin of beef, with each thin slice accompanied by a piece of undercut or chump cut moderately thick.

**Leg of lamb.** The bone is towards the carver and may be held with a napkin. Meat is first sliced on a slant or as a wedge, from ten o'clock across the joint, then slantwise onwards up to twelve o'clock. Then the whole of the thick part furthest from the carver, can be sliced and finally the inside of the leg may be carved. The slices from the thick part should be served accompanied with slices from the inside of the leg.

**Shoulder of lamb.** This is perhaps the most awkward joint to carve and anyone doubtful about it should hold the bone with a napkin instead of a fork. Put the bone towards the carver as when carving a leg and start carving in the same way. Then continue from one o'clock to two o'clock from the centre of the meat, and work downwards and also carve some pieces from underneath. The meat sliced from twelve o'clock to three downwards are from the prime cuts and a piece of each, perhaps with one from the blade itself should be served with each slice.

**Crown of lamb.** This is virtually a number of cutlets still joined together, bent in a circle and tied so that the bones stand up like a crown. The butcher will do this for you. The cutlets can be quickly divided with an ordinary carving knife and fork and any stuffing or vegetables placed in the centre of the crown are served with a spoon. Because, as with all cutlets, people may wish to eat the sweet bits of meat along the bone, the ends of the bone are often decorated with small paper cutlet frills, to keep the fingers clean.

**Loin of pork.** The bone must be "chined" or sawn through, and the crackling scored before the joint is cooked so that the meat may be carved intact in slices. Ask the butcher to do this if you are in any doubt.

**Veal.** Carve a knuckle of veal like a shoulder of lamb and a fillet of veal like a round of beef. Loin of veal is served either in chops or carved along its length.

**Ham and gammon.** A whole ham is carved like a leg of lamb and people usually like very thin slices. A gammon joint should be carved straight down whenever possible and a boned ham likewise.

**Poultry.** Chicken, pheasant, guinea-fowl: with the breast uppermost, the first stage of carving involves the removal of a leg which is divided into two portions if the bird is a big one. The wing is then removed at the joint, the breast sliced downwards and the wishbone cut off. With a very small bird carving may not be necessary if the bird can be split in two. Occasionally, a poulterer will truss a bird so that it is easier to sever a wing first. The sensible course is to do whatever is convenient.

**Turkey and goose.** Start carving by cutting slices from the top and bottom of one drumstick (leg), then the whole side of the breast is sliced, whether or not the drumstick is detached. A portion of stuffing should accompany each helping.

**Duck.** This can be an awkward bird to carve and the inexperienced are warned that it gives the impression of having more meat on it than may actually be there. Start by removing the wishbone, then slice down each side of the breast and remove a leg and part of the breast in whole portions. The leg and breast may then be divided up.

**Partridge, grouse, pigeons and other small birds.** These are usually served whole, but very large ones may be split in two. They are very often served sitting on a piece of bread fried in their own dripping.

If there is any doubt about how to carve or divide game, ask the advice of the poulterer or game merchant who supplied it.

**SERVICE.** The kind of service depends entirely on the domestic arrangements of the householders. In general, in a household with staff, the custom is for food to be either carved or divided into individual portions before it is brought into the dining room and then to be offered to each person at the table. This may be done (and saves time if host or hostess is not an adroit carver) even if people are going to hand dishes to each other. For family meals, the host and hostess do the serving, though a member of the family may act as "maid" by handing round plates and side dishes. It is important that food should not be allowed to get cold during the meal if second helpings are to be offered. Strictly, one helping only is offered at a very formal meal, but in a household where the cook is good, provision for second and even third helpings should always be made for family meals and informal occasions. At fairly formal dinners of three courses, however, it is not inhospitable to assume that people will only want one helping of the first course. When a dish is to be offered a second time, the ideal – with something like a pudding or attractively garnished piece of food – is to have a completely new one or at least have the remains of the first helping rearranged on another plate before being offered again.

Some people are under the impression that it is more elegant to offer all first courses and sweets in individual portions, but this is not so. Large portions of the best type of British food can be both appealing and often easier to prepare. Naturally, if large numbers of people have to help themselves from a single dish, item of serving is cut down by giving them individual portions.

**Sauces, gravies and cream.** Although in a household with several staff these are offered individually, they may also be set on the table for people to help themselves. With hot sauces it is often more convenient to have two or more sauce or gravy boats in use in relays, one always being kept hot. Provide a ladle or spoon or not, according to the consistency of the sauce – this also applies to mint sauce, redcurrant jelly, Cumberland sauce, and savoury and sweet butters.

**Mustard.** If this is served, it is thoughtful to offer French as well as English, and French mustard is always served from the jar in which it is bought.

**Coffee after meals.** Whether this is served at the table or away from it depends rather on the time available that people have to spare. At a banquet, of course, the coffee is served on the table, but in a private house after dinner it is usual to make a break at the end of the meal. This provides an opportunity for people to go and wash if they wish. Nowadays it is not invariable for the women to leave the dining room before the men, but if they do, the general practice is for coffee to be served to them in the drawing room with a second relay, freshly made, brought in when the men join them later – a period of time which may be five or ten minutes or half an hour.

Brandy and liqueurs may accompany the service of coffee on these fairly formal occasions, and if port is to be served, with the decanter circulating among the men left at the table, it is thoughtful to have another one left in the drawing room for the benefit of the women. But nowadays, especially among young people, the continental practice of everyone leaving the table together is usual.

After-dinner coffee cups are small and after-dinner coffee should be strong. Offer the choice of hot milk or cream as well as sugar, although it is not necessary to have special "coffee sugar". Coffee spoons must be small in proportion to the size of the cups.

Breakfast or mid-morning coffee is usually served accompanied by hot milk, offered separately, in case some people prefer it black. Medium or large sized cups are then used.

**Tea.** Tea is served in medium or large sized cups, according to the occasion and individual preferences. Some people prefer one really outsize cup to several small ones. Conventionally, an early morning cup and cups for afternoon tea are of medium size and breakfast cups slightly larger.

There are endless discussions about when the milk should be put in the teacup. Many people find that to put it in first gives a completely different taste from when it is added afterwards. At fairly formal drawing-room tea, the most considerate thing is to ask guests how they like it, if at all. China tea should be served from a china pot and many people like a slice of lemon put into the cup as well. Some people like lemon with Indian tea and many Americans prefer cream with it instead of cold milk.

Whether or not a slop basin is used is likewise a matter of personal preference and convenience. If a strainer is used when pouring tea, there should be no slop to empty away.

Sugar tongs are an obvious convenience when a hostess is serving tea to several people and they ask her to put in the sugar but there is currently a reaction away from the excessive refinement of former times when people would go to any lengths to avoid touching food with their fingers and many nowadays prefer to offer a sugar basin to people who can help themselves with their fingers. It is, however, more convenient as well as slightly more correct to have lump sugar, rather than loose sugar served with a spoon.

## TABLEWARE

Plate, china, everyday glassware and cutlery should be chosen with especial care, as unless several sets of table equipment can be afforded, it is important to choose items of this kind that will be suitable to both everyday and special occasions, and also that those which are breakable can be duplicated or replaced at need. Basic dishes should therefore be simple and many of the traditional designs of china go well with either very modern or old style tableware. White will probably always be the favourite background colour and pale cream is almost as effective. It is worth remembering, though, that the white of many British china manufacturers is not the same as the white of certain continental factories, and therefore if dishes are to be matched up the same sort of ground colour should be maintained. In choosing other colours, it should be considered whether the china is to be used largely under artificial light or in daylight and on what sort of table; last of all, brilliant colour or elaborate pattern on a small table can give an impression of restlessness and crowding. So when choosing a whole service, do not decide by merely looking at a single place setting, but have at least part of the service laid out on a table in the shop.

Pottery and informal china is extremely suitable for everyday use and for simple dishes. Casseroles, serving dishes, salad plates and soup bowls may be extras in the china cupboard and therefore should be selected so that they will go with other plates and dishes. It is frequently possible to mix different kinds of both fine china and pottery, providing that the different types have something in common, such as a basic shape or pattern, or a recurrent colour. But usually quality has to be teamed with quality and very fine china does not look well side by side with pottery that is ideal for, say, a spaghetti supper. If people are in doubt as to how their tableware will team up or if they are selecting a set of dishes for a wedding present, it is always safest to choose white, whether in porcelain, bone china, pottery or glass.

There are many excellent examples of tableware in plastic (such as melamine) at the present time, and the simple lines and clear colours make it perfectly correct for informal settings, especially from the practical point of view with large and young families. But it should be remembered that in general plastic will not stand up to great heat, and therefore these plates should not be put in the oven or on plate warmers.

Nowadays it is usual at all except the most formal meals to bring to the table dishes in which the food has been cooked. Glass, decorated porcelain and pottery, earthenware, copper, stainless steel and even the formerly humble enamelware can all be used in this way. For really formal occasions, and should silver serving dishes or those matching the dinner service not be available, plain white porcelain, copper, stainless steel or plain or transparent oven glass are perfectly acceptable. Should a serving dish not match the rest of the tableware, a degree of uniformity of appearance can be achieved by fastening a folded table napkin around it and securing this with pins or clips. Either white or (for informal occasions) brilliantly coloured napkins may be used.

**Cutlery.** This also must be chosen for practicality as well as appearance. Silver and plate are lifetime investments, but much stainless steel is now excellently designed and ideal for hard wear. It is not necessary to have all the cutlery around the table matching throughout the meal, although uniformity as regards basic knives, forks and spoons is desirable. When choosing cutlery with handles other than silver, plate, or stainless steel, thought should be given to how it is to be washed up; if a washing-up machine is used, some special care may need to be taken with certain handles.

A point to remember is that although antique silver and good plate looks well with either traditional china or the most severe of contemporary designs, any dinner service on which there is gold or silver on the china may not match up with the cutlery; for example, the "silver" of some stainless steel services is quite a different colour from that of sterling silver or silver plate or the silver used in certain traditional patterns of china. Another point to bear in mind when shopping for cutlery, is that antique or traditionally patterned knives and forks are always inclined to be bigger than those designed for today, so care should be observed in their selection if only a small table is in use. The pattern of cutlery, whether this is plain or elaborate, should also be selected so that it partners the china. Try and see both cutlery and tableware as part of the same setting before deciding on any major purchase.

**Other tableware.** (For glasses and glassware to do with the service of wine, see pp. 299–300).

Glasses give life to a table and glassware, whether plain, coloured, engraved or cut, is extremely useful for both formal and informal occasions. Glass sets of salt and pepper (ideally a pair for each place setting), butter dishes, sugar bowls and other small utensils are correct on even the most formal table should silverware not be available. (Plain porcelain, stainless steel and even wood can look highly decorative on all but the most elaborately set formal table, but "quaint" china and pottery are best kept for family and informal meals. If salads are to be mixed at table or by individuals to suit their own taste, then simply designed oil and vinegar or special salad sets are better than those that may be described as "peasanty".)

**Bread, butter and cheese.** For fairly formal meals a roll is either put on the side plate or in the napkin. Otherwise, people may help themselves or be helped from a bread basket or bread board.

Butter may either be put on a dish, a board or a platter. Large slabs of butter look well for all but the most formal meals and it is now possible to get butter moulds and hands which improve the appearance even more. For formal occasions, when individual butter dishes accompany place settings or are shared between dinner partners, the butter may either be in a single small slab, or in pats, slices, balls or curls, though unless these can be made expertly and kept cold until they are required, it is better just to put out a single small piece.

When cheese is offered, it should be arranged on a board with a sharp knife. If several cheeses of very different flavours and consistencies are served, it is helpful to have a different knife for each. A whole cheese, such as a whole Stilton, is wrapped in a napkin and presented on its own plate or slab. Runny cheeses, such as Brie, may be put on a little mat or piece of straw – such as that used for wrapping around wine bottles. If you use a cloth mat, be careful that the knife does not damage it. The conventional cheese knife is one with a sharp blade and curving tip with which the cheese may be picked up. For Stilton, a scoop is traditional, although many authorities advocate the horizontal slicing of this cheese. With Dutch cheese, a flat knife with a cutting edge set in the centre of a flat surface is used for paring off slivers. But an ordinary knife may be used for serving all cheeses, although a spoon and fork is often a convenience with those that are either very creamy or crumbly.

**Cloths, napkins and mats.** There is no rigid rule about the use of any of these today and an endless variety is available. Their choice and use is dictated by personal taste and practicality.

A table cloth should be chosen in relation to the shape and size of the table. A square one will, if about the same size, go on a round table and a round cloth on a square table, but with oval or elongated tables and very narrow tables, care must be taken, as the cloth may either overhang the edge of the table too much or not enough. It is probably most generally convenient if the overhang of the cloth reaches just to the seat of the dining chairs, or to the laps of the diners.

For fairly informal meals, a square or a rectangular cloth can be laid at an angle with its corners hanging down the sides of the table, but for a formal meal it usually looks best to have the cloth laid in line with the lines of the table, especially if there is a design on the cloth that needs to be shown off by its being laid in a regular way. With very small or narrow tables, a cloth reaching only just to the edge of the table without an overhang can be a convenience, and sideboard runners and even buffet cloths may even be used on the table for this purpose.

When using dinner cloths on a polished table, it is better to have an overall protective underlay of some kind rather than to set mats under the cloth. With very fine transparent cloths, the use of a coloured cloth underneath can be very attractive.

Linen will always remain the supreme table cloth material and white probably the most all-purpose colour. Linen damask is a superior background for fine tableware and silver. The use of colour, however, in both linen, organdie, appliqué, and so on is now perfectly correct on all occasions, but it is worth bearing in mind that a cloth with a lot of embroidery on it may make glasses and even plates unsteady. Formal dinner cloths often have a central runner or cloth laid on top of them; this can enhance the appearance of the table and protect the large cloth from any drips from candles or spills from sauces, etc., which may be put in the middle. The same applies to table mats set on top of a cloth. The use of contrasting colour can be very effective but of course the mat should not obscure the general appearance of a cloth that is beautiful in itself. The use of plain mats on a patterned cloth is a good idea when it is desirable to avoid patterned china being laid on a patterned cloth, and checked or striped mats on a plain cloth draw the different place settings closely together and make a table avoid seeming too large. Rayon damask, linen and cotton mixtures, and seersucker are nowadays of very high quality and often of outstanding design and can be used on all but the most formal of occasions. For nursery use, family breakfasts and buffet parties likely to be on the riotous side there are also excellent plastic cloths. Formerly, cloths were divided by categories into those for breakfast, luncheon, tea, dinner and supper, but nowadays few households would make such distinctions. Cloths for informal occasions may virtually be of any kind of material, colour or design.

**Napkins.** Napkins to match the cloth or the place settings are attractive, but not essential. A vivid contrast can look highly decorative, but for maximum effectiveness it is as well to have cloth and napkins of the same material – linen, cotton, damask and so on – and in the same weight as the cloth. Checked, striped, polka-dot or any patterned napkins can look fresh and gay with a plain cloth or vice versa but if a pattern of an overall nature is rather large or vivid then a plain napkin of the key colour of the cloth is probably best, and vice versa. Stripes or dots with checks and a mixture of patterns can merely look hectic.

Small napkins of a kind traditionally associated with afternoon tea at the table and also for bridge parties, are now only really useful for snack meals and a napkin that is to be of any practical use should be at least 10 inches by 8 inches minimum. An oblong napkin may, of course, do double duty as a place setting mat. Traditionally, dinner napkins are larger than luncheon napkins, but nowadays this depends entirely on the size of the table and tableware and the type of cloth used. If the napkins are to be folded so as to take little room, a smaller size is obviously more sensible. Large Victorian napkins, which could be folded into a variety of shapes when starched and ironed flat, are not practical for many contemporary tables, although a folded or pleated napkin can look decorative, as can napkins into which a single flower has been tucked or which are set on the table in rings or clips. If napkins are to be used by the family for more than one meal, then the use of napkin rings is practical, although the continental custom of putting the napkin in a small cloth bag – to match napkin and cloth – is probably more hygienic.

**Paper Napkins.** Nowadays the quality of these is much improved and the designs of many are so good that it is possible to make use of them for all but the most formal of meals. Plain, brilliantly coloured paper napkins can be most effective on a table and if a course is served which is going to be eaten with the fingers (such as asparagus and certain shellfish), after which the napkins will be changed, then it is extremely practical to provide a paper napkin which can be thrown away, after the immediate cleaning of the fingers, rather than risk staining fine damask or linen.

**Place Mats.** In the past it was traditional for mats only to be used at luncheon. They generally were set in twos or threes – one for the large plate, one for the glass and sometimes even one for the side plate, and were usually round or square. Nowadays mats of all kinds may be used for virtually any social occasion. Separate mats for separate plates and glasses, especially if the mats are light in texture and the table large are perfectly practical, but one large place setting mat, either oblong, oval or round is often more convenient, especially on small tables.

It is important when choosing and setting mats to consider the shape and proportions of the table. Round mats look well on round, oval, square and rectangular tables (unless rectangular plates are used, which may overlap the mats awkwardly) and oval mats are equally all-purpose and create an illusion of space on the table. Square and rectangular mats never look quite right on a round or oval table of small size. With a completely square table, oblong and rectangular mats minimise the squareness of the table surface. With a long narrow table, on which place setting mats take up a lot of room and possibly even meet across the middle, the impression of more space and better proportions is given if either the settings are laid only on one side of the table or if they are not laid directly opposite each other. In general, with tables of this kind, it is best to choose long and narrow mats and, if these are plain, to set them on a patterned cloth with the pattern running across the table to give the effect of breadth.

With a large table, the use of a central runner or central mat can be highly effective and provide a focal point for a vase of flowers, candles and small articles of tableware such as salts and peppers. Sometimes a complete contrast for this mat or runner can be striking, such as the use of a gold or silver centre for some special party or a flower patterned or brilliantly embroidered centrepiece on a table that may otherwise seem a little sombre. A centrepiece of this kind may be created with the use of several small mats or even napkins, overlapping or side by side, if one large mat or runner is not available.

The most striking effects will be obtained by the use of mats that contrast with the surface of the table – light coloured mats on dark wood or vice versa. Very pale mats can also look beautiful on a light coloured table or dark mats on dark wood but in general two soft colours do not look well together. For all but the most formal dinner parties it is also possible to use different colours or even different types of mat if more than one is to be used for each place setting. But as with the combination of different cloths and napkins, it is better to choose mats of the same sort of material. With mats laid on a cloth, the suggestions as regards the effectiveness of contrast against the background made in relation to tables (see above) should also be borne in mind. Otherwise, the only thing to remember is that the place setting mat is a background or frame for the tableware and cutlery and when choosing mats the size of all the equipment to go on them should be remembered.

**Monograms.** Either an initial or a monogram can look very handsome worked on linen or in cut-out embroidery or appliqué. With a napkin, the placing of a monogram or initial should be so planned that it shows when the napkin is folded, the most convenient way being for the monogram to be at an angle across one corner. With place mats large enough to be monogrammed in one corner, the monogram may either be at an angle or in line with the edges. If any of these are worked in contrasting colour from that of the fabric they will inevitably draw the eye and although this can look dramatic and pleasant, it can also look fussy. The advice of the embroiderer who is to do the work should be taken on this point or, if this is to be done at home, consultation with an expert in needlework is worth while before starting. For formal table linen, the embroidery is invariably in the same colour as the linen.

Mats used on the dessert plates when finger bowls are brought in and which are then put on the table above the place setting, need not match the place mats, though it is better that they should be of similar quality and material. But very often just a small lace-edged linen mat is used and plain linen or organdie mats, either round or square, are always likely to be suitable.

## CARE OF CHINA AND LINEN

Ideally, everything that goes on the table should be able to be washed. For certain very special lace or silk cloths, dry cleaning may be recommended, but lace can usually be washed by hand, though if it is very delicate it is an idea to tack it lightly to a sheet or piece of muslin. It should just have the soap squeezed gently through it and not be wrung or twisted. Lace and heavily embroidered cloths and mats are usually best ironed first on the wrong side, which brings up the pattern, and then finished on the right side.

With linen damask and cotton, a better finish is always produced when the material has been starched. All fabrics look better after ironing if some care has been given to getting them of a uniform dampness before using the iron. Do not iron creases hard into a cloth or, with a heavy one, put it away under a weight of other things, as this strains the fabric where the folds and creases come.

Very fine linen should usually and ideally be washed by hand, but a good washing machine should no do harm providing that a suitable detergent only is used and that very fragile fabrics are not subjected to great heat or agitation.

Soap will not harm the finest china, nor will most detergents, but soda or anything abrasive can damage certain delicate finishes, especially with antique china, so its use should be avoided. Where dishwashing machines are concerned, factors to consider are the type of detergent used (manufacturers of china will usually be able to say which kinds will not harm their products), the heat of the water and agitation of objects in the machine. Again ideally, fine china is most safely washed by hand. Washing up should never be done in a hurry; plates and cups should not be tumbled into the bowl, cups should never be held by the handle while being washed, nor should washing-up be piled on the edge of the draining board. A plastic washing-up bowl minimises breakages, as does a plastic draining rack. It is important to rinse tableware thoroughly before drying it, as sometimes smears of soap or detergent remain. It is better to soak off any food that may have hardened on plates or casseroles rather than try and scrape or rub it off; if the washing-up cannot be done directly after the meal, then even a hurried rinse with cold water will prevent the food from sticking badly.

When storing china, try to avoid stacking plates too high as the weight can strain those at the bottom and the pressure can cause slight damage to the glaze after a while. Cups that are stacked inside each other are bound to fall over at some time and are safer hung on hooks if there is not space to stand them on a shelf.

With cutlery, the main care is to see that, when the handles are not of the same material as the rest of the knife, fork or spoon, they should not be subjected to great heat or abrasion without the owner being sure they can stand this. Some synthetic handles can deteriorate in washing-up machines and the manufacturers' instructions should be checked when they are bought. Cutlery, like china, should not be stored haphazardly in a drawer, when one piece will scratch against another. As well as the many special polishes available for simplified silver cleaning and the tarnish-proof bags in which it can be kept, both silver and other cutlery can very easily be stored in polythene.

For care of wineglasses and decanters, see p. 298.

# LEGAL INFORMATION

## YOUR HOME

**Estate Agents.** If you are selling a house you are quite at liberty to advertise it yourself and find your own buyer, but you will probably employ an estate agent to do so for you. Make sure that you have a clear agreement with him covering:

    (a) what his commission will be;
    (b) in what event it becomes payable. The usual arrangement is for him to be paid only if someone actually completes the purchase of your house and for his commission then to be on a scale fixed by the surveyors' professional bodies – but this is not something laid down by law, it is a matter of arrangement.

If you are buying a house, you will almost always go to one or more estate agents to find what is available. Most agents are very helpful to purchasers and most are honest – but do bear in mind that, however helpful and however honest, he is not your agent but that of the man who is selling, and that he is paid to act in that man's interests and not in yours.

**Deposits.** The agent's job is to find a potential buyer and to agree a price with him. When that has been done he will very likely ask you for a deposit. If you are dealing with a reputable and well-established firm you may safely pay such a deposit, but you should get a receipt stating that you have agreed to buy the house "subject to contract" (these words are important) and that the agent is to hold the deposit "as stake-holder" (these words are also important). If you are in the slightest doubt you should at once consult your solicitor: many people have lost their deposits. Payment of a deposit shows you are in earnest: it does *not* mean that you have definitely got the house – either you or the vendor can still back out at any time until a written contract has been signed. However keen you are to clinch the deal do *not* sign any such document without first consulting your solicitor (and this applies to buying at auction also – if you are thinking of doing so you should consult your solicitor 2 or 3 weeks beforehand): otherwise you may find that you have bought something you did not expect.

## BUYING A HOUSE

In buying a house there are three things on the business side which you will be concerned about: 1, that you can find the money; 2, that the house is structurally sound; and 3, that you will get what you are paying for.

**1. Finance.** This will usually involve a mortgage and probably you will go to a building society for it. If you do not know a society or if for other reasons you want help in arranging finance, you should consult your bank manager, the vendor's estate agent, or your own solicitor. A mortgage on a life assurance endowment policy, in conjunction with the mortgage on the house, will in many cases be the best method of finding the money; this is something on which you ought to take advice.

**2. Survey.** This is a matter for a surveyor and again, if you do not know one, ask one of the people mentioned above. You may be able to judge the condition of property fairly well for yourself, but remember that the things which are likely to cause you trouble – and expense – are the things you are least likely to be able to see: the roof, the electric wiring and the drains. See that your surveyor is clearly instructed to investigate these three. If there is the slightest reason to suspect dry rot or woodworm it is worth getting the vendor's permission to lift floorboards, etc. and to call in one of the specialist firms: they will make a free and expert survey, but will of course charge for any treatment found to be necessary. Your surveyor will probably disclaim liability for any rot or worm which may exist, but which escapes his notice.

Do not think, because your building society makes a loan after sending a surveyor to see the house, that you need not have a survey done for yourself. The building society is concerned with the question: what will this house fetch in a forced sale? (i.e. if you default). But what you want to know is: what major repairs is this house going to need in the next few years? – quite a different question.

3. **Investigation of Title.** This is what you employ your solicitor for, but he will help also on the other two points. There is one thing however which you must usually check for yourself, and that is the plan of what you are buying. You may find that boundaries are inexactly shown or do not incorporate adjustments which have been made between neighbours in the past – and there is always the possibility of even more serious errors. If you happen to be buying a building plot or other land with an open boundary, ask your solicitor to insist that the vendor supplies a proper scale plan prepared by a surveyor: not one merely "by way of identification only". Even if the land or house has a registered title, insist that a plan is supplied: there is a growing bad habit of referring to registered properties by number alone although you cannot know what is registered under a particular number. It might not only involve wrong boundaries, but might be the wrong property altogether – so insist on seeing and checking a plan.

The most obvious aspect of ensuring that you get what you hope to buy is checking that the vendor does own the property. Apart from fraud (which because of our system of conveyancing is very rare) it is easy for there to be a perfectly innocent mistake about this. For example, the house may not be owned by Mr Smith who is selling it to you, but by Mr and Mrs Smith jointly, in which case it is no good taking a conveyance from Mr Smith alone.

But in addition to this obvious point, there are others which you need to check and they can be classified as follows:

1. Will you as owner of the house have any rights over the land of your neighbours?
2. Will your neighbours have any rights over your land?

These two questions are more often important with country property, but they cannot be ignored in buying a house in a built-up area. It is quite possible, for example, that your drains or pipes or wires run through your neighbour's garden, or his through yours; and if so, it is as well that you should know exactly what your rights and liabilities are. You may have a building, perhaps a garage, built right up to the boundary of your land and you will want to know whether you have any right to go on to your neighbour's land to repair or redecorate your flank wall. Rights of this kind over the land of someone else are technically known as "easements".

Another type of third party right commonly found in built-up areas is "restrictive covenants", which are agreements made by a previous owner restricting the use to which the property may be put, and which may or may not be binding on you.

3. Are public authorities likely to exercise their powers so as to affect the property?

You want to know, for example, that proper planning permission has been obtained for a new house and that the building bye-laws have been complied with. You want to know that neither the local highway authority nor the Ministry of Transport have plans for road-widening or for constructing an entirely new road which may eat away part of your garden or may even call for the demolition of the whole house.

4. Is there a tenancy of any part of the property?

You may be buying the house wholly or partly as an investment, in which case you obviously want to have full particulars of the tenancies which you will take over. Owing to the complex legislation on this subject (three systems of control relating to residential tenancies alone) a very careful investigation must be made. On the other hand, if you are not buying for investment but for your own occupation it is just as important to be sure that no one is going to claim that they have a tenancy of the top flat or the shed at the bottom of the garden or something of that sort.

5. What financial obligations will you have as owner or occupier of the property

You will expect to pay rates, but will want to know the rateable value and the current rate in the pound. Your solicitor will also enquire, as a matter of routine, whether there are any unusual outgoings, such as tithes or land tax (two taxes which are obsolescent, but which still exist in certain cases), or whether there is an outstanding liability to the local authority for making up the road or whether there is some potential liability to your neighbour for upkeep of a party wall and so on.

6. Are there any third party rights which must be removed before you complete your purchase or which would put you off it altogether?

The most obvious of these, of course, is your vendor's existing mortgage. This must be repaid and the lender's rights extinguished before you or your building society can safely put money into the property. There are other less likely dangers which must nevertheless be checked. For example, some previous owner may have granted an option to someone else to buy the property or take a lease over it, or the local authority may have passed a resolution for compulsory acquisition of land which includes the house in order to build a school or for some other public purpose.

All these are the things which are covered by the "scale fee" which your solicitor will charge, but he will also see that your mortgage money is available at the right time, and will co-ordinate the timing of the whole operation so that the vendor moves out in time for you to move in on the day you have arranged – not always easy when there is a chain-reaction of people buying and selling, all of them probably dependent on borrowed money.

**Registered and Unregistered Titles.** How does your solicitor or you, if you do it yourself, find out about all these things? It is impossible to give a "Do it yourself" guide to conveyancing in the space available here, but very briefly:

1. Perusal of the draft contract of sale prepared by the vendor will suggest points on which more information is required.

2. Many things (for example, ownership of boundaries) are found out by asking the vendor.

3. Local authorities keep a register of "local land charges": search in these registers (sometimes in one only, sometimes in two) and an enquiry directed to the authority or authorities concerned brings to light many important facts.

4. The title deeds of the property will establish the actual ownership and some of the third party rights and other matters, but it is also necessary to search (against the names of former owners) in the Land Charges Registry at Kidbrooke and in some cases in the Companies Registry in Old Street, London. If the title to the property is registered at H.M. Land Registry (which has various branches, each dealing with a different part of the country) this part of the investigation is simplified because investigation need be made only there and not at the Land Charges Registry nor Companies Registry.

**Joint or Common Ownership.** You may have your house conveyed not to you alone but to yourself and your wife (or husband). If this is done you may own the house either jointly (in which case it passes automatically to the survivor on the death of either of you) or in common (in which case you each own a definite share in the house – which need not necessarily be a half – and that share will pass under your Will and not automatically to the other party). It is commonly believed that there is less Estate Duty to be paid if a house is owned jointly between husband and wife but this is a great over-simplification of quite a complicated question. If you think of owning your house either jointly or in common you must consult your solicitor about it.

**Mortgages.** The mortgage deed which you will sign will be a formidable document and you are unlikely to be able to understand all of it even with the help of explanation from your solicitor. However, by far the greater part of it comes into play only if you default in your obligations in some way. So long as you make your repayments promptly what you need to know can be summed up as follows.

1. You cannot be prevented from repaying what you owe but you may agree not to repay within a certain time, or you may agree to do so only on penalty – perhaps three to six months extra interest. If you think you may be able to repay the loan fairly quickly you should enquire about this beforehand.

2. You will be responsible to the lender for keeping the property in good repair just as if you were a tenant and he were the landlord.

3. You are almost certain to be forbidden to let the property or any part of it without the lender's consent. The reason for this is that you might let at a low rent on a long lease, taking a premium which you put in your pocket, and the lender would then be left with a security much reduced in value. If you break this clause and do grant a tenancy in spite of it, the tenancy will be binding between you and the tenant but will not bind the lender. Therefore, when he finds out about it, he can eject the tenant and the tenant can claim damages from you.

**Expense.** The purely business expenses of moving house are:

*For the vendor* – his estate agent's commission for finding a purchaser and settling the price with him; and his solicitor's fee for preparing the contract of sale, satisfying the purchaser about the title to the property, third party rights and so on, and for seeing that the old mortgage is properly paid off.

*For the purchaser* – the fee of his lender's surveyor for valuing the pro-property; the fee of his own surveyor for inspecting the condition of the property; his solicitor's fee for doing the work shortly described above under Investigation of Title, for preparing the document of conveyance to the purchaser, for satisfying the lender about the title to the property, and for advising the purchaser about the mortgage; the Land Registry fee (if the title is regis-

tered) which is a commercial fee for the work done by the Registry; the fee of the lender's solicitor for ensuring on behalf of the lender that the title is in order, and for preparing the mortgage documents; and the stamp duty on the documents, which is a form of taxation.

The amount of all these varies with the circumstances, and in particular with the price of the property and the amount of the mortgage. The solicitors' fees also depend on whether the title is registered or unregistered, on whether the lender is a building society or not, and on whether one solicitor acts for more than one party to the transaction – it is cheaper if the same solicitor acts for purchaser and lender, but not cheaper if the same one acts for purchaser and vendor (which is generally inadvisable anyway).

Merely as an example, here are typical expenses which might be incurred on the sale of a house for £3,750 and a mortgage from a building society (who instruct the purchaser's solicitor to act for them also) for £3,000.

| | Registered Title | Unregistered Title |
|---|---|---|
| **Vendor** | | |
| Agent's Commision | £106 5 0 | £106 5 0 |
| Solicitor: sale | £38 15 0 | £58 2 6 |
|   repayment of mortgage | £5 5 0 | £5 5 0 |
| | £150 5 0 | £169 12 6 |
| **Purchaser** | | |
| Lender's Surveyor | £8 0 0 | £8 0 0 |
| Purchaser's Surveyor | £21 0 0 | £21 0 0 |
| Solicitor: purchase | £38 15 0 | £58 2 6 |
|   mortgage | £19 0 0 | £19 0 0 |
| Land Registry | £9 7 6 | — |
| Stamp Duty | £3 15 0 | £3 15 0 |
| | £99 17 6 | £109 17 6 |

**Compulsory Purchase.** Virtually any property, including your private house, can be compulsorily acquired by the local authority or by one of the agencies of the government. If this should happen to you, you ought at once to consult your solicitor: the authority may be exceeding its powers and in any case you have a right to object and to be heard at a public enquiry; if the acquisition goes ahead you must also consult a surveyor specialising in this type of work to ensure that at least you get all the compensation to which you are entitled. The subject is very complex, but put at its simplest you are entitled to the current market price of what is taken from you.

## Town and Country Planning

The general rule is that no land may be "developed" unless one has planning permission. "Development" means either:

1. building, engineering, mining, etc., operations;

or 2. a material change in the use to which property is put.

On the face of it this would prevent the private householder doing many quite normal things within his own boundary, but there are certain exceptions to the general rule. For example:

a) internal work, whether decorative or structural, is not development, nor is external work which does not materially affect the appearance.

b) the use of land or buildings within your own boundary for a purpose incidental to the enjoyment of your house as a house is not development.

c) you may enlarge your house (including the erection of a garage) within certain limits without getting planning permission, (although this is development), and you may also erect ancillary buildings, such as a garden shed and also walls and fences, without planning permission, but again, within certain limits.

d) the external painting of your house, although strictly speaking development, is covered by a general permission given by Ministerial Order.

You should note however that:

1. the conversion of your house into two or more units, for example by letting part of it as a separate flat, is development and requires planning permission;

2. in general the construction of any new access to a public highway requires permission;

3. in almost all cases of constructional work, quite apart from any planning permission that may be necessary, you

will also have to obtain the consent of the local authority under the building bye-laws.

If you do carry out some development without permission and go undetected for four years, the planning authority can take no steps against you.

If you require advice on town planning matters, the Town Planning Institute will give you the names and addresses of surveyors, architects and solicitors who specialise in this work.

**Boundaries.** People often think that the ownership of their boundary walls or fences will be shown by the title deeds to their property or by the Land Register. Generally speaking this is not so. It is often very difficult to decide which of two neighbours owns a particular boundary. The well-known rule of thumb that fence posts, wall buttresses etc. are built on the land of the man owning the boundary is sometimes of help.

The ownership of boundaries is particularly important because of two points which are frequently misunderstood.

1. You have no right to use a boundary fence or wall which belongs to your neighbour. Strictly speaking if you train your roses up it you are trespassing on his land. (There are special rules about party walls in London which do give neighbours a right to use each other's boundaries. This is a subject on which you will need to take advice from a solicitor or surveyor.)

2. You are under no obligation, generally speaking, to repair the walls or fences which you own. It follows, of course, that you cannot make your neighbour repair his, however unsightly the result or whatever the loss of privacy— you can always build another boundary on your own land, but of course at your own expense.

**Neighbours.** Your legal relations with your neighbours are governed by two fundamental principles in English law.

1. You can do what you like on your own property.

2. You may not enter upon nor in any

way interfere with your neighbour's property.

It follows, for example, that your neighbour may not come on your land for any purpose without your invitation (which may of course be implied) unless he has some special right to do so. He may have such a right if pipes or wires for services to his house pass through your garden. If he has a right for his pipes or wires to run through your land he will usually also have a right to enter your land for the purpose of repairing them. You are under no obligation to contribute to the repair of any such pipes or wires unless you yourself make use of them; the same rule applies to a right of way. You need not contribute to its upkeep unless you use it.

It also follows that if your neighbour's trees overgrow the boundary between you he is trespassing, because the air above the surface and the soil beneath are part of your property. If this does happen and if it is inconvenient to you, the courteous thing is to ask your neighbour to cut back the offending branches. If he does not do so you are at liberty to cut them yourself – provided that in doing so you do not yourself trespass on your neighbour's land – but the branches, and in particular any fruit that may be on them, continue to belong to your neighbour and not to you.

Again it follows from the same principle that (always subject to town planning or other public restrictions) you may open windows in any part of your house even if they overlook part of neighbouring gardens in such a way as to destroy their privacy. However the other side of this is that your neighbour is equally at liberty (again subject to town planning etc.) to erect a screen standing entirely on his own land which will effectively block out the view to your window. In some countries there is a right for a property owner to continue to enjoy a long established view, and in some there is a right to privacy. Neither of these rights exist in England.

Your freedom to do what you like on your own property obviously is affected by the other principle, that you must not interfere with your neighbour's property.

Apart from trespass, if you use your property in such a way as to cause unreasonable interference with the use or enjoyment by other people of their property, you commit the tort of Nuisance and your neighbour can bring proceedings to recover monetary damages from you and/or an injunction, *i.e.* an order of Court that you stop doing whatever gives rise to the Nuisance. You do not have to be a lawyer to realise that in most cases it is a question of degree whether or not there is a Nuisance and one which can be solved ultimately only by common sense. To take a common case: if your neighbour carries out extensive building operations next door, it is very likely to inconvenience you and to be a considerable nuisance, but that is not to say that it will amount to the tort of Nuisance. Just as it would be unreasonable for your neighbour to carry out his building in such a way as to cause unnecessary disturbance (perhaps by using pneumatic drills at night) so it would be unreasonable for you to claim that he must not build on his land at all in case it inconvenienced you.

If you think your neighbour is behaving so unreasonably that you have a cause of action against him you will have to take professional advice. The sort of thing your solicitor will want to know in advising you is: exact details of what is happening; how long it has been going on; whether requests have been made to your neighbour to do it in a less inconvenient way or at less inconvenient times, and how he has responded; whether the activity in question is one to be expected in your particular neighbourhood or not (for example, you cannot complain of the noise of factories in an industrial area although you could if somebody started a factory in a residential suburb).

## TENANCIES

**Leases and Tenancy Agreements.** In general the terms of your tenancy, whether you hold under a long lease or under a short term agreement – perhaps made by word of mouth – depend upon what you have agreed with your landlord; therefore if you have a dispute with him the first thing to do is to look at your agreement.

Rent Books do *not* necessarily contain a note of all the terms of the agreement. In weekly tenancies, the agreement is often by word of mouth and many points may not have been covered. A frequent instance is liability for repair. Suppose some part of your rented accommodation, say the back door, needs to be repaired. Who is responsible for it? The answer is, the person who has agreed to be. If neither you nor your landlord have agreed to be then neither is responsible. The practical effect is that if you want the door repaired, you will have to do it yourself, but your landlord cannot make you do so.

Like any general proposition of law, that is subject to exceptions. In the first place under any tenancy you, the tenant, must use the premises in a tenant-like manner: that is to say that you must not deliberately or by negligence damage them, but that does not make you responsible for normal wear and tear. In the second place, since 1961 under any residential tenancy for less than seven years (and this includes all tenancies from week to week, month to month, etc.) your landlord is responsible, whatever the agreement may say, for maintenance of the structure and also of the water, gas, electricity and sanitary services together with space and water heating apparatus (if any). Apart from that, your landlord is always responsible, (not to you, but to the local authority) under the Public Health Acts, for maintaining the property in a certain minimum state to the satisfaction of the Authority, which in practice means the satisfaction of its sanitary inspector. A tenant can sometimes indirectly make his landlord carry out work by asking the Local Authority to take action in this way.

So much for the case where nothing has been agreed about repairs. If there is something in the agreement about your, or your landlord's, responsibility for repair (and it may very often be divided between you) the rule to remember is that the condition in which you take over premises has no relevance unless (and this is exceptional) a "schedule of condition" was agreed at the beginning of the tenancy and you or the landlord, as the case may be, is only to repair up to that standard. The age of the premises is relevant, however; you do not have to make old property into new.

An important limitation on a landlord's right to enforce agreements about repair is that he cannot make his tenant pay for dilapidations, *i.e.* for disrepair, a sum of money greater than the damage to his reversion. This somewhat technical expression can perhaps best be understood by an example. The question is most likely to arise at the end of a long lease, under which the tenant is usually responsible for all repairs. The price for which the landlord could sell the vacated house in its actual state of repair might be, say, a thousand pounds less than if it were in good repair. That figure of a thousand pounds is the maximum claim he can make on the tenant even if the actual cost of carrying out the repairs is, say, fifteen hundred pounds. (In most cases the agreement will be modified still further by the 1954 Act: see below). There are also provisions which may relieve a tenant from having to carry out mere decoration, or from having to do any repairs before the last 3 years of his tenancy.

The other obligation under a tenancy which is often misunderstood is the tenant's obligation to pay rent. Many tenants think that if their landlord is doing something wrong (for example, failing to carry out repair for which he is responsible under their agreement) the tenant has a right to force his hand by stopping the rent. That is not so. The tenant must pay his rent whatever the landlord is doing. The proper way to make the landlord carry out his obligations is to take proceedings in the Court. However, despite this rule, in practice withholding the rent does often produce results.

**Protection from Eviction, etc.** The tenant of most types of property is now protected against various forms of unreasonable conduct by his landlord during the tenancy and against being required to leave at the end of the tenancy except for good reason. Different types of protection apply to different types of property. Agricultural tenancies are protected under the Agricultural Holdings Acts, the basic principle of which is that the tenant cannot be dispossessed so long as he farms properly; that he receives compensation when he has to go; and that so long as he remains he pays a proper market rent. Business tenancies are protected under an Act of 1954, the basic principle of which is that the tenant of a shop or office, etc. is entitled to a new lease when his existing lease expires provided he is willing to pay a proper market rent, but that the landlord can obtain possession if he needs the premises for his own business or in order to carry out extensive alterations or to rebuild.

**House on Ground Lease.** The same Act protects tenants of houses held on long lease (over 21 years) at ground rents. whose rateable value on 23 March 1965 was less than £401 (London) or £201 (elsewhere). Anyone who thinks he is affected should not only get professional advice but should do so early: the tenant may lose protection if certain time limits are not observed and the landlord too may lose his rights if he does not take the proper steps at the proper time.

The basic scheme of the Act is that the tenancy created by the long lease continues automatically even when the time agreed for the expiry of the lease comes to an end – until one party or the other takes steps to alter the position as laid down by the Act.

The tenant may want to leave. In that case, he can do so either by agreement with his landlord or by giving him one month's written notice.

If it is the landlord who wants the tenant to leave, he must give him notice in a particular form and must state his reasons: only certain reasons laid down by the Act are sufficient for this purpose. Examples are: that the property is to be redeveloped. that the tenant has failed to pay his rent, that the landlord needs the accommodation for himself or a near relative. The tenant may of course accept the reason which is given and go. If he disputes the matter, and an agreed solution cannot be negotiated, the landlord can refer the matter to the County Court which will decide whether the tenant is to go or to stay.

It often happens of course that the tenant wants to stay and the landlord is content for him to do so but wants a higher rent (this will usually be so when the former rent has been only a ground rent fixed many years ago), or wants possession of some part of the house no longer occupied by the tenant, or wants some other alteration in the terms of the former lease. In that case also, the landlord must give the tenant notice in a special form, saying exactly what he proposes; and again, if agreement cannot be reached by negotiation, the landlord can refer the matter to the County Court which will settle the disputed points.

The two things which usually cause difficulty are repairs and rent. Almost all long leases make the tenant completely responsible for repair of the whole house and this can be a heavy burden when the lease comes to an end and, probably, the house is 60 or 100 years old – although of course the tenant knew of the obligation when he took on the lease and got the house more cheaply because of it. However, the Act, by a rather complicated procedure, provides that in the cases where the tenant is to remain in the house he does not have to comply with the agreement in the lease about repairs, and cannot be made to pay for more than is necessary to put the house into good repair, having regard to its age, character and locality.

The rent obviously is bound to be greater than formerly but, if not agreed, is not to be more than a reasonable rent, having regard to the repairs which are to be done and to the other terms of the new tenancy.

A rather bewildering set of controls applies to short-term residential tenancies.

**Furnished or Shared Tenancies.** Furnished tenancies, or unfurnished tenancies which began before 6th July 1957 where a kitchen or living-room is shared with the landlord, come under the local Rent Tribunals and two sorts of protection are given to the tenant:

*a*) the Tribunal can reduce the rent if it is too high. If you think this is so in your case, you should apply to the Secretary of the local Rent Tribunal (it is probably best in the first instance to consult your nearest Citizens Advice Bureau);

*b*) if the tenancy is a periodic one, *i.e.* from month to month, quarter to quarter, or something of that sort, and the landlord serves notice bringing it to an end, the Tribunal has power to suspend the operation of the landlord's notice for up to six months at a time. *N.B.* This power does not exist in the case of a furnished tenancy for a length of time which was fixed at the outset; for example, a tenancy for one year – when the year expires you will either have to negotiate a new tenancy or leave.

**Controlled Tenancies.** Then there is the great number of unfurnished residential tenancies subject to the Rent Acts 1920–1957, commonly called "controlled tenancies". In fact there are two different categories of control broadly similar, but with minor differences.

1."Old Control" which applied until 1939 and which still does apply to some properties. With the passage of time these are dwindling in number.

2. "New Control" which was instituted on the outbreak of the 1939–1945 war and ended by the Rent Act of 1957. This continues to apply to a great number of properties and in particular to all tenancies (not subject to old control) granted before 6th July 1957, where the rateable value of the property on 7th November 1956 was less than £41 in London, or £31 elsewhere (you can find out the figures which apply in your case by asking the Rating Department of your local authority).

The basic features of both types of control are:

*a*) so long as the original tenancy agreement (whether in writing or merely by word of mouth) is not brought to an end, its terms continue to apply;

*b*) when the tenancy agreement is ended, whether by notice to quit or by expiry of the time for which it was agreed the tenancy should last, the tenant does not have to leave, but can continue in occupation of his home under what is known as a "statutory tenancy", *i.e.* a personal right (which cannot be sold or disposed of in any other way) to remain in the premises as his home. This statutory tenancy can be transmitted on the death of the first statutory tenant for two more generations, for example, first to a widow and then to a daughter;

*c*) the rent under the statutory tenancy may not be more than a figure laid down by the Acts and based on the gross value of the property for rating (*N.B. not* the rateable value; not the amount of rates paid). In many cases it will be twice this value. The landlord can (on proper notice) add the amount of the rates, if he pays them, and also $12\frac{1}{2}$ per cent of the cost of any improvements he has made to the property.

*d*) the landlord can get the tenant out only on a number of grounds laid down in the Acts, which basically are if the tenant fails to pay his rent or in some other way misbehaves in his capacity as tenant, if the landlord requires the premises for himself or a member of his family, or if there is suitable alternative accommodation to which the tenant can go.

Not only must the landlord prove one of these specified grounds but in every case the Court must think it reasonable to dispossess the tenant and readmit the landlord.

**Regulated Tenancies.** Lastly, there is the system of "regulated tenancies" introduced by the Act of 1965 which applies to unfurnished tenancies which do not fall within the scope of either of the previous controls, and where the rateable value of the property on 23rd March'1965 was less than £401, (London), or £201 (elsewhere). Under this system, the rules for security of tenure are approximately, but not exactly the same as for controlled tenancies. In particular, there is provision for owner-occupiers in certain circumstances to be able to regain possession of their homes if they have let them temporarily (which they would not be able to do under a controlled tenancy). However, the arrangements about rents are different.

1. On the expiry of the tenancy agreement the rent continues at the same level until either the landlord or the tenant (or both) applies to the local Rent Officer for it to be raised or lowered.

2. The Rent Officer determines a "fair rent"; this is not defined by the Act, but seems to mean the proper market rent without taking account of pure scarcity value.

3. If either party is dissatisfied, he can appeal to the local Rent Assessment Committee.

4. The "fair rent", once registered, will remain at that figure for 3 years; at the end of that time either party can apply to have it raised or lowered.

5. Most "unfurnished" tenants for whom rent increases were authorised on or after July 10 1968 enjoy further protection under the Prices and Incomes Act 1968. Their increases must be "phased" to a maximum of 10/- per week for the first year with a limit on the second. The local rent office can supply details.

6. The landlord can, as in a controlled tenancy, add to the rent the amount of the rates if he pays them, but if he wants a higher rent on account of any improvement he has made to the property he must apply to the Rent Officer.

**Unprotected Persons.** There are important categories of people who are not protected in respect of their homes, either as to rent or as to security of tenure. They are.: 1. Tenants of the Crown, local authorities, New Town Corporations or housing associations. 2. Tenants of public houses. 3. Tenants of furnished accommodation for a fixed time. 4. Occupants of homes which go with their job – see below. 5. Occupants of boarding houses or private hotels.

Tenants of part-residential part-business premises will usually be protected either under the Rent Acts (controlled tenancy) or under the 1954 Act (business tenancy); they are not protected under the 1965 Act (regulated tenancy).

**Boarding Houses and Service Occupancies.** There is a type of occupation known to the law which is less than a tenancy and called a "mere licence". That is what you have if you go to a

boarding house or hotel – you have no tenancy of the room you occupy, whether for one night or for a month or longer. You merely have the proprietor's permission to occupy it upon the terms as to payment, etc. which have been agreed between you. He cannot turn you out during the time you have agreed so long as you carry out your part of the agreement by payment, proper behaviour, and so on. But when the time comes to an end you get no protection from the various Acts mentioned above because you have no tenancy.

Exactly the same is true of a service occupancy. This is where an employee is required, as part of his terms of service, to occupy particular premises. This can apply to domestic servants, agricultural workers, caretakers, chauffeurs etc. – and the Prime Minister, Archbishop of Canterbury and others. Such a person has no tenancy at all and when his employment ends he has no right to continue in occupation of his quarters (subject to some special rules for agricultural tied cottages). That seems simple but it can cause a great deal of difficulty because such a situation is narrowly divided from a service tenancy. That is where the employee is a true tenant occupying his premises under an agreement separate from his service agreement and paying a rent in one form or another. The distinction between the two can be very fine, but it can be very important. If you find yourself in this sort of situation you must take competent professional advice.

## PET ANIMALS

There is a general rule that if you keep anything on your land which is not naturally there, and it escapes and causes damage to others, then you are liable for that damage. This rule has a particular application to animals and you will in general be liable for any damage caused by pets which stray across your boundary on to other people's property. There is also the very important general rule against causing injury or damage to others by your negligence and this can apply just as much to animals as to, for example, your motor car. So apart from all other rules on the subject you must not be negligent in control of your pets: for example, it would probably be negligent to allow your small son to take out your large mastiff for exercise because he would not be able to control the animal.

Apart from these general rules there are some which apply especially to animals. There is the Dogs Act of 1906 which makes you responsible, irrespective of the circumstances, for damage done by your dog to "cattle" (for this purpose including horses, sheep, goats and pigs), later extended also to poultry. Then if you choose to keep wild animals as pets, you will, again irrespective of the circumstances, be responsible for any damage to persons or property which they may cause.

All of this imposes a fairly heavy responsibility on pet owners, but there are some rules in their favour. The two most important are:

1. If there is no question of trespass, negligence etc., you are not responsible for damage done by ordinary domestic animals unless you knew that they were liable to cause that sort of damage. So you are not responsible if your pet dog bites the postman as he walks up your path, unless the dog has previously bitten somebody else.

2. You are not responsible for damage done by your pets even when they are trespassing if they are only doing something natural to that sort of animal. The most obvious case is that you are not responsible if your cat strays and kills someone else's tame pigeons, because it is the nature of cats to kill birds (but remember what is said above about the particular liability attaching to dogs under the 1906 Act).

What about somebody else injuring your pet? Here the position is simpler. Your pet is your property and the general rule applies that anyone who damages your property, either deliberately or negligently, must make good the value to you. (He may have a defence that it was necessary to injure or even kill your animal in order to protect animals etc. of his own). The motorist who runs over your pet is therefore responsible for paying you the value of it (provided the accident is his fault) and is under the same obligation to stop and give you his name and address, etc. as in the case of other road accidents – but note that this does not apply if it is poultry or a cat which has been killed.

## HUSBAND AND WIFE

It used to be said that under English law husband and wife were one person. For almost no purposes is that so today. They are two separate, independent persons with their own rights and obligations. The most important exceptions are:

1. That their two incomes are taxed as if they were both the income of the husband (see under Income Tax);

2. That the system of law which governs a wife, particularly her property rights and her rights about divorce, is settled by where the husband has his permanent home, irrespective of where she may live. What this can mean in practice is that (subject as always to important exceptions) if an Englishman deserts his wife and settles permanently in some foreign country, then so long as they are married the wife, although left behind in England, will be governed in many important respects by the law of the foreign country and not by that of England. It is not possible to explore the intricacies of what is called "Private International Law" in a book of this nature. Any problem of this sort will require advice at least from one lawyer and very likely from a lawyer from each of the countries concerned.

Legal difficulties between husband and wife most often concern either property or divorce.

PROPERTY. So far as property is concerned each has his or her own legal rights. Your house may be owned by the husband, it may be owned by the wife, or it may be owned jointly between you, in which case each has separate rights in it. In practice of course, married couples, particularly happy married couples, do not regard most of their property in this way but treat it as belonging in some vague and undefined way to both of them or even belonging

R—E.W.—L

to the family as a whole. That is not given legal recognition in England (although it is in some other countries) and when one of the couple dies the ownership of their goods and other property will have to be disentangled for estate duty and this may also have to be done if there is a divorce or separation. Basically, "who owns what" is decided between husband and wife by the same rules as would apply to other people, but there are some special rules.

1. Any savings made by the wife out of a housekeeping allowance from the husband, and anything purchased out of those savings, belongs to the spouses equally.

2. If a joint bank account is opened simply as a matter of convenience, but is supplied from the husband's income, any balance in the account is not joint property, but remains the property of the husband.

3. Wedding presents, if clearly given to one party (jewellery to the wife; cuff-links to the husband), are the property of that person, otherwise they are joint property. While they are both alive either party can insist on having his half share (either by division or by sale), but on death the presents pass automatically to the survivor.

4. In general it can be said that if husband or wife have agreed at the time of purchase what their respective rights in property are to be and this is clearly recorded then the Courts will give effect to what has been agreed. If there was no agreement or if it is too vague to be clearly proved, there is a presumption that a husband who puts property wholly or partly into his wife's name is doing so with the intention of making a gift of it, in whole or in part, to her, but that a wife who puts property into her husband's name has no such intention, so that he is to be merely a trustee for her. There is a growing tendency however for the Courts to decide that property is owned equally between the two, particularly where both have contributed financially although not necessarily equally. For example, if husband and wife buy a house in their joint names and expressly say in the conveyance that it is held as to one-third for the wife and as to two-thirds for the husband (or in some other defined proportions) then, no matter in what proportions they have contributed the purchase price, the division of ownership which they have agreed will be upheld by the Courts. If no such agreement is recorded in the deeds and the husband provides the whole of the money a joint purchase will be deemed, because of the presumption mentioned above, to belong to them jointly; but where the wife provides the whole of the money the property will be hers alone even if bought in joint names or even in that of the husband only. However, where as is common today both have contributed either to the initial deposit or to the repayment of mortgage money the Court is very likely to find, even with contributions that are unequal, that the property is owned jointly. The Court has to be invoked in such cases because of the very natural vagueness between husband and wife about such matters and because when these questions have to be decided they are often "at arms' length". The Court has a special power under Section 17 of the Married Women's Property Act of 1882 which does not apply to anyone except husband and wife, to decide these problems with what may be called "palm-tree justice" rather than by strict rules of law.

DIVORCE. If you are involved in what is called "unhappy matrimonial differences" you will have to go to a lawyer for advice and there is nothing to be gained by trying to summarise here the complicated body of divorce law and practice with which you may be involved. However, a few salient points may help you to keep your bearings when discussing matters with your solicitor and counsel. In the first place, husband and wife under English law are under a duty to cohabit, i.e. to live with each other, but neither can be made to do so against his or her will. There is a form of legal proceedings called "Restitution of Conjugal Rights", but success in that does not produce an order that the erring spouse *shall* come back; it produces only a declaration by the Court that he or she *ought* to come back. It is therefore of practical importance, in some cases, as a first step towards establishing the matrimonial offence of Desertion.

The policy of our law is that (at any rate at the time of writing) a divorce can be granted only:

*a*) on the petition of one spouse against the other;

*b*) on the ground that the other has committed a "matrimonial offence" against the petitioner.

In other words, a divorce cannot be granted because the parties want it, or because the marriage has irretrievably broken down, or at the request of the spouse who is in the wrong.

There are 5 matrimonial offences for which a divorce can be granted and another 5 for which the Court can annul the marriage; in addition, there are 5 grounds on which the Court can say the marriage has been a nullity from the outset, *i.e.* has never really taken place at all. Those which are of everyday importance are:

*For Divorce*:

Adultery.

Desertion – this does not simply mean leaving the matrimonial home; it means wrongfully bringing cohabitation to an end, which can be done by driving the innocent spouse from the home just as much as by the guilty spouse leaving the home.

Cruelty – this means conduct that injures or is likely to injure the health of the innocent spouse and it therefore includes what by American analogy is often called "mental cruelty".

*For Annulment*:

Wilful refusal or physical inability on the part of one spouse to consummate the marriage, *i.e.* to have sexual intercourse. *Note:* if this has taken place even once there is no question of nullity – although there might be a case of cruelty by improper refusal of intercourse.

Even if a matrimonial offence has been committed, the innocent party may not be able to get a divorce because there are a number of "bars", some absolute and some at the discretion of the Court. The two most commonly arising in practice are:

1. Adultery on the part of the petitioner. It obviously should not lie in the mouth of the spouse who has himself, or herself, committed adultery to ask for a divorce because the other spouse has done the same thing – yet this does in practice happen quite often. Notwithstanding the apparent anomaly the Court has power, in its discretion, to overlook the adultery of the petitioner and to grant a divorce because of the adultery of the respondent. All petitioners for divorce are under a duty to tell their solicitor whether they have committed adultery and, if they have done so, to give particulars to the Court in a document known as a "discretion statement".

2. Collusion – which means really two allied but distinct things:

*a*) agreement between the parties to present a false case to the Court; and

*b*) agreement whereby the acquiescence of one party is bought by the other.

Examples will make this clearer. It is collusion of the first kind if husband and wife arrange, in order to obtain a divorce, that she will present a petition against him on the ground of his adultery (which has taken place), but will suppress the fact of the adultery which she herself has committed. It is collusion of the second kind if husband and wife agree that he will petition on the ground of her cruelty and that she will not deny it because of a generous financial arrangement made beforehand. This type of collusion often used to lead to practical difficulty because it made it dangerous for the parties or even their lawyers to discuss financial arrangements in the early stages, although it is often desirable in the interests of the parties and even more of their children for this very thing to be done. The law therefore now permits the parties to make arrangements of this sort which are or may be collusive, to disclose them fully to the Court, and to get the approval of the Court, which says in effect: Although this is collusive, we think it is a proper arrangement to make and it will not be regarded as a bar if you now proceed to a divorce.

**CHILDREN.** The chief sufferers from a

broken marriage are the children and there is little that the law can do about this, but two important rules of English law seek to do what is possible.

1. In all matters concerning children the prime consideration for the Court is the well-being of the child and not any supposed rights or wrongs of either parent.

2. The Court is not allowed to grant a divorce until satisfactory arrangements have been made for the children of the marriage under the age of 16.

There are two terms used in this connection which can be confusing: "custody", which roughly means the power of decision in such matters as schooling, religious upbringing etc.; and "care and control" which means what custody is often thought to mean, *i.e.* the actual day to day care of the child. Another expression often used is "access", which means the right to see a child who is in the care and control of the other party, to take it out, to receive visits from it during holidays, and so on. It requires strong evidence nowadays to deprive either party of access to their children, whatever matrimonial offence they have committed.

**MAINTENANCE.** If a married couple part the problem of money for the wife and young children usually arises. A husband in England is responsible for maintaining his wife so long as she remains his wife and so long as she has not committed a matrimonial offence against him, and he is responsible for maintaining his children under the age of 21 whatever his wife does and whether he remarries or has another family. If agreement can be reached between the parties it should be recorded in a maintenance agreement (which should be professionally prepared). If agreement cannot be reached, the wife (on behalf of herself and/or her young children) can apply to the Magistrate's Court or to the High Court for an order that the husband shall pay a stated sum to her either for herself and/or the children. This again is obviously a matter for expert advice, but two practical aspects should be remembered. If a man, rich or poor, leaves his wife and sets up another

household – and especially if he starts another family – the money which is available has to go round more people. Therefore, there will be less for each, the innocent as well as the guilty. Secondly, it is one thing to have a right to money from someone, but often a very different thing actually to get that money from him. Unfortunately, our machinery for enforcing orders of the Court in this sort of case is very defective. The wife should also remember that if she has an income of her own, or if she is capable of earning money but chooses not to, her income or earning capacity will be taken into account.

It is always important to see that full account is taken of tax considerations. This is just as much so for the comparatively poor as the comparatively rich. If a husband is making "voluntary" payments to his wife (or ex-wife) or children, *i.e.* payments not under a proper and binding maintenance agreement or Order of Court, he is paying income tax (and surtax if applicable) on the total income from which all are being maintained. This must nearly always be extravagant. The tax on £$\frac{1}{2}$ X taken by itself, is usually less than half the tax on £X, taken as a whole. Therefore, if the total income which is available to the whole family (or ex-family) is split up for tax purposes, so that the wife bears some of the tax and each child bears some of the tax, the total net sum will be greater and there can be a little more for all. Not all divorce specialists are good at this: speak to your lawyer about it and see that he gets advice if he does not understand it himself.

## SUCCESSION ON DEATH

### WILLS

**Family Provision.** The most notable feature about the English law relating to Wills is that the Englishman (in which is included, of course, Englishwoman) can leave his property to whomever he pleases; he is under no obligation (at law) to leave a penny piece to his spouse or children. This is in marked contrast to countries whose law is based on Roman law (for example Scotland) where a certain minimum fraction of one's estate must be left to one's nearest and, it is presumed, dearest.

The only inroad on this principle which English law has permitted is under an Act of 1938 and subsequent amendments by which a dependent (*i.e.* a widow, or widower, an ex-spouse, a spinster daughter, or a child who cannot fend for himself) has a right, not to any specified fraction of the estate, but only to apply to the Court which may then make such provision for the dependent out of the deceased's estate as it thinks reasonable in the circumstances. There is a strict time-limit laid down by the Act within which a claim must be made and therefore if you think you have a claim of this sort it is essential that you take your solicitor's advice without delay. If on the other hand you are making a will and intend to cut out all members of your near family, you will be wise to explain the circumstances fully to your solicitor and ask him to prepare a statement of your reasons, to be left with the will. If a case is subsequently brought by one of your dependents you will not be available to answer it, and it is much more likely to be defeated if a proper statement of your reasons can be produced.

**Invalid Wills.** A will can be attacked from a different point of view: not that you receive nothing under it but that it is invalid. It may be in your interest to do this if you would then benefit under an earlier will or under the deceased's intestacy. There are three grounds on which the validity of a will can be disputed:

1. That it has not been properly executed. To be valid, an English will must be in writing and must be signed by the testator "at the foot or end thereof" in the presence of two witnesses together who must then sign in the testator's presence (there are special rules about wills executed abroad, including Scotland, which are too complicated for short summary). Neither of the witnesses nor their spouses

should be beneficiaries under the will because the gift to them will be forfeited. A soldier on actual military service or a sailor at sea can make a will informally, even by word of mouth, but it is desirable to make a formal one if possible.

2. That the will has been made under the improper influence of someone else. If you allege this, it is you who must prove it and it is obviously difficult to do so. Such an allegation should not be lightly made, but if after consideration you decide to do so, the advice of a solicitor is essential.

3. That the testator was not of mental capacity to make a will. The test for this is not the same as for medical insanity. The test is whether the testator understands

(*a*) that it is his will he is making;

(*b*) what he has to dispose of;

(*c*) the claims upon him to which he ought to give effect. Here again, if you think that someone did not know what they were doing when they made their will, it is for you to prove that this was so. The evidence of doctors who knew the deceased will be desirable and a lawyer's advice essential.

A person under 21 cannot make a valid will at all (except for soldiers and sailors as above).

**Home-made Wills.** On the making of your will the only sensible advice that can be given is; do not try to do it yourself. However simple your wishes, you are more likely than not to express them in a way which will cause trouble and expense to your family. However small your estate, your unguided wishes are quite likely not to be the best in your family's interests. It is simple to have your will professionally prepared by a solicitor and the few guineas it will cost is money well spent. When you consult him you should have in your mind:

*a*) the type of property of which your estate will consist and its approximate value;

*b*) the names and ages of your immediate family;

*c*) your wishes for them – be prepared to be advised about this;

*d*) who you want to be responsible for winding up your estate, *i.e.* your executors (see below);

*e*) any special wishes which you have about burial, funeral service, etc.

**Executors.** When you die someone has to:

1. account for and pay estate duty and capital gains tax on your death (any estate over £5,000 will be affected by one or both, so they are not for the rich only);

2. obtain probate of your will, *i.e.* have its validity recognised by the Probate Division of the High Court;

3. obtain control over all your assets and sell them as necessary to raise the cash which will be required;

4. pay your debts, including the expenses of your funeral (but not of any gravestone or any other memorial);

5. pay any legacies you have given in cash and hand over any you have given in kind;

6. either hand over your residuary estate to your residuary legatee or legatees, or continue to hold it as trustee if you have left it for a child who is under 21, or for two or more people in succession – for example, to your widow for her life and then to your children.

The person or persons who have to carry out these tasks are your executors. There is nothing against a beneficiary also being an executor: in fact in a simple case where you leave the whole of your property outright to one person, that person is the most suitable executor. It is perfectly possible for executors to carry out all their duties personally and they will find the officials of the Probate Registry, the Estate Duty Office and the Inspector of Taxes courteous and helpful. Most executors, however (including banks and insurance companies) prefer to delegate most of the work to their solicitor. If this is done, an executor is not, contrary to what you may read in advertisements, caused a great deal of personal trouble. All he will have to do personally is to take decisions, for example about what should be sold and what should be retained; to sign various documents all of which will be prepared for him; and to clear up the deceased's personal papers and other effects, which is essentially a personal task.

There is therefore no reason why you should not appoint friends or relations as executors, even in quite complicated cases. In some cases you may think it wise to appoint a professional executor to act with your friend or friends. Solicitors and accountants in particular are accustomed to acting as executors and so of course are the trustee departments of most banks and many insurance companies. It is an advantage to appoint one of these corporate trustees if your estate is going to be unusually complicated or if you have settled it on trusts which are likely to last beyond the lifetime of a reasonably young executor. But generally speaking banks and insurance companies should not be appointed in the case of the ordinary estate of reasonable size and no great complexity: remember that it costs a good deal more to do so as they (quite justifiably) charge substantial fees for their services which are payable in addition to the solicitor's bill.

**Intestacy.** If you die without leaving a valid will, you are intestate. The distribution of your estate will be, in accordance with the Administration of Estates Act 1925 (as subsequently amended) among your statutory "next of kin". The rules have to provide for a great number of different circumstances and it is not possible to reproduce them in full. However, by way of example, a surviving spouse gets the whole estate if there are no surviving parents, descendants, brothers, sisters, nephews or nieces; gets the first £8,750 plus the personal chattels and the income from half the rest of the estate if there are surviving descendants and gets the first £30,000 plus the personal chattels and the income from half the rest of the estate if there are no descendants, but there are surviving parents, brothers, sisters, nephews or nieces. Surviving children (or grandchildren whose parent is dead) who reach the age of 21 or marry younger, take the estate between them subject to the rights of the surviving spouse if there is one.

**Administrators.** As there is no will, there are no executors and therefore one or more of the persons entitled under the statutory rules has to be appointed by the Court as administrator to perform the same duties. This is a complication and expense which could have been avoided by leaving a will. It is said that even if the rules of intestacy are exactly what you yourself would wish (and of course that will not always be the case) there are thirteen separate reasons why you should make a will. One has already been mentioned. Another is that if you have made a will and appointed executors it is clear at once who they are and there cannot be any jockeying for position among various relations who may be equally entitled under the rules of intestacy to act as administrators. A third reason, of more importance than might appear, is that if you leave a will and lodge it, as you should, in the strong-room of your solicitor or bank, it can be produced at once when you die and your wishes will be at once known; but if you do not leave a will, there will be nothing to announce the fact and no one will at first be in charge of your affairs. Much time may be spent by various relations enquiring of banks, solicitors, accountants and friends if they have a will and searching among your papers for one; even at the end of the day when everyone has decided that you cannot have left one after all and it has been agreed that someone should apply for Letters of Administration, a will may turn up in some unforeseen place.

## SHOPS AND SALE OF GOODS

**GUARANTEES BY SHOPS.** When you buy many types of goods you will be accustomed to getting a guarantee from a manufacturer. If something subsequently goes wrong, you are probably familiar with the situation in which the shopkeeper says, or at any rate clearly implies by his attitude: "The fault is nothing to do with me; it is a matter for the manufacturer which you should take up with him, but if you like I will take it up for you." You perhaps imagine that this attitude correctly reflects your rights in the matter. It ought to be more widely realised that every shopkeeper guarantees everything he sells and that manufacturers' guarantees are as often matters of good will as of legal liability on their part.

Anyone who sells goods guarantees that they correspond with the description under which they have been sold. This applies to everyone and not only to shopkeepers; it applies to secondhand goods as much as to new ones. It is therefore of very wide application. For example, if a secondhand car is described as having done 10,000 miles only and in fact it has done 30,000 miles, then it does not comply with the description and the buyer can reject it or, if he is too late to do that, can recover from the seller the difference in value of the two cars. Of course not all goods are sold by description and in particular if you go into a shop and say "May I please have that one", there is no sale by description and no liability on the part of the shopkeeper, at least under this head.

But there are two more guarantees implied in many sales which apply particularly to shopkeepers dealing in the ordinary course of their business. If you make known expressly or by implication, the particular purpose for which you require the goods, seeking the shop's advice on their suitability, then the shop guarantees that what it sells is reasonably fit for your purpose. This rule is of wider application than might appear because the very slightest indication of your purpose will bring it in by implication. Thus if you go to buy a hot-water bottle you do not need to explain that you want it for heating your bed at night; that is implied. And if for some reason it is a very inefficient heater you may take it back to the shop and ask for your money back provided you do so immediately you find out that it is defective. Note, however, two qualifications on this rule:

1. The shopkeeper is guaranteeing only "reasonable" fitness for a purpose. He is not guaranteeing perfection.

2. The rule does not apply at all if you buy a specific article under its trade name. So if you have generally found Blank's razor blades satisfactory and you go and buy a packet of them by name, it is no good complaining to the shop that this particular packet does not come up to Blank's usual high standard; there is no guarantee of fitness for purpose by the shop in this instance, but you may have a claim under the next rule.

Goods sold in a shop by description are guaranteed to be "of merchantable quality". There is no exact definition of that term, but it can perhaps be summed up as meaning fit to be sold as goods of the type described. You will see that this rule has a wider application than the preceding rule, but does not impose quite so high a standard. So, to go back to the razor blades, although you might not be able to complain that the particular packet of Blank's blades were not up to the usual standard you could reject them if they were not fit to be sold as razor blades at all. The important qualification on this rule is that it does not apply when the buyer has inspected the goods and failed to notice obvious defects.

If you find you have bought defective goods, take them straight back to the shop from which you got them and insist on having your money back or on their replacement by sound goods. Do not listen if the shopkeeper says it has nothing to do with him and that is how he got them from the manufacturer. Do not listen even if the shopkeeper can show that the defect is something which he could not have discovered and could not have put right. That does not matter; he has guaranteed them. You will probably find that not only shop assistants, but even shop proprietors are quite ignorant of the obligations they take on simply by selling; you will have to persuade them that you know more of the law than they do. But remember one point. These guarantees do not cover cases where you yourself make a mistake and simply choose the wrong article for your purpose, or where you buy goods which are too cheap and of too low a quality.

## Manufacturer's Guarantees

Manufacturers' guarantees are more definite and precise in their wording than the general common-law guarantees referred to above, but they are less definite in their legal effect, because they have not been contested in the Courts. The views of leading lawyers about their effectiveness differ. This is important to you because these guarantees very commonly purport to do two things.

1. They offer you certain rights direct against the manufacturer and not against the shopkeeper, rights which may go beyond the shopkeeper's obligation in the particular case and, at any rate, are more clear and certain. For example, it is common for a manufacturer to undertake to replace faulty parts coming to light within, say, a year of purchase. Whatever may be the shopkeeper's obligations in the particular case, this is obviously something for which you would like to have the manufacturer's liability too.

2. They also commonly purport either to cut out altogether or to cut down your other rights in the matter. Those other rights are, first of all the shopkeeper's obligations which we have referred to above and secondly, the obligation of every manufacturer, whether or not he offers any guarantee, to compensate the consumer for any damage which the consumer suffers by reason of a defect in the goods which could not reasonably have been discovered by prior examination. For example, if you buy a car from your garage and you are seriously injured because of defective steering, you will not only have your rights as a buyer against the garage (because it has sold the car to you), but also direct against the manufacturer.

In many cases, you would be better off without the guarantee, because you may be giving up your valuable rights against the shopkeeper and because the rights which the manufacturer is offering may be very limited – in particular they may not cover the cost of labour or of collection and re-delivery of the faulty goods, which can be the greater part of the cost involved. So if you are offered a guarantee which you have to do something to accept, for example, by filling up and returning some form, what should you do? There is no universal answer, but very often the correct advice is: do not accept it. If the guarantee is legally effective, you are quite likely giving up more than you are getting; if it is not legally effective, the manufacturer may well honour his "obligations" under it simply as a matter of good business even if you have done nothing about it.

**Hire Purchase and Credit Sale.** Many goods today, of course, are not sold outright but are supplied either on hire purchase or on credit sale. In substance, both these types of transaction are a means of buying on credit, but owing to the defective nature of our law on the subject the form of hire purchase in particular does not correspond to the substance. The result is a great deal of tortuous legislation and practical difficulty. It will help if you can keep clearly in mind that a credit sale is just what its name says. You buy the goods but pay for them over a period and not at once; in the meantime they are your property. A hire purchase transaction on the other hand is not a sale at all. The goods remain the property of someone else (probably a finance company and not the shop from which you have got them) and you are hiring them for a period of time at the end of which, and only at the end of which, they will become your property.

The Hire Purchase Acts contain elaborate provisions to safeguard the person who enters into these transactions, and the Acts now apply to all motor vehicle transactions and to all other transactions with private individuals if the total hire-purchase price is under £2,001.

Among the important provisions of the Acts are:

1. In certain cases the customer can, within a limited time, back out of the agreement he (or often she) has made. This was intended to deal with agreements signed under pressure from door-to-door salesmen.

2. In general, the guarantee of fitness for purpose and of merchantable quality which are referred to above apply as in outright sales; in addition there are restrictions, peculiar to hire-purchase transactions, on the seller excluding these obligations by agreement.

3. Once you have paid a third of the total hire-purchase price, the owner of the goods can get them back, if you then default in further payments, only by action in the County Court and not by coming and taking them. The court has special powers in such cases to order modified future payments etc. in order to ensure, if possible, that you are not deprived of the benefit of the agreement which you have largely complied with.

4. If you want to end the agreement and return the goods, you may do so whatever you have agreed:
   a) by giving notice to the owner;
   b) by returning the goods;
you can then be made to pay (with what you have paid already) up to half of the agreed hire-purchase price, but no more.

**INSURANCE**

There are two types of insurance:

1. Life assurance: the distinguishing feature of which is that the Company agrees to pay a stated sum (or more) on the death of the life assured (or at some agreed earlier date). The person insured is therefore certain to be paid by the Company at some time or other. The uncertainty is only in the time and to some extent in the amount of the payment.

2. Risk Insurance: the distinguishing feature of which is that the Company agrees to pay the loss you suffer (not an agreed sum) if, and only if, a certain risk occurs. Such policies generally run only for a year at a time, and neither the insured nor the Company is under any obligation to renew.

**Life Assurance.** Life Assurance itself is of two main types – whole life, and endowment. Under a whole life policy the payment of the sum assured is made only on the death of the life assured. Under an endowment policy, payment is made on the death of the life assured *or* on a specified date (usually attainment by the life assured of a particular age or the expiry of a particular length of time from the commencement of the policy), if the life assured is still alive when that date comes.

Each of those two types can be further divided into policies "without profits" (*i.e.* where the sum assured is fixed from the outset) and "with profits" (where the sum eventually to be paid is made up of a basic fixed sum plus "bonuses" which are allocated by the Company from time to time out of its profits). Premiums on with-profits policies are higher than on those without profits, but owing to the competitive nature of the business and the investment skill of the companies, with-profits policies almost always show a better return at the end of the day.

No insurance contract of either type can be valid unless the insured has a proper interest in the risk to be covered (otherwise it would be mere gambling and therefore unenforceable). This means that you can insure only the life of a person from whose death you would suffer financial loss, for example, your partner in business. One can always insure one's own life, and that of one's spouse, for any amount.

It is quite common in life assurance for the life assured and the person to whom the policy belongs (the insured) to be different people. This can arise in more than one way. You may insure your own life and assign the policy, *e.g.* as a gift to a grown-up child; you may insure the life of someone else in whose life you have an insurable interest; or you may assure your own life, but for the benefit from the outset of someone else, for example your wife or your children.

There are many variations on the basic types of policy briefly described above – too many to make any useful summary of them. Very often they are designed to attract the young married man wishing to safeguard his family for the future, but whose means, particularly in the early days of marriage, are too small to enable him to take out straightaway the type of policy which he will

ultimately require. Advice on details must be sought from an insurance broker (whose business is advising on and selling insurance policies of all types) or an insurance agent (whose business is in some other field but who acts as an agent for one or more insurance companies; solicitors, accountants, bank managers and estate agents are often insurance agents).

When a few premiums have been paid on a life policy it acquires a "surrender value" (usually about 90 per cent of what has been paid) which the Company will pay if the policy is cancelled (surrendered). Alternatively, one can usually convert the policy to one which is "paid up", *i.e.* you pay no more premiums, but the policy is kept alive for a smaller insured sum instead of being cancelled.

You can use a policy which has a surrender value as security for a loan, usually either from the Company itself or from your bank. You can also use a life policy, even before it has a surrender value, as "collateral security" with some other asset, and this is very commonly done on buying a house. In fact up to early middle age it is often the best and cheapest way of raising a mortgage. Life policies are also a valuable means of saving; this is particularly so when they are operated in conjunction with a unit trust. Advice about all these aspects of life assurance can be obtained from a competent broker or agent. Lastly, life policies (and annuities) are very useful in mitigating the effect of Estate Duty. Your estate will pay duty if it is worth more than £5,000 and although the rates of tax are small to begin with they increase very steeply. Many people ought to think about the problem who would not by any means regard themselves as rich. In order to obtain proper help and advice, it is essential to go to someone who specialises in this type of work. Many so-called Estate Duty experts or Tax Advisers are knowledgeable only about one or two standard "dodges" which use life policies, and do not have the wider knowledge necessary to advise on other solutions. Probably it is best to consult a solicitor specialising in the field (and not all of them do so) and insist that he consults one of the firms of insurance brokers who also specialise in this field.

**Risk Insurance.** The risks which the ordinary insurance companies will cover are by now fairly standardised and so are the policies issued for the purpose. Unusual risks can sometimes be covered on special terms through Lloyds, which essentially is a working association of individual underwriters and not an insurance company in the ordinary sense. Typical policies are: household policies, which may be against fire only or against "comprehensive risks" and which may cover the structure only or may include the contents; "all risks" policies on valuables; public liability policies against your risk of becoming liable for damages to someone whom you injure negligently, for example, with the point of your umbrella in the street, personal accident policies against the risk of an accident to yourself; motor-car policies; and so on.

The terms used are a little misleading to the literal minded: "comprehensive" and "all risks" for example mean, not every risk, but those listed in the policy; the standard lists are wide, but do not include everything.

Risk insurance policies are what lawyers call "contracts of indemnity": that is, the insurance company is saying to you: "If you suffer a particular loss we will make it good to you; otherwise we pay nothing." Several important consequences follow. For one thing, the amount of the payment will be only the amount of your loss. So if your hearth-rug is damaged by a coal from the fire, you cannot get from the Company the cost of a new rug: if the damage is repairable you can get the cost of repair and if it is not repairable you can get the cost of a second-hand rug, because it is only a second-hand rug and not a new one which you have lost. If you want to insure something particularly valuable or something whose value may be difficult to establish when it has gone you should get a professional valuation, produce this to the insurance company, and ask them to insert it as an agreed value in the policy; then in the case of total loss or destruction you will recover that value without argument. In all other cases, the insured value is not a measure of what the company will pay you; it is the measure on which your premiums are calculated and fixes the *maximum* which the company will pay.

## TRAFFIC ACCIDENTS

The law so far as it especially affects motorists is fairly well-known to them and would, in any case, be impracticable to summarise here. We therefore deal only with three aspects of accidents:

1. insurance against the result of an accident;
2. what does the law require you to do if an accident occurs?
3. what should you do in your own interest after an accident?

**Car Insurance.** Every person driving a car is obliged by law to be insured against "Third Party Risks" which means his liability to pay damages to anyone whom he injures if the accident is in whole or in part his fault. The obligation is a personal one and if you are driving a friend's car it is *you* who are responsible that you are insured. Failure to be insured is a serious crime and can lead to disqualification from driving or to imprisonment. It is not enough to say in defence: "My friend said his policy would cover me", if your friend was mistaken. It is true that your friend has also committed a crime by allowing you to drive his car while uninsured, but that does not affect the offence that you have committed.

You are not obliged to be insured in respect of a passenger. Therefore if you are driving with your wife in the car and she is injured in an accident which is your fault she will not recover any compensation if you only have third party cover: she cannot recover from the other driver because he is not at fault and she cannot recover from your insurers because they are not covering this risk.

Nor does third party cover extend to property damage. Therefore if you have an accident (again your fault) in which the other driver's car is badly damaged you will have to pay those damages out of your own pocket.

It is, therefore, wise to see that your car policy covers injury to passengers and property damage (including damage to your own car). If it also covers you while driving other people's cars, you can do so with a quiet mind so far as compulsory insurance is concerned – but remember that although you may have a comprehensive cover while driving your own car, you may have third party cover only while driving someone else's car. There are no general rules about this and as with all insurance the only way to know what cover you have is to study your policy carefully.

**At an accident.** If you are involved in an accident in which any injury, however slight, is caused to another person, another vehicle, or an animal (other than cats or fowls) you have three duties.

1. You must stop.
2. You must give the other party your name and address, the number of your car and the name and address of the car owner.
3. If a person has been injured and not merely an animal or another vehicle, you must also produce your insurance certificate.

You must stop in all cases, but if you choose you need not give the particulars required by 2 and 3 above to the other party, but may instead give them to the police within 24 hours. Your obligation goes no further than that and you are under no duty to make any statement to the police about how the accident occurred – although    particularly if you think you are not at fault, it may often be wise to do this.

The requirements about stopping and giving particulars have nothing to do with the question of who was responsible for the accident: you must stop and you must supply the particulars in every case.

On the other hand if you have an accident, however serious, in which the only damage is either to your own car or to yourself or to someone else's property (not a vehicle) then there is no obligation

either to stop or to give any information – though again it may well be wise to do so.

**After an accident.** If you are involved in any sort of traffic accident in which you or your car has been injured you will want to recover the cost of the damage from someone else; if someone else or their vehicle has been injured, they may want to recover damages from you. The wise course in most cases is first of all to note down at the scene of the accident as much information as possible: names and addresses of witnesses; the exact position of the vehicles; the driving conditions (light, road surface, and so on); an accurate note of anything the other driver or his passenger(s) has said. Be circumspect yourself. Do not volunteer any statement to anyone and do not lose your temper; consider carefully before saying anything either to the police or the other driver which goes beyond your obligations as noted above.

If a claim is made against you, do not make any reply beyond an acknowledgement and the statement that you have passed the matter on to your insurance company. Do this immediately and your insurers will deal with the claim or will tell you if you are not covered; if that is the case, you should at once take advice from your solicitor.

On the other hand, if you feel that the accident was the fault of the other driver or of someone else, you have a choice: you may either claim against the other party, or you may claim against your own insurers. Too many people claim under their own insurance without thought and then are dismayed to find that they have lost their no-claim bonus, or even worse that the premium is increased. Remember that you need never claim on your own insurers; remember that if you do they will not claim from the other driver even if he was at fault (the "knock-for-knock" agreement); and remember that a no-claim bonus is exactly what it says – it is not a "no blame" bonus.

If you make a claim your insurers are entitled to forfeit the bonus even if you were in no way to blame. It is often wiser therefore simply to notify your insurers of the accident, emphasising that you are not making a claim against them, and then to make a claim against the other driver. He may pass that on to his insurers and they will make every effort to get from you the name of your insurers so that they may operate the knock-for-knock agreement. You must resist this and tell them that you are claiming against their insured and against him only. Of course if you follow this line you may be forced to take legal proceedings to make the other man (really, his insurers) pay up, and you will not necessarily win the case; that is why careful thought is necessary about which course to follow. You may think it wise to consult your solicitor at the outset.

## TAXES

This country has one of the most complicated systems of taxation in the world. We cannot do more here than indicate the outline of the five direct taxes with which most of us have to be concerned. In addition to these, there are other direct taxes such as stamp duty (on many documents) and corporation tax (on the profits of companies) and numerous indirect taxes such as customs duties, excise duties and purchase tax.

## RATES

Each rating authority levies a local tax, the "general rate", on the occupiers of all property (other than agricultural) in its area. So far as houses are concerned a gross rateable value is assessed for each property, the criterion of which is the rent at which it could be let on an annual tenancy under which the tenant pays the rates and the landlord carries out repairs. From this a statutory deduction is made for repairs to arrive at the net annual value. The tax is charged at a given "rate" of so much in the pound upon this net value.

The person who has to pay the rate is the occupier of the premises and not the owner. (It is for this reason that your solicitor will see that the rates are apportioned between you and the other party when you buy or sell a house.)

You may be a tenant at what is called an "inclusive rent" which means that although the authority could demand the rates from you, your landlord has agreed with you to pay them and in practice will pay them direct to the authority so that you have nothing more to pay than your rent to him.

If you think that the rateable value of your property is too high, you should first go and inspect the rating list at the local town hall – it is open to all – to see if your assessment is out of line with those of similar and nearby properties. If it is not out of line you have not much chance of an alteration, but if you still think it is wrong you should take the matter up with the local District Valuer. Certain surveyors specialise in this type of work and you can get professional assistance from one of them.

## INCOME TAX

This tax is charged on the income of every individual in the country except married women, whose income is treated for this purpose (only) as part of their husband's income.

To arrive at the figure of your net income, you first deduct from your gross income any expenses you have incurred in earning it. The artificiality of our tax laws is shown by the fact that you are not allowed to deduct all the things which common sense (or an accountant) would regard as an undoubted business expense, and by the further fact that if you are an employee, the rules are even more restrictive than if you are self employed.

Having arrived at your net income, you then deduct "charges" on income. This signifies money you pay which is regarded, for tax purposes, as income of the payee and not of you; for example, interest on loans, and certain payments under deeds of covenant.

Then you deduct certain allowances which are free of tax. For example, there is a personal allowance at different rates, depending on whether you are married or single, a child allowance for each child under the age of sixteen (or over that age and receiving full-time education), provided that the child does not have an independent income over a certain amount; and a special allowance if part of your taxable income is money earned by your wife. There are special reliefs for elderly persons and those with small incomes.

What remains after these deductions is your "taxable income". It is taxed at four different rates.

1. One or more "reduced rates" apply to the first two or three hundred pounds of taxable income; if your income includes money earned by your wife you will get the benefit of the reduced rates for the first part of her earnings as well as for the first part of what really is your own income, earned or not.

2. The next part of your income up to several thousands of pounds will, if earned, bear tax at one or more rates arrived at by deducting what is known as the "earned income relief" from the "standard rate of tax". In this, as in other respects, income which is directly earned is treated much more favourably than income derived from savings.

3. Any earned income above the limit for earned income relief or any unearned income above the limit for reduced rates will bear tax at what is called the standard rate, although in fact it applies in a minority of cases.

4. If your income is above a certain figure (considerably higher for earned income than unearned) you will pay additional tax known as "surtax" on a scale which increases steeply as your income rises.

Income tax is paid in one of two ways:

1. By direct assessment upon the tax payer and payment by him direct to the Revenue. This applies typically, for example, to the earnings of persons in business on their own.

2. By "deduction at source" whereby the person from whom your income comes deducts the tax and hands it over direct to the Revenue without it ever passing through your hands. This applies for example, to all dividends (tax on which at the standard rate is deducted by the company), to all payments under deeds of covenant (tax on which at the standard rate is deducted by the person paying it), and to the wages and salaries of all persons in employment (tax on

which is deducted by the employer under the system known as P.A.Y.E.). In this case, the tax is not deducted at the standard rate but in accordance with a "coding" based upon the tax circumstances of the individual employee which is intended to result in his having paid the correct tax after making allowance for all reliefs, charges, allowances, etc. in each complete tax year. P.A.Y.E. however is only a method of tax *collection*. It is not a method of tax *assessment*. Any person paying tax under this method is entitled to have a separate assessment from the Inspector of Taxes as if he were self-employed. If this assessment for a given year shows an amount of tax due which is different from that deducted under P.A.Y.E. the difference must, of course, be paid to or by the Revenue.

Similarly, deduction at source from dividends, etc. is merely a method of tax collection and as this is done throughout at the standard rate it will often happen that the individual will have paid by deduction at source more tax than is correct having regard to his personal circumstances. In such cases, it is up to him to make a claim to the Inspector of Taxes for repayment of the tax which has been overpaid.

## SHORT TERM CAPITAL GAINS

If a gain (or loss) is made on the disposal of certain assets within twelve months of acquisition the profit is treated as if it were income (and the loss is similarly deducted from income). This does not apply to the house in which you live, your private motor car, or articles of furniture and other chattels sold for less than £1,000 each. Other types of capital receipts, notably certain premiums on the grant of leases, are also treated for tax purposes as if they were income and taxed accordingly. The rules are complicated and advice should be sought from an accountant or solicitor.

## ESTATE DUTY

This is now the only "death duty" in the U.K. It is levied at a rate which depends on the amount of property passing on the death and does not depend upon the relationship of beneficiaries to the deceased.

The Duty is not payable simply on the amount of your property when you die: it is not as straightforward as that. The rate of Duty must first be found by "aggregation" of the value of all property which "passes" on your death, *i.e.* the ownership of which changes when you die, whether it belongs to you or not. A common example of property which changes ownership although you do not own it is a trust fund from which you have the income and the capital of which goes to someone else on your death. Although you have received only the income, the capital of the fund is aggregated with the other property passing on your death to form the total on which the rate of Duty is based (there is an important exception from this rule in favour of the survivor of two spouses). Another type of property which passes on your death although it does not form part of your estate is property which you own jointly with someone else, very often with your husband or wife or it may be with your partner in business. There is a good deal of misunderstanding about the effect of joint ownership upon Estate Duty – see "Joint or Common Ownership" on page 313. All that can be said here is that the rules are more complicated than you might expect and differ for different types of property, *e.g.* houses, bank accounts and shares.

The rate of Estate Duty depends upon the total value of all property passing on the death. It begins at £5,000 with 1 per cent and rises by various steps to a maximum rate of 80 per cent. The rates rise steeply above about £20,000 and as the tax can very largely be avoided by taking appropriate steps the family man who is likely to leave such a sum may feel under a duty to take advice in order to safeguard his dependants. Suggestions are made under "Life Assurance" about the best source of this kind of advice (page 330).

Estate Duty at the appropriate rate will be levied on each part of the total aggregated sum. Thus your executors will pay Duty at that rate upon your own estate, the trustees of any fund in which you had an interest will pay Duty at the same rate out of that fund and – a source of unpleasant surprise to many people – anyone who has received a substantial gift from you within 5 years before your death will also pay Duty at the same rate out of his own pocket (unless you have provided otherwise in your will).

This happens because, although gifts which a person has made before he dies do not really change ownership on his death, any within 5 years of death are artificially deemed to do so and therefore are included in the total upon which Estate Duty is to be paid (with a reducing scale of values after the first 2 years). Some gifts, however, are free of Estate Duty as soon as they are made. For example, any gifts up to a total of £500 to any person within the 5 years before death (this is why ordinary birthday and Christmas presents are not dutiable) and any gift made upon marriage. The marriage settlement was for many years a traditional part of the financial arrangements of the moneyed classes, but it has gone out of fashion. This seems strange because it has several advantages, of which one has just been mentioned, and these can be of value to people who would probably not consider themselves as well-to-do. Those who wish to make gifts in order to reduce the amount of Estate Duty when they die often think they can have their cake and eat it. The subject is one upon which advice should be taken, but the basic rule can be stated simply enough, and it is that if a gift is to be excluded (after 5 years) from your dutiable estate it must be an out-and-out gift from which you do not continue to get any benefit at all.

There is some property which, although it passes on the death, is not aggregated with the rest in order to arrive at the rate of Duty. It is treated as "an estate by itself" and therefore bears Duty at the (usually much lower) rate of Duty appropriate to that size of estate considered alone. A notable example is property in which the deceased never had an interest (which most people of course would not expect to be taxable at all on his death). It is use of this principle which enables the father of a family to reduce the burden of Estate Duty when he dies by means of life assurance policies for which he pays, but which belong to his wife and/or children: as he has "never had an interest" in them the rate of Duty on the policies is likely to be much less than on the rest of what he leaves, and may be nil.

Your executors will have to pay Estate Duty on all your property other than freehold land before they are even able to obtain probate of your will, and therefore before they are able to deal with any of your assets. The practical result is that before they can deal with your estate they must make a valuation of it and submit it to the Estate Duty Office, that office must assess the Duty, the amount of the Duty must be borrowed from your bank, and the duty paid. This can not only cause a hardship if values drop between the date of your death and the date when your executors can actually deal with your assets, but it causes weeks, and it may be months, of delay before the effective winding-up of your estate can begin.

## CAPITAL GAINS TAX

A new tax was introduced in 1965 which, in principle, taxes the profit (less losses) made when you dispose of any of your assets. This is the Capital Gains Tax. As it is new it is not so well understood as, for example, Income Tax, and it may be worth emphasising one or two points about it:

1. the tax does not apply to companies but they pay a different tax, Corporation Tax, on all their profits whether in the nature of income or of capital.

2. It is not all capital *receipts* which are taxed (*e.g.* you will not pay tax on a legacy which you get), but capital *gains*, *i.e.* the increase in value of assets since the "base date".

3. The base date is, primarily, 6th April 1965 or the date of acquisition by you, if later. There are special rules about assets which you owned on 6th April 1965, designed in general to avoid penalising you if there was a drop in value before that date but a rise after it.

4. The tax is not on *real* rises in value but on rises in terms of money; as money is always losing value (inflation) this means that in many cases the "gains" tax will be paid when there has been a loss. To take a simple example, if you invest £100 now in a unit trust and sell the units in 20 years' time for £170 you will have made a gain (in terms of money) of £70 and will be taxed accordingly – but if money has in the meantime halved in value you will have made a real loss (to break even you would have to sell for £200). But you will be taxed just the same.

5. The tax is not even confined to monetary gains: you may make a loss even in terms of money and still be taxed on a "gain". For example, if you buy a boat for £1,500 and sell it, 5 years later for £1,200 you have made a money loss of £300 – but the boat is a "wasting asset" (*i.e.* has a predictable life of less than 15 years) and its cost is therefore written-off for tax purposes over its predictable life; if that is 15 years in the case of your boat the cost will have been written-down to £1,000 by the date of your sale – so you will pay tax on a "gain" of £200.

6. The tax is not even confined to cases where there is any disposal of an asset for cash at all: it is payable in certain cases on gains which might have been made, but have not actually been made. For example:

*a*) the tax is payable by your executors when you die on the net gain (if more than £5,000) in value of your estate since the date of acquisition of each item in it (or since 6th April 1965).

*b*) if you make a gift worth more than £100, you will pay tax (as well as making the gift) as if you had *sold* the asset in question instead of giving it away. Therefore, give away assets which have *dropped*, so that you get the benefit of the notional loss.

*c*) tax is payable every 15 years on unrealised gains in funds of discretionary trusts or funds held for a child when it attains a certain age, *e.g.* 21 (in addition, of course, to tax on actual gains made on the switch of investments).

There are important exemptions from the tax, which will have the effect of allowing many of the commoner transactions of life to go free, but the ordinary man in the street (if there is such a thing) should not assume that the tax is not for him: it well may be.

Some of the exemptions are:

I. There is no tax on the disposal of your private residence (or principal residence, if you have more than one).

II. There is no tax on the disposal of investments in "national savings".

III. There is no tax on the proceeds of life assurance policies at maturity or on surrender.

IV. There is no tax on disposal of a chattel for less than £1,000 – this will cover sale of furniture etc. up to the value stated: a set of articles counts as one.

V. There is no tax on disposal of motor cars.

VI. There is no tax on gambling winnings (nor of course is there any allowable loss on disposal of your car or on your gambling losses – which is doubtless the reason for the exemption).

VII. Tax on the disposal of business assets which are replaced by others is deferred until final disposal of the replacements.

VIII. An individual over the age of 60 who disposes (by sale or gift) of his business or of shares in a family company in which he has been actively engaged for the past ten years is exempt from the tax on £2,000 of gain for every year of age over 60 up to a maximum of £10,000 tax free gain at age 65. It is possibly unintentional on the part of Parliament that to obtain this exemption the individual does not actually have to retire from the business. He has only to dispose of his interest in it.

IX. Transactions between husband and wife are ignored for purposes of the tax.

X There is no tax on making a gift under £101 in value.

The rate of tax is calculated in one of two ways: a standard flat rate (initially 30 per cent) is to be fixed annually by Parliament, but if it would be more beneficial to an individual to pay income tax at his top rate as for unearned income upon one half of his net capital gains (up to £5,000) in a given year, then that alternative basis is to apply to him instead of the flat rate.

## NATIONAL INSURANCE, ETC.

Part of the taxation required to pay for various social services is collected by means of stamps on national insurance cards and part is collected with income tax under P.A.Y.E.; the remainder of the money required for these services comes from general taxation.

The social services in question are:

1. The National Insurance Scheme.
2. The Industrial Injuries Scheme.
3. The National Health Service (of which approximately only one sixth of the cost comes from this source; the remainder comes from general taxation).
4. The Redundancy Payments Scheme.

For this purpose, tax payers are divided into three classes who are liable to different amounts of "contribution", as the tax is called, and who are entitled to different benefits. These are:

*Class 1:* Persons in employment. They are entitled to all benefits under the National Insurance Scheme, the Industrial Injuries Scheme and the Redundancy Payments Scheme. They are liable for "contributions" at a flat rate for the class, higher for men than for women (which includes an element attributable to the Industrial Injuries Scheme) plus, if their earnings are over a certain figure, a "graduated contribution" (varying with how much they earn) which goes towards graduated pension in addition to the standard Retirement Pension (but they may be "contracted out" of this part of the tax if their employer has arranged for them to have at least equivalent benefits from an ordinary pension scheme). The employer also pays a flat rate tax for persons in this class (including an element for both the Industrial Injuries and Redundancy Payments Schemes) and an amount equal to any graduated contributions payable by his employees (and of course Selective Employments Tax, which is a separate thing).

*Class 2:* Self-employed persons. They are not entitled to benefit under the Industrial Injuries Scheme to Redundancy Payments, nor to Unemployment

Benefit. They pay "contributions" at a flat rate for the class, higher for men than for women.

*Class 3:* Non-employed persons. They are not entitled to benefit under the Industrial Injuries Scheme, to Redundancy Payments, to Unemployment Benefit, nor to Sickness Benefit or Maternity Allowance. They, like class 2, are liable to contributions at a flat rate for the class, higher for men than for women.

Women as such are liable to the tax, but married women who work for an employer (class 1) have the choice of not paying the flat rate contribution in return for receiving lower benefits (they must pay the Industrial Injuries contribution and, if liable to it, the graduated contribution unless contracted out). Widows working for an employer are in a similar position. Married women who are self-employed have a choice of paying contributions in class 2 (to which they belong) or in class 3 or none at all, with of course different entitlements to benefit in each case. Married women who do not work have no liability, but in some circumstances can pay the contributions for class 3.

Special explanatory leaflets can be obtained from local Pensions and National Insurance Offices about married women and about others in special positions, such as widows, students, persons in classes 2 and 3 with very small incomes, persons employed part-time, seamen, airmen, members of the forces, persons from foreign countries which have similar schemes and with which reciprocal arrangements have been made, and persons over retirement age.

Persons who are ill, unemployed, etc. in general are not required to pay the tax, except that persons in class 1 must continue to pay graduated contribution if applicable.

## NATIONAL INSURANCE BENEFITS

Your entitlement to the benefits of the scheme in a particular case depends on whether you satisfy certain "contribution conditions", for details of which you should enquire at your local Pensions and National Insurance Office.

The amount which you will get will be, in some cases, increased if you have dependants and will be in some cases, reduced if you are in hospital.

The benefits are:

1. **Sickness Benefit,** When you are too ill to work, a weekly sum is paid after the first 3 days for the first year of incapacity.

2. **Unemployment Benefit.** This is payable (at the same rate as Sickness Benefit) if you are unable to get employment. It is a condition for receiving this benefit that you register at an employment exchange and are prepared to take suitable jobs which they find for you.

3. **Maternity Grant.** This is a lump sum payment on the birth of a child.

4. **Maternity Allowance.** This is a weekly sum payable for 11 weeks before the baby is expected and for 7 weeks after, but only to working women who have chosen to pay their own contributions.

5. **Retirement Pension.** This is a weekly sum paid, in the case of men, to those over age 70 whether retired or not; it is strictly speaking a "retirement" pension only for those who retire from work at the minimum age of 65. A certain amount of part-time work is ignored in deciding whether you have retired. If you earn more than a certain amount from work which is ignored in this way, your pension will be reduced. On the other hand, if you do not retire at the minimum age, but continue until the age of 70, you will have to continue paying contributions, but will get a higher pension when the time comes.

The ages are 5 years less in each case for women (strange, for what is really the stronger and longer-lived sex).

The pension for persons in class 1 is in two parts: a flat rate pension (at a lower rate for women who have not paid contributions on their own account), and a graduated additional pension corresponding to the graduated contributions (for women, this depends on their having paid contributions on their own account).

**6. Widow's Allowance.** This is a short term allowance for the first 13 weeks of widowhood at a rate higher than the other benefits.

**7. Widow's Pension.** This is a weekly sum payable to widows aged 50 or more who have been married for 3 years or more and which comes into effect 14 weeks after the husband dies (or on the expiry of the two allowances mentioned below if they are applicable).

**8. Widowed Mother's Allowance.** This is for (usually) younger widows who have dependent children and is a weekly sum for themselves and the children.

**8a. Widowed Mother's Personal Allowance** is a weekly sum for the widow alone while she has a child no longer officially dependent, but still living with her, if below a certain age.

**9. Widow's Basic Pension,** which is a smaller weekly sum, is a hang-over from the pre-1948 scheme and is for those not entitled under the current scheme.

The various widow's benefits are for widows and cease if they re-marry.

Retirement Pension is not payable in addition to widow's benefits; in general if she would be entitled to both the widow gets which ever is the higher.

**10. Guardian's Allowance.** This is a weekly sum for someone looking after a child both of whose parents are dead and one at least of whom has been insured under the scheme.

**11. Child's Special Allowance.** This is a weekly allowance, varying with the number of children, for a woman whose marriage has been dissolved or annulled, whose former husband is now dead, and who has dependent children towards whose maintenance the deceased former husband was contributing a certain minimum amount.

**12. Death Grant.** This is a lump sum payment made to the personal represent- atives or to the next of kin upon the death of a person insured under the scheme or of his or her spouse or child. A reduced sum is payable for a man born before 5th July 1893 and nothing at all for a man born before 5th July 1883 (similarly for women whose date of birth is 5 years later in each case).

## IND USTRIAL INJURIES BENEFITS

**1. Injury Benefit.** This is a weekly payment for persons in class 1, incapacitated for work by an injury at work or by an industrial disease. It is paid for the first 26 weeks of incapacity (other than the first three days) instead of Sickness Benefit.

**2. Disablement Benefit.** This may take the form either of a weekly payment or a lump sum payment, the amount of which depends upon the extent of disablement (as assessed by a medical Board) for persons in class 1 whose capacity for work is lessened by an accident at work or an industrial disease. It is payable when Injury Benefit ceases (or straightaway if no Injury Benefit is payable) and, unlike Injury Benefit, can be paid in addition to Sickness Benefit. There are various supplementary allowances for special hardship, permanent unfitness for work, need for a constant attendant and for hospital residence.

**3. Benefit for Widows and Dependants.** Amounts, varying with the circumstances and paid either weekly or in a lump sum, may be paid for the dependants of persons in class 1 who die as the result of an accident at work or an industrial disease.

## LEGAL AID AND ADVICE

We have said more than once that in various circumstances you ought to get advice from a solicitor or his assistance in doing something. One of the social services available in England is financial help to enable you to get such advice or such assistance.

There are four schemes.

1. **The official Advice Scheme.** This enables persons of small means to get advice at an interview with a solicitor on payment of 2/6 (free for those on National Assistance). For details ask your Citizen's Advice Bureau or the local Legal Aid Office.

2. **The voluntary Advice Scheme.** This is not strictly speaking a social service, because it is provided voluntarily by the legal profession itself and not by the State. Most solicitors are willing to give advice under the scheme at an interview, as under the official scheme in 1 above, at a charge of £1 per half hour. They will give this to anyone who applies for it without regard to their means. The scheme is, therefore, of universal application and ought to be used more than it is, particularly as the rate charged is only about one third to one quarter of the proper "rate for the job".

3. **Legal Aid for Claims.** This is available to persons of small means as in 1 above and enables them to have the assistance of a solicitor (for example in writing letters, speaking to the other party, etc.) in making a claim against someone else or in resisting a claim by someone else; in either case, short of court proceedings.

4. **Legal Aid for Proceedings.** This is probably the best known of the schemes and provides the services of a solicitor, barrister, expert witnesses, and enquiry agents, as necessary, to conduct or defend proceedings in nearly all courts of law (but *N.B.* not in the multitude of special tribunals which we now have). It is available to persons of greater financial means than under 1 and 3 above, but if you have more than a certain amount either of income or of savings, you will have to contribute towards your expenses. Even if you have to make a substantial contribution from your own pocket the scheme is still of advantage to you because your maximum contribution is fixed and known at the outset, but the State guarantees that it will pay the whole expense involved however high that may turn out to be. You should realise, however, that if

you win your case and recover money, whether for damages or for costs, from the other party, you will normally have to re-imburse to the Legal Aid Fund out of your winnings the whole of the expenses of your case.

If you lose your case and do not have legal aid, you normally have to pay the greater part of your opponent's expenses as well as your own; if you have legal aid, you have to pay towards your own expenses only the contribution as mentioned above and towards your opponent's expenses only what the judge considers reasonable in all the circumstances, including the manner in which your case has been conducted and your financial position.

Your financial eligibility for legal aid and the amount of your contribution are fixed by the National Assistance Board; a local Legal Aid Committee decides whether you have sufficiently good grounds in law to justify spending public money on your chances.

Legal aid is not available for libel, slander or breach of promise to marry or in the County Court, for judgement summonses and some minor matters.

The foregoing schemes apply to civil matters only. There are separate arrangements for legal aid in criminal matters, about which you should enquire at your local Magistrate's Court.

## CONTRACTS OF EMPLOYMENT

Basically, the terms upon which you are employed depend upon what you and your employer have agreed, that is to say upon your contract of employment. Such questions as the length of notice which you have to give or to receive to end the employment, the amount of holiday to which you are entitled, and so on, are matters for agreement between you, although in some cases wages and holidays may be governed by statute, for example by orders under the Wages Councils Act, 1959. Agreements between trade union and employers do not, strictly speaking, form part of your contract of employment, which is still in essence a personal matter between you and your employer – although, of course, any such contract may, and often does, incorporate terms which have been arrived at by collective bargaining.

Contracts of employment are often made by word of mouth only and probably for this reason attention is frequently not paid to some of the points which ought to be dealt with. The Contracts of Employment Act 1963 should have the effect of making both employers and employees give more thought to such matters because the Act requires employers to give all employees of more than 13 weeks standing written particulars of some of the principal terms of their employment (except in cases where the agreement itself is in writing and covers the same points). Particulars must be given of:

1. the identity of the parties;
2. the date the employment began and (when it is for a fixed term) the date on which it is to end, or (if not for a fixed term) the length of notice required on either side to terminate it;
3. the rate of remuneration and the intervals at which it is paid;
4. hours of work;
5. holidays and holiday pay;
6. sick pay and sick leave;
7. pensions and pension schemes.

Difficulties about terms of employment usually arise when it comes to an end. Sometimes an employee of quite long standing is unexpectedly dismissed without being given what he considers an adequate reason. Anyone in such a position should realise that (unless the employment is for a fixed length of time agreed at the outset) either party to the contract is at liberty at any time to bring it to an end with or without an adequate reason or any reason at all, provided only that he gives the proper length of notice to the other party. In this respect what is sauce for the goose is sauce for the gander; the employer no more requires to have a reason for terminating the employee's services than the employee does if it is he who wants to leave.

The length of notice which has to be given is, like the other terms of the employment, a matter for agreement at the outset, but whatever is agreed, it must not be less than the minima laid down by the Contracts of Employment Act 1963. The minima are: one week if notice is given by the employee, but if notice is given by the employer a length of time dependant on the employee's length of service, that is to say one week's notice after 26 weeks' service, two weeks' notice after 2 years' service, and four weeks' notice after 5 years' service (merely technical changes of employer, for example, on the sale of a business as a going concern, or changes of partners in a firm, do not interrupt continuous service for this purpose).

Serious misconduct on the part of the employee, for example, wilful disobedience of a reasonable order, will justify the employer in terminating the contract without the agreed length of notice, i.e. summary dismissal. Employers will, however, generally be careful before claiming to exercise this right, because summary dismissal which is unjustified gives the employee a right to damages. The same principle applies the other way round: if an employee leaves without giving proper notice he can be sued for damages by his employer. Although this has not been often done in the past, there seems to be an increasing tendency for employers to avail themselves of their rights.

The Contracts of Employment Act 1963, referred to above, does not apply in all cases. In particular, it does not apply to casual and short-term workers, police officers, merchant seamen, registered dock workers, nor to civil servants (but it does apply to employees of state corporations, such as the BBC, and to employees of local authorities).

When an employment has been ended, the employee often wants a reference from his employer to assist him in getting another job. Most employers are willing to give references and most will make them as favourable to the ex-employee as their consciences will permit. This, however, is a matter of grace on their part, because there is no obligation on an employer to give any reference at all. An employer who does give a reference and comments unfavourably on his ex-employee is not guilty of libel, provided he is expressing his honest opinion.

**REDUNDANCY PAYMENTS.** Another consequence of losing one's job will, in many cases, be receipt of a "redundancy payment" under the Redundancy Payments Act of 1965. Employees should note that this arises only when they receive notice from their employer and not where they give notice to their employer, even if they do so in consequence, for example, of a warning from him that their employment will soon have to be terminated because of a falling-off in work or some other reason.

If notice is given by the employer "by reason of redundancy" to an employee who has been in 2 years' continuous service after the age of 18, then the employee is entitled to a redundancy payment on the following scale: for service between the ages of 18 and 21 half a week's pay per year, for service between 21 and 40 one week's pay per year, for service between 40 and 65 (60 for women) one and a half week's pay per year, with a maximum of 20 weeks entitlement and £40 per week, *i.e.* a payment of £1,200. Merely technical changes of employment do not break continuity for this purpose, as under the Contracts of Employment Act 1963: there are special provisions about strikes and lock-outs.

Redundancy payments are not subject to Income Tax and it seems that they will not effect any right to Unemployment Benefit nor to damages for wrongful dismissal.

The employee will not be eligible for a redundancy payment in several cases, of which some of the more important are:

1. If the employer would have been entitled to dismiss him summarily for misconduct. Employers should note that if they give full notice, they must at the same time give notice that they would have been entitled to dismiss without notice (although they need not state the particular misconduct which would have constituted justification) otherwise they will find that they will still have to make a redundancy payment notwithstanding the employee's misconduct.

2. If the employee unreasonably refuses an offer of suitable alternative employment.

3. If the right to a payment is excluded by agreement in a contract of employment for a fixed term of two years or more – apart from this provision it is not possible, even if employer and employee agree, to contract out of the Act.

4. If the employer is his/her husband or wife (or certain other relations in the case of domestic service).

5. If he is in certain parts of the public service.

6. If he is in part-time work, which in this context means less than 21 hours per week.

7. If he is over the minimum pension age under National Insurance.

Employers can recover 66⅔ per cent (for employees aged 40 and below) or 70 per cent (in other cases) of redundancy payments from the Redundancy Fund which is financed by taxation collected from employers (not employees) as part of the National Insurance stamp.

**ACROSTICS.** The acrostic is a short poem in which, by taking the initial letter of each line in sequence, a name or sentence is formed. The word comes from the Greek, *akros*, at the point or end, and *stichos*, a line. The acrostic was formerly in vogue for valentine and love verses. When employed as a riddle it is called a *Rebus*, *which see*.

**ACROSTICS (Double).** This riddle is a double Rebus, the initial and final letters of a word or words selected making two names or two words. The usual plan is first to suggest the foundation words, and then to describe the separate words, whose initials and finals furnish the answer to the question. Thus:—

A Party to charm the young and erratic—
But likely to frighten the old and rheumatic.
1 The carriage in which the fair visitants came;
2 A very old tribe with a very old name;
3 A brave Prince of Wales free from scandal or shame

The answer is Picnic.

|   |   |         |   |
|---|---|---------|---|
| 1 | P | Phaeton | N |
| 2 | I | Iceni   | I |
| 3 | C | Caradoc | C |

**AFFINITIES.** To pair guests as partners for whist drives, supper, &c. Each guest is given a card bearing a name which is usually associated with another name in history or literature, &c., and each has to find his or her "affinity." Such pairs as Abelard and Heloise, Antony and Cleopatra, Dante and Beatrice, Darby and Joan, Paolo and Francesca, Paul and Virginia, Romeo and Juliet, Samson and Delilah, Tristram and Isolde, &c., will readily suggest themselves as appropriate affinities.

**ANAGRAMS** (from *ana*, backwards, and *gramma*, a letter) are formed by the transposition of the letters of words or sentences, or names of persons, so as to produce a word, sentence, or verse, of pertinent or of widely different meaning. The following are good examples:—

| Words | Transpositions |
|-------|----------------|
| Astronomers | No more stars |
| Catalogues | Got as a clue |
| Elegant | Neat leg. |
| Impatient | Tim in a pet |
| Immediately | I met my Delia |
| Masquerade | Queer as mad |
| Matrimony | Into my arm |
| Melodrama | Made moral |

**ARITHMOREMS.** The Arithmorem is made by substituting figures in a part of the word indicated for Roman numerals. The nature of the riddle – from the Greek *arithmos*, number, and the Latin *remanere*, stay behind – will be easily seen from the following example, which also forms a double acrostic:—

H   51 and *a tub* – a fine large fish
A   twice 50 and *gore* – a sprightly movement in music
R   5 and *be* – a part of speech
U   551 and *as an a* – a Spanish province
To  201 and *ran* – a stupefying drug
R   102 and *nt* – an acid
OU  250 and *paa* – a Mexican town.

The answer is *Havanna Tobacco*. Halibu*t*, *A*llegr*o*, *V*er*b*, *A*ndalusi*a*, *N*arcoti*c*, *N*itri*c*, *A*capulc*o*.

**BACKGAMMON**

A game of mingled chance and skill, played on a board marked with points. The board has twenty-four points, coloured alternately red and blue; the implements of play are fifteen draughtsmen on each side, and the movements of the men are determined by the throw of two dice; each player being provided with a dice box and dice. It is too elaborate to explain briefly. Handbooks to the game are easily procurable.

**BOOK TEAS.** Each invited guest comes representing the title of a well-known book, which the other guests have to guess.

The following examples may be given:—

| Book | Illustration |
|------|-------------|
| "A Safety Match" | — Match-box with one safety match |
| "Bleak House" | — — a B, a leek, and sketch of a house. |
| "Four Feathers" | — — Bunch of 4 feathers |
| "Talisman" | — — A charm |
| "Wild Wales" | — — Picture of infant crying |
| "Plain Tales from the Hills" | — — — Couple of rabbits' tails |
| "Our Mutual Friend" | — Portrait of someone well known to company |
| "Twenty Years After" | — Date of same day, 20 years later, on card |
| "Oliver Twist" | — — "All of a twist" – suitable drawing |
| "The White Company" | Business card, "John White, Bros.," Iron-founders |
| "Redgauntlet" | — — A red glove |

**CAPPING LINES.** In this game the company sit round the room, and one is selected as Head of the class, and reads or speaks a line of poetry. He or she then challenges the next player to give the following line, and the name of the author. If he cannot do either he pays *two* forfeits; but if he can cap the line or give the author's name, he only pays one, goes to the top of the class, and is exempted from all forfeits for the rest of the round. He then in his turn gives a line and so on through the game.

*Example:* (First player) "The way was long, the wind was cold"

(Second player) "The minstrel was infirm and old" (Scott).

**CHARADES (ACTED).** Characters dressed in costumes made up of handkerchiefs, coats, table-covers, &c., come on and perform an extempore play, usually in three acts, founded upon the parts of a word, and its *whole*. The word has to be guessed by the rest of the company. Some amount of preparation is essential, somebody must be chosen stage manager. He will assist in the choice of an effective word, and give the players, as speedily as he can, a notion of what each has to do. The following list of suitable words – which can, of course, be added to – will found helpful. But do not select too obvious words:—

| | | |
|---|---|---|
| Al-tar | Honey-moon | Over-charge |
| Bag-dad | Imp-lore | Plain-tiff |
| Band-age | In-no-cent | Pot-ash |
| Bride-cake | Kit-ten | Prop-a-gate |
| Friend-ship | Mis-take | Stair-case |
| Goose-berry | Neck-lace | Steer-age |

**CHESS**

The rules given below are those accepted by English chess players.

**i.** The board is to be so placed as to leave a white square at the right-hand end of the row nearest each player. The Queen always stands upon a square of her own colour at the beginning of the game.

**ii.** Any mistake in placing the board or the men may be rectified before the fourth move is completed but not after.

**iii.** The players draw lots, with a white and a black pawn, for the first move, and, in a series of games, take the first move alternately. White generally move first.

**iv.** The players move alternately. The piece touched must be moved. When the fingers of the player have once left the piece, it cannot be again removed from the square it occupies.

[Except the move be illegal, when the opponent can insist on the piece being moved in the proper manner, or for the player's King to be moved instead.]

**v.** In touching a piece simply to adjust it, the player must notify to his adversary that such is his intention.

**vi.** If a player touches one of his opponent's pieces and that piece is in a position to be taken, the opponent may insist on the player taking that piece, unless by doing so the player places his King in check. If the piece is not in a position to be taken, the player must move his King only, provided he can do so without placing it in check.

**vii.** A pawn may be played either one or two squares at a time when first moved.

[In the latter case it is liable to be taken *en passant*, i.e. with a pawn that could have taken it had it been played only one square].

**viii.** A player cannot castle in any of the following circumstances:—1. If he has moved either King or the Rook with which he proposes to castle. 2. If the King be in check. 3. If there be any piece between the King and the Rook. 4. If the King, in moving, pass over any square commanded by any opposing piece.

**ix.** If a player give a check without crying "check," the adversary need not take notice of the check. But if it is claimed on the next move, the pieces should be replaced, and the game properly played.

**x.** If a player say check without actually attacking the King, and his adversary move his King or take the piece, the latter may retract his move if it be done before the player has made his next move.

**xi.** If a player makes a false move, his opponent may compel him to move the piece falsely moved, or to move his King if it can be done without putting the King in check. If the next move has been made, neither side can recall the false move.

**xii. A Drawn Game** results:—
1. If neither player can checkmate his opponent's King.
2. If a player is unable to checkmate in 50 moves after being called upon to do so.
3. If a player whose King is not in check cannot move without putting his King in check. This is "Stalemate."
4. If each side is left with King only, or King and Knight, or King and Bishop.
5. If a player is perpetually checked, but can continue to get out of check.
6. If both players repeat the same moves thrice in succession, or if the same position occur more than twice.

**xiii.** Directly a pawn reaches its eighth square it must be exchanged for a piece of the same colour.

[It is usual to change the pawn for a Queen, but it may be replaced by a Rook, Bishop, or Knight, without reference to the pieces already on the board. In practice it would be changed for a Queen or a Knight, seeing that the Queen's moves include those of the Rook and Bishop. Thus you may have two or more Queens, three or more Rooks, Bishops, or Knights on the board at the end of the game].

## CHRONOGRAMS OR CHRONOGRAPHS

are riddles in which the letters of the Roman notation in a sentence or series of words are so arranged as to make up a date. The following is a good example:—

My Day Closed Is In Immortality

The initials MDCIII give 1603, the year of Queen Elizabeth's death. Sometimes the Chronogram is employed to express a date on coins or medals; but oftener it is simply used as a riddle:—A poet who in blindness wrote; another lived in Charles's reign; a third called the father of English verse; a Spanish dramatist; the scolding wife of Socrates; and the Prince of Latin poets – their initials give the year of the Great Plague – MDCLXV – 1665: Milton, Dryden, Chaucer, Lope-de-Vega, Xantippe, Virgil. The word comes from *chronos* time, and *gramma*, a letter.

## CLUEDO

An exciting proprietory board game for 2–6 players. A murder has been committed and all six members of the house party are suspect. With what sort of weapon? It could have been any one of six weapons found on the premises. In which room? The deed could have been done in any one of the nine rooms shown in the plan of Tudor Close. Which player can first link the guilty party, with the weapon used and with the room where the murder was done? Excellent for older youngsters.

**CONUNDRUMS.** These are simple catches, generally founded upon words capable of double meaning. The following are examples:—

Where did Charles the First's executioner dine, and what did he take?
*He took a chop at the King's Head.*
Why should a gouty man make his will?
*To have his legatees* (leg at ease).
Why are bankrupts more to be pitied than idiots?
*Because bankrupts are broken, while idiots are only cracked.*
Why is the treadmill like a true convert?
*Because its turning is the result of conviction.*
Why is a dog's tail like the heart of a tree?
*Because it's farthest from the bark.*
What was the difference between Noah's Ark and Joan of Arc?
*One was made of Gophir wood and the other Maid of Orleans.*

## CROWN AND ANCHOR

It is played with a board and dice. The board has a representation of a playing card at each corner, a heart, a diamond, a club, and a spade, and a crown and an anchor in the middle. Three special dice, each bearing the above six symbols, are used. The holder of the board – the banker – throws the three dice after the players have placed their stakes on the different symbols on the board. He pays the equivalent of their stakes to the players who have staked on the corresponding symbols to those turned up on the dice, and rakes in all other stakes. Should two crowns, &c., turn up he pays double stakes to the stakers on the crown, if three crowns, treble stakes, and so on.

**CRYPTOGRAPHY,** or secret writing – from the Greek *cryptos*, a secret, and *graphé*, a writing – has been largely employed in State despatches, commercial correspondence, love epistles, and riddles.

When one letter is always made to stand for another, the secret of a cryptograph is soon discovered, but when, as in the following example, the same letter does not invariably correspond to the letter for which it is a substitute, the difficulty of deciphering the cryptograph is manifestly increased:—

Ohs ya h sych oayarsa rr loucys syms
Osrh srore rrhmu h smsmsmah emshyr snms.

The translation of this can be made only by the possessor of the key – twenty-six letters which, when applied to the cryptograph, will give a couplet from Parnell's "Hermit":—

"Far in a wild, unknown to public view,
From youth to age a reverend hermit grew."

a b c d e f g h i j k l m n o p q r s t u v w x y z
h u s h m o n e y b y c h a r l e s h r o s s e s q

"Hush Money, by Charles H. Ross, Esq."

**DARTS**

An indoor game played on a circular board made of elm, 18 inches in diameter, and 2 inches thick. It is divided into twenty segments by wires nailed to the surface each segment numbered in irregular sequence from one to twenty. The bull's-eye is a half-inch circle in the middle counting fifty; round it is an outer circle counting twenty-five. The board is fixed with the bull's-eye 5 feet 8 inches from the ground.

Three darts are used, each player throwing all of them in turn. The most

common form of the game starts and finishes with the dart planted in the "double" strip – the outer circle, ⅜ of an inch wide, which traverses the circumference of the board. The players stand 9 feet from the board and the score required is 301, 501, 1,001, or other odd numbers decided upon. Each score obtained is subtracted from the agreed total and victory goes to the player or team which first reduces the total exactly to nothing with a "double."

**DECAPITATIONS AND CURTAILMENTS** are riddles somewhat of the nature of the Logogriph, *which see*. In the first, the omission of the successive initials produces new words as – Prelate, Relate, Elate, Late, Ate. In the curtailment the last letter of the word is taken away with a similar result, as – Patent, Paten, Pate, Pat, Pa.

**DOMINOES**

This game is played by two or more persons, with twenty-eight oblong pieces, plain on the back, but on the face divided by a black line in the middle, and indented with spots, from one to a double-six. Sometimes a double set is played with, of which double-nine is the highest.

**Method of Play.** The dominoes are well mixed together, with their faces upon the table. Each player draws one, and if four play, those who choose the two highest are partners against those who take the two lowest. Drawing the latter also serves to determine who is to lay down the first piece – a great advantage. Afterwards each player takes seven pieces at random.

The eldest hand having laid down one, the next must pair him at either end of the piece he may choose, according to the number of pips, or the blank in the compartment of the piece; but whenever anyone cannot match the part, either of the domino last put down, or of that unpaired at the other end of the row, then he says, "*Go*"; and the next is at liberty to play. Thus they play alternately, either until one party has played all his pieces, and thereby won the game, or till the game be *blocked*; that is, when neither party can play, by matching the pieces where unpaired at either end; then that player wins who has the smallest number of pips on the pieces remaining in his hand.

It is to the advantage of every player to dispossess himself as early as possible of the heavy pieces, such as a double-six, five, four, &c. Sometimes, when two persons play, they take each only three or five pieces, and agree to *play* or *draw – i.e.* when one cannot come in, or pair the pieces upon the board at the end unmatched, he draws from the pieces in stock till he finds one to suit. There are various other ways of playing dominoes; all'dependent on the matching of the pips.

## DRAUGHTS, RULES OF THE GAME

**i.** The board is to be so placed as to have the black double corners at the right hand of the player. The men are placed and played on the black squares.

**ii.** The first move is taken by agreement, and in all the subsequent games of the same sitting, the first move is taken alternately. Black always moves first.

**iii.** The man touched must be moved, but the men may be properly adjusted during any part of the game. After they are so placed, if either player, when it is his turn to play, touches a man he must move it or forfeit the game.

**iv.** If a player has one of his men in such a position that it can be taken, and his opponent fails to take it, and makes another move, the player may (*a*) compel his opponent to retract the move, and take the man; (*b*) allow the move to stand without penalty; or (*c*) allow the move to stand, but remove from the board the man that failed to take, and then make his own move. This is called "huff and move."

The "huff" must be claimed before the player makes his next move. A huff is not a move.

**v.** Five minutes is the longest time allowed to consider a move, which if not made within that time, forfeits the game, and where there is *only one* way of taking *one or more* pieces, one minute alone is allowed, or the game is forfeited.

**vi.** A player must take all the pieces he can legally take with the same move, otherwise he is liable to be "huffed" by his opponent. On making a King, however, the latter remains on his square till a move has been made by the opponent.

**vii.** A false move must be remedied as soon as it is discovered, or the maker of such move loses the game.

**viii.** When only a small number of men remain toward the end of the game, the possessor of the lesser number may call on his opponent to win within 40 of his own moves, or declare the game drawn. With two Kings to one, the game must be won in at most 20 moves on each side.

**The Losing Game.** A variety of the game is sometimes played, called "First off the board," in which the object is to make your opponent "take" all your men, the player who first succeeds in doing so winning the game.

**Draughts: Italian Game.** In this form of the game the board is set with the black square in the right-hand corner. A single man may not take a King, and if there is an alternative way of taking, the player must take in the way which causes him to take the greatest number of men.

**Draughts: Polish Game.** This game is played on a board of 100 squares with 20 men a side. In taking, the men move backwards as well as forwards. A man reaching the crown head goes on taking any men that are *en prise*, and does not stop to be crowned as in the English game. If no men are *en prise* at the crown head, the man becomes a Queen and can then move over any number of squares diagonally and must take all adverse men *en prise* on the lines she commands.

This form of the game is also played on a board of 144 squares and 30 men a side.

**Draughts: Spanish Game.** The board is set as in the Italian game. The largest possible number of men must be taken if there are alternative ways of taking open to a player. The King when crowned has the same powers of movement and capture as the Queen in the Polish game.

The game is sometimes played with 11 men and a King, or with 10 men and 2 Kings a side instead of 12 men.

**Draughts: Turkish Game.** The board has 64 squares and 16 men a side placed on adjacent squares on the second and third back rows. The men move forwards perpendicularly, and horizontally either to left or to right. A King when crowned can move any number of vacant squares perpendicularly or horizontally. Taking is compulsory and the greatest possible number must be taken, the men being removed from the board one by one as taken.

**ENIGMAS** are compositions of a different character, based upon *ideas*, rather than upon words. Enigmas may be founded upon simple catches, like Conundrums, in which form they are usually called "Riddles," such as:—

> "Though you set me on foot,
> I shall be on my head."

The answer is, *A nail in a shoe*. The celebrated Enigma, on the letter H, usually attributed to Lord Byron, commencing:

> "'Twas whispered in heaven, 'twas muttered in hell
> And echo caught faintly the sound as it fell";

is an admirable specimen.

**THE "EYES" GAME.** The curtains having been drawn close, the players except one go behind them. Those behind the curtains choose one of their number who looks between the curtains, showing only his eyes. The player who is left in the room has to guess who it is. If he is wrong he has to pay a forfeit. If right, he may go beind the curtain, and the one detected has to guess.

**HIDDEN WORDS.** A riddle in which names of towns, persons, rivers, &c., are hidden or arranged, without transposition, in the midst of sentences which convey no suggestion of their presence. In the following sentence, for instance, there are hidden six Christian names:—
Here is hid a skate where the land or alley ends. The names of course are Ida,

Kate, Ethel, Dora. Great varieties of riddles, known as Buried Cities, Hidden Towns, &c., are formed on this principle.

**LEXICON**
A useful and entertaining game for the family.

Ten lettered cards are dealt to each of the players. The remainder of the cards are placed in a heap face down on the table and the top card exposed and placed alongside. For five or more players it is necessary to use two packs.

The player on the left of the dealer commences. The next player on the left then plays and so on round the table. Each player, after examining his cards, can do one of four alternatives:

(*a*) Form one complete word and place it face up on the table.

(*b*) He can discard one of his cards and take either the exposed card or the blind one from the heap.

He must discard BEFORE taking up the exposed or blind card. The discarded card is placed on top of, or in the place of, the exposed card and this becomes the exposed card on the table.

(*c*) When a word is exposed on the table he can insert a card, or cards, in any such word. In doing this the order of the letters must not be disturbed or the word reversed. The other letters must be added at either end, or inserted. Only one word can be attacked at the same turn.

(*d*) When a word is exposed on the table he can take a card, or cards, out of his own hand and change it, or them, for a letter, or letters in a word provided the word left on the table is complete.

No player is allowed to PASS HIS TURN without doing one of these four alternatives, but he is not allowed to do more than one in the same turn.

A player's turn ceases when he has done one of the four actions "A", "B", "C" or "D".

The object of the game is to get rid of your cards as quickly as possible. The first player to do this ends the round and the other players count their scores from the numbers on the cards left in their hands. The score is then entered against that particular player's name and then the cards are dealt out for another round

The first player to reach 100 retires from the game, the others going on till by elimination one only is left – the winner. Lexicon is a proprietary game.

**LIPOGRAM** – from *leipo*, "I leave out," and *gramma*, a letter – is a riddle in which a name or sentence is written without its vowels, as Thprffthpddngsnthtng – The proof of the pudding is in the eating.

**LOGOGRIPH.** This is a riddle (*logos*, a word, and *griphos*, a riddle) in which a word is made to undergo several changes. These changes are brought about by the addition, substraction, omission, or substitution of a letter or letters. The following by Lord Macaulay is an excellent example:—

"Cut off my head, how singular I act
  Cut off my tail, and plural I appear.
Cut off my head and tail – most curious fact,
  Although my middle's left, there's nothing there
What is my head cut off? – a sounding sea
  What is my tail cut off? – a flowing river
Amid their mingling depths I fearless play
  Parent of softest sounds, though mute for ever "

The answer is *cod*. Cut off its head and it is *od* (odd, singular); its tail, and it is *Co.*, plural, for company; head and tail, and it is *o*, nothing. Its head is a sounding C (sea), its tail a flowing D (river Dee), and amid their depths the cod may "fearless play, parent of softest *sounds* yet mute for ever."

**METAGRAM**, a riddle in which the change of the initial letter produces a series of words of different meanings; from *meta*, implying change, and *gramma*, a letter. Thus:—

I cover your head; change my head, and I set you to sleep; change it again and again, and with every change comes a new idea. – Cap, Nap, Gap, Sap, Hap, Map, Lap, Pap, Rap, Tap.

This kind of riddle is also known as word-capping.

## MONOPOLY

"Monopoly", a popular board game for 2–6 players, contains 44 miniature Houses and Hotels, a thick wad of money, Title Deeds to famous streets, stations and other properties in London. You can buy famous sites and "develop" them by building "houses" or "hotels" – to yield steeply rising rents – or you may have to sell off your buildings and even mortgage the sites if times are lean. The idea of the game is to buy and rent or sell properties so profitably that one becomes the wealthiest player and eventual monopolist. "Monopoly" is a proprietary game of blended skill, luck and fun and is readily obtainable.

**PALINDROME**, from the Greek *palindromos*, running back again. This is a word, sentence, or verse that reads the same both forwards and backwards – as, madam, level, reviver; live on no evil; love your treasure and treasure your love; you provoked Harry before Harry provoked you; servants respect masters when masters respect servants. Perhaps the best example is the sentence which, referring to the first banishment of Napoleon, makes him say, as to his power to conquer Europe:—

"Able was I ere I saw Elba."

**PUZZLES** vary much. Upon the principle of the square-words, riddlers form Diagonals, Diamonds, Pyramids, Crosses, Stars, &c. These specimens will show their peculiarities:

**Oblique Puzzle.** Malice, eight, a church council, a Scottish river, what I write with, a decided negative, the capital of Ireland. The initials downward name a celebrated musician.

**Diagonal Puzzle.** A direction, a singer, a little bird, a lady's ring, a sharp shaver. Read from left to right and right to left, the centrals show two favourite novelists.

The following are the answers to these two puzzles.

| OBLIQUE | DIAGONAL |
|---------|----------|
| R E V E N G E | L A B E L |
| O C T A V E | T E N O R |
| S Y N O D | D I V E R |
| S P E Y | J E W E L |
| I N K | R A Z O R |
| N O | |
| I | |

**Diamond Puzzle.** The head of a mouse, what the mouse lives in, the county of calves, a town in Sussex, an Irish lough, a Transatlantic stream, a royal county, a

Yorkshire borough, Eve's temptation, our poor relation, myself. Centrals down and across, show a wide, wide, long river.

The construction of the Diamond Puzzle is exhibited in the following diagram, which is, at the same time the answer to it:

```
            DIAMOND
              M
            A I R
          E S S E X
        H O R S H A M
      KI L L I N U R E
    MIS S I S S I P P I
      B E R KS HI R E
        HAL I F A X
          A P P L E
            A P E
              I
```

**Boss: or Fifteen Puzzle.**

Apparently simple, this game is really difficult of solution. Fifteen cubes of wood, severally marked from 1 to 15, are placed indifferently in a box made to hold sixteen; thus:

| 9 | 11 | 3 | 7 |
|---|----|---|---|
| 8 | 14 | 10 | 15 |
| 6 | 12 | 13 | 2 |
| 5 | 1 | 4 | |

| 1 | 2 | 3 | 4 |
|---|---|---|---|
| 5 | 6 | 7 | 8 |
| 9 | 10 | 11 | 12 |
| 13 | 14 | 15 | |

The puzzle consists in sliding the cubes from square to square, without lifting them or removing them from the box, until they are placed in their natural order. It is easy enough to move the squares up to 12; but to get the last three into order is often a puzzle indeed. If the cubes fall in either of the following positions – 13, 15, 14; 14, 13, 15; or 15, 14, 13 – the problem is unsolvable; it follows, therefore, that the last row must be either 14, 15, 13; or 15, 13, 14. If you get the cubes into either of these positions, you can easily bring them right but if you cannot, the only way is to begin the game all over again.

**The Thirty-Four Puzzle.** Sixteen discs or squares, numbered from 1 to 16, are placed indifferently on the table – or they may be in the fifteen box; and the puzzle is to so arrange them as to make the sum of the figures add up to 34, whether counted up, down, across or diagonally. Here is the solution:

| 1 | 15 | 14 | 4 |
|---|----|----|---|
| 12 | 6 | 7 | 9 |
| 8 | 10 | 11 | 4 |
| 13 | 3 | 2 | 16 |

| 1 | 8 | 13 | 12 |
|---|---|----|----|
| 14 | 11 | 2 | 7 |
| 4 | 5 | 16 | 9 |
| 15 | 10 | 3 | 6 |

**REBUSES** form a class of Enigma generally formed by the first, sometimes the first and last, letters of words, or of transpositions of letters, or additions to words. Dr. Johnson, however, represented Rebus to be a word represented by a picture. And putting Johnson's definition and our own explanation together, the reader may obtain a good idea of the nature of the Rebus of which the following is an example:

> The father of the Grecian Jove;
>   A little boy who's blind;
> The foremost land in all the world;
>   The mother of mankind;
> A poet whose love-sonnets are
>   Still very much admired:–
> The *initial* letters will declare
>   A blessing to the tired.
> Answer – *Saturn*; *Love*; *England*; *Eve*; *Petrarch*.
> The initials form *sleep*.

**SQUARE WORDS.** A riddle, in which the letters of each word selected read both across and down. With four letters the making of the riddle is easy, but with five or six the difficulty increases. We give an example of each:

**i.** Inside, a thought, a liquid gem, a timid creature.

**ii.** To run out, odour, he sees, to loosen, unseen essence.

**iii.** Compensations, a court favourite, to assist, to bite slightly, Spanish money, sarcasms.

```
      i.              ii.
    P I T H        I S S U E
    I D E A        S C E N T
    T E A R        S E E T H
    H A R E        U N T I E
                   E T H E R
         iii.
      A M EN D S
      M I NI O N
      E N A B L E
      N I B B L E
      D O L L A R
      S NE E R S
```

With seven or eight letters the riddle becomes exceedingly difficult, especially if the selected words are of like character and syllables.

## ROULETTE

A gambling game, purely of chance, and is played on an oblong table covered with green cloth, having in the centre a circular space in which a numbered wheel revolves. On each side of the wheel the cloth is divided into exactly corresponding spaces, marked *passe*, *pair*, *manque*, *impair*, *rouge*, *noir*.

The wheel contains 37 compartments, coloured alternately black and red, and numbered irregularly from 1 to 36 and zero. Frequently a double zero (00) is added, in which case there are 38 compartments. The numbers from 1 to 18 are *manque*, those from 19 to 36 are *passe*. Even numbers are *pair*, odd numbers *impair*.

The minimum stake is fixed, but the methods of staking are innumerable.

One croupier sits on each side of the wheel, and one at each end of the table to help the players in making their stakes and getting their winnings. Behind each of the croupiers at the wheel, on a raised chair sits an official to supervise the play.

The croupier whose duty it is to set the wheel in motion, calls to the players to make their stakes, spins the wheel, and throws the ball into it in a direction contrary to that in which it is revolving. As the wheel slows down he calls out "*Rien ne va plus,*" after which no stakes may be made.

When the ball finally settles in a numbered compartment, he calls out the number and the chances that win, *e.g. noir*, *pair et passe*. The croupiers then rake in all the stakes that have been lost, and pay out to the winners the amounts they have gained.

At the beginning of play a certain sum of money is supplied to those in charge of the table, and if this sum is exhausted during the course of play the bank is said to be broken.

## SCRABBLE

An entertaining and useful word-making proprietory game, played on a board with lettered and numbered pieces. Seven letters are drawn to start and each player in turn endeavours to make words. The score is reckoned on the value of the letters used and by the indications on the board. 2–4 players.

## CARD GAMES
## BANKER

A gambling game played with an ordinary pack of cards, usually by 5 or 6 players, each paying into a pool a fixed stake.

The dealer (or banker) gives three cards to each player, and turns up one card. If the turned-up card is not lower than an eight he goes on turning up cards until one lower than eight appears. The player on the dealer's left may now bet up to the amount of the pool that among his cards there is one of higher value in the same suit than the turned-up card, but he may not touch or look at his cards before betting. If he wins he takes the amount of his bet from the pool; if he loses he pays the amount into the pool. The next player on the left then makes his bet and so on, the dealer being last.

Whenever the pool is exhausted a fresh pool is made, and after a full round of the table the deal passes to the next player on the left of the dealer.

Should any player touch or look at his cards before he has made his bet he is fined twice the amount of the stake, and loses his right to bet during that round.

**Another Method.** The dealer (banker) cuts the cards into as many packs or portions as there are players, including himself, taking care that the bottom card of the original pack is not at the bottom of any of the small packs. The players then place the amount of their stakes, up to a fixed limit, agreed upon before play begins, upon the pack they select to bet on.

When all stakes have been made on one or other, or all, of the packs, except the banker's, the dealer turns up the packs – his own last – and pays the amount of their stakes to all those who have staked upon packs whose bottom cards are of higher value than his own, and collects the stakes of those who have staked on packs whose bottom cards are of equal or lower value. The "bank" changes hands only when the banker has to pay everybody, and the person holding the highest card then becomes banker.

## BEGGAR MY NEIGHBOUR

An exciting juvenile game requiring no effort from two players, to whom a pack of ordinary playing cards is equally dealt. The idea is for one of the players to win the whole pack. The players hold the cards face downwards and in turn play them face upwards on to one pile. When an ace, king, queen or jack is played, the other player plays, respectively, four, three, two or one cards. If he himself is unable to turn up one of the above cards his opponent takes the pile.

## BÉZIQUE

This game for two players is played with two packs of cards, from which the twos, threes, fours, fives, and sixes have been discarded. The remaining sixty-four cards, shuffled well together, are then dealt out, eight to each player, either one at a time, or by threes, twos, and threes; the seventeenth turned up for trump, and the rest (called the "talon" or "stock") left, face downwards, on the table, above the exposed trump card.

If the trump card be a seven, the dealer scores ten points. An incorrect deal or an exposed card necessitates a new deal, which passes to the other player. The non-dealer has the lead. A trump card takes any card of another suit. Except trumping, the higher card, whether of the same suit or not, takes the trick – the ace ranking highest, the ten next, and then the king, queen, knave, nine, &c.

When two cards of equal value are played, the first wins. *Some players require the winning card to be of the same suit as that led, unless trumped.* After each trick is taken, an additional card is drawn by each player from the top of the pack – the taker of the last trick drawing first, and so on till all the pack is exhausted, including the trump card.

Players are not obliged to follow suit or trump until all the cards have been drawn from the pack. Tricks are of no value, except for the aces and tens they may contain. Tricks should not be looked at till the end of the deal, except by mutual consent.

When a player plays without drawing, he must draw two cards next time, and his opponent scores ten. When a player draws out of turn, his opponent scores ten, if he has not drawn a card himself. When a player draws two cards instead of one, his opponent may decide which card is to be returned to the pack, and it should not be placed at the top, but towards the middle of the pack.

A player discovering his opponent holding more than eight cards, while he only holds eight, adds 100 to his score. Should both have more than their proper number there is no penalty, but each must play without drawing.

**Terms and counting used in Bézique.—i.** *A Declaration* is the exhibition on the table of any cards or combination of cards, as follows:

**ii.** *Bézique* is the queen of spades and knave of diamonds, for which the holder scores 40 points.

[A variation provides that when the trump is either spades or diamonds, Bézique may be queen of clubs and knave of hearts.]

**iii.** *Double Bézique* – Bézique having been declared, may be again used to form Double Bézique, two queens of spades and two knaves of diamonds. All four cards must be visible on the table together – 500 points.

**iv.** *Sequence* is ace, ten, king, queen, and knave of trumps – 250 points.

**v.** *Royal Marriage* is the king and queen of trumps – 40 points.

**vi.** *Common Marriage* is the king and queen of any suit, except trumps – 20 points.

**vii.** *Four aces* are the aces of any suits – 100 points.

**viii.** *Four kings* are the kings of any suits – 80 points.

**ix.** *Four queens* are the queens of any suits – 60 points.

**x.** *Four knaves* are the knaves of any suits – 40 points.

**xi.** Playing the seven of trumps – except in the last eight tricks – 10; exchanging the seven of trumps for the trump card – 10; the last trick – 10; each ace and ten in the tricks at the end of each deal – 10.

**xii.** The game is 1,000, 2,000, or 4,000 up. Markers are sold with the cards.

## Mode of Playing Bézique

**i.** Play is commenced by the non-dealer, whose card is played to by the dealer. Immediately after taking a trick, and then only, a player can make a declaration; but he must do so before drawing another card. Only one declaration can be made after each trick.

**ii.** If, in making a declaration, a player puts down a wrong card or cards, either in addition to or in the place of any card or cards of that declaration he is not allowed to score until he has taken another trick. Moreover, he must resume the cards, subject to their being called for as "faced" cards.

**iii.** The seven of trumps may be exchanged for the trump card, and for this exchange ten is scored. This exchange is made immediately after he has taken a trick, but he may make a declaration at the same time, the card exchanged not being used in such declaration.

**iv.** Whenever the seven of trumps is played, except in the last eight tricks, the player scores ten for it, no matter whether he wins the trick or not.

**v.** When all the cards are drawn from the pack, the players take up their eight cards. No more declarations can be made, and the play proceeds as at Whist, except that the ten ranks higher than the king.

**vi.** In the last eight tricks the player is obliged to follow suit, and he must win the trick if possible, either by playing a higher card, or, if he has not a card of the same suit, by playing a trump.

**vii.** A player who revokes in the last eight tricks, or omits to take when he can, forfeits the eight tricks to his opponent.

**viii.** The last trick is the thirty-second, for which the winner scores ten.

[The game may be varied by making the last trick the twenty-fourth – the next before the last eight tricks. It is an unimportant point, but one that should be agreed upon before the game is commenced.]

**ix.** After the last eight tricks are played, each player examines his cards, and for each ace and ten that he holds he scores ten.

**x.** The non-dealer scores aces and tens first; and in case of a tie, the player scoring the highest number of points, less the aces and tens in the last deal, wins the game. If still a tie, the taker of the last trick wins.

**xi.** All cards played in error are liable to be called for as "faced" cards at any period of the game, except during the last eight tricks.

**xii.** In counting forfeits a player may either add the points to his own score or deduct them from the score of his opponent.

## Marriages, Sequences, &c.

**i.** The cards forming the declarations are placed on the table to show that they are properly scored, and the cards may thence be played into tricks as if in your hand.

**ii.** Kings and queens once married cannot be re-married, but can be used while they remain on the table, to make up four kings, four queens, or a sequence.

**iii.** The king and queen used in a sequence cannot afterwards be declared as a royal marriage.

**iv.** If four knaves have been declared, the knave of diamonds may be used again for a bézique, or to complete a sequence.

**v.** If four aces have been declared, the ace of trumps may be again used to perfect a sequence.

**vi.** If the queen of spades has been married, she may be again used to form a bézique, and vice versa, and again for four queens.

**Forfeits at Bézique.** The following are Forfeits:

For drawing out of turn, 10; for playing out of turn, 10; for playing without drawing, 10; for overdrawing, 100; for a revoke in the last eight tricks, all the eight tricks.

**Cautions in Bézique.** In playing Bézique, it is best to keep your tens till you can make them count; to retain your sequence cards as long as possible; to watch your opponent's play; to declare a royal marriage previous to declaring a sequence of double bézique; to make sure of the last trick but one in order to prevent your opponent from declaring; to declare as soon as you have an opportunity.

## THREE-HANDED BÉZIQUE

i. The above rules hold good in the case of three-handed games – treble bézique counting 1,500. An extra pack of cards is required for the third player; so that, in the case of three, the trump card is the twenty-fifth.

ii. The game is always played from left to right, the first player on the left of the dealer commencing. The game is usually 2,000 up.

## FOUR-HANDED BÉZIQUE

i. Four-handed Bézique may be played by partners decided either by choice or cutting. Partners sit opposite each other, one collecting the tricks of both, and the other keeping the score, or each may keep his own score, which is preferable.

ii. A player may make a declaration immediately after his partner has taken a trick, and may inquire of his partner if he has anything to declare, before drawing.

iii. Declarations must be made by each player separately, as in two-handed bézique.

## BRIDGE

The game is played by four persons, who cut for partners. The cards are dealt in the ordinary way, except that the last card must not be turned up. Nor does a misdeal forfeit the deal.

Each player having examined his or her "hand," the dealer declares the trump suit, unless he elects for no-trumps, or passes his right to his partner. No remark must be made by any player, beyond the formal "To you, partner." The partner must make a declaration. The suit (or no suit) having been declared, the player on the dealer's left says to his partner, "Shall we to – (naming the suit), partner?" or he may "double," which means making the

value of the suit declared double its normal value. His partner then says "content," or may "double" if the first player has not already done so. The dealer then has the option of either expressing content or of redoubling.

There are five honours in Bridge – ace, king, queen, knave, ten, named in the order of their power. Each game consists of 30 points, the rubber being the best of three games. The scores are made up as follows:

Each trick above six tricks counts:

2 in spades
4 in clubs
6 in diamonds
8 in hearts
12 in no-trumps

If the partners hold between them three honours they count twice the value of the trick; if four honours, four times the value; if all the honours, five times the value. If a player hold in his own hand four honours, he scores four honours in addition to the score for conjoint honours. If a player hold the five honours he scores ten times the trick value of the suit. In no-trumps if the partners hold between them three aces, they score 30; if they hold the four aces they score 100. If a player does not hold a single trump card he scores for "chicane," as this condition is called, twice the value of a trick in the suit. When one side takes all the tricks, this is known as a "grand slam" and counts 40; 12 tricks, a "little slam" and counts 20.

The winners of the rubber add 100 points to their score. One player keeps their score. Scoring-sheets are generally supplied in packets, and the value of the different tricks is printed on them.

## AUCTION BRIDGE

As Bridge when first introduced largely superseded whist so did Auction Bridge take the place of ordinary or "straight" Bridge. In ordinary Bridge the restriction of the "declaration" to the dealer and his partner was found to be the occasion for the spoiling of many a good hand. So "Auction" was evolved. In its turn it has been superseded by "Contract".

## CONTRACT BRIDGE

An extension of Auction Bridge. The outstanding difference in the two games is that at Contract the declarer may score, below the line, only as many odd tricks (i.e. tricks beyond the "book" of six tricks) as he has contracted to win. It is necessary, therefore, for partners to arrive at the exact valuation and expectancy of their combined hands in the course of the bidding.

The bidding starts with the dealer, and the player making the highest bid becomes the declarer. The play is similar to Whist except that the first lead is made by the player on the declarer's left, and after the first lead declarer's partner (dummy) spreads his hand face upwards on the table and declarer plays the cards from dummy.

The laws of Contract Bridge, as revised and adopted by the Committee of the Portland Club, are the standard authority on the game.

*The Scoring.* 27. (1) Points are scored in respect of odd tricks and slams bid and won, overtricks, undertricks, honours and rubber.

(2) Points scored in respect of odd tricks bid and won are scored in a trick score; all other points are scored separately in a premium score. (*Tricks transferred to pay the revoke penalty are scored as tricks won.*)

28. (1) A game is won by the side which, in one or more hands, first scores 100 points for odd tricks bid and won.

(2) The hand in which a side wins a game is played out, and all points won therein are scored; but no trick score obtained by either side in that hand, or in any preceding hand, can assist towards winning the next game.

29. The side which wins the first game becomes vulnerable for the remainder of the rubber. If the other side wins the second game, it also becomes vulnerable for the remainder of the rubber. Vulnerability affects the number of points scored for doubled overtricks, undertricks and slams, in the manner described in the laws 31, 32, and 34.

30. If the declarer fulfils his contract, his side scores for odd tricks bid and won:

When clubs or diamonds are trumps, 20 points per trick;

When hearts or spades are trumps, 30 points per trick.

When there are no-trumps, 40 points for the first trick, and 30 points each subsequent trick.

These points are doubled in the case of a doubled contract, and are quadrupled in the case of a redoubled contract.

31. If the declarer, in addition to fulfilling his contract, wins one or more overtricks, his side scores for each overtrick:

When undoubled, a premium equal to the trick points he would have scored if he had contracted to win the trick;

Doubled – Twice the trick points.

32. If the declarer fails to fulfil his contract, his side scores nothing for the tricks won by him, and the opponents score:

In not vulnerable contracts:

Undoubled – 50 points for each undertrick;

Doubled – 100 points for the first undertrick and 200 for each subsequent undertrick.

Redoubled – twice the doubled points;

In vulnerable contracts:

Undoubled – 100 points per trick;

Doubled – 200 points for the first trick and 300 for each subsequent trick.

Redoubled – twice the doubled points.

33. Either side scores for honours, as follows:

If there is a trump suit:—

For four honours held in one hand, 100 points;

For five honours held in one hand, 150 points.

If there are no trumps:—

For four aces held in one hand, 150 points.

34. If the declarer:—

(*a*) Bids and makes a little slam, his side scores for a little slam, if not vulnerable, 500 points; if vulnerable, 750 points;

(*b*) Bids and makes a grand slam, his side scores, if not vulnerable, 1,000 points, if vulnerable, 1,500 points.

The contracting side, having contracted to make seven odd tricks and failed, cannot score a little slam.

35. (1) The rubber ends when one side has won two games, and the winners of the final game add to their score 500 points if their opponents have won one game, and 700 if their opponents have not won a game.

(2) Where a rubber ends by arrangement before either side has won two games, a side which has won one game adds 300 points to its score.

36. At the end of the rubber the trick and premium score of each side is added up; the side with the larger total score wins the rubber, and the difference between the two totals represent the number of points won.

## CRIBBAGE

This game is played with the full pack of cards, often by four persons, but it is a better game for two. There are also different modes of playing – with five, six, or eight cards; but the best games are those with five or six cards.

### Terms Used in Cribbage

i. *Crib.* The crib is composed of the cards thrown out by each player, and the dealer is entitled to score whatever points are made by them.

ii. *Pairs* are two similar cards, as two aces or two kings. Whether in hand or play they reckon for two points.

iii. *Pairs-Royal* are three similar cards, and reckon for six points, whether in hand or play.

iv. *Double Pairs-Royal* are four similar cards and reckon for twelve points, whether in hand or play. The points gained by pairs, pairs-royal and double pairs-royal, in playing, are thus effected: Your opponent having played a seven and you another, constitutes a pair, and entitled you to score two points; your opponent then playing a third seven, makes a pairs-royal, and he marks six; and your playing a fourth is a double pairs-royal, and entitles you to twelve points.

v. *Fifteens.* Every fifteen reckons for two points, whether in hand or play. In hand they are formed either by two or more cards. If in play, such cards as

together make fifteen are played, the player whose card completes that number, scores two points.

vi. *Sequences* are three, four or more successive cards, and reckon for an equal number of points, either in hand or play. In playing a sequence, it is of no consequence which card is thrown down first; as thus: your opponent playing an ace, you a five, he a three, you a two, then he a four – he counts five for sequence.

vii. *Flush.* When the cards are all of one suit, they reckon for as many points as there are cards. For a flush in the crib, the turned up card must be of the same suit as those put out.

viii. *His Nob.* The knave of the suit turned up reckons for one point.

ix. *His Heels.* The knave when turned up reckons for two points, but is only once counted.

x. *The Go.* The point scored by the last player, if he make under thirty-one; if he makes thirty-one exactly, he marks two.

xi. *Last.* Three points taken at the commencement of the game of five-card cribbage by the non-dealer.

### Rules of Cribbage

i. The players cut for deal. The ace is lowest in cutting. In case of a tie they cut again. The holder of the lowest card deals either five, six or eight cards each, as arranged.

ii. A cut must consist of not fewer than four cards.

iii. Too many or too few cards dealt constitutes a misdeal, the penalty for which is the taking of two points by the non-dealer.

iv. A faced card, or a card exposed during the act of dealing, necessitates a new deal, without penalty.

v. The dealer shuffles the cards and the non-dealer cuts them for the "start".

vi. If the non-dealer touch the cards (except to cut them for the turn-up) after they have been cut for the start, he forfeits two points.

vii. In cutting for the start, not fewer than four cards must be lifted from the pack or left on the table.

viii. The non-dealer throws out for the

crib before the dealer. A card once laid out cannot be recalled, nor must either party touch the crib till the hand is played out. Either player confusing the crib cards with his hand is liable to a penalty of three points.

[In three- and four-hand cribbage the left-hand player throws out first the the crib, then the next, the dealer last. The usual and best way is for the non-dealer to throw his crib over to the dealer's side of the board; on these two cards the dealer places his own, and hands the pack over to be cut. The pack is then at the right side of the board for the next deal.]

**ix.** The player who takes more points than those to which he is entitled, either in play or in reckoning hand or crib, is liable to be "pegged"; that is, to be put back as many points as he has over-scored, and have the points added to his opponent's side.

[In pegging you must not remove your opponents' *front* peg till you have given him another. In order "to take him down," you remove *your own back peg* and place it *where his front peg ought to be;* you then take his *wrongly placed peg* and put it *in front of your own front,* as many holes as he has forfeited by wrongly scoring.]

**x.** No penalty attaches to the taking of too few points in play, hand or crib.

**xi.** When a player has once taken his hand or crib, he cannot amend his score.

**xii.** When a knave is turned up, "two for his heels" must be scored before the dealer's own card can be played, or they cannot be taken.

**xiii.** A player cannot demand the assistance of his adversary in reckoning hand and crib.

**xiv.** A player may not, except to "peg him," touch his adversary's pegs, under a penalty of two points. If the foremost peg has been displaced by accident, it must be placed in the hole behind the peg standing on the board.

**xv.** The peg once holed cannot be removed by either player till another point or points be gained.

**xvi.** The player who scores a game as won when, in fact, it is not won, loses it.

**xvii.** A *lurch* – scoring the whole sixty-one before your adversary has scored thirty-one – is equivalent to a double game, if agreed to previous to the commencement of the game.

**xviii.** A card that may be legally played cannot be withdrawn after it has been once thrown face upwards on the table.

**xix.** If a player neglect to score his hand, crib, or any point or points of the game, he cannot score them after the cards are packed or the next card played.

**xx.** The player who throws up his cards and refuses to score, forfeits the game.

**xxi.** If a player neglect to play when he can play a card within the prescribed thirty-one, he forfeits two holes.

**xxii.** Each player's hand and crib must be plainly thrown down on the table and not mixed with the pack, under penalty of the forfeiture of the game.

**FIVE-CARD CRIBBAGE** is played in the same way, five cards only being dealt to each player, of which they each lay out two for crib.

**SIX-CARD CRIBBAGE.** In this the sixty-one points or holes on the cribbage-board mark the game. The player cutting the lowest card deals; after which, each player lays out, face downwards, two of his six cards for the crib, which belong to the dealer. The adversary cuts the remainder of the pack, and the dealer turns up and lays upon the crib the uppermost card, which is called the *turn-up.* If it be a knave, he marks two points. The card turned up is reckoned by both in counting their hands or crib. The eldest hand then plays a card, which the other should endeavour to pair, or find one, the pips of which, reckoned with the first, will make fifteen; then the non-dealer plays another card, and so on alternately, until the pips on the cards played make thirty-one or the nearest possible number under that. (The Court cards count as ten each in all games of cribbage.)

**Counting for Game in Cribbage.** When he whose turn it is to play cannot produce a card that makes thirty-one, or under that number, he says, "Go," and his opponent scores one, or plays any card or cards he may have that will make exactly thirty-one, he takes two points. Such cards as remain after this are not played, but each player then counts and scores his hand, the non-dealer first. The dealer then marks the points for his hand, and also for his crib, each reckoning the cards every way they can possibly be varied, and always including the turned-up card.

| | Points |
|---|---|
| For every fifteen .. .. .. | 2 |
| For a sequence of 3 or 4 cards .. | 3 or 4 |
| For a pair (2 of a kind) .. .. | 2 |
| For a royal pair (3 of a kind) .. | 6 |
| For a double pairs-royal (4 of a kind) | 12 |
| Knave of the suit turned up .. | 1 |

For a flush in hand, that is, cards all of one suit, or for a full flush, when the cards in hand and the turn-up are of the same suit, 1 for each card.

The highest number that can be counted from five cards is 29 – made from four fives and a knave; that is, three fives and a knave of the suit turned up, and a five on the pack – for the combination of the four fives, 16; for the double pairs-royal, 12; his nob, 1 = 29.

**Maxims for Laying Out the Crib Cards.** In laying out cards for the crib, the player should consider not only his own hand, put also to whom the crib belongs, as well as the state of the game; for what might be right in one situation would be wrong in another. Possessing a pairs-royal it is generally advisable to lay out the other cards for crib, unless it belongs to the opponent. Avoid giving him two fives, a deuce and a trois, five and six, seven and eight, five and any other tenth card.

When he does not thereby materially injure his hand, the player should for his own crib lay out close cards in hopes of making a sequence; or two of a suit, in expectation of a flush; or cards that of themselves reckoned with others will count fifteen.

When the opponent is nearly up, it may be expedient to keep such cards as may prevent him from gaining at play. The rule is to baulk his crib by laying out cards not likely to prove of advantage to him, and to lay out favourably for your own crib. This applies to a stag of the game when it may be of consequence to keep in hand cards likely to tell in play, or when the non-dealer would be either out by his hand, or has reason for thinking the crib of little moment. A king and a nine is the best baulk, as none can form a sequence behind it; king or queen, with an ace,

six, seven, eight, or nine are good ones to put out.

Low cards are generally the most likely to gain at play; the flushes and sequences, particularly if the latter be also flushes, are eligible hands, as thereby the player will often be enabled either to assist his own crib, or baulk that of his opponent; a knave should never be put out for his crib, if it can be retained in hand.

**THREE- OR FOUR-HAND CRIBBAGE** differs little from the preceding. The players put out but one card each to the crib, and when thirty-one, or the nearest to that has been made, the next eldest hand leads, and the players go on again in rotation, with the remaining cards, till all are played out, before they proceed to show hands and crib. For three-handed cribbage triangular boards are used.

**ÉCARTÉ.** This game is played by two persons with a pack of cards from which the twos, threes, fours, fives, and sixes have been discarded. It is usual to play with two packs, used alternately.

The players cut for deal, the highest card deals. The pack is shuffled and the non-dealer cuts. The dealer then from the united pack gives five cards to each in the manner described in Rule v., beginning with his adversary. The eleventh card is turned up for trump. If the turn-up be a king, the dealer marks one point; five points being game.

The non-dealer looks at his cards, and if he be dissatisfied with them, he may propose – that is, change any or all of them for others from the *stock*, or remainder of the pack on the table. Should he propose, he says, "I propose," or "cards," and it is in the option of the dealer to give or refuse cards. When he decides to give, he says, "I accept," or "How many?" Should he refuse to change, he says, "I decline," or "Play." The dealer may, if he accept the proposal, change any or all the cards in his own hand. Sometimes a second discard is allowed, but that must be by previous agreement. Of course the non-dealer may play without discarding, in which case the dealer must play his own hand without changing any of his cards.

When the hands are arranged the non-dealer plays a card, which is won or lost by the playing of a superior card of the suit led. The second must follow suit, or win the trick if he can; otherwise he may throw any card he chooses.

The order in value of the cards is – king, queen, knave, ace, ten, nine, eight, seven. Trumps win other suits. The winner of the trick leads for the next trick, and so on till the five cards on each side are played. The winner of three tricks scores one point; if he win the whole five tricks – the *vôle* – he scores two points; if he hold the king, he names it before playing his first card – "I mark king." Should the non-dealer play without proposing, and fail to make three tricks, his opponent marks two points; should the dealer refuse to accept and fail to win three tricks, his opponent scores two.

The game is five up; that is, the player who first makes five points wins. The score is marked by two cards, a three and a two, or by counting. The deal is taken alternately; but when the play is for rubbers it is usual to cut for deal at the end of each rubber. A player holding the king should not announce it till the last moment. The non-dealer should not declare the king until immediately before playing his first card, unless that card be the king, when he is entitled to call and mark it before it is played to; and the dealer should not announce the king till after his opponent has led.

## THREE-HANDED ÉCARTÉ

If *three* persons wish to form a game they can play a *pool*, each contributing an equal amount to the pool. They all cut, the lowest being out, and the other two playing the first game. The loser puts into the pool a sum equal to that which he originally put in, and the person who was out takes his place. Should the winner of the first game lose the second, he puts a stake in the pool, stands out, and so on until one player wins two consecutive games, when he takes the pool.

## Rules of Écarté

i. Each player has the right to shuffle the cards *above* the table; but the dealer shall have the right to do so last.

ii. The cut must not be fewer than two cards off the pack, and at least two cards must be left on the table.

iii. When more than one card is exposed in cutting, there must be a new deal.

iv. The highest écarté card cut secures the deal, which holds good even though the pack be imperfect.

v. The dealer must give five cards to each by three and two, or by two and three, at a time, which plan must not be changed during the game.

vi. An incorrect deal, playing out of turn, or a faced card, necessitates a new deal.

vii. The eleventh card must be turned up for trumps; and the remaining cards placed, face downwards, on the table.

viii. The king turned up must be marked by the dealer before the trump of the next deal is turned up.

ix. A king of trumps held in hand must be announced and marked before the player lays down his first card, or he loses his right to mark it. If played in the first trick, it must be announced before it is played to.

x. A proposal or acceptance cannot be retraced or altered.

xi. Before taking cards, the player must place his discarded cards, face downwards, on the table, and neither look at nor touch them till the round be over.

xii. The player holding king marks one point; making three tricks, one point; five tricks, two points.

xiii. The non-dealer playing without proposing and failing to win the point, gives two tricks to his opponent.

xiv. The dealer who refuses the first proposal and fails to win the point (three tricks), gives his opponent two points.

xv. An admitted overscore or underscore may be amended without penalty before the cards are dealt for the following round.

**HEARTS** is played by four persons, with a full pack. The cards rank as in Whist, to which this game has some resemblance; there is, however, no partnership, no trump suit, and although tricks are made, the object is to avoid winning any trick which contains a card of the heart suit.

The deal having been cut for, the cards are shuffled and dealt as at whist, but the last card is *not* turned up. Each player is bound to follow suit if possible. If he cannot, he may play any card he chooses, getting rid of any hearts he may have. Each hand is game.

At the finish of the hand, the tricks are turned up, and the hearts counted. Supposing that of the 13 hearts A has 3, B 1, C 4, and D 5. Here B wins, having the smallest number and each of the other players pays him one counter (or as agreed on) for each heart they hold. If there is a tie, as where A and B have 2 hearts each, C 4, and D 5, C and D pay 9 counters and A and B divide them; but as this cannot be done equally the odd counter is put in the middle of the table to await the result of the next game.

Where there are three players, one of the black deuces is generally taken out; or the complete pack may be used, leaving the last card face downwards in the centre of the table at each deal.

**SLIPPERY ANN** is a variant of above game in which the Queen of Spades (Slippery Ann) counts 15; the Knave of Diamonds (Silly Billy) counts 11; Ace of Hearts 5, King 4, Queen 3, Knave 2, all other hearts 1 each.

**NAPOLEON OR NAP.** Played by four, five, or six persons, with a full pack, which take the same value as in Whist. The object of the game is to make tricks, which are paid to or received from the declarer at a fixed rate, a penny or more a trick, as previously arranged.

The deal being decided in the usual way, the pack is cut and five cards are dealt one at a time to each player, beginning at the left. After every round the deal passes. Each player looks at his cards, the one to the left of the dealer being the first to declare. When he thinks he can make two or three tricks he says, "I go two," or "I go three." The

next may perhaps think he can make four tricks; and if the fourth believes he can do better he declares "Napoleon," and undertakes to win the whole five tricks. The players declare or pass in the order in which they sit; and a declaration once made cannot be recalled. The player making the highest declaration leads; the first card played becomes the trump suit; and to win a trick, a higher card of the suit led or a trump must be played. The winner of the first trick leads for the second, and so on till each of the five tricks is played out. Each player must follow suit, but he is not bound to head the trick or to trump. Each card as played remains face upwards on the table in front of the player.

Supposing the stake to be a penny a trick, the declarer, if he win all the tricks he declared, receives from each of his adversaries a penny for each of the declared tricks; but if he fail to win the required number, he pays to each of them a penny a trick. For "Napoleon" he receives double stakes from each player; but failing to win the five tricks he pays them single stakes.

The game, though simple, requires good judgement and memory to play it well. The aim of the players is to cooperate to prevent the declarer winning the number of tricks he declared.

Sometimes it is varied by the introduction of a "Wellington," which is a superior call after the Napoleon, and the player pays double if he loses; also a "Blücher," the loser paying triple stakes; or "Misere," in which the player undertakes to lose all his tricks. The value of this call may vary according to arrangement before play begins. Each player may Pass, or decline to make a declaration; and when all the players pass, the deal is void, and the stakes are usually doubled for the following deal.

Occasionally a pool or kitty is made by each dealer paying a half stake; or the players may purchase new cards from the pack. In either case, the pool is taken by the winner of the first Napoleon, or divided according to arrangement at the close of play.

**NEWMARKET.** A very similar game to Pope Joan, but requires no special board.

The eight of diamonds having been taken out of the pack, the game is played with the remaining cards. The ace of spades, king of diamonds, queen of hearts, and knave of clubs, or any similar combination of the four principal cards of different suits, from another pack are laid in the centre of the table face upwards in the form of a square. Each player stakes an agreed number of counters, dividing his counters among the four exposed cards as he chooses. The dealer pays double stakes, also distributed as he chooses.

The cards are dealt one at a time, an extra hand also being dealt in order to form a like number of "stops." There are no trumps.

The player on the dealer's left leads any suit he likes, but *must* lead the lowest he holds (ace ranks lowest), at the same time naming the card. The player having the next highest card of the same suit plays and names it, and so on till a "stop" is reached, when the person playing the stop leads to the next round.

The game continues till a player has played all his cards. The winner receives from the losers one counter for each card remaining in their hands; and when during the game, a card corresponding with one of the pool cards is played, the person playing it receives all the counters staked on that card.

## PATIENCE

A game for single players, the varieties of which are innumerable. One of the best-known is Demon patience.

It is played with a full pack of cards in the following manner:

Shuffle the pack thoroughly. Count out thirteen cards and lay them on one side in a stack face upwards. This forms the stock. Place the next four cards from the pack face upwards in a row to form the heads of columns. The next card is then turned up and placed above one of the columns, forming the base upon which to build. The other three cards of the same value are placed, as they turn up, above the other three columns. The bases are built upwards in suits, and the columns downwards in sequence of alternate colours. Thus a red four is placed above a black five, and so on.

When a vacancy occurs in the row of columns, that is to say, when all the cards in a column have been built on to the bases, or have been transferred to another column, the vacancy is filled by the top card of the stock, until the stock is exhausted, and afterwards from the top card of the pack in hand.

After the four cards forming the heads of columns, and a fifth card determining the base have been laid out, the procedure is as follows:

Take three cards in order together from the pack and lay them in a packet face upwards on the table. If the exposed card of the three can be used, either on the base or on one of the column cards, place it accordingly, always playing to the base first. Use the next card of the three in the same way if suitable; if not, take the next three cards from the pack, and put them face upwards on the packet, using such as are suitable, always keeping an eye on the stock for cards that fit.

When you have turned all the cards of the pack in threes in this way, take up the unused cards, and use as the pack again, always taking three cards. If there are only two cards left in the pack you may use them singly. Continue to turn the pack as long as you can play. If you have gone through the pack without finding a card you can use, the game is lost, unless by borrowing a top card from one of the bases you can, by placing it on one of the columns, continue the game. This privilege may be used once only.

**POKER, OR DRAW POKER.** This game is known in several varieties, e.g. Straight Poker, Stud Poker, Whisky Poker, etc. The game is of American origin in the above forms. It is an elaboration of the game of *Brag*.

The game is played with an ordinary pack. Any number of players up to seven may take part, but five or six is probably the best number.

Five cards are dealt one at a time to each player, and each in turn has the option of coming in or of not playing after looking at his cards. Those who decide to come in put so many chips into the pool, and can then discard any or all of their cards, and receive in exchange (or "draw" as it is called) an equal number. When all who are to play have drawn the betting begins.

A limit is put on the amount that may be bet at a time, each player, when his turn comes, having the right to bet any amount up to the limit.

The player on the left of the dealer is called the "age," and he puts into the pool an amount known as the "ante," which is usually a small fixed proportion of the limit. The player on the left of the "age," having seen his cards, is asked by the dealer, "Do you play?" If he elects to play he puts into the pool twice the amount of the ante, if not, he throws his cards face down on the table, and the player on his left has his turn, and so on, till it comes round to the "age," who is the last to be asked if he plays or not. Then the dealer, beginning with the "age," asks each player in turn how many cards are wanted, and the exchanges are made, he being himself the last to draw.

The player on the left of the "age" has his first bet. He can bet whatever he thinks his hand is worth, from the amount of the ante up to the limit, or, he may throw in his cards face downwards without betting, the right to bet passing to the player on his left. Thus the betting or throwing in goes round the table to the "age." If no one has made a bet till it comes to his turn, he collects the pool without having to make a bet or to show his cards. When any player makes a bet, the player on his left can "see" the bet, or raise it, or he can throw in. If one or more players "see" the original bet, i.e. put into the pool an amount equal to it, and no one raises the bet, then the original betting hand shows his cards, and if none of the others can show a better hand he takes the pool, otherwise the best hand wins. If, however, any player raises the bet he must put into the pool the amount of the bet plus the amount by which he raises it, which may be anything up to the limit. Whoever wishes to "see" this raise must put in an equal amount, and may further raise it by the limit and so

on till the last raise is seen, when the best hand wins as before, or if no player sees it the last raiser takes the pool without having to show his cards.

The values of the hands from the best downwards, are as under:—

1. *Straight Flush.* 5 cards of the same suit in sequence, e.g. ace, king, queen, knave, ten of hearts.

2. *Fours.* 4 cards of the same denomination, e.g. 4 kings, with one other card.

3. *Full House.* 3 cards of the same denomination, with 2 others also of the same denomination, e.g. 3 tens with 2 eights.

4. *Flush.* 5 cards of the same suit not in sequence, e.g. 5 diamonds.

5. *Straight.* 5 cards of different suits in sequence, e.g. an ace, a king, a queen, a knave, and a ten.

6. *Threes.* 3 cards of the same denomination, e.g. 3 knaves, with 2 other cards of different values.

7. *Two pairs.* e.g. 2 nines and 2 sevens and one other card.

8. *One pair.* 2 cards of the same denomination and 3 other cards of different values.

9. *Highest card.* 5 cards of different denominations, one being a high card, say, an ace.

With similar hands that having the highest card wins, e.g. a Flush with an ace in it, beats a Flush the highest card of which is a king; a Straight, queen high, beats a Straight, knave high. Three tens beats three nines. Three tens and two nines beats three nines and two aces. A pair of nines with a king, &c., beats a pair of nines with a queen, &c. If the hands are identical, the pool is divided.

The object in the draw is to improve the hand if possible, and much useful information as to the composition of your opponents' hands may be gained by noting carefully the number of cards drawn. If a player asks for three cards he is most likely drawing to a pair, if he asks for two he probably has threes in his hand. If he draws only one card he may have two pairs, or four cards of a flush or of a straight, or fours; if he declines to draw any he is likely to have one of the strongest combinations in his hand.

**PONTOON or VINGT-ET-UN.** The game of *Vingt-et-un*, or Twenty-one, may be played by two or more; and, as the deal is advantageous, and often continues long with the same person, it is usual to determine it at the commencement by turning up the first ace, or knave.

**Counting in Vingt-et-un.** Ace counts either one or eleven, court cards ten each, and the other cards according to the number of pips.

**Method of Playing.** The dealer first deals one card round, each player then looks at his card, and, with the exception of the dealer, stakes what he chooses on it. The dealer also looks at his card, and if it is a good one he may double the stakes of the other players; a second card is then dealt round, after which the dealer asks each player in rotation, beginning with the eldest hand on the left, whether he stands or chooses another card. If he needs another card, it must be given from the top of the pack, face upwards, and afterwards another, or more, if desired, till the points of the additional card or cards, added to those dealt, exceed or make Vingt-et-un, or twenty-one exactly, or such a number less than twenty-one as the player thinks fit to stand upon.

When the points on the player's cards exceed twenty-one, he throws the cards on the table, face downwards, and pays the stake. Having satisfied all the other players, the dealer exposes his own two cards, and is, in turn, entitled to draw additional cards, and on making a Vingt-et-un, receives double stakes from all who stand the game, except such as have made twenty-one, who only pay a single stake. Should the dealer in taking additional cards overdraw he pays all who are standing.

When any player has a Vingt-et-un, and the dealer not, or if the dealer has overdrawn, then the opponent so having twenty-one, wins double stakes from him. In other cases, except a natural Vingt-et-un happen, the dealer pays single stakes to all whose numbers under twenty-one are higher than his own, and receives from those who have equal or

lower numbers. In some companies ties pay the dealer.

Should a player receive for his first two cards two of the same denomination, two aces, two eights, &c., he may elect to stake a separate amount on each, and after placing his stakes he gets from the dealer two other cards to complete the two hands, and then obtains additional cards for each hand until he stands or is overdrawn.

**Natural Vingt-et-un.** Twenty-one, when dealt in a player's first two cards, is styled a *Natural*. It should be declared at once, and entitles the holder to double stakes from the dealer, and to the deal, except it be agreed to pass the deal round. If the dealer turns up a natural he takes double stakes from all the players and retains the deal. If there be more than one natural, all after the first receive single stakes only.

**FRENCH VINGT-ET-UN OR VARIATIONS.** There are eight rounds in this game, each played differently, thus:—

1. As in ordinary Vingt-et-un.

2. (*Imaginary Tens.*) Each of the players stakes before receiving a card. Ten points are added to the value of his card, and the holder decides, according to the amount then made, to draw or otherwise.

3. (*Blind Vingt-et-un.*) Each of the players, having staked, receives two cards, but must not look at them. He may, if he chooses, draw one or more cards, doing so haphazard.

4. (*Sympathy and Antipathy.*) Each of the players, having staked, is called on to elect for Sympathy or Antipathy. Having elected, he receives two cards. If they are the same colour Sympathy wins; if different Antipathy. The player receives or pays as he has chosen correctly or not.

5. (*Rouge et noir.*) Each player, having staked, declares for either red or black, and receives a card. If he has chosen correctly he wins, or vice versa.

6. (*Self and Company.*) The players stake, and the dealer deals two cards, face upwards, one for himself and the other for the company. If they are alike he wins. If not, he keeps on dealing the

cards one by one, face upwards, until a card is dealt which pairs either of the two first dealt. If that for "self" is paired, the dealer wins; and vice versa.

7. (*Differences.*) Two cards are dealt, face upwards, to each player, and two to the dealer. The latter pays all who are higher, and receives from all who are lower, at an agreed amount for each unit of difference. Ties cancel, and aces count *one* only.

8. (*The Clock.*) The cards being shuffled and cut, the dealer commences to deal the cards, face upwards, saying as he deals the first, "One," – as he deals the second, "Two," and so on up to king. If a card turned up agrees with the number called out, he wins the stakes. If he reaches thirteen without any card agreeing, he pays the other players.

## RUMMY OR COON-CAN

Card game of American origin for two to six players. It is played with one pack of cards (containing a joker) if not more than three players are engaged; if four to six play two packs (mixed) are required. With only two players the game is known as Rummy.

Ten cards are dealt to each person, and the next card is turned up on the table; the remainder of the pack is placed beside it face down.

The object of the game is to get rid of all the cards in your hand by making sequences of three or more cards (in suits only), or sets of three cards of the same value in different suits. When such sequences or sets have been formed, the player holding them, when his turn comes to play, lays them face upwards on the table. The sequences may be added to at either end, or the sets may be completed by any player holding the proper cards when his turn to play comes.

The player on the left of the dealer begins, and may take up either the exposed card or the top card of the pack. He then declares any set or sequence which he may hold, and discards one card from his hand face upwards. Next player on his left then proceeds in the same way, and a heap of discarded cards is thus built up alongside the pack.

If a set of three has been laid down and a player afterwards gets the fourth he may use it either to complete the set or to form part of a sequence in his hand. But a card already laid down as part of a sequence or set cannot afterwards be used in another combination.

If the pack has all been used before any of the players has got rid of all his cards, the discarded heap is turned face down and becomes the pack, and play continues.

The joker may be used to represent any card to form part of a sequence provided the card so represented is not already exposed on the table. Any player who holds the card so represented may substitute it for the joker and may then use the joker himself; but this can be done once only in the same game.

The ace may be reckoned as "1" or as "ace" in forming sequences.

When a complete hand has been laid down by a player his opponents have to pay him the value of all cards in their hands, viz., 10 for each court card; 11 for each ace; 15 for the joker and face value for the rest. The joker is not essential to the game, but adds to the interest. Counters or scoring cards are required.

## SNAP

A simple game for children played with ordinary playing cards, which are shuffled and dealt equally – usually to two players. Cards are held face downward and played face upward in turn, each player on to his own pile. When cards of the same value appear on each pile, the first player to shout "snap" takes both piles. The object is to win the whole of your opponent's cards.

## WHIST

Four persons cut for partners; the two highest are against the two lowest. The partners sit opposite to each other, and he who cuts the lowest card is entitled to the deal. The ace is the lowest in cutting.

**i. Shuffling.** Each player has a right to shuffle the cards before the deal; but it is usual for the elder hand only; and the dealer after.

**ii. Dealing.** The pack is then cut by the right-hand adversary; and the dealer distributes the cards, one by one, to each of the players, beginning with the player on his left, until he comes to the last card which he turns up for trump, and leaves on the table till the first trick be played.

[*Note.* – A better plan than turning up the last card and thus exposing one of the dealer's hand, is to determine the trump by cutting before commencing each deal.]

**iii. First Play.** The eldest hand, the player on the left of the dealer, plays first. The winner of the trick plays again; and so on till all the cards are played out.

**iv. Mistakes.** No intimations or signs are permitted between the partners.

**v. Collecting Tricks.** The tricks belonging to each player should be turned and collected by one of the partners only. Each trick, above six, counts one point.

**vi. Honours.** The ace, king, queen, and knave of trumps are called honours; and when a player and his partner hold three honours, either separately or between them, they count two points towards the game; if they have four honours, they count four points.

**vii. Game.** The Game consists of Five Points. One for a Single – 5 to 3 or 4; Two for a Double – 5 to 1 or 2; Three for a Triple – 5 to love. A Rubber – two Games successively won, or the two best Games out of three – counts for Two Points. Thus, if the first Game be won by 5 to 4, the Points are 1 to love; the second Game won by the opposite side by 5 to 1, the Points are then 1 to 2; the third Game won by the side which won first, by 5 to love. The Points are then 6 to 2 – a balance of 4. This is arrived at thus: the Single in the first Game, 1; the Triple in the third Game, 3; the Rubber (two Games of three), 2; together, 6. From this deduct 2, for the Double gained by the opponents in the second Game, which leaves 4, as above.

## Terms Used in Whist

**i.** *Finessing* is the attempt to gain an advantage; thus: If you have the best and third best card of the suit led, you put on the third best, and run the risk of your opponent having the second best; if he has it not (and it is two to one against his having it), you are then certain of gaining a trick.

**ii.** *Forcing* is playing the suit of which your partner or adversary has not any, and which he must trump in order to win.

**iii.** *Long Cards* are cards of any suit left in one hand, when the rest of the suit has been played. The *long trump* being the last trump in is of great value.

**iv.** *Loose Card,* a card of no value, and the most proper to throw away.

**v.** *Points.* Five make the game; the units of the score are called *points,* and are made either by tricks or honours.

**vi.** *Quarte,* four successive cards in suit.

**vii.** *Quarte Major,* a sequence of ace, king, queen, and knave.

**viii.** *Quint,* five successive cards in suit.

**ix.** *Quint Major* is a sequence of ace, king, queen, knave, and ten.

**x.** *Ruffing.* Trumping a plain suit.

**xi.** *See-saw* is when each partner trumps a suit, and when they play those suits to each other for that purpose.

**xii.** *Score* is the number of points set up.

**xiii.** *Slam* is when either side win every trick.

**xiv.** *Tenace* is the combination in the same hand of the best and third best cards that are still in of any suit.

**xv.** *Tierce* a sequence of three cards in suit.

**xvi.** *Tierce Major,* a sequence of ace, king, and queen.

## Rules of Whist

**i.** The deal is determined by cutting-in. Cutting-in and cutting-out must be by pairs.

[Less than three cards, above or below, is not a cut. Ace is lowest. Ties cut again. Lowest deals. Each player may shuffle, the dealer last. The right-hand adversary cuts to dealer.]

**ii.** If a card be exposed, a fresh deal may be demanded.

**iii.** Dealer must not look at bottom card; and the trump-card must be left, face upwards, on the table till the first trick be turned, or opponents may call a fresh deal.

**iv.** Too many or too few cards is a misdeal – an exposed or face card. In either case, a fresh deal may be demanded.

[In cases of a misdeal, the deal passes to the next player.]

**v.** After the first round has been played, no fresh deal can be called.

[If the first player holds fewer than thirteen cards, the other hands being right, the deal stands.]

**vi.** If two cards be dealt to the same player, the dealer may rectify his error before dealing another card.

[The dealer must not touch the cards after they have left his hand; but he may count those remaining in the pack if he suspect a misdeal, or he may ask the players to count their cards. One partner may not deal for another without the consent of opponents.]

**vii.** If the trump-card be not taken into the dealer's hand at the expiration of the first round, it may be treated as an exposed card, and called.

[After this, no one has a right to ask what was the trump-card, but he may ask "What are Trumps?"]

**viii.** If the third hand play before the second, the fourth has a right to play before his partner; or if the fourth hand play before the second, or third, the cards so played must stand, and the second be compelled to win the trick if he can.

**ix.** If a player lead out of his turn, or otherwise expose a card, that card may be called, if the playing of it does not cause a revoke.

[Calling a card is the insisting on its being played when the suit comes round, or when it may be played.]

**x.** If a player trump by mistake, he may recall his card, and play to the suit, if the card be not covered; but he may be compelled to play the highest or lowest of the suit led, and to play the exposed trump when it is called by his adversaries.

**xi.** If, before a trick be turned, a player discovers that he has not followed suit, he may recall his card; but the card played in error can be called when the suit is played.

**xii.** Before a trick is turned, the player who made it may see the preceding trick.

[Only *one* trick is to be shown; not more, as is sometimes erroneously believed.]

**xiii.** Before he plays, a player may require his partner to "draw his card," or he may have each card in the trick claimed before the trick be turned.

**xiv.** When a player does not follow suit his partner is allowed to ask him whether he has any card of the suit led.

**xv.** The penalty for a revoke – either by wrongfully trumping the suit led, or by playing a card of another suit – is the loss of three tricks; but no revoke can be claimed till the cards are abandoned, and the trick turned.

[Revokes forfeit three tricks from the hand or score, or opponents may add three to their score; partner may ask and correct a trick if not turned; the revoking side cannot score out in that deal.]

**xvi.** No revoke can be claimed after the tricks are gathered up, or after the cards are cut for the next deal.

[The wilful mixing up of the cards in such case loses the game.]

**xvii.** The proof of a revoke lies with the claimants, who may examine each trick on the completion of the round.

**xviii.** If a revoke occur on both sides there must be a new deal.

**xix.** Honours cannot be counted unless they are claimed previous to the next deal.

[No omission to score honours can be rectified after the cards are packed; but an overscore, if proved, must be deducted.]

**Canadian Whist.** A game for two players. All the cards are used, and in dealing are placed in pairs, face downwards on the table. Each player then turns over the top card of twelve of the thirteen pairs dealt to him, taking the other two cards (which are called "blinds") into his hands. The non-dealer has the choice of trumps, after having seen all the exposed cards, and the game proceeds as at Whist; it is optional to take a trick, but a led suit must be followed, even from the "blinds." As each exposed card is played the under card must be exposed. Counting commences after either hand has taken thirteen tricks, each trick beyond thirteen counting one. Eleven is the usual game, but any number is optional as agreed upon before starting.

**Dummy Whist** affords facilities for a "hand" at whist when only three players are present. Double Dummy is no doubt occasionally resorted to *pour passer le temps*, but as a rule two persons deem it better to take to cribbage, bézique, chess, or draughts, rather than fall back upon this variation. Dummy Whist, on the other hand, provides quite a good game, especially when the players are evenly matched. Since the player who has dummy for a partner has a slight advantage the partnership should be changed every rubber, unless the other pair object. Virtually the laws of ordinary whist apply to Dummy, with the single exception which gives the game its name. Trumps are shown either by turning up the last card dealt, or by cutting from a second or spare pack, or, in the absence of a second, by disclosing a card in the course of shuffling. Dummy's cards are exposed on the table and play proceeds in the usual manner. Dummy's partner playing both Dummy's hand and his own, as well as dealing for him.

**Progressive Whist.** In playing this game three or more tables, according to the number present, should be arranged, with four players at each table. The cards are dealt and played as in ordinary whist. The tables should be numbered consecutively from 1 upward, each table having in its centre a card bearing its distinctive number.

After playing the first hand the two winning players "progress" to the next table – i.e. from No. 1 table to No. 2 table, from No. 2 to No. 3, No. 3 to No. 4, No. 4 to No. 1, and so on), being careful to *change partners* at each successive table, that is to say the winning lady of table 1 will have as partner the losing gentleman at table 2, and so on. The same method of "progressing" is followed after each hand; and the game may consist of any number of deals.

After playing each hand, each player marks on his or her scoring card the total number of tricks *taken as partners*, and at the end of the evening the lady and gentleman having the highest totals are awarded the prizes of merit, while the lady and gentleman having the lowest totals receive the consolation or "booby" prizes. The method of progressing is often varied: sometimes the winning lady goes up, and the winning gentleman goes down, and sometimes the losing couples move.

Printed scoring cards are obtainable. The trump suit for each deal is printed thereon, but it is usual for someone in charge of the game to announce the trumps for each deal before play begins. There are various odd methods of scoring for a proportion of the deals, such as "Klondyke" when the winners score double; "Kimberley," diamonds trumps; "Misere," score opponents' tricks; "Workhouse," losers score half; "Mystery," the thirteen cards dealt to each player are left on the table face down. Losing lady plays her top card, which becomes trumps; the other players play their top cards. The winner of the trick plays the next card on his or her pile, and the others follow by playing their top cards, and so on.

**Solo Whist.** This game is played by two, three, or four persons with an ordinary pack of fifty-two cards. When five persons wish to play, the one on the right of the dealer neither joins in the current round nor pays any stakes. Pools or Kitties should not be formed when there are five players. The regular and best game is with four players.

The deal, as in Whist, is taken by the players in rotation, and is decided by the lowest of the four cards turned up. (In cutting for deal the ace is lowest, and the king is highest.) The cards are dealt *three at a time* to each player in rotation, beginning with the person at the dealer's left. When forty-eight cards have been dealt, twelve to each player, the remaining four are dealt singly, the last being turned up to indicate the trump suit.

A better plan, however, is to cut the trump suit from another pack instead of turning up and exposing the last card, and this is recommended, as it not infrequently occurs that an exposed card spoils a Misère déclarée, e.g. if an ace or king be exposed in an otherwise perfect Misère hand it becomes a dangerous card to the holder and may prevent a call; if not exposed he may have a chance to discard.

**Objects in Solo Whist.** Every game is played with a specific object in view, that object being declared beforehand. This is known as a "Call" or "Declaration." There are six objects or calls in Solo Whist, each of them having a different scope and value. They are as follows:

i. *Proposal and Acceptance*, where two players in partnership essay to make eight or more tricks between them against the others. The first caller, the player on the dealer's left, may accept a proposition after having originally passed, as he would otherwise be debarred the chance of accepting; but in all other instances a player who has once passed cannot accept or make any other declaration.

ii. *Solo*. The making of not less than five tricks by a player out of his own hand, against the other three players.

iii. *Misère*. The attempt by the caller to lose all thirteen tricks, the other players trying to force him to win a trick. (There are no trumps in a misère.)

iv. *Abondance*. Where the player declaring endeavours to make not less than nine tricks against the other three players. The person playing the abondance selects any suit he pleases for trumps, but does not announce such selection until it appears evident that no other player can announce a superior call, the trump suit then being named. An abondance with the original turn-up suit declared as trumps, takes precedence of an abondance in another suit.

v. *Misère ouverte*. This is the same as ordinary misère with this difference, that after the first trick has been played the caller exposes his remaining cards on the table.

vi. *Abondance déclarée*. The highest call at Solo, the caller having to make all thirteen tricks. There are no trumps, each suit being of equal value, and the caller, no matter where he sits, always leads out first; as the leader cannot make overtricks he is not liable to pay for undertricks should he fail, but is only liable for the stakes, the game being ended directly he loses a trick.

**Solo Whist – Mode of Play.** Every round

at Solo is complete in itself and is played to attain one of these six objects, and there is no scoring. Honours are not counted as at ordinary Whist, and court cards in trumps are useful only for the tricks they make.

The players having examined their cards, the eldest hand (the player on the dealer's left) declares first. If he holds a superlative hand and sees a likelihood of winning all the tricks, he declares *Abondance déclarée*, and cannot be stopped by any player who has subsequently to declare.

If he has an exceptionally bad hand consisting almost entirely of small cards, he declares *Misère ouverte*, the next highest call. Should he have a very strong hand in trumps, and thinks he can win nine tricks, he goes *Abondance*. It is rarely, however, that a player gets a sufficiently strong hand to make *nine* tricks, much less *thirteen*, or a sufficiently weak hand to make *Misère ouverte*. He then has four courses open to him. If he has a bad hand, he may declare a *Misère* or he may refuse to declare (saying "I pass"). If he has a pretty strong hand, he may either declare *Solo*, or he may make a *Proposal*.

The eldest hand having declared, the second makes his declaration, and then the third and fourth. A proposing hand not finding an accepter, can alter his call to one of the superior calls, viz. solo, misère, or abondance; and any caller, who has not passed, even if he be only an accepter, if overcalled, can make any higher declaration he chooses.

If all the hands pass the deal is void, the cards are thrown in and redealt by the next dealer, each player contributing a certain sum (generally half or a quarter the proposed stake), and the first player who makes a successful independent call (a call other than a proposition and acceptance) takes the pool, or if unsuccessful *doubles it*.

Frequently, instead of throwing up the hands, a "general" or "general misère" is played, the hand being played in the usual way and the player taking the last trick having to pay an amount agreed on (half the proposed stake, as a rule) to each of his opponents. There are no trumps in a "general."

It is usual to pay double price for overtricks (but not double for the stake) when the declaring side makes a "slam" of all thirteen tricks.

There is no penalty for a misdeal, the cards being simply redealt by the same player.

If, on an independent call being made, any player make a remark directly or indirectly conveying an intimation as to the state of the hands, the caller may demand that the offender pay the stakes to the side that wins, or he can throw up his hand and claim a redeal.

A player revoking forfeits for every revoke three tricks, which are deducted from the score of his own side and added to that of his opponents; when both sides revoke, the whole deal is invalidated and neither side can win.

**Stakes.** The stakes at Solo Whist are not invariable, and should always be settled before play begins.

**Solo Whist for three players.** There are two methods of playing solo with three players. The first and preferable way is by taking out the twos, threes, and fours; the turn-up card only being used to denote trumps. The other system is to discard one entire suit, and play the remaining three. In this case there is no odd card, the turn-up being the dealer's.

In the three-players' game there are no proposals and acceptances, and the lowest call is a *solo* of six tricks. As there is very frequently a general "pass," it is usual to call solos in "flying colours" (*see* the Kimberley Game), the second solo being one of six tricks.

**Solo Whist for two players.** Here, again, the pack consists of forty cards, the twos, threes, and fours being eliminated, and the turn-up card not being used except to denote the trump suit. Deal the cards into three lots, the one to the dealer's left being used as a dummy, and not looked at until a call is decided on. It is then opened, sorted out, and exposed on the table *to the left of the caller.* The caller's opponent then plays dummy's cards with his own against the declaration. The hand to the dealer's left (whether dummy or caller) invariably having first lead.

The lowest call is a solo of *five* tricks; the order being solo, abondance, misère, and abondance déclarée.

Abondance is double the price of solo; misère three times the price of solo; and abondance déclarée four times the price of solo.

There is necessarily no misère ouverte, the ordinary misère being more exposed than in any other variation of the game (for not only are the caller's cards known, but also those of his adversaries). This game also is played with "flying colours," solo in the second suit being of *five* tricks.

**Solo Whist. The Kimberley Game.** This game is Solo Whist without propositions and acceptances. A solo is therefore the lowest call, and if all the players pass, a pool is formed, the first person making a successful call taking it, or doubling it if unsuccessful.

The Kimberley Game is played with "flying colours," that is to say, when every one passes a second chance of calling is given to them in regular rotation. This second call must be a solo of *six* tricks, the caller selecting and naming his own trump suit, but it must not be the original suit. A solo only can be called in "flying colours," and the over or undertricks are counted from *six.*

**BILLIARDS**

This well-known game of skill is played on a rectangular table measuring 12 feet long by 6 feet 1½ inches broad, and 2 feet 9½ to 10½ inches high, with pockets at the corners and at the middle of the longer sides. The game is played to the rules of the Billiards Association and Control Council, 15 Exeter Street, London, W.C.

The Baulk line is drawn 29 inches from the face of the bottom cushion and parallel to it. The "D" is a semicircle described in Baulk with a radius of 11½ inches and having its centre at the middle of the baulk line.

The following spots are marked on the table: (a) the Spot, 12½ inches from the face of the top cushion; (b) the Centre Spot, half-way between the middle pockets; (c) the Pyramid Spot, half-way between the Centre Spot and the face of the top cushion; (d) the middle of the baulk line, all four being on the centre longitudinal line of the table.

The game is played with three ivory balls – plain white, spot-white and red, the object being to drive one or the other of them into any of the six pockets (making a hazard), and to strike one ball against the two others (making a cannon). The instrument for striking at the ball is a long tapering leather-tipped stick called a cue; and the game is scored by hazards, cannons and penalties. The ball struck with the cue is known as the striker's ball; the ball played at as the object ball. A ball, other than the striker's ball, struck into a pocket is a winning hazard; the striker's ball falling into a pocket after contact with the white or red, is a losing hazard.

**English Billiards** is usually played 100 up. The points are thus reckoned – three for each red hazard, two for each white hazard, and two for each cannon.

For a miss the opponent scores one point; if, in consequence of a miss, the striker's ball goes into a pocket (known as "running a coup"), or is forced off the table, the opponent scores three points. If, after contact with another ball, the striker's or any other ball is forced off the table the opponent scores two points.

The game commences by stringing or tossing for lead and choice of balls. The red ball is placed on the spot at the top of the table, and the first player either strikes at it with his own ball, playing from baulk, or gives a miss.

A player may not make two misses in successive turns unless he or the opponent scores after the first miss. A miss given when the striker is in hand, and there is no ball out of baulk, does not count as one of the two misses.

Every time the red ball is pocketed it is replaced on the spot. When the striker's ball is pocketed it is said to be "in hand", and must be played from baulk. When the opponent's ball is pocketed it remains in hand until his turn comes to play.

A ball in baulk cannot be played on direct by a player whose ball is in hand.

The striker must play his ball from within the "D," and must play it out of baulk; he may strike any point of a ball or cushion out of baulk, or may play against a cushion in baulk to strike a ball out of baulk.

He who makes a hazard or cannon goes on playing till he fails to score. Then the other goes on, and so they play alternately till one or other completes the required number of points, and wins the game.

The referee, or in his absence the marker, is the sole judge of fair or unfair play, and he may, of his own initiative, intervene if he observes any contravention of the rules.

**Pyramids** is a game played by two persons, or by four – two a side. Fifteen red balls are arranged in the form of a triangle or pyramid, *actually touching one another*, with the apex towards the player and with the base parallel to the top cushion. The centre of the apex ball covers the pyramid spot.

The game consists entirely of winning hazards, and he who succeeds in pocketing the greatest number of balls wins.

The first player plays at the pyramid with the white ball from baulk, and if he succeeds in pocketing one of the coloured balls scores one point and proceeds to play with the white ball upon any other ball until he fails to pocket one, when his opponent continues the game until he also fails to score.

If a player pockets the white ball, forces any ball off the table, or misses the other balls he forfeits one point, loses his turn, and cannot score any points he may have made in the stroke.

When only one red ball remains on the table should the striker playing on the last red make no score nor incur a forfeit, his opponent plays with the red ball from where it has come to rest, to strike the white, and so on alternately until a score or forfeit ends the game.

## POOL

A game played by several persons, consisting of winning hazards only. Each player subscribes a certain stake called the major stake to form a pool or gross sum, and at starting has three chances or lives called the minor stakes. He then draws haphazard from a bag one of a series of marked or coloured balls, and the game proceeds thus: The white ball is placed on the spot, and the red is played on to it from baulk. If the player pocket the white he receives the price of a life from the owner of that ball; but if he fail, the next player (yellow) plays on the red; and so on alternately till all have played, or till a ball is pocketed. When a ball is pocketed the striker plays at the ball nearest his own, and goes on playing as long as he can score.

The first player who loses his three lives can *star*: that is, he can, by paying into the pool the value of three lives, purchase as many lives as then remain to the player (or players) with the lowest number.

The order of play is white, red, yellow, green, brown, blue, pink, spot-white, spot-red, etc. (as usually given on the Pool marking board); and this order is retained so long as all the original players remain in the game.

In pools of fewer than four players the game is continued until all the players but one have lost all their lives (including extra lives under the star). The surviving player takes the whole pool.

In pools of four or more players, when the number of players is reduced to two, with an equality of lives, they divide the pool; or they may by agreement play out the game for the entire pool. A striker who has lawfully pocketed a ball has the option of continuing his break or dividing.

Any number of balls may be pocketed by the same stroke, if the first impact of the cue-ball strikes the ball *on*. If two balls are struck simultaneously the stroke is a foul.

The striker is entitled to have a ball intervening between his ball and the ball he is playing on, removed until the stroke is played, after which it must be replaced.

## SNOOKER

Snooker (or Snooker's Pool) is a combi-nation of Pyramids and Pool. It may be played by two or more persons either as sides or independently.

1. The pool balls used are yellow, green, brown, blue, pink and black, with the white as cue-ball.

2. The fifteen reds (pyramid balls) are placed as in the game of Pyramids. The black pool ball is placed on the billiard spot; the pink on the centre line of the table and touching the apex ball of the pyramid, the blue on the centre spot; the brown on the middle spot of the baulk line; the green on the left and the yellow on the right-hand corners of the D.

3. The values of the balls are: each red 1; yellow, 2; green, 3; brown, 4; blue, 5; pink, 6; black, 7.

4. Baulk is no protection.

5. Players must first determine by lot, or otherwise, the order of their turn, which must remain unaltered through-out the game. The first player must play from baulk. The cue-ball must strike a red as the first stroke of each turn, until all the reds are off the table. The value of each red, lawfully pocketed by the same stroke, is scored. For the next stroke (if a score is made) the cue-ball must strike a pool ball, the value of which (if lawfully pocketed) is scored. The game is continued by pocketing reds and pool balls alternately. If the striker fails to score, the player next in turn plays from where the cue-ball came to rest. If the cue-ball is pocketed or forced off the table, the next player plays from hand. Each pool ball pocketed or forced off the table must be respotted before the next stroke, until finally pocketed under the rules. If the player who law-fully pockets the last red pocket any pool ball with his next stroke, that ball is re-spotted. The pool balls must then be struck by the cue-ball in the progressive order of their value, and are not re-spotted. The striker must nominate which pool ball he is *on* if requested by an opponent, and may so nominate for his own protection.

6. When the proper spot for a pool ball is occupied when it requires to be re-spotted, the ball shall be placed on the next unoccupied spot following the order of value in rule 2. If all the spots

are occupied it shall be placed as near its own spot as possible between that spot and the nearest part of the top cushion.

7. Two balls (other than two reds) must not be pocketed by the same stroke; nor two balls (other than two reds) be struck simultaneously.

8. If the cue-ball is touching another ball it must be played away from the touching ball without moving it.

9. When only the black ball is left the first score or forfeit ends the game, unless the scores are equal, in which case the black must be spotted and the players shall draw lots for the choice of playing at the black from hand. The next score or forfeit ends the game.

10. After a foul, if the next player be snookered for all reds or the pool ball he is *on*, he may nominate any ball to play on.

11. If the cue-ball is angled it must be played from where it lies, but if angled after a foul, it must be played from hand.

12. In addition to ordinary fouls in the game of billiards the following are fouls in the snooker game:—

(a) Making a losing hazard.

(b) Causing the cue-ball to strike a ball he is not *on*.

(c) Making a miss.

13. If, during a stroke, any rule is broken, the striker cannot score; loses his turn; loses the right of snookering his opponent; and forfeits points, which are added to the opponent's score.

For a miss, four points, or the value of the ball he is *on*.

For striking with the cue-ball a pool ball when *on* a red; or for striking the wrong pool ball; or for forcing a coloured ball (or the cue-ball after impact) off the table; or for a losing hazard the value of the ball struck, or the value of the ball he was *on*, or the value of any ball pocketed or forced off the table.

For pocketing more than one ball (other than reds) by the same stroke, or for striking more than one ball (other than reds) simultaneously, he forfeits the value of any ball so pocketed or struck.

For other fouls he forfeits four points, or the value of the ball fouled or pocketed, or the value of the ball he was *on*.

**Volunteer Snooker.** The game is played as at Snooker until a red is lawfully pocketed. In all subsequent strokes of any turn, the cue-ball may strike any ball (except two reds in succession) that the player may nominate. Such a ball is a free ball, provided that red balls and pool balls are played on alternately as in Snooker, otherwise it is a penalty ball, and if the striker fail to pocket a penalty ball, the stroke is foul. If pocketed its value is scored and the foul condoned, provided that if any pool ball be pocketed from the same spot three times in succession in the same turn it shall remain in the pocket until after the next stroke, from which any ball is a free ball.

Every pool ball pocketed, or forced off the table, must otherwise be re-spotted before the next stroke until finally pocketed. The game is continued until all the reds are off the table. If the player who pockets the last red, pocket any pool ball with his next stroke that ball is re-spotted. *Free* balls after this are not re-spotted, and the pool balls must be played on in the progressive order of value, when they are *free*, otherwise they are *penalty* balls.

After a foul, if the next player be snookered, he is *on* the nearest ball, as a *free* ball, or he may *volunteer*.

The striker is said to *volunteer* if the cue-ball strikes a pool ball which is not *on*, after the first stroke.

A *penalty ball* is a pool ball for which the striker forfeits its value, if he fail to pocket it.

A *free ball* is a red or pool ball for which the striker incurs no penalty for failing to pocket it.

The penalties are the same as in ordinary Snooker.

## MODERN BALLROOM DANCING

Any reader who wishes to learn the latest steps in modern ballroom dancing or old time dancing would be well advised to obtain a copy of *Modern Ballroom Dancing* by Victor Silvester and *The Complete Old Time Dancer* by Walter Whitman.

Below are set out the more important points to remember concerning ballroom dancing of the present day.

1. The feet should always be perfectly straight; the toes must not be allowed to turn outwards.

2. Step easily from the hips.

3. When moving forward, the weight of the body should be forward. When moving backward the weight of the body should be forward.

4. Move easily and naturally. Keep the muscles under control but do not hold them tense.

5. Always dance in time to the music.

## THE SLOW FOX-TROT

The Slow Fox-trot is danced to four-four time, the gentleman advancing.

*The Walk Forward.* Take a long step straight from the hip, skimming the foot lightly over the floor. Keep the weight forward. Repeat with the other leg.

*The Walk Backward.* Swing the leg back from the hip, keeping the weight on the front foot. Continuing, the weight should be carried between both feet, gradually transferring the weight to the ball of the back foot. Repeat with opposite leg.

## THE THREE-STEP

As the name suggests, this consists of three steps taken forward or backward, which are fitted to four beats of the music and counted quick, quick, slow. The first step is taken on the first beat, the second step on the second beat, the third step on the third beat and carried over to the fourth.

The other steps in this dance are the Feather Step, the Natural Turn, the Reverse Turn, the Reverse Wave, the Change of Direction, the Telemark, the Impetus Turn, and the Open Telemark.

## THE QUICK-STEP

The Quick-Step is danced to four-four time. There are two fundamental steps in this dance – the Walk and the Chassé. Every standardized figure is made up of these two steps.

*The Walk Forward.* This is the same as in the Slow Fox-trot, but quicker. Take a gliding step straight from the hips, skimming the foot lightly over the floor. At the full stretch of stride the weight should be on the heel of the front foot; immediately lower on to the flat foot. The back foot should now be on the toes before it is released to move forward. Repeat for the opposite leg. Keep moving forward continuously, and do not release the back foot until the last possible moment.

*The Walk Backward.* This is the same as in the Slow Fox-trot, but quicker. Swing the leg back from the hip, going on to the toes first and keeping the weight on the front foot. Continuing, the weight should be carried between the two feet, the toes of the front foot should leave the floor so that the pressure is on the front heel. The weight is then transferred to the ball of the back foot. Do not lower the back heel until the other foot passes it. Repeat with the opposite leg. With the weight forward, keep moving backwards continuously, and do not release the front foot hurriedly; draw it back with pressure on the heel.

*The Chassés.* These may be taken in different ways, but it is always a step with one foot, close the other foot up to it, and then move the original foot again. The Chassé is counted quick, quick, slow, and takes four beats of the music.

The other steps to be learned are the Natural Turn, the Natural Pivot Turn, the Reverse Turn, the Chassé Reverse Turn, the Quarter Turn, the Zig-zag, the Cross Chassé, the Drag, the Change of Direction, the Double Reverse Skim, the Running Zig-zag, the Natural Spin Turn, the Corté, the Check Finish, the Running Finish, the Cross Swivel, the Impetus Turn, the Running Right Turn, and the Side Step.

## THE TANGO

The "track" of the Tango is to curve forward and backward steps inwards – slightly towards the middle of the floor. It differs from other dances in three respects. One's partner is held slightly more to one's side; the man's left forearm is bent inwards a little more, and his right hand is placed farther round his partner. The Tango is the only dance in which the feet are picked up from the floor; the movements are not gliding as in other dances, and for this reason the knees are relaxed slightly more than usual. There is no rise and fall; Tango must be kept quite flat throughout.

*The Walk Forward.* Take a natural step forward, picking the foot up slightly; when out to full extent place it down, heel first, going immediately on to the flat foot. Keep the back foot behind you until the last possible moment before stepping forward with it. Repeat with the opposite leg.

*The Walk Backward.* Swing the leg back from the hip. When out to the full extent, the toes should meet the floor first immediately lowering the ball of the foot with the heel off the floor. The weight should be evenly balanced between the two feet, the toes of the front foot should be off the floor slightly so that the pressure is on the front heel. The weight is then transferred to the ball of the back foot. Hold the front foot in front of you until the last possible moment before moving it back.

Dancers wishing to learn the great variety of steps which make up this dance are recommended to study Victor Silvester's *Modern Ballroom Dancing* in which the following steps are described in detail, and are illustrated with carefully-prepared drawings: The Progressive Side Step, the Basic Reverse Turn, the Closed Promenade, the Back Corté, the Natural Turn, the Open Reverse Turn, the Open Promenade, the Natural Promenade Turn, the Rock, and the Progressive Side Step Reverse Turn.

## THE WALTZ

The modern Waltz serves as a splendid example to contradict those people who say that modern dancing is always changing. Apart from the fact that the turns are taken on what is known as diagonal lines, the fundamental figures remain the same now as they were many years ago. There are but three fundamental figures – the Natural Turn, the Reverse Turn, and the Changes, that is, changing from the Natural Turn to the Reverse Turn and vice versa. In the Turns and the Forward Changes it is essential that the feet be closed together on the third beat of the music. Another important feature which it is necessary to observe in order to obtain the correct rhythm, swing and lilt, is the rise. Rise at the end of the first step, continue rising on the second step, coming up on to the toes on the third step, and drop again as you take the first step. This rise must be inserted throughout the dance. The Turns and Changes are taken on diagonal lines. This means to say that instead of beginning the figures facing the line of dance they are commenced either diagonally to the wall, as in the case with the Natural Turn, or diagonally to the middle of the room, as is the case of the Reverse Turn. On each turn only three-quarters of a turn is made instead of a full turn. This makes the turns much easier to perform.

The essential steps of this dance and the many variations are fully described in Victor Silvester's *Modern Ballroom Dancing*. These include: the Natural Turn, the Reverse Turn, the Forward Change, the Backward Change, the Natural Spin, the Reverse Corté, the Hesitation Change, the Double Reverse Spin, the Outside Spin, and the Open Telemark.

## OLD-FASHIONED DANCES
## LANCERS

**i.** *First figure.* First lady and second gentleman advance and retire, advance, turn with both hands, retiring to places. First couple lead through centre set to corners and turn with both hands. Second lady and first gentleman, then third lady and fourth gentleman, and fourth lady and third gentleman repeat.

**ii.** *Second figure.* First couple advance twice, leaving the lady in the centre with her back to opposite couple – set in the centre – turn to places – all advance in two lines – all turn partners. Other couples repeat.

**iii.** *Third figure.* First lady advances and stops, opposite gentleman advances and bows, lady curtsies – both retire to places – ladies chain (twice). Other couples repeat.

**iv.** *Fourth figure.* First couple advance and salute couple on right – cross over and salute couple on left – change places with partners, and set, and pirouette to places – right and left with opposite couple. Each couple in turn repeats.

**v.** *Fifth figure.* The grand chain. The first couple advance and turn facing the top; then the couple at right advance behind the top couple; then the couple at left and the opposite couple do the same, forming two lines. All change places with partners and back again. The ladies file off to the right, the gentlemen to the left. Gentlemen take ladies' left hands in their right hands. Fall back to form two lines, the ladies in one line, the gentlemen in the other. Advance and retire in lines. Turn partners with both hands to places. Second, third, and fourth couples repeat. Finish with the grand chain.

## POLKA

This dance may still occasionally be seen in the modern ballroom. The gentleman and lady place themselves in position as in the waltz. The lady steps to the right with the right foot, draws the left foot up to it and springs lightly on the right foot; then steps to the left with the left foot, draws the right foot up to it and springs lightly on the left foot, at the same time turning to the right. Care should be taken to mark each *third* step as indicated by the music. The gentleman's step is exactly the same as the lady's, but of course he commences with the left foot.

## EIGHTSOME REEL

Danced by four couples. All join hands and circle round to left, set and turn partners. Gentleman's arm round lady's waist, ladies give right hand across. Chassé half round to left, gentlemen give left hand and chassé back to places. Set and turn partners, then grand chain.

First lady in centre dancing reel step, others circle round. The lady sets and turns with her own partner, then with opposite partner and they dance the reel of three. All circle round again with the same lady in the centre, then she sets and turns with gentleman on her left, and afterwards with the gentleman on her right; they dance the reel of three, and

the lady goes back to her own place. The second, third, and fourth ladies in turn go into the centre, and dance as the first lady.

The gentlemen then begin and dance in the centre as the ladies did. When all have been in the centre, all join hands and circle round as at the beginning, finishing with grand chain.

## THE HIGHLAND REEL

This dance is performed by the company arranged in parties of three, along the room in the following manner: a lady between two gentlemen, in double rows. All advance and retire – each lady then performs the reel with the gentleman on her right hand, and retires with the opposite gentleman to places – hands three round and back again – all six advance and retire – then lead through to the next trio, and continue the figure to the end of the room. Adopt the Highland step, and music of three-four time.

## THE HIGHLAND SCOTTISCHE

Danced in two parts:
*First part.* Partners face each other, a short distance apart, and dance independently.

(*a*) Spring with both feet, alighting on the left, the right pointing in the second position.

(*b*) Hop on left foot, at the same time raising the right behind.

(*c*) Hop on left foot, right pointing in second position.

(*d*) Repeat (*b*).

(*e*) Repeat the whole, commencing with the opposite foot. This brings the dancers facing each other again.

*Second part.* With right arms linked, and left arms raised, partners hop twice on left foot, twice on right, twice on left, twice on right, raising the opposite feet and circling round each other.

Repeat in the opposite direction, linking left arms and raising right arms.

## WALTZ COTILLON

First couple waltz round inside; first and second ladies advance twice and cross over, turning twice; first and second gentlemen do the same; third and fourth couples the same; first and second couples waltz to places, third and fourth do the same; all waltz to partners, and turn half round with both hands, meeting the next lady; perform this figure until in your places; form two side lines, all advance twice and cross over, turning twice; the same returning; all waltz round; the whole repeated four times.

## SIR ROGER DE COVERLEY

All form two lines, the gentlemen facing the ladies. Top lady and bottom gentleman advance to centre, present right hands and pass quickly round each other to places, top gentleman and bottom lady do the same, then top lady and bottom gentleman advance, give left hands and pass quickly round to places, top gentleman and bottom lady the same. The beginning couple advance and give both hands, turning round to places, following couple the same. The top lady and bottom gentleman advance to centre and turn round each other back to back without touching, the other couple do the same; first lady and bottom gentleman then advance, bow to each other and retire, first gentleman and bottom lady the same. The top gentleman then turns outwards to his right, and the lady turns outwards to her left; each leading down to the bottom of the room, followed by the other gentlemen and ladies. The top couple meet at the bottom, join hands, holding them up as an arch for the other couples to dance through to places, but remaining themselves at the bottom. The figure is then repeated by the other couples in succession.

## SPORTS AND GAMES

There is an unprecedented increase in sports and games facilities today. Most enthusiasts have the opportunity to play the games of their choice, receive coaching, or merely watch the games without much difficulty. However, it is not always easy to find out about the facilities existing locally. If an enquiry at the local library or Citizen's Advice Bureau does not produce the answer, or if information on the rules of a game is sought then it is wise to write to the suitable representative organization to ask for advice.

Most sports and games have representative bodies only too glad to give help. The addresses of some of them are as follows:

**Angling.**
National Federation of Anglers, 47 Lindon Drive, Alvaston, Derby.

**Association Football.**
The Football Association, 22 Lancaster Gate, London W.2.

**Athletics.**
Amateur Athletic Association, 26 Park Crescent, London W.1.

**Badminton.**
Badminton Association of England, 4 Madeira Avenue, Bromley, Kent.

**Basket Ball.**
Amateur Basket Ball Association, Dept. of Physical Education, The University, Leeds 2.

**Billiards.**
Billiards Association and Control Council, 15 Exeter Street, Strand, London W.C.2.

**Bowls.**
English Bowling Association, 2 Roseford Road, Cambridge.

**Boxing.**
Amateur Boxing Association, Clutha House, 10 Storey's Gate, London S.W.1.

**Canoeing.**
British Canoe Union, 26–29 Park Crescent, London W.1.

**Cricket.**
Marylebone Cricket Club, Lord's Ground, London N.W.8.

**Cycling.**
British Cycling Federation, 26 Park Crescent, London W.1.

**Fencing.**
Ladies' Amateur Fencing Union, 58a Ridgmount Gardens, London W.C.1.

**Golf.**
English Golf Union, 35 Broad Street, Wokingham, Berks.

**Hockey.**
Hockey Association, 26 Park Crescent, London W.1.
All England Women's Hockey Association, 45 Doughty Street, London W.C.1.

**Judo.**
British Judo Association, 26–29 Park Crescent, London W.1.

**Motor Cycling.**
Auto-Cycle Union, 31 Belgrave Square, London S.W.1.

**Mountaineering.**
British Mountaineering Council, c/o Alpine Club, 74 South Audley Street, London W.1.

**Netball.**
All England Netball Association, 26–29 Park Crescent, London W.1.

**Rugby Football.**
The Rugby Football Union, Whitton Road, Twickenham, Middx.

**Rugby Football.**
The Rugby Football League, 180 Chapeltown Road, Leeds 7.

**Shooting.**
National Rifle Association, Bisley Camp, Brookwood, Woking, Surrey.
National Small-bore Association, Codrington House, 113 Southwark Street, London S.E.1.

**Skating.**
National Skating Association of Great Britain, Charterhouse, London E.C.1.

**Ski-ing.**
National Ski Federation of Great Britain, 118 Eaton Square, London S.W.1.

**Swimming.**
Amateur Swimming Association, 64 Cannon Street, London E.C.4.
**Table Tennis.**
English Table Tennis Association, 26 Park Crescent, London W.1.
**Tennis.**
Lawn Tennis Association, Palliser Road, Barons Court, West Kensington, London W.14.
**Wrestling.**
British Amateur Wrestling Association, 60 Calabria Road, London N.5.

## MOTORING ORGANIZATIONS

The two principal motoring organizations in Britain are the Automobile Association and The Royal Automobile Club. You can become a member upon payment of the annual subscription.

Amongst the many invaluable services provided to members are the following:

Breakdown assistance
Road patrols
Roadside telephone boxes
Service centres
Mobile offices
Rescue Services
Free legal and technical advice
Favourable insurance rates
Caravanning and camping service

## TOURING AT HOME AND ABROAD

The A.A. and the R.A.C. route planning service provides routes and advice and, if required, notes on interesting things to see and do in each area. They also give members all information about taking vehicles abroad, making sea and air reservations, and issue free route and touring brochures.

Full details of services offered to members can be obtained from the Automobile Association, Fanum House, Leicester Square, London W.C.2 and the Royal Automobile Club, 83–85 Pall Mall, London S.W.1.

## DRIVER'S LICENCE

Application for a licence (or a provisional licence) has to be made to the Council of the County or County Borough in which the applicant resides.

For a driving test, application has to be made to the Clerk to the Traffic Area (Ministry of Transport) in which the applicant lives.

## DRIVING TESTS

However little you mean to drive, if you pass the test you will get a licence allowing you to drive anywhere in Britain, town or country. The Examiner must therefore be satisfied that, whatever the traffic conditions, you can handle your vehicle with safety and with consideration for all road users, in the spirit of the Highway Code.

Remember:

(i) you *must* have a *current* driving licence which covers the type of vehicle on which you take the test;
(ii) you *must* while driving before and on test be fully covered by insurance against third-party risks.

## REGISTRATION OF CARS

When a car is first licensed it is also entered in a register kept by the local authority which issues the licence: the register contains particulars of the vehicle, the name and address of the person who keeps and uses the car (the "registered owner", but not necessarily the real owner), and the registration number allotted to the vehicle – which the vehicle must exhibit on its number plates. The registration will be moved from time to time as necessary to the register of the local authority in whose area the car is normally kept.

Anyone who has "reasonable cause" to do so can obtain the name of the "owner" and other registered particulars on payment of 1/- to the registering authority. If you are involved in an accident, for example, you can by this means get on the track of the driver of another vehicle if you managed only to make a note of its registration number at the time.

When a car is sold, the registration book (issued by the registering authority and containing a copy of the registered particulars) must be handed over to the new owner and the change of ownership must be notified to the authority. The absence of the "log book", as it is commonly called, is therefore a suspicious circumstance and you should never buy a car if the log book is not produced and handed over. The converse unhappily is not true: the fact that the seller does produce the log book and that it has his name in it does not prove that he owns the car – he may, for example, have it only on hire-purchase. There is, in fact, no way of checking with reasonable certainty that the seller of a car (or any chattel – a valuable painting or manuscript, for example) is the owner of it; no way of "investigating title" as there is for a house or land. Because of this lack many people are swindled every year.

## CAR TEST CERTIFICATES

A number of detailed requirements are laid down in the Motor Vehicles (Construction and Use) Regulations 1955 with which all motor cars must comply to ensure that they are roadworthy. Any car may at any time be stopped by a policeman to see that it complies with these regulations. It is a criminal offence if the regulations are not complied with.

In addition, in respect of three of the more important matters dealt with by the Regulations (the brakes, the steering and the lights) cars over a certain age (which is reduced from time to time) cannot get a road traffic licence unless a certificate is produced to show they have been tested by an approved garage and comply with the Regulations. It is important to realise that the certificate is for the purpose of obtaining a car licence and that is all; if you have a car successfully tested and a few weeks later you are stopped for a spot check under the Regulations the car must still pass the spot test; it is no answer to produce the earlier test certificate. You have to pay the garage which does the test for the certificate (but the amount they may charge is from time to time prescribed by regulations), but you will not have to pay for a spot test if stopped by the police.

# NEW ROAD SIGNS

*These are some of the new road signs which will be introduced on all-purpose roads*

## DEFINITE INSTRUCTIONS

Stop and Give Way

Give Way

No Overtaking

No U-Turns

All Motor Vehicles Prohibited

Turn Right

Turn Left at Junction

No Entry

No Right Turn

No Waiting

No Stopping (Clearway)

Keep Left

## WARNING

Dual Carriageway Ends

Road Narrows

Pedestrian Crossing Ahead

Children

Low Flying Aircraft or Sudden Aircraft Noise

Other Danger

Road Works

Steep Hill Downwards

Traffic Merges

Height Limit

## INFORMATORY

Cyclists and Moped Riders Only

No Through Road

Hospital

Entrance to Parking-Meter Zone

Exit from Parking-Meter Zone

Ring Road (Repeater)

# FLOWER DECORATION

## CUTTING AND THE CARE OF FLOWERS

Flowers, says Jean De Valon in her *Flower Decoration*, should never be cut during the heat of the day. The best times for cutting are early morning and late afternoon, when the stems are filled with moisture. Blooms that are just emerging from the tight-bud stage should be selected since they will last several days longer than those already open and also retain their colour better.

Neither the buying nor the cutting of flowers should be a haphazard affair. Before entering the florist's shop or stepping out into the garden, it is necessary to have a clear idea of what you propose to do. The room or rooms in which an arrangement is to be placed and its position in the room will have a distinct bearing on the nature, shape and size of the arrangement. Whether the blooms are home-grown or purchased, plunge them almost up to their necks in a deep container of cold water immediately you get them into the house Then let them stand in a cool room for at least an hour.

When your flowers have been properly hardened off, you are one step nearer the actual arranging of them. The next step is to remove all leaves, side-shoots and buds from that part of the stem which will be below the water line. All such material left below the surface will quickly start to deteriorate and decay, making the water foul and dirty. Careful cleaning at this stage obviates the necessity for frequent changes of water. In fact, if the cleaning is properly done, no water changes should be needed at all. Your container will merely require a regular topping-up to ensure that a sufficient water level is maintained.

## CONTAINERS AND HOLDERS

Apart from vases, pots and bowls expressly made for the purpose, there is an almost limitless fund of likely containers to be found in your own home. Old jugs, soup tureens, oven dishes, biscuit tins and the like can all be utilized.

It cannot be too strongly stressed that the container is an essential part of the arrangement. In colour, shape, size, and the material from which it is made, it must be in harmony with the flowers it is to hold and the background against which they will be seen. Therefore, even though the choice of container may be wide it should not be indiscriminate.

Autumn foliage and chrysanthemums look perfect in copper containers – and copper is said to prolong the life of the flowers by destroying bacteria in the water; roses, lilies, carnations, and all elegant flowers, look their best in silver. The homely flowers of the cottage garden – geraniums, pinks, sweet williams – are seen to advantage in pottery.

Every flower arrangement needs, of course, to be firmly secured in its container. To this end, there are three methods in general use: pinholders, wire mesh (or chicken wire), and a proprietary product.

## COLOUR

*Black* is the absence of colour; *white* is the mixing of all colour; *grey* is neutral colour. Black, white and grey are, therefore, ideal for containers as they complement all colours and never distract the eyes from the actual arrangement.

Another quality of colour is that it suggests weight. Dark colours *look* heavy, while light colours appear to be light in weight. This is the reason why light coloured flowers are better placed at the top of a design, with the darker ones near the base. For even though two flowers may be identical in all respects other than colour, the darker one will appear to be heavier than the other.

A similar illusion created by colour relates to temperature. Red and yellow, and their many combinations, give an impression of warmth and cheerfulness and are therefore ideal for sick-room arrangements. The blues, living up to their colloquial name, have just the opposite effect. They seem to be cool – cold, even – and emotionally unexciting. Green conveys an atmosphere of freshness, serenity and restfulness.

## BASIC FLOWER DESIGNS
The designs are identified by the following names: Symmetrical, Asymmetrical, Vertical, Horizontal, Radiating, Round, Crescent, and Hogarth.

**1. Symmetrical.** As its name implies, this is an arrangement having a perfect, regular balance – one side matching the other. It is also known as the *Formal* or *Mass* arrangement.

In this type of arrangement it is customary to use wire mesh as the support, and when you have fitted it into your container you will be ready to begin.

**2. Asymmetrical.** As opposed to the Symmetrical, this is a design having no formal balance. That is to say, there is

no matching of one side against the other. The container used is usually of the low, shallow variety, but not too shallow. It is usual to employ a pinholder to support an arrangement of this nature, and the container must be able to hold sufficient water to cover the pinholder.

Never use a round bowl for this type of arrangement, for its symmetry would be strongly at variance with the off-centre design. An entree dish, or any type of low, oval bowl, would make a suitable container.

**3. Vertical.** This is where the narrow-necked vase comes into its own.

Since the nature of the vase does not allow for a great deal of material, your flowers for this design should be carefully chosen. Unlike a mass arrangement, they will attract individual attention.

Each piece must be placed as close as possible to the first placement, the lengths of stems decreasing progressively.

**4. Horizontal** This perhaps is the most useful design of all. It is the basis of all luncheon or dining-table arrangements and is perfect, less formally, for just *any* table. Regarding the container used, it should be shallow; apart from that, the field is open.

Although pinholders can be used, it is much simpler to use wire mesh for this type of arrangement. In which case, you will wire your container with four thicknesses.

It is *not* necessary for the two sides of the arrangement to duplicate each other, though each must be equally good. Dissimilar sides, in fact, make for a

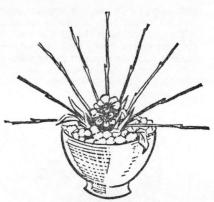

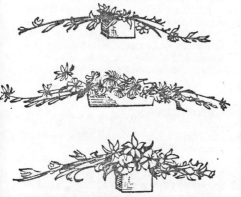

more interesting design. Unlike the foregoing designs, this one will be seen from above and on all sides. For this reason, particular attention should be paid to the grouping of colours and attractiveness of outline.

**5. Radiating.** This is a most economical design because it requires so little material to obtain a striking effect. It is particularly useful during the autumn and winter months when one's choice of material is, in any event, more limited. With just leaves – magnolia leaves, perhaps, or laurel leaves – a really delightful arrangement can be achieved.

The most suitable container would be a round bowl, for the pattern of the arrangement is symmetrical. With a deep bowl, wire mesh can be used for support; but for a shallow bowl a pinholder is preferable, being easier to conceal. The pinholder should be in the centre of the bowl, slightly towards the back.

Contrary to all other designs, the

material used here should be roughly of *equal* length. For in actual fact this pattern is more truly symmetrical than the design bearing that name.

The first placement stands dead centre in the wire or on the pinholder, while the second and third placements are inserted almost horizontally to either side. The remainder of your material is added evenly on either side to form a fan shape.

**6. Round.** A round design requires a round container. If you use a glass bowl, a pinholder *must* be used to give support; but if the bowl is opaque, use mesh wire. It is much simpler to work with on a design of this nature.

With the key placements in position, you proceed to fill in with whatever flowers and foliage you have. Instead of reaching around or across the bowl, you turn it as you add each piece. The turning of the bowl ensures that the arrangement has no bare patches but is well filled and of an even appearance from every angle.

Practically any material is suitable for the round design, and it can be done in bowls of any size. It is a very pleasing arrangement to look down upon, which makes it ideal for coffee tables or other low tables.

**7. Crescent.** A low container – but not a round one if it can be avoided – should be used for this design, in conjunction with a pinholder.

The pinholder should be placed well off centre towards the back of the container. (Wire mesh is impracticable because it would be difficult to conceal.)

To commence the design it is best to outline the crescent with pliable material such as Scotch broom or pussy willow.

When the outline is ready, fix it firmly on the pinholder, off-centre and to the back. One piece should rise and curve towards the opposite side of the container, its tip being almost in line with that side, while the other piece should curve upwards from the container level. There should be an appreciable distance between the tips of these two pieces as they curve towards each other. They most certainly must never meet or the crescent shape would be lost.

The added flowers must carefully follow the crescent line.

**8. Hogarth.** This design is named after William Hogarth the painter, whose contention it was that the "S" curve is the line of beauty. We have, therefore, a design which upholds his belief that it is easier for the eye to follow the lazy "S" curve than to follow a pattern made up of straight lines.

To gain the full effect of the design use a tall, slender, narrow-necked container. Wire mesh, folded into a loose pencil-shape as for a vertical arrangement, should be used for support.

For the focal point use a large flower, a rosette of small flowers, or even some attractive foliage. Its position will be immediately in front of where the upward and downward sweeps meet. – *Flower Decoration* by Jean De Valon.

## JAPANESE FLOWER ARRANGEMENT

In her standard work *The Art of Japanese Flower Arrangement*, Stella Coe – one of the foremost exponents of the art in the West – explains that to the Japanese there is more to flower arranging than merely achieving a pleasant decorative effect for the home. It embraces a symbolism which gives new meaning and subtle depth to the many ways in which branches and flowers can be used together in scenic and pictorial representations.

*Ikebana*, which is generally accepted as meaning "flower arrangement", is properly interpreted as "the arrangement of living plant material" and is the key to the essential differences between Japanese and Western styles. Whereas Western arrangements generally favour a mass of flowers and a combination of colours, the Japanese concept calls for restraint in the use of material, with colour being of the smallest importance. The prescribed angles at which flowers and branches incline in the basic arrangements and their infinite variations provide the three-dimensional effect which gives Japanese flower arrangements their breathtaking and lifelike quality.

# CHILDREN: EMPLOYMENT AND ADOPTION

## FAMILY ALLOWANCES

These cash payments made to a family with more than one child are not part of the National Insurance scheme but are provided wholly out of general taxation; there are therefore no contribution conditions and everyone with more than one child which is maintained by him or her is eligible. The allowances are subject to income tax and surtax as earned income, as also are National Insurance benefits (but not Unemployment, Sickness and Maternity Benefits and Death Grants, which are not taxable). They may be claimed for children under school leaving age with an extension to the age of sixteen for certain incapacitated children and to the age of nineteen for those undergoing education up to that age (including certain apprentices). Claim forms may be obtained from any local Pensions and National Insurance office, and you will need the child's birth certificate.

## EMPLOYMENT OF CHILDREN

Under the Children and Young Persons Act 1933 no child of compulsory school age may be employed

(a) until within two years of leaving school, or

(b) before the end of school hours on any school day, or

(c) between 8 p.m. and 6 a.m., or

(d) for more than two hours on any school day or Sunday, or

(e) to perform any tasks likely, to cause injury.

These rules may be extended by local bye-laws. There are in addition particular restrictions on the employment of children for purposes of entertainment. The detailed rules are complicated but the general principle is that no child under twelve may be so employed, and the licence of the local authority must be obtained for the employment of a child over that age if a charge is made to the public (these requirements do not apply to certain BBC performances nor do they apply to choristers). There are similar requirements about a licence for the employment of any young person under the age of 18 for the purpose of entertainment abroad.

Another Act, the Young Persons (Employment) Act 1938 imposes further regulations, also quite complicated in their detail, about the employment of young persons over school age but below 18 as errand or messenger boys or girls.

Apart from these general rules there are particular restrictions on the employment of children or young persons in a number of fields, notably in industrial undertakings, factories, sea-going ships (including registered fishing-boats), shops, mines and quarries.

## ADOPTION

The adoption of children so as to make them in law members of a family to which they do not belong by nature, although a well-known concept in Roman law, is a comparatively recent one in English law having been introduced to this country only in 1926.

Adoption is effected by an order of the High Court, a County Court or a Magistrate's Court. The effect of such an order is that the natural parents of the child (whether legitimate or illegitimate) cease in law to be its parents and the adoptive parents step into their shoes. Thus, to take a fairly striking example, if grandparents adopt their daughter's son he becomes the brother of his own mother. The effect, of course, is not only in terms of family relationship but also in property; an adopted child in general succeeds to property as if it were the natural child of its adoptive parents. In order to enable persons making wills, settlements etc. to exclude adopted children if they wish to do so an adopted child, however, will not succeed to property under a will or settlement if the document was made before the adoption order; for this purpose a will is "made" on the date of death. Contrary to the general rule titles, and property settled to devolve with titles, descend to natural children only and not to adopted children.

**Fostering.** It will be seen that adoption must be distinguished from mere fostering (although this is sometimes loosely called adoption) because fostering creates no legal relationship whereas adoption, in law, transfers the child wholly out of one family and into another.

**Adoption Safeguards.** Naturally the practice of adoption has to be safeguarded in various ways: there are, for example, rules to prevent trafficking in children (particularly necessary because, strange though it may seem, the demand for children exceeds the supply of them); and there are also rules to ensure that the adopter is of proper age and sex etc. to become an adoptive parent and to ensure that a married couple both consent if a child is to be adopted by one of them. It is worth noting that there is nothing to prevent the natural father or mother adopting their own child. There are circumstances in which it is desirable that they should do so.

Because by adoption the child's natural parents cease in law to be its parents an adoption order cannot be made without the consent of the legal parents, legal guardian or the mother of an illegitimate child. This requirement can be overridden if consent is withheld unreasonably. Usually in matters concerning children the principle of English law is that the child's welfare is paramount, but in this particular case what is "reasonable" is considered not from the child's point of view but from the parents' point of view.

**Adoption Order.** Before an adoption order is made the child must have been in the care and possession of the applicant for three continuous months after it is over the age of six weeks old. Three months' notice of intention to apply for the order must be given to the local authority (unless the applicant is the natural parent of the child) and the authority has certain supervisory powers and duties during that period. The object of both these rules is of course to ensure so far as possible that the adoptive parent and the child are suited to each other, and that the adoptive parent is a suitable person.

**Adoption procedure.** If you wish to adopt a child the easiest place at which to get information is the Children's Department of your local authority. County Councils and County Borough Councils and also registered Adoption Societies are legally authorized to arrange adoptions.

# MUSIC AND ART

## MUSIC

Music has often been called "the universal language because it speaks to the minds and hearts of men irrespective of differences in spoken language. The language of music can be read and understood by people of all cultures once they know its symbols and the sounds they represent.

Musical sounds are called *notes* and each note has a fixed duration and pitch in relation to other notes in the same piece of music. The note's *duration* is indicated by its shape and its *pitch* by its position on a system of lines called a *staff*. The shapes of the various notes, from the longest to the shortest are shown below. Each note lasts half the time of the one which precedes it in the following list.

| | English Name | American Name |
|---|---|---|
| •𝅜 | Breve | Double whole note |
| 𝅝 | Semibreve | Whole note |
| 𝅗𝅥 or ρ | Minim | Half note |
| 𝅘𝅥 or ρ | Crotchet | Quarter note |
| 𝅘𝅥𝅮 or ƒ | Quaver | Eighth note |
| 𝅘𝅥𝅯 or ƒ | Semiquaver | Sixteenth note |
| 𝅘𝅥𝅰 or ƒ | Demisemiquaver | Thirty-second note |

The duration of a *rest*, or period of silence, is indicated by the following signs:

a breve rest

a semibreve

a minim

a crotchet

a quaver

a semiquaver

a demisemiquaver

The time of the music is written at the beginning of a piece. It takes the form of a *time signature* which tells how many beats there are to each *bar* or *measure* of beats. For example, if there are four beats to the bar, the upper figure of the time signature will be 4. The lower figure indicates the duration of each beat. If each beat is a minim in duration, the lower figure will be 2 (or a half note); if it is a crotchet, it will be 4 (a quarter note). Thus a time signature for six quaver beats in a bar would be written $\frac{6}{8}$.

The *tempo*, or speed, at which the music is played is usually suggested by the composer by means of an Italian word written at the top of the music. Some of the commonest of these terms are:

*Adagio* . . . in a leisurely fashion.
*Andante* . . . at a walking pace.
*Allegro* . . . fast.
*Allegretto* . . . not so fast as Allegro.
*Largo* . . . slow.

*Lento* ... very slow.
*Moderato* ... at a moderate pace.
*Presto* ... quick
*Prestissimo* ... very quick.
*Vivace* ... at a lively pace.

The pitch of one note in relation to another is shown by its position on or between the lines of the staff. If notes are required beyond those which can be shown within the range of the staff, short lines called *ledger lines* are added above or below the staff. The actual pitch of the notes is fixed by adding a *clef* sign at the beginning of each staff. The clef gives a definite pitch to one line of the staff and the other lines and the spaces rise or fall alphabetically from this fixed point. For example, the treble or G clef fixes the note G on the second line from the bottom of the staff. Thus, the space above will be A and the space below will be F.

The principal clefs are as follows:

Treble (G) clef

The C clef

Bass (F) clef

Composers of many nations have contributed to the musical repertoire we enjoy today. Some of the greatest of these musicians were:
Palestrina (*c*1526–1594)
William Byrd (1543–1623)
Monteverdi (1568–1643)
Jean Baptiste Lully (1632–1687)
Archangelo Corelli (1653–1713)
Alessandro Scarlatti (1659–1725)
Henry Purcell (1659–1695)
Johann Sebastian Bach (1685–1750)
George Frederic Handel (1685–1759)
C. P. E. Bach (1714–1788)
Christopher Willibald Gluck (1714–1787)

Joseph Haydn (1732–1809)
Wolfgang Amadeus Mozart (1756–1791)
Ludwig van Beethoven (1770–1827)
Gioacchino Rossini (1792–1868)
Franz Schubert (1797–1828)
Hector Berlioz (1803–1869)
Felix Mendelssohn-Bartholdy (1809–1847)
Frédéric Chopin (1810–1849)
Robert Schumann (1810–1856)
Franz Liszt (1811–1886)
Richard Wagner (1813–1883)
Giuseppe Verdi (1813–1901)
Charles Gounod (1818–1893)
Johannes Brahms (1833–1897)
Alexander Borodin (1834–1887)
Georges Bizet (1838–1875)
Peter Tchaikowsky (1840–1893)
Anton Dvořák (1841–1904)
Arthur Sullivan (1842–1900)
Edward Elgar (1857–1934)
Giacomo Puccini (1858–1924)
Gustav Mahler (1860–1911)
Claude Debussy (1862–1918)
Richard Strauss (1864–1949)
Jan Sibelius (1865–1957)
Ralph Vaughan Williams (1872–1958)
Sergei Rachmaninov (1873–1943)
Arnold Schönberg (1874–1951)
Béla Bartók (1881–1945)

## ARTISTS

The known history of the visual arts, painting, modelling and sculpture stretches back into prehistory. Mural paintings of animals and votive statues of fertility goddesses reveal man's early attempts to realise in paint, clay and stone, the physical and spiritual world about him. Among the great artists of historical times whose works we have grown to admire and love are:
Phidias (*c*490–*c*420 B.C.)
Praxiteles (*c*300s B.C.)
Giotto (*c*1266–1337)
Fra Angelico (1387–1455)
Piero della Francesca (*c*1416–1492)
Sandro Botticelli (1444–1510)
Hieronymus Bosch (*c*1450–1516)
Leonardo da Vinci (1452–1519)
Albrecht Dürer (1471–1528)
Michelangelo (1475–1564)
Titian (1477–1576)
Raphael (1483–1520)
Hans Holbein (1497–1543)

Tintoretto (1518–1594)
Gian Lorenzo Bernini (1598–1680)
Luca della Robbia (1400–1483)
Donatello (c1386–1466)
Benvenuto Cellini (1500–1571)
Pieter Bruegle (1525–1568)
El Greco (1541–1614)
Peter Paul Rubens (1577–1640)
Franz Hals (c1580–1666)
Anthony Vandyke (1599–1641)
Diego Velasquez (1599–1660)
Rembrandt (1606–1669)
Jan Vermeer (1632–1675)
Antoine Watteau (1684–1721)
Giovanni Battista Tiepolo (1696–1770)

William Hogarth (1697–1764)
Francisco Goya (1746–1828)
Joseph Turner (1775–1851)
Edgar Degas (1834–1917)
Paul Cézanne (1839–1906)
Pierre Auguste Renoir (1841–1919)
John Singer Sargent (1856–1926)
Georges Seurat (1859–1891)
Toulouse-Lautrec (1864–1901)
Vincent van Gogh (1853–1890)
Auguste Rodin (1840–1917)
Paul Gaugin (1848–1903)
Henri Rousseau (1844–1910)
Amedeo Modigliani (1884–1920)
Henri Matisse (1869–1954)

## SCOUTS

Headquarters: 25 Buckingham Palace Road, London SW1.
Chief Scout: Sir Charles Maclean Bt., JP.
UK membership 555,222.
Age Limits: Cub Scouts – 8 to 11 years
Scouts – 11 to 16 years
Venture Scouts – 16 to 20 years.

The scout movement may be said to have begun during the siege of Mafeking in the South African War.

Lord Baden-Powell had, for some years before the outbreak of that war, been running classes for training the soldiers under his command in scouting and campaigning, with a view to developing character as well as efficiency in the individual soldier. When his troops were beleaguered in Mafeking, his Chief staff officer, Major Lord Edward Cecil, set about organizing the boys of the town as a general utility corps on scout lines.

The boys were divided into patrols of six each, with a leader. Baden-Powell's belief that boys will learn readily and take responsibility if trusted and put upon their honour was amply justified by the excellent manner in which they carried out the duties allotted to them.

So successful was the scheme that Baden-Powell later adopted the patrol system in training the South African Constabulary for field work. The uniform chosen for scouts was the now familiar cowboy hat, shirt, green tie and shorts, and badges were awarded for efficiency in various kinds of work.

The first trial camp for scout training for boys was held in 1907, and its success was so pronounced that Baden-Powell was led to take the idea further. In 1908, he published the scout's vademecum, *Scouting for Boys*, which led to the formation of troops of scouts in a number of centres throughout the United Kingdom.

So rapidly did the movement spread that in 1910 Baden-Powell decided to leave the army and devote himself to the Boy Scouts. He became Chief Scout, and threw himself with characteristic zeal into all scout activities; camp life, pioneering, boat work, nature study, etc. His idea was to supply the boys with what was frequently wanting in their ordinary school training – guidance on character training, general knowledge, handicraft skill, physical development and knowledge of the laws of health, and to imbue them with the idea of service for others and for the State – in short, to train them to become good citizens.

The Scout movement is non-military and non-political, and boys of all classes and denominations are to be found in its ranks. The boys are taught self-discipline, but each scout has to promise on his honour to carry out, so far as he can, the Scout Law, and to fulfil the Scout obligation of doing a good turn every day. The boys are taught how to track and follow signs, how to signal, how to build a shack, light a fire and cook their food, and other details of scout-craft.

There are special opportunities for those boys interested in sea scouting and air scouting. Handicapped boys may join the Extension Branch where activities are specially devised for their needs.

The movement has spread all over the world, as was shown in the great Scout Rally held at Olympia in 1920, in the International Scout Conference held in Paris in 1922 and jamborees held since.

Officially, the scheme in this country is under the control of the Boy Scouts' Association, incorporated by Royal Charter in 1912. The organization consists of Chief Scout and Council, County Commissioners with County Scout Councils, and District Commissioners.

In 1966, the Chief Scout's *Advance*

*Party Report* made revolutionary recommendations. These included changes in the Scout Law, in titles of the parts of the movement and changes in uniform. The Association accepted the recommendations almost without exception.

Recognised Cub Scout Packs, Scout Troops and Venture Scout Groups are under the immediate control of a Local Association from the secretary of which, detailed information may be obtained. The work is entirely voluntary and those willing to help should communicate with the Local Association or with Headquarters.

## GUIDES

Headquarters: 17–19 Buckingham Palace Road, London SW1.
Chief Guide: Olave Lady Baden-Powell, GBE.
Commonwealth Commissioner: Mrs Derek Parker Bowles.
UK membership: 644,234
Age limits: Brownie Guides – 7 to 11 years
Guides – 10 to 16 years
Ranger Guides – 16 to 20 years

Guiding is a training in citizenship for girls, organized on parallel lines to those of the Boy Scouts' Association, though the two movements are run separately. The organization is decentralized as far as possible, the local administration being in the hands of the District, Division and County Commissioners. They are appointed by the Executive Committee of the Council, which is responsible for the general policy of the movement throughout the Commonwealth.

In the early days of the scout movement, girls began to register as scouts. In order to cater for these girls, Lord Baden-Powell asked his sister to adapt scout principles and training to the requirements of girls. In 1910, the movement received the name of guides. Through the years, various modifications to the original movement have been made. The latest of these being contained in the recommendations of the guide "Working Party". These included amendments to the Promise and the Law, changes in the names of the guide organizations and in the uniforms.

Membership of the guide movement is open to all girls within the age groups 7 to 20, irrespective of colour, class or creed, provided they are willing to make the Guide Promise and to carry it out in their daily lives. The Promise, made by every guide on her enrolment, is to do her duty to God and the Queen, to help other people at all times, and to obey the Guide Law. The Guide Law is a simple ethical code, embodying honour, loyalty, usefulness, friendliness, courtesy, kindness to animals, obedience, cheerfulness, thrift and cleanness of life.

Guide training makes a particular appeal to young people by its practical methods and approach. Learning by doing rather than by theory is its keynote, and is carried through the various series of tests, which give every guide the opportunity to develop her special interests and talents. Outdoor activities are particularly emphasized, and it is the aim of every guide to become an expert camper. The patrol system, by which each company is divided into patrols of six or eight girls who appoint a leader from among themselves, gives a valuable training in democratic self-government, and this is further developed in the Ranger Guide Company.

Guiding is not confined to those who are physically active. Through the Extension Section it embraces the blind, the deaf, cripples and invalids and high grade mental defectives, who, in spite of their handicaps, take their full place in the Guide organization. Some tests have to be adapted to meet their particular needs, but they join in all guide functions, including camps and other activities, on the same level as other girls.

Specialized interests are catered for, particularly in the Ranger Branch which has sections for Sea and Air Rangers. This enables girls with a love of the sea to gain practice in sailing and rowing, to learn sea lore and methods of navigation; air-minded girls can similarly study air routes and air navigation, and eventually test their skill in gliders and aeroplanes.

Guiding has the same enthusiastic

following throughout the Commonwealth as it has in Great Britain, and has spread to twenty-eight countries throughout the world. The world membership is now approximately three million. Each country has its own national organization, and close contact between them is maintained through the World Association of Girl Guides and Girl Scouts. International camps and conferences are held frequently, and individual companies of different nationalities are encouraged to correspond with each other and if possible to exchange visits.

For further information on Guiding, see *The Story of the Girl Guides*, by Rose Kerr, published by the Girl Guides' Association.

## BOYS' BRIGADE

Headquarters: Brigade House, Parson's Green, London SW6.
Brigade President: The Lord Bruce, JP, DL.
UK membership: 142,600 boys.
Age limits: Junior Section – 8 to 12 years
Company Section – 12 to 16 years
Senior Section – 16 to 19 years.

The Boys' Brigade is the pioneer organization for boys, having been founded in Glasgow, in October, 1883, by Mr (afterwards Sir) Wm. A. Smith, who died in 1914. The object of the Brigade, as laid down in its constitution, is "The advancement of Christ's Kingdom among boys and the promotion of habits of obedience, reverence, discipline, self-respect, and all that tends towards a true Christian manliness."

The Brigade is composed of companies each of which is connected with a church mission, or other religious organization, which is responsible, through the officers, for the religious instruction given to the boys. The Brigade develops every side of a boy's life. The leading features of BB work include Bible-class, club-rooms, drill, first-aid, life-saving, swimming, physical training, cricket, football, scouting, signalling, music, and summer camps.

The movement has spread to all parts of the world, and the Brigade system has been adopted by the Church Lads' Brigade and the Jewish Lads' Brigade, all of which are run on very similar lines.

Particulars regarding the formation and enrolment of companies may be had from the Brigade Headquarters. Additional information may also be found in the book *The Story of the Boys' Brigade*, by Austin E. Birch, published by Muller.

## GIRLS' BRIGADE

Headquarters: Brigade House, 8 Parson's Green, London SW6.
President: Lady MacDermott.
UK membership: 65,066
Age limits: Explorers – 5 to 8 years
Juniors – 8 to 11 years
Seniors – 11 to 14 years
Brigaders – 14 upwards.

The Girls' Brigade is the counterpart of the Boys' Brigade and companies of the two organizations share some of their activities. The GB aims "To help girls to become followers of the Lord Jesus Christ, and through self-control, reverence, and a sense of responsibility to find true enrichment of life."

The GB leaders are appointed by the local church and they run various activities, such as camping, Bible study, nature study, crafts, singing, service projects, home making, cookery, and many others.

## CHURCH LADS' BRIGADE

Headquarters: 58 Gloucester Place, London W1.
President: His Grace the Lord Bishop of Canterbury.
Age limits: Young Boys' Corps – 8 to 10 years
Junior Training Corps – 10 to 13 years
Senior Corps – 13 to 21 years.

This is an organization with similar aims and methods to those of the Boys' Brigade. The CLB was founded by Col. W. M. Gee in 1891. Its membership is confined to the Church of England and its aim, to "... extend the Kingdom of Christ among lads and to make them faithful members of the Church", is pursued by means of drill, Bible study, games, camping singing, and others.

Further information about the CLB may be found in the booklets *General Information About CLB*; and *The CLB Object and Method* which may be obtained from the Headquarters.

## CHURCH GIRLS' BRIGADE

Headquarters: 90 Deansgate, Manchester 3.

This organization is the counterpart, for girls, of the Church Lads' Brigade. The two organizations share similar aims and systems of control.

## JEWISH LADS' BRIGADE

Headquarters: 33 Henriques Street, London E1.
Commandant: Brigade Colonel, the Rt Hon Lord Swaythling, OBE, JP.
Age limits: 11 years 3 months to 19 years.

The Jewish Lads' Brigade was formed in 1895 by Col. A. E. W. Goldsmit MVO with the intention of providing for Jewish boys the benefits seen to be provided by other Brigades of the time. The JLB's aim is so ". . . to train its members in loyalty, honour, discipline and self-respect, that they shall become worthy and useful citizens and a credit to their Country and Community."

## JEWISH GIRLS' BRIGADE

This organization, which was founded in 1963, is incorporated in the Jewish Lads' Brigade. The JGB shares the aims and methods of the JLB and together they have a membership of about 2,500.

## NATIONAL ASSOCIATION OF BOYS' CLUBS

Headquarters: 17 Bedford Square, London WC1.
President: HRH The Duke of Gloucester, KG, Kt.
UK membership: clubs – 2,034
   boys – 158,119
Age limit: 14 to 20 years.

This association was founded in 1925 in order to bring under one administration the Federation of Boys' Clubs in such places as London, Liverpool, Birmingham and Bristol. The aim of the NABC is to provide opportunities for the fulfilment of the mental, physical, artistic and religious needs of boys.

Further information on the association may be found in the NABC quarterly magazine *Challenge* which may be obtained from the Headquarters.

## NATIONAL ASSOCIATION OF YOUTH CLUBS

Headquarters: Devonshire Street House, 30 Devonshire Street, London W1.
Presidents: Her Grace the Duchess of Buccleugh and Queensberry, The Rt Hon Lord Hunt of Llanvair Waterdine, CBE, DSO.
UK membership: clubs – 3,244
    girls – 105,958
    boys – 132,620
Age limit: approximately 14 to 21 years.

This association was formed in 1911. The NAYC today aims ". . . to help young people through leisure-time activities so to develop their physical, mental and spiritual capacities that they grow to maturity as individuals and members of society." Its clubs are to be found in all parts of the country.

Further information on the association may be obtained either direct from the Headquarters, from their *Annual Report*, or from their booklet, *What is the NAYC?*

BIRDS' EGGS. In selecting eggs for a cabinet, always choose those which are newly-laid. Prick a small hole in the least beautiful side of the egg with a needle, then insert a small steel drill and make a round smooth hole. The contents may then be either sucked up through a fine glass tube into a bulb, or blown out by holding the point of the blowpipe a little distance from the hole, but not in it. A syringe or pressure-ball held in the hand, or a small bellows may be used. Gently wash out the inside of the shell with a mild detergent, making sure it is thoroughly clean, and then rinse with warm water.

R—E.W.—O

When the shell is drained dry, cut a small round patch of paper and paste over the hole.

The eggs of some birds are protected by law and it is a punishable offence to steal them from the nest. Where the serious ornithologist wishes to make a collection of eggs, he should confine himself to those birds which are not protected by law and never take more than one egg from a nest. If the collector is in any doubt about which eggs he may take, he should consult the Royal Society for the Protection of Birds, The Lodge, Sandy, Bedfordshire: Telephone, Sandy 111.

## TO DRY BOTANICAL SPECIMENS FOR PRESERVATION.

The main points to be observed are to preserve the plants in such a way that the moisture may be quickly absorbed, the colours preserved as far as possible, and sufficient pressure maintained so that they do not curl up in drying.

Pressing between sheets of common brown paper is best except for very delicate plants which require a smoother and more absorbent paper. Blotting-paper is apt to absorb the moisture too rapidly.

The paper should be cut to folio size – the British Museum Herbarium paper measures $17\frac{1}{2}$ inches by $11\frac{1}{2}$ inches.

Two boards should be made for the top and bottom of the sheets, and pressure may be applied by a weight of any kind placed on the top board.

If the plants are small, gather them root and stem, if large, cut off branches about a foot in length. Place them side by side on the same sheet, never on top of each other, and lay over them one or more sheets according to the thickness and nature of the plants. – *British Museum Handbook for Collectors*.

## TO PRESERVE FLOWERS.

Dip them, whilst fresh gathered, in gum water. Let them drain for a few minutes and place them in a vase. The gum will then produce a thin coating on the stems and leaves, thus preserving their shape and colour.

Faded flowers may be restored by dipping them in very hot water half-way up the stems, then lay them by until the water cools. The portions of the stems which have been immersed must then be cut off and the flowers placed in clean cold water.

A little charcoal in the glass in which cut flowers are placed helps to keep them fresh for a long time. A piece of camphor dissolved in the water has a similar effect.

Another method of preserving the form and colour of flowers for winter decoration is to stick them upright in a lump of clay in the bottom of a large box or jar, and then to pour in slowly and carefully sufficient fine dry sand to completely cover the flower in such a way that its shape will be retained. Keep in a dry, warm place for two or three weeks. Flowers preserved in this way will keep their natural colour and shape for a long time.

## TO PRESERVE SEAWEEDS.

First wash the seaweed in fresh water, then take a plate or dish (the larger the better), cut your paper to the size required, place it in the plate with fresh water and, with a good sized camel hair pencil, spread out the plant in a natural form (picking out with a pin gives the seaweed an unnatural appearance, and destroys the characteristic fall of the branches); then gently raise the paper with the specimen out of the water, placing it in a slanting position for a few moments so as to allow the superfluous water to run off; after which place it in the press.

The press is made with either thin pieces of board or pasteboard. Lay on the first board two sheets of blotting-paper; on that lay your specimens; place straight and smooth over them a piece of old muslin, fine cambric, or linen; then some more blotting paper, and place another board on the top of that, and continue in the same way. The blotting-paper and the muslin should be carefully removed and dried every day, and then replaced; at the same time, those specimens that are sufficiently dry may be taken away.

You can either gum the specimens in a scrapbook, or fix them in, as drawings are often fastened, by making four slits in the page, and inserting each corner. This is by far the best plan, as it allows their removal without injury to the page. Some of the large algae will not adhere to the paper, and consequently require gumming. After careful cleaning and pressing, brush the coarser kinds over with spirits of turpentine, in which two or three small lumps of gum mastic have been dissolved by shaking in a warm place; two thirds of a small phial is the proper proportion, and this will make the specimens retain a fresh appearance.

**TO MAKE SKELETON LEAVES.** The leaves should be put into an earthen or glass bowl, and a large quantity of rain water poured over them; after this they must be left in the open air, and to the heat of the sun, without covering the bowl. As the water evaporates and the leaves become dry, more water must be added; the leaves will by this means putrefy, but the time required for this varies; some plants will be finished in a month, others will require two months or longer, according to the toughness of their parenchyma.

When they have been in a state of putrefaction for some time, the two membranes will begin to separate, and the green part of the leaf will become fluid; then the operation of clearing is to be performed. The leaf is to be put upon a flat white earthen plate, and covered with clear water; and being gently squeezed with the finger, the membranes will begin to open, and the green substance will come out at the edges; the membranes must be carefully taken off with the finger, and great caution must be used in separating them near the middle rib. When once there is an opening towards this separation the whole membrane follows easily; when both membranes are taken off, the skeleton is finished, and it has to be washed clean with water, and then dried between the leaves of a scrapbook.

**TO TAKE IMPRESSIONS OF LEAVES.** Prepare two rubbers by tying up wool or any other soft substance in wash-leather; then prepare the colours in which you wish to print leaves. The colours may be artists' oils, poster paint of a stiff consistency or printer's ink. Get a number of leaves the size and kind you wish to stamp, then dip the rubbers into the paint, and rub them one over the other, so that you have only a small quantity of the composition on the rubbers. Having warmed a leaf between your hands, to make it pliable, place it upon one rubber and moisten it gently with the other; take the leaf off and apply it to the substance on which you wish to make the imprint; upon the leaf, place a piece of white paper, press gently, and a beautiful impression of all the veins of the leaf will be obtained.

**Another Method of Taking Leaf Impressions.** Hold oiled paper in the smoke of a lamp or a candle, until it becomes coated with the soot; to this paper apply the leaf, having previously warmed it between your hands, so that it may be pliable. Place the lower surface of the leaf upon the blackened surface of the oil-paper, so that the numerous veins, which are so prominent on this side, may receive from the paper a coating of soot. Lay a paper over the leaf, and then press it gently upon the smoked paper with the fingers, or with a small roller covered with woollen cloth, or some similarly soft material, so that every part of the underside of the leaf may come in contact with the sooted oil-paper. A coating of the carbon (soot) will adhere to the leaf. Then remove the leaf carefully, and place the blackened surface on a sheet of white paper, or in a book prepared for the purpose, covering the leaf with a clean slip of paper, and pressing upon it with the fingers, or roller, as before. With care, excellent impressions may be obtained in this way.

**TO MAKE LINO-CUTS.** Lino-cuts may be used to produce attractive designs on greetings cards, repeating patterns on fabrics and to decorate many other articles.

Decide on a simple design or stylized picture and draw it on a sheet of paper. Take a piece of thick lino and glue it to a flat piece of wood. The lino should be painted with a white, water-based paint so that the design can be traced onto the lino block and seen clearly. Decide on which part of the design is to print and which is to leave the paper blank. Using lino cutters, which may be bought at any art shop for a few shillings, gouge out the portion of the design to be left blank. This will leave the design to be printed in relief.

Before printing, clean the block thoroughly. On a small sheet of glass, roll a blob of printing ink to and fro until it is smooth and even. Clean the roller (which also costs a few shillings from an art shop) and then roll it over the glass a few times to pick up an even layer of ink. Spread the ink which is on the roller over the design, using the roller at various angles. Carefully place a sheet of paper on the block and press down firmly, burnishing it with the back of a large spoon. Peel off the paper and you will see your design clearly printed.

The block should be cleaned after each use. Various coloured inks and papers may be tried for effect, but it is wise to use a fairly stiff, porous paper, such as cartridge paper.

## TO MAKE BRASS-RUBBINGS.

Many old churches have fine brass plates on graves set into the floors of the aisles or on the walls above the graves. These brasses are often beautifully engraved with a likeness of the dead man or woman. It is possible, with patience, to transfer the design on the brass to a sheet of paper. The result makes a rich and striking picture.

The materials required for making a brass-rubbing are simple. You need a large sheet of tough, but fairly thin paper – most art shops will advise which is the most suitable they have in stock – a couple of weights, a roll of Sellotape, a large piece of cobbler's heel, and a spray varnish as used by artists to "fix" charcoal sketches.

When you have discovered the brass which you want to copy, it is important to have a word with an official of the church, the verger or the vicar, and ask permission to make the rubbing. Usually permission is given graciously and a small gift in the poor box is received gratefully.

Before taking the rubbing, dust the brass carefully to remove any grit, then unroll the paper, securing it with the weights and Sellotape. This should be done thoroughly since it is most irritating to have completed half the rubbing only to discover that the paper has either moved or rolled up.

Having secured the paper, take the cobbler's heel and begin to rub gently round the outline of the brass, taking care not to leave surplus blacking outside the design. When the outline is clear, work down the brass, from head to foot, filling in as strongly as you like. Some people like "grainy" rubbings, while others prefer hard, shiny, black ones. When the rubbing is complete, place a sheet of tracing paper over it and roll them up together to prevent smudging. When the rubbing is safely home, unroll it carefully and spray it with the "fixer". The top of the rubbing may be secured round a rod of half or three-quarter inch dowel. An eyelet screwed into each end of the rod and a ribbon or cord threaded through them will allow the brass-rubbing to be hung on the wall.

## COLLECTING STAMPS.

So many countries issue a large variety of postage stamps that a collector is wise if he restricts his collection to stamps of one country or of a group of countries. For example, some collectors specialize in stamps of the Commonwealth countries, others are even more specialized, collecting only stamps of the United Kingdom.

Stamps should be carefully mounted in an album. A loose-leaf album is usually best for the purpose, because it allows the collection to be increased without difficulty. The stamps are stuck on to the pages of the album by means of small pieces of gummed paper called stamp hinges. On no account should stamps be stuck down directly on to the page. Stamps should always be stored in a dry place to prevent them sticking to one another and becoming damaged.

There are several great stamp collections in the world, the greatest being that which belongs to the Queen. Occasionally, part of this collection may be seen by the public. Advice on beginning your own collection of stamps may be obtained from the book *Your Book of Stamps*, by James Watson (Faber and Faber).

Objects, other than stamps, which are collected by enthusiasts include matchboxes, cheese labels, wine bottle labels, printers' ephemera (anything printed, from bus tickets to commemorative programmes, medicine labels to bookplates). In fact, there are no limits to what may form an interesting collection without great expense.

## ROTARY CLUBS

The Rotary movement, started in Chicago in 1905, has for its objects the encouragement of a high ethical standard in business transactions, and the promotion of social intercourse. Only one representative of any trade or profession is admitted to full membership of a particular club, thus ensuring variety of interest and experience, and avoiding the possibility of the domination of any one interest. These clubs are now established in all the principal cities and towns, and there is a British Association of Rotary Clubs.

## SEVEN WONDERS OF THE ANCIENT WORLD

A Greek poet, Antipater of Sidon, chose seven wonders of the world sometime during the 100s B.C. These wonders have fascinated men ever since. The wonders which Antipater chose were:

1. The pyramids of Egypt.
2. The hanging gardens of Babylon, built by Nebuchadnezzar for his wife. She was a princess from the mountains and he devised for her great terraces of flowers and shrubs to create an illusion of mountain sides.
3. The statue of Zeus at Olympia which was carved by the Greek sculptor Pheidias about 450 B.C. It stood about

40 feet high and was inlaid with ivory, gold and precious stones.

4. The temple of Diana at Ephesus which was of great beauty and measured 400 feet in length.
5. The mausoleum at Halicarnassus, built at the command of Queen Artemisia as a monument to her husband, King Mausolus of Caria, about 353 B.C.
6. The Colossus of Rhodes, an enormous statue which is said to have straddled the harbour at Rhodes. It was probably built by Chares of Lindus and was destroyed by an earthquake in 224 B.C.
7. The pharos at Alexandria, a lighthouse which was said to be about 400 feet high. It was built on the orders of Ptolemy Philadelphus who commanded that a beacon be kept burning on the summit as a guide to sailors.

## PALMISTRY

Palmistry or cheiromancy is the art of delineating the character and destiny of an individual from the lines and markings of the palm of the hand.

Cheirogonomy, a branch of palmistry, deals with the shapes of the hands and fingers.

The following are the principal lines of the palm:

1. The line of head, or the indications of mentality.
2. The line of life.
3. The line of Mars, or inner life line.
4. The line of destiny or fate.
5. The line of the sun or success.
6. The line of heart, indicating the affections and emotions.
7. The line of marriage.
8. The line of health.
9. The Girdle of Venus.
10. The line of intuition.

1. The line of head is the most important line on the hand. The two hands should be carefully compared – the left showing the inherited tendencies, the right the developed or cultivated qualities. A poor or non-developed line of head in the right hand indicates lack of purpose or ambition. A clean-cut deep line of head indicates strong mentality.

2. The line of life is that line which

runs round the base of the thumb. The broad life line seems to belong to people who have more robust animal strength, whereas the finer and deeper line relates to people who have more nerve or will-force.

3. The line of Mars is found only on some hands encircling the Mount of Venus (the ball of the thumb) inside the line of life.

4. The line of destiny, or fate, is another important line. It indicates the main events of one's career. It runs straight up the centre of the palm from the wrist towards the fingers.

5. The line of the sun, the line of success or brilliancy. A good line of the sun denotes good luck and a bright and happy disposition. It runs up the palm to the base of the third finger.

6. The line of heart runs across the hand under the fingers, and generally rises under the base of the first, and runs off the side of the hand under the base of the little finger.

7. The line of marriage is a short line between the base of the little finger and the heart line.

8. The line of health rises at the base of the little finger and crosses the hand in a diagonal direction.

9. The girdle of Venus is a broken or sometimes unbroken semi-circular line from the base of the first finger to the base of the fourth finger.

10. The line of intuition is a semi-circular line from the base of the fourth finger to the base of the hand, and indicates a highly-strung temperament.

**Cheirognomy.** – There are seven types or shapes of hands:

1. The elementary, or lowest type.
2. The square, or useful hand.
3. The spatulate, or nervous, active type.
4. The philosophic, or jointed hand.
5. The conic, or artistic type.
6. The psychic, or idealistic hand.
7. The mixed hand.

For fuller details consult *The Language of the Hand*, and other works on the subject, by Cheiro (Herbert Jenkins).

**NATIONAL MARRIAGE GUIDANCE COUNCIL.** This council helps people to overcome problems in marriage and offers information which is useful both before and during marriage. The council publishes leaflets and booklets of information and the counsellors are always ready to discuss and help with individual difficulties. They also send Education Counsellors to schools to lead Group Discussions on personal relationships in general.

The council may be contacted through their headquarters at 58 Queen Anne Street, London W1, or through any of their 116 branches whose addresses may be found in local telephone directories under Marriage Guidance.

**CITIZENS ADVICE BUREAUX.** National Headquarters: 26 Bedford Square, London WC1.

The Citizens Advice Bureau is a centre for providing information on any subject. For example, they will answer questions on house purchase and rents, legal aid, consumer problems, personal and matrimonial problems, orders for eviction, financial problems and appeals against the decisions of statutory departments. The staff have the resources of their national headquarters, the advice of the Law Society and of social and voluntary organizations to guide them in their answers.

There are more than 450 bureaux in Britain and the address of your local bureau may be found in the telephone directory.

**VOLUNTARY ORGANIZATIONS**
There are many voluntary organizations in Britain. They offer advice and help to people who ask for it and welcome offers of assistance from the public. The London headquarters addresses of a few organizations follow. A fuller list may be found in the booklet *A Guide to Voluntary Service*, by David Hobman (HMSO).

British Diabetic Association, 152 Harley Street, W1. WELbeck 6001.

British Epilepsy Association, 27 Nassau Street, W1. LANgham 2704.

British Polio Fellowship, Clifton House, Euston Road, NW1. EUSton 5851.

British Red Cross Society (Headquarters), 14 Grosvenor Crescent, SW1. BELgravia 5454.

Central Council for the Disabled, 34 Eccleston Square, SW1. VICtoria 0747.

Family Planning Association, 231 Tottenham Court Road, W1. MUSeum 9135.

Family Welfare Association (Central Office), 296 Vauxhall Bridge Road, SW1. VICtoria 7334.

Invalid Children's Aid Association (Central Office), 4 Palace Gate, W8. KNIghtsbridge 8222.

Muscular Distrophy Association, 26 Borough High Street, SE1. HOP 5116.

National Association for Maternal and Child Welfare, B.M.A. House, Tavistock Square, WC1. EUSton 1874.

National Association for Mental Health, 39 Queen Anne Street, W1. WELbeck 1272.

National Children's Home, 85 Highbury Park, N5. CANonbury 2033.

National Council for the Unmarried Mother and Her Child, 255 Kentish Town Road, NW5. GULliver 8383.

National Deaf Children's Society, 31 Gloucester Place, W1. HUNter 3251.

OXFAM, 12 Crane Street, EC4. FLEet Street 5701.

Royal National Institute for the Blind, 224 Great Portland Street, W1. EUSton 5251.

Royal Society for the Prevention of Cruelty to Animals, 105 Jermyn Street, SW1. WHItehall 7177.

Save the Children Fund, 29 Queen Anne's Gate, SW1. WHItehall 2461.

Spastics Society (Head Office), 12 Park Crescent, W1. MUSeum 5020.

## CONSUMER SAFEGUARDS

The Consumer Council, set up in 1963, provides customers with advice and guidance which may be obtained through the Citizen's Advice Bureaux (see page 398).

Although the Council cannot take up complaints on behalf of individuals and cannot enforce the standards which it considers desirable, it does advise manufacturers and suppliers and promotes action to achieve those standards.

Customers with individual complaints should consult their solicitor or the Consumer's Association. The Association is an independent non-profit-making company with about 500,000 members. It publishes, in its monthly magazine *Which*, a report on comparative tests made on various goods. The Association also publishes other reports of a specialized nature, such as their bulletin on drugs, their guide to good food, etc.

## TELEVISION

The inventor, John Logie Baird, first showed television to the public in 1925. Eleven years later, in 1936, the first regular television service in the world was begun by the BBC. During World War II, the service was discontinued, but it began again in 1946. In 1954, an Act of Parliament established the Independent Television Authority (ITA) which controls the commercial TV Companies.

The first live pictures from Russia were shown, by way of the Eurovision link, in 1961. And, in 1962, the BBC further increased its range when they showed pictures from the USA by using the space satellite, Telstar.

The BBC and ITV transmit 405-line pictures, but the BBC added another channel in 1964 which transmits 625-line pictures. The United Kingdom is served by the BBC, by the companies controlled by the ITA and, in the Republic of Ireland, by Telefis Eireann.

The BBC's broadcasting time of more than 3,000 hours every year may be divided into the following categories: 2% music; 2% sports; 4% special presentations; 4% religion; 6% news; 8% schools broadcasts; 8% light entertainment; 9% children's broadcasts; 11% drama; 13% films and features; 15% outside broadcasts; 18% documentaries.

The ITA arranges transmission of more than 3,300 hours of broadcasting every year to its various regions. Their programmes may be divided as follows: 1% music; 2% panel games and quizzes; 3% schools programmes; 4% Welsh language programmes; 5% children's broadcasts; 8% religion; 9% drama; 11% news; 12% sports; 15% light entertainment; 30% documentaries.

## POSTAL INFORMATION

**Letters.** – The Post Office offers two levels of service for all letters, irrespective of content:
1st Class letters and packets (costing 5d. for the first 4 ozs.) are normally delivered the day after posting. 2nd Class letters and packets (costing 4d. for the first 4 ozs.) usually follow up to 24 hours later. Since the Post Office no longer lays down conditions for the contents of any class of letter mail (such as "Printed Paper" etc.) all letters may be sealed in both services but they can be sent unsealed if preferred.
**Postcards** may be sent by either service at the appropriate letter rate.
**Packets** weighing more than 1 lb. 8 ozs. cannot be sent by the second class letter service.
(For further information see Post Office Leaflet PL 274 5/68.)

**Post Office Preferred (POP) sizes**
Under this Post Office regulation, envelopes of a size above a maximum of $4\frac{3}{4}$ ins $\times$ $9\frac{1}{4}$ ins, and envelopes below a minimum of $3\frac{1}{2}$ ins $\times$ $5\frac{1}{2}$ ins will be liable to an additional charge.
Envelopes outside the POP range may still be used, and mail weighing more than 4 oz. will be unaffected by the choice of envelope. But mail weighing up to 4 oz., posted in envelopes outside the POP range, will be liable to an additional charge. (See *Post Office Guide* for full details.)
If a letter contains something valuable, it may be registered so that, in case of loss, the sender may claim compensation from the Post Office, but in the case of a registered letter sent overseas the maximum compensation payable is £2 18s. 0d. If a sender wants a record of delivery of a letter sent in the internal service of this country, he can send it by recorded delivery. In this case, the recipient will be asked to sign a receipt when the postman delivers the letter. In the registration and recorded delivery services, for a small additional fee, the sender can obtain confirmation that the letter has been delivered. The PO arranges for urgent letters to be specially delivered, after their arrival at delivery offices, whenever this ensures earlier

delivery. An extra fee is charged for this.
**Airmail.**–Air letters, either the stamped Air Letter forms or ordinary airmail letters (at varying postage rates) can be sent to all countries outside Europe. There are special rates and conditions for airmail to members of Her Majesty's forces.

**Parcel Post.** – Bear in mind that the Post Office will not accept parcels which exceed certain dimensions and weight. These can be ascertained at the nearest office or from the *Post Office Guide*. It is desirable that parcels should be securely done up, as they cannot be handled with much delicacy and care; it would be quite unreasonable to expect it. Registered parcels must be fastened with wax, gum or other adhesive substance, string alone is not sufficient; for such parcels you should take care to obtain a receipt. When sending articles that might be damaged, be sure to pack them in a box or other receptacle, using at least two inches of soft material to absorb knocks and shock. The words FRAGILE WITH CARE should be written clearly by the address.
Parcels for HM forces abroad have special rates. Parcels sent to countries overseas are subject to restrictions and to possible customs charges. They cannot be registered, but may be insured on payment of a small fee.

**Cash on Delivery.** – The sender can specify the amount of money to be collected from the recipient on delivery of a parcel, or a registered letter. The Post Office returns this amount to the sender.

**Telegrams.** – Write out the whole telegram on the form provided by the Post Office. The address should be sufficient to enable the telegram to be delivered without reference to directories or other sources of information. The name and address of the sender must be filled in. One may use a telephone to dictate messages to the Post Office for onward transmission as telegrams at any time. Radio-telegrams can be sent to and from most British and foreign ships. Specially designed telegrams are available for 21st Birthday, Wedding, Baby and all purpose greetings. The charge per word for all types of telegrams and the scope of the services available can be ascertained at the Post Office.

**Telephone.** – The Post Office controls the telephone system of the whole of Great Britain (except in the City of Hull), Northern Ireland and the Isle of Man. Enquiries concerning the service should be addressed to the Telephone Manager, whose address is given in the preface of the local telephone directory.

In the directory preface, the section entitled "How to Make a Call" indicates briefly the manner in which the telephone should be used. The directory preface also gives details of call charges, special call facilities and the recorded information services available; the latter include the Speaking Clock, Weather, Road Weather, Recipe, Test Match Information and Teletourist. The rentals for various classes of service and types of equipment can be obtained from the local Telephone Manager. In those areas where Subscriber Trunk Dialling (STD) is available, a list of dialling codes and charges are provided and replacements or further copies may be obtained from the Telephone Manager.

Details of inland and international telephone services, and ships and air-craft radio-telephone services may be found in the *Post Office Guide*.

**Money Orders.** – Inland Money Orders are issued by, and are payable at, all money order offices in the United Kingdom and are also payable in the Irish Republic. Orders issued in the Irish Republic are payable in the United Kingdom. The amount of a money order may not exceed a prescribed sum which may be ascertained at the Post Office, where the requisite form is obtainable. The full name of the payee and of the remitter should be entered on the form. The remitter may state on the form if the order is to be paid only through a bank. Before an order can be paid at a Post Office, it must be signed by the payee who must give the remitter's name correctly. The rates and conditions for overseas money orders are given in the *Post Office Guide* which also gives the terms and scope of telegraphed money orders.

**Postal Orders.** – These may be purchased at, and are payable at, most post offices throughout Great Britain, Northern Ireland, the Channel Islands and the Isle of Man. They are also paid in the Irish Republic. Postal orders are issued from 1s. 0d. up to 5s. in sixpenny steps, by one shilling steps to 21s., and by one pound steps to £5. A commission, called *poundage*, is charged according to value. Postal orders may be crossed for payment through a bank and must bear the name of the payee. The counterfoil should be retained by the sender and not forwarded with the order.

**Post Office Savings Bank.** – See section on *Money, Investment and Pensions*, page 185.

**Post Office Guide** – is available at post offices for reference by the public. It gives information about post office services, how they can be used, their cost, scope, limitations (*e.g.*, as to size or weight of postal packets), etc. This book is on sale at post offices, Government bookshops or through any book-seller, and a Free Supplement Service is available to anyone who fills in the Supplement Order card contained in the Guide and sends it to his local Head or District Postmaster.

## SOME IMPORTANT MUSEUMS AND ART GALLERIES

Most cities and large towns in the United Kingdom have a museum and art gallery. Most of the smaller museums show collections which are mainly of local interest; these can be absorbing to the enquiring visitor. Larger museums have, in many instances, collections of broader interest and importance. Some museums have specialized collections, such as the Maidstone Museum of Carriages, others are more general in their policy, collecting a great variety of objects, such as those seen in the Sheffield City Museum.

The following is a list of nationally known museums. The times of opening and closing vary, in many cases, from season to season and it is wise to telephone before your visit to make sure that the museum will be open.

**Aberdeen Art Gallery & Industrial Museum**, School Hill (tel. 23456 ext. 57). Regional museum of North-East Scotland.

**Museum of Welsh Antiquities**, College Road, Bangor (2501). History of North Wales, its prehistory and culture.

**Museum of Costume**, Assembly Rooms, Bath. Every kind of costume since the 1600s.

**Montague Motor Museum**, Palace House Beaulieu (374). Veteran and vintage motor cars and motor cycles.

**Ulster Museum**, Stranmillis (668259). Antiquities, history and culture of the Ulster area.

**Birmingham City Museum & Art Gallery**, Congrave Street, Birmingham 3 (CENtral 7000). Large collection of art, antiquities and natural history specimens from all parts of the world.

**Fitzwilliam Museum**, Trumpington Street, Cambridge (50023). Old and modern paintings, antiquities, collections of music and medieval manuscripts.

**National Museum of Wales**, Cathys Park, Cardiff (26241). Art, industrial and general collections.

**The Manx Museum**, Windsor Road, Douglas, Isle of Man (522). Folklore, archeology and natural history collections.

**National Museum of Ireland**, Kildare Street, Dublin, Republic of Ireland (65521). National collection of antiquities, folklore, botany, zoology and fine arts.

**Gulbenkian Museum of Oriental Art and Archeology**, Elevet Hill, Durham (2872). Oriental fine arts collection.

**Royal Scottish Museum**, Chambers Street, Edinburgh (Caledonian 7534). Collections of art, archeology, natural history, children's gallery, geology, technology.

**Abbey House Museum**, Kinkstall, Leeds (55821). Folk museum of Yorkshire with full-sized houses, work places and streets.

**Walker Art Gallery**, William Brown Street, Liverpool (NORth 1371). European paintings.

**British Museum**, Great Russell Street, London WC1 (MUSeum 1555). National museum of antiquities, art, archeology, prints, drawings, books.

**British Museum of Natural History**, Cromwell Road, South Kensington, London SW7 (KENsington 6323). National collection of plants, animals, rocks and minerals.

**The Museum of British Transport**, Triangle Place, Clapham, London SW4 (MACauley 3241). Collection of historical vehicles of all kinds.

**National Gallery**, Trafalgar Square, London WC2 (WHItehall 7618). National collection of European paintings.

**National Portrait Gallery**, St. Martins Place, Trafalgar Square, London WC2 (WHItehall 6511). Portraits of British men and women.

**Royal Academy of Art**, Burlington House, Piccadilly, London W1 (REGent 7981). Exhibitions of contemporary and old masters.

**Science Museum**, Exhibition Road, South Kensington, London SW7 (KENsington 6371). Collection of scientific instruments, machines, and other scientific materials.

**Tate Gallery**, Millbank, London SW1 (TATe Gallery 4444). National collection of British painting, modern French painting and modern sculpture.

**Tower of London**, Tower Hill, London EC3 (ROYal 2195). Crown jewels, collection of armour and weapons.

**Victoria and Albert Museum**, Cromwell Road, South Kensington, London SW7 (KENsington 6371). Arts of all kinds.

**Wallace Collection**, Manchester Square, London W1 (WELbeck 0687). European painting, sculpture, furniture, European and oriental armour, weapons and ceramics.

**City Art Gallery**, Moseley Street, Manchester (Central 2391). Pictures, miniatures, sculpture.

**Ashmolean Museum of Art and Archeology**, Beaumont Street, Oxford (57522). Archeology, European painting, coins, English silver.

**English Rural Life Museum**, Whiteknights Park, Reading (82088). History of the English countryside and domestic life.

**York Castle Museum**, Tower Street, York (53611). Collection of domestic and agricultural equipment, toys and costumes.

For information on most collections in Britain see *Museums and Galleries in Great Britain and Ireland* (Index Publishers Ltd.).

## SUMMER TIME

For a number of years prior to 1914 the late William Willett urged the adoption of the principle of saving daylight in the summer months by advancing all time-keepers throughout the United Kingdom.

The imperative need for increased production as well as the desirability of more extended hours of daylight for the recreation of workers during the war, led to the passing of the first Summer Time Act in 1916. On May 21st in that year the clocks were advanced one hour, and Greenwich time was restored on September 30th.

From 1917 to 1924 the change to and from summer time took place at varying dates. By the Summer Time Act, 1925, the duration of summer time was made permanent, beginning at 2 o'clock Greenwich mean time in the morning of the next day to follow the third Saturday in April, or, if that day be Easter Day, the next day to follow the second Saturday in April, and ending at 2 a.m. on the next day to follow the first Saturday in October.

As from February 18th, 1968, Summer Time was fixed at one hour ahead of Greenwich Mean Time. It is intended there is to be no reversion to G.M.T. towards the end of each year thereafter, as had normally obtained prior to that date. Under this arrangement the standard time of Great Britain conforms to Central European Time.

## GREENWICH TIME

Greenwich time is now used throughout the British Islands, Algeria, Belgium, France, Gibraltar, Spain, Portugal and the Faroe Islands. Austria, Denmark, Germany, Italy, Malta, Nigeria, Norway, Sweden, Switzerland and the Western Balkan peninsula use Mid-European time, namely, 1 hour fast of Greenwich time. Eastern-European time (2 hours fast of Greenwich) is used in the Eastern Balkan peninsula, including Greece. Russia keeps 2 hours 1 minute fast of Greenwich. Holland keeps Amsterdam time, 19 minutes 40 seconds slow of Greenwich.

It should be noted that in the list of towns that follows later the times given fast or slow of Greenwich are the local times calculated according to the difference in longitude between Greenwich and the places mentioned. The legal times (i.e. the times shown on the clocks at these places) are not those given.

### TOWNS EAST OF GREENWICH.

| Town | Greenwich Noon is Here |
|------|------------------------|
| Adelaide | 9.16 p.m. |
| Alexandria | 2.00 ,, |
| Algiers | 12.12 ,, |
| Amsterdam | 12.20 ,, |
| Athens | 1.35 ,, |
| Bangkok | 6.40 ,, |
| Belgrade | 1.22 ,, |
| Berlin | 12.54 ,, |
| Berne | 12.30 ,, |
| Bombay | 4.50 ,, |
| Brisbane | 10.08 ,, |
| Brussels | 12.17 ,, |
| Budapest | 1.16 ,, |
| Cabul | 4.35 ,, |
| Calais | 12.07 ,, |
| Calcutta | 5.54 ,, |
| Cape Town | 1.14 ,, |
| Christiania | 12.43 ,, |
| Copenhagen | 12.50 ,, |
| Dover | 12.05 ,, |
| Durban | 2.04 ,, |
| Hamburg | 12.40 ,, |
| Hobart | 9.50 ,, |
| Hong-Kong | 7.37 ,, |
| Istanbul | 1.55 ,, |
| Jerusalem | 2.21 ,, |
| Khartoum | 1.32 ,, |
| Leningrad | 2.03 ,, |
| Madras | 5.21 ,, |
| Malta | 12.58 ,, |
| Marseilles | 12.21 ,, |
| Melbourne | 9.40 ,, |
| Milan | 12.36 ,, |
| Moscow | 2.30 ,, |
| Naples | 12.56 ,, |
| Odessa | 2.03 ,, |
| Paris | 12.09 ,, |
| Peking | 7.45 ,, |
| Port Elizabeth | 1.42 ,, |
| Rome | 12.50 ,, |
| Shanghai | 8.06 ,, |
| Stockholm | 1.12 ,, |
| Suez | 2.10 ,, |
| Sydney | 10.05 ,, |
| Tokio | 9.19 ,, |
| Venice | 12.50 ,, |
| Vienna | 1.06 ,, |
| Warsaw | 1.22 ,, |
| Wellington, N.Z. | 11.39 ,, |

## Towns Slow of Greenwich.

| Town | Greenwich Noon is Here |
|------|------------------------|
| Aberdeen .. .. .. | 11.52 a.m. |
| Baltimore .. .. .. | 6.55 ,, |
| Belfast .. .. .. | 11.35 ,, |
| Bermuda .. .. .. | 7.40 ,, |
| Birmingham .. .. | 11.53 ,, |
| Bordeaux .. .. | 11.58 ,, |
| Boston, U.S. .. .. | 7.15 ,, |
| Brighton .. .. .. | 11.59 ,, |
| Bristol .. .. .. | 11.50 ,, |
| Buenos Aires .. .. | 8.07 ,, |
| Cadiz .. .. .. | 11.35 ,, |
| Cardiff .. .. .. | 11.47 ,, |
| Chicago .. .. .. | 6.10 ,, |
| Dublin .. .. .. | 11.35 ,, |
| Edinburgh .. .. | 11.47 ,, |
| Gibraltar .. .. | 11.40 ,, |
| Glasgow .. .. | 11.43 ,, |
| Havana .. .. | 6.30 ,, |
| Holyhead .. .. | 11.41 ,, |
| Kingston, Jamaica | 6.53 ,, |
| Leeds .. .. .. | 11.54 ,, |
| Lisbon .. .. .. | 11.25 ,, |
| Liverpool .. .. | 11.48 ,, |
| Madrid .. .. .. | 11.45 ,, |
| Manchester .. .. | 11.51 ,, |
| Monte Video .. .. | 8.12 ,, |
| Montreal .. .. | 7.06 ,, |
| Newcastle .. .. | 11.54 ,, |
| New Orleans .. .. | 5.58 ,, |
| New York .. .. | 7.04 ,, |
| Ottawa .. .. | 6.57 ,, |
| Philadelphia .. .. | 7.00 ,, |
| Plymouth .. .. | 11.43 ,, |
| Portsmouth .. .. | 11.56 ,, |
| Quebec .. .. | 7.15 ,, |
| Rio de Janeiro .. | 9.07 ,, |
| San Francisco .. .. | 3.50 ,, |
| Southampton .. .. | 11.53 ,, |
| Toronto .. .. | 6.42 ,, |
| Victoria, B.C. .. .. | 3.45 ,, |
| Washington, D.C. .. | 6.50 ,, |

## THE INTERNATIONAL DATE LINE

Astronomers have calculated that the sun *appears* to move over the surface of Earth at 15° per hour. At 180° longitude west (half-way round the world from Greenwich, which is 0° longitude), time is twelve hours in advance of Greenwich. In other words, at midday in Greenwich the day is just ending at 180° longitude west and just beginning at 180° longitude east.

The international date line (IDL) itself is an imaginary line, arranged by international agreement, marking on the map the place where a new calendar day commences. The IDL follows the 180th meridian most of the way round the world and it runs, for a large part of this distance through the Pacific Ocean. However, the line has several kinks

in it in order to avoid land; it would obviously be inconvenient to have two calendar dates in operation in one country. If a man sails across the line from east to west, he loses a day; from west to east, he gains a day.

## TIME MEASURE

| | |
|---|---|
| 60 seconds .................. | = 1 minute. |
| 60 minutes .................. | = 1 hour. |
| 24 hours .................... | = 1 day. |
| 7 days ...................... | = 1 week. |
| 4 weeks (28 days)............ | = 1 month (lunar). |
| 28, 30, or 31 days ........... | = 1 month (calendar). |
| 13 lunar months ............ | = 1 year (solar). |
| 12 calendar months .......... | = 1 year. |
| 52 weeks .................... | = 1 year. |
| 354 days .................... | = 1 year (lunar). |
| 365 days .................... | = 1 year (solar). |
| 366 days .................... | = 1 leap year |
| 100 years................... | = 1 century. |
| 1,000 years ................. | = 1 millenium |

Thirty days hath September,
April, June and November.
All the rest have thirty-one,
Excepting February alone.
Which hath but twenty-eight days clear,
And twenty-nine in each leap year.

## THE SEASONS

| | | | | |
|---|---|---|---|---|
| Spring commences | .. | .. | March 21st. |
| Summer ,, | .. | .. | June 22nd. |
| Autumn ,, | .. | .. | Sept. 24th. |
| Winter ,, | .. | .. | Dec. 22nd. |

## QUARTERLY TERMS

### ENGLAND

| | | | | |
|---|---|---|---|---|
| Lady Day | .. | .. | .. | .. March 25th. |
| Midsummer | .. | .. | .. | June 24th. |
| Michaelmas | .. | .. | .. | Sept. 29th. |
| Christmas | .. | .. | .. | Dec. 25th. |

### SCOTLAND

| | | | | |
|---|---|---|---|---|
| Candlemas | .. | .. | .. | Feb. 2nd. |
| Whit-Sunday | .. | .. | .. | May 15th. |
| Lammas | .. | .. | .. | Aug. 1st. |
| Martinmas | .. | .. | .. | Nov. 11th. |

The removal terms in Scotland are 28th May and 28th November, or the following day if these fall on a Sunday.

## BANK HOLIDAYS

### ENGLAND AND IRELAND
Good Friday.
Easter Monday.
Spring Holiday.
Summer Holiday.
Christmas Day.
Boxing Day.
St. Partick's Day (Ireland).
Orangeman's Day (N. Ireland).

### SCOTLAND
New Year's Day
Good Friday.
First Monday in May.
First Monday in August.
Christmas Day.

Stock Exchange Extra Holidays,
January 1st, May 1st, August 1st.

## THE PULSE AT DIFFERENT AGES

| Age. | Beats per minute |
|---|---|
| Newly born | 130 to 140 |
| 1st Year | 115 to 130 |
| 2nd ,, | 100 to 115 |
| 3rd ,, | 95 to 105 |
| 7 to 14 | 80 to 90 |
| 14 to 21 | 75 to 85 |
| 21 to 60 | 70 to 75 |
| Over 60 | 75 to 85 |

## DISTANCES OF SUN, MOON AND PLANETS FROM EARTH

| | |
|---|---|
| Sun | 92,957,000 miles |
| Moon | 238,000 ,, |
| Mercury | 92,957,000 ,, |
| Venus | 92,957,000 ,, |
| Mars | 141,640,000 ,, |
| Jupiter | 483,640,000 ,, |
| Saturn | 886,700,000 ,, |
| Uranus | 1,783,100,000 ,, |
| Neptune | 2,793,100,000 ,, |
| Pluto | 3,673,500,000 ,, |

## TABLE OF THE NUMBER OF DAYS, FROM ANY DAY OF ONE MONTH TO THE SAME DAY OF ANY OTHER MONTH

| From | Jan. | Feb. | Mar. | Apr. | May | June | July | Aug. | Sept. | Oct. | Nov. | Dec. |
|---|---|---|---|---|---|---|---|---|---|---|---|---|
| To January | 365 | 334 | 306 | 275 | 245 | 214 | 184 | 153 | 122 | 92 | 61 | 31 |
| February | 31 | 365 | 337 | 306 | 276 | 245 | 215 | 184 | 153 | 123 | 92 | 62 |
| March | 59 | 28 | 365 | 334 | 304 | 273 | 243 | 212 | 181 | 151 | 120 | 90 |
| April | 90 | 59 | 31 | 365 | 335 | 304 | 274 | 243 | 212 | 182 | 151 | 121 |
| May | 120 | 89 | 61 | 30 | 365 | 334 | 304 | 273 | 242 | 212 | 181 | 151 |
| June | 151 | 120 | 92 | 61 | 31 | 365 | 335 | 304 | 273 | 243 | 212 | 182 |
| July | 181 | 150 | 122 | 91 | 61 | 30 | 365 | 334 | 303 | 273 | 242 | 212 |
| August | 212 | 181 | 153 | 122 | 92 | 61 | 31 | 365 | 334 | 304 | 273 | 243 |
| September | 243 | 212 | 184 | 153 | 123 | 92 | 62 | 31 | 365 | 335 | 304 | 274 |
| October | 273 | 242 | 214 | 183 | 153 | 122 | 92 | 61 | 30 | 365 | 334 | 304 |
| November | 304 | 273 | 244 | 214 | 184 | 153 | 123 | 92 | 61 | 31 | 365 | 335 |
| December | 334 | 303 | 275 | 244 | 214 | 183 | 153 | 122 | 91 | 61 | 30 | 365 |

### USE OF THE ABOVE TABLE.

What is the number of days from 10th of October to 10th July?
Look in the upper line for October, let your eye descend down that column till you come opposite to July and you will find 273 days, the exact number of days required.
Again, what is the number of days from 16th February to 14th August?

| | |
|---|---|
| Under February, and opposite to August, is | 181 days. |
| From which subtract the difference between 14 and 16 | 2 days. |
| The exact number of days required is | 179 days. |

N.B.—In Leap Year, if the last day of February comes between, add one day for the day over to the number in the Table.

## SIGNS OF THE ZODIAC

The Zodiac is a belt of the heavens confined to about 8° on each side of the Ecliptic in which revolves the sun and principal planets. The Zodiac is divided into twelve parts, known by their signs:—

Spring—
   *Aries*, the Ram ♈
   *Taurus*, the Bull ♉
   *Gemini*, the Twins ♊

Summer—
   *Cancer*, the Crab ♋
   *Leo*, the Lion ♌
   *Virgo*, the Virgin ♍

Autumn—
   *Libra*, the Balance ♎
   *Scorpio*, the Scorpion ♏
   *Sagittarius*, the Archer ♐

Winter—
   *Capricornus*, the Sea Goat ♑
   *Acquarius*, the Water Bearer ♒
   *Pisces*, the Fishes ♓

## SIGNS OF THE WEATHER

**i. Dew.**—If the dew lies plentifully on the grass after a fair day, it is a sign of another fair day. If not, and there is no wind, rain must follow. A red evening portends fine weather; but if the redness spreads too far upwards from the horizon in the evening, and especially in the morning, it foretells wind or rain, or both.

**ii. Colour of Sky.**—When the sky, in rainy weather, is tinged with sea green, the rain will increase; if with deep blue, it will be showery.

**iii. Clouds.**—If you wish to know what sort of weather you may expect, go out and choose the smallest cloud you can see. Watch it, and if it grows smaller and finally disappears, you may be pretty sure of fine weather; or the opposite, if the cloud grows larger. The reason is that when the air is becoming charged with electricity each cloud attracts smaller ones, until it passes off in rain; but if rain is diffusing itself, a large cloud breaks up and dissolves. Before heavy rain, the clouds grow bigger, and increase very fast, especially before thunder. When the clouds are formed like fleeces, but dense in the middle and bright towards the edges, with the sky bright, they are signs of a frost, with hail, snow or rain. If clouds form high in the air, in thin white trains like locks of wool, they portend wind, and probably rain. When a general cloudiness covers the sky, and small black fragments of clouds fly underneath, they are a sure sign of rain, and probably will be lasting. Two currents of clouds always portend rain and, in summer, thunder.

**iv. Heavenly bodies.**—A haziness in the air, which dims the sun's light, and makes the orb appear whitish or ill-defined—or at night, if the moon and stars grow dim, and a ring encircles the moon, rain will follow. If the sun's rays appear like Moses' horns—if white at setting or shorn of his rays, or if it goes down into a bank of clouds in the horizon, bad weather is to be expected. If the moon looks pale and dim, we expect rain; if red, wind; if it is her natural colour, with a clear sky, fair weather. If the moon is rainy throughout, it will clear at the change, and, perhaps, the rain return a few days after. If fair throughout, and wet at the change, the fair weather will probably return on the fourth or fifth day.

## WEATHER SAYINGS AND QUOTATIONS

Full moon brings fair weather, pale moon doth rain.

Morning sun never lasts a day.

If the sun goes pale to bed,
'Twill rain tomorrow, it is said.

If wind follows sun's course, expect fair weather.

When the wind's in the west, the weather's at the best.

Red sky in the morning
Is a shepherd's warning:
Red sky at night
Is a shepherd's delight.

A summerish January;
A winterish spring

February fill dyke
Be it black or be it white;
But if it be white,
It's the better to like.

April showers being forth May flowers.

April blows his horn (thunders),
When it's good both for hay and corn.

Dry May and dripping June.

If the first of July, it be rainy weather,
'Twill rain more or less for four weeks together

If the twenty-fourth of August be fair,
Then hope for a good Autumn that year.

There is really no such thing as bad weather, only different kinds of good weather.—Lord Aveberry.

'Tis the hard grey weather
Breeds hard English men.—
                                    Charles Kingsley.

'Tis very warm weather when one's in bed.—Jonathan Swift.

## THE BEAUFORT SCALE

Wind force is expressed by means of the *Beaufort Scale*, a numerical scale devised by Admiral Sir Francis Beaufort in 1808, which has been revised from time to time. This scale is used for logging the wind force in a ship's deck log, for ship's weather reports to shore meteorological authorities and in weather broadcasts.

The wind speed corresponding to any Beaufort number according to the table given below is the wind speed at 33 feet above the surface in an open situation.

| Beaufort Number, International | Speed of wind in Nautical Miles Per Hour | Beaufort Description of Wind, International |
|---|---|---|
| 0 | less than 1 | Calm. |
| 1 | 1–3 | Light air. |
| 2 | 4–6 | Light breeze. |
| 3 | 7–10 | Gentle breeze. |
| 4 | 11–16 | Moderate breeze |
| 5 | 17–21 | Fresh breeze. |
| 6 | 22–27 | Strong breeze. |
| 7 | 28–33 | Strong wind. |
| 8 | 34–40 | Fresh gale. |
| 9 | 41–47 | Strong gale. |
| 10 | 48–55 | Whole gale. |
| 11 | 56–65 | Storm. |
| 12 | above 65 | Hurricane. |

## NAUTICAL MEASURE

| | |
|---|---|
| 6 feet | = 1 fathom. |
| 120 fathoms | = 1 cable's length. |
| 2,027·3 yards | = 1 knot (nautical mile) |
| 3 knots | = 1 league (nautical). |
| 60 knots | = 1 degree. |
| 69·121 statute miles | |
| 360 degrees | = the earth's circumference. |

## MONARCHS OF ENGLAND

| House of Normandy. | | | | | Reign |
|---|---|---|---|---|---|
| William I | .. | .. | .. | .. | .. 1066–1087 |
| William II | .. | .. | .. | .. | .. 1087–1100 |
| Henry I | .. | .. | .. | .. | .. 1100–1135 |
| Stephen | .. | .. | .. | .. | .. 1135–1154 |

| House of Plantagenet. | | | | | |
|---|---|---|---|---|---|
| Henry II | .. | .. | .. | .. | .. 1154–1189 |
| Richard I | .. | .. | .. | .. | .. 1189–1199 |
| John | .. | .. | .. | .. | .. 1199–1216 |
| Henry III | .. | .. | .. | .. | .. 1216–1272 |
| Edward I | .. | .. | .. | .. | .. 1272–1307 |
| Edward II | .. | .. | .. | .. | .. 1307–1327 |
| Edward III | .. | .. | .. | .. | .. 1327–1377 |
| Richard II | .. | .. | .. | .. | .. 1377–1399 (Deposed) |

| House of Lancaster. | | | | | |
|---|---|---|---|---|---|
| Henry IV | .. | .. | .. | .. | .. 1399–1413 |
| Henry V | .. | .. | .. | .. | .. 1413–1422 |
| Henry VI | .. | .. | .. | .. | .. 1422–1461 (Deposed |

| House of York. | | | | | |
|---|---|---|---|---|---|
| Edward IV | .. | .. | .. | .. | .. 1461–1483 |
| Edward V | .. | .. | .. | .. | .. 1483–1483 |
| Richard III | .. | .. | .. | .. | .. 1483–1485 |

| House of Tudor. | | | | | |
|---|---|---|---|---|---|
| Henry VII | .. | .. | .. | .. | .. 1485–1509 |
| Henry VIII | .. | .. | .. | .. | .. 1509–1547 |
| Edward VI | .. | .. | .. | .. | .. 1547–1553 |
| Mary I | .. | .. | .. | .. | .. 1553–1558 |
| Elizabeth I | .. | .. | .. | .. | .. 1558–1603 |

| House of Stuart. | | | | | |
|---|---|---|---|---|---|
| James I | .. | .. | .. | .. | .. 1603–1526 |
| Charles I | .. | .. | .. | .. | .. 1625–1649 (Beheaded) |
| (Commonwealth) | .. | .. | .. | .. 1649–1660 |
| Charles II | .. | .. | .. | .. | .. 1660–1685 |
| James II | .. | .. | .. | .. | .. 1685–1688 (Deposed) |
| William III | .. | .. | .. | .. 1689–1702 |
| Mary II | .. | .. | .. | .. | .. 1689–1694 |
| Anne | .. | .. | .. | .. | .. 1702–1714 |

| House of Hanover. | | | | | |
|---|---|---|---|---|---|
| George I | .. | .. | .. | .. | .. 1714–1727 |
| George II | .. | .. | .. | .. | .. 1727–1760 |
| George III | .. | .. | .. | .. | .. 1760–1820 |
| George IV | .. | .. | .. | .. | .. 1820–1830 |
| William IV | .. | .. | .. | .. | .. 1830–1837 |
| Victoria | .. | .. | .. | .. | .. 1837–1901 |

| House of Saxe-Coburg-Gotha. | | | | | |
|---|---|---|---|---|---|
| Edward VII | .. | .. | .. | 1901–1910 |

| House of Windsor. | | | | | |
|---|---|---|---|---|---|
| George V | .. | .. | .. | .. | .. 1910–1936 |
| Edward VIII | .. | .. | .. | .. 1936–1936 Abdicated |
| George VI | .. | .. | .. | .. | .. 1936–1952 |
| Elizabeth II | .. | .. | .. | 1952– |
| (Heir apparent—Prince Charles) | | | | | |

## MORSE CODE

The code of signalling devised by Professor Samuel Morse is, now universally used. The complete alphabet is as follows:—

| | | | |
|---|---|---|---|
| A . — | | N — . |
| B — . . . | | O — — — |
| C — . — . | | P . — — . |
| D — . . | | Q — — . — |
| E . | | R . — . |
| F . . — . | | S . . . |
| G — — . | | T — |
| H . . . . | | U . . — |
| I . . | | V . . . — |
| J . — — — | | W . — — |
| K — . — | | X — . . — |
| L . — . . | | Y — . — — |
| M — — | | Z — — . . |

Figures are represented as follows:—

| International Code. | Army Signalling Code. |
|---|---|
| 1 . — — — — | 1 . — |
| 2 . . — — — | 2 . . — |
| 3 . . . — — | 3 . . . — |
| 4 . . . . — | 4 . . . . — |
| 5 . . . . . | 5 . . . . . |
| 6 — . . . . | 6 — . . . . |
| 7 — — . . . | 7 — . . . |
| 8 — — — . . | 8 — . . |
| 9 — — — — . | 9 — . |
| 0 — — — — — | 0 — |

. . . . . .
, . — . — . —
; — . — . — .
: — — — . . .
? . . — — . .
! — — . . — —

## WORLD CUP WINNERS

1930 Uruguay
1934 Italy
1938 Italy

1950 Uruguay
1954 W. Germany
1958 Brazil
1962 Brazil
1966 England

## FRENCH WEIGHTS AND MEASURES AND THEIR ENGLISH EQUIVALENTS

| Metres to Yards | | Kilometres to Miles | | Grammes to Grains | | Kilogrammes to Pounds | |
|---|---|---|---|---|---|---|---|
| Metres | Yards | Kms. | Miles | Grams | Grains | Kilo-grms. | Pounds Avoirdupois |
| 1 | 1·093 | 1 | ·621 | 1 | 15·432 | 1 | 2·204 |
| 2 | 2·187 | 2 | 1·243 | 2 | 30·865 | 2 | 4·409 |
| 3 | 3·280 | 3 | 1·864 | 3 | 46·297 | 3 | 6·614 |
| 4 | 4·374 | 4 | 2·486 | 4 | 61·729 | 4 | 8·818 |
| 5 | 5·468 | 5 | 3·107 | 5 | 77·162 | 5 | 11·023 |
| 6 | 6·561 | 6 | 3·728 | 6 | 92·594 | 6 | 13·228 |
| 7 | 7·655 | 7 | 4·350 | 7 | 108·026 | 7 | 15·432 |
| 8 | 8·749 | 8 | 4·971 | 8 | 123·459 | 8 | 17·637 |
| 9 | 9·842 | 9 | 5·592 | 9 | 138·891 | 9 | 19·842 |
| 10 | 10·936 | 10 | 6·214 | 10 | 154·323 | 10 | 22·046 |
| 11 | 12·030 | 11 | 6·835 | 11 | 169·756 | 11 | 24·250 |
| 12 | 13·123 | 12 | 7·456 | 12 | 185·188 | 12 | 26·455 |
| 13 | 14·217 | 13 | 8·072 | 13 | 200·620 | 13 | 28·660 |
| 14 | 15·310 | 14 | 8·699 | 14 | 216·053 | 14 | 30·865 |
| 15 | 16·404 | 15 | 9·321 | 15 | 231·485 | 15 | 33·069 |
| 16 | 17·498 | 16 | 9·942 | 16 | 246·917 | 16 | 35·274 |
| 17 | 18·591 | 17 | 10·563 | 17 | 262·350 | 17 | 37·478 |
| 18 | 19·685 | 18 | 11·185 | 18 | 277·782 | 18 | 39·683 |
| 19 | 20·779 | 19 | 11·806 | 19 | 293·214 | 19 | 41·888 |
| 20 | 21·872 | 20 | 12·428 | 20 | 308·647 | 20 | 44·092 |
| 30 | 32·808 | 30 | 18·641 | 30 | 462·971 | 30 | 66·139 |
| 40 | 43·745 | 40 | 24·855 | 40 | 617·294 | 40 | 88·185 |
| 50 | 54·681 | 50 | 31·069 | 50 | 771·617 | 50 | 110·231 |

1 Metre........................ = 39⅜ inches
1 Kilometre .................. = 1093⅜ yards.   1 Yard ...................... = 91½ centimetres

Although the gramme is the established unit of weight, the kilogramme is most frequently used.

## LENGTH: METRIC AND ENGLISH EQUIVALENTS

| Metric | Symbol | |
|---|---|---|
| Angstrom | Å | =0.00000000394 inches |
| Millimicron | mμ=10Å | =0·00000003937 ,, |
| Micron | μ=1,000mμ | =0·00003937 ,, |
| Millimetre | mm=1,000μ | =0·03937 ,, |
| Centimetre | cm=10mm | =0·3937 ,, |
| Decimetre | dm=10cm | =3·937 ,, |
| Metre | m=10dm | =39·37 ,, |
| Decametre | dkm=10m | =10·936 yards |
| Hectametre | hm=10dkm | =109·363 ,, |
| Kilometre | km=10hm | =0·621 miles |
| Myriametre | mym=10km | =6·214 ,, |

The unit of length is the metre, and is the ten-millionth part of a meridian arc from the pole to the equator.

To reduce kilometres to miles (roughly), multiply by 6 and cut off the last figure; thus 27 × 6 kms= 162 miles cut off the 2=16 miles.

## MEASURES OF CAPACITY AND WEIGHT

| French | | English Equiv |
|---|---|---|
| Décistère (10th of a stere) .... | = | 3·5317 cu. ft. |
| Stère (cubic metre) .......... | = | 35·3166 ,, |
| Milligramme (100th of a grm.) | = | 0·0154 grns. |
| Centigramme (1000th of a grm.) | = | 0·1544 ,, |
| Décigramme (10th of a grm.) .. | = | 1·5440 ,, |
| Gramme (the unit of weight) .. | = | 15·4323 ,, |
| Décagramme (10 grammes) .. | = | 154·3234 ,, |
| Hectogramme (100 grms.) .. | = | 3·5291 oz. av. |
| Kilogramme (1000 grms.) .. | = | 2·2057 lbs. ,, |

| 1 Ounce Troy | .............. | = 31·1 grammes. |
|---|---|---|
| 1 Ounce Avoir. | .............. | = 28½ grammes. |
| 1 Pound ,, | ................. | = 453½ grammes. |
| 1 Quarter ,, | ................. | = 12·70 kgs. |
| 1 Ton ,, | ................. | = 1016 kgs. |

## TABLE OF EXPENSES, INCOME AND WAGES

*Showing at one view what any sum, from £1 to £1,000 per Annum, is per Day, Week, or Month.*

| Per Year | Per Month | Per Week | Per Day | Per Year | Per Month | Per Week | Per Day | Per Year | Per Month | Per Week | Per Day |
|---|---|---|---|---|---|---|---|---|---|---|---|
| £ s. | s. d. | s. d. | d. | £ s. | £ s. d. | s. d. | s. d. | £ s. | £ s. d. | £ s. d. | £ s. d. |
| 1 0 | 1 8 | 0 4½ | 0¾ | 8 8 | 0 14 0 | 3 2¾ | 0 5½ | 18 18 | 1 11 6 | 0 7 3¼ | 0 1 0½ |
| 1 10 | 2 6 | 0 7 | 1 | 8 10 | 0 14 2 | 3 3¼ | 0 5½ | 19 0 | 1 11 8 | 0 7 3½ | 0 1 0½ |
| 2 0 | 3 4 | 0 9¼ | 1¼ | 9 0 | 0 15 0 | 3 5½ | 0 6 | 20 0 | 1 13 4 | 0 7 8¼ | 0 1 1¼ |
| 2 2 | 3 6 | 0 9¾ | 1½ | 9 9 | 0 15 9 | 3 7½ | 0 6¼ | 25 0 | 2 1 8 | 0 9 7 | 0 1 4½ |
| 2 10 | 4 2 | 0 11½ | 1¾ | 10 0 | 0 16 8 | 3 10¼ | 0 6½ | 30 0 | 2 10 0 | 0 11 6½ | 0 1 7¾ |
| 3 0 | 5 0 | 1 1¾ | 2 | 10 10 | 0 17 6 | 4 0½ | 0 7 | 40 0 | 3 6 8 | 0 15 4½ | 0 2 2¼ |
| 3 3 | 5 3 | 1 2½ | 2 | 11 0 | 0 18 4 | 4 3¾ | 0 7¼ | 50 0 | 4 3 4 | 0 19 2¾ | 0 2 9 |
| 3 10 | 5 10 | 1 4¼ | 2¼ | 11 11 | 0 19 3 | 4 5¼ | 0 7½ | 60 0 | 5 0 0 | 1 3 1 | 0 3 3½ |
| 4 0 | 6 8 | 1 6½ | 2¾ | 12 0 | 1 0 0 | 4 7½ | 0 8 | 70 0 | 5 16 8 | 1 6 11 | 0 3 10 |
| 4 4 | 7 0 | 1 7½ | 2¾ | 12 12 | 1 1 0 | 4 10¼ | 0 8¼ | 80 0 | 6 13 4 | 1 10 9¼ | 0 4 4½ |
| 4 10 | 7 6 | 1 8¾ | 3 | 13 0 | 1 1 8 | 5 0 | 0 8½ | 90 0 | 7 10 0 | 1 14 7½ | 0 4 11¼ |
| 5 0 | 8 4 | 1 11 | 3¼ | 13 13 | 1 2 9 | 5 3 | 0 9 | 100 0 | 8 6 8 | 1 18 5½ | 0 5 5¾ |
| 5 5 | 8 9 | 2 0¼ | 3½ | 14 0 | 1 3 4 | 5 4½ | 0 9¼ | 200 0 | 16 13 4 | 3 16 11 | 0 0 11½ |
| 5 10 | 9 2 | 2 1½ | 3¾ | 14 14 | 1 4 6 | 5 7¾ | 0 9¾ | 300 0 | 25 0 0 | 5 15 4½ | 0 16 5¼ |
| 6 0 | 10 0 | 2 3¾ | 4 | 15 0 | 1 5 0 | 5 9¾ | 0 9¾ | 400 0 | 33 6 8 | 7 13 10¼ | 1 1 11 |
| 6 6 | 10 6 | 2 5 | 4¼ | 15 15 | 1 6 3 | 6 0¾ | 0 10¼ | 500 0 | 41 13 4 | 9 12 3¾ | 1 7 4¾ |
| 6 10 | 10 10 | 2 6 | 4¼ | 16 0 | 1 6 8 | 6 1¾ | 0 10½ | 600 0 | 50 0 0 | 11 10 9¼ | 1 12 10½ |
| 7 0 | 11 8 | 2 8¼ | 4½ | 16 16 | 1 8 0 | 6 5½ | 0 11 | 700 0 | 58 6 8 | 13 9 2¾ | 1 18 4¼ |
| 7 7 | 12 3 | 2 10 | 4¾ | 17 0 | 1 8 4 | 6 6½ | 0 11¼ | 800 0 | 66 13 4 | 15 7 8¼ | 2 3 10 |
| 7 10 | 12 6 | 2 10½ | 5 | 17 17 | 1 9 0 | 6 10½ | 0 11¾ | 900 0 | 75 0 0 | 17 6 1¾ | 2 9 3¾ |
| 8 0 | 13 4 | 3 1 | 5¼ | 18 0 | 1 10 0 | 6 11 | 0 11¾ | 1000 0 | 83 6 8 | 19 4 7¼ | 2 14 9½ |

## INTEREST TABLE FOR ONE YEAR

*By this Table, unlimited calculations may be made. Thus, to find interest on £1,250 per annum, add sums given for £1,000, £200, and 50. 2 per cent. is found by taking half of 4 p.c.; 8 p.c. by doubling 4 p.c.; 7½ p.c., by adding 5 to 2½ p.c., and so on.*

| Principal | 2½ p.c. | 3 p.c. | 3½ p.c. | 4 p.c. | 5 p.c. | Principla | 2½ p.c. | 3 p.c. | 3½ p.c. | 4 p.c. | 5 p.c. |
|---|---|---|---|---|---|---|---|---|---|---|---|
| £ | £ s. d. | £ s. d. | £ s. d. | £ s. d. | £ s. | £ | £ s. | £ s. | £ s. | £ s. | £ s. |
| 1 | 0 0 6 | 0 0 7¼ | 0 0 8½ | 0 0 9½ | 0 1 | 60 | 1 10 | 1 16 | 2 2 | 2 8 | 3 0 |
| 2 | 0 1 0 | 0 1 2½ | 0 1 4¾ | 0 1 7¼ | 0 2 | 70 | 1 15 | 2 2 | 2 9 | 2 16 | 3 10 |
| 3 | 0 1 6 | 0 1 9½ | 0 2 1¼ | 0 2 4¾ | 0 3 | 80 | 2 0 | 2 8 | 2 16 | 3 4 | 4 0 |
| 4 | 0 2 0 | 0 2 4¾ | 0 2 9½ | 0 3 2½ | 0 4 | 90 | 2 5 | 2 14 | 3 3 | 3 12 | 4 10 |
| 5 | 0 2 6 | 0 3 0 | 0 3 6 | 0 4 0 | 0 5 | 100 | 2 10 | 3 0 | 3 10 | 4 0 | 5 0 |
| 6 | 0 3 0 | 0 3 7¼ | 0 4 2½ | 0 4 9½ | 0 6 | 200 | 6 0 | 6 0 | 7 0 | 8 0 | 10 0 |
| 7 | 0 3 6 | 0 4 2½ | 0 4 10¾ | 0 5 7½ | 0 7 | 300 | 7 10 | 9 0 | 10 10 | 12 0 | 15 0 |
| 8 | 0 4 0 | 0 4 9½ | 0 5 7¼ | 0 6 4¾ | 0 8 | 400 | 10 0 | 12 0 | 14 0 | 16 0 | 20 0 |
| 9 | 0 4 6 | 0 5 4¾ | 0 6 3½ | 0 7 2½ | 0 9 | 500 | 12 10 | 15 0 | 17 10 | 20 0 | 25 0 |
| 10 | 0 5 0 | 0 6 0 | 0 7 0 | 0 8 0 | 0 10 | 600 | 15 0 | 18 0 | 21 0 | 24 0 | 30 0 |
| 20 | 0 10 0 | 0 12 0 | 0 14 0 | 0 16 0 | 1 0 | 700 | 17 10 | 21 0 | 24 10 | 28 0 | 35 0 |
| 30 | 0 15 0 | 0 18 0 | 1 1 0 | 1 4 0 | 1 10 | 800 | 20 0 | 24 0 | 28 0 | 32 0 | 40 0 |
| 40 | 1 0 0 | 1 4 0 | 1 8 0 | 1 12 0 | 2 0 | 900 | 22 10 | 27 0 | 21 10 | 36 0 | 45 0 |
| 50 | 1 5 0 | 1 10 0 | 1 15 0 | 2 0 0 | 2 10 | 1000 | 25 0 | 30 0 | 35 0 | 40 0 | 50 0 |

## COMPOUND INTEREST

To find how long it will take for a sum of money to be doubled at compound interest, divide 70 by the rate of interest:

$\frac{70}{\text{rate}}$ = Number of years. $\frac{70}{5} = 14$.

A sum of money at 5 per cent interest will be doubled in 14 years.

## PERCENTAGES OR DISCOUNTS

Showing the Reduction per £ on Discounts allowed for Cash Purchases, at Rates ranging from 1 to 50 per cent.

| | | *s.* | *d.* | | | | *s.* | *d.* | |
|---|---|---|---|---|---|---|---|---|---|
| 0½ | p.c. is | 0 | 1 | per £ | 11 | p.c. is | 2 | 2½ | per £ |
| 1 | ,, | 0 | 2½ | ,, | 12 | ,, | 2 | 5 | ,, |
| 1½ | ,, | 0 | 3½ | ,, | 12½ | ,, | 2 | 6 | ,, |
| 2 | ,, | 0 | 5 | ,, | 13 | ,, | 2 | 7 | ,, |
| 2½ | ,, | 0 | 6 | ,, | 14 | ,, | 2 | 9½ | ,, |
| 3 | ,, | 0 | 7 | ,, | 15 | ,, | 3 | 0 | ,, |
| 3½ | ,, | 0 | 8½ | ,, | 17½ | ,, | 3 | 6 | ,, |
| 4 | ,, | 0 | 9½ | ,, | 20 | ,, | 4 | 0 | ,, |
| 4½ | ,, | 0 | 11 | ,, | 22½ | ,, | 4 | 6 | ,, |
| 5 | ,, | 1 | 0 | ,, | 25 | ,, | 5 | 0 | ,, |
| 5½ | ,, | 1 | 1 | ,, | 27½ | ,, | 5 | 6 | ,, |
| 6 | ,, | 1 | 2½ | ,, | 30 | ,, | 6 | 0 | ,, |
| 6½ | ,, | 1 | 3½ | ,, | 32½ | ,, | 6 | 6 | ,, |
| 7 | ,, | 1 | 5 | ,, | 35 | ,, | 7 | 0 | ,, |
| 7½ | ,, | 1 | 6 | ,, | 37½ | ,, | 7 | 6 | ,, |
| 8 | ,, | 1 | 7 | ,, | 40 | ,, | 8 | 0 | ,, |
| 8½ | ,, | 1 | 8½ | ,, | 42½ | ,, | 8 | 6 | ,, |
| 9 | ,, | 1 | 9½ | ,, | 45 | ,, | 0 | 9 | ,, |
| 9½ | ,, | 1 | 11 | ,, | 47½ | ,, | 9 | 6 | ,, |
| 10 | ,, | 2 | 0 | ,, | 50 | ,, | 10 | 0 | ,, |

## VALUES OF FOREIGN CURRENCY

NOTE: This information was correct at the time of going to press, but due to the frequent fluctuations in the exchange rate of various currencies, these figures must be taken as approximate only. Accurate, up-to-the-minute figures may be obtained from a bank.

| | | | | |
|---|---|---|---|---|
| Argentine | Peso=100 centavos | 0 | 0 | 0½ |
| Australia | Dollar=100 cents | 0 | 8 | 11 |
| Austria | Schilling=10 groschen | 0 | 0 | 4 |
| Belgium | Franc=100 centimes | 0 | 0 | 2 |
| Bulgaria | Lev=100 stolinki | 0 | 5 | 8 |
| Canada | Dollar=100 cents | 0 | 6 | 8 |
| Czechoslovakia | Koruna=100 hater | 0 | 0 | 6 |
| Denmark | Krone=100 öre | 0 | 1 | 1 |
| Finland | Markka=100 pennies | 0 | 2 | 0 |
| France | Franc=100 centimes | 0 | 1 | 8 |
| Germany (East) | Deutsche Mark=100 pfennig | 0 | 3 | 0 |
| Germany (Federal Republic of) | Deutsche Mark=100 pfennig | 0 | 2 | 1 |
| Greece | Drachma=100 lepla | 0 | 0 | 3 |
| Holland | Guilder=100 cents | | 2 | 4 |
| Hungary | Florint=100 filler | 0 | 0 | 7¼ |
| India | Rupee=100 paise | 0 | 1 | 6 |
| Italy | Lira=100 centesimi (10 Lira) | | | 1½ |
| Jamaica | Pound=20 shillings | 1 | 0 | 0 |
| Japan | Yen=100 sen | | | ¼ |
| Luxembourg | Franc=100 centimes | 0 | 0 | 1¾ |
| Netherlands | Florin=100 cents | 0 | 2 | 4 |
| New Zealand | Dollar=100 cents | 0 | 9 | 4 |
| Norway | Krone=100 öre | 0 | 1 | 2 |
| Pakistan | Rupee=100 paisa | 0 | 1 | 6 |
| Poland | Zloty=100 groszy | 0 | 1 | 9½ |
| Portugal | Escudo=100 centavos | 0 | 0 | 3 |
| Rhodesia | Pound=20 shillings | 1 | 0 | 0 |
| Rumania | Leu=100 bani | 0 | 1 | 2¼ |
| Russia | Rouble=100 copecks | 0 | 7 | 11¼ |
| South Africa | Rand=100 cents | 0 | 10 | 6 |
| Spain | Peseta=100 céntimos | | | 1½ |
| Sweden | Krona=100 öre | 0 | 1 | 8 |
| Switzerland | Franc=100 centimes | 0 | 1 | 11 |
| U.S.A. | Dollar=100 cents | 0 | 8 | 4 |
| West Indies, The | Dollar=100 cents | 0 | 4 | 2 |
| Yugoslavia | Dinar=100 pavas | 0 | 0 | 8 |

## CENTIGRADE/FAHRENHEIT TABLE

To convert Centigrade to Fahrenheit: Multiply the number of degrees by $\frac{9}{5}$ and add 32 to the result. To convert Fahrenheit to Centigrade: Subtract 32 from the number of degrees and multiply by $\frac{5}{9}$.

| *Centigrade* | *Fahrenheit* |
|---|---|
| 100 | 212 |
| 95 | 203 |
| 90 | 194 |
| 85 | 185 |
| 78·9 | 174 |
| 75 | 167 |
| 70 | 158 |
| 65 | 149 |
| 60 | 140 |
| 55 | 131 |
| 52·8 | 127 |
| 50 | 122 |
| 45 | 113 |
| 42·2 | 108 |
| 40 | 104 |
| 36·7 | 98 |
| 35 | 95 |
| 32·2 | 90 |
| 30 | 86 |
| 26·7 | 80 |
| 25 | 77 |
| 20 | 68 |
| 15·5 | 60 |
| 12·8 | 55 |
| 10 | 50 |
| 7·2 | 45 |
| 5 | 41 |
| 1·7 | 35 |
| 0 | 32 |
| −1·1 | 30 |
| −5 | 23 |
| −6·7 | 20 |
| −10 | 14 |
| −12·2 | 10 |
| −15 | 5 |
| −17·8 | 0 |
| −20 | −4 |
| −25 | −13 |
| −30 | −22 |
| −35 | −31 |
| −40 | −40 |

Boiling point is 100°C; 212°F.
Freezing point is 0°C; 32°F.

## LONG MEASURE

| | |
|---|---|
| 12 lines | = 1 inch. |
| 12 inches | = 1 foot. |
| 3 feet | = 1 yard. |
| 5½ yards (16½ feet) | = 1 pole or rod. |
| 4 poles (22 yards) | = 1 chain. |
| 40 poles (10 chains) | = 1 furlong. |
| 8 furlongs (1,760 yards) | = 1 mile. |
| 3 miles | = 1 league. |

| | |
|---|---|
| 3 barleycorns | = 1 inch. |
| 2¼ inches | = 1 nail. |
| 3 inches | = 1 palm. |
| 4 inches | = 1 hand. (height of horses). |
| 9 inches | = 1 span. |
| 18 inches | = 1 cubit. |
| 2½ feet | = 1 pace (military). |
| 5 feet | = 1 pace (geometrical). |

## LAND MEASURES

| | |
|---|---|
| 7·92 inches | = 1 link. |
| 25 links | = 1 pole or rod. |
| 4 poles (22 yds. or 100 links) | = 1 chain. |
| 80 chains | = 1 mile. |

| | |
|---|---|
| 62·7264 sq. inches | = 1 sq. link. |
| 6·5 square links | = 1 sq. pole. |
| 16 square poles | = 1 sq. chain. |
| 10 square chains | = 1 acre. |
| 30 acres | = 1 yd. of land. |
| 100 acres | = 1 hide of land. |
| 40 hides | = 1 barony. |

NOTE.—The United Kingdom has a land area of 93,000 sq. miles.

## SQUARE MEASURE

| | |
|---|---|
| 144 square inches | = 1 sq. foot. |
| 9 square feet | = 1 sq. yard. |
| 30¼ square yards | = 1 sq. pole, rod, or perch. |
| 40 square poles | = 1 rood. |
| 4 roods | = 1 acre. |
| 640 acres (43,560 sq. ft.) | = 1 sq. mile. |

NOTE.—Earth has an area of 196 million sq. miles; 55 million sq. miles of land. With a total population of about 3,135 million; population density per sq. mile is about 57 people.

## CUBIC MEASURE

| | |
|---|---|
| 1,728 cubic inches | = 1 cubic foot. |
| 27 cubic feet | = 1 cubic yard. |
| 16 cubic feet | = 1 cord foot. |
| 8 cord ft. (128 cub. ft.) | = 1 cord. |

## LIQUID MEASURE

| | |
|---|---|
| 4 gills | = 1 pint. |
| 2 pints | = 1 quart. |
| 4 quarts | = 1 gallon. |
| 9 gallons | = 1 firkin. |
| 10 gallons | = 1 anker. |
| 2 firkins (18 gals.) | = 1 kilderkin. |
| 2 kilderkins | = 1 barrel. |
| 1½ barrels | = 1 hogshead |
| 2 hogsheads | = 1 butt. |
| 2 butts | = 1 tun. |

## DRY MEASURE

| | |
|---|---|
| 4 gills | = 1 pint. |
| 2 pints | = 1 quart. |
| 4 quarts | = 1 gallon. |

| | |
|---|---|
| 2 gallons | = 1 peck. |
| 4 pecks | = 1 bushel. |
| 3 bushels | = 1 bag. |
| 4 bushels | = 1 coomb. |
| 5 bushels | = 1 sack (flour). |
| 8 bushels | = 1 quarter. |
| 36 bushels (12 bags) | = 1 chaldron. |
| 40 bushels (5 quarters) | = 1 wey (horse-load) |
| 2 weys | = 1 last. |

## CIRCULAR MEASURE

Used in astronomical and geographical calculations.

| | |
|---|---|
| 60 seconds (") | = 1 minute ('). |
| 60 minutes | = 1 degree (°). |
| 30 degrees | = 1 sign (zodiac). |
| 60 degrees | = 1 sextant. |
| 90 degrees | = 1 quadrant. |
| 360 degrees | = 1 circle. |

## TROY WEIGHT

| | |
|---|---|
| 3·17 grains | = 1 carat |
| 24 grains | = 1 pennyweight. (dwt.) |
| 20 pennyweights | = 1 ounce |
| 12 ounces | = 1 pound (lb.). |
| 100 pounds | = 1 hundred-weight (cwt.). |

NOTE.—The carat is not a measure of weight, but the proportion of gold in the alloy composing the article. Articles of gold are reckoned as constituting of 24 carats, of which so many (usually 9, 15, 18, or 22) are of pure gold, and the rest alloy. An article stamped 9 carats is 9 parts gold and 15 parts alloy. A sovereign is 22 carat gold.

## APOTHECARIES' WEIGHT

Used in Medical prescriptions.

| | |
|---|---|
| 20 grains | = 1 scruple (℈) |
| 3 scruples | = 1 drachm (ʒ) |
| 8 drachms | = 1 ounce (℥) |
| 12 ounces | = 1 pound |

## AVOIRDUPOIS WEIGHT

| | |
|---|---|
| 16 drams | = 1 ounce (oz.) |
| 16 ounces | = 1 pound (lb.) |
| 14 pounds | = 1 stone (st.) |
| 28 pounds | = 1 quarter (qr.) |
| 4 quarters (112 pounds) | = 1 hundredweight (cwt.). |
| 20 hundredweights | = 1 ton. |

NOTE.—In the United States, 100 pounds = hundredweight.

## PAPER MEASURE

| | |
|---|---|
| 24 sheets | = 1 quire. |
| 20 quires (480 sheets) | = 1 ream. |
| 516 sheets | = 1 printer's ream. |
| 2 reams | = 1 bundle. |
| 10 reams | = 1 bale. |

## 'A' SERIES OF TRIMMED PAPER SIZES

| | mm. | inches |
|---|---|---|
| A0 | 841 × 1189 | 33·11 × 46·81 |
| A1 | 594 × 841 | 23·39 × 33·11 |
| A2 | 420 × 594 | 16·54 × 23·39 |
| A3 | 297 × 420 | 11·69 × 16·54 |
| A4 | 210 × 297 | 8·27 × 11·69 |
| A5 | 148 × 210 | 5·83 × 8·27 |
| A6 | 105 × 148 | 4·13 × 5·83 |
| A7 | 74 × 105 | 2·91 × 4·13 |
| A8 | 52 × 74 | 2·05 × 2·91 |
| A9 | 37 × 52 | 1·46 × 2·05 |
| A10 | 26 × 37 | 1·02 × 1·46 |

## 'B' SERIES OF TRIMMED PAPER SIZES

| | mm. | inches |
|---|---|---|
| B0 | 1000 × 1414 | 39·37 × 55·67 |
| B1 | 707 × 1000 | 27·83 × 39·37 |
| B2 | 500 × 707 | 19·68 × 27·83 |
| B3 | 353 × 500 | 13·90 × 19·68 |
| B4 | 250 × 353 | 9·84 × 13·90 |
| B5 | 176 × 250 | 6·93 × 9·84 |
| B6 | 125 × 176 | 4·92 × 6·93 |
| B7 | 88 × 125 | 3·46 × 4·92 |
| B8 | 62 × 88 | 2·44 × 3·46 |
| B9 | 44 × 62 | 1·73 × 2·44 |
| B10 | 31 × 44 | 1·22 × 1·73 |

## SIZES OF PRINTING PAPERS

| *Name* | *Inches* |
|---|---|
| Double Royal .. .. | 40 × 25 |
| Double Demy .. .. | 35 × 22½ |
| Double Post .. .. .. | 31½ × 19½ |
| Double Crown .. .. | 30 × 20 |
| Elephant .. .. .. | 30 × 23 |
| Imperial .. .. .. | 30 × 22 |
| Super Royal .. .. .. | 27½ × 20½ |
| Royal .. .. .. .. | 25 × 20 |
| Medium .. .. .. | 24 × 19 |
| Demy .. .. .. .. | 22½ × 17½ |

## SIZES OF WRITING PAPERS.

| *Name* | *Inches* |
|---|---|
| Imperial .. .. .. | 30 × 22 |
| Cartridge .. .. .. | 26 × 21 |
| Royal .. .. .. .. | 24 × 19 |
| Medium .. .. .. | 22 × 17½ |
| Demy .. .. .. .. | 20 × 15½ |
| Large Post .. .. .. | 21 × 16½ |
| Post .. .. .. .. | 19 × 15¼ |
| Foolscap .. .. .. | 16¾ × 13¼ |
| Copy .. .. .. .. | 20¼ × 16 |
| Pott .. .. .. .. | 15 × 12½ |

## SIZES OF BOOKS

| *Size* | *Height and breadth in inches* |
|---|---|
| Royal Folio .. .. .. | 19 × 12 |
| Demy Folio .. .. .. | 18 × 11 |
| Imperial Quarto .. .. | 15½ × 13 |
| Royal Quarto .. .. | 12½ × 10 |
| Demy Quarto .. .. | 11½ × 8½ |
| Crown Quarto .. .. | 11 × 8 |
| Royal Octavo .. .. | 10 × 6½ |
| Medium Octavo .. .. | 9½ × 6 |
| Demy Octavo .. .. | 9 × 5¾ |
| Crown Octavo .. .. | 7½ × 5 |
| Foolscap Octavo .. .. | 7 × 4½ |
| 12mo. .. .. .. | 7 × 4 |
| 16mo. .. .. .. | 6½ × 4 |
| Royal 32mo. .. .. | 5 × 3 |

## TABLE OF DISTANCE ONE CAN SEE

A rough method of calculating the distance to the visible horizon is to take the square root of one and a half times the height in feet of the observer above sea-level and the result is a near approximation to the distance of the visible horizon in miles.

| *Height in feet* | *Distance in miles* |
|---|---|
| 0·582 | 1 |
| 1 | 1·31 |
| 2 | 1·87 |
| 3 | 2·29 |
| 4 | 2·63 |
| 5 | 2·96 |
| 6 | 3·24 |
| 7 | 3·49 |
| 8 | 3·73 |
| 9 | 3·96 |
| 10 | 4·18 |
| 11 | 4·39 |
| 12 | 4·58 |
| 13 | 4·77 |
| 15 | 5·12 |
| 20 | 5·92 |
| 25 | 6·61 |
| 30 | 7·25 |
| 40 | 8·37 |
| 50 | 9·35 |
| 60 | 9·65 |
| 70 | 11·07 |
| 80 | 11·83 |
| 90 | 12·25 |
| 100 | 13·23 |
| 200 | 18·72 |
| 300 | 22·91 |
| 500 | 29·58 |
| 1,000 | 32·41 |
| 2,000 | 59·2 |
| 3,000 | 72·5 |
| 4,000 | 83·7 |
| 5,000 | 93·5 |
| (1 mile) 5,280 | 96·1 |

# AWARDS, HONOURS AND TITLES

A.B.—*Artium Baccalaureus*, Bachelor of Arts; Able Bodied Seaman.
A.C.A.—Associate of the Institute of Chartered Accountants.
A.C.P.—Associate of the College of Preceptors.
A.D.G.—Assistant-Director-General.
A.D.M.S.—Assistant-Director of Medical Services.
A.F.A.—Associate of the Faculty of Actuaries in Scotland.
A.F.M.—Air Force Medal.
A.G.S.M.—Associate of the Guildhall School of Music.
A.I.A.—Associate of the Institute of Actuaries.
A.I.C.—Associate of the Institute of Chemistry.
A.I.G.—Adjutant Inspector General.
A.M.—Albert Medal; *Artium Magister*, Master of Arts.
A.M.I.E.E.—Associate Member of the Institution of Electrical Engineers.
A.M.I.M.E.—Associate Member of the Institute of Mining Engineers.
A.M.I.Mech.E.—Associate Member of the Institution of Mechanical Engineers.
A.M.Inst.C.E.—Associate Member of the Institution of Civil Engineers.
M.A.Inst.Gas E.—Associate Member of the Institution of Gas Engineers.
A.P.S.—Associate of the Pharmaceutical Society.
A.R.C.M.—Associate of the Royal College of Music.
A.R.C.O.—Associate of the Royal College of Organists.
A.R.A.—Associate of the Royal Academy.
A.R.E.—Associate of the Royal Society of Painter Etchers.
A.R.I.B.A.—Associate of the Royal Institute of British Architects.
A.R.M.C.M.—Associate of the Royal Manchester College of Music.
A.R.S.A.—Associate of the Royal Scottish Academy; Associate of the Royal Society of Arts.
A.R.S.M.—Associate of the Royal School of Mines (Royal College of Science).
A.S.A.A.—Associate of the Society of Accountants and Auditors.
A.S.A.M.—Associate of the National Society of Art Masters.
A.T.C.L.—Associate of Trinity College, London (Music.)

B.A.—*Baccalaureus Artium*, Bachelor of Arts; British Academy; British Association.
B.Agric.—Bachelor of Agriculture.
B.Ch.—*Baccalaureus Chirurgiæ*, Bachelor of Surgery.
B.Ch.D.—Bachelor of Dental Surgery.
B.C.L.—Bachelor of Canon Law; Bachelor Civil Law.
B.Com.—Bachelor of Commerce.
B.D.—Bachelor of Divinity.
B.D.S.—Bachelor of Dental Surgery.
B.Eng.—Bachelor of Engineering.
B.Hy.—Bachelor of Hygiene.
B.L.—Bachelor of Laws.
B.Lit.—Bachelor of Literature.
B.Litt.—Bachelor of Letters.
B.M.—Bachelor of Medicine.
B.M.E.—Bachelor of Mining Engineering.
B.Met.—Bachelor of Metallurgy.
B.Mus.—Bachelor of Music.
B.Ph., B.Phil.—Bachelor of Philosophy.
B.Sc.—Bachelor of Science.
B.Th.—Bachelor of Theology.

C.B.—Companion (of the Order) of the Bath.
C.B.E.—Commander (of the Order) of the British Empire.
C.G.M.—Conspicuous Gallantry Medal (Naval).
C.G.S.—Chief of the General Staff.
C.H.—Companion of Honour.
Ch.B.—*Chirurgiæ Baccalaureus*, Bachelor in Surgery.
Ch.M.—*Chirurgiæ Magister*, Master in Surgery.
C.I.—Imperial Order of the Crown of India.

C.I.G.S.—Chief of the Imperial General Staff.
C.-in-C.—Commander in Chief.
C.L.—Commander of the Order of Leopold.
C.M.—Certificated Master; *Chirurgiæ Magister*, Master in Surgery.
C.M.G.—Companion of the Order of St. Michael and St. George.
C.O.—Commanding Officer.
C.P.C.—Clerk of the Privy Council.
C.P.S.—*Custos Privati Sigilli*, Keeper of the Privy Seal.
C.R.—*Custos Rotulorum*, Keeper of the Rolls.
C.S.—Clerk of Session; Clerk to the Signet; Common Sergeant; *Custos Sigilli*, Keeper of the Seal.
C.S.C.—Conspicuous Service Cross.
C.S.I.—Companion of the Order of the Star of India.
C.S.O.—Chief Signals Officer; Chief Staff Officer.
C.V.O.—Commander of the Royal Victorian Order.

D.B.E.—Dame of the Order of the British Empire.
D.C.—Deputy Consul.
D.C.L.—Doctor of Civil Law.
D.C.M.—Distinguished Conduct Medal.
D.D.—Doctor of Divinity.
D.D.S.—Doctor of Dental Surgery.
D.Eng.—Doctor of Engineering
D.F.C.—Distinguished Flying Cross.
D.F.M.—Distinguished Flying Medal.
D.G.—Director-General.
D.Hy.—Doctor of Hygiene.
D.I.C.—Diploma of the Imperial College of Science and Technology.
D.Lit.—Doctor of Literature.
D.Litt.—Doctor of Letters.
D.M.D.—Doctor of Dental Medicine.
D.P.H.—Diploma of Public Health.
D.Ph.—Doctor of Philosophy.
D.Sc.—Doctor of Science.
D.S.C.—Distinguished Service Cross (Naval).
D.S.M.—Distinguished Service Medal (Naval).
D.S.O.—Companion of the Distinguished Service Order.
D.Th.—Doctor of Theology.
D.Z.—Doctor of Zoology.

F.A.I.—Fellow of the Auctioneers' Institute.
F.C.A.—Fellow of the Institute of Chartered Accountants.
F.C.I.—Fellow of the Institute of Commerce.
F.C.P.—Fellow of the College of Preceptors.
F.E.S.—Fellow of the Entomological, or Ethnological Society.
F.F.A.—Fellow of the Faculty of Actuaries.
F.F.P.S.—Fellow of the Faculty of Physicians and Surgeons.
F.F.P.S.G.—Fellow of the Faculty of Physicians and Surgeons of Glasgow.
F.G.S.—Fellow of the Geological Society.
F.I.A.—Fellow of the Institute of Actuaries.
F.I.C.—Fellow of the Institute of Chemistry.
Fid.Def.—*Fidei Defensor*, Defender of the Faith.
F.I.H.—Fellow of the Institute of Hygiene.
F.L.A.—Fellow of the Library Association.
F.P.S.—Fellow of the Philharmonic Society; Fellow of the Philosophical Society.
F.Phys.S.—Fellow of the Physical Society.
F.R.A.I.—Fellow of the Royal Anthropological Institute.
F.R.A.S.—Fellow of the Royal Astronomical Society.
F.R.C.O.—Fellow of the Royal College of Organists.
F.R.C.S.L.—Fellow of the Royal College of Surgeons, London.
F.R.Econ.S.—Fellow of the Royal Economic Society.
F.R.Hist.S.—Fellow of the Royal Historical Society.
F.R.Hort.S.—Fellow of the Royal Horticultural Society.
F.R.Met.S—Fellow of the Meteorological Society.
F.R.N.S.A.—Fellow of the Royal School of Naval Architecture.
F.R.P.S.—Fellow of the Royal Photographic Society.
F.R.S.—Fellow of the Royal Society.
F.R.S.A.—Fellow of the Royal Society of Arts.
F.R.S.L.—Fellow of the Royal Society of Literature; Fellow of the Royal Society of London.

**F.R.S.S.A.**—Fellow of the Royal Scottish Society of Arts.
**F.S.A.**—Fellow of the Society of Antiquaries.
**F.S.A.A.**—Fellow of the Society of Accountants and Auditors.
**F.S.I.**—Fellow of the Surveyors' Institution.
**F.Z.S.**—Fellow of the Zoological Society.

**G.B.E.**—Knight or Dame Grand Cross (Order of the) British Empire.
**G.C.**—George Cross.
**G.C.B.**—Knight Grand Cross of the Bath.
**G.C.I.E.**—Knight Grand Commander of the Indian Empire.
**G.C.M.G.**—Knight Grand Cross of St. Michael and St. George.
**G.C.S.I.**—Knight Grand Commander of the Star of India.
**G.C.V.O.**—Knight Grand Cross of the Royal Victorian Order.
**G.M.**—George Medal.
**G.O.C.**—General Officer Commanding.
**G.O.C.-in-C.**—General Officer Commanding in-Chief.
**G.P.**—General Practitioner.
**G.S.O.**—General Staff Officer.

**H.M.I.S.**—Her Majesty's Inspector of Schools.
**H.R.S.A.**—Honorary Member of the Royal Scottish Academy.
**I.S.O.**—Imperial Service Order.

**J.P.**—Justice of the Peace.

**K.B.**—Knight Bachelor; Knight of the Bath.
**K.B.E.**—Knight Commander (of the Order) of the British Empire.
**K.C.B.**—Knight Commander of the Bath.
**K.C.H.**—Knight Commander (of the Order) of Hanover.
**K.C.I.E.**—Knight Commander (of the Order) of the Indian Empire.
**K.C.M.G.**—Knight Commander of St. Michael and St. George.
**K.C.S.I.**—Knight Commander of the Star of India.
**K.C.V.O.**—Knight Commander of Royal Victorian Order.
**K.G.**—Knight of the Garter.
**K.H.**—Knight of the Order of Hanover.
**K.S.G.**—Knight of St. Gregory.
**K.T.**—Knight of the Order of the Thistle.

**L.A.**—Literature in Arts.
**L.Ch.**—Licentiate in Surgery.
**L.C.J.**—Lord Chief Justice.
**L.C.P.**—Licentiate of the College of Preceptors.
**L.Div.**—Licentiate in Divinity.
**L.D.S.**—Licentiate in Dental Surgery.
**L.F.P.S.**—Licentiate of the Faculty of Physicians and Surgeons.
**Litt.D.**—Doctor of Letters.
**L.L.A.**—Lady Literate in Arts.
**LL.B.**—*Legum Baccalaureus*, Bachelor of Laws.
**LL.D.**—*Legum Doctor*, Doctor of Laws.
**L.L.I.**—Lord Lieutenant of Ireland.
**LL.M.**—*Legum Magister*, Master of Civil and Canon Law.
**L.M.**—Licentiate in Medicine; Licentiate in Midwifery
**L.M.R.C.P.**—Licentiate in Midwifery, Royal College of Physicians.
**L.M.S.**—Licentiate in Medicine and Surgery.
**L.M.S.S.A.**—Licentiate in Medicine and Surgery Society of Apothecaries, London.
**L.P.S.**—Lord Privy Seal.
**L.R.A.M.**—Licentiate of the Royal Academy of Music.
**L.R.C.P.**—Licentiate of the Royal College of Physicians.
**L.S.A.**—Licentiate of the Society of Apothecaries.
**L.S.Sc.**—Licentiate in Sanitary Science.

**M.A.**—Master of Arts.
**M.A.O.**—Master of (the Art of) Obstetrics.

**M.B.**—*Medicinæ Baccalaureus*, Bachelor of Medicine.
**M.B.C.P.E.**—Member of the British College of Physical Education.
**M.B.E.**—Member (of the Order) of the British Empire.
**M.C.**—Master of Chemistry; Military Cross.
**M.Ch.**—*Magister Chirurgiæ*, Master of Surgery.
**M.Ch.D.**—Master of Dental Surgery.
**M.Com.**—Master of Commerce.
**M.C.P.**—Member of the College of Preceptors.
**M.D.**—*Medicinæ Doctor*, Doctor of Medicine.
**M.D.S.**—Master of Dental Surgery.
**M.Eng.**—Master of Engineering.
**M.F.H.**—Master of Foxhounds.
**M.G.T.I.**—Member of the Gymnastic Teachers' Institute.
**M.H.K.**—Member of the House of Keys (Isle of Man).
**M.H.R.**—Member of the House of Representatives.
**M.Hy.**—Master of Hygiene.
**M.I.E.E.**—Member of the Institution of Electrical Engineers.
**M.I.J.**—Member of the Institute of Journalists.
**M.I.M.E.**—Member of the Institute of Mining Engineers.
**M.I.Mech.E.**—Member of the Institution of Mechanical Engineers.
**M.I.M.M.**—Member of the Institute of Mining and Metallurgy.
**M.I.N.A.**—Member of the Institute of Naval Architects.
**M.Inst.C.E.**—Member of the Institution of Civil Engineers.
**M.Inst.Gas.E.**—Member of the Institution of Gas Engineers.
**M.I.S.T.M.**—Member of the Incorporated Society of Trained Masseuses.
**M.L.**—Licentiate in Medicine; Licentiate in Midwifery.
**M.L.A.**—Member of the Legislative Assembly; Member of the Library Association.
**M.L.C.**—Member of the Legislative Council.
**Mlle.**—Mademoiselle.
**M.M.**—Master Mason; Military Medal.
**Mme., Mmes.**—Madame; Mesdames.
**M.N.A.S.**—Member of the National Academy of Sciences.
**M.N.S.P.E.**—Member of the National Society of Physical Education.
**M.O.**—Medical Officer.
**M.O.H.**—Medical Officer of Health.
**M.P.**—Member of Parliament.
**M.P.S.**—Member of the Pharmaceutical Society; Member of the Philological Society.
**M.R.A.S.**—Member of the Royal Asiatic Society; Member of the Royal Academy of Science.
**M.R.C.C.**—Member of the Royal College of Chemistry.
**M.R.C.O.**—Member of the Royal College of Organists.
**M.R.C.P.**—Member of the Royal College of Physicians.
**M.R.C.S.**—Member of the Royal College of Surgeons.
**M.R.C.V.S.**—Member of the Royal College of Veterinary Surgeons.
**M.R.I.**—Member of the Royal Institution.
**M.R.I.A.**—Member of the Royal Irish Academy.
**M.R.S.A.**—Member of the Royal Society of Arts.
**M.R.S.L.**—Member of the Royal Society of Literature.
**M.S.**—Master of Science; Master of Surgery.
**M.S.A.**—Member of the Society of Apothecaries; Member of the Society of Arts.
**M.Sc.**—Master of Science.
**M.S.H.**—Master of Staghounds.
**Mus.B.; Mus.Bac.**—*Musicæ Baccalaureus*. Bachelor of Music.
**Mus.D.; Mus.Doc.**—*Musicæ Doctor*, Doctor of Music.
**Mus.M.**—*Musicæ Magister*, Master of Music.
**M.V.O.**—Member of the Royal Victorian Order.

**N.C.O.**—Non-commissioned Officer.
**N.P.**—Notary Public.

O.B.E.—Officer of the Order of the British Empire.
O.C.—Officer Commanding.
O.L.—Officer of the Order of Leopold.
O.M.—Order of Merit.
O.R.C.—Order of the Red Cross.
O.S.—Ordinary Seaman.
O.S.A.—Order of Saint Augustine.
O.S.B.—Order of Saint Benedict.
O.S.F.—Order of Saint Francis.
O.S.M.A.—Order of Saint Michael and All Angels.

Ph.B.—*Philosophiæ Baccalaureus*, Bachelor of Philosophy.
P.C.—Perpetual Curate; Police Constable; Privy Councillor.
Ph.D.—*Philosophiæ Doctor*, Doctor of Philosophy.
P.M.G.—Postmaster-General; Paymaster General.
P.O.—Petty Officer.
P.R.A.—President of the Royal Academy.
P.R.I.—President of the Royal Institute of Painters in Watercolours.
P.R.I.B.A.—President of the Royal Institute of British Architects.
P.R.S.—President of the Royal Society.
P.R.S.A.—President of the Royal Scottish Academy.
P.R.S.E.—President of the Royal Society of Edinburgh.

Q.C.—Queen's Council.
Q.M.—Quarter-Master.
Q.M.S.—Quarter-Master-Sergeant.

R.A.—Rear Admiral; Royal Academician.
R.D.—Rural Dean.
R.H.—Royal Highness.
R.M.—Resident Magistrate.
R.P.—Regius Professor.
R.S.M.—Regimental Sergeant Major.
R.S.S.—*Regiæ Societatis Socius*, Fellow of the Royal Society.
R.W.—Right Worshipful; Right Worthy.

S.A.S.—*Societatis Antiquariorum Socius*, Fellow of the Society of Antiquaries.
Sc.B.—*Scientiæ Baccalaureus*, Bachelor of Science.
Sc.D.—*Scientiæ Doctor*, Doctor of Science.
S.M.Lond.Soc.—*Societatis Medicæ Londinensis Socius*, Fellow of the London Medical Society.
S.S.C.—Solicitor before the Supreme Courts (Scotland).
SS.D.—*Sanctissimus Dominus*, Most Holy Lord (The Pope).

T.D.—Territorial Officers' Decoration.

U.J.D.—*Utriusque Juris Doctor*, Doctor of Civil and Canon Law.
U.K.A.—Ulster King of Arms.

V.A.—Vice-Admiral; Royal Order of Victoria and Albert.
V.C.—Victoria Cross.
V.D.—Volunteer Officers' Decoration.
V.O.—Victorian Order.

## MISCELLANEOUS ABBREVIATIONS

A1.—First-class (Lloyd's Register of ships); First rate (slang).
A.A.—Athletic Association; Automobile Association.
A.A.A.—Amateur Athletic Association.
A.B.A.—Amateur Boxing Association.
A.B.C.—Aerated Bread Company; Associated British Cinemas.
A.C.—Alternating Current.
A.C.U.—Auto-Cycle Union.
A.D.—*Anno Domini*, In the Year of Our Lord.
A.D.C.—Aide-de-camp.
Ad hoc.—For this special purpose.
Ad lib.—*Ad libitum*, At pleasure, to any extent.
Ad val.—*Ad valorem*, According to value.

A.E.U.—Amalgamated Engineering Union.
A.F.A.—Amateur Fencing Association; Amateur Football Association.
A.F.A.M.—Ancient Free and Accepted Masons.
A.H.—*Anno Hegiræ*, In the year of Hegira (Mohammedan Era).
A.H.M.—Association of Head Mistresses.
A.I.D.—Aircraft Inspection Department; Army Intelligence Department.
A.I.F.—Australian Imperial Force.
A.L.A.M.—Association of Licensed Automobile Manufacturers.
A.M.—*Alpes Maritimes*; *Anno Mundi*, In the year of the world; *Ante Meridian*, Before midday; *Ave Maria*, Hail Mary.
A.N.Z.A.C.—Australian and New Zealand Army Corps; an Australian or New Zealand soldier.
A.O.D.—Ancient Order of Druids.
A.O.F.—Ancient Order of Foresters.
A.O.F.G.—Ancient Order of Free Gardeners.
A.O.H.—Ancient Order of Hibernians.
A.O.S.—Agricultural Organization Society; Ancient Order of Shepherds.
A.P.S.—Aborigines Protection Society; American Peace Society; American Protestant Society.
A.S.A.—Amateur Swimming Association.
A.S.E.—Amalgamated Society of Engineers.
A.S.G.B.—Aeronautical Society of Great Britain.
A.T.D.S.—Association of Teachers of Domestic Science.
A.U.W.T.—Association of University Women Teachers.
A.V.—Authorised Version of the Bible.

B.A.R.—Book Auction Records.
B.B.A.—British Beekeepers' Association.
B.B.C.—British Broadcasting Corporation.
B.C.—Before Christ; Board of Control; British Columbia.
B.C.P.E.—British College of Physical Education.
B.Ed.—Bachelor of Education.
B.L.—Black Letter.
B.M.A.—British Medical Association.
B.M.J.—British Medical Journal.
B.O.A.—British Olympic Association; British Optical Association.
B.A.O.R.—British Army of the Rhine.
B.O.U.—British Ornithologists' Union.
B.P.—British Pharmacopœia.
B.S.A.—Birmingham Small Arms Co.
B.S.L.—Botanical Society of London.
B.S.T.—British Summer Time.
B.Th.U.—British Thermal Unit.
B.T.U.—Board of Trade Unit.
B.W.T.A.—British Women's Temperance Association.

C.—Centigrade.
C.A.—Chartered Accountant.
C.C.—Chamber of Commerce; Circuit Court; County Council, -lor: County Court.
c.c.—cubic centimetres.
C.D.Acts.—Contagious Diseases Acts.
C.E.T.S.—Church of England Temperance Society.
C.E.W.H.S.—Church of England Women's Help Society.
C.E.W.M.S.—Church of England Working Men's Society.
cf.—*confer*, compare.
C.G.—Coast Guard.
C.G.S.—Centimetre-gramme-second (unit of length mass and time).
C.I.—Channel Islands.
C.I.D.—Criminal Investigation Department.
C.M.—Common Metre; Court Martial.
cm.—centimetre.
C.M.S.—Church Missionary Society.
C.M.U.A.—Commerical Motor Users' Association.
c/o.—Care of.
C.O.D.—Cash on Delivery.
C.P.R.—Canadian Pacific Railway.
cres.—crescendo.
C.S.—Chemical Society; Civil Service; Court of Session.

C.Ss.R.—*Congregatio Sanctissimi Redemptoris*, Redemptorist Fathers.
C.T.C.—Cyclists' Touring Club.
C.U.—Coalition Unionist; Cambridge University.
C.U.P.—Cambridge University Press.
C.W.S.—Co-operative Wholesale Society.

D.C.—District Court; District of Columbia; Direct Current.
D.C.L.—Distillers Company Limited.
D.C.L.I.—Duke of Cornwall's Light Infantry.
D.D.T.—Dichlor-diphenyl-trichlorethane (insecticide)
deg.—Degree.
D.F.—Direction Finding (or Finder).
D.G.—*Dei gratia*, By the grace of God; Dragoon Guards.
dg.—decigram.
dim.—diminuendo.
dkg.—decagram.
dkl—decalitre.
dkm.—decametre.
dl.—decilitre.
D.L.I.—Durham Light Infantry.
D.L.O.—Dead Letter Office.
dm.—decimetre.
D.N.B.—Dictionary of National Biography.
D.P.—Displaced Person.
D.R. —Dead Reckoning.
D.S.—*Dal Segno*, Repeat from the mark.
dwt.—pennyweight.

e. & o.e.—errors and omissions excepted.
E.C.U.—English Church Union.
E.D.D.—English Dialect Dictionary.
E.H.A.—Educational Handwork Association.
E.I.S.—Educational Institute of Scotland.
E.L.U.—English Lacrosse Union.
E.P.N.S.—Electroplated Nickel Silver.
E.T.U.—Electrical Trades Union.
E.U.—Evangelical Union.
*ex.div.*—Without dividend.
*ex.int.*—without interest.

F.—Fahrenheit.
F.A.—Football Association.
F.B.I.—Federal Bureau of Investigation; Federation of British Industries.
F.G.—Foot Guards.
F.M.S.—Federated Malay States.
F.P.—Fine paper.

G.F.S.—Girls' Friendly Society.
G.H.Q.—General Headquarters.
gm.—gramme.
G.M.T.—Greenwich Mean Time.
G.P.—General paralysis.
G.P.O.—General Post Office.
gr.—grain.
grm.—gramme.

h. & c.—hot and cold.
hhd.—hogshead.
hl.—hectolitre.
H.L.I.—Highland Light Infantry.
hm.—hectometre.
H.M.S.—Her Majesty's Ship; Her Majesty's Service.

*Ib.* or *Ibid.*—*Ibidem*, In the same place.
I.D.B.—Illicit diamond buying.
I.D.L.—International Date Line.
I.H.S.—(*Greek* 'IH), Jesus.
I.L.P.—Independent Labour Party.
inc.—incorporated.
I.N.R.I.—*Jesus Nazarenus, Rex Iudæorum*, Jesus of Nazareth King of the Jews.
I.O.F.—Independent Order of Foresters.
I.O.G.T.Independent Order of Good Templars.
I.O.O.F.—Independent Order of Oddfellows.
I.O.P.—Institute of Painters in Oil-Colours.
I.O.U.—I Owe You.
I.Q.—Intelligence Quotient.
I.R.A.—Irish Republican Army.
I.W.W.—Industrial Workers of the World.

kc.—kilocycles.
K.C.L.—King's College, London.
kg.—kilogramme.
kl.—kilolitre.
km.—kilometre.
K.O.S.B.—King's Own Scottish Borderers.
K.R.R.—King's Royal Rifles.
kv.—kilovolt.
kw.—kilowatt.

L.A.—Library Association.
lb.—*libra*, pound (weight).
L.G.U.—Ladies' Golfing Union.
L.I.—Light Infantry.
L.K.A.—Ladies' Kennel Association.
L.M.S.—London Missionary Society.
L.T.A.—Lawn Tennis Association; London Teachers' Association.
L.W.L.—Load Water Line.

m.—metre; mile; million.
M.A.—Military Academy.
M.A.A.Ltd.—Motor Agents' Association, Limited.
M.B.T.A.—MetropolitanⒷBoard Teachers' Association
M.C.C.—Marylebone Cricket Club; Middlesex County County.
Med. Jur.—Medical Jurisprudence.
M.F.B.—Metropolitan Fire Brigade.
mg.—milligram.
M.I.—Military Intelligence.
misc.—miscellaneous.
ml.—millilitre.
M.L.A.—Modern Language Association.
mm.—millimetre.
M.O.—Money Order.
M.P.—Metropolitan Police; Mounted Police.
MS.; MSS.—Manuscript; Manuscripts.
M.T.A.—Motor Trade Association; Music Teachers' Association.
M.U.—Mother's Union; Motor Union.

N.A.A.—National Artillery Association.
N.A.A.F.I.—Navy, Army and Air Force Institute.
N.A.L.G.O.—National Association of Local Government Officers.
N.B.—New Brunswick; North British; *Nota bene* (note well).
N.C.C.—National Coursing Club.
N.C.U.—National Cyclists' Union.
N.E.—New England.
N.E.D.—New i.e. Oxford English Dictionary.
nem.con.—*Nemine contradicente*, No one contradicting.
Nem.diss.—*Nemine dissentiente*, No one dissenting.
N.F.U.—National Froebel Union.
N.F.W.T.—National Federation of Women Teachers.
N.H.C.—National Hunt Committee.
N.H.S.—National Health Service.
N.I.D.—Naval Intelligence Division.
N.L.—Navy League; North Latitude.
N.L.C.—National Liberal Club.
N.L.F.—National Liberal Federation.
N.L.I.—National Life-boat Institution.
N.O.D.—Naval Ordnance Department.
nom.—nominal.
Non-con.—Nonconformist.
*non seq.*—*non sequitur*, it does not follow.
N.P.L.—National Physical Laboratory.
N.R.A.—National Rifle Association.
N.S.—New Series; New Style; Nova Scotia; Numismatic Society.
N.S.A.M.—National Society of Art Masters.
N.S.P.E.—National Society of Physical Education.
N.S.W.—New South Wales.
N.T.—New Testament; Northern Territory (Australia).
N.U.R.—National Union of Railwaymen.
N.U.S.E.C.—National Union of Societies for Equal Citizenship.
N.U.T.—National Union of Teachers.
N.U.W.S.S.—National Union of Women's Suffrage Societies.
N.U.W.T.—National Union of Women Teachers.
N.U.W.W.—National Union of Women Workers.
N.Y.H.S.—New York Historical Society.

O.C.—Old Carthusian; **Old Catholic.**
o.c.—*opere citato,* In the work cited.
O.D.—*Ordnance Datum;* Old Dutch.
O.E.D.—Oxford English Dictionary.
O.H.L.—Oxford Higher Local Examinations.
O.H.M.S.—On Her Majesty's Service.
O.H.S.—Oxford Historical Society.
O.L.—Old Latin.
O.M.S.—Organisation for the Maintenance of Supplies.
O.P.—*Ordo Prædictaorum,* Dominican Order; Out of Print (books); Opposite Prompt (theatre).
op.—opus.
O.S.—Old Saxon; Old Style; Ordnance Survey; Original Series; Outsize.
O.S.N.C.—Orient Steam Navigation Company.
O.T.C.—Officers' Training Corps.
O.U.—Oxford University.
O.U.D.S.—Oxford University Dramatic Society.
O.U.P.—Oxford University Press.
oz.—ounce.

P.A.—**Protestant Alliance.**
p.a.—*per annum,* yearly.
P. & O.—Peninsular and Oriental.
P.B.—Plymouth Brethren; Prayer Book; Primitive Baptists.
P.C.—Parish Council; *Patres Conscripti,* Conscript Fathers; Perpetual Curate; Privy Council.
p.c.—per cent; postcard.
P.C.C.—Prerogative Court of Canterbury.
P.E.—Protestant Episcopal.
p.m.—*post meridiem,* afternoon.
P.M.G.—Pall Mall Gazette.
P.N.E.U.—Parents' National Educational Union.
P.O.—Post Office; Postal Order.
P.O.O.—Post Office Order.
P.R.B.—Pre-Raphaelite Brotherhood.
P.S.—Postscript.
p.s.—prompt side (theatre).
P.S.A.—Pleasant Sunday Afternoon.
P.S.N.C.—Pacific Steam Navigation Company.
P.W.D.—Public Works Department.

Q.A.B.—Queen Anne's Bounty.
Q.A.I.M.N.S.—Queen Alexandra's Imperial Military Nursing Service.
Q.A.M.F.N.S.—Queen Alexandra's Military Families Nursing Service.
Q.A.R.N.N.S.—Queen Alexandra's Royal Naval Nursing Service.
Q.C.—Queen's College.
Q.M.A.A.C.—Queen Mary's Army Auxiliary Corps.
Q.S.—Quarter Sessions.
qt.—quart.
Q.U.I.—Queen's University of Ireland.

R.A.—Right Ascension; Royal Academy; Royal Artillery.
R.A.A.—Royal Academy of Arts.
R.A.C.—Royal Agricultural College; Royal Arch Chapter; Royal Automobile Club.
R.A.E.—Royal Aircraft Establishment.
R.A.F.—Royal Air Force.
R.A.G.C.—Royal and Ancient Gold Club.
R.A.M.—Royal Academy of Music.
R.A.M.C.—Royal Army Medical Corps.
R.A.O.B.—Royal Antediluvian Order of Buffaloes.
R.A.O.C.—Royal Army Ordnance Corps.
R.A.S.—Royal Agricultural Society; Royal Astronomical Society; Royal Asiatic Society.
R.B.A.—Royal Society of British Artists.
R.C.—Red Cross; Roman Catholic.
R.C.A.—Royal Cambrian Academy; Royal College of Art.
R.C.C.—Representative Church Council; Roman Catholic Church.
R.C.I.—Royal Colonial Institute.
R.C.M.—Royal College of Music.
R.C.O.—Royal College or Organists.
R.C.P.—Royal College of Physicians; Royal College of Preceptors.
R.C.S.—Royal College of Surgeons; Royal Corps of Signals.

R.C.V.S.—Royal College of Veterinary Surgeons.
R.D.C.—Rural District Council.
R.D.S.—Royal Dublin Society.
R.E.—Royal Engineers; Royal Society o f Painter Etchers.
R.F.C.—Royal Flying Corps.
R.G.G.—Royal Grenadier Guards.
R.G.S.—Royal Geographical Society.
R.H.—Royal Highlanders.
R.H.A.—Royal Hibernian Academy; Royal Horse Artillery.
R.H.S.—Royal Humane Society.
R.I.—Rhode Island; Royal Institution; Royal Institute of Painters in Water Colours.
R.I.A.—Royal Irish Academy.
R.I.A.M.—Royal Irish Academy of Music.
R.I.B.A.—Royal Institute of British Architects.
R.I.C.—Royal Irish Constabulary.
R.I.P.—*Requiescat in pace,* May he (she) rest in peace.
R.L.O.—Returned Letter Office.
R.M.—Royal Mail; Royal Marines.
R.M.A.—Royal Military Academy.
R.M.C.—Royal Military College.
R.Met.S.—Royal Meteorological Society.
R.M.S.—Royal Mail Service; Royal Mail Steamer; Royal Microscopical Society; Royal Society of Miniature Painters.
R.N. Royal Navy.
R.N.D.—Royal Naval Division.
R.N.R.—Royal Naval Reserve.
R.N.V.R.—Royal Naval Volunteer Reserve.
R.O.—Receiving Office; Recruiting Office; Royal Observatory.
R.O.I.—Royal Institute of Oil Painters.
R.P.—Reformed Presbyterian; Rules of Procedure; Reprinting (books).
R.P.A.—Rationalist Press Association.
R.P.E.—Reformed Protestant Episcopal.
R.R.C.—Royal Red Cross.
R.S.—Royal Society; Revised Statutes.
R.S.A.—Royal Scottish Academy; Royal Society of Antiquaries; Royal Society of Arts.
R.S.D.—Royal Society of Dublin.
R.S.E.—Royal Society of Edinburgh.
R.S.F.—Royal Scottish Fusiliers.
R.S.L.—Royal Society of Literature; Royal Society of London.
R.S.M.—Royal School of Medicine; Royal School of Mines.
R.S.P.C.A.—Royal Society for the Prevention of Cruelty to Animals.
R.S.V.P.—*Repondez s'il vous plait.* Please reply.
R.S.W.—Royal Scottish Society of Painters in Water-Colours.
R.T.S.—Religious Tract Society; Royal Toxophilite Society.
R.T.Y.C.—Royal Thames Yacht Club.
R.U.—Rugby Union.
R.U.S.I.—Royal United Service Institution.
R.W.—Royal Warrant.
R.W.A.—Royal West of England Academy.
R.W.S.—Royal Society of Painters in Water-Colours.
R.Y.S.—Royal Yacht Squadron.

S.A.A.A.—Scottish Amateur Athletic Association.
S.A.E.—Society of Automobile Engineers.
S.A.S.—Special Air Service.
S.B.A.—Scottish Bowling Association; Society of Biblical Archaeology.
S.C.M.—State Certified Midwife.
S.C.M.U.A.—Scottish Commerical Motor Users' Association.
S.C.U.—Scottish Cyclists' Union.
S.D.F.—Social Democratic Federation.
S.F.A.—Scottish Football Association.
S.J.—Society of Jesus.
S.M.E.—School of Military Engineering.
S.M.M.& T.—Society of Motor Manufacturers and Traders.
S.M.T.A.—Scottish Motor Trade Association.

S.O.S.—Morse Code Signal of Distress at Sea, "Save our Souls".
S.P.C.K.—Society for Promoting Christian Knowledge.
S.P.G.—Society for the Propagation of the Gospel.
S.P.R.—Society for Psychical Research.
S.P.R.L.—Society for the Promotion of Religion and Learning.
S.P.V.D.—Society for the Prevention of Venereal Disease.
S.R.C.—Students' Representative Council.
S.S.C.—*Societas Sanctæ Crucis*, Society of the Holy Cross.
S.S.U.—Sunday School Union.
S.W.B.—South Wales Borderers.

T.A.—Territorial Army.
T.A.B.—Total Abstinence Brotherhood.
T.A.R.C.—Thames Amateur Rowing Club.
T.C.A.—Training College Association.
T.C.D.—Trinity College, Dublin.
T.C.O.—Trinity College, Oxford.
T.F.—Territorial Forces.
T.F.N.S.—Territorial Force Nursing Society.
T.N.T.—Trinitrotoluene (high explosive).
T.N.X.—Trinitroxylol (high explosive).
T.O.—Telegraph Office; Turn Over.
Toc. H.—Talbot House.
T.P.C.—Thames Punting Club.
T.R.C.—Teachers' Registration Council; Thames Rowing Club; Tithe Rent Charge.
T.T.—Teetotaller.
T.U.C.—Trade Union Congress.

U.C.—University College.

U.D.C.—Urban District Council.
U.F.C.—United Free Church of Scotland.
U.K.A.—United Kingdom Alliance.
U.S.A.—United States of America.
U.S.C.—United States of Colombia.
U.S.I.—United Service Institution.
U.U.—University Union.

V. & A. Mus.—Victoria and Albert Museum.
V.C.—Vice-Chairman; -Chancellor; -Consul.
V.I.P.—Very Important Person.

w.—watt.
W.D.—War Department.
W.E.A.—Workers Educational Association.
W.E.U.—Women's Educational Union.
W.F.L.—Women's Freedom League.
W.H.M.A.—Women's Home Missionary Association.
W.L.F.—Women's Liberal Federation.
W.O.—War Office; Walk-over (sport).
W.R.I.—Women's Rural Institute.
W.S.P.U.—Women's Social and Political Union.
W.U.S.L.—Women's United Service League.
W.V.S.—Women's Volunteer Service.

Y.M.C.A.—Young Men's Christian Association.
Y.M.Cath.A.—Young Men's Catholic Association.
Y.M.C.U.—Young Men's Christian Union.
Y.M.F.S.—Young Men's Friendly Society.
Y.W.C.A.—Young Women's Christian Association.
Y.W.C.T.U.—Young Women's Christian Temperance Union.
Y.W.S.—Young Wales Society.

Z.S.—Zoological Society.

## PERPETUAL CALENDAR, 1752-1980

| | Common Years | | | | | | | Leap Years | | | | | | |
|---|---|---|---|---|---|---|---|---|---|---|---|---|---|---|
| | 1761 | 1762 | 1757 | 1754 | 1755 | 1758 | 1753 | 1764 | 1768 | 1772 | 1776 | 1780 | 1756 | 1760 |
| | 1767 | 1773 | 1763 | 1765 | 1766 | 1769 | 1759 | 1792 | 1796 | 1812 | 1816 | 1820 | 1784 | 1788 |
| | 1778 | 1779 | 1774 | 1771 | 1777 | 1775 | 1770 | 1804 | 1808 | 1840 | 1844 | 1848 | 1824 | 1828 |
| | 1789 | 1790 | 1785 | 1782 | 1783 | 1786 | 1781 | 1832 | 1836 | 1868 | 1872 | 1876 | 1852 | 1856 |
| | 1795 | 1802 | 1791 | 1793 | 1794 | 1797 | 1787 | 1860 | 1864 | 1896 | 1912 | 1916 | 1880 | 1884 |
| | 1801 | 1813 | 1803 | 1799 | 1800 | 1809 | 1798 | 1888 | 1892 | 1908 | 1940 | 1944 | 1920 | 1924 |
| | 1807 | 1819 | 1814 | 1805 | 1806 | 1815 | 1810 | 1928 | 1904 | 1936 | 1968 | 1972 | 1948 | 1952 |
| | 1818 | 1830 | 1825 | 1811 | 1817 | 1826 | 1821 | 1956 | 1932 | 1964 | | | 1976 | 1980 |
| | 1829 | 1841 | 1831 | 1822 | 1823 | 1837 | 1827 | | 1960 | | | | | |
| | 1835 | 1847 | 1842 | 1833 | 1834 | 1843 | 1838 | | | | | | | |
| | 1846 | 1858 | 1853 | 1839 | 1845 | 1854 | 1849 | | | | | | | |
| | 1857 | 1869 | 1859 | 1850 | 1851 | 1865 | 1855 | | | | | | | |
| | 1863 | 1875 | 1870 | 1861 | 1862 | 1871 | 1866 | | | | | | | |
| | 1874 | 1886 | 1881 | 1867 | 1873 | 1882 | 1877 | | | | | | | |
| | 1885 | 1897 | 1887 | 1878 | 1879 | 1893 | 1883 | | | | | | | |
| | 1891 | 1909 | 1898 | 1889 | 1890 | 1899 | 1894 | | | | | | | |
| | 1903 | 1915 | 1910 | 1895 | 1902 | 1905 | 1900 | | | | | | | |
| | 1914 | 1926 | 1921 | 1901 | 1913 | 1911 | 1906 | | | | | | | |
| | 1925 | 1937 | 1927 | 1907 | 1919 | 1922 | 1917 | | | | | | | |
| | 1931 | 1943 | 1938 | 1918 | 1930 | 1933 | 1923 | | | | | | | |
| | 1942 | 1954 | 1949 | 1929 | 1941 | 1939 | 1934 | | | | | | | |
| | 1953 | 1965 | 1955 | 1935 | 1947 | 1950 | 1945 | | | | | | | |
| | 1959 | | 1966 | 1946 | 1958 | 1961 | 1951 | | | | | | | |
| | | | | 1957 | | 1967 | 1962 | | | | | | | |
| | | | | 1963 | | | | | | | | | | |
| Jan. | 4 | 5 | 6 | 2 | 3 | 7 | 1 | 7 | 5 | 3 | 1 | 6 | 4 | 2 |
| Feb. | 7 | 1 | 2 | 5 | 6 | 3 | 4 | 3 | 1 | 6 | 4 | 2 | 7 | 5 |
| Mar. | 7 | 1 | 2 | 5 | 6 | 3 | 4 | 4 | 2 | 7 | 5 | 3 | 1 | 6 |
| Apr. | 3 | 4 | 5 | 1 | 2 | 6 | 7 | 7 | 5 | 3 | 1 | 6 | 4 | 2 |
| May | 5 | 6 | 7 | 3 | 4 | 1 | 2 | 2 | 7 | 5 | 3 | 1 | 6 | 4 |
| June | 1 | 2 | 3 | 6 | 7 | 4 | 5 | 5 | 3 | 1 | 6 | 4 | 2 | 7 |
| July | 3 | 4 | 5 | 1 | 2 | 6 | 7 | 7 | 5 | 3 | 1 | 6 | 4 | 2 |
| Aug. | 6 | 7 | 1 | 4 | 5 | 2 | 3 | 3 | 1 | 6 | 4 | 2 | 7 | 5 |
| Sep. | 2 | 3 | 4 | 7 | 1 | 5 | 6 | 6 | 4 | 2 | 7 | 5 | 3 | 1 |
| Oct. | 4 | 5 | 6 | 2 | 3 | 7 | 1 | 1 | 6 | 4 | 2 | 7 | 5 | 3 |
| Nov. | 7 | 1 | 2 | 5 | 6 | 3 | 4 | 4 | 2 | 7 | 5 | 3 | 1 | 6 |
| Dec. | 2 | 3 | 4 | 7 | 1 | 5 | 6 | 6 | 4 | 2 | 7 | 5 | 3 | 1 |

NOTE.—To find the day of the week on which a date fell or will fall in a specified year, e.g. 8th October 1863, look for the column in which the year 1863 occurs, viz. column 1, follow the column down to the month October; the figure 4 occurs. Now look in line 4 of the table on page opposite, and along it to figure 8, and at the top of that column you will find the day, Thursday — the 8th Oct, 1863, was a Thursday.

| 7 | 6 | 5 | 4 | 3 | 2 | 1 | |
|---|---|---|---|---|---|---|---|
|   |   |   |   |   |   | 1 | Mon. |
|   |   |   |   |   | 1 | 2 | Tues. |
|   |   |   |   | 1 | 2 | 3 | Wed. |
|   |   |   | 1 | 2 | 3 | 4 | Thurs. |
|   |   | 1 | 2 | 3 | 4 | 5 | Fri. |
|   | 1 | 2 | 3 | 4 | 5 | 6 | Sat. |
| 1 | 2 | 3 | 4 | 5 | 6 | 7 | Sun. |
| 2 | 3 | 4 | 5 | 6 | 7 | 8 | Mon. |
| 3 | 4 | 5 | 6 | 7 | 8 | 9 | Tues. |
| 4 | 5 | 6 | 7 | 8 | 9 | 10 | Wed. |
| 5 | 6 | 7 | 8 | 9 | 10 | 11 | Thurs. |
| 6 | 7 | 8 | 9 | 10 | 11 | 12 | Fri. |
| 7 | 8 | 9 | 10 | 11 | 12 | 13 | Sat. |
| 8 | 9 | 10 | 11 | 12 | 13 | 14 | Sun. |
| 9 | 10 | 11 | 12 | 13 | 14 | 15 | Mon. |
| 10 | 11 | 12 | 13 | 14 | 15 | 16 | Tues. |
| 11 | 12 | 13 | 14 | 15 | 16 | 17 | Wed. |
| 12 | 13 | 14 | 15 | 16 | 17 | 18 | Thurs. |
| 13 | 14 | 15 | 16 | 17 | 18 | 19 | Fri. |
| 14 | 15 | 16 | 17 | 18 | 19 | 20 | Sat. |
| 15 | 16 | 17 | 18 | 19 | 20 | 21 | Sun. |
| 16 | 17 | 18 | 19 | 20 | 21 | 22 | Mon. |
| 17 | 18 | 19 | 20 | 21 | 22 | 23 | Tues. |
| 18 | 19 | 20 | 21 | 22 | 23 | 24 | Wed. |
| 19 | 20 | 21 | 22 | 23 | 24 | 25 | Thurs. |
| 20 | 21 | 22 | 23 | 24 | 25 | 26 | Fri. |
| 21 | 22 | 23 | 24 | 25 | 26 | 27 | Sat. |
| 22 | 23 | 24 | 25 | 26 | 27 | 28 | Sun. |
| 23 | 24 | 25 | 26 | 27 | 28 | 29 | Mon. |
| 24 | 25 | 26 | 27 | 28 | 29 | 30 | Tues. |
| 25 | 26 | 27 | 28 | 29 | 30 | 31 | Wed. |
| 26 | 27 | 28 | 29 | 30 | 31 |   | Thurs. |
| 27 | 28 | 29 | 30 | 31 |   |   | Fri. |
| 28 | 29 | 30 | 31 |   |   |   | Sat. |
| 29 | 30 | 31 |   |   |   |   | Sun. |
| 30 | 31 |   |   |   |   |   | Mon. |
| 31 |   |   |   |   |   |   | Tues. |

## READY RECKONER.

### ⅛d.

| No. | £ | s. | d. | No. | £ | s. | d. | No. | £ | s. | d. |
|---|---|---|---|---|---|---|---|---|---|---|---|
| 2 | — | — | — ¼ | 36 | — | — | 4½ | 70 | — | — | 8¾ |
| 3 | — | — | — ⅜ | 37 | — | — | 4⅝ | 71 | — | — | 8⅞ |
| 4 | — | — | — ½ | 38 | — | — | 4¾ | 72 | — | — | 9 |
| 5 | — | — | — ⅝ | 39 | — | — | 4⅞ | 73 | — | — | 9⅛ |
| 6 | — | — | — ¾ | 40 | — | — | 5 | 74 | — | — | 9¼ |
| 7 | — | — | — ⅞ | 41 | — | — | 5⅛ | 75 | — | — | 9⅜ |
| 8 | — | — | 1 | 42 | — | — | 5¼ | 76 | — | — | 9½ |
| 9 | — | — | 1⅛ | 43 | — | — | 5⅜ | 77 | — | — | 9⅝ |
| 10 | — | — | 1¼ | 44 | — | — | 5½ | 78 | — | — | 9¾ |
| 11 | — | — | 1⅜ | 45 | — | — | 5⅝ | 79 | — | — | 9⅞ |
| 12 | — | — | 1½ | 46 | — | — | 5¾ | 80 | — | — | 10 |
| 13 | — | — | 1⅝ | 47 | — | — | 5⅞ | 81 | — | — | 10⅛ |
| 14 | — | — | 1¾ | 48 | — | — | 6 | 82 | — | — | 10¼ |
| 15 | — | — | 1⅞ | 49 | — | — | 6⅛ | 83 | — | — | 10⅜ |
| 16 | — | — | 2 | 50 | — | — | 6¼ | 84 | — | — | 10½ |
| 17 | — | — | 2⅛ | 51 | — | — | 6⅜ | 85 | — | — | 10⅝ |
| 18 | — | — | 2¼ | 52 | — | — | 6½ | 86 | — | — | 10¾ |
| 19 | — | — | 2⅜ | 53 | — | — | 6⅝ | 87 | — | — | 10⅞ |
| 20 | — | — | 2½ | 54 | — | — | 6¾ | 88 | — | — | 11 |
| 21 | — | — | 2⅝ | 55 | — | — | 6⅞ | 89 | — | — | 11⅛ |
| 22 | — | — | 2¾ | 56 | — | — | 7 | 90 | — | — | 11¼ |
| 23 | — | — | 2⅞ | 57 | — | — | 7⅛ | 91 | — | — | 11⅜ |
| 24 | — | — | 3 | 58 | — | — | 7¼ | 92 | — | — | 11½ |
| 25 | — | — | 3⅛ | 59 | — | — | 7⅜ | 93 | — | — | 11⅝ |
| 26 | — | — | 3¼ | 60 | — | — | 7½ | 94 | — | — | 11¾ |
| 27 | — | — | 3⅜ | 61 | — | — | 7⅝ | 95 | — | — | 11⅞ |
| 28 | — | — | 3½ | 62 | — | — | 7¾ | 96 | — | 1 | 0 |
| 29 | — | — | 3⅝ | 63 | — | — | 7⅞ | 97 | — | 1 | 0⅛ |
| 30 | — | — | 3¾ | 64 | — | — | 8 | 98 | — | 1 | 0¼ |
| 31 | — | — | 3⅞ | 65 | — | — | 8⅛ | 99 | — | 1 | 0⅜ |
| 32 | — | — | 4 | 66 | — | — | 8¼ | 100 | — | 1 | 0½ |
| 33 | — | — | 4⅛ | 67 | — | — | 8⅜ | 144 | — | 1 | 6 |
| 34 | — | — | 4¼ | 68 | — | — | 8½ | 500 | — | 5 | 2½ |
| 35 | — | — | 4⅜ | 69 | — | — | 8⅝ | 750 | — | 7 | 9¾ |

### ¼d.

| No. | £ | s. | d. | No. | £ | s. | d. | No. | £ | s. | d. |
|---|---|---|---|---|---|---|---|---|---|---|---|
| 2 | — | — | — ½ | 36 | — | — | 9 | 70 | — | 1 | 5½ |
| 3 | — | — | — ¾ | 37 | — | — | 9¼ | 71 | — | 1 | 5¾ |
| 4 | — | — | 1 | 38 | — | — | 9½ | 72 | — | 1 | 6 |
| 5 | — | — | 1¼ | 39 | — | — | 9¾ | 73 | — | 1 | 6¼ |
| 6 | — | — | 1½ | 40 | — | — | 10 | 74 | — | 1 | 6½ |
| 7 | — | — | 1¾ | 41 | — | — | 10¼ | 75 | — | 1 | 6¾ |
| 8 | — | — | 2 | 42 | — | — | 10½ | 76 | — | 1 | 7 |
| 9 | — | — | 2¼ | 43 | — | — | 10¾ | 77 | — | 1 | 7¼ |
| 10 | — | — | 2½ | 44 | — | — | 11 | 78 | — | 1 | 7½ |
| 11 | — | — | 2¾ | 45 | — | — | 11¼ | 79 | — | 1 | 7¾ |
| 12 | — | — | 3 | 46 | — | — | 11½ | 80 | — | 1 | 8 |
| 13 | — | — | 3¼ | 47 | — | — | 11¾ | 81 | — | 1 | 8¼ |
| 14 | — | — | 3½ | 48 | — | 1 | 0 | 82 | — | 1 | 8½ |
| 15 | — | — | 3¾ | 49 | — | 1 | 0¼ | 83 | — | 1 | 8¾ |
| 16 | — | — | 4 | 50 | — | 1 | 0½ | 84 | — | 1 | 9 |
| 17 | — | — | 4¼ | 51 | — | 1 | 0¾ | 85 | — | 1 | 9¼ |
| 18 | — | — | 4½ | 52 | — | 1 | 1 | 86 | — | 1 | 9½ |
| 19 | — | — | 4¾ | 53 | — | 1 | 1¼ | 87 | — | 1 | 9¾ |
| 20 | — | — | 5 | 54 | — | 1 | 1½ | 88 | — | 1 | 10 |
| 21 | — | — | 5¼ | 55 | — | 1 | 1¾ | 89 | — | 1 | 10¼ |
| 22 | — | — | 5½ | 56 | — | 1 | 2 | 90 | — | 1 | 10½ |
| 23 | — | — | 5¾ | 57 | — | 1 | 2¼ | 91 | — | 1 | 10¾ |
| 24 | — | — | 6 | 58 | — | 1 | 2½ | 92 | — | 1 | 11 |
| 25 | — | — | 6¼ | 59 | — | 1 | 2¾ | 93 | — | 1 | 11¼ |
| 26 | — | — | 6½ | 60 | — | 1 | 3 | 94 | — | 1 | 11½ |
| 27 | — | — | 6¾ | 61 | — | 1 | 3¼ | 95 | — | 1 | 11¾ |
| 28 | — | — | 7 | 62 | — | 1 | 3½ | 96 | — | 2 | 0 |
| 29 | — | — | 7¼ | 63 | — | 1 | 3¾ | 97 | — | 2 | 0¼ |
| 30 | — | — | 7½ | 64 | — | 1 | 4 | 98 | — | 2 | 0½ |
| 31 | — | — | 7¾ | 65 | — | 1 | 4¼ | 99 | — | 2 | 0¾ |
| 32 | — | — | 8 | 66 | — | 1 | 4½ | 100 | — | 2 | 1 |
| 33 | — | — | 8¼ | 67 | — | 1 | 4¾ | 144 | — | 3 | 0 |
| 34 | — | — | 8½ | 68 | — | 1 | 5 | 500 | — | 10 | 5 |
| 35 | — | — | 8¾ | 69 | — | 1 | 5¼ | 750 | — | 15 | 7½ |

### ½d.

| No. | £ | s. | d. | No. | £ | s. | d. | No. | £ | s. | d. |
|---|---|---|---|---|---|---|---|---|---|---|---|
| 2 | — | — | 1 | 36 | — | 1 | 6 | 70 | — | 2 | 11 |
| 3 | — | — | 1½ | 37 | — | 1 | 6½ | 71 | — | 2 | 11½ |
| 4 | — | — | 2 | 38 | — | 1 | 7 | 72 | — | 3 | 0 |
| 5 | — | — | 2½ | 39 | — | 1 | 7½ | 73 | — | 3 | 0½ |
| 6 | — | — | 3 | 40 | — | 1 | 8 | 74 | — | 3 | 1 |
| 7 | — | — | 3½ | 41 | — | 1 | 8½ | 75 | — | 3 | 1½ |
| 8 | — | — | 4 | 42 | — | 1 | 9 | 76 | — | 3 | 2 |
| 9 | — | — | 4½ | 43 | — | 1 | 9½ | 77 | — | 3 | 2½ |
| 10 | — | — | 5 | 44 | — | 1 | 10 | 78 | — | 3 | 3 |
| 11 | — | — | 5½ | 45 | — | 1 | 10½ | 79 | — | 3 | 3½ |
| 12 | — | — | 6 | 46 | — | 1 | 11 | 80 | — | 3 | 4 |
| 13 | — | — | 6½ | 47 | — | 1 | 11½ | 81 | — | 3 | 4½ |
| 14 | — | — | 7 | 48 | — | 2 | 0 | 82 | — | 3 | 5 |
| 15 | — | — | 7½ | 49 | — | 2 | 0½ | 83 | — | 3 | 5½ |
| 16 | — | — | 8 | 50 | — | 2 | 1 | 84 | — | 3 | 6 |
| 17 | — | — | 8½ | 51 | — | 2 | 1½ | 85 | — | 3 | 6½ |
| 18 | — | — | 9 | 52 | — | 2 | 2 | 86 | — | 3 | 7 |
| 19 | — | — | 9½ | 53 | — | 2 | 2½ | 87 | — | 3 | 7½ |
| 20 | — | — | 10 | 54 | — | 2 | 3 | 88 | — | 3 | 8 |
| 21 | — | — | 10½ | 55 | — | 2 | 3½ | 89 | — | 3 | 8½ |
| 22 | — | — | 11 | 56 | — | 2 | 4 | 90 | — | 3 | 9 |
| 23 | — | — | 11½ | 57 | — | 2 | 4½ | 91 | — | 3 | 9½ |
| 24 | — | 1 | 0 | 58 | — | 2 | 5 | 92 | — | 3 | 10 |
| 25 | — | 1 | 0½ | 59 | — | 2 | 5½ | 93 | — | 3 | 10½ |
| 26 | — | 1 | 1 | 60 | — | 2 | 6 | 94 | — | 3 | 11 |
| 27 | — | 1 | 1½ | 61 | — | 2 | 6½ | 95 | — | 3 | 11½ |
| 28 | — | 1 | 2 | 62 | — | 2 | 7 | 96 | — | 4 | 0 |
| 29 | — | 1 | 2½ | 63 | — | 2 | 7½ | 97 | — | 4 | 0½ |
| 30 | — | 1 | 3 | 64 | — | 2 | 8 | 98 | — | 4 | 1 |
| 31 | — | 1 | 3½ | 65 | — | 2 | 8½ | 99 | — | 4 | 1½ |
| 32 | — | 1 | 4 | 66 | — | 2 | 9 | 100 | — | 4 | 2 |
| 33 | — | 1 | 4½ | 67 | — | 2 | 9½ | 144 | — | 6 | 0 |
| 34 | — | 1 | 5 | 68 | — | 2 | 10 | 500 | 1 | 0 | 10 |
| 35 | — | 1 | 5½ | 69 | — | 2 | 10½ | 750 | 1 | 11 | 3 |

### ¾d.

| No. | £ | s. | d. | No. | £ | s. | d. | No. | £ | s. | d. |
|---|---|---|---|---|---|---|---|---|---|---|---|
| 2 | — | — | 1½ | 36 | — | 2 | 3 | 70 | — | 4 | 4½ |
| 3 | — | — | 2¼ | 37 | — | 2 | 3¾ | 71 | — | 4 | 5¼ |
| 4 | — | — | 3 | 38 | — | 2 | 4½ | 72 | — | 4 | 6 |
| 5 | — | — | 3¾ | 39 | — | 2 | 5¼ | 73 | — | 4 | 6¾ |
| 6 | — | — | 4½ | 40 | — | 2 | 6 | 74 | — | 4 | 7½ |
| 7 | — | — | 5¼ | 41 | — | 2 | 6¾ | 75 | — | 4 | 8¼ |
| 8 | — | — | 6 | 42 | — | 2 | 7½ | 76 | — | 4 | 9 |
| 9 | — | — | 6¾ | 43 | — | 2 | 8¼ | 77 | — | 4 | 9¾ |
| 10 | — | — | 7½ | 44 | — | 2 | 9 | 78 | — | 4 | 10½ |
| 11 | — | — | 8¼ | 45 | — | 2 | 9¾ | 79 | — | 4 | 11¼ |
| 12 | — | — | 9 | 46 | — | 2 | 10½ | 80 | — | 5 | 0 |
| 13 | — | — | 9¾ | 47 | — | 2 | 11¼ | 81 | — | 5 | 0¾ |
| 14 | — | — | 10½ | 48 | — | 3 | 0 | 82 | — | 5 | 1½ |
| 15 | — | — | 11¼ | 49 | — | 3 | 0¾ | 83 | — | 5 | 2¼ |
| 16 | — | 1 | 0 | 50 | — | 3 | 1½ | 84 | — | 5 | 3 |
| 17 | — | 1 | 0¾ | 51 | — | 3 | 2¼ | 85 | — | 5 | 3¾ |
| 18 | — | 1 | 1½ | 52 | — | 3 | 3 | 86 | — | 5 | 4½ |
| 19 | — | 1 | 2¼ | 53 | — | 3 | 3¾ | 87 | — | 5 | 5¼ |
| 20 | — | 1 | 3 | 54 | — | 3 | 4½ | 88 | — | 5 | 6 |
| 21 | — | 1 | 3¾ | 55 | — | 3 | 5¼ | 89 | — | 5 | 6¾ |
| 22 | — | 1 | 4½ | 56 | — | 3 | 6 | 90 | — | 5 | 7½ |
| 23 | — | 1 | 5¼ | 57 | — | 3 | 6¾ | 91 | — | 5 | 8¼ |
| 24 | — | 1 | 6 | 58 | — | 3 | 7½ | 92 | — | 5 | 9 |
| 25 | — | 1 | 6¾ | 59 | — | 3 | 8¼ | 93 | — | 5 | 9¾ |
| 26 | — | 1 | 7½ | 60 | — | 3 | 9 | 94 | — | 5 | 10½ |
| 27 | — | 1 | 8¼ | 61 | — | 3 | 9¾ | 95 | — | 5 | 11¼ |
| 28 | — | 1 | 9 | 62 | — | 3 | 10½ | 96 | — | 6 | 0 |
| 29 | — | 1 | 9¾ | 63 | — | 3 | 11¼ | 97 | — | 6 | 0¾ |
| 30 | — | 1 | 10½ | 64 | — | 4 | 0 | 98 | — | 6 | 1½ |
| 31 | — | 1 | 11¼ | 65 | — | 4 | 0¾ | 99 | — | 6 | 2¼ |
| 32 | — | 2 | 0 | 66 | — | 4 | 1½ | 100 | — | 6 | 3 |
| 33 | — | 2 | 0¾ | 67 | — | 4 | 2¼ | 144 | — | 9 | 0 |
| 34 | — | 2 | 1½ | 68 | — | 4 | 3 | 500 | 1 | 11 | 3 |
| 35 | — | 2 | 2¼ | 69 | — | 4 | 3¾ | 750 | 2 | 6 | 10½ |

# READY RECKONER.

## 1d.

| No. | £ | s. | d. | No. | £ | s. | d. | No. | £ | s. | d. |
|---|---|---|---|---|---|---|---|---|---|---|---|
| 2 | – | – | 2 | 36 | – | 3 | 0 | 70 | – | 5 | 10 |
| 3 | – | – | 3 | 37 | – | 3 | 1 | 71 | – | 5 | 11 |
| 4 | – | – | 4 | 38 | – | 3 | 2 | 72 | – | 6 | 0 |
| 5 | – | – | 5 | 39 | – | 3 | 3 | 73 | – | 6 | 1 |
| 6 | – | – | 6 | 40 | – | 3 | 4 | 74 | – | 6 | 2 |
| 7 | – | – | 7 | 41 | – | 3 | 5 | 75 | – | 6 | 3 |
| 8 | – | – | 8 | 42 | – | 3 | 6 | 76 | – | 6 | 4 |
| 9 | – | – | 9 | 43 | – | 3 | 7 | 77 | – | 6 | 5 |
| 10 | – | – | 10 | 44 | – | 3 | 8 | 78 | – | 6 | 6 |
| 11 | – | – | 11 | 45 | – | 3 | 9 | 79 | – | 6 | 7 |
| 12 | – | 1 | 0 | 46 | – | 3 | 10 | 80 | – | 6 | 8 |
| 13 | – | 1 | 1 | 47 | – | 3 | 11 | 81 | – | 6 | 9 |
| 14 | – | 1 | 2 | 48 | – | 4 | 0 | 82 | – | 6 | 10 |
| 15 | – | 1 | 3 | 49 | – | 4 | 1 | 83 | – | 6 | 11 |
| 16 | – | 1 | 4 | 50 | – | 4 | 2 | 84 | – | 7 | 0 |
| 17 | – | 1 | 5 | 51 | – | 4 | 3 | 85 | – | 7 | 1 |
| 18 | – | 1 | 6 | 52 | – | 4 | 4 | 86 | – | 7 | 2 |
| 19 | – | 1 | 7 | 53 | – | 4 | 5 | 87 | – | 7 | 3 |
| 20 | – | 1 | 8 | 54 | – | 4 | 6 | 88 | – | 7 | 4 |
| 21 | – | 1 | 9 | 55 | – | 4 | 7 | 89 | – | 7 | 5 |
| 22 | – | 1 | 10 | 56 | – | 4 | 8 | 90 | – | 7 | 6 |
| 23 | – | 1 | 11 | 57 | – | 4 | 9 | 91 | – | 7 | 7 |
| 24 | – | 2 | 0 | 58 | – | 4 | 10 | 92 | – | 7 | 8 |
| 25 | – | 2 | 1 | 59 | – | 4 | 11 | 93 | – | 7 | 9 |
| 26 | – | 2 | 2 | 60 | – | 5 | 0 | 94 | – | 7 | 10 |
| 27 | – | 2 | 3 | 61 | – | 5 | 1 | 95 | – | 7 | 11 |
| 28 | – | 2 | 4 | 62 | – | 5 | 2 | 96 | – | 8 | 0 |
| 29 | – | 2 | 5 | 63 | – | 5 | 3 | 97 | – | 8 | 1 |
| 30 | – | 2 | 6 | 64 | – | 5 | 4 | 98 | – | 8 | 2 |
| 31 | – | 2 | 7 | 65 | – | 5 | 5 | 99 | – | 8 | 3 |
| 32 | – | 2 | 8 | 66 | – | 5 | 6 | 100 | – | 8 | 4 |
| 33 | – | 2 | 9 | 67 | – | 5 | 7 | 144 | – | 12 | 0 |
| 34 | – | 2 | 10 | 68 | – | 5 | 8 | 500 | 2 | 1 | 8 |
| 35 | – | 2 | 11 | 69 | – | 5 | 9 | 750 | 3 | 2 | 6 |

## 1¼d.

| No. | £ | s. | d. | No. | £ | s. | d. | No. | £ | s. | d. |
|---|---|---|---|---|---|---|---|---|---|---|---|
| 2 | – | – | 2½ | 36 | – | 3 | 9 | 70 | – | 7 | 3½ |
| 3 | – | – | 3¾ | 37 | – | 3 | 10¼ | 71 | – | 7 | 4¾ |
| 4 | – | – | 5 | 38 | – | 3 | 11½ | 72 | – | 7 | 6 |
| 5 | – | – | 6¼ | 39 | – | 4 | 0¾ | 73 | – | 7 | 7¼ |
| 6 | – | – | 7½ | 40 | – | 4 | 2 | 74 | – | 7 | 8½ |
| 7 | – | – | 8¾ | 41 | – | 4 | 3¼ | 75 | – | 7 | 9¾ |
| 8 | – | – | 10 | 42 | – | 4 | 4½ | 76 | – | 7 | 11 |
| 9 | – | – | 11¼ | 43 | – | 4 | 5¾ | 77 | – | 8 | 0¼ |
| 10 | – | 1 | 0½ | 44 | – | 4 | 7 | 78 | – | 8 | 1½ |
| 11 | – | 1 | 1¾ | 45 | – | 4 | 8¼ | 79 | – | 8 | 2¾ |
| 12 | – | 1 | 3 | 46 | – | 4 | 9½ | 80 | – | 8 | 4 |
| 13 | – | 1 | 4¼ | 47 | – | 4 | 10¾ | 81 | – | 8 | 5¼ |
| 14 | – | 1 | 5½ | 48 | – | 5 | 0 | 82 | – | 8 | 6½ |
| 15 | – | 1 | 6¾ | 49 | – | 5 | 1¼ | 83 | – | 8 | 7¾ |
| 16 | – | 1 | 8 | 50 | – | 5 | 2½ | 84 | – | 8 | 9 |
| 17 | – | 1 | 9¼ | 51 | – | 5 | 3¾ | 85 | – | 8 | 10¼ |
| 18 | – | 1 | 10½ | 52 | – | 5 | 5 | 86 | – | 8 | 11½ |
| 19 | – | 1 | 11¾ | 53 | – | 5 | 6¼ | 87 | – | 9 | 0¾ |
| 20 | – | 2 | 1 | 54 | – | 5 | 7½ | 88 | – | 9 | 2 |
| 21 | – | 2 | 2¼ | 55 | – | 5 | 8¾ | 89 | – | 9 | 3¼ |
| 22 | – | 2 | 3½ | 56 | – | 5 | 10 | 90 | – | 9 | 4½ |
| 23 | – | 2 | 4¾ | 57 | – | 5 | 11¼ | 91 | – | 9 | 5¾ |
| 24 | – | 2 | 6 | 58 | – | 6 | 0½ | 92 | – | 9 | 7 |
| 25 | – | 2 | 7¼ | 59 | – | 6 | 1¾ | 93 | – | 9 | 8¼ |
| 26 | – | 2 | 8½ | 60 | – | 6 | 3 | 94 | – | 9 | 9½ |
| 27 | – | 2 | 9¾ | 61 | – | 6 | 4¼ | 95 | – | 9 | 10¾ |
| 28 | – | 2 | 11 | 62 | – | 6 | 5½ | 96 | – | 10 | 0 |
| 29 | – | 3 | 0¼ | 63 | – | 6 | 6¾ | 97 | – | 10 | 1¼ |
| 30 | – | 3 | 1½ | 64 | – | 6 | 8 | 98 | – | 10 | 2½ |
| 31 | – | 3 | 2¾ | 65 | – | 6 | 9¼ | 99 | – | 10 | 3¾ |
| 32 | – | 3 | 4 | 66 | – | 6 | 10½ | 100 | – | 10 | 5 |
| 33 | – | 3 | 5¼ | 67 | – | 6 | 11¾ | 144 | – | 15 | 0 |
| 34 | – | 3 | 6½ | 68 | – | 7 | 1 | 500 | 2 | 12 | 1 |
| 35 | – | 3 | 7¾ | 69 | – | 7 | 2¼ | 750 | 3 | 18 | 1½ |

## 1½d.

| No. | £ | s. | d. | No. | £ | s. | d. | No. | £ | s. | d. |
|---|---|---|---|---|---|---|---|---|---|---|---|
| 2 | – | – | 3 | 36 | – | 4 | 6 | 70 | – | 8 | 9 |
| 3 | – | – | 4½ | 37 | – | 4 | 7½ | 71 | – | 8 | 10½ |
| 4 | – | – | 6 | 38 | – | 4 | 9 | 72 | – | 9 | 0 |
| 5 | – | – | 7½ | 39 | – | 4 | 10½ | 73 | – | 9 | 1½ |
| 6 | – | – | 9 | 40 | – | 5 | 0 | 74 | – | 9 | 3 |
| 7 | – | – | 10½ | 41 | – | 5 | 1½ | 75 | – | 9 | 4½ |
| 8 | – | 1 | 0 | 42 | – | 5 | 3 | 76 | – | 9 | 6 |
| 9 | – | 1 | 1½ | 43 | – | 5 | 4½ | 77 | – | 9 | 7½ |
| 10 | – | 1 | 3 | 44 | – | 5 | 6 | 78 | – | 9 | 9 |
| 11 | – | 1 | 4½ | 45 | – | 5 | 7½ | 79 | – | 9 | 10½ |
| 12 | – | 1 | 6 | 46 | – | 5 | 9 | 80 | – | 10 | 0 |
| 13 | – | 1 | 7½ | 47 | – | 5 | 10½ | 81 | – | 10 | 1½ |
| 14 | – | 1 | 9 | 48 | – | 6 | 0 | 82 | – | 10 | 3 |
| 15 | – | 1 | 10½ | 49 | – | 6 | 1½ | 83 | – | 10 | 4½ |
| 16 | – | 2 | 0 | 50 | – | 6 | 3 | 84 | – | 10 | 6 |
| 17 | – | 2 | 1½ | 51 | – | 6 | 4½ | 85 | – | 10 | 7½ |
| 18 | – | 2 | 3 | 52 | – | 6 | 6 | 86 | – | 10 | 9 |
| 19 | – | 2 | 4½ | 53 | – | 6 | 7½ | 87 | – | 10 | 10½ |
| 20 | – | 2 | 6 | 54 | – | 6 | 9 | 88 | – | 11 | 0 |
| 21 | – | 2 | 7½ | 55 | – | 6 | 10½ | 89 | – | 11 | 1½ |
| 22 | – | 2 | 9 | 56 | – | 7 | 0 | 90 | – | 11 | 3 |
| 23 | – | 2 | 10½ | 57 | – | 7 | 1½ | 91 | – | 11 | 4½ |
| 24 | – | 3 | 0 | 58 | – | 7 | 3 | 92 | – | 11 | 6 |
| 25 | – | 3 | 1½ | 59 | – | 7 | 4½ | 93 | – | 11 | 7½ |
| 26 | – | 3 | 3 | 60 | – | 7 | 6 | 94 | – | 11 | 9 |
| 27 | – | 3 | 4½ | 61 | – | 7 | 7½ | 95 | – | 11 | 10½ |
| 28 | – | 3 | 6 | 62 | – | 7 | 9 | 96 | – | 12 | 0 |
| 29 | – | 3 | 7½ | 63 | – | 7 | 10½ | 97 | – | 12 | 1½ |
| 30 | – | 3 | 9 | 64 | – | 8 | 0 | 98 | – | 12 | 3 |
| 31 | – | 3 | 10½ | 65 | – | 8 | 1½ | 99 | – | 12 | 4½ |
| 32 | – | 4 | 0 | 66 | – | 8 | 3 | 100 | – | 12 | 6 |
| 33 | – | 4 | 1½ | 67 | – | 8 | 4½ | 144 | – | 18 | 0 |
| 34 | – | 4 | 3 | 68 | – | 8 | 6 | 500 | 3 | 2 | 6 |
| 35 | – | 4 | 4½ | 69 | – | 8 | 7½ | 750 | 4 | 13 | 9 |

## 1¾d.

| No. | £ | s. | d. | No. | £ | s. | d. | No. | £ | s. | d. |
|---|---|---|---|---|---|---|---|---|---|---|---|
| 2 | – | – | 3½ | 36 | – | 5 | 3 | 70 | – | 10 | 2½ |
| 3 | – | – | 5¼ | 37 | – | 5 | 4¾ | 71 | – | 10 | 4¼ |
| 4 | – | – | 7 | 38 | – | 5 | 6½ | 72 | – | 10 | 6 |
| 5 | – | – | 8¾ | 39 | – | 5 | 8¼ | 73 | – | 10 | 7¾ |
| 6 | – | – | 10½ | 40 | – | 5 | 10 | 74 | – | 10 | 9½ |
| 7 | – | 1 | 0¼ | 41 | – | 5 | 11¾ | 75 | – | 10 | 11¼ |
| 8 | – | 1 | 2 | 42 | – | 6 | 1½ | 76 | – | 11 | 1 |
| 9 | – | 1 | 3¾ | 43 | – | 6 | 3¼ | 77 | – | 11 | 2¾ |
| 10 | – | 1 | 5½ | 44 | – | 6 | 5 | 78 | – | 11 | 4½ |
| 11 | – | 1 | 7¼ | 45 | – | 6 | 6¾ | 79 | – | 11 | 6¼ |
| 12 | – | 1 | 9 | 46 | – | 6 | 8½ | 80 | – | 11 | 8 |
| 13 | – | 1 | 10¾ | 47 | – | 6 | 10¼ | 81 | – | 11 | 9¾ |
| 14 | – | 2 | 0½ | 48 | – | 7 | 0 | 82 | – | 11 | 11½ |
| 15 | – | 2 | 2¼ | 49 | – | 7 | 1¾ | 83 | – | 12 | 1¼ |
| 16 | – | 2 | 4 | 50 | – | 7 | 3½ | 84 | – | 12 | 3 |
| 17 | – | 2 | 5¾ | 51 | – | 7 | 5¼ | 85 | – | 12 | 4¾ |
| 18 | – | 2 | 7½ | 52 | – | 7 | 7 | 86 | – | 12 | 6½ |
| 19 | – | 2 | 9¼ | 53 | – | 7 | 8¾ | 87 | – | 12 | 8¼ |
| 20 | – | 2 | 11 | 54 | – | 7 | 10½ | 88 | – | 12 | 10 |
| 21 | – | 3 | 0¾ | 55 | – | 8 | 0¼ | 89 | – | 12 | 11¾ |
| 22 | – | 3 | 2½ | 56 | – | 8 | 2 | 90 | – | 13 | 1½ |
| 23 | – | 3 | 4¼ | 57 | – | 8 | 3¾ | 91 | – | 13 | 3¼ |
| 24 | – | 3 | 6 | 58 | – | 8 | 5½ | 92 | – | 13 | 5 |
| 25 | – | 3 | 7¾ | 59 | – | 8 | 7¼ | 93 | – | 13 | 6¾ |
| 26 | – | 3 | 9½ | 60 | – | 8 | 9 | 94 | – | 13 | 8½ |
| 27 | – | 3 | 11¼ | 61 | – | 8 | 10¾ | 95 | – | 13 | 10¼ |
| 28 | – | 4 | 1 | 62 | – | 9 | 0½ | 96 | – | 14 | 0 |
| 29 | – | 4 | 2¾ | 63 | – | 9 | 2¼ | 97 | – | 14 | 1¾ |
| 30 | – | 4 | 4½ | 64 | – | 9 | 4 | 98 | – | 14 | 3½ |
| 31 | – | 4 | 6¼ | 65 | – | 9 | 5¾ | 99 | – | 14 | 5¼ |
| 32 | – | 4 | 8 | 66 | – | 9 | 7½ | 100 | – | 14 | 7 |
| 33 | – | 4 | 9¾ | 67 | – | 9 | 9¼ | 144 | 1 | 1 | 0 |
| 34 | – | 4 | 11½ | 68 | – | 9 | 11 | 500 | 3 | 12 | 11 |
| 35 | – | 5 | 1¼ | 69 | – | 10 | 0¾ | 750 | 5 | 9 | 4½ |

# READY RECKONER.

## 2d.

| No. | £ | s. | d. | No | £ | s. | d. | No. | £ | s. | d. |
|---|---|---|---|---|---|---|---|---|---|---|---|
| 2 | - | - | 4 | 36 | - | 6 | 0 | 70 | - | 11 | 8 |
| 3 | - | - | 6 | 37 | - | 6 | 2 | 71 | - | 11 | 10 |
| 4 | - | - | 8 | 38 | - | 6 | 4 | 72 | - | 12 | 0 |
| 5 | - | - | 10 | 39 | - | 6 | 6 | 73 | - | 12 | 2 |
| 6 | - | 1 | 0 | 40 | - | 6 | 8 | 74 | - | 12 | 4 |
| 7 | - | 1 | 2 | 41 | - | 6 | 10 | 75 | - | 12 | 6 |
| 8 | - | 1 | 4 | 42 | - | 7 | 0 | 76 | - | 12 | 8 |
| 9 | - | 1 | 6 | 43 | - | 7 | 2 | 77 | - | 12 | 10 |
| 10 | - | 1 | 8 | 44 | - | 7 | 4 | 78 | - | 13 | 0 |
| 11 | - | 1 | 10 | 45 | - | 7 | 6 | 79 | - | 13 | 2 |
| 12 | - | 2 | 0 | 46 | - | 7 | 8 | 80 | - | 13 | 4 |
| 13 | - | 2 | 2 | 47 | - | 7 | 10 | 81 | - | 13 | 6 |
| 14 | - | 2 | 4 | 48 | - | 8 | 0 | 82 | - | 13 | 8 |
| 15 | - | 2 | 6 | 49 | - | 8 | 2 | 83 | - | 13 | 10 |
| 16 | - | 2 | 8 | 50 | - | 8 | 4 | 84 | - | 14 | 0 |
| 17 | - | 2 | 10 | 51 | - | 8 | 6 | 85 | - | 14 | 2 |
| 18 | - | 3 | 0 | 52 | - | 8 | 8 | 86 | - | 14 | 4 |
| 19 | - | 3 | 2 | 53 | - | 8 | 10 | 87 | - | 14 | 6 |
| 20 | - | 3 | 4 | 54 | - | 9 | 0 | 88 | - | 14 | 8 |
| 21 | - | 3 | 6 | 55 | - | 9 | 2 | 89 | - | 14 | 10 |
| 22 | - | 3 | 8 | 56 | - | 9 | 4 | 90 | - | 15 | 0 |
| 23 | - | 3 | 10 | 57 | - | 9 | 6 | 91 | - | 15 | 2 |
| 24 | - | 4 | 0 | 58 | - | 9 | 8 | 92 | - | 15 | 4 |
| 25 | - | 4 | 2 | 59 | - | 9 | 10 | 93 | - | 15 | 6 |
| 26 | - | 4 | 4 | 60 | - | 10 | 0 | 94 | - | 15 | 8 |
| 27 | - | 4 | 6 | 61 | - | 10 | 2 | 95 | - | 15 | 10 |
| 28 | - | 4 | 8 | 62 | - | 10 | 4 | 96 | - | 16 | 0 |
| 29 | - | 4 | 10 | 63 | - | 10 | 6 | 97 | - | 16 | 2 |
| 30 | - | 5 | 0 | 64 | - | 10 | 8 | 98 | - | 16 | 4 |
| 31 | - | 5 | 2 | 65 | - | 10 | 10 | 99 | - | 16 | 6 |
| 32 | - | 5 | 4 | 66 | - | 11 | 0 | 100 | - | 16 | 8 |
| 33 | - | 5 | 6 | 67 | - | 11 | 2 | 144 | 1 | 4 | 0 |
| 34 | - | 5 | 8 | 68 | - | 11 | 4 | 500 | 4 | 3 | 4 |
| 35 | - | 5 | 10 | 69 | - | 11 | 6 | 750 | 6 | 5 | 0 |

## 2¼d.

| No. | £ | s. | d. | No. | £ | s. | d. | No. | £ | s. | d. |
|---|---|---|---|---|---|---|---|---|---|---|---|
| 2 | - | - | 4½ | 36 | - | 6 | 9 | 70 | - | 13 | 1½ |
| 3 | - | - | 6¾ | 37 | - | 6 | 11¼ | 71 | - | 13 | 3¾ |
| 4 | - | - | 9 | 38 | - | 7 | 1½ | 72 | - | 13 | 6 |
| 5 | - | - | 11¼ | 39 | - | 7 | 3¾ | 73 | - | 13 | 8¼ |
| 6 | - | 1 | 1½ | 40 | - | 7 | 6 | 74 | - | 13 | 10½ |
| 7 | - | 1 | 3¾ | 41 | - | 7 | 8¼ | 75 | - | 14 | 0¾ |
| 8 | - | 1 | 6 | 42 | - | 7 | 10½ | 76 | - | 14 | 3 |
| 9 | - | 1 | 8¼ | 43 | - | 8 | 0¾ | 77 | - | 14 | 5¼ |
| 10 | - | 1 | 10½ | 44 | - | 8 | 3 | 78 | - | 14 | 7½ |
| 11 | - | 2 | 0¾ | 45 | - | 8 | 5¼ | 79 | - | 14 | 9¾ |
| 12 | - | 2 | 3 | 46 | - | 8 | 7½ | 80 | - | 15 | 0 |
| 13 | - | 2 | 5¼ | 47 | - | 8 | 9¾ | 81 | - | 15 | 2¼ |
| 14 | - | 2 | 7½ | 48 | - | 9 | 0 | 82 | - | 15 | 4½ |
| 15 | - | 2 | 9¾ | 49 | - | 9 | 2¼ | 83 | - | 15 | 6¾ |
| 16 | - | 3 | 0 | 50 | - | 9 | 4½ | 84 | - | 15 | 9 |
| 17 | - | 3 | 2¼ | 51 | - | 9 | 6¾ | 85 | - | 15 | 11¼ |
| 18 | - | 3 | 4½ | 52 | - | 9 | 9 | 86 | - | 16 | 1½ |
| 19 | - | 3 | 6¾ | 53 | - | 9 | 11¼ | 87 | - | 16 | 3¾ |
| 20 | - | 3 | 9 | 54 | - | 10 | 1½ | 88 | - | 16 | 6 |
| 21 | - | 3 | 11¼ | 55 | - | 10 | 3¾ | 89 | - | 16 | 8¼ |
| 22 | - | 4 | 1½ | 56 | - | 10 | 6 | 90 | - | 16 | 10½ |
| 23 | - | 4 | 3¾ | 57 | - | 10 | 8¼ | 91 | - | 17 | 0¾ |
| 24 | - | 4 | 6 | 58 | - | 10 | 10½ | 92 | - | 17 | 3 |
| 25 | - | 4 | 8¼ | 59 | - | 11 | 0¾ | 93 | - | 17 | 5¼ |
| 26 | - | 4 | 10½ | 60 | - | 11 | 3 | 94 | - | 17 | 7½ |
| 27 | - | 5 | 0¾ | 61 | - | 11 | 5¼ | 95 | - | 17 | 9¾ |
| 28 | - | 5 | 3 | 62 | - | 11 | 7½ | 96 | - | 18 | 0 |
| 29 | - | 5 | 5¼ | 63 | - | 11 | 9¾ | 97 | - | 18 | 2¼ |
| 30 | - | 5 | 7½ | 64 | - | 12 | 0 | 98 | - | 18 | 4½ |
| 31 | - | 5 | 9¾ | 65 | - | 12 | 2¼ | 99 | - | 18 | 6¾ |
| 32 | - | 6 | 0 | 66 | - | 12 | 4½ | 100 | - | 18 | 9 |
| 33 | - | 6 | 2¼ | 67 | - | 12 | 6¾ | 144 | 1 | 7 | 0 |
| 34 | - | 6 | 4½ | 68 | - | 12 | 9 | 500 | 4 | 13 | 9 |
| 35 | - | 6 | 6¾ | 69 | - | 12 | 11¼ | 750 | 7 | 0 | 7½ |

## 2½d.

| No. | £ | s. | d. | No. | £ | s. | d. | No. | £ | s. | d. |
|---|---|---|---|---|---|---|---|---|---|---|---|
| 2 | - | - | 5 | 36 | - | 7 | 6 | 70 | - | 14 | 7 |
| 3 | - | - | 7½ | 37 | - | 7 | 8½ | 71 | - | 14 | 9½ |
| 4 | - | - | 10 | 38 | - | 7 | 11 | 72 | - | 15 | 0 |
| 5 | - | 1 | 0½ | 39 | - | 8 | 1½ | 73 | - | 15 | 2½ |
| 6 | - | 1 | 3 | 40 | - | 8 | 4 | 74 | - | 15 | 5 |
| 7 | - | 1 | 5½ | 41 | - | 8 | 6½ | 75 | - | 15 | 7½ |
| 8 | - | 1 | 8 | 42 | - | 8 | 9 | 76 | - | 15 | 10 |
| 9 | - | 1 | 10½ | 43 | - | 8 | 11½ | 77 | - | 16 | 0½ |
| 10 | - | 2 | 1 | 44 | - | 9 | 2 | 78 | - | 16 | 3 |
| 11 | - | 2 | 3½ | 45 | - | 9 | 4½ | 79 | - | 16 | 5½ |
| 12 | - | 2 | 6 | 46 | - | 9 | 7 | 80 | - | 16 | 8 |
| 13 | - | 2 | 8½ | 47 | - | 9 | 9½ | 81 | - | 16 | 10½ |
| 14 | - | 2 | 11 | 48 | - | 10 | 0 | 82 | - | 17 | 1 |
| 15 | - | 3 | 1½ | 49 | - | 10 | 2½ | 83 | - | 17 | 3½ |
| 16 | - | 3 | 4 | 50 | - | 10 | 5 | 84 | - | 17 | 6 |
| 17 | - | 3 | 6½ | 51 | - | 10 | 7½ | 85 | - | 17 | 8½ |
| 18 | - | 3 | 9 | 52 | - | 10 | 10 | 86 | - | 17 | 11 |
| 19 | - | 3 | 11½ | 53 | - | 11 | 0½ | 87 | - | 18 | 1½ |
| 20 | - | 4 | 2 | 54 | - | 11 | 3 | 88 | - | 18 | 4 |
| 21 | - | 4 | 4½ | 55 | - | 11 | 5½ | 89 | - | 18 | 6½ |
| 22 | - | 4 | 7 | 56 | - | 11 | 8 | 90 | - | 18 | 9 |
| 23 | - | 4 | 9½ | 57 | - | 11 | 10½ | 91 | - | 18 | 11½ |
| 24 | - | 5 | 0 | 58 | - | 12 | 1 | 92 | - | 19 | 2 |
| 25 | - | 5 | 2½ | 59 | - | 12 | 3½ | 93 | - | 19 | 4½ |
| 26 | - | 5 | 5 | 60 | - | 12 | 6 | 94 | - | 19 | 7 |
| 27 | - | 5 | 7½ | 61 | - | 12 | 8½ | 95 | - | 19 | 9½ |
| 28 | - | 5 | 10 | 62 | - | 12 | 11 | 96 | 1 | 0 | 0 |
| 29 | - | 6 | 0½ | 63 | - | 13 | 1½ | 97 | 1 | 0 | 2½ |
| 30 | - | 6 | 3 | 64 | - | 13 | 4 | 98 | 1 | 0 | 5 |
| 31 | - | 6 | 5½ | 65 | - | 13 | 6½ | 99 | 1 | 0 | 7½ |
| 32 | - | 6 | 8 | 66 | - | 13 | 9 | 100 | 1 | 0 | 10 |
| 33 | - | 6 | 10½ | 67 | - | 13 | 11½ | 144 | 1 | 10 | 0 |
| 34 | - | 7 | 1 | 68 | - | 14 | 2 | 500 | 5 | 4 | 2 |
| 35 | - | 7 | 3½ | 69 | - | 14 | 4½ | 750 | 7 | 16 | 3 |

## 2¾d.

| No. | £ | s. | d. | No. | £ | s. | d. | No. | £ | s. | d. |
|---|---|---|---|---|---|---|---|---|---|---|---|
| 2 | - | - | 5½ | 36 | - | 8 | 3 | 70 | - | 16 | 0½ |
| 3 | - | - | 8¼ | 37 | - | 8 | 5¾ | 71 | - | 16 | 3¼ |
| 4 | - | - | 11 | 38 | - | 8 | 8½ | 72 | - | 16 | 6 |
| 5 | - | 1 | 1¾ | 39 | - | 8 | 11¼ | 73 | - | 16 | 8¾ |
| 6 | - | 1 | 4½ | 40 | - | 9 | 2 | 74 | - | 16 | 11½ |
| 7 | - | 1 | 7¼ | 41 | - | 9 | 4¾ | 75 | - | 17 | 2¼ |
| 8 | - | 1 | 10 | 42 | - | 9 | 7½ | 76 | - | 17 | 5 |
| 9 | - | 2 | 0¾ | 43 | - | 9 | 10¼ | 77 | - | 17 | 7¾ |
| 10 | - | 2 | 3½ | 44 | - | 10 | 1 | 78 | - | 17 | 10½ |
| 11 | - | 2 | 6¼ | 45 | - | 10 | 3¾ | 79 | - | 18 | 1¼ |
| 12 | - | 2 | 9 | 46 | - | 10 | 6½ | 80 | - | 18 | 4 |
| 13 | - | 2 | 11¾ | 47 | - | 10 | 9¼ | 81 | - | 18 | 6¾ |
| 14 | - | 3 | 2½ | 48 | - | 11 | 0 | 82 | - | 18 | 9½ |
| 15 | - | 3 | 5¼ | 49 | - | 11 | 2¾ | 83 | - | 19 | 0¼ |
| 16 | - | 3 | 8 | 50 | - | 11 | 5½ | 84 | - | 19 | 3 |
| 17 | - | 3 | 10¾ | 51 | - | 11 | 8¼ | 85 | - | 19 | 5¾ |
| 18 | - | 4 | 1½ | 52 | - | 11 | 11 | 86 | - | 19 | 8½ |
| 19 | - | 4 | 4¼ | 53 | - | 12 | 1¾ | 87 | - | 19 | 11¼ |
| 20 | - | 4 | 7 | 54 | - | 12 | 4½ | 88 | 1 | 0 | 2 |
| 21 | - | 4 | 9¾ | 55 | - | 12 | 7¼ | 89 | 1 | 0 | 4¾ |
| 22 | - | 5 | 0½ | 56 | - | 12 | 10 | 90 | 1 | 0 | 7½ |
| 23 | - | 5 | 3¼ | 57 | - | 13 | 0¾ | 91 | 1 | 0 | 10¼ |
| 24 | - | 5 | 6 | 58 | - | 13 | 3½ | 92 | 1 | 1 | 1 |
| 25 | - | 5 | 8¾ | 59 | - | 13 | 6¼ | 93 | 1 | 1 | 3¾ |
| 26 | - | 5 | 11½ | 60 | - | 13 | 9 | 94 | 1 | 1 | 6½ |
| 27 | - | 6 | 2¼ | 61 | - | 13 | 11¾ | 95 | 1 | 1 | 9¼ |
| 28 | - | 6 | 5 | 62 | - | 14 | 2½ | 96 | 1 | 2 | 0 |
| 29 | - | 6 | 7¾ | 63 | - | 14 | 5¼ | 97 | 1 | 2 | 2¾ |
| 30 | - | 6 | 10½ | 64 | - | 14 | 8 | 98 | 1 | 2 | 5½ |
| 31 | - | 7 | 1¼ | 65 | - | 14 | 10¾ | 99 | 1 | 2 | 8¼ |
| 32 | - | 7 | 4 | 66 | - | 15 | 1½ | 100 | 1 | 2 | 11 |
| 33 | - | 7 | 6¾ | 67 | - | 15 | 4¼ | 144 | 1 | 13 | 0 |
| 34 | - | 7 | 9½ | 68 | - | 15 | 7 | 500 | 5 | 14 | 7 |
| 35 | - | 8 | 0¼ | 69 | - | 15 | 9¾ | 750 | 8 | 11 | 10½ |

# READY RECKONER.

## 3d.

| No. | £ | s. | d. | No. | £ | s. | d. | No. | £ | s. | d. |
|---|---|---|---|---|---|---|---|---|---|---|---|
| 2 | – | – | 6 | 36 | – | 9 | 0 | 70 | – | 17 | 6 |
| 3 | – | – | 9 | 37 | – | 9 | 3 | 71 | – | 17 | 9 |
| 4 | – | 1 | 0 | 38 | – | 9 | 6 | 72 | – | 18 | 0 |
| 5 | – | 1 | 3 | 39 | – | 9 | 9 | 73 | – | 18 | 3 |
| 6 | – | 1 | 6 | 40 | – | 10 | 0 | 74 | – | 18 | 6 |
| 7 | – | 1 | 9 | 41 | – | 10 | 3 | 75 | – | 18 | 9 |
| 8 | – | 2 | 0 | 42 | – | 10 | 6 | 76 | – | 19 | 0 |
| 9 | – | 2 | 3 | 43 | – | 10 | 9 | 77 | – | 19 | 3 |
| 10 | – | 2 | 6 | 44 | – | 11 | 0 | 78 | – | 19 | 6 |
| 11 | – | 2 | 9 | 45 | – | 11 | 3 | 79 | – | 19 | 9 |
| 12 | – | 3 | 0 | 46 | – | 11 | 6 | 80 | 1 | 0 | 0 |
| 13 | – | 3 | 3 | 47 | – | 11 | 9 | 81 | 1 | 0 | 3 |
| 14 | – | 3 | 6 | 48 | – | 12 | 0 | 82 | 1 | 0 | 6 |
| 15 | – | 3 | 9 | 49 | – | 12 | 3 | 83 | 1 | 0 | 9 |
| 16 | – | 4 | 0 | 50 | – | 12 | 6 | 84 | 1 | 1 | 0 |
| 17 | – | 4 | 3 | 51 | – | 12 | 9 | 85 | 1 | 1 | 3 |
| 18 | – | 4 | 6 | 52 | – | 13 | 0 | 86 | 1 | 1 | 6 |
| 19 | – | 4 | 9 | 53 | – | 13 | 3 | 87 | 1 | 1 | 9 |
| 20 | – | 5 | 0 | 54 | – | 13 | 6 | 88 | 1 | 2 | 0 |
| 21 | – | 5 | 3 | 55 | – | 13 | 9 | 89 | 1 | 2 | 3 |
| 22 | – | 5 | 6 | 56 | – | 14 | 0 | 90 | 1 | 2 | 6 |
| 23 | – | 5 | 9 | 57 | – | 14 | 3 | 91 | 1 | 2 | 9 |
| 24 | – | 6 | 0 | 58 | – | 14 | 6 | 92 | 1 | 3 | 0 |
| 25 | – | 6 | 3 | 59 | – | 14 | 9 | 93 | 1 | 3 | 3 |
| 26 | – | 6 | 6 | 60 | – | 15 | 0 | 94 | 1 | 3 | 6 |
| 27 | – | 6 | 9 | 61 | – | 15 | 3 | 95 | 1 | 3 | 9 |
| 28 | – | 7 | 0 | 62 | – | 15 | 6 | 96 | 1 | 4 | 0 |
| 29 | – | 7 | 3 | 63 | – | 15 | 9 | 97 | 1 | 4 | 3 |
| 30 | – | 7 | 6 | 64 | – | 16 | 0 | 98 | 1 | 4 | 6 |
| 31 | – | 7 | 9 | 65 | – | 16 | 3 | 99 | 1 | 4 | 9 |
| 32 | – | 8 | 0 | 66 | – | 16 | 6 | 100 | 1 | 5 | 0 |
| 33 | – | 8 | 3 | 67 | – | 16 | 9 | 144 | 1 | 16 | 0 |
| 34 | – | 8 | 6 | 68 | – | 17 | 0 | 500 | 6 | 5 | 0 |
| 35 | – | 8 | 9 | 69 | – | 17 | 3 | 750 | 9 | 7 | 6 |

## 3¼d.

| No. | £ | s. | d. | No. | £ | s. | d. | No. | £ | s. | d. |
|---|---|---|---|---|---|---|---|---|---|---|---|
| 2 | – | – | 6½ | 36 | – | 9 | 9 | 70 | – | 18 | 11½ |
| 3 | – | – | 9¾ | 37 | – | 10 | 0¼ | 71 | – | 19 | 2¾ |
| 4 | – | 1 | 1 | 38 | – | 10 | 3½ | 72 | – | 19 | 6 |
| 5 | – | 1 | 4¼ | 39 | – | 10 | 6¾ | 73 | – | 19 | 9¼ |
| 6 | – | 1 | 7½ | 40 | – | 10 | 10 | 74 | 1 | 0 | 0½ |
| 7 | – | 1 | 10¾ | 41 | – | 11 | 1¼ | 75 | 1 | 0 | 3¾ |
| 8 | – | 2 | 2 | 42 | – | 11 | 4½ | 76 | 1 | 0 | 7 |
| 9 | – | 2 | 5¼ | 43 | – | 11 | 7¾ | 77 | 1 | 0 | 10¼ |
| 10 | – | 2 | 8½ | 44 | – | 11 | 11 | 78 | 1 | 1 | 1½ |
| 11 | – | 2 | 11¾ | 45 | – | 12 | 2¼ | 79 | 1 | 1 | 4¾ |
| 12 | – | 3 | 3 | 46 | – | 12 | 5½ | 80 | 1 | 1 | 8 |
| 13 | – | 3 | 6¼ | 47 | – | 12 | 8¾ | 81 | 1 | 1 | 11¼ |
| 14 | – | 3 | 9½ | 48 | – | 13 | 0 | 82 | 1 | 2 | 2½ |
| 15 | – | 4 | 0¾ | 49 | – | 13 | 3¼ | 83 | 1 | 2 | 5¾ |
| 16 | – | 4 | 4 | 50 | – | 13 | 6½ | 84 | 1 | 2 | 9 |
| 17 | – | 4 | 7¼ | 51 | – | 13 | 9¾ | 85 | 1 | 3 | 0¼ |
| 18 | – | 4 | 10½ | 52 | – | 14 | 1 | 86 | 1 | 3 | 3½ |
| 19 | – | 5 | 1¾ | 53 | – | 14 | 4¼ | 87 | 1 | 3 | 6¾ |
| 20 | – | 5 | 5 | 54 | – | 14 | 7½ | 88 | 1 | 3 | 10 |
| 21 | – | 5 | 8¼ | 55 | – | 14 | 10¾ | 89 | 1 | 4 | 1¼ |
| 22 | – | 5 | 11½ | 56 | – | 15 | 2 | 90 | 1 | 4 | 4½ |
| 23 | – | 6 | 2¾ | 57 | – | 15 | 5¼ | 91 | 1 | 4 | 7¾ |
| 24 | – | 6 | 6 | 58 | – | 15 | 8½ | 92 | 1 | 4 | 11 |
| 25 | – | 6 | 9¼ | 59 | – | 15 | 11¾ | 93 | 1 | 5 | 2¼ |
| 26 | – | 7 | 0½ | 60 | – | 16 | 3 | 94 | 1 | 5 | 5½ |
| 27 | – | 7 | 3¾ | 61 | – | 16 | 6¼ | 95 | 1 | 5 | 8¾ |
| 28 | – | 7 | 7 | 62 | – | 16 | 9½ | 96 | 1 | 6 | 0 |
| 29 | – | 7 | 10¼ | 63 | – | 17 | 0¾ | 97 | 1 | 6 | 3¼ |
| 30 | – | 8 | 1½ | 64 | – | 17 | 4 | 98 | 1 | 6 | 6½ |
| 31 | – | 8 | 4¾ | 65 | – | 17 | 7¼ | 99 | 1 | 6 | 9¾ |
| 32 | – | 8 | 8 | 66 | – | 17 | 10½ | 100 | 1 | 7 | 1 |
| 33 | – | 8 | 11¼ | 67 | – | 18 | 1¾ | 144 | 1 | 19 | 0 |
| 34 | – | 9 | 2½ | 68 | – | 18 | 5 | 500 | 6 | 15 | 5 |
| 35 | – | 9 | 5¾ | 69 | – | 18 | 8¼ | 750 | 10 | 3 | 1½ |

## 3½d.

| No. | £ | s. | d. | No. | £ | s. | d. | No. | £ | s. | d. |
|---|---|---|---|---|---|---|---|---|---|---|---|
| 2 | – | – | 7 | 36 | – | 10 | 6 | 70 | 1 | 0 | 5 |
| 3 | – | – | 10½ | 37 | – | 10 | 9½ | 71 | 1 | 0 | 8½ |
| 4 | – | 1 | 2 | 38 | – | 11 | 1 | 72 | 1 | 1 | 0 |
| 5 | – | 1 | 5½ | 39 | – | 11 | 4½ | 73 | 1 | 1 | 3½ |
| 6 | – | 1 | 9 | 40 | – | 11 | 8 | 74 | 1 | 1 | 7 |
| 7 | – | 2 | 0½ | 41 | – | 11 | 11½ | 75 | 1 | 1 | 10½ |
| 8 | – | 2 | 4 | 42 | – | 12 | 3 | 76 | 1 | 2 | 2 |
| 9 | – | 2 | 7½ | 43 | – | 12 | 6½ | 77 | 1 | 2 | 5½ |
| 10 | – | 2 | 11 | 44 | – | 12 | 10 | 78 | 1 | 2 | 9 |
| 11 | – | 3 | 2½ | 45 | – | 13 | 1½ | 79 | 1 | 3 | 0½ |
| 12 | – | 3 | 6 | 46 | – | 13 | 5 | 80 | 1 | 3 | 4 |
| 13 | – | 3 | 9½ | 47 | – | 13 | 8½ | 81 | 1 | 3 | 7½ |
| 14 | – | 4 | 1 | 48 | – | 14 | 0 | 82 | 1 | 3 | 11 |
| 15 | – | 4 | 4½ | 49 | – | 14 | 3½ | 83 | 1 | 4 | 2½ |
| 16 | – | 4 | 8 | 50 | – | 14 | 7 | 84 | 1 | 4 | 6 |
| 17 | – | 4 | 11½ | 51 | – | 14 | 10½ | 85 | 1 | 4 | 9½ |
| 18 | – | 5 | 3 | 52 | – | 15 | 2 | 86 | 1 | 5 | 1 |
| 19 | – | 5 | 6½ | 53 | – | 15 | 5½ | 87 | 1 | 5 | 4½ |
| 20 | – | 5 | 10 | 54 | – | 15 | 9 | 88 | 1 | 5 | 8 |
| 21 | – | 6 | 1½ | 55 | – | 16 | 0½ | 89 | 1 | 5 | 11½ |
| 22 | – | 6 | 5 | 56 | – | 16 | 4 | 90 | 1 | 6 | 3 |
| 23 | – | 6 | 8½ | 57 | – | 16 | 7½ | 91 | 1 | 6 | 6½ |
| 24 | – | 7 | 0 | 58 | – | 16 | 11 | 92 | 1 | 6 | 10 |
| 25 | – | 7 | 3½ | 59 | – | 17 | 2½ | 93 | 1 | 7 | 1½ |
| 26 | – | 7 | 7 | 60 | – | 17 | 6 | 94 | 1 | 7 | 5 |
| 27 | – | 7 | 10½ | 61 | – | 17 | 9½ | 95 | 1 | 7 | 8½ |
| 28 | – | 8 | 2 | 62 | – | 18 | 1 | 96 | 1 | 8 | 0 |
| 29 | – | 8 | 5½ | 63 | – | 18 | 4½ | 97 | 1 | 8 | 3½ |
| 30 | – | 8 | 9 | 64 | – | 18 | 8 | 98 | 1 | 8 | 7 |
| 31 | – | 9 | 0½ | 65 | – | 18 | 11½ | 99 | 1 | 8 | 10½ |
| 32 | – | 9 | 4 | 66 | – | 19 | 3 | 100 | 1 | 9 | 2 |
| 33 | – | 9 | 7½ | 67 | – | 19 | 6½ | 144 | 2 | 2 | 0 |
| 34 | – | 9 | 11 | 68 | – | 19 | 10 | 500 | 7 | 5 | 10 |
| 35 | – | 10 | 2½ | 69 | 1 | 0 | 1½ | 750 | 10 | 18 | 9 |

## 3¾d.

| No. | £ | s. | d. | No. | £ | s. | d. | No. | £ | s. | d. |
|---|---|---|---|---|---|---|---|---|---|---|---|
| 2 | – | – | 7½ | 36 | – | 11 | 3 | 70 | 1 | 1 | 10½ |
| 3 | – | – | 11¼ | 37 | – | 11 | 6¾ | 71 | 1 | 2 | 2¼ |
| 4 | – | 1 | 3 | 38 | – | 11 | 10½ | 72 | 1 | 2 | 6 |
| 5 | – | 1 | 6¾ | 39 | – | 12 | 2¼ | 73 | 1 | 2 | 9¾ |
| 6 | – | 1 | 10½ | 40 | – | 12 | 6 | 74 | 1 | 3 | 1½ |
| 7 | – | 2 | 2¼ | 41 | – | 12 | 9¾ | 75 | 1 | 3 | 5¼ |
| 8 | – | 2 | 6 | 42 | – | 13 | 1½ | 76 | 1 | 3 | 9 |
| 9 | – | 2 | 9¾ | 43 | – | 13 | 5¼ | 77 | 1 | 4 | 0¾ |
| 10 | – | 3 | 1½ | 44 | – | 13 | 9 | 78 | 1 | 4 | 4½ |
| 11 | – | 3 | 5¼ | 45 | – | 14 | 0¾ | 79 | 1 | 4 | 8¼ |
| 12 | – | 3 | 9 | 46 | – | 14 | 4½ | 80 | 1 | 5 | 0 |
| 13 | – | 4 | 0¾ | 47 | – | 14 | 8¼ | 81 | 1 | 5 | 3¾ |
| 14 | – | 4 | 4½ | 48 | – | 15 | 0 | 82 | 1 | 5 | 7½ |
| 15 | – | 4 | 8¼ | 49 | – | 15 | 3¾ | 83 | 1 | 5 | 11¼ |
| 16 | – | 5 | 0 | 50 | – | 15 | 7½ | 84 | 1 | 6 | 3 |
| 17 | – | 5 | 3¾ | 51 | – | 15 | 11¼ | 85 | 1 | 6 | 6¾ |
| 18 | – | 5 | 7½ | 52 | – | 16 | 3 | 86 | 1 | 6 | 10½ |
| 19 | – | 5 | 11¼ | 53 | – | 16 | 6¾ | 87 | 1 | 7 | 2¼ |
| 20 | – | 6 | 3 | 54 | – | 16 | 10½ | 88 | 1 | 7 | 6 |
| 21 | – | 6 | 6¾ | 55 | – | 17 | 2¼ | 89 | 1 | 7 | 9¾ |
| 22 | – | 6 | 10½ | 56 | – | 17 | 6 | 90 | 1 | 8 | 1½ |
| 23 | – | 7 | 2¼ | 57 | – | 17 | 9¾ | 91 | 1 | 8 | 5¼ |
| 24 | – | 7 | 6 | 58 | – | 18 | 1½ | 92 | 1 | 8 | 9 |
| 25 | – | 7 | 9¾ | 59 | – | 18 | 5¼ | 93 | 1 | 9 | 0¾ |
| 26 | – | 8 | 1½ | 60 | – | 18 | 9 | 94 | 1 | 9 | 4½ |
| 27 | – | 8 | 5¼ | 61 | – | 19 | 0¾ | 95 | 1 | 9 | 8¼ |
| 28 | – | 8 | 9 | 62 | – | 19 | 4½ | 96 | 1 | 10 | 0 |
| 29 | – | 9 | 0¾ | 63 | – | 19 | 8¼ | 97 | 1 | 10 | 3¾ |
| 30 | – | 9 | 4½ | 64 | 1 | 0 | 0 | 98 | 1 | 10 | 7½ |
| 31 | – | 9 | 8¼ | 65 | 1 | 0 | 3¾ | 99 | 1 | 10 | 11¼ |
| 32 | – | 10 | 0 | 66 | 1 | 0 | 7½ | 100 | 1 | 11 | 3 |
| 33 | – | 10 | 3¾ | 67 | 1 | 0 | 11¼ | 144 | 2 | 5 | 0 |
| 34 | – | 10 | 7½ | 68 | 1 | 1 | 3 | 500 | 7 | 16 | 3 |
| 35 | – | 10 | 11¼ | 69 | 1 | 1 | 6¾ | 750 | 11 | 14 | 4½ |

# READY RECKONER.

## 4d.

| No. | £ | s. | d. | No. | £ | s. | d. | No. | £ | s. | d. |
|---|---|---|---|---|---|---|---|---|---|---|---|
| 2 | – | – | 8 | 36 | – | 12 | 0 | 70 | 1 | 3 | 4 |
| 3 | – | 1 | 0 | 37 | – | 12 | 4 | 71 | 1 | 3 | 8 |
| 4 | – | 1 | 4 | 38 | – | 12 | 8 | 72 | 1 | 4 | 0 |
| 5 | – | 1 | 8 | 39 | – | 13 | 0 | 73 | 1 | 4 | 4 |
| 6 | – | 2 | 0 | 40 | – | 13 | 4 | 74 | 1 | 4 | 8 |
| 7 | – | 2 | 4 | 41 | – | 13 | 8 | 75 | 1 | 5 | 0 |
| 8 | – | 2 | 8 | 42 | – | 14 | 0 | 76 | 1 | 5 | 4 |
| 9 | – | 3 | 0 | 43 | – | 14 | 4 | 77 | 1 | 5 | 8 |
| 10 | – | 3 | 4 | 44 | – | 14 | 8 | 78 | 1 | 6 | 0 |
| 11 | – | 3 | 8 | 45 | – | 15 | 0 | 79 | 1 | 6 | 4 |
| 12 | – | 4 | 0 | 46 | – | 15 | 4 | 80 | 1 | 6 | 8 |
| 13 | – | 4 | 4 | 47 | – | 15 | 8 | 81 | 1 | 7 | 0 |
| 14 | – | 4 | 8 | 48 | – | 16 | 0 | 82 | 1 | 7 | 4 |
| 15 | – | 5 | 0 | 49 | – | 16 | 4 | 83 | 1 | 7 | 8 |
| 16 | – | 5 | 4 | 50 | – | 16 | 8 | 84 | 1 | 8 | 0 |
| 17 | – | 5 | 8 | 51 | – | 17 | 0 | 85 | 1 | 8 | 4 |
| 18 | – | 6 | 0 | 52 | – | 17 | 4 | 86 | 1 | 8 | 8 |
| 19 | – | 6 | 4 | 53 | – | 17 | 8 | 87 | 1 | 9 | 0 |
| 20 | – | 6 | 8 | 54 | – | 18 | 0 | 88 | 1 | 9 | 4 |
| 21 | – | 7 | 0 | 55 | – | 18 | 4 | 89 | 1 | 9 | 8 |
| 22 | – | 7 | 4 | 56 | – | 18 | 8 | 90 | 1 | 10 | 0 |
| 23 | – | 7 | 8 | 57 | – | 19 | 0 | 91 | 1 | 10 | 4 |
| 24 | – | 8 | 0 | 58 | – | 19 | 4 | 92 | 1 | 10 | 8 |
| 25 | – | 8 | 4 | 59 | – | 19 | 8 | 93 | 1 | 11 | 0 |
| 26 | – | 8 | 8 | 60 | 1 | 0 | 0 | 94 | 1 | 11 | 4 |
| 27 | – | 9 | 0 | 61 | 1 | 0 | 4 | 95 | 1 | 11 | 8 |
| 28 | – | 9 | 4 | 62 | 1 | 0 | 8 | 96 | 1 | 12 | 0 |
| 29 | – | 9 | 8 | 63 | 1 | 1 | 0 | 97 | 1 | 12 | 4 |
| 30 | – | 10 | 0 | 64 | 1 | 1 | 4 | 98 | 1 | 12 | 8 |
| 31 | – | 10 | 4 | 65 | 1 | 1 | 8 | 99 | 1 | 13 | 0 |
| 32 | – | 10 | 8 | 66 | 1 | 2 | 0 | 100 | 1 | 13 | 4 |
| 33 | – | 11 | 0 | 67 | 1 | 2 | 4 | 144 | 2 | 8 | 0 |
| 34 | – | 11 | 4 | 68 | 1 | 2 | 8 | 500 | 8 | 6 | 8 |
| 35 | – | 11 | 8 | 69 | 1 | 3 | 0 | 750 | 12 | 10 | 0 |

## 4¼d.

| No. | £ | s. | d. | No. | £ | s. | d. | No. | £ | s. | d. |
|---|---|---|---|---|---|---|---|---|---|---|---|
| 2 | – | – | 8½ | 36 | – | 12 | 9 | 70 | 1 | 4 | 9½ |
| 3 | – | 1 | 0¾ | 37 | – | 13 | 1¼ | 71 | 1 | 5 | 1¾ |
| 4 | – | 1 | 5 | 38 | – | 13 | 5½ | 72 | 1 | 5 | 6 |
| 5 | – | 1 | 9¼ | 39 | – | 13 | 9¾ | 73 | 1 | 5 | 10¼ |
| 6 | – | 2 | 1½ | 40 | – | 14 | 2 | 74 | 1 | 6 | 2½ |
| 7 | – | 2 | 5¾ | 41 | – | 14 | 6¼ | 75 | 1 | 6 | 6¾ |
| 8 | – | 2 | 10 | 42 | – | 14 | 10½ | 76 | 1 | 6 | 11 |
| 9 | – | 3 | 2¼ | 43 | – | 15 | 2¾ | 77 | 1 | 7 | 3¼ |
| 10 | – | 3 | 6½ | 44 | – | 15 | 7 | 78 | 1 | 7 | 7½ |
| 11 | – | 3 | 10¾ | 45 | – | 15 | 11¼ | 79 | 1 | 7 | 11¾ |
| 12 | – | 4 | 3 | 46 | – | 16 | 3½ | 80 | 1 | 8 | 4 |
| 13 | – | 4 | 7¼ | 47 | – | 16 | 7¾ | 81 | 1 | 8 | 8¼ |
| 14 | – | 4 | 11½ | 48 | – | 17 | 0 | 82 | 1 | 9 | 0½ |
| 15 | – | 5 | 3¾ | 49 | – | 17 | 4¼ | 83 | 1 | 9 | 4¾ |
| 16 | – | 5 | 8 | 50 | – | 17 | 8½ | 84 | 1 | 9 | 9 |
| 17 | – | 6 | 0¼ | 51 | – | 18 | 0¾ | 85 | 1 | 10 | 1¼ |
| 18 | – | 6 | 4½ | 52 | – | 18 | 5 | 86 | 1 | 10 | 5½ |
| 19 | – | 6 | 8¾ | 53 | – | 18 | 9¼ | 87 | 1 | 10 | 9¾ |
| 20 | – | 7 | 1 | 54 | – | 19 | 1½ | 88 | 1 | 11 | 2 |
| 21 | – | 7 | 5¼ | 55 | – | 19 | 5¾ | 89 | 1 | 11 | 6¼ |
| 22 | – | 7 | 9½ | 56 | – | 19 | 10 | 90 | 1 | 11 | 10½ |
| 23 | – | 8 | 1¾ | 57 | 1 | 0 | 2¼ | 91 | 1 | 12 | 2¾ |
| 24 | – | 8 | 6 | 58 | 1 | 0 | 6½ | 92 | 1 | 12 | 7 |
| 25 | – | 8 | 10¼ | 59 | 1 | 0 | 10¾ | 93 | 1 | 12 | 11¼ |
| 26 | – | 9 | 2½ | 60 | 1 | 1 | 3 | 94 | 1 | 13 | 3½ |
| 27 | – | 9 | 6¾ | 61 | 1 | 1 | 7¼ | 95 | 1 | 13 | 7¾ |
| 28 | – | 9 | 11 | 62 | 1 | 1 | 11½ | 96 | 1 | 14 | 0 |
| 29 | – | 10 | 3¼ | 63 | 1 | 2 | 3¾ | 97 | 1 | 14 | 4¼ |
| 30 | – | 10 | 7½ | 64 | 1 | 2 | 8 | 98 | 1 | 14 | 8½ |
| 31 | – | 10 | 11¾ | 65 | 1 | 3 | 0¼ | 99 | 1 | 15 | 0¾ |
| 32 | – | 11 | 4 | 66 | 1 | 3 | 4½ | 100 | 1 | 15 | 5 |
| 33 | – | 11 | 8¼ | 67 | 1 | 3 | 8¾ | 144 | 2 | 11 | 0 |
| 34 | – | 12 | 0½ | 68 | 1 | 4 | 1 | 500 | 8 | 17 | 1 |
| 35 | – | 12 | 4¾ | 69 | 1 | 4 | 5¼ | 750 | 13 | 5 | 7½ |

## 4½d.

| No. | £ | s. | d. | No. | £ | s. | d. | No. | £ | s. | d. |
|---|---|---|---|---|---|---|---|---|---|---|---|
| 2 | – | – | 9 | 36 | – | 13 | 6 | 70 | 1 | 6 | 3 |
| 3 | – | 1 | 1½ | 37 | – | 13 | 10½ | 71 | 1 | 6 | 7½ |
| 4 | – | 1 | 6 | 38 | – | 14 | 3 | 72 | 1 | 7 | 0 |
| 5 | – | 1 | 10½ | 39 | – | 14 | 7½ | 73 | 1 | 7 | 4½ |
| 6 | – | 2 | 3 | 40 | – | 15 | 0 | 74 | 1 | 7 | 9 |
| 7 | – | 2 | 7½ | 41 | – | 15 | 4½ | 75 | 1 | 8 | 1½ |
| 8 | – | 3 | 0 | 42 | – | 15 | 9 | 76 | 1 | 8 | 6 |
| 9 | – | 3 | 4½ | 43 | – | 16 | 1½ | 77 | 1 | 8 | 10½ |
| 10 | – | 3 | 9 | 44 | – | 16 | 6 | 78 | 1 | 9 | 3 |
| 11 | – | 4 | 1½ | 45 | – | 16 | 10½ | 79 | 1 | 9 | 7½ |
| 12 | – | 4 | 6 | 46 | – | 17 | 3 | 80 | 1 | 10 | 0 |
| 13 | – | 4 | 10½ | 47 | – | 17 | 7½ | 81 | 1 | 10 | 4½ |
| 14 | – | 5 | 3 | 48 | – | 18 | 0 | 82 | 1 | 10 | 9 |
| 15 | – | 5 | 7½ | 49 | – | 18 | 4½ | 83 | 1 | 11 | 1½ |
| 16 | – | 6 | 0 | 50 | – | 18 | 9 | 84 | 1 | 11 | 6 |
| 17 | – | 6 | 4½ | 51 | – | 19 | 1½ | 85 | 1 | 11 | 10½ |
| 18 | – | 6 | 9 | 52 | – | 19 | 6 | 86 | 1 | 12 | 3 |
| 19 | – | 7 | 1½ | 53 | – | 19 | 10½ | 87 | 1 | 12 | 7½ |
| 20 | – | 7 | 6 | 54 | 1 | 0 | 3 | 88 | 1 | 13 | 0 |
| 21 | – | 7 | 10½ | 55 | 1 | 0 | 7½ | 89 | 1 | 13 | 4½ |
| 22 | – | 8 | 3 | 56 | 1 | 1 | 0 | 90 | 1 | 13 | 9 |
| 23 | – | 8 | 7½ | 57 | 1 | 1 | 4½ | 91 | 1 | 14 | 1½ |
| 24 | – | 9 | 0 | 58 | 1 | 1 | 9 | 92 | 1 | 14 | 6 |
| 25 | – | 9 | 4½ | 59 | 1 | 2 | 1½ | 93 | 1 | 14 | 10½ |
| 26 | – | 9 | 9 | 60 | 1 | 2 | 6 | 94 | 1 | 15 | 3 |
| 27 | – | 10 | 1½ | 61 | 1 | 2 | 10½ | 95 | 1 | 15 | 7½ |
| 28 | – | 10 | 6 | 62 | 1 | 3 | 3 | 96 | 1 | 16 | 0 |
| 29 | – | 10 | 10½ | 63 | 1 | 3 | 7½ | 97 | 1 | 16 | 4½ |
| 30 | – | 11 | 3 | 64 | 1 | 4 | 0 | 98 | 1 | 16 | 9 |
| 31 | – | 11 | 7½ | 65 | 1 | 4 | 4½ | 99 | 1 | 17 | 1½ |
| 32 | – | 12 | 0 | 66 | 1 | 4 | 9 | 100 | 1 | 17 | 6 |
| 33 | – | 12 | 4½ | 67 | 1 | 5 | 1½ | 144 | 2 | 14 | 0 |
| 34 | – | 12 | 9 | 68 | 1 | 5 | 6 | 500 | 9 | 7 | 6 |
| 35 | – | 13 | 1½ | 69 | 1 | 5 | 10½ | 750 | 14 | 1 | 3 |

## 4¾d.

| No. | £ | s. | d. | No. | £ | s. | d. | No. | £ | s. | d. |
|---|---|---|---|---|---|---|---|---|---|---|---|
| 2 | – | – | 9½ | 36 | – | 14 | 3 | 70 | 1 | 7 | 8½ |
| 3 | – | 1 | 2¼ | 37 | – | 14 | 7¾ | 71 | 1 | 8 | 1¼ |
| 4 | – | 1 | 7 | 38 | – | 15 | 0½ | 72 | 1 | 8 | 6 |
| 5 | – | 1 | 11¾ | 39 | – | 15 | 5¼ | 73 | 1 | 8 | 10¾ |
| 6 | – | 2 | 4½ | 40 | – | 15 | 10 | 74 | 1 | 9 | 3½ |
| 7 | – | 2 | 9¼ | 41 | – | 16 | 2¾ | 75 | 1 | 9 | 8¼ |
| 8 | – | 3 | 2 | 42 | – | 16 | 7½ | 76 | 1 | 10 | 1 |
| 9 | – | 3 | 6¾ | 43 | – | 17 | 0¼ | 77 | 1 | 10 | 5¾ |
| 10 | – | 3 | 11½ | 44 | – | 17 | 5 | 78 | 1 | 10 | 10½ |
| 11 | – | 4 | 4¼ | 45 | – | 17 | 9¾ | 79 | 1 | 11 | 3¼ |
| 12 | – | 4 | 9 | 46 | – | 18 | 2½ | 80 | 1 | 11 | 8 |
| 13 | – | 5 | 1¾ | 47 | – | 18 | 7¼ | 81 | 1 | 12 | 0¾ |
| 14 | – | 5 | 6½ | 48 | – | 19 | 0 | 82 | 1 | 12 | 5½ |
| 15 | – | 5 | 11¼ | 49 | – | 19 | 4¾ | 83 | 1 | 12 | 10¼ |
| 16 | – | 6 | 4 | 50 | – | 19 | 9½ | 84 | 1 | 13 | 3 |
| 17 | – | 6 | 8¾ | 51 | 1 | 0 | 2¼ | 85 | 1 | 13 | 7¾ |
| 18 | – | 7 | 1½ | 52 | 1 | 0 | 7 | 86 | 1 | 14 | 0½ |
| 19 | – | 7 | 6¼ | 53 | 1 | 0 | 11¾ | 87 | 1 | 14 | 5¼ |
| 20 | – | 7 | 11 | 54 | 1 | 1 | 4½ | 88 | 1 | 14 | 10 |
| 21 | – | 8 | 3¾ | 55 | 1 | 1 | 9¼ | 89 | 1 | 15 | 2¾ |
| 22 | – | 8 | 8½ | 56 | 1 | 2 | 2 | 90 | 1 | 15 | 7½ |
| 23 | – | 9 | 1¼ | 57 | 1 | 2 | 6¾ | 91 | 1 | 16 | 0¼ |
| 24 | – | 9 | 6 | 58 | 1 | 2 | 11½ | 92 | 1 | 16 | 5 |
| 25 | – | 9 | 10¾ | 59 | 1 | 3 | 4¼ | 93 | 1 | 16 | 9¾ |
| 26 | – | 10 | 3½ | 60 | 1 | 3 | 9 | 94 | 1 | 17 | 2½ |
| 27 | – | 10 | 8¼ | 61 | 1 | 4 | 1¾ | 95 | 1 | 17 | 7¼ |
| 28 | – | 11 | 1 | 62 | 1 | 4 | 6½ | 96 | 1 | 18 | 0 |
| 29 | – | 11 | 5¾ | 63 | 1 | 4 | 11¼ | 97 | 1 | 18 | 4¾ |
| 30 | – | 11 | 10½ | 64 | 1 | 5 | 4 | 98 | 1 | 18 | 9½ |
| 31 | – | 12 | 3¼ | 65 | 1 | 5 | 8¾ | 99 | 1 | 19 | 2¼ |
| 32 | – | 12 | 8 | 66 | 1 | 6 | 1½ | 100 | 1 | 19 | 7 |
| 33 | – | 13 | 0¾ | 67 | 1 | 6 | 6¼ | 144 | 2 | 17 | 0 |
| 34 | – | 13 | 5½ | 68 | 1 | 6 | 11 | 500 | 9 | 17 | 11 |
| 35 | – | 13 | 10¼ | 69 | 1 | 7 | 3¾ | 750 | 14 | 16 | 10½ |

# READY RECKONER.

## 5d.

| No. | £ | s. | d. | No. | £ | s. | d. | No. | £ | s. | d. |
|---|---|---|---|---|---|---|---|---|---|---|---|
| 2 | – | – | 10 | 36 | – | 15 | 0 | 70 | 1 | 9 | 2 |
| 3 | – | 1 | 3 | 37 | – | 15 | 5 | 71 | 1 | 9 | 7 |
| 4 | – | 1 | 8 | 38 | – | 15 | 10 | 72 | 1 | 10 | 0 |
| 5 | – | 2 | 1 | 39 | – | 16 | 3 | 73 | 1 | 10 | 5 |
| 6 | – | 2 | 6 | 40 | – | 16 | 8 | 74 | 1 | 10 | 10 |
| 7 | – | 2 | 11 | 41 | – | 17 | 1 | 75 | 1 | 11 | 3 |
| 8 | – | 3 | 4 | 42 | – | 17 | 6 | 76 | 1 | 11 | 8 |
| 9 | – | 3 | 9 | 43 | – | 17 | 11 | 77 | 1 | 12 | 1 |
| 10 | – | 4 | 2 | 44 | – | 18 | 4 | 78 | 1 | 12 | 6 |
| 11 | – | 4 | 7 | 45 | – | 18 | 9 | 79 | 1 | 12 | 11 |
| 12 | – | 5 | 0 | 46 | – | 19 | 2 | 80 | 1 | 13 | 4 |
| 13 | – | 5 | 5 | 47 | – | 19 | 7 | 81 | 1 | 13 | 9 |
| 14 | – | 5 | 10 | 48 | 1 | 0 | 0 | 82 | 1 | 14 | 2 |
| 15 | – | 6 | 3 | 49 | 1 | 0 | 5 | 83 | 1 | 14 | 7 |
| 16 | – | 6 | 8 | 50 | 1 | 0 | 10 | 84 | 1 | 15 | 0 |
| 17 | – | 7 | 1 | 51 | 1 | 1 | 3 | 85 | 1 | 15 | 5 |
| 18 | – | 7 | 6 | 52 | 1 | 1 | 8 | 86 | 1 | 15 | 10 |
| 19 | – | 7 | 11 | 53 | 1 | 2 | 1 | 87 | 1 | 16 | 3 |
| 20 | – | 8 | 4 | 54 | 1 | 2 | 6 | 88 | 1 | 16 | 8 |
| 21 | – | 8 | 9 | 55 | 1 | 2 | 11 | 89 | 1 | 17 | 1 |
| 22 | – | 9 | 2 | 56 | 1 | 3 | 4 | 90 | 1 | 17 | 6 |
| 23 | – | 9 | 7 | 57 | 1 | 3 | 9 | 91 | 1 | 17 | 11 |
| 24 | – | 10 | 0 | 58 | 1 | 4 | 2 | 92 | 1 | 18 | 4 |
| 25 | – | 10 | 5 | 59 | 1 | 4 | 7 | 93 | 1 | 18 | 9 |
| 26 | – | 10 | 10 | 60 | 1 | 5 | 0 | 94 | 1 | 19 | 2 |
| 27 | – | 11 | 3 | 61 | 1 | 5 | 5 | 95 | 1 | 19 | 7 |
| 28 | – | 11 | 8 | 62 | 1 | 5 | 10 | 96 | 2 | 0 | 0 |
| 29 | – | 12 | 1 | 63 | 1 | 6 | 3 | 97 | 2 | 0 | 5 |
| 30 | – | 12 | 6 | 64 | 1 | 6 | 8 | 98 | 2 | 0 | 10 |
| 31 | – | 12 | 11 | 65 | 1 | 7 | 1 | 99 | 2 | 1 | 3 |
| 32 | – | 13 | 4 | 66 | 1 | 7 | 6 | 100 | 2 | 1 | 8 |
| 33 | – | 13 | 9 | 67 | 1 | 7 | 11 | 144 | 3 | 0 | 0 |
| 34 | – | 14 | 2 | 68 | 1 | 8 | 4 | 500 | 10 | 8 | 4 |
| 35 | – | 14 | 7 | 69 | 1 | 8 | 9 | 750 | 15 | 12 | 6 |

## 5¼d.

| No. | £ | s. | d. | No. | £ | s. | d. | No. | £ | s. | d. |
|---|---|---|---|---|---|---|---|---|---|---|---|
| 2 | – | – | 10½ | 36 | – | 15 | 9 | 70 | 1 | 10 | 7½ |
| 3 | – | 1 | 3¾ | 37 | – | 16 | 2¼ | 71 | 1 | 11 | 0¾ |
| 4 | – | 1 | 9 | 38 | – | 16 | 7½ | 72 | 1 | 11 | 6 |
| 5 | – | 2 | 2¼ | 39 | – | 17 | 0¾ | 73 | 1 | 11 | 11¼ |
| 6 | – | 2 | 7½ | 40 | – | 17 | 6 | 74 | 1 | 12 | 4½ |
| 7 | – | 3 | 0¾ | 41 | – | 17 | 11¼ | 75 | 1 | 12 | 9¾ |
| 8 | – | 3 | 6 | 42 | – | 18 | 4½ | 76 | 1 | 13 | 3 |
| 9 | – | 3 | 11¼ | 43 | – | 18 | 9¾ | 77 | 1 | 13 | 8¼ |
| 10 | – | 4 | 4½ | 44 | – | 19 | 3 | 78 | 1 | 14 | 1½ |
| 11 | – | 4 | 9¾ | 45 | – | 19 | 8¼ | 79 | 1 | 14 | 6¾ |
| 12 | – | 5 | 3 | 46 | 1 | 0 | 1½ | 80 | 1 | 15 | 0 |
| 13 | – | 5 | 8¼ | 47 | 1 | 0 | 6¾ | 81 | 1 | 15 | 5¼ |
| 14 | – | 6 | 1½ | 48 | 1 | 1 | 0 | 82 | 1 | 15 | 10½ |
| 15 | – | 6 | 6¾ | 49 | 1 | 1 | 5¼ | 83 | 1 | 16 | 3¾ |
| 16 | – | 7 | 0 | 50 | 1 | 1 | 10½ | 84 | 1 | 16 | 9 |
| 17 | – | 7 | 5¼ | 51 | 1 | 2 | 3¾ | 85 | 1 | 17 | 2¼ |
| 18 | – | 7 | 10½ | 52 | 1 | 2 | 9 | 86 | 1 | 17 | 7½ |
| 19 | – | 8 | 3¾ | 53 | 1 | 3 | 2¼ | 87 | 1 | 18 | 0¾ |
| 20 | – | 8 | 9 | 54 | 1 | 3 | 7½ | 88 | 1 | 18 | 6 |
| 21 | – | 9 | 2¼ | 55 | 1 | 4 | 0¾ | 89 | 1 | 18 | 11¼ |
| 22 | – | 9 | 7½ | 56 | 1 | 4 | 6 | 90 | 1 | 19 | 4½ |
| 23 | – | 10 | 0¾ | 57 | 1 | 4 | 11¼ | 91 | 1 | 19 | 9¾ |
| 24 | – | 10 | 6 | 58 | 1 | 5 | 4½ | 92 | 2 | 0 | 3 |
| 25 | – | 10 | 11¼ | 59 | 1 | 5 | 9¾ | 93 | 2 | 0 | 8¼ |
| 26 | – | 11 | 4½ | 60 | 1 | 6 | 3 | 94 | 2 | 1 | 1½ |
| 27 | – | 11 | 9¾ | 61 | 1 | 6 | 8¼ | 95 | 2 | 1 | 6¾ |
| 28 | – | 12 | 3 | 62 | 1 | 7 | 1½ | 96 | 2 | 2 | 0 |
| 29 | – | 12 | 8¼ | 63 | 1 | 7 | 6¾ | 97 | 2 | 2 | 5¼ |
| 30 | – | 13 | 1½ | 64 | 1 | 8 | 0 | 98 | 2 | 2 | 10½ |
| 31 | – | 13 | 6¾ | 65 | 1 | 8 | 5¼ | 99 | 2 | 3 | 3¾ |
| 32 | – | 14 | 0 | 66 | 1 | 8 | 10½ | 100 | 2 | 3 | 9 |
| 33 | – | 14 | 5¼ | 67 | 1 | 9 | 3¾ | 144 | 3 | 3 | 0 |
| 34 | – | 14 | 10½ | 68 | 1 | 9 | 9 | 500 | 10 | 18 | 9 |
| 35 | – | 15 | 3¾ | 69 | 1 | 10 | 2¼ | 750 | 16 | 8 | 1½ |

## 5½d.

| No. | £ | s. | d. | No. | £ | s. | d. | No. | £ | s. | d. |
|---|---|---|---|---|---|---|---|---|---|---|---|
| 2 | – | – | 11 | 36 | – | 16 | 6 | 70 | 1 | 12 | 1 |
| 3 | – | 1 | 4½ | 37 | – | 16 | 11½ | 71 | 1 | 12 | 6½ |
| 4 | – | 1 | 10 | 38 | – | 17 | 5 | 72 | 1 | 13 | 0 |
| 5 | – | 2 | 3½ | 39 | – | 17 | 10½ | 73 | 1 | 13 | 5½ |
| 6 | – | 2 | 9 | 40 | – | 18 | 4 | 74 | 1 | 13 | 11 |
| 7 | – | 3 | 2½ | 41 | – | 18 | 9½ | 75 | 1 | 14 | 4½ |
| 8 | – | 3 | 8 | 42 | – | 19 | 3 | 76 | 1 | 14 | 10 |
| 9 | – | 4 | 1½ | 43 | – | 19 | 8½ | 77 | 1 | 15 | 3½ |
| 10 | – | 4 | 7 | 44 | 1 | 0 | 2 | 78 | 1 | 15 | 9 |
| 11 | – | 5 | 0½ | 45 | 1 | 0 | 7½ | 79 | 1 | 16 | 2½ |
| 12 | – | 5 | 6 | 46 | 1 | 1 | 1 | 80 | 1 | 16 | 8 |
| 13 | – | 5 | 11½ | 47 | 1 | 1 | 6½ | 81 | 1 | 17 | 1½ |
| 14 | – | 6 | 5 | 48 | 1 | 2 | 0 | 82 | 1 | 17 | 7 |
| 15 | – | 6 | 10½ | 49 | 1 | 2 | 5½ | 83 | 1 | 18 | 0½ |
| 16 | – | 7 | 4 | 50 | 1 | 2 | 11 | 84 | 1 | 18 | 6 |
| 17 | – | 7 | 9½ | 51 | 1 | 3 | 4½ | 85 | 1 | 18 | 11½ |
| 18 | – | 8 | 3 | 52 | 1 | 3 | 10 | 86 | 1 | 19 | 5 |
| 19 | – | 8 | 8½ | 53 | 1 | 4 | 3½ | 87 | 1 | 19 | 10½ |
| 20 | – | 9 | 2 | 54 | 1 | 4 | 9 | 88 | 2 | 0 | 4 |
| 21 | – | 9 | 7½ | 55 | 1 | 5 | 2½ | 89 | 2 | 0 | 9½ |
| 22 | – | 10 | 1 | 56 | 1 | 5 | 8 | 90 | 2 | 1 | 3 |
| 23 | – | 10 | 6½ | 57 | 1 | 6 | 1½ | 91 | 2 | 1 | 8½ |
| 24 | – | 11 | 0 | 58 | 1 | 6 | 7 | 92 | 2 | 2 | 2 |
| 25 | – | 11 | 5½ | 59 | 1 | 7 | 0½ | 93 | 2 | 2 | 7½ |
| 26 | – | 11 | 11 | 60 | 1 | 7 | 6 | 94 | 2 | 3 | 1 |
| 27 | – | 12 | 4½ | 61 | 1 | 7 | 11½ | 95 | 2 | 3 | 6½ |
| 28 | – | 12 | 10 | 62 | 1 | 8 | 5 | 96 | 2 | 4 | 0 |
| 29 | – | 13 | 3½ | 63 | 1 | 8 | 10½ | 97 | 2 | 4 | 5½ |
| 30 | – | 13 | 9 | 64 | 1 | 9 | 4 | 98 | 2 | 4 | 11 |
| 31 | – | 14 | 2½ | 65 | 1 | 9 | 9½ | 99 | 2 | 5 | 4½ |
| 32 | – | 14 | 8 | 66 | 1 | 10 | 3 | 100 | 2 | 5 | 10 |
| 33 | – | 15 | 1½ | 67 | 1 | 10 | 8½ | 144 | 3 | 6 | 0 |
| 34 | – | 15 | 7 | 68 | 1 | 11 | 2 | 500 | 11 | 9 | 2 |
| 35 | – | 16 | 0½ | 69 | 1 | 11 | 7½ | 750 | 17 | 3 | 9 |

## 5¾d.

| No. | £ | s. | d. | No. | £ | s. | d. | No. | £ | s. | d. |
|---|---|---|---|---|---|---|---|---|---|---|---|
| 2 | – | – | 11½ | 36 | – | 17 | 3 | 70 | 1 | 13 | 6½ |
| 3 | – | 1 | 5¼ | 37 | – | 17 | 8¾ | 71 | 1 | 14 | 0¼ |
| 4 | – | 1 | 11 | 38 | – | 18 | 2½ | 72 | 1 | 14 | 6 |
| 5 | – | 2 | 4¾ | 39 | – | 18 | 8¼ | 73 | 1 | 14 | 11¾ |
| 6 | – | 2 | 10½ | 40 | – | 19 | 2 | 74 | 1 | 15 | 5½ |
| 7 | – | 3 | 4¼ | 41 | – | 19 | 7¾ | 75 | 1 | 15 | 11¼ |
| 8 | – | 3 | 10 | 42 | 1 | 0 | 1½ | 76 | 1 | 16 | 5 |
| 9 | – | 4 | 3¾ | 43 | 1 | 0 | 7¼ | 77 | 1 | 16 | 10¾ |
| 10 | – | 4 | 9½ | 44 | 1 | 1 | 1 | 78 | 1 | 17 | 4½ |
| 11 | – | 5 | 3¼ | 45 | 1 | 1 | 6¾ | 79 | 1 | 17 | 10¼ |
| 12 | – | 5 | 9 | 46 | 1 | 2 | 0½ | 80 | 1 | 18 | 4 |
| 13 | – | 6 | 2¾ | 47 | 1 | 2 | 6¼ | 81 | 1 | 18 | 9¾ |
| 14 | – | 6 | 8½ | 48 | 1 | 3 | 0 | 82 | 1 | 19 | 3½ |
| 15 | – | 7 | 2¼ | 49 | 1 | 3 | 5¾ | 83 | 1 | 19 | 9¼ |
| 16 | – | 7 | 8 | 50 | 1 | 3 | 11½ | 84 | 2 | 0 | 3 |
| 17 | – | 8 | 1¾ | 51 | 1 | 4 | 5¼ | 85 | 2 | 0 | 8¾ |
| 18 | – | 8 | 7½ | 52 | 1 | 4 | 11 | 86 | 2 | 1 | 2½ |
| 19 | – | 9 | 1¼ | 53 | 1 | 5 | 4¾ | 87 | 2 | 1 | 8¼ |
| 20 | – | 9 | 7 | 54 | 1 | 5 | 10½ | 88 | 2 | 2 | 2 |
| 21 | – | 10 | 0¾ | 55 | 1 | 6 | 4¼ | 89 | 2 | 2 | 7¾ |
| 22 | – | 10 | 6½ | 56 | 1 | 6 | 10 | 90 | 2 | 3 | 1½ |
| 23 | – | 11 | 0¼ | 57 | 1 | 7 | 3¾ | 91 | 2 | 3 | 7¼ |
| 24 | – | 11 | 6 | 58 | 1 | 7 | 9½ | 92 | 2 | 4 | 1 |
| 25 | – | 11 | 11¾ | 59 | 1 | 8 | 3¼ | 93 | 2 | 4 | 6¾ |
| 26 | – | 12 | 5½ | 60 | 1 | 8 | 9 | 94 | 2 | 5 | 0½ |
| 27 | – | 12 | 11¼ | 61 | 1 | 9 | 2¾ | 95 | 2 | 5 | 6¼ |
| 28 | – | 13 | 5 | 62 | 1 | 9 | 8½ | 96 | 2 | 6 | 0 |
| 29 | – | 13 | 10¾ | 63 | 1 | 10 | 2¼ | 97 | 2 | 6 | 5¾ |
| 30 | – | 14 | 4½ | 64 | 1 | 10 | 8 | 98 | 2 | 6 | 11½ |
| 31 | – | 14 | 10¼ | 65 | 1 | 11 | 1¾ | 99 | 2 | 7 | 5¼ |
| 32 | – | 15 | 4 | 66 | 1 | 11 | 7½ | 100 | 2 | 7 | 11 |
| 33 | – | 15 | 9¾ | 67 | 1 | 12 | 1¼ | 144 | 3 | 9 | 0 |
| 34 | – | 16 | 3½ | 68 | 1 | 12 | 7 | 500 | 11 | 19 | 7 |
| 35 | – | 16 | 9¼ | 69 | 1 | 13 | 0¾ | 750 | 17 | 19 | 4½ |

# READY RECKONER.

## 6d.

| No. | £ | s. | d. | No. | £ | s. | d. | No. | £ | s. | d. |
|---|---|---|---|---|---|---|---|---|---|---|---|
| 2 | – | 1 | 0 | 36 | – | 18 | 0 | 70 | 1 | 15 | 0 |
| 3 | – | 1 | 6 | 37 | – | 18 | 6 | 71 | 1 | 15 | 6 |
| 4 | – | 2 | 0 | 38 | – | 19 | 0 | 72 | 1 | 16 | 0 |
| 5 | – | 2 | 6 | 39 | – | 19 | 6 | 73 | 1 | 16 | 6 |
| 6 | – | 3 | 0 | 40 | 1 | 0 | 0 | 74 | 1 | 17 | 0 |
| 7 | – | 3 | 6 | 41 | 1 | 0 | 6 | 75 | 1 | 17 | 6 |
| 8 | – | 4 | 0 | 42 | 1 | 1 | 0 | 76 | 1 | 18 | 0 |
| 9 | – | 4 | 6 | 43 | 1 | 1 | 6 | 77 | 1 | 18 | 6 |
| 10 | – | 5 | 0 | 44 | 1 | 2 | 0 | 78 | 1 | 19 | 0 |
| 11 | – | 5 | 6 | 45 | 1 | 2 | 6 | 79 | 1 | 19 | 6 |
| 12 | – | 6 | 0 | 46 | 1 | 3 | 0 | 80 | 2 | 0 | 0 |
| 13 | – | 6 | 6 | 47 | 1 | 3 | 6 | 81 | 2 | 0 | 6 |
| 14 | – | 7 | 0 | 48 | 1 | 4 | 0 | 82 | 2 | 1 | 0 |
| 15 | – | 7 | 6 | 49 | 1 | 4 | 6 | 83 | 2 | 1 | 6 |
| 16 | – | 8 | 0 | 50 | 1 | 5 | 0 | 84 | 2 | 2 | 0 |
| 17 | – | 8 | 6 | 51 | 1 | 5 | 6 | 85 | 2 | 2 | 6 |
| 18 | – | 9 | 0 | 52 | 1 | 6 | 0 | 86 | 2 | 3 | 0 |
| 19 | – | 9 | 6 | 53 | 1 | 6 | 6 | 87 | 2 | 3 | 6 |
| 20 | – | 10 | 0 | 54 | 1 | 7 | 0 | 88 | 2 | 4 | 0 |
| 21 | – | 10 | 6 | 55 | 1 | 7 | 6 | 89 | 2 | 4 | 6 |
| 22 | – | 11 | 0 | 56 | 1 | 8 | 0 | 90 | 2 | 5 | 0 |
| 23 | – | 11 | 6 | 57 | 1 | 8 | 6 | 91 | 2 | 5 | 6 |
| 24 | – | 12 | 0 | 58 | 1 | 9 | 0 | 92 | 2 | 6 | 0 |
| 25 | – | 12 | 6 | 59 | 1 | 9 | 6 | 93 | 2 | 6 | 6 |
| 36 | – | 13 | 0 | 60 | 1 | 10 | 0 | 94 | 2 | 7 | 0 |
| 27 | – | 13 | 6 | 61 | 1 | 10 | 6 | 95 | 2 | 7 | 6 |
| 28 | – | 14 | 0 | 62 | 1 | 11 | 0 | 96 | 2 | 8 | 0 |
| 29 | – | 14 | 6 | 63 | 1 | 11 | 6 | 97 | 2 | 8 | 6 |
| 30 | – | 15 | 0 | 64 | 1 | 12 | 0 | 98 | 2 | 9 | 0 |
| 31 | – | 15 | 6 | 65 | 1 | 12 | 6 | 99 | 2 | 9 | 6 |
| 32 | – | 16 | 0 | 66 | 1 | 13 | 0 | 100 | 2 | 10 | 0 |
| 33 | – | 16 | 6 | 67 | 1 | 13 | 6 | 144 | 3 | 12 | 0 |
| 34 | – | 17 | 0 | 68 | 1 | 14 | 0 | 500 | 12 | 10 | 0 |
| 35 | – | 17 | 6 | 69 | 1 | 14 | 6 | 750 | 18 | 15 | 0 |

## 6¼d.

| No. | £ | s. | d. | No. | £ | s. | d. | No. | £ | s. | d. |
|---|---|---|---|---|---|---|---|---|---|---|---|
| 2 | – | 1 | 0½ | 36 | – | 18 | 9 | 70 | 1 | 16 | 5½ |
| 3 | – | 1 | 6¾ | 37 | – | 19 | 3¼ | 71 | 1 | 16 | 11¾ |
| 4 | – | 2 | 1 | 38 | – | 19 | 9½ | 72 | 1 | 17 | 6 |
| 5 | – | 2 | 7¼ | 39 | 1 | 0 | 3¾ | 73 | 1 | 18 | 0¼ |
| 6 | – | 3 | 1½ | 40 | 1 | 0 | 10 | 74 | 1 | 18 | 6½ |
| 7 | – | 3 | 7¾ | 41 | 1 | 1 | 4¼ | 75 | 1 | 19 | 0¾ |
| 8 | – | 4 | 2 | 42 | 1 | 1 | 10½ | 76 | 1 | 19 | 7 |
| 9 | – | 4 | 8¼ | 43 | 1 | 2 | 4¾ | 77 | 2 | 0 | 1¼ |
| 10 | – | 5 | 2½ | 44 | 1 | 2 | 11 | 78 | 2 | 0 | 7½ |
| 11 | – | 5 | 8¾ | 45 | 1 | 3 | 5¼ | 79 | 2 | 1 | 1¾ |
| 12 | – | 6 | 3 | 46 | 1 | 3 | 11½ | 80 | 2 | 1 | 8 |
| 13 | – | 6 | 9¼ | 47 | 1 | 4 | 5¾ | 81 | 2 | 2 | 2¼ |
| 14 | – | 7 | 3½ | 48 | 1 | 5 | 0 | 82 | 2 | 2 | 8½ |
| 15 | – | 7 | 9¾ | 49 | 1 | 5 | 6¼ | 83 | 2 | 3 | 2¾ |
| 16 | – | 8 | 4 | 50 | 1 | 6 | 0½ | 84 | 2 | 3 | 9 |
| 17 | – | 8 | 10¼ | 51 | 1 | 6 | 6¾ | 85 | 2 | 4 | 3¼ |
| 18 | – | 9 | 4½ | 52 | 1 | 7 | 1 | 86 | 2 | 4 | 9½ |
| 19 | – | 9 | 10¾ | 53 | 1 | 7 | 7¼ | 87 | 2 | 5 | 3¾ |
| 20 | – | 10 | 5 | 54 | 1 | 8 | 1½ | 88 | 2 | 5 | 10 |
| 21 | – | 10 | 11¼ | 55 | 1 | 8 | 7¾ | 89 | 2 | 6 | 4¼ |
| 22 | – | 11 | 5½ | 56 | 1 | 9 | 2 | 90 | 2 | 6 | 10½ |
| 23 | – | 11 | 11¾ | 57 | 1 | 9 | 8¼ | 91 | 2 | 7 | 4¾ |
| 24 | – | 12 | 6 | 58 | 1 | 10 | 2½ | 92 | 2 | 7 | 11 |
| 25 | – | 13 | 0¼ | 59 | 1 | 10 | 8¾ | 93 | 2 | 8 | 5¼ |
| 26 | – | 13 | 6½ | 60 | 1 | 11 | 3 | 94 | 2 | 8 | 11½ |
| 27 | – | 14 | 0¾ | 61 | 1 | 11 | 9¼ | 95 | 2 | 9 | 5¾ |
| 28 | – | 14 | 7 | 62 | 1 | 12 | 3½ | 96 | 2 | 10 | 0 |
| 29 | – | 15 | 1¼ | 63 | 1 | 12 | 9¾ | 97 | 2 | 10 | 6¼ |
| 30 | – | 15 | 7½ | 64 | 1 | 13 | 4 | 98 | 2 | 11 | 0½ |
| 31 | – | 16 | 1¾ | 65 | 1 | 13 | 10¼ | 99 | 2 | 11 | 6¾ |
| 32 | – | 16 | 8 | 66 | 1 | 14 | 4½ | 100 | 2 | 12 | 1 |
| 33 | – | 17 | 2¼ | 67 | 1 | 14 | 10¾ | 144 | 3 | 15 | 0 |
| 34 | – | 17 | 8½ | 68 | 1 | 15 | 5 | 500 | 13 | 0 | 5 |
| 35 | – | 18 | 2¾ | 69 | 1 | 15 | 11¼ | 750 | 19 | 10 | 7½ |

## 6½d.

| No. | £ | s. | d. | No. | £ | s. | d. | No. | £ | s. | d. |
|---|---|---|---|---|---|---|---|---|---|---|---|
| 2 | – | 1 | 1 | 36 | – | 19 | 6 | 70 | 1 | 17 | 11 |
| 3 | – | 1 | 7½ | 37 | 1 | 0 | 0½ | 71 | 1 | 18 | 5½ |
| 4 | – | 2 | 2 | 38 | 1 | 0 | 7 | 72 | 1 | 19 | 0 |
| 5 | – | 2 | 8½ | 39 | 1 | 1 | 1½ | 73 | 1 | 19 | 6½ |
| 6 | – | 3 | 3 | 40 | 1 | 1 | 8 | 74 | 2 | 0 | 1 |
| 7 | – | 3 | 9½ | 41 | 1 | 2 | 2½ | 75 | 2 | 0 | 7½ |
| 8 | – | 4 | 4 | 42 | 1 | 2 | 9 | 76 | 2 | 1 | 2 |
| 9 | – | 4 | 10½ | 43 | 1 | 3 | 3½ | 77 | 2 | 1 | 8½ |
| 10 | – | 5 | 5 | 44 | 1 | 3 | 10 | 78 | 2 | 2 | 3 |
| 11 | – | 5 | 11½ | 45 | 1 | 4 | 4½ | 79 | 2 | 2 | 9½ |
| 12 | – | 6 | 6 | 46 | 1 | 4 | 11 | 80 | 2 | 3 | 4 |
| 13 | – | 7 | 0½ | 47 | 1 | 5 | 5½ | 81 | 2 | 3 | 10½ |
| 14 | – | 7 | 7 | 48 | 1 | 6 | 0 | 82 | 2 | 4 | 5 |
| 15 | – | 8 | 1½ | 49 | 1 | 6 | 6½ | 83 | 2 | 4 | 11½ |
| 16 | – | 8 | 8 | 50 | 1 | 7 | 1 | 84 | 2 | 5 | 6 |
| 17 | – | 9 | 2½ | 51 | 1 | 7 | 7½ | 85 | 2 | 6 | 0½ |
| 18 | – | 9 | 9 | 52 | 1 | 8 | 2 | 86 | 2 | 6 | 7 |
| 19 | – | 10 | 3½ | 53 | 1 | 8 | 8½ | 87 | 2 | 7 | 1½ |
| 20 | – | 10 | 10 | 54 | 1 | 9 | 3 | 88 | 2 | 7 | 8 |
| 21 | – | 11 | 4½ | 55 | 1 | 9 | 9½ | 89 | 2 | 8 | 2½ |
| 22 | – | 11 | 11 | 56 | 1 | 10 | 4 | 90 | 2 | 8 | 9 |
| 23 | – | 12 | 5½ | 57 | 1 | 10 | 10½ | 91 | 2 | 9 | 3½ |
| 24 | – | 13 | 0 | 58 | 1 | 11 | 5 | 92 | 2 | 9 | 10 |
| 25 | – | 13 | 6½ | 59 | 1 | 11 | 11½ | 93 | 2 | 10 | 4½ |
| 26 | – | 14 | 1 | 60 | 1 | 12 | 6 | 94 | 2 | 10 | 11 |
| 27 | – | 14 | 7½ | 61 | 1 | 13 | 0½ | 95 | 2 | 11 | 5½ |
| 28 | – | 15 | 2 | 62 | 1 | 13 | 7 | 96 | 2 | 12 | 0 |
| 29 | – | 15 | 8½ | 63 | 1 | 14 | 1½ | 97 | 2 | 12 | 6½ |
| 30 | – | 16 | 3 | 64 | 1 | 14 | 8 | 98 | 2 | 13 | 1 |
| 31 | – | 16 | 9½ | 65 | 1 | 15 | 2½ | 99 | 2 | 13 | 7½ |
| 32 | – | 17 | 4 | 66 | 1 | 15 | 9 | 100 | 2 | 14 | 2 |
| 33 | – | 17 | 10½ | 67 | 1 | 16 | 3½ | 144 | 3 | 18 | 0 |
| 34 | – | 18 | 5 | 68 | 1 | 16 | 10 | 500 | 13 | 10 | 10 |
| 35 | – | 18 | 11½ | 69 | 1 | 17 | 4½ | 750 | 20 | 6 | 3 |

## 6¾d.

| No. | £ | s. | d. | No. | £ | s. | d. | No. | £ | s. | d. |
|---|---|---|---|---|---|---|---|---|---|---|---|
| 2 | – | 1 | 1½ | 36 | 1 | 0 | 3 | 70 | 1 | 19 | 4½ |
| 3 | – | 1 | 8¼ | 37 | 1 | 0 | 9¾ | 71 | 1 | 19 | 11¼ |
| 4 | – | 2 | 3 | 38 | 1 | 1 | 4½ | 72 | 2 | 0 | 6 |
| 5 | – | 2 | 9¾ | 39 | 1 | 1 | 11¼ | 73 | 2 | 1 | 0¾ |
| 6 | – | 3 | 4½ | 40 | 1 | 2 | 6 | 74 | 2 | 1 | 7½ |
| 7 | – | 3 | 11¼ | 41 | 1 | 3 | 0¾ | 75 | 2 | 2 | 2¼ |
| 8 | – | 4 | 6 | 42 | 1 | 3 | 7½ | 76 | 2 | 2 | 9 |
| 9 | – | 5 | 0¾ | 43 | 1 | 4 | 2¼ | 77 | 2 | 3 | 3¾ |
| 10 | – | 5 | 7½ | 44 | 1 | 4 | 9 | 78 | 2 | 3 | 10½ |
| 11 | – | 6 | 2¼ | 45 | 1 | 5 | 3¾ | 79 | 2 | 4 | 5¼ |
| 12 | – | 6 | 9 | 46 | 1 | 5 | 10½ | 80 | 2 | 5 | 0 |
| 13 | – | 7 | 3¾ | 47 | 1 | 6 | 5¼ | 81 | 2 | 5 | 6¾ |
| 14 | – | 7 | 10½ | 48 | 1 | 7 | 0 | 82 | 2 | 6 | 1½ |
| 15 | – | 8 | 5¼ | 49 | 1 | 7 | 6¾ | 83 | 2 | 6 | 8¼ |
| 16 | – | 9 | 0 | 50 | 1 | 8 | 1½ | 84 | 2 | 7 | 3 |
| 17 | – | 9 | 6¾ | 51 | 1 | 8 | 8¼ | 85 | 2 | 7 | 9¾ |
| 18 | – | 10 | 1½ | 52 | 1 | 9 | 3 | 86 | 2 | 8 | 4½ |
| 19 | – | 10 | 8¼ | 53 | 1 | 9 | 9¾ | 87 | 2 | 8 | 11¼ |
| 20 | – | 11 | 3 | 54 | 1 | 10 | 4½ | 88 | 2 | 9 | 6 |
| 21 | – | 11 | 9¾ | 55 | 1 | 10 | 11¼ | 89 | 2 | 10 | 0¾ |
| 22 | – | 12 | 4½ | 56 | 1 | 11 | 6 | 90 | 2 | 10 | 7½ |
| 23 | – | 12 | 11¼ | 57 | 1 | 12 | 0¾ | 91 | 2 | 11 | 2¼ |
| 24 | – | 13 | 6 | 58 | 1 | 12 | 7½ | 92 | 2 | 11 | 9 |
| 25 | – | 14 | 0¾ | 59 | 1 | 13 | 2¼ | 93 | 2 | 12 | 3¾ |
| 26 | – | 14 | 7½ | 60 | 1 | 13 | 9 | 94 | 2 | 12 | 10½ |
| 27 | – | 15 | 2¼ | 61 | 1 | 14 | 3¾ | 95 | 2 | 13 | 5¼ |
| 28 | – | 15 | 9 | 62 | 1 | 14 | 10½ | 96 | 2 | 14 | 0 |
| 29 | – | 16 | 3¾ | 63 | 1 | 15 | 5¼ | 97 | 2 | 14 | 6¾ |
| 30 | – | 16 | 10½ | 64 | 1 | 16 | 0 | 98 | 2 | 15 | 1½ |
| 31 | – | 17 | 5¼ | 65 | 1 | 16 | 6¾ | 99 | 2 | 15 | 8¼ |
| 32 | – | 18 | 0 | 66 | 1 | 17 | 1½ | 100 | 2 | 16 | 3 |
| 33 | – | 18 | 6¾ | 67 | 1 | 17 | 8¼ | 144 | 4 | 1 | 0 |
| 34 | – | 19 | 1½ | 68 | 1 | 18 | 3 | 500 | 14 | 1 | 3 |
| 35 | – | 19 | 8¼ | 69 | 1 | 18 | 9¾ | 750 | 21 | 1 | 10½ |

# READY RECKONER.

## 7d.

| No. | £ | s. | d. | No. | £ | s. | d. | No. | £ | s. | d. |
|---|---|---|---|---|---|---|---|---|---|---|---|
| 2 | - | 1 | 2 | 36 | 1 | 1 | 0 | 70 | 2 | 0 | 10 |
| 3 | - | 1 | 9 | 37 | 1 | 1 | 7 | 71 | 2 | 1 | 5 |
| 4 | - | 2 | 4 | 38 | 1 | 2 | 2 | 72 | 2 | 2 | 0 |
| 5 | - | 2 | 11 | 39 | 1 | 2 | 9 | 73 | 2 | 2 | 7 |
| 6 | - | 3 | 6 | 40 | 1 | 3 | 4 | 74 | 2 | 3 | 2 |
| 7 | - | 4 | 1 | 41 | 1 | 3 | 11 | 75 | 2 | 3 | 9 |
| 8 | - | 4 | 8 | 42 | 1 | 4 | 6 | 76 | 2 | 4 | 4 |
| 9 | - | 5 | 3 | 43 | 1 | 5 | 1 | 77 | 2 | 4 | 11 |
| 10 | - | 5 | 10 | 44 | 1 | 5 | 8 | 78 | 2 | 5 | 6 |
| 11 | - | 6 | 5 | 45 | 1 | 6 | 3 | 79 | 2 | 6 | 1 |
| 12 | - | 7 | 0 | 46 | 1 | 6 | 10 | 80 | 2 | 6 | 8 |
| 13 | - | 7 | 7 | 47 | 1 | 7 | 5 | 81 | 2 | 7 | 3 |
| 14 | - | 8 | 2 | 48 | 1 | 8 | 0 | 82 | 2 | 7 | 10 |
| 15 | - | 8 | 9 | 49 | 1 | 8 | 7 | 83 | 2 | 8 | 5 |
| 16 | - | 9 | 4 | 50 | 1 | 9 | 2 | 84 | 2 | 9 | 0 |
| 17 | - | 9 | 11 | 51 | 1 | 9 | 9 | 85 | 2 | 9 | 7 |
| 18 | - | 10 | 6 | 52 | 1 | 10 | 4 | 86 | 2 | 10 | 2 |
| 19 | - | 11 | 1 | 53 | 1 | 10 | 11 | 87 | 2 | 10 | 9 |
| 20 | - | 11 | 8 | 54 | 1 | 11 | 6 | 88 | 2 | 11 | 4 |
| 21 | - | 12 | 3 | 55 | 1 | 12 | 1 | 89 | 2 | 11 | 11 |
| 22 | - | 12 | 10 | 56 | 1 | 12 | 8 | 90 | 2 | 12 | 6 |
| 23 | - | 13 | 5 | 57 | 1 | 13 | 3 | 91 | 2 | 13 | 1 |
| 24 | - | 14 | 0 | 58 | 1 | 13 | 10 | 92 | 2 | 13 | 8 |
| 25 | - | 14 | 7 | 59 | 1 | 14 | 5 | 93 | 2 | 14 | 3 |
| 26 | - | 15 | 2 | 60 | 1 | 15 | 0 | 94 | 2 | 14 | 10 |
| 27 | - | 15 | 9 | 61 | 1 | 15 | 7 | 95 | 2 | 15 | 5 |
| 28 | - | 16 | 4 | 62 | 1 | 16 | 2 | 96 | 2 | 16 | 0 |
| 29 | - | 16 | 11 | 63 | 1 | 16 | 9 | 97 | 2 | 16 | 7 |
| 30 | - | 17 | 6 | 64 | 1 | 17 | 4 | 98 | 2 | 17 | 2 |
| 31 | - | 18 | 1 | 65 | 1 | 17 | 11 | 99 | 2 | 17 | 9 |
| 32 | - | 18 | 8 | 66 | 1 | 18 | 6 | 100 | 2 | 18 | 4 |
| 33 | - | 19 | 3 | 67 | 1 | 19 | 1 | 144 | 4 | 4 | 0 |
| 34 | - | 19 | 10 | 68 | 1 | 19 | 8 | 500 | 14 | 11 | 8 |
| 35 | 1 | 0 | 5 | 69 | 2 | 0 | 3 | 750 | 21 | 17 | 6 |

## 7¼d.

| No. | £ | s. | d. | No. | £ | s. | d. | No. | £ | s. | d. |
|---|---|---|---|---|---|---|---|---|---|---|---|
| 2 | - | 1 | 2½ | 36 | 1 | 1 | 9 | 70 | 2 | 2 | 3½ |
| 3 | - | 1 | 9¾ | 37 | 1 | 2 | 4¼ | 71 | 2 | 2 | 10¾ |
| 4 | - | 2 | 5 | 38 | 1 | 2 | 11½ | 72 | 2 | 3 | 6 |
| 5 | - | 3 | 0¼ | 39 | 1 | 3 | 6¾ | 73 | 2 | 4 | 1¼ |
| 6 | - | 3 | 7½ | 40 | 1 | 4 | 2 | 74 | 2 | 4 | 8½ |
| 7 | - | 4 | 2¾ | 41 | 1 | 4 | 9¼ | 75 | 2 | 5 | 3¾ |
| 8 | - | 4 | 10 | 42 | 1 | 5 | 4½ | 76 | 2 | 5 | 11 |
| 9 | - | 5 | 5¼ | 43 | 1 | 5 | 11¾ | 77 | 2 | 6 | 6¼ |
| 10 | - | 6 | 0½ | 44 | 1 | 6 | 7 | 78 | 2 | 7 | 1½ |
| 11 | - | 6 | 7¾ | 45 | 1 | 7 | 2¼ | 79 | 2 | 7 | 8¾ |
| 12 | - | 7 | 3 | 46 | 1 | 7 | 9½ | 80 | 2 | 8 | 4 |
| 13 | - | 7 | 10¼ | 47 | 1 | 8 | 4¾ | 81 | 2 | 8 | 11¼ |
| 14 | - | 8 | 5½ | 48 | 1 | 9 | 0 | 82 | 2 | 9 | 6½ |
| 15 | - | 9 | 0¾ | 49 | 1 | 9 | 7¼ | 83 | 2 | 10 | 1¾ |
| 16 | - | 9 | 8 | 50 | 1 | 10 | 2½ | 84 | 2 | 10 | 9 |
| 17 | - | 10 | 3¼ | 51 | 1 | 10 | 9¾ | 85 | 2 | 11 | 4¼ |
| 18 | - | 10 | 10½ | 52 | 1 | 11 | 5 | 86 | 2 | 11 | 11½ |
| 19 | - | 11 | 5¾ | 53 | 1 | 12 | 0¼ | 87 | 2 | 12 | 6¾ |
| 20 | - | 12 | 1 | 54 | 1 | 12 | 7½ | 88 | 2 | 13 | 2 |
| 21 | - | 12 | 8¼ | 55 | 1 | 13 | 2¾ | 89 | 2 | 13 | 9¼ |
| 22 | - | 13 | 3½ | 56 | 1 | 13 | 10 | 90 | 2 | 14 | 4½ |
| 23 | - | 13 | 10¾ | 57 | 1 | 14 | 5¼ | 91 | 2 | 14 | 11¾ |
| 24 | - | 14 | 6 | 58 | 1 | 15 | 0½ | 92 | 2 | 15 | 7 |
| 25 | - | 15 | 1¼ | 59 | 1 | 15 | 7¾ | 93 | 2 | 16 | 2¼ |
| 26 | - | 15 | 8½ | 60 | 1 | 16 | 3 | 94 | 2 | 16 | 9½ |
| 27 | - | 16 | 3¾ | 61 | 1 | 16 | 10¼ | 95 | 2 | 17 | 4¾ |
| 28 | - | 16 | 11 | 62 | 1 | 17 | 5½ | 96 | 2 | 18 | 0 |
| 29 | - | 17 | 6¼ | 63 | 1 | 18 | 0¾ | 97 | 2 | 18 | 7¼ |
| 30 | - | 18 | 1½ | 64 | 1 | 18 | 8 | 98 | 2 | 19 | 2½ |
| 31 | - | 18 | 8¾ | 65 | 1 | 19 | 3¼ | 99 | 2 | 19 | 9¾ |
| 32 | - | 19 | 4 | 66 | 1 | 19 | 10½ | 100 | 3 | 0 | 5 |
| 33 | - | 19 | 11¼ | 67 | 2 | 0 | 5¾ | 144 | 4 | 7 | 0 |
| 34 | 1 | 0 | 6½ | 68 | 2 | 1 | 1 | 500 | 15 | 2 | 1 |
| 35 | 1 | 1 | 1¾ | 69 | 2 | 1 | 8¼ | 750 | 22 | 13 | 1½ |

## 7½d.

| No. | £ | s. | d. | No. | £ | s. | d. | No. | £ | s. | d. |
|---|---|---|---|---|---|---|---|---|---|---|---|
| 2 | - | 1 | 3 | 36 | 1 | 2 | 6 | 70 | 2 | 3 | 9 |
| 3 | - | 1 | 10½ | 37 | 1 | 3 | 1½ | 71 | 2 | 4 | 4½ |
| 4 | - | 2 | 6 | 38 | 1 | 3 | 9 | 72 | 2 | 5 | 0 |
| 5 | - | 3 | 1½ | 39 | 1 | 4 | 4½ | 73 | 2 | 5 | 7½ |
| 6 | - | 3 | 9 | 40 | 1 | 5 | 0 | 74 | 2 | 6 | 3 |
| 7 | - | 4 | 4½ | 41 | 1 | 5 | 7½ | 75 | 2 | 6 | 10½ |
| 8 | - | 5 | 0 | 42 | 1 | 6 | 3 | 76 | 2 | 7 | 6 |
| 9 | - | 5 | 7½ | 43 | 1 | 6 | 10½ | 77 | 2 | 8 | 1½ |
| 10 | - | 6 | 3 | 44 | 1 | 7 | 6 | 78 | 2 | 8 | 9 |
| 11 | - | 6 | 10½ | 45 | 1 | 8 | 1½ | 79 | 2 | 9 | 4½ |
| 12 | - | 7 | 6 | 46 | 1 | 8 | 9 | 80 | 2 | 10 | 0 |
| 13 | - | 8 | 1½ | 47 | 1 | 9 | 4½ | 81 | 2 | 10 | 7½ |
| 14 | - | 8 | 9 | 48 | 1 | 10 | 0 | 82 | 2 | 11 | 3 |
| 15 | - | 9 | 4½ | 49 | 1 | 10 | 7½ | 83 | 2 | 11 | 10½ |
| 16 | - | 10 | 0 | 50 | 1 | 11 | 3 | 84 | 2 | 12 | 6 |
| 17 | - | 10 | 7½ | 51 | 1 | 11 | 10½ | 85 | 2 | 13 | 1½ |
| 18 | - | 11 | 3 | 52 | 1 | 12 | 6 | 86 | 2 | 13 | 9 |
| 19 | - | 11 | 10½ | 53 | 1 | 13 | 1½ | 87 | 2 | 14 | 4½ |
| 20 | - | 12 | 6 | 54 | 1 | 13 | 9 | 88 | 2 | 15 | 0 |
| 21 | - | 13 | 1½ | 55 | 1 | 14 | 4½ | 89 | 2 | 15 | 7½ |
| 22 | - | 13 | 9 | 56 | 1 | 15 | 0 | 90 | 2 | 16 | 3 |
| 23 | - | 14 | 4½ | 57 | 1 | 15 | 7½ | 91 | 2 | 16 | 10½ |
| 24 | - | 15 | 0 | 58 | 1 | 16 | 3 | 92 | 2 | 17 | 6 |
| 25 | - | 15 | 7½ | 59 | 1 | 16 | 10½ | 93 | 2 | 18 | 1½ |
| 26 | - | 16 | 3 | 60 | 1 | 17 | 6 | 94 | 2 | 18 | 9 |
| 27 | - | 16 | 10½ | 61 | 1 | 18 | 1½ | 95 | 2 | 19 | 4½ |
| 28 | - | 17 | 6 | 62 | 1 | 18 | 9 | 96 | 3 | 0 | 0 |
| 29 | - | 18 | 1½ | 63 | 1 | 19 | 4½ | 97 | 3 | 0 | 7½ |
| 30 | - | 18 | 9 | 64 | 2 | 0 | 0 | 98 | 3 | 1 | 3 |
| 31 | - | 19 | 4½ | 65 | 2 | 0 | 7½ | 99 | 3 | 1 | 10½ |
| 32 | 1 | 0 | 0 | 66 | 2 | 1 | 3 | 100 | 3 | 2 | 6 |
| 33 | 1 | 0 | 7½ | 67 | 2 | 1 | 10½ | 144 | 4 | 10 | 0 |
| 34 | 1 | 1 | 3 | 68 | 2 | 2 | 6 | 500 | 15 | 12 | 6 |
| 35 | 1 | 1 | 10½ | 69 | 2 | 3 | 1½ | 750 | 23 | 8 | 9 |

## 7¾d.

| No. | £ | s. | d. | No. | £ | s. | d. | No. | £ | s. | d. |
|---|---|---|---|---|---|---|---|---|---|---|---|
| 2 | - | 1 | 3½ | 36 | 1 | 3 | 3 | 70 | 2 | 5 | 2½ |
| 3 | - | 1 | 11¼ | 37 | 1 | 3 | 10¾ | 71 | 2 | 5 | 10¼ |
| 4 | - | 2 | 7 | 38 | 1 | 4 | 6½ | 72 | 2 | 6 | 6 |
| 5 | - | 3 | 2¾ | 39 | 1 | 5 | 2¼ | 73 | 2 | 7 | 1¾ |
| 6 | - | 3 | 10½ | 40 | 1 | 5 | 10 | 74 | 2 | 7 | 9½ |
| 7 | - | 4 | 6¼ | 41 | 1 | 6 | 5¾ | 75 | 2 | 8 | 5¼ |
| 8 | - | 5 | 2 | 42 | 1 | 7 | 1½ | 76 | 2 | 9 | 1 |
| 9 | - | 5 | 9¾ | 43 | 1 | 7 | 9¼ | 77 | 2 | 9 | 8¾ |
| 10 | - | 6 | 5½ | 44 | 1 | 8 | 5 | 78 | 2 | 10 | 4½ |
| 11 | - | 7 | 1¼ | 45 | 1 | 9 | 0¾ | 79 | 2 | 11 | 0¼ |
| 12 | - | 7 | 9 | 46 | 1 | 9 | 8½ | 80 | 2 | 11 | 8 |
| 13 | - | 8 | 4¾ | 47 | 1 | 10 | 4¼ | 81 | 2 | 12 | 3¾ |
| 14 | - | 9 | 0½ | 48 | 1 | 11 | 0 | 82 | 2 | 12 | 11½ |
| 15 | - | 9 | 8¼ | 49 | 1 | 11 | 7¾ | 83 | 2 | 13 | 7¼ |
| 16 | - | 10 | 4 | 50 | 1 | 12 | 3½ | 84 | 2 | 14 | 3 |
| 17 | - | 10 | 11¾ | 51 | 1 | 12 | 11¼ | 85 | 2 | 14 | 10¾ |
| 18 | - | 11 | 7½ | 52 | 1 | 13 | 7 | 86 | 2 | 15 | 6½ |
| 19 | - | 12 | 3¼ | 53 | 1 | 14 | 2¾ | 87 | 2 | 16 | 2¼ |
| 20 | - | 12 | 11 | 54 | 1 | 14 | 10½ | 88 | 2 | 16 | 10 |
| 21 | - | 13 | 6¾ | 55 | 1 | 15 | 6¼ | 89 | 2 | 17 | 5¾ |
| 22 | - | 14 | 2½ | 56 | 1 | 16 | 2 | 90 | 2 | 18 | 1½ |
| 23 | - | 14 | 10¼ | 57 | 1 | 16 | 9¾ | 91 | 2 | 18 | 9¼ |
| 24 | - | 15 | 6 | 58 | 1 | 17 | 5½ | 92 | 2 | 19 | 5 |
| 25 | - | 16 | 1¾ | 59 | 1 | 18 | 1¼ | 93 | 3 | 0 | 0¾ |
| 26 | - | 16 | 9½ | 60 | 1 | 18 | 9 | 94 | 3 | 0 | 8½ |
| 27 | - | 17 | 5¼ | 61 | 1 | 19 | 4¾ | 95 | 3 | 1 | 4¼ |
| 28 | - | 18 | 1 | 62 | 2 | 0 | 0½ | 96 | 3 | 2 | 0 |
| 29 | - | 18 | 8¾ | 63 | 2 | 0 | 8¼ | 97 | 3 | 2 | 7¾ |
| 30 | - | 19 | 4½ | 64 | 2 | 1 | 4 | 98 | 3 | 3 | 3½ |
| 31 | 1 | 0 | 0¼ | 65 | 2 | 1 | 11¾ | 99 | 3 | 3 | 11¼ |
| 32 | 1 | 0 | 8 | 66 | 2 | 2 | 7½ | 100 | 3 | 4 | 7 |
| 33 | 1 | 1 | 3¾ | 67 | 2 | 3 | 3¼ | 144 | 4 | 13 | 0 |
| 34 | 1 | 1 | 11½ | 68 | 2 | 3 | 11 | 500 | 16 | 2 | 11 |
| 35 | 1 | 2 | 7¼ | 69 | 2 | 4 | 6¾ | 750 | 24 | 4 | 4½ |

# READY RECKONER.

## 8d.

| No. | £ | s. | d. | No. | £ | s. | d. | No. | £ | s. | d. |
|---|---|---|---|---|---|---|---|---|---|---|---|
| 2 | – | 1 | 4 | 36 | 1 | 4 | 0 | 70 | 2 | 6 | 8 |
| 3 | – | 2 | 0 | 37 | 1 | 4 | 8 | 71 | 2 | 7 | 4 |
| 4 | – | 2 | 8 | 38 | 1 | 5 | 4 | 72 | 2 | 8 | 0 |
| 5 | – | 3 | 4 | 39 | 1 | 6 | 0 | 73 | 2 | 8 | 8 |
| 6 | – | 4 | 0 | 40 | 1 | 6 | 8 | 74 | 2 | 9 | 4 |
| 7 | – | 4 | 8 | 41 | 1 | 7 | 4 | 75 | 2 | 10 | 0 |
| 8 | – | 5 | 4 | 42 | 1 | 8 | 0 | 76 | 2 | 10 | 8 |
| 9 | – | 6 | 0 | 43 | 1 | 8 | 8 | 77 | 2 | 11 | 4 |
| 10 | – | 6 | 8 | 44 | 1 | 9 | 4 | 78 | 2 | 12 | 0 |
| 11 | – | 7 | 4 | 45 | 1 | 10 | 0 | 79 | 2 | 12 | 8 |
| 12 | – | 8 | 0 | 46 | 1 | 10 | 8 | 80 | 2 | 13 | 4 |
| 13 | – | 8 | 8 | 47 | 1 | 11 | 4 | 81 | 2 | 14 | 0 |
| 14 | – | 9 | 4 | 48 | 1 | 12 | 0 | 82 | 2 | 14 | 8 |
| 15 | – | 10 | 0 | 49 | 1 | 12 | 8 | 83 | 2 | 15 | 4 |
| 16 | – | 10 | 8 | 50 | 1 | 13 | 4 | 84 | 2 | 16 | 0 |
| 17 | – | 11 | 4 | 51 | 1 | 14 | 0 | 85 | 2 | 16 | 8 |
| 18 | – | 12 | 0 | 52 | 1 | 14 | 8 | 86 | 2 | 17 | 4 |
| 19 | – | 12 | 8 | 53 | 1 | 15 | 4 | 87 | 2 | 18 | 0 |
| 20 | – | 13 | 4 | 54 | 1 | 16 | 0 | 88 | 2 | 18 | 8 |
| 21 | – | 14 | 0 | 55 | 1 | 16 | 8 | 89 | 2 | 19 | 4 |
| 22 | – | 14 | 8 | 56 | 1 | 17 | 4 | 90 | 3 | 0 | 0 |
| 23 | – | 15 | 4 | 57 | 1 | 18 | 0 | 91 | 3 | 0 | 8 |
| 24 | – | 16 | 0 | 58 | 1 | 18 | 8 | 92 | 3 | 1 | 4 |
| 25 | – | 16 | 8 | 59 | 1 | 19 | 4 | 93 | 3 | 2 | 0 |
| 26 | – | 17 | 4 | 60 | 2 | 0 | 0 | 94 | 3 | 2 | 8 |
| 27 | – | 18 | 0 | 61 | 2 | 0 | 8 | 95 | 3 | 3 | 4 |
| 28 | – | 18 | 8 | 62 | 2 | 1 | 4 | 96 | 3 | 4 | 0 |
| 29 | – | 19 | 4 | 63 | 2 | 2 | 0 | 97 | 3 | 4 | 8 |
| 30 | 1 | 0 | 0 | 64 | 2 | 2 | 8 | 98 | 3 | 5 | 4 |
| 31 | 1 | 0 | 8 | 65 | 2 | 3 | 4 | 99 | 3 | 6 | 0 |
| 32 | 1 | 1 | 4 | 66 | 2 | 4 | 0 | 100 | 3 | 6 | 8 |
| 33 | 1 | 2 | 0 | 67 | 2 | 4 | 8 | 144 | 4 | 16 | 0 |
| 34 | 1 | 2 | 8 | 68 | 2 | 5 | 4 | 500 | 16 | 13 | 4 |
| 35 | 1 | 3 | 4 | 69 | 2 | 6 | 0 | 750 | 25 | 0 | 0 |

## 8¼d.

| No. | £ | s. | d. | No. | £ | s. | d. | No. | £ | s. | d. |
|---|---|---|---|---|---|---|---|---|---|---|---|
| 2 | – | 1 | 4½ | 36 | 1 | 4 | 9 | 70 | 2 | 8 | 1½ |
| 3 | – | 2 | 0¾ | 37 | 1 | 5 | 5¼ | 71 | 2 | 8 | 9¾ |
| 4 | – | 2 | 9 | 38 | 1 | 6 | 1½ | 72 | 2 | 9 | 6 |
| 5 | – | 3 | 5¼ | 39 | 1 | 6 | 9¾ | 73 | 2 | 10 | 2¼ |
| 6 | – | 4 | 1½ | 40 | 1 | 7 | 6 | 74 | 2 | 10 | 10½ |
| 7 | – | 4 | 9¾ | 41 | 1 | 8 | 2¼ | 75 | 2 | 11 | 6¾ |
| 8 | – | 5 | 6 | 42 | 1 | 8 | 10½ | 76 | 2 | 12 | 3 |
| 9 | – | 6 | 2¼ | 43 | 1 | 9 | 6¾ | 77 | 2 | 12 | 11¼ |
| 10 | – | 6 | 10½ | 44 | 1 | 10 | 3 | 78 | 2 | 13 | 7½ |
| 11 | – | 7 | 6¾ | 45 | 1 | 10 | 11¼ | 79 | 2 | 14 | 3¾ |
| 12 | – | 8 | 3 | 46 | 1 | 11 | 7½ | 80 | 2 | 15 | 0 |
| 13 | – | 8 | 11¼ | 47 | 1 | 12 | 3¾ | 81 | 2 | 15 | 8¼ |
| 14 | – | 9 | 7½ | 48 | 1 | 13 | 0 | 82 | 2 | 16 | 4½ |
| 15 | – | 10 | 3¾ | 49 | 1 | 13 | 8¼ | 83 | 2 | 17 | 0¾ |
| 16 | – | 11 | 0 | 50 | 1 | 14 | 4½ | 84 | 2 | 17 | 9 |
| 17 | – | 11 | 8¼ | 51 | 1 | 15 | 0¾ | 85 | 2 | 18 | 5¼ |
| 18 | – | 12 | 4½ | 52 | 1 | 15 | 9 | 86 | 2 | 19 | 1½ |
| 19 | – | 13 | 0¾ | 53 | 1 | 16 | 5¼ | 87 | 2 | 19 | 9¾ |
| 20 | – | 13 | 9 | 54 | 1 | 17 | 1½ | 88 | 3 | 0 | 6 |
| 21 | – | 14 | 5¼ | 55 | 1 | 17 | 9¾ | 89 | 3 | 1 | 2¼ |
| 22 | – | 15 | 1½ | 56 | 1 | 18 | 6 | 90 | 3 | 1 | 10½ |
| 23 | – | 15 | 9¾ | 57 | 1 | 19 | 2¼ | 91 | 3 | 2 | 6¾ |
| 24 | – | 16 | 6 | 58 | 1 | 19 | 10½ | 92 | 3 | 3 | 3 |
| 25 | – | 17 | 2¼ | 59 | 2 | 0 | 6¾ | 93 | 3 | 3 | 11¼ |
| 26 | – | 17 | 10½ | 60 | 2 | 1 | 3 | 94 | 3 | 4 | 7½ |
| 27 | – | 18 | 6¾ | 61 | 2 | 1 | 11¼ | 95 | 3 | 5 | 3¾ |
| 28 | – | 19 | 3 | 62 | 2 | 2 | 7½ | 96 | 3 | 6 | 0 |
| 29 | – | 19 | 11¼ | 63 | 2 | 3 | 3¾ | 97 | 3 | 6 | 8¼ |
| 30 | 1 | 0 | 7½ | 64 | 2 | 4 | 0 | 98 | 3 | 7 | 4½ |
| 31 | 1 | 1 | 3¾ | 65 | 2 | 4 | 8¼ | 99 | 3 | 8 | 0¾ |
| 32 | 1 | 2 | 0 | 66 | 2 | 5 | 4½ | 100 | 3 | 8 | 9 |
| 33 | 1 | 2 | 8¼ | 67 | 2 | 6 | 0¾ | 144 | 4 | 19 | 0 |
| 34 | 1 | 3 | 4½ | 68 | 2 | 6 | 9 | 500 | 17 | 3 | 9 |
| 35 | 1 | 4 | 0¾ | 69 | 2 | 7 | 5¼ | 750 | 25 | 15 | 7½ |

## 8½d.

| No. | £ | s. | d. | No. | £ | s. | d. | No. | £ | s. | d. |
|---|---|---|---|---|---|---|---|---|---|---|---|
| 2 | – | 1 | 5 | 36 | 1 | 5 | 6 | 70 | 2 | 9 | 7 |
| 3 | – | 2 | 1½ | 37 | 1 | 6 | 2½ | 71 | 2 | 10 | 3½ |
| 4 | – | 2 | 10 | 38 | 1 | 6 | 11 | 72 | 2 | 11 | 0 |
| 5 | – | 3 | 6½ | 39 | 1 | 7 | 7½ | 73 | 2 | 11 | 8½ |
| 6 | – | 4 | 3 | 40 | 1 | 8 | 4 | 74 | 2 | 12 | 5 |
| 7 | – | 4 | 11½ | 41 | 1 | 9 | 0½ | 75 | 2 | 13 | 1½ |
| 8 | – | 5 | 8 | 42 | 1 | 9 | 9 | 76 | 2 | 13 | 10 |
| 9 | – | 6 | 4½ | 43 | 1 | 10 | 5½ | 77 | 2 | 14 | 6½ |
| 10 | – | 7 | 1 | 44 | 1 | 11 | 2 | 78 | 2 | 15 | 3 |
| 11 | – | 7 | 9½ | 45 | 1 | 11 | 10½ | 79 | 2 | 15 | 11½ |
| 12 | – | 8 | 6 | 46 | 1 | 12 | 7 | 80 | 2 | 16 | 8 |
| 13 | – | 9 | 2½ | 47 | 1 | 13 | 3½ | 81 | 2 | 17 | 4½ |
| 14 | – | 9 | 11 | 48 | 1 | 14 | 0 | 82 | 2 | 18 | 1 |
| 15 | – | 10 | 7½ | 49 | 1 | 14 | 8½ | 83 | 2 | 18 | 9½ |
| 16 | – | 11 | 4 | 50 | 1 | 15 | 5 | 84 | 2 | 19 | 6 |
| 17 | – | 12 | 0½ | 51 | 1 | 16 | 1½ | 85 | 3 | 0 | 2½ |
| 18 | – | 12 | 9 | 52 | 1 | 16 | 10 | 86 | 3 | 0 | 11 |
| 19 | – | 13 | 5½ | 53 | 1 | 17 | 6½ | 87 | 3 | 1 | 7½ |
| 20 | – | 14 | 2 | 54 | 1 | 18 | 3 | 88 | 3 | 2 | 4 |
| 21 | – | 14 | 10½ | 55 | 1 | 18 | 11½ | 89 | 3 | 3 | 0½ |
| 22 | – | 15 | 7 | 56 | 1 | 19 | 8 | 90 | 3 | 3 | 9 |
| 23 | – | 16 | 3½ | 57 | 2 | 0 | 4½ | 91 | 3 | 4 | 5½ |
| 24 | – | 17 | 0 | 58 | 2 | 1 | 1 | 92 | 3 | 5 | 2 |
| 25 | – | 17 | 8½ | 59 | 2 | 1 | 9½ | 93 | 3 | 5 | 10½ |
| 26 | – | 18 | 5 | 60 | 2 | 2 | 6 | 94 | 3 | 6 | 7 |
| 27 | – | 19 | 1½ | 61 | 2 | 3 | 2½ | 95 | 3 | 7 | 3½ |
| 28 | – | 19 | 10 | 62 | 2 | 3 | 11 | 96 | 3 | 8 | 0 |
| 29 | 1 | 0 | 6½ | 63 | 2 | 4 | 7½ | 97 | 3 | 8 | 8½ |
| 30 | 1 | 1 | 3 | 64 | 2 | 5 | 4 | 98 | 3 | 9 | 5 |
| 31 | 1 | 1 | 11½ | 65 | 2 | 6 | 0½ | 99 | 3 | 10 | 1½ |
| 32 | 1 | 2 | 8 | 66 | 2 | 6 | 9 | 100 | 3 | 10 | 10 |
| 33 | 1 | 3 | 4½ | 67 | 2 | 7 | 5½ | 144 | 5 | 2 | 0 |
| 34 | 1 | 4 | 1 | 68 | 2 | 8 | 2 | 500 | 17 | 14 | 2 |
| 35 | 1 | 4 | 9½ | 69 | 2 | 8 | 10½ | 750 | 26 | 11 | 3 |

## 8¾d.

| No. | £ | s. | d. | No. | £ | s. | d. | No. | £ | s. | d. |
|---|---|---|---|---|---|---|---|---|---|---|---|
| 2 | – | 1 | 5½ | 36 | 1 | 6 | 3 | 70 | 2 | 11 | 0½ |
| 3 | – | 2 | 2¼ | 37 | 1 | 6 | 11¾ | 71 | 2 | 11 | 9¼ |
| 4 | – | 2 | 11 | 38 | 1 | 7 | 8½ | 72 | 2 | 12 | 6 |
| 5 | – | 3 | 7¾ | 39 | 1 | 8 | 5¼ | 73 | 2 | 13 | 2¾ |
| 6 | – | 4 | 4½ | 40 | 1 | 9 | 2 | 74 | 2 | 13 | 11½ |
| 7 | – | 5 | 1¼ | 41 | 1 | 9 | 10¾ | 75 | 2 | 14 | 8¼ |
| 8 | – | 5 | 10 | 42 | 1 | 10 | 7½ | 76 | 2 | 15 | 5 |
| 9 | – | 6 | 6¾ | 43 | 1 | 11 | 4¼ | 77 | 2 | 16 | 1¾ |
| 10 | – | 7 | 3½ | 44 | 1 | 12 | 1 | 78 | 2 | 16 | 10½ |
| 11 | – | 8 | 0¼ | 45 | 1 | 12 | 9¾ | 79 | 2 | 17 | 7¼ |
| 12 | – | 8 | 9 | 46 | 1 | 13 | 6½ | 80 | 2 | 18 | 4 |
| 13 | – | 9 | 5¾ | 47 | 1 | 14 | 3¼ | 81 | 2 | 19 | 0¾ |
| 14 | – | 10 | 2½ | 48 | 1 | 15 | 0 | 82 | 2 | 19 | 9½ |
| 15 | – | 10 | 11¼ | 49 | 1 | 15 | 8¾ | 83 | 3 | 0 | 6¼ |
| 16 | – | 11 | 8 | 50 | 1 | 16 | 5½ | 84 | 3 | 1 | 3 |
| 17 | – | 12 | 4¾ | 51 | 1 | 17 | 2¼ | 85 | 3 | 1 | 11¾ |
| 18 | – | 13 | 1½ | 52 | 1 | 17 | 11 | 86 | 3 | 2 | 8½ |
| 19 | – | 13 | 10¼ | 53 | 1 | 18 | 7¾ | 87 | 3 | 3 | 5¼ |
| 20 | – | 14 | 7 | 54 | 1 | 19 | 4½ | 88 | 3 | 4 | 2 |
| 21 | – | 15 | 3¾ | 55 | 2 | 0 | 1¼ | 89 | 3 | 4 | 10¾ |
| 22 | – | 16 | 0½ | 56 | 2 | 0 | 10 | 90 | 3 | 5 | 7½ |
| 23 | – | 16 | 9¼ | 57 | 2 | 1 | 6¾ | 91 | 3 | 6 | 4¼ |
| 24 | – | 17 | 6 | 58 | 2 | 2 | 3½ | 92 | 3 | 7 | 1 |
| 25 | – | 18 | 2¾ | 59 | 2 | 3 | 0¼ | 93 | 3 | 7 | 9¾ |
| 26 | – | 18 | 11½ | 60 | 2 | 3 | 9 | 94 | 3 | 8 | 6½ |
| 27 | – | 19 | 8¼ | 61 | 2 | 4 | 5¾ | 95 | 3 | 9 | 3¼ |
| 28 | 1 | 0 | 5 | 62 | 2 | 5 | 2½ | 96 | 3 | 10 | 0 |
| 29 | 1 | 1 | 1¾ | 63 | 2 | 5 | 11¼ | 97 | 3 | 10 | 8¾ |
| 30 | 1 | 1 | 10½ | 64 | 2 | 6 | 8 | 98 | 3 | 11 | 5½ |
| 31 | 1 | 2 | 7¼ | 65 | 2 | 7 | 4¾ | 99 | 3 | 12 | 2¼ |
| 32 | 1 | 3 | 4 | 66 | 2 | 8 | 1½ | 100 | 3 | 12 | 11 |
| 33 | 1 | 4 | 0¾ | 67 | 2 | 8 | 10¼ | 144 | 5 | 5 | 0 |
| 34 | 1 | 4 | 9½ | 68 | 2 | 9 | 7 | 500 | 18 | 4 | 7 |
| 35 | 1 | 5 | 6¼ | 69 | 2 | 10 | 3¾ | 750 | 27 | 6 | 10½ |

# READY RECKONER.

## 9d.

| No. | £ | s. | d. | No. | £ | s. | d. | No. | £ | s. | d. |
|---|---|---|---|---|---|---|---|---|---|---|---|
| 2 | – | 1 | 6 | 36 | 1 | 7 | 0 | 70 | 2 | 12 | 6 |
| 3 | – | 2 | 3 | 37 | 1 | 7 | 9 | 71 | 2 | 13 | 3 |
| 4 | – | 3 | 0 | 38 | 1 | 8 | 6 | 72 | 2 | 14 | 0 |
| 5 | – | 3 | 9 | 39 | 1 | 9 | 3 | 73 | 2 | 14 | 9 |
| 6 | – | 4 | 6 | 40 | 1 | 10 | 0 | 74 | 2 | 15 | 6 |
| 7 | – | 5 | 3 | 41 | 1 | 10 | 9 | 75 | 2 | 16 | 3 |
| 8 | – | 6 | 0 | 42 | 1 | 11 | 6 | 76 | 2 | 17 | 0 |
| 9 | – | 6 | 9 | 43 | 1 | 12 | 3 | 77 | 2 | 17 | 9 |
| 10 | – | 7 | 6 | 44 | 1 | 13 | 0 | 78 | 2 | 18 | 6 |
| 11 | – | 8 | 3 | 45 | 1 | 13 | 9 | 79 | 2 | 19 | 3 |
| 12 | – | 9 | 0 | 46 | 1 | 14 | 6 | 80 | 3 | 0 | 0 |
| 13 | – | 9 | 9 | 47 | 1 | 15 | 3 | 81 | 3 | 0 | 9 |
| 14 | – | 10 | 6 | 48 | 1 | 16 | 0 | 82 | 3 | 1 | 6 |
| 15 | – | 11 | 3 | 49 | 1 | 16 | 9 | 83 | 3 | 2 | 3 |
| 16 | – | 12 | 0 | 50 | 1 | 17 | 6 | 84 | 3 | 3 | 0 |
| 17 | – | 12 | 9 | 51 | 1 | 18 | 3 | 85 | 3 | 3 | 9 |
| 18 | – | 13 | 6 | 52 | 1 | 19 | 0 | 86 | 3 | 4 | 6 |
| 19 | – | 14 | 3 | 53 | 1 | 19 | 9 | 87 | 3 | 5 | 3 |
| 20 | – | 15 | 0 | 54 | 2 | 0 | 6 | 88 | 3 | 6 | 0 |
| 21 | – | 15 | 9 | 55 | 2 | 1 | 3 | 89 | 3 | 6 | 9 |
| 22 | – | 16 | 6 | 56 | 2 | 2 | 0 | 90 | 3 | 7 | 6 |
| 23 | – | 17 | 3 | 57 | 2 | 2 | 9 | 91 | 3 | 8 | 3 |
| 24 | – | 18 | 0 | 58 | 2 | 3 | 6 | 92 | 3 | 9 | 0 |
| 25 | – | 18 | 9 | 59 | 2 | 4 | 3 | 93 | 3 | 9 | 9 |
| 26 | – | 19 | 6 | 60 | 2 | 5 | 0 | 94 | 3 | 10 | 6 |
| 27 | 1 | 0 | 3 | 61 | 2 | 5 | 9 | 95 | 3 | 11 | 3 |
| 28 | 1 | 1 | 0 | 62 | 2 | 6 | 6 | 96 | 3 | 12 | 0 |
| 29 | 1 | 1 | 9 | 63 | 2 | 7 | 3 | 97 | 3 | 12 | 9 |
| 30 | 1 | 2 | 6 | 64 | 2 | 8 | 0 | 98 | 3 | 13 | 6 |
| 31 | 1 | 3 | 3 | 65 | 2 | 8 | 9 | 99 | 3 | 14 | 3 |
| 32 | 1 | 4 | 0 | 66 | 2 | 9 | 6 | 100 | 3 | 15 | 0 |
| 33 | 1 | 4 | 9 | 67 | 2 | 10 | 3 | 144 | 5 | 8 | 0 |
| 34 | 1 | 5 | 6 | 68 | 2 | 11 | 0 | 500 | 18 | 15 | 0 |
| 35 | 1 | 6 | 3 | 69 | 2 | 11 | 9 | 750 | 28 | 2 | 6 |

## 9¼d.

| No. | £ | s. | d. | No. | £ | s. | d. | No. | £ | s. | d. |
|---|---|---|---|---|---|---|---|---|---|---|---|
| 2 | – | 1 | 6½ | 36 | 1 | 7 | 9 | 70 | 2 | 13 | 11½ |
| 3 | – | 2 | 3¾ | 37 | 1 | 8 | 6¼ | 71 | 2 | 14 | 8¾ |
| 4 | – | 3 | 1 | 38 | 1 | 9 | 3½ | 72 | 2 | 15 | 6 |
| 5 | – | 3 | 10¼ | 39 | 1 | 10 | 0¾ | 73 | 2 | 16 | 3¼ |
| 6 | – | 4 | 7½ | 40 | 1 | 10 | 10 | 74 | 2 | 17 | 0½ |
| 7 | – | 5 | 4¾ | 41 | 1 | 11 | 7¼ | 75 | 2 | 17 | 9¾ |
| 8 | – | 6 | 2 | 42 | 1 | 12 | 4½ | 76 | 2 | 18 | 7 |
| 9 | – | 6 | 11¼ | 43 | 1 | 13 | 1¾ | 77 | 2 | 19 | 4¼ |
| 10 | – | 7 | 8½ | 44 | 1 | 13 | 11 | 78 | 3 | 0 | 1½ |
| 11 | – | 8 | 5¾ | 45 | 1 | 14 | 8¼ | 79 | 3 | 0 | 10¾ |
| 12 | – | 9 | 3 | 46 | 1 | 15 | 5½ | 80 | 3 | 1 | 8 |
| 13 | – | 10 | 0¼ | 47 | 1 | 16 | 2¾ | 81 | 3 | 2 | 5¼ |
| 14 | – | 10 | 9½ | 48 | 1 | 17 | 0 | 82 | 3 | 3 | 2½ |
| 15 | – | 11 | 6¾ | 49 | 1 | 17 | 9¼ | 83 | 3 | 3 | 11¾ |
| 16 | – | 12 | 4 | 50 | 1 | 18 | 6½ | 84 | 3 | 4 | 9 |
| 17 | – | 13 | 1¼ | 51 | 1 | 19 | 3¾ | 85 | 3 | 5 | 6¼ |
| 18 | – | 13 | 10½ | 52 | 2 | 0 | 1 | 86 | 3 | 6 | 3½ |
| 19 | – | 14 | 7¾ | 53 | 2 | 0 | 10¼ | 87 | 3 | 7 | 0¾ |
| 20 | – | 15 | 5 | 54 | 2 | 1 | 7½ | 88 | 3 | 7 | 10 |
| 21 | – | 16 | 2¼ | 55 | 2 | 2 | 4¾ | 89 | 3 | 8 | 7¼ |
| 22 | – | 16 | 11½ | 56 | 2 | 3 | 2 | 90 | 3 | 9 | 4½ |
| 23 | – | 17 | 8¾ | 57 | 2 | 3 | 11¼ | 91 | 3 | 10 | 1¾ |
| 24 | – | 18 | 6 | 58 | 2 | 4 | 8½ | 92 | 3 | 10 | 11 |
| 25 | – | 19 | 3¼ | 59 | 2 | 5 | 5¾ | 93 | 3 | 11 | 8¼ |
| 26 | 1 | 0 | 0½ | 60 | 2 | 6 | 3 | 94 | 3 | 12 | 5½ |
| 27 | 1 | 0 | 9¾ | 61 | 2 | 7 | 0¼ | 95 | 3 | 13 | 2¾ |
| 28 | 1 | 1 | 7 | 62 | 2 | 7 | 9½ | 96 | 3 | 14 | 0 |
| 29 | 1 | 2 | 4¼ | 63 | 2 | 8 | 6¾ | 97 | 3 | 14 | 9¼ |
| 30 | 1 | 3 | 1½ | 64 | 2 | 9 | 4 | 98 | 3 | 15 | 6½ |
| 31 | 1 | 3 | 10¾ | 65 | 2 | 10 | 1¼ | 99 | 3 | 16 | 3¾ |
| 32 | 1 | 4 | 8 | 66 | 2 | 10 | 10½ | 100 | 3 | 17 | 1 |
| 33 | 1 | 5 | 5¼ | 67 | 2 | 11 | 7¾ | 144 | 5 | 11 | 0 |
| 34 | 1 | 6 | 2½ | 68 | 2 | 12 | 5 | 500 | 19 | 5 | 5 |
| 35 | 1 | 6 | 11¾ | 69 | 2 | 13 | 2¼ | 750 | 28 | 18 | 1½ |

## 9½d.

| No. | £ | s. | d. | No. | £ | s. | d. | No. | £ | s. | d. |
|---|---|---|---|---|---|---|---|---|---|---|---|
| 2 | – | 1 | 7 | 36 | 1 | 8 | 6 | 70 | 2 | 15 | 5 |
| 3 | – | 2 | 4½ | 37 | 1 | 9 | 3½ | 71 | 2 | 16 | 2½ |
| 4 | – | 3 | 2 | 38 | 1 | 10 | 1 | 72 | 2 | 17 | 0 |
| 5 | – | 3 | 11½ | 39 | 1 | 10 | 10½ | 73 | 2 | 17 | 9½ |
| 6 | – | 4 | 9 | 40 | 1 | 11 | 8 | 74 | 2 | 18 | 7 |
| 7 | – | 5 | 6½ | 41 | 1 | 12 | 5½ | 75 | 2 | 19 | 4½ |
| 8 | – | 6 | 4 | 42 | 1 | 13 | 3 | 76 | 3 | 0 | 2 |
| 9 | – | 7 | 1½ | 43 | 1 | 14 | 0½ | 77 | 3 | 0 | 11½ |
| 10 | – | 7 | 11 | 44 | 1 | 14 | 10 | 78 | 3 | 1 | 9 |
| 11 | – | 8 | 8½ | 45 | 1 | 15 | 7½ | 79 | 3 | 2 | 6½ |
| 12 | – | 9 | 6 | 46 | 1 | 16 | 5 | 80 | 3 | 3 | 4 |
| 13 | – | 10 | 3½ | 47 | 1 | 17 | 2½ | 81 | 3 | 4 | 1½ |
| 14 | – | 11 | 1 | 48 | 1 | 18 | 0 | 82 | 3 | 4 | 11 |
| 15 | – | 11 | 10½ | 49 | 1 | 18 | 9½ | 83 | 3 | 5 | 8½ |
| 16 | – | 12 | 8 | 50 | 1 | 19 | 7 | 84 | 3 | 6 | 6 |
| 17 | – | 13 | 5½ | 51 | 2 | 0 | 4½ | 85 | 3 | 7 | 3½ |
| 18 | – | 14 | 3 | 52 | 2 | 1 | 2 | 86 | 3 | 8 | 1 |
| 19 | – | 15 | 0½ | 53 | 2 | 1 | 11½ | 87 | 3 | 8 | 10½ |
| 20 | – | 15 | 10 | 54 | 2 | 2 | 9 | 88 | 3 | 9 | 8 |
| 21 | – | 16 | 7½ | 55 | 2 | 3 | 6½ | 89 | 3 | 10 | 5½ |
| 22 | – | 17 | 5 | 56 | 2 | 4 | 4 | 90 | 3 | 11 | 3 |
| 23 | – | 18 | 2½ | 57 | 2 | 5 | 1½ | 91 | 3 | 12 | 0½ |
| 24 | – | 19 | 0 | 58 | 2 | 5 | 11 | 92 | 3 | 12 | 10 |
| 25 | – | 19 | 9½ | 59 | 2 | 6 | 8½ | 93 | 3 | 13 | 7½ |
| 26 | 1 | 0 | 7 | 60 | 2 | 7 | 6 | 94 | 3 | 14 | 5 |
| 27 | 1 | 1 | 4½ | 61 | 2 | 8 | 3½ | 95 | 3 | 15 | 2½ |
| 28 | 1 | 2 | 2 | 62 | 2 | 9 | 1 | 96 | 3 | 16 | 0 |
| 29 | 1 | 2 | 11½ | 63 | 2 | 9 | 10½ | 97 | 3 | 16 | 9½ |
| 30 | 1 | 3 | 9 | 64 | 2 | 10 | 8 | 98 | 3 | 17 | 7 |
| 31 | 1 | 4 | 6½ | 65 | 2 | 11 | 5½ | 99 | 3 | 18 | 4½ |
| 32 | 1 | 5 | 4 | 66 | 2 | 12 | 3 | 100 | 3 | 19 | 2 |
| 33 | 1 | 6 | 1½ | 67 | 2 | 13 | 0½ | 144 | 5 | 14 | 0 |
| 34 | 1 | 6 | 11 | 68 | 2 | 13 | 10 | 500 | 19 | 15 | 10 |
| 35 | 1 | 7 | 8½ | 69 | 2 | 14 | 7½ | 750 | 29 | 13 | 9 |

## 9¾d.

| No. | £ | s. | d. | No. | £ | s. | d. | No. | £ | s. | d. |
|---|---|---|---|---|---|---|---|---|---|---|---|
| 2 | – | 1 | 7½ | 36 | 1 | 9 | 3 | 70 | 2 | 16 | 10½ |
| 3 | – | 2 | 5¼ | 37 | 1 | 10 | 0¾ | 71 | 2 | 17 | 8¼ |
| 4 | – | 3 | 3 | 38 | 1 | 10 | 10½ | 72 | 2 | 18 | 6 |
| 5 | – | 4 | 0¾ | 39 | 1 | 11 | 8¼ | 73 | 2 | 19 | 3¾ |
| 6 | – | 4 | 10½ | 40 | 1 | 12 | 6 | 74 | 3 | 0 | 1½ |
| 7 | – | 5 | 8¼ | 41 | 1 | 13 | 3¾ | 75 | 3 | 0 | 11¼ |
| 8 | – | 6 | 6 | 42 | 1 | 14 | 1½ | 76 | 3 | 1 | 9 |
| 9 | – | 7 | 3¾ | 43 | 1 | 14 | 11¼ | 77 | 3 | 2 | 6¾ |
| 10 | – | 8 | 1½ | 44 | 1 | 15 | 9 | 78 | 3 | 3 | 4½ |
| 11 | – | 8 | 11¼ | 45 | 1 | 16 | 6¾ | 79 | 3 | 4 | 2¼ |
| 12 | – | 9 | 9 | 46 | 1 | 17 | 4½ | 80 | 3 | 5 | 0 |
| 13 | – | 10 | 6¾ | 47 | 1 | 18 | 2¼ | 81 | 3 | 5 | 9¾ |
| 14 | – | 11 | 4½ | 48 | 1 | 19 | 0 | 82 | 3 | 6 | 7½ |
| 15 | – | 12 | 2¼ | 49 | 1 | 19 | 9¾ | 83 | 3 | 7 | 5¼ |
| 16 | – | 13 | 0 | 50 | 2 | 0 | 7½ | 84 | 3 | 8 | 3 |
| 17 | – | 13 | 9¾ | 51 | 2 | 1 | 5¼ | 85 | 3 | 9 | 0¾ |
| 18 | – | 14 | 7½ | 52 | 2 | 2 | 3 | 86 | 3 | 9 | 10½ |
| 19 | – | 15 | 5¼ | 53 | 2 | 3 | 0¾ | 87 | 3 | 10 | 8¼ |
| 20 | – | 16 | 3 | 54 | 2 | 3 | 10½ | 88 | 3 | 11 | 6 |
| 21 | – | 17 | 0¾ | 55 | 2 | 4 | 8¼ | 89 | 3 | 12 | 3¾ |
| 22 | – | 17 | 10½ | 56 | 2 | 5 | 6 | 90 | 3 | 13 | 1½ |
| 23 | – | 18 | 8¼ | 57 | 2 | 6 | 3¾ | 91 | 3 | 13 | 11¼ |
| 24 | – | 19 | 6 | 58 | 2 | 7 | 1½ | 92 | 3 | 14 | 9 |
| 25 | 1 | 0 | 3¾ | 59 | 2 | 7 | 11¼ | 93 | 3 | 15 | 6¾ |
| 26 | 1 | 1 | 1½ | 60 | 2 | 8 | 9 | 94 | 3 | 16 | 4½ |
| 27 | 1 | 1 | 11¼ | 61 | 2 | 9 | 6¾ | 95 | 3 | 17 | 2¼ |
| 28 | 1 | 2 | 9 | 62 | 2 | 10 | 4½ | 96 | 3 | 18 | 0 |
| 29 | 1 | 3 | 6¾ | 63 | 2 | 11 | 2¼ | 97 | 3 | 18 | 9¾ |
| 30 | 1 | 4 | 4½ | 64 | 2 | 12 | 0 | 98 | 3 | 19 | 7½ |
| 31 | 1 | 5 | 2¼ | 65 | 2 | 12 | 9¾ | 99 | 4 | 0 | 5¼ |
| 32 | 1 | 6 | 0 | 66 | 2 | 13 | 7½ | 100 | 4 | 1 | 3 |
| 33 | 1 | 6 | 9¾ | 67 | 2 | 14 | 5¼ | 144 | 5 | 17 | 0 |
| 34 | 1 | 7 | 7½ | 68 | 2 | 15 | 3 | 500 | 20 | 6 | 3 |
| 35 | 1 | 8 | 5¼ | 69 | 2 | 16 | 0¾ | 750 | 30 | 9 | 4½ |

# READY RECKONER.

## 10d.

| No. | £ | s. | d. | No. | £ | s. | d. | No. | £ | s. | d. |
|---|---|---|---|---|---|---|---|---|---|---|---|
| 2 | – | 1 | 8 | 36 | 1 | 10 | 0 | 70 | 2 | 18 | 4 |
| 3 | – | 2 | 6 | 37 | 1 | 10 | 10 | 71 | 2 | 19 | 2 |
| 4 | – | 3 | 4 | 38 | 1 | 11 | 8 | 72 | 3 | 0 | 0 |
| 5 | – | 4 | 2 | 39 | 1 | 12 | 6 | 73 | 3 | 0 | 10 |
| 6 | – | 5 | 0 | 40 | 1 | 13 | 4 | 74 | 3 | 1 | 8 |
| 7 | – | 5 | 10 | 41 | 1 | 14 | 2 | 75 | 3 | 2 | 6 |
| 8 | – | 6 | 8 | 42 | 1 | 15 | 0 | 76 | 3 | 3 | 4 |
| 9 | – | 7 | 6 | 43 | 1 | 15 | 10 | 77 | 3 | 4 | 2 |
| 10 | – | 8 | 4 | 44 | 1 | 16 | 8 | 78 | 3 | 5 | 0 |
| 11 | – | 9 | 2 | 45 | 1 | 17 | 6 | 79 | 3 | 5 | 10 |
| 12 | – | 10 | 0 | 46 | 1 | 18 | 4 | 80 | 3 | 6 | 8 |
| 13 | – | 10 | 10 | 47 | 1 | 19 | 2 | 81 | 3 | 7 | 6 |
| 14 | – | 11 | 8 | 48 | 2 | 0 | 0 | 82 | 3 | 8 | 4 |
| 15 | – | 12 | 6 | 49 | 2 | 0 | 10 | 83 | 3 | 9 | 2 |
| 16 | – | 13 | 4 | 50 | 2 | 1 | 8 | 84 | 3 | 10 | 0 |
| 17 | – | 14 | 2 | 51 | 2 | 2 | 6 | 85 | 3 | 10 | 10 |
| 18 | – | 15 | 0 | 52 | 2 | 3 | 4 | 86 | 3 | 11 | 8 |
| 19 | – | 15 | 10 | 53 | 2 | 4 | 2 | 87 | 3 | 12 | 6 |
| 20 | – | 16 | 8 | 54 | 2 | 5 | 0 | 88 | 3 | 13 | 4 |
| 21 | – | 17 | 6 | 55 | 2 | 5 | 10 | 89 | 3 | 14 | 2 |
| 22 | – | 18 | 4 | 56 | 2 | 6 | 8 | 90 | 3 | 15 | 0 |
| 23 | – | 19 | 2 | 57 | 2 | 7 | 6 | 91 | 3 | 15 | 10 |
| 24 | 1 | 0 | 0 | 58 | 2 | 8 | 4 | 92 | 3 | 16 | 8 |
| 25 | 1 | 0 | 10 | 59 | 2 | 9 | 2 | 93 | 3 | 17 | 6 |
| 26 | 1 | 1 | 8 | 60 | 2 | 10 | 0 | 94 | 3 | 18 | 4 |
| 27 | 1 | 2 | 6 | 61 | 2 | 10 | 10 | 95 | 3 | 19 | 2 |
| 28 | 1 | 3 | 4 | 62 | 2 | 11 | 8 | 96 | 4 | 0 | 0 |
| 29 | 1 | 4 | 2 | 63 | 2 | 12 | 6 | 97 | 4 | 0 | 10 |
| 30 | 1 | 5 | 0 | 64 | 2 | 13 | 4 | 98 | 4 | 1 | 8 |
| 31 | 1 | 5 | 10 | 65 | 2 | 14 | 2 | 99 | 4 | 2 | 6 |
| 32 | 1 | 6 | 8 | 66 | 2 | 15 | 0 | 100 | 4 | 3 | 4 |
| 33 | 1 | 7 | 6 | 67 | 2 | 15 | 10 | 144 | 6 | 0 | 0 |
| 34 | 1 | 8 | 4 | 68 | 2 | 16 | 8 | 500 | 20 | 16 | 8 |
| 35 | 1 | 9 | 2 | 69 | 2 | 17 | 6 | 750 | 31 | 5 | 0 |

## 10¼d.

| No. | £ | s. | d. | No. | £ | s. | d. | No. | £ | s. | d. |
|---|---|---|---|---|---|---|---|---|---|---|---|
| 2 | – | 1 | 8½ | 36 | 1 | 10 | 9 | 70 | 2 | 19 | 9½ |
| 3 | – | 2 | 6¾ | 37 | 1 | 11 | 7¼ | 71 | 3 | 0 | 7¾ |
| 4 | – | 3 | 5 | 38 | 1 | 12 | 5½ | 72 | 3 | 1 | 6 |
| 5 | – | 4 | 3¼ | 39 | 1 | 13 | 3¾ | 73 | 3 | 2 | 4¼ |
| 6 | – | 5 | 1½ | 40 | 1 | 14 | 2 | 74 | 3 | 3 | 2½ |
| 7 | – | 5 | 11¾ | 41 | 1 | 15 | 0¼ | 75 | 3 | 4 | 0¾ |
| 8 | – | 6 | 10 | 42 | 1 | 15 | 10½ | 76 | 3 | 4 | 11 |
| 9 | – | 7 | 8¼ | 43 | 1 | 16 | 8¾ | 77 | 3 | 5 | 9¼ |
| 10 | – | 8 | 6½ | 44 | 1 | 17 | 7 | 78 | 3 | 6 | 7½ |
| 11 | – | 9 | 4¾ | 45 | 1 | 18 | 5¼ | 79 | 3 | 7 | 5¾ |
| 12 | – | 10 | 3 | 46 | 1 | 19 | 3½ | 80 | 3 | 8 | 4 |
| 13 | – | 11 | 1¼ | 47 | 2 | 0 | 1¾ | 81 | 3 | 9 | 2¼ |
| 14 | – | 11 | 11½ | 48 | 2 | 1 | 0 | 82 | 3 | 10 | 0½ |
| 15 | – | 12 | 9¾ | 49 | 2 | 1 | 10¼ | 83 | 3 | 10 | 10¾ |
| 16 | – | 13 | 8 | 50 | 2 | 2 | 8½ | 84 | 3 | 11 | 9 |
| 17 | – | 14 | 6¼ | 51 | 2 | 3 | 6¾ | 85 | 3 | 12 | 7¼ |
| 18 | – | 15 | 4½ | 52 | 2 | 4 | 5 | 86 | 3 | 13 | 5½ |
| 19 | – | 16 | 2¾ | 53 | 2 | 5 | 3¼ | 87 | 3 | 14 | 3¾ |
| 20 | – | 17 | 1 | 54 | 2 | 6 | 1½ | 88 | 3 | 15 | 2 |
| 21 | – | 17 | 11¼ | 55 | 2 | 6 | 11¾ | 89 | 3 | 16 | 0¼ |
| 22 | – | 18 | 9½ | 56 | 2 | 7 | 10 | 90 | 3 | 16 | 10½ |
| 23 | – | 19 | 7¾ | 57 | 2 | 8 | 8¼ | 91 | 3 | 17 | 8¾ |
| 24 | 1 | 0 | 6 | 58 | 2 | 9 | 6½ | 92 | 3 | 18 | 7 |
| 25 | 1 | 1 | 4¼ | 59 | 2 | 10 | 4¾ | 93 | 3 | 19 | 5¼ |
| 26 | 1 | 2 | 2½ | 60 | 2 | 11 | 3 | 94 | 4 | 0 | 3½ |
| 27 | 1 | 3 | 0¾ | 61 | 2 | 12 | 1¼ | 95 | 4 | 1 | 1¾ |
| 28 | 1 | 3 | 11 | 62 | 2 | 12 | 11½ | 96 | 4 | 2 | 0 |
| 29 | 1 | 4 | 9¼ | 63 | 2 | 13 | 9¾ | 97 | 4 | 2 | 10¼ |
| 30 | 1 | 5 | 7½ | 64 | 2 | 14 | 8 | 98 | 4 | 3 | 8½ |
| 31 | 1 | 6 | 5¾ | 65 | 2 | 15 | 6¼ | 99 | 4 | 4 | 6¾ |
| 32 | 1 | 7 | 4 | 66 | 2 | 16 | 4½ | 100 | 4 | 5 | 5 |
| 33 | 1 | 8 | 2¼ | 67 | 2 | 17 | 2¾ | 144 | 6 | 3 | 0 |
| 34 | 1 | 9 | 0½ | 68 | 2 | 18 | 1 | 500 | 21 | 7 | 1 |
| 35 | 1 | 9 | 10¾ | 69 | 2 | 18 | 11¼ | 750 | 32 | 0 | 7½ |

## 10½d.

| No. | £ | s. | d. | No. | £ | s. | d. | No. | £ | s. | d. |
|---|---|---|---|---|---|---|---|---|---|---|---|
| 2 | – | 1 | 9 | 36 | 1 | 11 | 6 | 70 | 3 | 1 | 3 |
| 3 | – | 2 | 7½ | 37 | 1 | 12 | 4½ | 71 | 3 | 2 | 1½ |
| 4 | – | 3 | 6 | 38 | 1 | 13 | 3 | 72 | 3 | 3 | 0 |
| 5 | – | 4 | 4½ | 39 | 1 | 14 | 1½ | 73 | 3 | 3 | 10½ |
| 6 | – | 5 | 3 | 40 | 1 | 15 | 0 | 74 | 3 | 4 | 9 |
| 7 | – | 6 | 1½ | 41 | 1 | 15 | 10½ | 75 | 3 | 5 | 7½ |
| 8 | – | 7 | 0 | 42 | 1 | 16 | 9 | 76 | 3 | 6 | 6 |
| 9 | – | 7 | 10½ | 43 | 1 | 17 | 7½ | 77 | 3 | 7 | 4½ |
| 10 | – | 8 | 9 | 44 | 1 | 18 | 6 | 78 | 3 | 8 | 3 |
| 11 | – | 9 | 7½ | 45 | 1 | 19 | 4½ | 79 | 3 | 9 | 1½ |
| 12 | – | 10 | 6 | 46 | 2 | 0 | 3 | 80 | 3 | 10 | 0 |
| 13 | – | 11 | 4½ | 47 | 2 | 1 | 1½ | 81 | 3 | 10 | 10½ |
| 14 | – | 12 | 3 | 48 | 2 | 2 | 0 | 82 | 3 | 11 | 9 |
| 15 | – | 13 | 1½ | 49 | 2 | 2 | 10½ | 83 | 3 | 12 | 7½ |
| 16 | – | 14 | 0 | 50 | 2 | 3 | 9 | 84 | 3 | 13 | 6 |
| 17 | – | 14 | 10½ | 51 | 2 | 4 | 7½ | 85 | 3 | 14 | 4½ |
| 18 | – | 15 | 9 | 52 | 2 | 5 | 6 | 86 | 3 | 15 | 3 |
| 19 | – | 16 | 7½ | 53 | 2 | 6 | 4½ | 87 | 3 | 16 | 1½ |
| 20 | – | 17 | 6 | 54 | 2 | 7 | 3 | 88 | 3 | 17 | 0 |
| 21 | – | 18 | 4½ | 55 | 2 | 8 | 1½ | 89 | 3 | 17 | 10½ |
| 22 | – | 19 | 3 | 56 | 2 | 9 | 0 | 90 | 3 | 18 | 9 |
| 23 | 1 | 0 | 1½ | 57 | 2 | 9 | 10½ | 91 | 3 | 19 | 7½ |
| 24 | 1 | 1 | 0 | 58 | 2 | 10 | 9 | 92 | 4 | 0 | 6 |
| 25 | 1 | 1 | 10½ | 59 | 2 | 11 | 7½ | 93 | 4 | 1 | 4½ |
| 26 | 1 | 2 | 9 | 60 | 2 | 12 | 6 | 94 | 4 | 2 | 3 |
| 27 | 1 | 3 | 7½ | 61 | 2 | 13 | 4½ | 95 | 4 | 3 | 1½ |
| 28 | 1 | 4 | 6 | 62 | 2 | 14 | 3 | 96 | 4 | 4 | 0 |
| 29 | 1 | 5 | 4½ | 63 | 2 | 15 | 1½ | 97 | 4 | 4 | 10½ |
| 30 | 1 | 6 | 3 | 64 | 2 | 16 | 0 | 98 | 4 | 5 | 9 |
| 31 | 1 | 7 | 1½ | 65 | 2 | 16 | 10½ | 99 | 4 | 6 | 7½ |
| 32 | 1 | 8 | 0 | 66 | 2 | 17 | 9 | 100 | 4 | 7 | 6 |
| 33 | 1 | 8 | 10½ | 67 | 2 | 18 | 7½ | 144 | 6 | 6 | 0 |
| 34 | 1 | 9 | 9 | 68 | 2 | 19 | 6 | 500 | 21 | 17 | 6 |
| 35 | 1 | 10 | 7½ | 69 | 3 | 0 | 4½ | 750 | 32 | 16 | 3 |

## 10¾d.

| No. | £ | s. | d. | No. | £ | s. | d. | No. | £ | s. | d. |
|---|---|---|---|---|---|---|---|---|---|---|---|
| 2 | – | 1 | 9½ | 36 | 1 | 12 | 3 | 70 | 3 | 2 | 8½ |
| 3 | – | 2 | 8¼ | 37 | 1 | 13 | 1¾ | 71 | 3 | 3 | 7¼ |
| 4 | – | 3 | 7 | 38 | 1 | 14 | 0½ | 72 | 3 | 4 | 6 |
| 5 | – | 4 | 5¾ | 39 | 1 | 14 | 11¼ | 73 | 3 | 5 | 4¾ |
| 6 | – | 5 | 4½ | 40 | 1 | 15 | 10 | 74 | 3 | 6 | 3½ |
| 7 | – | 6 | 3¼ | 41 | 1 | 16 | 8¾ | 75 | 3 | 7 | 2¼ |
| 8 | – | 7 | 2 | 42 | 1 | 17 | 7½ | 76 | 3 | 8 | 1 |
| 9 | – | 8 | 0¾ | 43 | 1 | 18 | 6¼ | 77 | 3 | 8 | 11¾ |
| 10 | – | 8 | 11½ | 44 | 1 | 19 | 5 | 78 | 3 | 9 | 10½ |
| 11 | – | 9 | 10¼ | 45 | 2 | 0 | 3¾ | 79 | 3 | 10 | 9¼ |
| 12 | – | 10 | 9 | 46 | 2 | 1 | 2½ | 80 | 3 | 11 | 8 |
| 13 | – | 11 | 7¾ | 47 | 2 | 2 | 1¼ | 81 | 3 | 12 | 6¾ |
| 14 | – | 12 | 6½ | 48 | 2 | 3 | 0 | 82 | 3 | 13 | 5½ |
| 15 | – | 13 | 5¼ | 49 | 2 | 3 | 10¾ | 83 | 3 | 14 | 4¼ |
| 16 | – | 14 | 4 | 50 | 2 | 4 | 9½ | 84 | 3 | 15 | 3 |
| 17 | – | 15 | 2¾ | 51 | 2 | 5 | 8¼ | 85 | 3 | 16 | 1¾ |
| 18 | – | 16 | 1½ | 52 | 2 | 6 | 7 | 86 | 3 | 17 | 0½ |
| 19 | – | 17 | 0¼ | 53 | 2 | 7 | 5¾ | 87 | 3 | 17 | 11¼ |
| 20 | – | 17 | 11 | 54 | 2 | 8 | 4½ | 88 | 3 | 18 | 10 |
| 21 | – | 18 | 9¾ | 55 | 2 | 9 | 3¼ | 89 | 3 | 19 | 8¾ |
| 22 | – | 19 | 8½ | 56 | 2 | 10 | 2 | 90 | 4 | 0 | 7½ |
| 23 | 1 | 0 | 7¼ | 57 | 2 | 11 | 0¾ | 91 | 4 | 1 | 6¼ |
| 24 | 1 | 1 | 6 | 58 | 2 | 11 | 11½ | 92 | 4 | 2 | 5 |
| 25 | 1 | 2 | 4¾ | 59 | 2 | 12 | 10¼ | 93 | 4 | 3 | 3¾ |
| 26 | 1 | 3 | 3½ | 60 | 2 | 13 | 9 | 94 | 4 | 4 | 2½ |
| 27 | 1 | 4 | 2¼ | 61 | 2 | 14 | 7¾ | 95 | 4 | 5 | 1¼ |
| 28 | 1 | 5 | 1 | 62 | 2 | 15 | 6½ | 96 | 4 | 6 | 0 |
| 29 | 1 | 5 | 11¾ | 63 | 2 | 16 | 5¼ | 97 | 4 | 6 | 10¾ |
| 30 | 1 | 6 | 10½ | 64 | 2 | 17 | 4 | 98 | 4 | 7 | 9½ |
| 31 | 1 | 7 | 9¼ | 65 | 2 | 18 | 2¾ | 99 | 4 | 8 | 8¼ |
| 32 | 1 | 8 | 8 | 66 | 2 | 19 | 1½ | 100 | 4 | 9 | 7 |
| 33 | 1 | 9 | 6¾ | 67 | 3 | 0 | 0¼ | 144 | 6 | 9 | 0 |
| 34 | 1 | 10 | 5½ | 68 | 3 | 0 | 11 | 500 | 22 | 7 | 11 |
| 35 | 1 | 11 | 4¼ | 69 | 3 | 1 | 9¾ | 750 | 33 | 11 | 10½ |

# READY RECKONER.

## 11d.

| No. | £ | s. | d. | No. | £ | s. | d. | No. | £ | s. | d. |
|---|---|---|---|---|---|---|---|---|---|---|---|
| 2 | – | 1 | 10 | 36 | 1 | 13 | 0 | 70 | 3 | 4 | 2 |
| 3 | – | 2 | 9 | 37 | 1 | 13 | 11 | 71 | 3 | 5 | 1 |
| 4 | – | 3 | 8 | 38 | 1 | 14 | 10 | 72 | 3 | 6 | 0 |
| 5 | – | 4 | 7 | 39 | 1 | 15 | 9 | 73 | 3 | 6 | 11 |
| 6 | – | 5 | 6 | 40 | 1 | 16 | 8 | 74 | 3 | 7 | 10 |
| 7 | – | 6 | 5 | 41 | 1 | 17 | 7 | 75 | 3 | 8 | 9 |
| 8 | – | 7 | 4 | 42 | 1 | 18 | 6 | 76 | 3 | 9 | 8 |
| 9 | – | 8 | 3 | 43 | 1 | 19 | 5 | 77 | 3 | 10 | 7 |
| 10 | – | 9 | 2 | 44 | 2 | 0 | 4 | 78 | 3 | 11 | 6 |
| 11 | – | 10 | 1 | 45 | 2 | 1 | 3 | 79 | 3 | 12 | 5 |
| 12 | – | 11 | 0 | 46 | 2 | 2 | 2 | 80 | 3 | 13 | 4 |
| 13 | – | 11 | 11 | 47 | 2 | 3 | 1 | 81 | 3 | 14 | 3 |
| 14 | – | 12 | 10 | 48 | 2 | 4 | 0 | 82 | 3 | 15 | 2 |
| 15 | – | 13 | 9 | 49 | 2 | 4 | 11 | 83 | 3 | 16 | 1 |
| 16 | – | 14 | 8 | 50 | 2 | 5 | 10 | 84 | 3 | 17 | 0 |
| 17 | – | 15 | 7 | 51 | 2 | 6 | 9 | 85 | 3 | 17 | 11 |
| 18 | – | 16 | 6 | 52 | 2 | 7 | 8 | 86 | 3 | 18 | 10 |
| 19 | – | 17 | 5 | 53 | 2 | 8 | 7 | 87 | 3 | 19 | 9 |
| 20 | – | 18 | 4 | 54 | 2 | 9 | 6 | 88 | 4 | 0 | 8 |
| 21 | – | 19 | 3 | 55 | 2 | 10 | 5 | 89 | 4 | 1 | 7 |
| 22 | 1 | 0 | 2 | 56 | 2 | 11 | 4 | 90 | 4 | 2 | 6 |
| 23 | 1 | 1 | 1 | 57 | 2 | 12 | 3 | 91 | 4 | 3 | 5 |
| 24 | 1 | 2 | 0 | 58 | 2 | 13 | 2 | 92 | 4 | 4 | 4 |
| 25 | 1 | 2 | 11 | 59 | 2 | 14 | 1 | 93 | 4 | 5 | 3 |
| 26 | 1 | 3 | 10 | 60 | 2 | 15 | 0 | 94 | 4 | 6 | 2 |
| 27 | 1 | 4 | 9 | 61 | 2 | 15 | 11 | 95 | 4 | 7 | 1 |
| 28 | 1 | 5 | 8 | 62 | 2 | 16 | 10 | 96 | 4 | 8 | 0 |
| 29 | 1 | 6 | 7 | 63 | 2 | 17 | 9 | 97 | 4 | 8 | 11 |
| 30 | 1 | 7 | 6 | 64 | 2 | 18 | 8 | 98 | 4 | 9 | 10 |
| 31 | 1 | 8 | 5 | 65 | 2 | 19 | 7 | 99 | 4 | 10 | 9 |
| 32 | 1 | 9 | 4 | 66 | 3 | 0 | 6 | 100 | 4 | 11 | 8 |
| 33 | 1 | 10 | 3 | 67 | 3 | 1 | 5 | 144 | 6 | 12 | 0 |
| 34 | 1 | 11 | 2 | 68 | 3 | 2 | 4 | 500 | 22 | 18 | 4 |
| 35 | 1 | 12 | 1 | 69 | 3 | 3 | 3 | 750 | 34 | 7 | 6 |

## 11¼d.

| No. | £ | s. | d. | No. | £ | s. | d. | No. | £ | s. | d. |
|---|---|---|---|---|---|---|---|---|---|---|---|
| 2 | – | 1 | 10½ | 36 | 1 | 13 | 9 | 70 | 3 | 5 | 7½ |
| 3 | – | 2 | 9¾ | 37 | 1 | 14 | 8¼ | 71 | 3 | 6 | 6¾ |
| 4 | – | 3 | 9 | 38 | 1 | 15 | 7½ | 72 | 3 | 7 | 6 |
| 5 | – | 4 | 8¼ | 39 | 1 | 16 | 6¾ | 73 | 3 | 8 | 5¼ |
| 6 | – | 5 | 7½ | 40 | 1 | 17 | 6 | 74 | 3 | 9 | 4½ |
| 7 | – | 6 | 6¾ | 41 | 1 | 18 | 5¼ | 75 | 3 | 10 | 3¾ |
| 8 | – | 7 | 6 | 42 | 1 | 19 | 4½ | 76 | 3 | 11 | 3 |
| 9 | – | 8 | 5¼ | 43 | 2 | 0 | 3¾ | 77 | 3 | 12 | 2¼ |
| 10 | – | 9 | 4½ | 44 | 2 | 1 | 3 | 78 | 3 | 13 | 1½ |
| 11 | – | 10 | 3¾ | 45 | 2 | 2 | 2¼ | 79 | 3 | 14 | 0¾ |
| 12 | – | 11 | 3 | 46 | 2 | 3 | 1½ | 80 | 3 | 15 | 0 |
| 13 | – | 12 | 2¼ | 47 | 2 | 4 | 0¾ | 81 | 3 | 15 | 11¼ |
| 14 | – | 13 | 1½ | 48 | 2 | 5 | 0 | 82 | 3 | 16 | 10½ |
| 15 | – | 14 | 0¾ | 49 | 2 | 5 | 11¼ | 83 | 3 | 17 | 9¾ |
| 16 | – | 15 | 0 | 50 | 2 | 6 | 10½ | 84 | 3 | 18 | 9 |
| 17 | – | 15 | 11¼ | 51 | 2 | 7 | 9¾ | 85 | 3 | 19 | 8¼ |
| 18 | – | 16 | 10½ | 52 | 2 | 8 | 9 | 86 | 4 | 0 | 7½ |
| 19 | – | 17 | 9¾ | 53 | 2 | 9 | 8¼ | 87 | 4 | 1 | 6¾ |
| 20 | – | 18 | 9 | 54 | 2 | 10 | 7½ | 88 | 4 | 2 | 6 |
| 21 | – | 19 | 8¼ | 55 | 2 | 11 | 6¾ | 89 | 4 | 3 | 5¼ |
| 22 | 1 | 0 | 7½ | 56 | 2 | 12 | 6 | 90 | 4 | 4 | 4½ |
| 23 | 1 | 1 | 6¾ | 57 | 2 | 13 | 5¼ | 91 | 4 | 5 | 3¾ |
| 24 | 1 | 2 | 6 | 58 | 2 | 14 | 4½ | 92 | 4 | 6 | 3 |
| 25 | 1 | 3 | 5¼ | 59 | 2 | 15 | 3¾ | 93 | 4 | 7 | 2¼ |
| 26 | 1 | 4 | 4½ | 60 | 2 | 16 | 3 | 94 | 4 | 8 | 1½ |
| 27 | 1 | 5 | 3¾ | 61 | 2 | 17 | 2¼ | 95 | 4 | 9 | 0¾ |
| 28 | 1 | 6 | 3 | 62 | 2 | 18 | 1½ | 96 | 4 | 10 | 0 |
| 29 | 1 | 7 | 2¼ | 63 | 2 | 19 | 0¾ | 97 | 4 | 10 | 11¼ |
| 30 | 1 | 8 | 1½ | 64 | 3 | 0 | 0 | 98 | 4 | 11 | 10½ |
| 31 | 1 | 9 | 0¾ | 65 | 3 | 0 | 11¼ | 99 | 4 | 12 | 9¾ |
| 32 | 1 | 10 | 0 | 66 | 3 | 1 | 10½ | 100 | 4 | 13 | 9 |
| 33 | 1 | 10 | 11¼ | 67 | 3 | 2 | 9¾ | 144 | 6 | 15 | 0 |
| 34 | 1 | 11 | 10½ | 68 | 3 | 3 | 9 | 500 | 23 | 8 | 9 |
| 35 | 1 | 12 | 9¾ | 69 | 3 | 4 | 8¼ | 750 | 35 | 3 | 1½ |

## 11½d.

| No. | £ | s. | d. | No. | £ | s. | d. | No. | £ | s. | d. |
|---|---|---|---|---|---|---|---|---|---|---|---|
| 2 | – | 1 | 11 | 36 | 1 | 14 | 6 | 70 | 3 | 7 | 1 |
| 3 | – | 2 | 10½ | 37 | 1 | 15 | 5½ | 71 | 3 | 8 | 0½ |
| 4 | – | 3 | 10 | 38 | 1 | 16 | 5 | 72 | 3 | 9 | 0 |
| 5 | – | 4 | 9½ | 39 | 1 | 17 | 4½ | 73 | 3 | 9 | 11½ |
| 6 | – | 5 | 9 | 40 | 1 | 18 | 4 | 74 | 3 | 10 | 11 |
| 7 | – | 6 | 8½ | 41 | 1 | 19 | 3½ | 75 | 3 | 11 | 10½ |
| 8 | – | 7 | 8 | 42 | 2 | 0 | 3 | 76 | 3 | 12 | 10 |
| 9 | – | 8 | 7½ | 43 | 2 | 1 | 2½ | 77 | 3 | 13 | 9½ |
| 10 | – | 9 | 7 | 44 | 2 | 2 | 2 | 78 | 3 | 14 | 9 |
| 11 | – | 10 | 6½ | 45 | 2 | 3 | 1½ | 79 | 3 | 15 | 8½ |
| 12 | – | 11 | 6 | 46 | 2 | 4 | 1 | 80 | 3 | 16 | 8 |
| 13 | – | 12 | 5½ | 47 | 2 | 5 | 0½ | 81 | 3 | 17 | 7½ |
| 14 | – | 13 | 5 | 48 | 2 | 6 | 0 | 82 | 3 | 18 | 7 |
| 15 | – | 14 | 4½ | 49 | 2 | 6 | 11½ | 83 | 3 | 19 | 6½ |
| 16 | – | 15 | 4 | 50 | 2 | 7 | 11 | 84 | 4 | 0 | 6 |
| 17 | – | 16 | 3½ | 51 | 2 | 8 | 10½ | 85 | 4 | 1 | 5½ |
| 18 | – | 17 | 3 | 52 | 2 | 9 | 10 | 86 | 4 | 2 | 5 |
| 19 | – | 18 | 2½ | 53 | 2 | 10 | 9½ | 87 | 4 | 3 | 4½ |
| 20 | – | 19 | 2 | 54 | 2 | 11 | 9 | 88 | 4 | 4 | 4 |
| 21 | 1 | 0 | 1½ | 55 | 2 | 12 | 8½ | 89 | 4 | 5 | 3½ |
| 22 | 1 | 1 | 1 | 56 | 2 | 13 | 8 | 90 | 4 | 6 | 3 |
| 23 | 1 | 2 | 0½ | 57 | 2 | 14 | 7½ | 91 | 4 | 7 | 2½ |
| 24 | 1 | 3 | 0 | 58 | 2 | 15 | 7 | 92 | 4 | 8 | 2 |
| 25 | 1 | 3 | 11½ | 59 | 2 | 16 | 6½ | 93 | 4 | 9 | 1½ |
| 26 | 1 | 4 | 11 | 60 | 2 | 17 | 6 | 94 | 4 | 10 | 1 |
| 27 | 1 | 5 | 10½ | 61 | 2 | 18 | 5½ | 95 | 4 | 11 | 0½ |
| 28 | 1 | 6 | 10 | 62 | 2 | 19 | 5 | 96 | 4 | 12 | 0 |
| 29 | 1 | 7 | 9½ | 63 | 3 | 0 | 4½ | 97 | 4 | 12 | 11½ |
| 30 | 1 | 8 | 9 | 64 | 3 | 1 | 4 | 98 | 4 | 13 | 11 |
| 31 | 1 | 9 | 8½ | 65 | 3 | 2 | 3½ | 99 | 4 | 14 | 10½ |
| 32 | 1 | 10 | 8 | 66 | 3 | 3 | 3 | 100 | 4 | 15 | 10 |
| 33 | 1 | 11 | 7½ | 67 | 3 | 4 | 2½ | 144 | 6 | 18 | 0 |
| 34 | 1 | 12 | 7 | 68 | 3 | 5 | 2 | 500 | 23 | 19 | 2 |
| 35 | 1 | 13 | 6½ | 69 | 3 | 6 | 1½ | 750 | 35 | 18 | 9 |

## 11¾d.

| No. | £ | s. | d. | No. | £ | s. | d. | No. | £ | s. | d. |
|---|---|---|---|---|---|---|---|---|---|---|---|
| 2 | – | 1 | 11½ | 36 | 1 | 15 | 3 | 70 | 3 | 8 | 6½ |
| 3 | – | 2 | 11¼ | 37 | 1 | 16 | 2¾ | 71 | 3 | 9 | 6¼ |
| 4 | – | 3 | 11 | 38 | 1 | 17 | 2½ | 72 | 3 | 10 | 6 |
| 5 | – | 4 | 10¾ | 39 | 1 | 18 | 2¼ | 73 | 3 | 11 | 5¾ |
| 6 | – | 5 | 10½ | 40 | 1 | 19 | 2 | 74 | 3 | 12 | 5½ |
| 7 | – | 6 | 10¼ | 41 | 2 | 0 | 1¾ | 75 | 3 | 13 | 5¼ |
| 8 | – | 7 | 10 | 42 | 2 | 1 | 1½ | 76 | 3 | 14 | 5 |
| 9 | – | 8 | 9¾ | 43 | 2 | 2 | 1¼ | 77 | 3 | 15 | 4¾ |
| 10 | – | 9 | 9½ | 44 | 2 | 3 | 1 | 78 | 3 | 16 | 4½ |
| 11 | – | 10 | 9¼ | 45 | 2 | 4 | 0¾ | 79 | 3 | 17 | 4¼ |
| 12 | – | 11 | 9 | 46 | 2 | 5 | 0½ | 80 | 3 | 18 | 4 |
| 13 | – | 12 | 8¾ | 47 | 2 | 6 | 0¼ | 81 | 3 | 19 | 3¾ |
| 14 | – | 13 | 8½ | 48 | 2 | 7 | 0 | 82 | 4 | 0 | 3½ |
| 15 | – | 14 | 8¼ | 49 | 2 | 7 | 11¾ | 83 | 4 | 1 | 3¼ |
| 16 | – | 15 | 8 | 50 | 2 | 8 | 11½ | 84 | 4 | 2 | 3 |
| 17 | – | 16 | 7¾ | 51 | 2 | 9 | 11¼ | 85 | 4 | 3 | 2¾ |
| 18 | – | 17 | 7½ | 52 | 2 | 10 | 11 | 86 | 4 | 4 | 2½ |
| 19 | – | 18 | 7¼ | 53 | 2 | 11 | 10¾ | 87 | 4 | 5 | 2¼ |
| 20 | – | 19 | 7 | 54 | 2 | 12 | 10½ | 88 | 4 | 6 | 2 |
| 21 | 1 | 0 | 6¾ | 55 | 2 | 13 | 10¼ | 89 | 4 | 7 | 1¾ |
| 22 | 1 | 1 | 6½ | 56 | 2 | 14 | 10 | 90 | 4 | 8 | 1½ |
| 23 | 1 | 2 | 6¼ | 57 | 2 | 15 | 9¾ | 91 | 4 | 9 | 1¼ |
| 24 | 1 | 3 | 6 | 58 | 2 | 16 | 9½ | 92 | 4 | 10 | 1 |
| 25 | 1 | 4 | 5¾ | 59 | 2 | 17 | 9¼ | 93 | 4 | 11 | 0¾ |
| 26 | 1 | 5 | 5½ | 60 | 2 | 18 | 9 | 94 | 4 | 12 | 0½ |
| 27 | 1 | 6 | 5¼ | 61 | 2 | 19 | 8¾ | 95 | 4 | 13 | 0¼ |
| 28 | 1 | 7 | 5 | 62 | 3 | 0 | 8½ | 96 | 4 | 14 | 0 |
| 29 | 1 | 8 | 4¾ | 63 | 3 | 1 | 8¼ | 97 | 4 | 14 | 11¾ |
| 30 | 1 | 9 | 4½ | 64 | 3 | 2 | 8 | 98 | 4 | 15 | 11½ |
| 31 | 1 | 10 | 4¼ | 65 | 3 | 3 | 7¾ | 99 | 4 | 16 | 11¼ |
| 32 | 1 | 11 | 4 | 66 | 3 | 4 | 7½ | 100 | 4 | 17 | 11 |
| 33 | 1 | 12 | 3¾ | 67 | 3 | 5 | 7¼ | 144 | 7 | 1 | 0 |
| 34 | 1 | 13 | 3½ | 68 | 3 | 6 | 7 | 500 | 24 | 9 | 7 |
| 35 | 1 | 14 | 3¼ | 69 | 3 | 7 | 6¾ | 750 | 36 | 14 | 4½ |

## READY RECKONER.

### 1/-

| No. | £ | s. | d. | No. | £ | s. | d. | No. | £ | s. | d. |
|---|---|---|---|---|---|---|---|---|---|---|---|
| 2 | – | 2 | 0 | 36 | 1 | 16 | 0 | 70 | 3 | 10 | 0 |
| 3 | – | 3 | 0 | 37 | 1 | 17 | 0 | 71 | 3 | 11 | 0 |
| 4 | – | 4 | 0 | 38 | 1 | 18 | 0 | 72 | 3 | 12 | 0 |
| 5 | – | 5 | 0 | 39 | 1 | 19 | 0 | 73 | 3 | 13 | 0 |
| 6 | – | 6 | 0 | 40 | 2 | 0 | 0 | 74 | 3 | 14 | 0 |
| 7 | – | 7 | 0 | 41 | 2 | 1 | 0 | 75 | 3 | 15 | 0 |
| 8 | – | 8 | 0 | 42 | 2 | 2 | 0 | 76 | 3 | 16 | 0 |
| 9 | – | 9 | 0 | 43 | 2 | 3 | 0 | 77 | 3 | 17 | 0 |
| 10 | – | 10 | 0 | 44 | 2 | 4 | 0 | 78 | 3 | 18 | 0 |
| 11 | – | 11 | 0 | 45 | 2 | 5 | 0 | 79 | 3 | 19 | 0 |
| 12 | – | 12 | 0 | 46 | 2 | 6 | 0 | 80 | 4 | 0 | 0 |
| 13 | – | 13 | 0 | 47 | 2 | 7 | 0 | 81 | 4 | 1 | 0 |
| 14 | – | 14 | 0 | 48 | 2 | 8 | 0 | 82 | 4 | 2 | 0 |
| 15 | – | 15 | 0 | 49 | 2 | 9 | 0 | 83 | 4 | 3 | 0 |
| 16 | – | 16 | 0 | 50 | 2 | 10 | 0 | 84 | 4 | 4 | 0 |
| 17 | – | 17 | 0 | 51 | 2 | 11 | 0 | 85 | 4 | 5 | 0 |
| 18 | – | 18 | 0 | 52 | 2 | 12 | 0 | 86 | 4 | 6 | 0 |
| 19 | – | 19 | 0 | 53 | 2 | 13 | 0 | 87 | 4 | 7 | 0 |
| 20 | 1 | 0 | 0 | 54 | 2 | 14 | 0 | 88 | 4 | 8 | 0 |
| 21 | 1 | 1 | 0 | 55 | 2 | 15 | 0 | 89 | 4 | 9 | 0 |
| 22 | 1 | 2 | 0 | 56 | 2 | 16 | 0 | 90 | 4 | 10 | 0 |
| 23 | 1 | 3 | 0 | 57 | 2 | 17 | 0 | 91 | 4 | 11 | 0 |
| 24 | 1 | 4 | 0 | 58 | 2 | 18 | 0 | 92 | 4 | 12 | 0 |
| 25 | 1 | 5 | 0 | 59 | 2 | 19 | 0 | 93 | 4 | 13 | 0 |
| 26 | 1 | 6 | 0 | 60 | 3 | 0 | 0 | 94 | 4 | 14 | 0 |
| 27 | 1 | 7 | 0 | 61 | 3 | 1 | 0 | 95 | 4 | 15 | 0 |
| 28 | 1 | 8 | 0 | 62 | 3 | 2 | 0 | 96 | 4 | 16 | 0 |
| 29 | 1 | 9 | 0 | 63 | 3 | 3 | 0 | 97 | 4 | 17 | 0 |
| 30 | 1 | 10 | 0 | 64 | 3 | 4 | 0 | 98 | 4 | 18 | 0 |
| 31 | 1 | 11 | 0 | 65 | 3 | 5 | 0 | 99 | 4 | 19 | 0 |
| 32 | 1 | 12 | 0 | 66 | 3 | 6 | 0 | 100 | 5 | 0 | 0 |
| 33 | 1 | 13 | 0 | 67 | 3 | 7 | 0 | 144 | 7 | 4 | 0 |
| 34 | 1 | 14 | 0 | 68 | 3 | 8 | 0 | 500 | 25 | 0 | 0 |
| 35 | 1 | 15 | 0 | 69 | 3 | 9 | 0 | 750 | 37 | 10 | 0 |

### 1/3

| No. | £ | s. | d. | No | £ | s. | d. | No. | £ | s. | d. |
|---|---|---|---|---|---|---|---|---|---|---|---|
| 2 | – | 2 | 6 | 36 | 2 | 5 | 0 | 70 | 4 | 7 | 6 |
| 3 | – | 3 | 9 | 37 | 2 | 6 | 3 | 71 | 4 | 8 | 9 |
| 4 | – | 5 | 0 | 38 | 2 | 7 | 6 | 72 | 4 | 10 | 0 |
| 5 | – | 6 | 3 | 39 | 2 | 8 | 9 | 73 | 4 | 11 | 3 |
| 6 | – | 7 | 6 | 40 | 2 | 10 | 0 | 74 | 4 | 12 | 6 |
| 7 | – | 8 | 9 | 41 | 2 | 11 | 3 | 75 | 4 | 13 | 9 |
| 8 | – | 10 | 0 | 42 | 2 | 12 | 6 | 76 | 4 | 15 | 0 |
| 9 | – | 11 | 3 | 43 | 2 | 13 | 9 | 77 | 4 | 16 | 3 |
| 10 | – | 12 | 6 | 44 | 2 | 15 | 0 | 78 | 4 | 17 | 6 |
| 11 | – | 13 | 9 | 45 | 2 | 16 | 3 | 79 | 4 | 18 | 9 |
| 12 | – | 15 | 0 | 46 | 2 | 17 | 6 | 80 | 5 | 0 | 0 |
| 13 | – | 16 | 3 | 47 | 2 | 18 | 9 | 81 | 5 | 1 | 3 |
| 14 | – | 17 | 6 | 48 | 3 | 0 | 0 | 82 | 5 | 2 | 6 |
| 15 | – | 18 | 9 | 49 | 3 | 1 | 3 | 83 | 5 | 3 | 9 |
| 16 | 1 | 0 | 0 | 50 | 3 | 2 | 6 | 84 | 5 | 5 | 0 |
| 17 | 1 | 1 | 3 | 51 | 3 | 3 | 9 | 85 | 5 | 6 | 3 |
| 18 | 1 | 2 | 6 | 52 | 3 | 5 | 0 | 86 | 5 | 7 | 6 |
| 19 | 1 | 3 | 9 | 53 | 3 | 6 | 3 | 87 | 5 | 8 | 9 |
| 20 | 1 | 5 | 0 | 54 | 3 | 7 | 6 | 88 | 5 | 10 | 0 |
| 21 | 1 | 6 | 3 | 55 | 3 | 8 | 9 | 89 | 5 | 11 | 3 |
| 22 | 1 | 7 | 6 | 56 | 3 | 10 | 0 | 90 | 5 | 12 | 6 |
| 23 | 1 | 8 | 9 | 57 | 3 | 11 | 3 | 91 | 5 | 13 | 9 |
| 24 | 1 | 10 | 0 | 58 | 3 | 12 | 6 | 92 | 5 | 15 | 0 |
| 25 | 1 | 11 | 3 | 59 | 3 | 13 | 9 | 93 | 5 | 16 | 3 |
| 26 | 1 | 12 | 6 | 60 | 3 | 15 | 0 | 94 | 5 | 17 | 6 |
| 27 | 1 | 13 | 9 | 61 | 3 | 16 | 3 | 95 | 5 | 18 | 9 |
| 28 | 1 | 15 | 0 | 62 | 3 | 17 | 6 | 96 | 6 | 0 | 0 |
| 29 | 1 | 16 | 3 | 63 | 3 | 18 | 9 | 97 | 6 | 1 | 3 |
| 30 | 1 | 17 | 6 | 64 | 4 | 0 | 0 | 98 | 6 | 2 | 6 |
| 31 | 1 | 18 | 9 | 65 | 4 | 1 | 3 | 99 | 6 | 3 | 9 |
| 32 | 2 | 0 | 0 | 66 | 4 | 2 | 6 | 100 | 6 | 5 | 0 |
| 33 | 2 | 1 | 3 | 67 | 4 | 3 | 9 | 144 | 9 | 0 | 0 |
| 34 | 2 | 2 | 6 | 68 | 4 | 5 | 0 | 500 | 31 | 5 | 0 |
| 35 | 2 | 3 | 9 | 69 | 4 | 6 | 3 | 750 | 46 | 17 | 6 |

### 1/6

| No. | £ | s. | d. | No. | £ | s. | d. | No. | £ | s. | d. |
|---|---|---|---|---|---|---|---|---|---|---|---|
| 2 | – | 3 | 0 | 36 | 2 | 14 | 0 | 70 | 5 | 5 | 0 |
| 3 | – | 4 | 6 | 37 | 2 | 15 | 6 | 71 | 5 | 6 | 6 |
| 4 | – | 6 | 0 | 38 | 2 | 17 | 0 | 72 | 5 | 8 | 0 |
| 5 | – | 7 | 6 | 39 | 2 | 18 | 6 | 73 | 5 | 9 | 6 |
| 6 | – | 9 | 0 | 40 | 3 | 0 | 0 | 74 | 5 | 11 | 0 |
| 7 | – | 10 | 6 | 41 | 3 | 1 | 6 | 75 | 5 | 12 | 6 |
| 8 | – | 12 | 0 | 42 | 3 | 3 | 0 | 76 | 5 | 14 | 0 |
| 9 | – | 13 | 6 | 43 | 3 | 4 | 6 | 77 | 5 | 15 | 6 |
| 10 | – | 15 | 0 | 44 | 3 | 6 | 0 | 78 | 5 | 17 | 0 |
| 11 | – | 16 | 6 | 45 | 3 | 7 | 6 | 79 | 5 | 18 | 6 |
| 12 | – | 18 | 0 | 46 | 3 | 9 | 0 | 80 | 6 | 0 | 0 |
| 13 | – | 19 | 6 | 47 | 3 | 10 | 6 | 81 | 6 | 1 | 6 |
| 14 | 1 | 1 | 0 | 48 | 3 | 12 | 0 | 82 | 6 | 3 | 0 |
| 15 | 1 | 2 | 6 | 49 | 3 | 13 | 6 | 83 | 6 | 4 | 6 |
| 16 | 1 | 4 | 0 | 50 | 3 | 15 | 0 | 84 | 6 | 6 | 0 |
| 17 | 1 | 5 | 6 | 51 | 3 | 16 | 6 | 85 | 6 | 7 | 6 |
| 18 | 1 | 7 | 0 | 52 | 3 | 18 | 0 | 86 | 6 | 9 | 0 |
| 19 | 1 | 8 | 6 | 53 | 3 | 19 | 6 | 87 | 6 | 10 | 6 |
| 20 | 1 | 10 | 0 | 54 | 4 | 1 | 0 | 88 | 6 | 12 | 0 |
| 21 | 1 | 11 | 6 | 55 | 4 | 2 | 6 | 89 | 6 | 13 | 6 |
| 22 | 1 | 13 | 0 | 56 | 4 | 4 | 0 | 90 | 6 | 15 | 0 |
| 23 | 1 | 14 | 6 | 57 | 4 | 5 | 6 | 91 | 6 | 16 | 6 |
| 24 | 1 | 16 | 0 | 58 | 4 | 7 | 0 | 92 | 6 | 18 | 0 |
| 25 | 1 | 17 | 6 | 59 | 4 | 8 | 6 | 93 | 6 | 19 | 6 |
| 26 | 1 | 19 | 0 | 60 | 4 | 10 | 0 | 94 | 7 | 1 | 0 |
| 27 | 2 | 0 | 6 | 61 | 4 | 11 | 6 | 95 | 7 | 2 | 6 |
| 28 | 2 | 2 | 0 | 62 | 4 | 13 | 0 | 96 | 7 | 4 | 0 |
| 29 | 2 | 3 | 6 | 63 | 4 | 14 | 6 | 97 | 7 | 5 | 6 |
| 30 | 2 | 5 | 0 | 64 | 4 | 16 | 0 | 98 | 7 | 7 | 0 |
| 31 | 2 | 6 | 6 | 65 | 4 | 17 | 6 | 99 | 7 | 8 | 6 |
| 32 | 2 | 8 | 0 | 66 | 4 | 19 | 0 | 100 | 7 | 10 | 0 |
| 33 | 2 | 9 | 6 | 67 | 5 | 0 | 6 | 144 | 10 | 16 | 0 |
| 34 | 2 | 11 | 0 | 68 | 5 | 2 | 0 | 500 | 37 | 10 | 0 |
| 35 | 2 | 12 | 6 | 69 | 5 | 3 | 6 | 750 | 56 | 5 | 0 |

### 1/9

| No. | £ | s. | d. | No. | £ | s. | d. | No. | £ | s. | d. |
|---|---|---|---|---|---|---|---|---|---|---|---|
| 2 | – | 3 | 6 | 36 | 3 | 3 | 0 | 70 | 6 | 2 | 6 |
| 3 | – | 5 | 3 | 37 | 3 | 4 | 9 | 71 | 6 | 4 | 3 |
| 4 | – | 7 | 0 | 38 | 3 | 6 | 6 | 72 | 6 | 6 | 0 |
| 5 | – | 8 | 9 | 39 | 3 | 8 | 3 | 73 | 6 | 7 | 9 |
| 6 | – | 10 | 6 | 40 | 3 | 10 | 0 | 74 | 6 | 9 | 6 |
| 7 | – | 12 | 3 | 41 | 3 | 11 | 9 | 75 | 6 | 11 | 3 |
| 8 | – | 14 | 0 | 42 | 3 | 13 | 6 | 76 | 6 | 13 | 0 |
| 9 | – | 15 | 9 | 43 | 3 | 15 | 3 | 77 | 6 | 14 | 9 |
| 10 | – | 17 | 6 | 44 | 3 | 17 | 0 | 78 | 6 | 16 | 6 |
| 11 | – | 19 | 3 | 45 | 3 | 18 | 9 | 79 | 6 | 18 | 3 |
| 12 | 1 | 1 | 0 | 46 | 4 | 0 | 6 | 80 | 7 | 0 | 0 |
| 13 | 1 | 2 | 9 | 47 | 4 | 2 | 3 | 81 | 7 | 1 | 9 |
| 14 | 1 | 4 | 6 | 48 | 4 | 4 | 0 | 82 | 7 | 3 | 6 |
| 15 | 1 | 6 | 3 | 49 | 4 | 5 | 9 | 83 | 7 | 5 | 3 |
| 16 | 1 | 8 | 0 | 50 | 4 | 7 | 6 | 84 | 7 | 7 | 0 |
| 17 | 1 | 9 | 9 | 51 | 4 | 9 | 3 | 85 | 7 | 8 | 9 |
| 18 | 1 | 11 | 6 | 52 | 4 | 11 | 0 | 86 | 7 | 10 | 6 |
| 19 | 1 | 13 | 3 | 53 | 4 | 12 | 9 | 87 | 7 | 12 | 3 |
| 20 | 1 | 15 | 0 | 54 | 4 | 14 | 6 | 88 | 7 | 14 | 0 |
| 21 | 1 | 16 | 9 | 55 | 4 | 16 | 3 | 89 | 7 | 15 | 9 |
| 22 | 1 | 18 | 6 | 56 | 4 | 18 | 0 | 90 | 7 | 17 | 6 |
| 23 | 2 | 0 | 3 | 57 | 4 | 19 | 9 | 91 | 7 | 19 | 3 |
| 24 | 2 | 2 | 0 | 58 | 5 | 1 | 6 | 92 | 8 | 1 | 0 |
| 25 | 2 | 3 | 9 | 59 | 5 | 3 | 3 | 93 | 8 | 2 | 9 |
| 26 | 2 | 5 | 6 | 60 | 5 | 5 | 0 | 94 | 8 | 4 | 6 |
| 27 | 2 | 7 | 3 | 61 | 5 | 6 | 9 | 95 | 8 | 6 | 3 |
| 28 | 2 | 9 | 0 | 62 | 5 | 8 | 6 | 96 | 8 | 8 | 0 |
| 29 | 2 | 10 | 9 | 63 | 5 | 10 | 3 | 97 | 8 | 9 | 9 |
| 30 | 2 | 12 | 6 | 64 | 5 | 12 | 0 | 98 | 8 | 11 | 6 |
| 31 | 2 | 14 | 3 | 65 | 5 | 13 | 9 | 99 | 8 | 13 | 3 |
| 32 | 2 | 16 | 0 | 66 | 5 | 15 | 6 | 100 | 8 | 15 | 0 |
| 33 | 2 | 17 | 9 | 67 | 5 | 17 | 3 | 144 | 12 | 12 | 0 |
| 34 | 2 | 19 | 6 | 68 | 5 | 19 | 0 | 500 | 43 | 15 | 0 |
| 35 | 3 | 1 | 3 | 69 | 6 | 0 | 9 | 750 | 65 | 12 | 6 |

## READY RECKONER.

### 2/3

| No. | £ | s. | d. | No. | £ | s. | d. | No. | £ | s. | d. |
|---|---|---|---|---|---|---|---|---|---|---|---|
| 2 | – | 4 | 6 | 36 | 4 | 1 | 0 | 70 | 7 | 17 | 6 |
| 3 | – | 6 | 9 | 37 | 4 | 3 | 3 | 71 | 7 | 19 | 9 |
| 4 | – | 9 | 0 | 38 | 4 | 5 | 6 | 72 | 8 | 2 | 0 |
| 5 | – | 11 | 3 | 39 | 4 | 7 | 9 | 73 | 8 | 4 | 3 |
| 6 | – | 13 | 6 | 40 | 4 | 10 | 0 | 74 | 8 | 6 | 6 |
| 7 | – | 15 | 9 | 41 | 4 | 12 | 3 | 75 | 8 | 8 | 9 |
| 8 | – | 18 | 0 | 42 | 4 | 14 | 6 | 76 | 8 | 11 | 0 |
| 9 | 1 | 0 | 3 | 43 | 4 | 16 | 9 | 77 | 8 | 13 | 3 |
| 10 | 1 | 2 | 6 | 44 | 4 | 19 | 0 | 78 | 8 | 15 | 6 |
| 11 | 1 | 4 | 9 | 45 | 5 | 1 | 3 | 79 | 8 | 17 | 9 |
| 12 | 1 | 7 | 0 | 46 | 5 | 3 | 6 | 80 | 9 | 0 | 0 |
| 13 | 1 | 9 | 3 | 47 | 5 | 5 | 9 | 81 | 9 | 2 | 3 |
| 14 | 1 | 11 | 6 | 48 | 5 | 8 | 0 | 82 | 9 | 4 | 6 |
| 15 | 1 | 13 | 9 | 49 | 5 | 10 | 3 | 83 | 9 | 6 | 9 |
| 16 | 1 | 16 | 0 | 50 | 5 | 12 | 6 | 84 | 9 | 9 | 0 |
| 17 | 1 | 18 | 3 | 51 | 5 | 14 | 9 | 85 | 9 | 11 | 3 |
| 18 | 2 | 0 | 6 | 52 | 5 | 17 | 0 | 86 | 9 | 13 | 6 |
| 19 | 2 | 2 | 9 | 53 | 5 | 19 | 3 | ·87 | 9 | 15 | 9 |
| 20 | 2 | 5 | 0 | 54 | 6 | 1 | 6 | 88 | 9 | 18 | 0 |
| 21 | 2 | 7 | 3 | 55 | 6 | 3 | 9 | 89 | 10 | 0 | 3 |
| 22 | 2 | 9 | 6 | 56 | 6 | 6 | 0 | 90 | 10 | 2 | 6 |
| 23 | 2 | 11 | 9 | 57 | 6 | 8 | 3 | 91 | 10 | 4 | 9 |
| 24 | 2 | 14 | 0 | 58 | 6 | 10 | 6 | 92 | 10 | 7 | 0 |
| 25 | 2 | 16 | 3 | 59 | 6 | 12 | 9 | 93 | 10 | 9 | 3 |
| 26 | 2 | 18 | 6 | 60 | 6 | 15 | 0 | 94 | 10 | 11 | 6 |
| 27 | 3 | 0 | 9 | 61 | 6 | 17 | 3 | 95 | 10 | 13 | 9 |
| 28 | 3 | 3 | 0 | 62 | 6 | 19 | 6 | 96 | 10 | 16 | 0 |
| 29 | 3 | 5 | 3 | 63 | 7 | 1 | 9 | 97 | 10 | 18 | 3 |
| 30 | 3 | 7 | 6 | 64 | 7 | 4 | 0 | 98 | 11 | 0 | 6 |
| 31 | 3 | 9 | 9 | 65 | 7 | 6 | 3 | 99 | 11 | 2 | 9 |
| 32 | 3 | 12 | 0 | 66 | 7 | 8 | 6 | 100 | 11 | 5 | 0 |
| 33 | 3 | 14 | 3 | 67 | 7 | 10 | 9 | 144 | 16 | 4 | 0 |
| 34 | 3 | 16 | 6 | 68 | 7 | 13 | 0 | 500 | 56 | 5 | 0 |
| 35 | 3 | 18 | 9 | 69 | 7 | 15 | 3 | 750 | 84 | 7 | 6 |

### 2/6

| No. | £ | s. | d. | No. | £ | s. | d. | No. | £ | s. | d. |
|---|---|---|---|---|---|---|---|---|---|---|---|
| 2 | – | 5 | 0 | 36 | 4 | 10 | 0 | 70 | 8 | 15 | 0 |
| 3 | – | 7 | 6 | 37 | 4 | 12 | 6 | 71 | 8 | 17 | 6 |
| 4 | – | 10 | 0 | 38 | 4 | 15 | 0 | 72 | 9 | 0 | 0 |
| 5 | – | 12 | 6 | 39 | 4 | 17 | 6 | 73 | 9 | 2 | 6 |
| 6 | – | 15 | 0 | 40 | 5 | 0 | 0 | 74 | 9 | 5 | 0 |
| 7 | – | 17 | 6 | 41 | 5 | 2 | 6 | 75 | 9 | 7 | 6 |
| 8 | 1 | 0 | 0 | 42 | 5 | 5 | 0 | 76 | 9 | 10 | 0 |
| 9 | 1 | 2 | 6 | 43 | 5 | 7 | 6 | 77 | 9 | 12 | 6 |
| 10 | 1 | 5 | 0 | 44 | 5 | 10 | 0 | 78 | 9 | 15 | 0 |
| 11 | 1 | 7 | 6 | 45 | 5 | 12 | 6 | 79 | 9 | 17 | 6 |
| 12 | 1 | 10 | 0 | 46 | 5 | 15 | 0 | 80 | 10 | 0 | 0 |
| 13 | 1 | 12 | 6 | 47 | 5 | 17 | 6 | 81 | 10 | 2 | 6 |
| 14 | 1 | 15 | 0 | 48 | 6 | 0 | 0 | 82 | 10 | 5 | 0 |
| 15 | 1 | 17 | 6 | 49 | 6 | 2 | 6 | 83 | 10 | 7 | 6 |
| 16 | 2 | 0 | 0 | 50 | 6 | 5 | 0 | 84 | 10 | 10 | 0 |
| 17 | 2 | 2 | 6 | 51 | 6 | 7 | 6 | 85 | 10 | 12 | 6 |
| 18 | 2 | 5 | 0 | 52 | 6 | 10 | 0 | 86 | 10 | 15 | 0 |
| 19 | 2 | 7 | 6 | 53 | 6 | 12 | 6 | 87 | 10 | 17 | 6 |
| 20 | 2 | 10 | 0 | 54 | 6 | 15 | 0 | 88 | 11 | 0 | 0 |
| 21 | 2 | 12 | 6 | 55 | 6 | 17 | 6 | 89 | 11 | 2 | 6 |
| 22 | 2 | 15 | 0 | 56 | 7 | 0 | 0 | 90 | 11 | 5 | 0 |
| 23 | 2 | 17 | 6 | 57 | 7 | 2 | 6 | 91 | 11 | 7 | 6 |
| 24 | 3 | 0 | 0 | 58 | 7 | 5 | 0 | 92 | 11 | 10 | 0 |
| 25 | 3 | 2 | 6 | 59 | 7 | 7 | 6 | 93 | 11 | 12 | 6 |
| 26 | 3 | 5 | 0 | 60 | 7 | 10 | 0 | 94 | 11 | 15 | 0 |
| 27 | 3 | 7 | 6 | 61 | 7 | 12 | 6 | 95 | 11 | 17 | 6 |
| 28 | 3 | 10 | 0 | 62 | 7 | 15 | 0 | 96 | 12 | 0 | 0 |
| 29 | 3 | 12 | 6 | 63 | 7 | 17 | 6 | 97 | 12 | 2 | 6 |
| 30 | 3 | 15 | 0 | 64 | 8 | 0 | 0 | 98 | 12 | 5 | 0 |
| 31 | 3 | 17 | 6 | 65 | 8 | 2 | 6 | 99 | 12 | 7 | 6 |
| 32 | 4 | 0 | 0 | 66 | 8 | 5 | 0 | 100 | 12 | 10 | 0 |
| 33 | 4 | 2 | 6 | 67 | 8 | 7 | 6 | 144 | 18 | 0 | 0 |
| 34 | 4 | 5 | 0 | 68 | 8 | 10 | 0 | 500 | 62 | 10 | 0 |
| 35 | 4 | 7 | 6 | 69 | 8 | 12 | 6 | 750 | 93 | 15 | 0 |

### 2/9

| No. | £ | s. | d. | No. | £ | s. | d. | No. | £ | s. | d. |
|---|---|---|---|---|---|---|---|---|---|---|---|
| 2 | – | 5 | 6 | 36 | 4 | 19 | 0 | 70 | 9 | 12 | 6 |
| 3 | – | 8 | 3 | 37 | 5 | 1 | 9 | 71 | 9 | 15 | 3 |
| 4 | – | 11 | 0 | 38 | 5 | 4 | 6 | 72 | 9 | 18 | 0 |
| 5 | – | 13 | 9 | 39 | 5 | 7 | 3 | 73 | 10 | 0 | 9 |
| 6 | – | 16 | 6 | 40 | 5 | 10 | 0 | 74 | 10 | 3 | 6 |
| 7 | – | 19 | 3 | 41 | 5 | 12 | 9 | 75 | 10 | 6 | 3 |
| 8 | 1 | 2 | 0 | 42 | 5 | 15 | 6 | 76 | 10 | 9 | 0 |
| 9 | 1 | 4 | 9 | 43 | 5 | 18 | 3 | 77 | 10 | 11 | 9 |
| 10 | 1 | 7 | 6 | 44 | 6 | 1 | 0 | 78 | 10 | 14 | 6 |
| 11 | 1 | 10 | 3 | 45 | 6 | 3 | 9 | 79 | 10 | 17 | 3 |
| 12 | 1 | 13 | 0 | 46 | 6 | 6 | 6 | 80 | 11 | 0 | 0 |
| 13 | 1 | 15 | 9 | 47 | 6 | 9 | 3 | 81 | 11 | 2 | 9 |
| 14 | 1 | 18 | 6 | 48 | 6 | 12 | 0 | 82 | 11 | 5 | 6 |
| 15 | 2 | 1 | 3 | 49 | 6 | 14 | 9 | 83 | 11 | 8 | 3 |
| 16 | 2 | 4 | 0 | 50 | 6 | 17 | 6 | 84 | 11 | 11 | 0 |
| 17 | 2 | 6 | 9 | 51 | 7 | 0 | 3 | 85 | 11 | 13 | 9 |
| 18 | 2 | 9 | 6 | 52 | 7 | 3 | 0 | 86 | 11 | 16 | 6 |
| 19 | 2 | 12 | 3 | 53 | 7 | 5 | 9 | 87 | 11 | 19 | 3 |
| 20 | 2 | 15 | 0 | 54 | 7 | 8 | 6 | 88 | 12 | 2 | 0 |
| 21 | 2 | 17 | 9 | 55 | 7 | 11 | 3 | 89 | 12 | 4 | 9 |
| 22 | 3 | 0 | 6 | 56 | 7 | 14 | 0 | 90 | 12 | 7 | 6 |
| 23 | 3 | 3 | 3 | 57 | 7 | 16 | 9 | 91 | 12 | 10 | 3 |
| 24 | 3 | 6 | 0 | 58 | 7 | 19 | 6 | 92 | 12 | 13 | 0 |
| 25 | 3 | 8 | 9 | 59 | 8 | 2 | 3 | 93 | 12 | 15 | 9 |
| 26 | 3 | 11 | 6 | 60 | 8 | 5 | 0 | 94 | 12 | 18 | 6 |
| 27 | 3 | 14 | 3 | 61 | 8 | 7 | 9 | 95 | 13 | 1 | 3 |
| 28 | 3 | 17 | 0 | 62 | 8 | 10 | 6 | 96 | 13 | 4 | 0 |
| 29 | 3 | 19 | 9 | 63 | 8 | 13 | 3 | 97 | 13 | 6 | 9 |
| 30 | 4 | 2 | 6 | 64 | 8 | 16 | 0 | 98 | 13 | 9 | 6 |
| 31 | 4 | 5 | 3 | 65 | 8 | 18 | 9 | 99 | 13 | 12 | 3 |
| 32 | 4 | 8 | 0 | 66 | 9 | 1 | 6 | 100 | 13 | 15 | 0 |
| 33 | 4 | 10 | 9 | 67 | 9 | 4 | 3 | 144 | 19 | 16 | 0 |
| 34 | 4 | 13 | 6 | 68 | 9 | 7 | 0 | 500 | 68 | 15 | 0 |
| 35 | 4 | 16 | 3 | 69 | 9 | 9 | 9 | 750 | 103 | 2 | 6 |

### 3/6

| No. | £ | s. | d. | No. | £ | s. | d. | No. | £ | s. | d. |
|---|---|---|---|---|---|---|---|---|---|---|---|
| 2 | – | 7 | 0 | 36 | 6 | 6 | 0 | 70 | 12 | 5 | 0 |
| 3 | – | 10 | 6 | 37 | 6 | 9 | 6 | 71 | 12 | 8 | 6 |
| 4 | – | 14 | 0 | 38 | 6 | 13 | 0 | 72 | 12 | 12 | 0 |
| 5 | – | 17 | 6 | 39 | 6 | 16 | 6 | 73 | 12 | 15 | 6 |
| 6 | 1 | 1 | 0 | 40 | 7 | 0 | 0 | 74 | 12 | 19 | 0 |
| 7 | 1 | 4 | 6 | 41 | 7 | 3 | 6 | 75 | 13 | 2 | 6 |
| 8 | 1 | 8 | 0 | 42 | 7 | 7 | 0 | 76 | 13 | 6 | 0 |
| 9 | 1 | 11 | 6 | 43 | 7 | 10 | 6 | 77 | 13 | 9 | 6 |
| 10 | 1 | 15 | 0 | 44 | 7 | 14 | 0 | 78 | 13 | 13 | 0 |
| 11 | 1 | 18 | 6 | 45 | 7 | 17 | 6 | 79 | 13 | 16 | 6 |
| 12 | 2 | 2 | 0 | 46 | 8 | 1 | 0 | 80 | 14 | 0 | 0 |
| 13 | 2 | 5 | 6 | 47 | 8 | 4 | 6 | 81 | 14 | 3 | 6 |
| 14 | 2 | 9 | 0 | 48 | 8 | 8 | 0 | 82 | 14 | 7 | 0 |
| 15 | 2 | 12 | 6 | 49 | 8 | 11 | 6 | 83 | 14 | 10 | 6 |
| 16 | 2 | 16 | 0 | 50 | 8 | 15 | 0 | 84 | 14 | 14 | 0 |
| 17 | 2 | 19 | 6 | 51 | 8 | 18 | 6 | 85 | 14 | 17 | 6 |
| 18 | 3 | 3 | 0 | 52 | 9 | 2 | 0 | 86 | 15 | 1 | 0 |
| 19 | 3 | 6 | 6 | 53 | 9 | 5 | 6 | 87 | 15 | 4 | 6 |
| 20 | 3 | 10 | 0 | 54 | 9 | 9 | 0 | 88 | 15 | 8 | 0 |
| 21 | 3 | 13 | 6 | 55 | 9 | 12 | 6 | 89 | 15 | 11 | 6 |
| 22 | 3 | 17 | 0 | 56 | 9 | 16 | 0 | 90 | 15 | 15 | 0 |
| 23 | 4 | 0 | 6 | 57 | 9 | 19 | 6 | 91 | 15 | 18 | 6 |
| 24 | 4 | 4 | 0 | 58 | 10 | 3 | 0 | 92 | 16 | 2 | 0 |
| 25 | 4 | 7 | 6 | 59 | 10 | 6 | 6 | 93 | 16 | 5 | 6 |
| 26 | 4 | 11 | 0 | 60 | 10 | 10 | 0 | 94 | 16 | 9 | 0 |
| 27 | 4 | 14 | 6 | 61 | 10 | 13 | 6 | 95 | 16 | 12 | 6 |
| 28 | 4 | 18 | 0 | 62 | 10 | 17 | 0 | 96 | 16 | 16 | 0 |
| 29 | 5 | 1 | 6 | 63 | 11 | 0 | 6 | 97 | 16 | 19 | 6 |
| 30 | 5 | 5 | 0 | 64 | 11 | 4 | 0 | 98 | 17 | 3 | 0 |
| 31 | 5 | 8 | 6 | 65 | 11 | 7 | 6 | 99 | 17 | 6 | 6 |
| 32 | 5 | 12 | 0 | 66 | 11 | 11 | 0 | 100 | 17 | 10 | 0 |
| 33 | 5 | 15 | 6 | 67 | 11 | 14 | 6 | 144 | 25 | 4 | 0 |
| 34 | 5 | 19 | 0 | 68 | 11 | 18 | 0 | 500 | 87 | 10 | 0 |
| 35 | 6 | 2 | 6 | 69 | 12 | 1 | 6 | 750 | 131 | 5 | 0 |

# DECIMAL CURRENCY

*The information given here about decimal currency and its establishment in the United Kingdom is compiled exclusively from three publications of the Decimal Currency Board, namely* Britain's New Coins, Decimal Currency: Three Years To Go, Decimal Currency: Expressions of Amounts In Printing, Writing and in Speech (*H.M.S.O.*) *and from* Decimal Currency: the Change Over (*H.M.S.O.*)

## The system

The Decimal Currency Act, which was passed on 14 July 1967, finally decided which decimal currency system was to be established in the United Kingdom. The decimal system, like the present money system, will be based on the pound sterling. But from 1971 the pound will be divided into 100 new pence instead of 20 shillings each of 12 pence. There will be a new halfpenny as the lowest value coin.

Hitherto we have used three units to measure money values: the pound, the shilling and the penny. Under the decimal system we shall use only two: the pound and the new penny. We can call the decimal system a "pound-new penny" system as against the present "pounds, shilling and pence" system.

Photographs of each of the selected designs, with background notes and other facts about the coins, are given in *Britain's New Coins.*

## Phasing the coinage changes

The familiar £sd coins will not all be replaced on D Day (see below) by the decimal coins described. The changes are being phased over about four years so that we can get accustomed to them

The coinage:

There will be six decimal coins:

| Denomination | £ s. d. value | Metal | Approx. Diameter (mms.) | Type of Edge | Reverse Design |
|---|---|---|---|---|---|
| ½p | 1·2d. | Bronze | 17·1 | Plain | The Royal Crown. |
| 1p | 2·4d. | Bronze | 20·3 | Plain | Portcullis with chains royally crowned. |
| 2p | 4·8d. | Bronze | 25·9 | Plain | The badge of the Prince of Wales. |
| 5p | 1 shilling | Cupro-nickel | 23·6 | Milled | The badge of Scotland. A thistle royally crowned. |
| 10p | 2 shillings | Cupro-nickel | 28·5 | Milled | Lion passant guardant royally crowned. |
| 50p | 10 shillings | Cupro-nickel | 30·0 | Plain | Britannia. |

*Reproduced from* Decimal Currency: The Changeover (H.M.S.O.).

one by one. Full details are given in *Decimal Currency: Three Years to go – Facts and forecasts*. A summary of the changes is as follows:

**Spring 1968**

5p and 10p coins started to come into circulation to be used as shillings and florins.

**1 August 1969**

the halfpenny will be demonetised.

**October 1969**

the 50p coin will begin to replace the 10s. note.

**1 January 1970**

the halfcrown will be demonetised.

**15 February 1971 (D Day)**

½p, 1p and 2p coins will come into circulation.

**After the change-over period**

1d, 3d and 6d will be demonetised.

Pennies, threepenny bits and six-pences will continue to circulate during the changeover period; they will quickly decline in usefulness and will be de-monetised at the end of this period.

Decimalisation on the basis of the £ makes it possible to retain our present £1, £5 and £10 bank-notes. They will be replaced eventually by smaller notes with new designs but the changes will not start until 1972.

**Decimal Day**

On 15 February 1971, the £-new penny system will become our official cur-rency. The new bronze coins will be-come legal tender and we shall get them as change when we make purchases.

Banks will work wholly in the new currency. Accounts will be in decimal. All cheques and other bank documents will have to be written in decimals. Special arrangements will have to be made to handle £sd cheques not cleared before D Day, and to sell £sd coins to those who still need them.

Clearing banks will be closed for

normal public business from Thursday to Sunday, 11–14 February inclusive. This will give the banks time to make a complete and immediate changeover, to clear cheques in the pipeline, and to balance and convert accounts. Re-stricted services will be available to ensure the safeguarding of cash and to meet the needs of travellers.

**Income Tax: Postage Rates**

Most Government departments will change over to decimal currency on D Day so that income tax deductions and social security benefits will be decimal-ised. The Post Office will change over: postage rates and postal orders will be decimal. Many shops and offices will also make the change.

**The Changeover Period**

D Day will be followed by a changeover period during which shops and offices gradually switch to decimals as their essential machines are converted or re-placed. We do not know how long this period will be. Two years was commonly forecast at one time, but it is in every-one's interest to make the change-over period much shorter than that.

During the changeover period £sd will remain in use for some purposes, and the old pennies, threepenny bits and sixpences will continue to circulate, but in rapidly dwindling numbers. Some shops will still operate in £sd, quoting £sd prices, using £sd cash registers and giving £sd low-value coins as change. The shops which have gone decimal will quote decimal prices, use decimal cash registers and give decimal coins as change.

**Equivalents**

Although two currency systems will be in use together during the changeover period, most of our notes and coins will be common to both systems. It is only below sixpence that the old and new coins will not have exact equivalents. Bank-notes will be unchanged, and the 50, 10 and 5 new penny pieces will be familiar to the public, who will already have been using them as 10, 2 and 1 shilling pieces. The sixpence will be usable as a 2½ new penny piece. Only the ½d, 1p and 2p decimal coins and the £sd pennies and threepenny bits will not be interchangeable. But even these low-value coins will be usable in multiples of sixpence or 2½ new pence. For example, a decimal ½p coin and a 2p coin could be used together for a sixpenny purchase and a threepenny bit and three pennies could be used for a 2½p purchase.

## Shopping

Detailed arrangements for shopping and other cash transactions during the changeover period have still to be worked out, but it is likely that for some time before D Day and afterwards shops will show both £sd and decimal price labels to help customers. The predominant price on the price ticket will be in the currency used by the shop; the other price will be for guidance only.

## Conversion of prices and other £sd amounts

A sum which consists only of pounds is, of course, the same in decimal currency as in £sd. And converting a sum which involves shillings is easy. A shilling is exactly 5p, so to convert any shilling amount we do no more than apply an extended "five times" multiplication table. Thus:

| | | |
|---|---|---|
| 2/-=10p | 8/-=40p | 14/-=70p |
| 3/-=15p | 9/-=45p | 15/-=75p |
| 4/-=20p | 10/-=50p | 16/-=80p |
| 5/-=25p | 11/-=55p | 17/-=85p |
| 6/-=30p | 12/-=60p | 18/-=90p |
| 7/-=35p | 13/-=65p | 19/-=95p |

When pence are involved as well as pounds and shillings, conversion is less easy. Just as no £sd coin below sixpence has an exact decimal equivalent, so no £sd price or amount that is not a multiple of sixpence has an exact decimal equivalent. A penny is 5/12 of a new penny (or £0·00416 recurring), and many conversions will be made on that basis. But when we decimalise, a large number of £sd amounts, including prices in shops, will have to be adjusted

slightly by rounding upwards or downwards.

## OFFICIAL CONVERSION TABLES

### Table A: New Halfpenny Table

This table has been recommended by the Decimal Currency Board and accepted by the Government for converting £ s. d. amounts to the nearest new halfpenny amounts. The use of this table for price conversion will not be mandatory, but all concerned with the retail prices of goods and services are expected to use it wherever practicable.

| Pence | | | | New Pence |
|---|---|---|---|---|
| 1d. ... | ... | ... | ... | ½p |
| 2d. ... | ... | ... | ... | 1p |
| 3d. ... | ... | ... | ... | 1p |
| 4d. ... | ... | ... | ... | 1½p |
| 5d. ... | ... | ... | ... | 2p |
| 6d. ... | ... | ... | ... | 2½p |
| 7d. ... | ... | ... | ... | 3p |
| 8d. ... | ... | ... | ... | 3½p |
| 9d. ... | ... | ... | ... | 4p |
| 10d. ... | ... | ... | ... | 4p |
| 11d. ... | ... | ... | ... | 4½p |
| 1/- ... | ... | ... | ... | 5p |

In this table, only 6d. and 1/- convert exactly. The other ten amounts are rounded – five of them upwards (1d., 2d., 7d., 8d., 9d.) and five of them downwards (3d., 4d., 5d., 10d., 11d.). The effect of this is that, if the table is applied consistently to a large number of randomly selected amounts, there is no overall gain for either buyer or seller. If conversion tables of this kind are used, decimalisation will not affect the cost of living.

A second conversion table will be needed to give decimal equivalents in whole new pence because banks will not use the new halfpenny and many organisations will follow suit in their accounting. This is the whole new penny table:

### Table B: Whole New Penny Table

This table has been recommended by the Decimal Currency Board and accepted by the Government for converting £ s. d. amounts to the nearest whole new penny amounts in banking and accounting transactions where the new halfpenny will not be used.

| Shillings and Pence | | | | New Pence |
|---|---|---|---|---|
| 1d. | ... | ... | ... | 0p |
| 2d. | ... | ... | ... | 1p |
| 3d. | ... | ... | ... | 1p |
| 4d. | ... | ... | ... | 2p |
| 5d. | ... | ... | ... | 2p |
| 6d. | ... | ... | ... | 3p |
| 7d. | ... | ... | ... | 3p |
| 8d. | ... | ... | ... | 3p |
| 9d. | ... | ... | ... | 4p |
| 10d. | ... | ... | ... | 4p |
| 11d. | ... | ... | ... | 5p |
| 1/- | ... | ... | ... | 5p |
| 1/1d. | ... | ... | ... | 5p |
| 1/2d. | ... | ... | ... | 6p |
| 1/3d. | ... | ... | ... | 6p |
| 1/4d. | ... | ... | ... | 7p |
| 1/5d. | ... | ... | ... | 7p |
| 1/6d. | ... | ... | ... | 7p |
| 1/7d. | ... | ... | ... | 8p |
| 1/8d. | ... | ... | ... | 8p |
| 1/9d. | ... | ... | ... | 9p |
| 1/10d. | ... | ... | ... | 9p |
| 1/11d. | ... | ... | ... | 10p |
| 2/- | ... | ... | ... | 10p |

*Decimal Currency: The Change-over* (H.M.S.O.)

## Decimal Currency in Printing, Writing, and Speech

The letter p will be the recognised abbreviation for new penny or new pence and it should be placed after the amount. We should write 4p, 27p, 53½p and so on. No full stop should be used after the p unless it ends a sentence.

### The Decimal Point

The decimal point will be the normal decimal sign for amounts of currency and the following rules should be followed:

(*a*) In printed and handwritten documents the decimal point should generally be opposite the middle of the figure (not on the base line). This accords with BSI standards.

(*b*) In typewritten and other documents produced on machines which have no decimal point, the use of a stop on the base line (a full stop) is the acceptable alternative.

(*c*) The £ symbol should always appear when the point is used, and the p abbreviation should never appear when the point is used. Thus the £ and p should never appear in the same expression.

### Writing amounts in pounds only

The standard method of expression is to have the £ sign followed by a number: £5, or £2,750. A permissible alternative, mainly useful in accounting, is £5·00 or £2,750·00. If the decimal point is used it should be followed by two noughts, not just one.

### Writing amounts in new pence only

Two methods of expression are clear and acceptable:

| First method | Second method |
|---|---|
| 97p | £0·97 |
| 6p | £0·06 |
| ½p | £0·00½ |

The first method is probably more acceptable for everyday use and for price labels in shops. The second will be required in accounting. (See also preceding column.)

### Writing mixed amounts of pounds and new pence

With mixed amounts the decimal sign and the £ symbol should always be used. It is wrong to use the £ symbol and the new penny abbreviation, or to use both with a decimal point.

| Wrong | Right |
|---|---|
| | £1·10 |
| £29 27p | £29·27 |
| and | £877·80 |
| £29·27p | £25,397·69 |

Rules (*b*) and (*c*) in paragraph 15 still apply. (Preceding column.)

### The new halfpenny

The new halfpenny should generally be expressed as a vulgar fraction: ½. It should not be expressed as a third place of decimals. Ours will be a £-new penny-½ system, not a £-mil system with a

5 mil lowest value circulating coin. Both the following methods are correct:

| First method | Second method |
|---|---|
| 3½p | £0·03½ |
| 98½p | £0·98½ |
| ½p | £0·00½ |
| | £10·85½ |
| | £42·67½ |

## Oral expression

In speaking of decimal amounts, various methods will no doubt be used and variety will not greatly matter. On the other hand, if abbreviation goes too far it can be confusing. "Two seventy-five" is ambiguous. It is better to get into the habit of using the word "pound". Thus, "two pounds seventy-five" and "ninety-three pounds fifty-two".

## Expression of amounts in column form

Guidance may be useful on the expression of decimal amounts in columns or in statistical tables. The normal style should be:

| Amounts in pounds and new pence | Amounts in exact pounds |
|---|---|
| £ | £ |
| 20·05½ | 5,000 |
| 123·45 | 39 |
| 5·10 | 123 |
| 0·02½ | 23,521 |
| 1,000·0 | 6 |

The columns should in both cases be headed simply £ (not £p).

## ADVICE TO CUSTOMERS OF BANKS

### How to write decimal amounts

#### When handwritten

| Figures | Words |
|---|---|
| £29-00 | Twenty-nine pounds |
| £29-26 | Twenty-nine pounds 26 |
| £29-08 | Twenty-nine pounds 08 |
| £0-26 | Twenty-six pence |

Use a hyphen instead of the decimal point.

#### When printed

| Figures | Words |
|---|---|
| £29·08 | Twenty-nine pounds 08 |
| £0·26 | Twenty-six pence |

#### When typed

| Figures | Words |
|---|---|
| £29·00 | Twenty-nine pounds |
| £29·26 | Twenty-nine pounds 26 |

#### Note:

Always have at least one figure (a nought if necessary) between the pound sign and the hyphen (or decimal point when printed or typed), e.g. £0·75.

Always have two figures after the hyphen (or decimal point when printed or typed), e.g. £7·80, £32·06.

# THE METRIC SYSTEM (SI)

*Much of the information given in this section is based on or quoted from material issued by the Ministry of Technology, the Central Office of Information, the Ministry of Public Buildings and Works, the British Standards Institute and the Design Centre.*

There seems every prospect that by the mid-1970s most British institutions will have changed over to what is now generally considered to be the best form of the metric system of weights and measures – the so-called SI system.

## What is the Metric System?

It is a system of measurement in which (for example) two of the basic units are the metre, for measuring length, and the kilogramme, for measuring weight and mass. Larger or smaller quantities are derived by multiplying or dividing these units by 10, 100, 1,000 and so on.

Thus:

1 kilometre (km) = 1,000 metres (m)

1 millimetre (mm) = $\dfrac{1}{1,000}$ metre (m)

Calculations in the metric system will be much easier than in the imperial system because there are fewer units. For instance, length will be measured in metres, or parts or multiples of metres, instead of inches, feet, yards, chains, furlongs and miles.

## The Language of Metric

The main metric descriptions are:

| | | |
|---|---|---|
| *the metre* | (m) | for length |
| *the litre* | (l) | for capacity |
| *the gramme* | (g) | for weight (mass) |
| *the newton* | (N) | for force |
| *the joule* | (J) | for energy |
| *the watt* | (W) | for power |

They are preceded by these expressions to multiply or divide them:

| | |
|---|---|
| *mega* | for a million times |
| *kilo* | for a thousand times |
| *centi* | for a hundredth |
| *milli* | for a thousandth |
| *micro* | for a millionth |

Thus a megawatt is a million watts, a kilometre is a thousand metres, a centi-metre is a hundredth of a metre and a millilitre is a thousandth part of a litre.

Two other descriptions may be used occasionally. These are:

the *hectare* which is ten thousand square metres; the *tonne* which is one thousand kilogrammes.

## Metric Memo

### Lengths

Use kilometres (km) for distances, metres (m) for your height and millimetres (mm) for smaller lengths.

### Areas

Use square metres ($m^2$) for large areas like rooms and square millimetres for small objects ($mm^2$).

### Volumes

Use cubic metres ($m^3$), litres (l) and millilitres (ml).

### Weights

Use kilogrammes (kg) and grammes (g) Your weight in kilogrammes.

## The Change-over

In education, commerce and science the metric system will be taught and practised. In industry, by 1972, designers and draughtsmen will have to do calculations and produce drawings in metric units, and shop floor staff will have to work to metric drawings. New rules, gauges and other measuring devices will be necessary, and in some cases metric indexing dials will be provided on existing machine tools. Staff at all levels will have to become familiar with the metric units used in their jobs, and courses of retraining will be given where necessary.

## Time

Under the SI system, the unit of time is the second, minutes, hours, days, etc., and will be used as hitherto.

## Temperature (*Centigrade*)

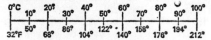

0°C is the freezing point of water
15°C is the temperature on a warm spring day
30°C is the temperature on a very hot summer's day
37°C is normal body temperature.
100°C is the boiling point of water.

## Comparisons

A 1-in screw is about 25 mm long

A 4-in nail is about 100 mm long

A 12-in tile measures about 300 mm

4 cu yd is about 3 cu m

1 cwt is about 50 kg

*Diagrams from Ministry of Public Building and Works leaflet, "Going Metric".*

## Metric Scale already in use

"For the help of teachers the following are some examples of the use of metric measures in Britain at the present time:

BMC have used the metric scale in manufacture of parts for many years (Morris as far back as 1939). Other examples in which the changeover has already begun are: nuts and bolts, plywood, tyres on toy model cars, canned foods, drills, car engine sizes, car and caravan lengths, sparking plugs, spanners, screw threads, films in common use (cine: 8mm and 16mm; camera: 35mm), weapons (especially guns), building components." – *Change For a Pound: A Teaching Guide for the Introduction of Decimal Currency and the Adoption of Metric Measures* (H.M.S.O.).

## International Paper Sizes (ISO)
### 'A' Series of Trimmed Paper Sizes

|     | mm. | inches |
|-----|-----|--------|
| A0  | 841 × 1189 | 33·11 × 46·81 |
| A1  | 594 × 841 | 23·39 × 33·11 |
| A2  | 420 × 594 | 16·54 × 23·39 |
| A3  | 297 × 420 | 11·69 × 16·54 |
| A4  | 210 × 297 | 8·27 × 11·69 |
| A5  | 148 × 210 | 5·83 × 8·27 |
| A6  | 105 × 148 | 4·13 × 5·83 |
| A7  | 74 × 105 | 2·91 × 4·13 |
| A8  | 52 × 74 | 2·05 × 2·91 |
| A9  | 37 × 52 | 1·46 × 2·05 |
| A10 | 26 × 37 | 1·02 × 1·46 |

### 'B' Series of Trimmed Paper Sizes

|     | mm. | inches |
|-----|-----|--------|
| B0  | 1000 × 1414 | 39·37 × 55·67 |
| B1  | 707 × 1000 | 27·83 × 39·37 |
| B2  | 500 × 707 | 19·68 × 27·83 |
| B3  | 353 × 500 | 13·90 × 19·68 |
| B4  | 250 × 353 | 9·84 × 13·90 |
| B5  | 176 × 250 | 6·93 × 9·84 |
| B6  | 125 × 176 | 4·92 × 6·93 |
| B7  | 88 × 125 | 3·46 × 4·92 |
| B8  | 62 × 88 | 2·44 × 3·46 |
| B9  | 44 × 62 | 1·73 × 2·44 |
| B10 | 31 × 44 | 1·22 × 1·73 |

## THE SHAPE OF THINGS TO COME

*From an article, "Living By The Litre," reproduced by courtesy of* Drive Magazine

### The Metric Motorist

"You'll have a collar size of 38·1 centimetres and you'll fill your pipe from a 50-gramme tin of tobacco. If you buy a new sports saloon you'll find it has a metric gearbox and a whole range of metric nuts and bolts – all given a chemical treatment which turns them bright yellow for easy identification, as well as making them three times as resistant to rust.

"When you decide to have a new garage built, it will have been designed in metres and centimetres instead of feet and inches. Petrol will be bought by value or in units of five litres, equivalent to 1·1 gallons. Tyre pressure gauges will register 1·7 bars instead of 24 pounds per square inch.

"Power output will be measured in watts rather than brake horsepower.

"All Britain's motor manufacturers are gradually redesigning to the metric scale. But to save the immense cost of retooling, old designs and components carried forward to new models will remain in inches . . .

"Fuel economy will be measured in different terms. Metric countries reckon in terms of litres per 100 kilometres. And if you're carrying a load on your roof-rack, mind your head – bridge clearances will be marked in metres."

### The Metric Mother

"You, madam, will have to learn how to cook all over again. You will need new kitchen scales and measuring jugs and another set of cookery books; all those ounces and gills will soon be obsolete. When manufacturers settle on a replacement for the half-pound pack of butter, you will no longer be able to measure ounce portions by progressive halving.

"You will buy the family drinks in cubic centimetres, gas in megajoules, curtain widths in metres and solid fuel by the quintal, which is 3¼ lb. less than two hundredweight. By 1972 jam will come in half-kilo jars, flour and sugar by the kilo bag.

"Dairies will probably settle for a 600 cc bottle, the same height as the present pint but with raised shoulders so that it will still fit into your refrigerator.

"Saucepans, kettles and liquidisers will have capacities marked in millilitres. The diameter of your cake tin will be measured in centimetres and the oven temperature in degrees Celsius.

"You're the family gardener? The roses will have to be planted half a metre apart, and by 1971 you'll be diluting sprays and weedkillers by metric quantities. The capacity of your watering can will be measured in litres. Some cut flowers are already packed in tens.

"If all this has given you a headache, take a metric aspirin – the standard tablet has already changed from five grains to 300 milligrams – or lie down on your new double bed. It measures 2 m by 1½ m, which will give you three square feet more space than the 6 ft. by 4 ft. 6in. bed you had to put up with in the old days."

### The Metric Teenager

"As girls will have noticed, cosmetics have already gone metric. Moisture cream comes in 70-gramme jars, talc in 85-gramme puffers, deep cleanser in 125 cc bottles. Soon, a girl's ideal vital statistics will be a frightening 91-61-91 – but in centimetres, not inches. To keep trim, she will have to watch the joules instead of the calories. And each morning she will weigh in on bathroom scales marked in kilos.

"Newlyweds who qualify for a new council house after 1972 will find it built entirely to metric specifications. The density of houses will be related to the hectare, not to the acre."

### Medicine

"Nurses will measure out medicine in cubic centimetre doses. There will be no tablespoonsful of castor oil, just metric teaspoons of 5 cc each. Dressmakers will buy material in metres.

"If you're driven to drink, order a tot of whisky in millilitres. And don't ask for 'a half of bitter' – unless you want half a litre, which is almost a pint.

"If you take a walk in the country, you'll plan your route on a map scaled to kilometres, nibble sweets bought by the gramme and take tea from a flask measured in millilitres, not fluid ounces.

The size of records and television screens will change, and from 1972 all photographs will be in centimetres or millimetres. A tennis racquet will be sized in grammes, a bicycle frame in centimetres, and a 16-hand horse will measure up at 162·56 centimetres ..."

## Sport

"There is hardly any leisure activity which will not somehow be affected by the changeover. Every sports pitch, goal post and netball stand will be redesigned to metric standards. The 22 yards of a cricket pitch will convert to an impossible 20·1168 metres; even the ball, bails and stumps will change size."
*Living By The Litre* by Keith Ellis in *Drive, the AA Magazine.*

## CONVERSION TABLE: SI Units to British: British to SI

### Length (Metric)
| | | |
|---|---|---|
| 1 kilometre (km) | = | 0·621 371 mile |
| 1 metre (m) | = | 1·093 61 yd |
| 1 centimetre (cm) | = | 0·393 701 in |
| 1 millimetre (mm) | = | 0·039 370 1 in |
| 1 $\mu$m | = | 39·370 1 $\mu$in |

### Length
| | | |
|---|---|---|
| 1 mile | = | 1·609 34 km |
| 1 furlong | = | 0·201 168 km |
| 1 chain | = | 20·116 8 m |
| 1 yd | = | 0·914 4 m |
| 1 ft | = | 0·304 8 m |
| 1 in | = | 25·4 mm = 2·54 cm |
| 1 milli-inch ("thou") | = | 25·4 $\mu$m |
| 1 $\mu$in (0.000 001 in) | = | 0·025 4 $\mu$m |
| 1 nautical mile | = | 1·853 18 km |
| 1 fathom | = | 1·828 8 m |

### Area (Metric)
| | | |
|---|---|---|
| 1 sq kilometre (km²) | = | 247·105 acres |
| 1 sq metre (m²) | = | 1·195 99 yd² |
| 1 sq centimetre (cm²) | = | 0·155 000 in² |

### Area
| | | |
|---|---|---|
| 1 sq mile | = | 2·589 99 km² =258·999 ha† |
| 1 acre | = | 4046·86 m² =0·404 686 ha |
| 1 rood | = | 1011·71 m² |
| 1 yd² (sq yard) | = | 0·836 127 m² |

| | | |
|---|---|---|
| 1 ft² (sq foot) | = | 0·092 903 0 m²= 929·030 cm² |
| 1 in² (sq inch) | = | 645·16 mm² = 6·451 6 cm² |

### Volume
| | | |
|---|---|---|
| 1 yd³ (cubic yd) | = | 0·764 555 m³ |
| 1 ft³ (cubic foot) | = | 28·316 8 dm³ |
| 1 in³ (cubic inch) | = | 16·387 1 cm³ |

### Volume (Metric)
| | | |
|---|---|---|
| 1 cu metre (m³†) | = | 1·307 95 yd³ |
| 1 cu decimetre (dm³) | = | 0·035 314 7 ft³ |
| 1 cu centimetre (cm³) | = | 0·061 023 7 in³ |
| 1 l (litre) | = | 0·220 0 gal |
| 1 l (litre) | = | 0·264 2 USgal |

### Capacity (Metric)
| | | |
|---|---|---|
| 1 cu centimetre | = | 0·061 cu in |
| 1 cu metre | = | 1·30795 cu yd |
| 1 litre (l) | = | 1·7598 pint |
| 1 hectolitre (hl) | = | 2·749 bushels |

### Capacity
| | | |
|---|---|---|
| 1 bu (bushel) | = | 36·368 7 dm³ |
| 1 pk (peck) | = | 9·092 18 dm³ |
| 1 gal | = | 4·546 09 dm³ =4·546 litres (l) |
| 1 USgal | = | 3·785 41 dm³ =3·785 litres |
| 1 qt (quart) | = | 1·136 52 dm³ =1·737 litres |
| 1 pt (pint) | = | 0·568 261 dm³ =0·568 litre |
| 1 gill | = | 0·142 065 dm³ =0·142 litre |
| 1 fl oz | = | 28·413 1 cm³ |
| 1 fluid drachm | = | 3·551 63 cm³ |
| 1 minim | = | 59·193 9 mm³ |

### Weight (Metric)
| | | |
|---|---|---|
| 1 kilogram (kg) | = | 2·204 62 lb |
| 1 gram (g) | = | 0·035 274 0 oz |
| | = | 15·432 4 gr (grain) |

### Weight
| | | |
|---|---|---|
| 1 ton | = | 1016·05 kg =1·016 05 t |
| 1 cwt | = | 50·802 3 kg |
| 1 ctl | = | 45·359 2 kg |

† 1 hectare (ha) = 10 000 m²

**Weight** (*continued*)

| | | | | | |
|---|---|---|---|---|---|
| 1 quarter | = | 12·700 6 kg | **1 oz apoth** | | |
| 1 stone | = | 6·350 29 kg | = 1 oz tr | = | 31·103 5 g |
| 1 lb | = | 0·453 592 37 kg | 1 drachm | = | 3·887 93 g |
| 1 oz | = | 28·349 5 g | 1 scruple | = | 1·295 98 g |
| 1 dr (dram) | = | 1·771 85 g | 1 dwt (penny- | | |
| 1 gr (grain) | = | 64·798 9 mg = | weight) | = | 1·555 17 g |
| | | 0·323 995 | 1 slug | = | 14·593 9 kg |
| | | metric carat | | | |

For further conversion factors, symbols and definitions the reader is referred to *Changing to the Metric System* by Pamela Anderton and P. H. Bigg (H.M.S.O.)

### METRIC WEIGHTS AND MEASURES AND THEIR EQUIVALENTS

| Metres to yards | | Kilometres to miles | | Grammes to grains | | Kilogrammes to pounds | |
|---|---|---|---|---|---|---|---|
| Metres | Yards | Kms. | Miles | Grams | Grains | Kilo-grms. | Pounds Avoirdupois |
| 1 | 1·093 | 1 | ·621 | 1 | 15·432 | 1 | 2·204 |
| 2 | 2·187 | 2 | 1·243 | 2 | 30·865 | 2 | 4·409 |
| 3 | 3·280 | 3 | 1·864 | 3 | 46·297 | 3 | 6·614 |
| 4 | 4·374 | 4 | 2·486 | 4 | 61·729 | 4 | 8·818 |
| 5 | 5·468 | 5 | 3·107 | 5 | 77·162 | 5 | 11·023 |
| 6 | 6·561 | 6 | 3·728 | 6 | 92·594 | 6 | 13·228 |
| 7 | 7·655 | 7 | 4·350 | 7 | 108·026 | 7 | 15·432 |
| 8 | 8·749 | 8 | 4·971 | 8 | 123·459 | 8 | 17·637 |
| 9 | 9·842 | 9 | 5·592 | 9 | 138·891 | 9 | 19·842 |
| 10 | 10·936 | 10 | 6·214 | 10 | 154·323 | 10 | 22·046 |
| 11 | 12·030 | 11 | 6·835 | 11 | 169·756 | 11 | 24·250 |
| 12 | 13·123 | 12 | 7·456 | 12 | 185·188 | 12 | 26·455 |
| 13 | 14·217 | 13 | 8·072 | 13 | 200·620 | 13 | 28·660 |
| 14 | 15·310 | 14 | 8·699 | 14 | 216·053 | 14 | 30·865 |
| 15 | 16·404 | 15 | 9·321 | 15 | 231·485 | 15 | 33·069 |
| 16 | 17·498 | 16 | 9·942 | 16 | 246·917 | 16 | 35·274 |
| 17 | 18·591 | 17 | 10·563 | 17 | 262·350 | 17 | 37·478 |
| 18 | 19·685 | 18 | 11·185 | 18 | 277·782 | 18 | 39·683 |
| 19 | 20·779 | 19 | 11·806 | 19 | 293·214 | 19 | 41·888 |
| 20 | 21·872 | 20 | 12·428 | 20 | 308·647 | 20 | 44·092 |
| 30 | 32·808 | 30 | 18·641 | 30 | 462·971 | 30 | 66·139 |
| 40 | 43·745 | 40 | 24·855 | 40 | 617·294 | 40 | 88·185 |
| 50 | 54·681 | 50 | 31·069 | 50 | 771·617 | 50 | 110·231 |

# INDEX